Ways of Reading

AN ANTHOLOGY FOR WRITERS

Ways of Reading

AN ANTHOLOGY FOR WRITERS

ELEVENTH EDITION

David Bartholomae
UNIVERSITY OF PITTSBURGH

Anthony Petrosky
UNIVERSITY OF PITTSBURGH

Stacey Waite
UNIVERSITY OF NEBRASKA–LINCOLN

bedford/st.martin's
Macmillan Learning
Boston • New York

Ways of Reading

AN ANTHOLOGY FOR WRITERS

ELEVENTH EDITION

David Bartholomae

UNIVERSITY OF PITTSBURGH

Anthony Petrosky

UNIVERSITY OF PITTSBURGH

Stacey Waite

UNIVERSITY OF NEBRASKA–LINCOLN

bedford/st.martin's

Macmillan Learning

Boston | New York

For Bedford/St. Martin's

Vice President, Editorial, Macmillan Learning Humanities: Edwin Hill
Editorial Director, English: Karen S. Henry
Senior Publisher for Composition, Business and Technical Writing, Developmental Writing: Leasa Burton
Executive Editor: John E. Sullivan III
Senior Developmental Editor: Caroline Thompson
Senior Production Editor: Harold Chester
Media Producer: Rand Thomas
Production Supervisor: Lisa McDowell
Executive Marketing Manager: Joy Fisher Williams
Copy Editor: Jennifer Brett Greenstein
Senior Photo Editor: Martha Friedman
Photo Researcher: Kerri Wilson, Lumina Datamatics, Inc.
Permissions Manager: Kalina Ingham
Permissions Editor: Jenn Kennett
Senior Art Director: Anna Palchik
Text Design: Tom Carling
Cover Design: John Callahan
Cover Image: Matej Krén, *Idiom* — detail of the interior of the sculpture, Municipal Library of Prague, 1998. *Photograph:* Gabriel Urbánek
Composition: Jouve
Printing and Binding: LSC Communications

Manufactured in the United States of America.

1 0 9 8 7
f e d c b

For information, write: Bedford/St. Martin's, 75 Arlington Street, Boston, MA 02116
(617-399-4000)

ISBN 978-1-319-04014-7

Acknowledgments

Text acknowledgments and copyrights appear at the back of the book on pages 722–23, which constitute an extension of the copyright page. Art acknowledgments and copyrights appear on the same page as the art selections they cover.

Preface

Ways of Reading is designed for a course in which students are given the opportunity to work on what they read, and to work on it by writing. When we began developing such courses, we realized that the problems our students had when asked to write or talk about what they read were not "reading problems," at least not as these are strictly defined. Our students knew how to move from one page to the next. They could read sentences. They had, obviously, been able to carry out many of the versions of reading required for their education — skimming textbooks, cramming for tests, strip-mining books for term papers.

Our students, however, felt powerless in the face of serious writing, in the face of long and complicated texts — the kinds of texts we thought they should find interesting and challenging. We thought (as many teachers have thought) that if we just, finally, gave them something good to read — something rich and meaty — they would change forever their ways of thinking about English. It didn't work, of course. The issue is not only *what* students read but what they can learn to *do* with what they read. We learned that the problems our students had lay not in the reading material (it was too hard) or in the students (they were poorly prepared) but in the classroom — in the ways we and they imagined what it meant to work on an essay.

There is no better place to work on reading than in a writing course, and this book is intended to provide occasions for readers to write. You will find a number of distinctive features in *Ways of Reading*. For one thing, it contains selections you don't usually see in a college reader: long, powerful, mysterious, and difficult pieces like Kwame Anthony Appiah's "Racial Identities," John Berger's "Ways of Seeing," Judith Butler's "Beside Oneself: On the Limits of Sexual Autonomy," Michel Foucault's "Panopticism," Susan Griffin's "Our Secret," Edward Said's "States," and John Edgar Wideman's "Our Time." These are the sorts of readings we talk about when we talk with our colleagues. We have learned that we can talk about them with our students as well.

When we chose the essays, we were looking for "readable" texts — that is, texts that leave some work for a reader to do. We wanted selections that invite students to be active, critical readers, that present powerful readings of common experience, that open up the familiar world and make it puzzling, rich, and problematic. We wanted to choose selections that invite students to take responsibility for their acts of interpretation. So we avoided the short set pieces you find in so many anthologies. In a sense, those short selections misrepresent the act of reading. They can be read in a single sitting; they make arguments that can be easily paraphrased; they solve all the problems they raise; they wrap up life and put it into a box; and so they turn reading into an act of appreciation, in which the most that seems to be required is a nod of the head. And they suggest that a writer's job is to do just that, to write a piece that is similarly tight and neat and self-contained. We wanted to avoid pieces that were so plainly written or tightly bound that there was little for students to do but "get the point."

We learned that if our students had reading problems when faced with long and complex texts, the problems lay in the way they imagined a reader — the role a reader plays, what a reader does, why a reader reads (if not simply to satisfy the requirements of a course). When, for example, our students were puzzled by what they read, they took this as a sign of failure. ("It doesn't make any sense," they would say, as though the sense was supposed to be waiting on the page, ready for them the first time they read through.) And our students were haunted by the thought that they couldn't remember everything they had read (as though one could store all of Judith Butler's "Beside Oneself: On the Limits of Sexual Autonomy" in memory); or if they did remember bits and pieces, they felt that the fragmented text they possessed was evidence that they could not do what they were supposed to do. Our students were confronting the experience of reading, in other words, but they were taking the problems of reading — problems all readers face — and concluding that there was nothing for them to do but give up.

As expert readers, we have all learned what to do with a complex text. We know that we can go back to a text; we don't have to remember it — in fact, we've learned to mark up a text to ease that reentry. We know that a reader is a person who puts together fragments. The coherent readings we construct begin with confusion and puzzlement, and we construct these readings by writing and rewriting — by working on a text.

These are the lessons our students need to learn, and this is why a course in reading is also a course in writing. Our students need to learn that there is something they can do once they have first read through a complicated text; successful reading is not just a matter of "getting" an essay the first time. In a very real sense, you can't begin to feel the power a reader has until you realize the problems, until you realize that no one "gets" Appiah or Butler or Wideman all at once. You work on what you read, and then what you have at the end is something that is yours, something you made. And this is what the teaching apparatus in *Ways of Reading* is designed to do. In a sense, it says to students, "OK, let's get to work on these essays; let's see what you can make of them."

This, then, is the second distinctive feature you will find in *Ways of Reading*: reading and writing assignments designed to give students access to the essays. After each selection, for example, you will find "Questions for a Second Reading." We wanted to acknowledge that rereading is a natural way of carrying out the work of a reader, just as rewriting is a natural way of completing the work of a writer. It is not something done out of despair or as a punishment for not getting things right the first time. The questions we have written highlight what we see as central textual or interpretive problems. These questions might serve as preparations for class discussion or ways of directing students' work in journals. Whatever the case, they both honor and direct the work of rereading.

Each selection is also followed by two sets of writing assignments, "Assignments for Writing" and "Making Connections." The first set directs students back into the work they have just read. While the assignments vary, there are some basic principles behind them. They ask students to work on the essay by focusing on difficult or problematic moments in the text; they ask students to work on the author's examples, extending and testing his or her methods of analysis; or they ask students to apply the method of the essay (its way of seeing and understanding the world) to settings or experiences of their own. The last assignments, "Making Connections," invite students to read one essay in the context of another, to see, for example, if Mary Louise Pratt's account of the "literate arts of the contact zone" can be used to frame a reading of Gloria Anzaldúa's prose or Richard E. Miller's account of education. In a sense, then, the essays are offered as models, but not as "prose models" in the strictest sense. What they model is a way of seeing or reading the world, of both imagining problems and imagining methods to make those problems available to a writer.

At the end of the book, we have included several assignment sequences. A single sequence provides structure for an entire course. (There are a number of additional sequences included in the Instructor's Manual.) Most of the sequences include more than one essay in the anthology and require a series of separate drafts and revisions. Alternative essays and assignments are included with the sequences. In academic life, readers seldom read single essays in isolation, as though one could be "finished" with Judith Butler after a week or two. Rather, they read with a purpose — with a project in mind or a problem to solve. The assignment sequences are designed to give students a feel for the rhythm and texture of an extended academic project. They offer, that is, one more way of reading and writing. Because these sequences lead students through intellectual projects proceeding from one week to the next, they enable them to develop authority as specialists, to feel the difference between being an expert and being a "common" reader on a single subject. And, with the luxury of time available for self-reflection, students can look back on what they have done, not only to revise what they know, but also to take stock and comment on the value and direction of their work.

Because of their diversity, it is difficult to summarize the assignment sequences. Perhaps the best way to see what we have done is to turn to the back of the book and look at them. They are meant not only to frame a project for students but to leave open possibilities for new directions. You should feel free to add or drop readings, to mix sequences, and to revise the assignments to fit your course and your schedule.

You will also notice that there are few "glosses" appended to the essays. We have not added many editors' notes to define difficult words or to identify names or allusions to other authors or artists. We've omitted them because their presence suggests something we feel is false about reading. They suggest that good readers know all the words or pick up all the allusions or recognize every name that is mentioned. This is not true. Good readers do what they can and try their best to fill in the blanks; they ignore seemingly unimportant references and look up the important ones. There is no reason for students to feel they lack the knowledge necessary to complete a reading of these texts. We have translated some foreign phrases, but we have kept the selections as clean and open as possible.

We have been asked on several occasions whether the readings aren't finally just too hard for students. The answer is no. Students will have to work on the selections, but that is the point of the course and the reason, as we said before, why a reading course is also a course in writing. College students want to believe that they can strike out on their own, make their mark, do something they have never done before. They want to *be* experts, not just hear from them. This is the great pleasure, as well as the great challenge, of undergraduate instruction. It is not hard to convince students they ought to be able to speak alongside of (or even speak back to) Judith Butler or Edward Said. And, if a teacher is patient and forgiving — willing, that is, to let a student work out a reading of Butler or Said, willing to keep from saying, "No, that's not it," and filling the silence with the "right" reading — then students can, with care and assistance, learn to speak for themselves. It takes a certain kind of classroom, to be sure. A teacher who teaches this book will have to be comfortable turning the essays over to the students, even with the knowledge that they will not do immediately on their own what a professional could do — at least not completely, or with the same grace and authority.

In our own teaching, we have learned that we do not have to be experts on every figure or every area of inquiry represented in this book. We can have intelligent, responsible conversations about Appiah's "Racial Identities" without being experts on Appiah's work or current work on race and identity. We needed to prepare ourselves to engage and direct students as readers, but we did not have to prepare ourselves to lecture on Foucault or Butler, on poststructuralism and gender theory. The classes we have been teaching, and they have been some of the most exciting we have ever taught, have been classes where students — together and with their instructors — work on what these essays might mean.

So here we are, imagining students working shoulder to shoulder with Said, Butler, and Foucault, even talking back to them as the occasion arises. There is a wonderful Emersonian bravado in all this. But such is the case with strong and active readers. If we allow students to work on powerful texts, they will want to share the power. This is the heady fun of academic life, the real pleasure of thinking, reading, and writing. There is no reason to keep it secret from our students.

NEW TO THE ELEVENTH EDITION

More than a third of the selections in the eleventh edition of *Ways of Reading* are new. Our principle of selection remained the same — we were looking for "readable" texts, pieces that instructors and students would find challenging and compelling, pieces that offer powerful readings of ordinary experiences, pieces worth extended work.

There are new selections by Ruth Behar, Gloria Bird, Joy Castro, Ta-Nehisi Coates, Atul Gawande, Ben Lerner, Michael Pollan, and Michael Specter, and a new selection from W. E. B. Du Bois that will be familiar to instructors who taught one of the earlier editions of *Ways of Reading*. In this edition, in addition to chapter-length selections, we explored some shorter essays that take on some complex subject matter that students can examine closely. In our contemporary moment, we thought it imperative to bring new voices into this edition that might lead students to think more deeply about language, identity, and politics. These new selections come from authors working in a variety of areas such as anthropology, nutrition science, genetics, memoir, critical theory, and creative writing. In these new texts, students will, indeed, revisit many of the critical questions that have been at the heart of *Ways of Reading* since its first edition — questions of being, questions of power, questions of education, questions of interpretation and composition. We believe it is crucial — perhaps now more than ever—for students to come to think of themselves as generative intellectuals, as writers who have the agency and ability to intervene in the public rhetorics that construct our world.

We have developed three new assignment sequences. Two of these new sequences—"The Art of Argument" and "On Difficulty"—appear in the textbook itself. A third new sequence, "Examinations of Race and Racism," appears in the Instructor's Manual, which you can download from **macmillanlearning.com**. We had hoped this third sequence, which relies heavily on the work of Ta-Nehisi Coates, would appear in the textbook, but our permissions process was delayed, and we only had time to add this new sequence to the Instructor's Manual. We have revised the existing sequences, some to incorporate the new selections, others because, after teaching them again, we thought about them differently. In addition to sequences focusing on academic writing, we have continued to offer sequences focusing on autobiographical writing and the personal essay. While there have always been assignments in *Ways of Reading* that ask students to use their experience as subject matter, these assignments invite students to look critically and historically at the autobiographical genre and position reading and thinking as part of one's "personal" experience. The new texts by writers like Gloria Bird, Joy Castro, and Ruth Behar, for example, have much to offer students in terms of how they might study and imitate this personal and intellectual work. We remain convinced that this kind of imitative work helps students think about sentences, rhetorical choices, and style in dynamic and useful ways. We continue to focus attention on prose models that challenge conventional forms and on writers who complicate the usual ways of thinking about and representing knowledge and experience. There are several assignment sequences that ask students to write as though they too could participate in such revisionary work.

ACKNOWLEDGMENTS

With our colleagues, we have taught most of the selections in this book, including the new ones. Several of us worked together to prepare the assignment sequences; most of these, too, have been tested in class. As we have traveled around giving talks, we've met many people who have used *Ways of Reading*. We have been delighted to hear them speak about how it has served their teaching, and we have learned much from their advice and example. It is an unusual and exciting experience to see our course turned into a text, to see our work read, critiqued, revised, and expanded. We have many people to thank. The list that follows can't begin to name all those to whom we owe a debt. And it can't begin to express our gratitude.

We owe much to the friendship and wisdom of our colleagues and students at both the University of Pittsburgh and the University of Nebraska–Lincoln. It is an honor and a pleasure to work together with such colleagues and students; we have learned much from their example, their critiques, and their suggestions. We owe much to the graduate students at the University of Nebraska–Lincoln, especially Zach Beare and Kirby Little, who have written assignments and done research for this particular edition. We wish to thank old friends and colleagues with whom we have worked for a very long time: Jean Ferguson Carr, Steve Carr,

Nick Coles, Jean Grace, Paul Kameen, Geeta Kothari, Jennifer Lee, Beth Matway, and Brenda Whitney. Thanks to all who have followed our work with interest and offered their support and criticism. We are grateful for the notes, letters, and student papers.

We were fortunate to have a number of outstanding reviewers on the project: Scott Campbell, University of Connecticut; Sheila L. Carter-Tod, Virginia Tech University; Lois Lake Church, Quinnipiac University; Leslie Dennen, University of San Francisco; Jordan Dominy, Savannah State University; Ana Douglass, Truckee Meadows Community College; Chris Featherman, Northeastern University; Laura Headley, Monterey Peninsula College; John Holland, San Francisco State University; Devon Holmes, University of San Francisco; Allen Johnson, Christian Brothers University; Adam Katz, Quinnipiac University; Melissa Lenos, Donnelly College; Jenn McCollum, Landmark College; Chris Murray, Texas A&M University; Glenda Pritchett, Quinnipiac University; Alison Reynolds, University of Florida; Lori Robison, University of North Dakota; Catherine Rogers, Savannah State University; Roberta Stagnaro, Southwestern College; Deborah Torkko, Vancouver Island University; Jeff Wheeler, Long Beach City College; and Kyle Wiggins, Boston University.

Chuck Christensen and Joan Feinberg, the founders of Bedford/St. Martin's, helped shape this project from its very beginning. They remain fine and thoughtful friends as well as fine and thoughtful editors. We thank Edwin Hill, Karen Henry, Leasa Burton, and John Sullivan for their continued guidance. John joined the group for the fifth edition. He had taught from an earlier edition of *Ways of Reading* and had, for us, a wonderful sense of the book's approach to reading, writing, and teaching. John is organized, resourceful, generous, quick to offer suggestions and to take on extra work. He soon became as much a collaborator as an editor. It was a real pleasure to work with him. We owe special thanks to Sarah Macomber, who solicited reviews and gathered new readings, and Caroline Thompson, who played a major role in helping to shape this new edition. Jennifer Kennett and Kerri Wilson handled permissions under the able guidance of Kalina Ingham and Martha Friedman. Cara Kaufman assisted with many details. Harold Chester expertly guided the manuscript through production. Jennifer Brett Greenstein was an excellent copy editor, sensitive to the quirks of our prose and attentive to detail.

And, finally, we are grateful to Joyce, to Vivian and Brie, and to Jesse, Dan, Kate, Matthew, and Ben, for their love and support.

ABOUT THE COVER

The covers for the eleven editions of *Ways of Reading* have all alluded to the history of the book. Our very first cover reproduced the marbled endpapers common in nineteenth-century book production.

The cover for this edition comes from *Idiom*, a sculptured environment by Slovakian artist Matej Krén (b. 1958). Krén is known for several large-scale structures (towers, cells, rotundas, dwellings) made entirely of books. *Idiom* (1995) was constructed for the International Biennial of São Paulo, Brazil. In 1998, it was installed in the Prague Municipal Library (Czech Republic).

Idiom is a tower made of hundreds of books, a cylinder that stands floor to ceiling with a large ten-foot gash in the front. There are mirrors at the top and bottom. When you look inside, you enter a tunnel leading to worlds far beyond the library.

In an era when texts circulate digitally, when the physical book is under threat, we were taken by Krén's work: walls and tunnels and fortifications, all made of bound books — as though books had gathered themselves for defense and protection, offering safe havens or routes of escape.

GET THE MOST OUT OF YOUR COURSE WITH *WAYS OF READING*

At Bedford/St. Martin's, providing support to teachers and their students who choose our books and digital tools is our first priority. The Bedford/St. Martin's English Community is now our home for professional resources, featuring Bedford *Bits*, our popular blog site offering new ideas for the composition class-room and composition teachers. In addition, you'll find an expanding collection of resources that support your teaching. Download titles from our professional resource series to support your teaching, review projects in the pipeline, sign up for professional development webinars, start a discussion, ask a question, and follow your favorite members. Join us to connect with other instructors at **community.macmillan.com**.

To learn more about or to order any of the following products, contact your Bedford/St. Martin's sales representative, e-mail sales support (**sales_support@ bfwpub.com**), or visit the website at **macmillanlearning.com**.

Choose from Alternative Formats of *Ways of Reading*

Bedford/St. Martin's offers a range of affordable formats, allowing students to choose the one that works best for them. For details, visit **macmillanlearning.com**.

- **Paperback.** To order the paperback edition, use ISBN 978-1-319-04014-7.
- **Other popular e-book formats.** For details about our e-book partners, visit **macmillanlearning.com/ebooks**.

Select Value Packages

Add value to your text by packaging one of the following resources with *Ways of Reading*. To learn more about package options for any of the following products, contact your Bedford/St. Martin's sales representative or visit **macmillanlearning.com**.

Writer's Help 2.0 is a powerful online writing resource that helps students find answers whether they are searching for writing advice on their own or as part of an assignment.

- **Smart search.** Built on research with more than 1,600 student writers, the smart search in Writer's Help 2.0 provides reliable results even when students use nov-ice terms, such as *flow* and *unstuck*.
- **Trusted content from our best-selling handbooks.** Choose *Writer's Help 2.0, Hacker Version* or *Writer's Help 2.0, Lunsford Version* and ensure that students have clear advice and examples for all of their writing questions.

- **Adaptive exercises that engage students.** Writer's Help 2.0 includes *Learning-Curve*, game-like online quizzing that adapts to what students already know and helps them focus on what they need to learn.

Student access is packaged with *Ways of Reading* at a significant discount. Order ISBN 978-1-319-10420-7 for *Writer's Help 2.0, Hacker Version* or ISBN 978-1-319-10416-0 for *Writer's Help 2.0, Lunsford Version* to ensure your students have easy access to online writing support. Students who rent a book or buy a used book can purchase access to Writer's Help 2.0 at **macmillanlearning.com/writershelp2**.

Instructors may request free access to Writer's Help 2.0 by registering as an instructor at **macmillanlearning.com/writershelp2**. For technical support, visit **macmillanlearning.com/getsupport**.

LaunchPad Solo for Readers and Writers allows students to work on whatever they need help with the most. At home or in class, students learn at their own pace, with instruction tailored to each student's unique needs. *LaunchPad Solo for Readers and Writers* includes the following features:

- **Pre-built units that support a learning arc.** Each easy-to-assign unit comprises a pre-test check, multimedia instruction and assessment, and a post-test that assesses what students have learned about critical reading, writing process, using sources, grammar, style, mechanics, and help for multilingual writers.
- **A video introduction to many topics.** Introductions offer an overview of the unit's topic, and many include a brief, accessible video to illustrate the concepts at hand.
- **Adaptive quizzing for targeted learning.** Most units include *LearningCurve*, game-like adaptive quizzing that focuses on the areas in which each student needs the most help.
- **The ability to monitor student progress.** Use our Gradebook to see which students are on track and which need additional help with specific topics.

LaunchPad Solo for Readers and Writers can be packaged **at a significant discount**. To ensure your students can take full advantage, contact your sales representative for a package ISBN. Visit **macmillanlearning.com/readwrite** for more information.

WriterKey. Built around best practices for feedback and revision, *WriterKey* puts student writers at the center of your course. Robust review tools allow you to quickly comment on assignments — using voice or text — and link to a flexible rubric and comment library all from one screen. Students use the same tools to reflect, ask for feedback on specific areas, and review each other's work. Powerful analytics, tied to instructor comments, show writers' strengths and areas for improvement. A side-by-side view of drafts lets students revise their work while they apply teacher and reviewer feedback. After revised drafts are submitted, instructors can compare drafts and view analytic data to see revision in action. For more, visit **ml.writerkey.com**.

Instructor Resources
macmillanlearning.com

You have a lot to do in your course. Bedford/St. Martin's wants to make it easy for you to find the support you need — and to get it quickly.

   Resources for Teaching Ways of Reading, an instructor's manual written by the authors of the textbook, is available as a PDF that can be downloaded from the Bedford/St. Martin's online catalog at the URL above. Visit the instructor resources tab for *Ways of Reading*. The manual includes ideas for teaching each selection and assignment sequence, a set of additional assignment sequences, and a collection of pedagogical essays written by instructors who have used *Ways of Reading*. An extensive overview offers answers to questions frequently asked about the book's approach, suggestions for including the book in TA training programs, and a "ToolKit" section with activities, assignments, and guidance for class work that bridges the gap between the challenging essays in the text and the realities of the composition classroom.

Contents

Introduction: Ways of Reading   1

The Readings   23

GLORIA ANZALDÚA, HOW TO TAME A WILD TONGUE   26

"So, if you really want to hurt me, talk badly about my language. Ethnic identity is twin skin to linguistic identity — I am my language. Until I can

"I have not kept my place. Like my mother and grandmother, I chose the earth — but the real earth, complicated and torn, not a post-Armageddon fantasy purveyed by a global religious organization with its own political and financial ends. I chose education, although, growing up, I knew no one who had graduated from college, aside from my schoolteachers and, briefly, my father's lawyer."

"At the time, I didn't realize that these small incidents were negotiations of power, contests over whose perspectives mattered and whose voices would be permitted and welcomed at the table."

[SELECTIONS FROM *Island of Bones*]

"Americans believe in the reality of 'race' as a defined, indubitable feature of the natural world. Racism — the need to ascribe bone-deep features to people and then humiliate, reduce, and destroy them — inevitably follows from this inalterable condition. In this way, racism is rendered as the innocent daughter of Mother Nature, and one is left to deplore the Middle Passage or the Trail of Tears the way one deplores an earthquake, a tornado, or any other phenomenon that can be cast as beyond the handiwork of men."

[FROM *Between the World and Me*]

"The ten years that follow youth, the years when first the realization comes that life is leading somewhere, — these were the years that passed after I left my little school."

"The function of the university is not simply to teach breadwinning, or to furnish teachers for the public schools, or to be a centre of polite society; it is, above all, to be the organ of that fine adjustment between real life and the growing knowledge of life, an adjustment which forms the secret of civilization."

"But when we have vaguely said that Education will set this tangle straight, what have we uttered but a truism? Training for life teaches living; but what training for the profitable living together of black men and white?"

[SELECTIONS FROM *The Souls of Black Folk*]

"Our society is one not of spectacle, but of surveillance; under the surface of images, one invests bodies in depth; behind the great abstraction of exchange, there continues the meticulous, concrete training of useful forces; the circuits of communication are the supports of an accumulation and a centralization of knowledge; the play of signs defines the anchorages of power; it is not that the beautiful totality of the individual is amputated, repressed, altered by our social order, it is rather that the individual is carefully fabricated in it, according to a whole technique of force and bodies."

[FROM *Discipline and Punish*]

"In our era of electronic communications, we've come to expect that important innovations will spread quickly. Plenty do: think of in-vitro fertilization, genomics, and communications technologies themselves. But there's an equally long list of vital innovations that have failed to catch on. The puzzle is why."

[FIRST APPEARED IN *The New Yorker*]

"The nightmare images of the German child-rearing practices that one discovers . . . call to mind the catastrophic events of recent German history. I first encountered this pedagogy in the writing of Alice Miller. At one time a psychoanalyst, she was haunted by a question, *What could make a person conceive the plan of gassing millions of human beings to death?* In her work, she traces the origins of this violence to childhood. Of course there cannot be one answer to such a monumental riddle, nor does any event in history have a single cause. Rather a field exists. . . ."

[FROM *A Chorus of Stones*]

"The first few seconds of a speech might sound more or less like oratory, but soon the competitors will be accelerating to nearly unintelligible speeds, pitch and volume rising, spit and sweat flying as they attempt to 'spread' their opponents — that is, to make more arguments and marshal more evidence than the other team can respond to within the allotted time, the rule being that a 'dropped argument,' no matter its quality, is conceded."

[FIRST APPEARED IN *Harper's Magazine*]

"Can secular institutions of higher education be taught to use writing to foster a kind of critical optimism that is able to transform idle feelings of hope into viable plans for sustainable action? Can the first year writing course become a place where we engage productively with the dark realities of our time: violence, suicide, war, and terrorism, as well as fraudulence, complicity, and trauma? Can teachers of first year writing be moved beyond praising students for generating arguments without consequence, thought with no interest in action?"

[FROM *Writing at the End of the World*]

"When a caste system becomes absolute, envy disappears. Yet the caste of layman-expert is not the fault of the expert. It is due altogether to the eager surrender of sovereignty by the layman so that he may take up the role not of the person but of the consumer."

[FROM *The Message in the Bottle*]

"Since nutrients, as compared with foods, are invisible and therefore slightly mysterious, it falls to the scientists (and to the journalists through whom the scientists reach the public) to explain the hidden reality of foods to us. In form this is a quasireligious idea, suggesting the visible world is not the one that really matters, which implies the need for a priesthood. For to enter the world where your dietary salvation depends on unseen nutrients, you need plenty of expert help."

[FROM *In Defense of Food: An Eater's Manifesto*]

"I use this term [contact zone] to refer to social spaces where cultures meet, clash, and grapple with each other, often in contexts of highly asymmetrical relations of power, such as colonialism, slavery, or their aftermaths as they are lived out in many parts of the world today. Eventually I will use the term to reconsider the models of community that many of us rely on in teaching and theorizing and that are under challenge today."

[FIRST APPEARED IN *Profession* 91]

"What I am about to say to you has taken me more than twenty years to admit: *A primary reason for my success in the classroom was that I couldn't forget that schooling was changing me and separating me from the life I enjoyed before becoming a student.* That simple realization! For years I never spoke to anyone about it. Never mentioned a thing to my family or my teachers or classmates."

[FROM *Hunger of Memory*]

"Exile is a series of portraits without names, without contexts. Images that are largely unexplained, nameless, mute. I look at them without precise anecdotal knowledge, but their realistic exactness nevertheless makes a deeper impression than mere information. I cannot reach the actual people who were photographed, except through a European photographer who saw them for me."

[FROM *After the Last Sky*]

"CRISPR technology offers a new outlet for the inchoate fear of tinkering with the fundamentals of life. There are many valid reasons to worry. But it is essential to assess both the risks and the benefits of any new technology. Most people would consider it dangerous to fundamentally alter the human gene pool to treat a disease like AIDS if we could cure it with medicine or a vaccine. But risks always depend on the potential result. If CRISPR helps unravel the mysteries of autism, contributes to a cure for a form of cancer, or makes it easier for farmers to grow more nutritious food while reducing environmental damage, the fears, like the many others before them, will almost certainly disappear."

[FIRST APPEARED IN *The New Yorker*]

"The hardest habit to break, since it was a habit of a lifetime, would be listening to myself listening to him. That habit would destroy any chance of seeing my brother on his terms; and seeing him in his terms, learning his terms, seemed the whole point of learning his story. However numerous and comforting the similarities, we were different. The world had seized on the difference, allowed me room to thrive, while he'd been forced into a cage. Why did it work out that way? What was the nature of the difference? Why did it haunt me? Temporarily at least, to answer these questions, I had to root my fiction-writing self out of our exchanges. I had to teach myself to listen."

[FROM *Brothers and Keepers*]

Assignment Sequences   663

Ways of Reading

AN ANTHOLOGY FOR WRITERS

Introduction:
Ways of Reading

MAKING A MARK

Reading involves a fair measure of push and shove. You make your mark on a text, and it makes its mark on you. Reading is not simply a matter of hanging back and waiting for a piece, or its author, to tell you what the writing has to say. In fact, one of the difficult things about reading is that the pages before you will begin to speak only when the authors are silent and you begin to speak in their place, sometimes for them — doing their work, continuing their projects — and sometimes for yourself, following your own agenda.

This is an unusual way to talk about reading, we know. We have not mentioned finding information or locating an author's purpose or identifying main ideas, useful though these skills are, because the purpose of our book is to offer you occasions to imagine other ways of reading. We think of reading as a social interaction. We need only look to the complex social interactions we engage in every day to imagine the multiple possibilities for reading — sometimes peaceful and polite, sometimes contentious, sometimes hesitant and difficult. If you imagine your reading as a particular kind of social interaction, then you might be able to imagine, for example, a text you might feel shy around, perhaps because it is behaving in a way you find unusual or difficult. You might imagine a text that encourages you, like a friend might — or a text that provokes you like an older brother. Thinking about reading this way means, of course, that you have to do your part of the interaction. Engaging with reading in these ways is an essential part of engaging with reading *as a writer*.

We'd like you to imagine that when you read the works we've collected here, somebody is saying something to you, and we'd like you to imagine that you are in a position to speak back, to say something of your own in turn. In other words, we are not presenting our book as a miniature library (a place to find information), and we do not think of you, the reader, as a term-paper writer (a person looking for information to summarize or report).

When you read, you hear an author's voice as you move along; you believe a person with something to say is talking to you. You pay attention, even when you don't completely understand what is being said, and you attempt to relate what the author says to what you already know or expect to hear or learn, trusting that it will all make sense in the end. Even if you don't quite grasp everything you are reading at every moment (and you won't), and even if you don't remember everything you've read (no reader does — at least not in long, complex pieces), you begin to see the outlines of the author's project, the patterns and rhythms of that particular way of seeing and interpreting the world.

When you stop to talk or write about what you've read, the author is silent; you take over — it is your turn to write, to begin responding to what the author said. At that point, this author and his or her text become something you construct out of what you remember or what you notice as you go back through the text a second time, working from passages or examples, but filtering them through your own predisposition to see or read in particular ways.

In "The Achievement of Desire," one of the essays in this book, Richard Rodriguez tells the story of his education, of how he was drawn to imitate his teachers because of his desire to think and speak like them. His is not a simple story of hard work and success, however. In a sense, Rodriguez's education gave him what he wanted — status, knowledge, a way of understanding himself and his position in the world. At the same time, his education made it difficult to talk to his parents, to share their point of view; and to a degree, he felt himself becoming consumed by the powerful ways of seeing and understanding represented by his reading and his education. The essay can be seen as Rodriguez's attempt to weigh what he has gained against what he has lost.

If ten of us read his essay, each would begin with the same words on the page, but when we discuss or write about the essay, each will retell and interpret Rodriguez's story differently; we will emphasize different sections — some, for instance, might want to discuss the strange way Rodriguez learned to read, others might be taken by his difficult and changing relations to his teachers, and still others might want to think about Rodriguez's remarks about his mother and father.

Each of us will come to his or her own sense of what is significant, of what the point is, and the odds are good that what each of us makes of the essay will vary. We will all understand Rodriguez's story in our own ways, even though we read the same piece. At the same time, if we are working with Rodriguez's essay (and not putting it aside or ignoring its peculiar way of thinking about education), we will be working within a framework he has established, one that makes education stand, metaphorically, for a complicated interplay between permanence and change, imitation and freedom, loss and achievement.

In "The Achievement of Desire," Rodriguez tells of reading a book by Richard Hoggart, *The Uses of Literacy*. He was captivated by a section of this book in which

Hoggart defines a particular kind of student, the "scholarship boy." Here is what Rodriguez says:

> Then one day, leafing through Richard Hoggart's *The Uses of Literacy*, I found, in his description of the scholarship boy, myself. For the first time I realized that there were other students like me, and so I was able to frame the meaning of my academic success, its consequent price — the loss. (p. 535)

For Rodriguez, this phrase, "scholarship boy," became the focus of Hoggart's book. Other people, to be sure, would read that book and take different phrases or sections as the key to what Hoggart has to say. Some might argue that Rodriguez misread the book, that it is really about something else, about British culture, for example, or about the class system in England. The power and value of Rodriguez's reading, however, are represented by what he was able to *do* with what he read, not record information or summarize main ideas but, as he says, "frame the meaning of my academic success." Hoggart provided a frame, a way for Rodriguez to think and talk about his own history as a student. As he goes on in his essay, Rodriguez not only uses this frame to talk about his experience, but he resists it, argues with it. He casts his experience in Hoggart's terms, but then makes those terms work for him by seeing both what they can and what they cannot do. This combination of reading, thinking, and writing is what we mean by *active reading*, a way of reading we like to encourage in our students, a way of reading that invites students to think of themselves as strong readers, readers capable of creating their own unique and innovative readings even when they are not experts on the subject an author undertakes.

When we have taught "The Achievement of Desire" to our students, it has been almost impossible for them not to see themselves in Rodriguez's description of the scholarship boy (and this was true of students who were not minority students and not literally on scholarships). They, too, have found a way of framing (even inventing) their own lives as students — students whose histories involve both success and loss. When we have asked our students to write about this essay, however, some students have argued, and quite convincingly, that Rodriguez had to either abandon his family and culture or remain ignorant. Other students have argued equally convincingly that Rodriguez's anguish was destructive and self-serving, that he was trapped into seeing his situation in terms that he might have replaced with others. He did not necessarily have to turn his back on his family. Some have contended that Rodriguez's problems with his family had nothing to do with what he says about education, that he himself shows how imitation need not blindly lead a person away from his culture, and these student essays, too, have been convincing. And some students have imagined Rodriguez's piece as raising complex questions rather than inviting us to come to particular conclusions about education, culture, or family. Interacting with texts might mean, at times, making arguments or drawing conclusions about that text. But sometimes it can also mean recognizing the aspects of a text that might be posing unanswerable and complicated questions, questions that invite us to explore or inquire rather than to take a stance. When you begin to speak, what you have to say might not be a statement; it might be a question, an unsolvable problem, or a way of extending the work you see the author doing.

Reading, in other words, can be the occasion for you to put things together, to notice this idea or theme rather than that one, to follow a writer's announced or secret ends while simultaneously following your own, to articulate or acknowledge what you think the set of questions an author raises invites you to ask. When this happens, when you forge a reading of a story or an essay, you make your mark on it, casting it in your terms. But the story makes its mark on you as well, teaching you not only about a subject (Rodriguez's struggles with his teachers and his parents, for example) but also about a way of seeing and understanding a subject. The text provides the opportunity for you to see through someone else's powerful language, to imagine your own familiar settings through the images, metaphors, and ideas of others. Rodriguez's essay, in other words, can make its mark on readers, but they, too, if they are active readers, can make theirs on it. Just as you engage in various ways of reading while you read "The Achievement of Desire," Rodriguez, through his writing, also engages in ways of reading; he offers you his angle of looking; his writing invites you to see as he sees, to take up what it might mean to see the world from his viewpoint. An active reader tries, in her first reading, to understand the way of reading enacted by an author. Understanding the angle from which Rodriguez sees and reads the world helps an active reader respond more powerfully as a writer.

Readers learn to put things together by writing. This is not something you can do, at least not to any degree, while you are reading. It requires that you work on what you have read, and this work best takes shape when you sit down to write. We will have more to say about this kind of thinking in a later section of the introduction, but for now let us say that writing gives you a way of going to work on the text you have read. To write about a story or an essay, you go back to what you have read to find phrases or passages that define what for you are the key moments, those that help you interpret sections that seem difficult or troublesome or mysterious. If you are writing an essay of your own, the work that you are doing gives a purpose and a structure to that rereading.

READERS LEARN TO PUT THINGS TOGETHER BY WRITING.

Writing also, however, gives you a way of going back to work on the text of your own reading. It allows you to be self-critical and self-reflexive. You can revise not just to make your essay neat or tight or tidy but to see what kind of reader you have been, to examine the pattern and consequences in the choices you have made. Revision, in other words, gives you the chance to work on your essay, but it also gives you an opportunity to work on your reading—to qualify or extend or question your interpretation of, say, "The Achievement of Desire."

We can describe this process of "re-vision," or re-seeing, fairly simply. You should not expect to read "The Achievement of Desire" once and completely understand the essay or know what you want to say. You will work out what you have to say while you write. And once you have constructed a reading—once you have completed a draft of your essay, in other words—you can step back, see what you have done, and go back to work on it. Through this activity—writing and rewriting—we have seen our students become active and critical readers.

Not everything a reader reads is worth that kind of effort. The pieces we have chosen for this book all provide, we feel, powerful ways of seeing (or framing) our common experience. The selections cannot be quickly summarized. They are striking, surprising, sometimes troubling in how they challenge common ways of seeing the world. Some of them have captured and altered the way our culture sees and understands daily experience. The essays have changed the ways people think and write. In fact, every selection in the book is one that has given us, our students, and our colleagues that dramatic experience, almost like a discovery, when we suddenly saw things as we had never seen them before and, as a consequence, we had to work hard to understand what had happened and how our thinking had changed.

If we recall, for example, the first time we read Susan Griffin's "Our Secret" or John Edgar Wideman's "Our Time," we know that they have radically shaped our thinking. We carry these essays with us in our minds, mulling over them, working through them, hearing Griffin and Wideman in sentences we write or read. We introduce the essays in classes we teach whenever we can; we are surprised, reading them for the third or fourth time, to find things we didn't see before. It's not that we failed to "get" these essays the first time around. In fact, we're not sure we have captured them yet, at least not in any final sense, and we disagree in basic ways about what Griffin and Wideman are saying, about what questions are central to their inquiry, or about how these essays might best be used. Essays like these are not the sort that you can "get" like a loaf of bread at the store. We're each convinced that the essays are ours in that we know best what's going on in them, and yet we have also become theirs, creatures of these essays, because of the ways they have come to influence our seeing, talking, reading, and writing. This power of influence is something we welcome, yet it is also something we resist.

Our experience with these texts is a remarkable one and certainly hard to provide for others, but the challenges and surprises are reasons we read — we hope to be taken and changed in just these ways. Or, to be more accurate, it is why we read outside the daily requirements to keep up with the news or conduct our business. And it is why we bring reading into our writing courses.

WAYS OF READING

Before explaining how we organized this book, we would like to say more about the purpose and place of the kind of active, labor-intensive reading we've been referring to.

Readers face many kinds of experiences, and certain texts are written with specific situations in mind and invite specific ways of reading. Some texts, for instance, serve very practical purposes — they give directions or information. Others, like the short descriptive essays often used in English textbooks and anthologies, celebrate common and conventional ways of thinking and ask primarily to be admired. These texts seem self-contained; they announce their own meanings with little effort and ask little from the reader, making it clear how they want to be read and what they have to say. They ask only for a nod of the head or for the reader to take notes and give a sigh of admiration ("yes, that was very well said"). They are clear and direct. It is as though the authors could anticipate all the questions their essays might raise and solve all the problems a reader might imagine. There is not much work for a reader to do, in other words, except perhaps to take notes and, in the case of textbooks, to work step-by-step, trying to remember as much as possible. These readings mostly require us to behave ourselves, to accept what they offer and recall it later.

This is how assigned readings are often presented in university classrooms. Introductory textbooks (in biology or business, for instance) are good examples of books that ask to be read dutifully and passively. In these texts the writers are experts, and your job, as novice, is to digest what they have to say. And, perhaps appropriately at times, the task set before you is to summarize — so you can speak again to what the author said, so you can better remember what you read. Essay tests are an example of the writing tasks that often follow this kind of reading. You might, for instance, study the human nervous system through textbook readings and lectures and then be asked to write a summary of what you know from both sources. Or a teacher might ask you during a class discussion to paraphrase a paragraph from a textbook describing chemical cell communication to see if you understand what you've read.

Another typical classroom form of reading is reading for main ideas. With this kind of reading you are expected to figure out what most people (or most people within a certain specialized group of readers) would take as the main idea of a selection. There are good reasons to read for main ideas. For one, it is a way to learn how to imagine and anticipate the values and habits of a particular group — test-makers or, if you're studying business, Keynesian economists, perhaps. If you are studying business, to continue this example, you must learn to notice what Keynesian economists notice — for instance, when they analyze the problems of growing government debt — to share key terms, to know the theoretical positions they take, and to adopt for yourself their common examples and interpretations, their jargon, and their established findings.

There is certainly nothing wrong with reading for information or reading to learn what experts have to say about their fields of inquiry. These are not, however, the only ways to read, although they are the ones most often taught. Perhaps because we think of ourselves as writing teachers, we are concerned with presenting other ways of reading in the college and university curriculum.

A danger arises in assuming that reading is only a search for information or main ideas. There are ways of thinking through problems and working with written texts that are essential to our academic, professional, and personal lives, but that are not represented by summary and paraphrase or by note-taking and essay exams.

Student readers, for example, can take responsibility for determining the meaning of the text. They can work as though they were doing something other than finding ideas already there on the page, and they can be guided by their own impressions or questions as they read. We are not, now, talking about finding hidden meanings. If such things as hidden meanings can be said to exist, they are hidden by readers' habits and prejudices (by readers' assumptions that what they read should tell them what they already know) or by readers' timidity and passivity (by their unwillingness to take the responsibility to say what they notice or to pose their own questions).

Reading to locate meaning in the text places a premium on memory, yet an active reader is not necessarily a person with a good memory. This point may seem minor, but we have seen too many students haunted because they could not remember everything they read or retain a complete essay in their minds. A reader could set herself the task of remembering as much as she could from Walker Percy's "The Loss of the Creature," an essay filled with stories about tourists at the Grand Canyon and students in a biology class, but a reader could also do other things with that essay; a reader might figure out, for example, how students and tourists might be said to have a common problem seeing what they want to see. Students who read Percy's essay as a memory test end up worrying about bits and pieces (bits and pieces they could go back and find, if they had to) and turn their attention away from the more pressing problem of how to make sense of a difficult and often ambiguous essay.

A reader who needs to have access to something in the essay can use simple memory aids. A reader can go back and scan, for one thing, to find passages or examples that might be worth reconsidering. Or a reader can construct a personal index, making marks in the margin or underlining passages that seem interesting or mysterious or difficult. A mark is a way of saying, "This is something I might want to work on later." If you mark the selections in this book as you read them, you will give yourself a working record of what, at the first moment of reading, you felt might be worth a second reading.

If Percy's essay presents problems for a reader, they are problems of a different order from summary and recall. The essay is not the sort that tells you what it says. You would have difficulty finding one sentence that sums up or announces, in a loud and clear voice, what Percy is talking about. In fact, Percy's essay is challenging reading in part because it does not have a single easily identifiable main idea. A reader could infer that it has several points to make, none of which can be said easily, and some of which, perhaps, are contradictory. To search for information, or to ignore the rough edges in search of a single, paraphrasable idea, is to divert attention from the task at hand, which is not to remember what Percy says, but to speak about the essay and what it means to you, the reader. In this sense, the Percy essay is not the sum of its individual parts; it is, more accurately, what its readers make of it.

A reader could go to an expert on Percy to solve the problem of what to make of the essay — perhaps to a teacher, perhaps to the Internet or to a book in the library. And if the reader pays attention, he could remember what the expert said, or she could take notes. But in doing either, the reader only rehearses the thoughts of others, abandoning the responsibility to make the essay meaningful, to become invested in the essay for one's own purposes. There are ways of reading, in other words, in which Percy's essay "The Loss of the Creature" is not what it means to the experts but what it means to you as a reader willing to take the chance to construct a reading. You can be the authority on Percy; you don't have to turn to others. The meaning of the essay, then, is something you develop as you go along, something for which you must take final responsibility. The meaning is forged from reading the essay, to be sure, but it is determined by what you *do* with the essay, by the connections you can make and your explanation of why those connections are important. This version of Percy's essay will finally be yours;

it will not be exactly what Percy said. (Only his words in the order he wrote them would say exactly what he said.) You will choose the path to take through his essay.

You'll notice (and we will discuss later) that we offer some "Questions for a Second Reading" once you've read through a piece one time. But what about that first reading, that first time you read a challenging and multidimensional piece of writing like the ones you find here? There are many ways to engage with a text as you read it for the first time. It's important to have a way to write on the text itself — not just to highlight sections you find interesting, troubling, or confusing (though you might do that, too), but to keep notes to yourself in the margins, perhaps writing questions that come up for you as you read, or writing down key words that will help you remember why you marked that particular place. Sometimes, with particularly difficult readings, we ask students to mark words, names, or phrases that they think would be useful hyperlinks — moments in the text where you wish you could click on the word or phrase in order to find out more. If you try this on your first read-through, you might learn something important; you might learn what you don't yet know about the text. Oftentimes, being an engaged reader means paying attention both to what is familiar and what is unfamiliar about what you are reading.

If an essay or a story is not the sum of its parts but something you as a reader create by putting together those parts that seem to matter to you, then the way to begin, once you have read a selection in this collection, is by reviewing what you recall, by going back to those places that stick in your memory — or, perhaps, to those sections you marked with checks or notes in the margins. You can even return to those moments in which you *didn't* know exactly where the text was trying to lead you.

You begin by seeing what you can make of these memories and notes. You should realize that with essays as long and complex as those we've included in this book, you will never feel, after a single reading, as though you have command of everything you read. This is not a problem. After four or five readings (should you give any single essay that much attention), you may still feel that there are parts you missed or don't understand. This sense of incompleteness is part of the experience of reading. And it is part of the experience of an active reader. No reader could retain one of these essays in her mind, no matter how proficient her memory or how experienced she might be. No reader, at least no reader we would trust, would claim that he understood everything that Michel Foucault or Judith Butler or Edward Said had to say. What engaged and active readers know is that they have to begin, and they have to begin regardless of their doubts or hesitations. After your first reading of an essay, you have a starting place, and you begin with your marked passages or examples or notes, with questions to answer, or with problems to solve. Active readings, in other words, put a premium on individual acts of attention and composition.

ENGAGED READERS, ENGAGING TEXTS

We chose pieces for this book that invite engaged readings. Our selections require more attention (or a different form of attention) than a written summary, a reduction to gist, or a recitation of main ideas. These are not "easy" reading. The challenges they present, however, do not make them inaccessible to college students. The essays are not specialized studies; they have interested, pleased, or piqued general and specialist audiences alike. To say that they are challenging is to say, then, that they leave some work for a reader to do. They are designed to teach a reader new ways to read (or to step outside habitual ways of reading), and they anticipate readers willing to take the time to learn. These readers need not be experts on the subject matter. Perhaps the most difficult problem for students is to believe that this is true.

You do not need experts to explain these stories and essays, although you could probably go to the library and find an expert guide to most of the selections we've included. Let's take, for example, John Berger's essay "Ways of Seeing." You could go to the library to find out how Berger is understood and regarded by experts, by literary critics or art historians, for example; you could learn how his work fits into an established body of work on art and representation. You could see what others have said about the writers he cites — Walter Benjamin, for example. You could see how others have read and made use of Berger. You could track one of his key terms, like "mystification."

Though it is often important to seek out other texts and to know what other people are saying or have said, it is often necessary and even desirable to begin on your own. Berger can also be read outside any official system of interpretation. He is talking, after all, about our daily experience. And when he addresses the reader, he addresses a person — not a five-paragraph formula writer. When he says, "The way we see things is affected by what we know and what we believe," *you* are part of that construction, part of the "we" he is invoking.

The primary question, then, is not what Berger's words might mean to an art historian or to those with credentials as professors or as cultural critics. The question is what you, the reader, can make of those words given your own experience, your goals, and the work you do with what he has written. In this sense, "Ways of Seeing" is not what it means to others (those who have already decided what it means) but what it means to you, and this meaning is something you compose when you write about the essay, even if the meaning you construct is tentative or uncertain.

I. A. Richards, a teacher, poet, and critic we admire, once said, "Read as though it made sense and perhaps it will." To take command of complex material like the selections in this book, you need not subordinate yourself to experts; you can assume the authority to provide such a reading on your own. This means you must allow yourself a certain tentativeness and recognize your limits. You should not assume that it is your job to solve all the problems these essays present. You can speak with authority while still acknowledging that complex issues *are* complex.

In "The American Scholar," Ralph Waldo Emerson says, "Meek young men grow up in libraries, believing it their duty to accept the views, which Cicero, which Locke, which Bacon, have given, forgetful that Cicero, Locke, and Bacon were only young men in libraries when they wrote these books." What Emerson offers here is not a fact but an attitude. There is creative reading, he says, as well as creative writing. It is up to you to treat authors as your equals, as people who will allow you to speak, too. At the same time, you must respect the difficulty and complexity of their texts and of the issues and questions they examine. Little is to be gained, in other words, by turning a complex essay into a message that would fit on a poster in a dorm room: "Be Yourself" or "Stand on Your Own Two Feet."

READING WITH AND AGAINST THE GRAIN

Reading, then, requires a difficult mix of authority and humility. On the one hand, a reader takes charge of a text; on the other, a reader gives generous attention to someone else's (a writer's) key terms and methods, commits his time to her examples, tries to think in her language, and imagines that this strange work is important and compelling, at least for the moment. If, as we suggested earlier, reading is a kind of social interaction, this means you are equally a listener and a responder. It might help to think about what it really means to listen to another person, to try to understand his or her point of view, before offering your own response.

Most of the questions in *Ways of Reading* will have you moving back and forth in these two modes, reading with and against the grain of a text, reproducing an author's methods, questioning his or her direction and authority. With Susan Bordo's essay "Beauty (Re)discovers the Male Body," for example, we have asked students to look at images from the contemporary media, to think about them in terms of her argument, and to write about them as she might — to see them and to understand them in her terms, through the lens of her essay. We have asked students to give themselves over to this essay, in other words — recognizing that this is not necessarily an easy thing to do. Notice what she would notice. Ask the questions she would ask. Try out her conclusions.

To read generously, to work inside someone else's system, to see your world in someone else's terms — we call this "reading with the grain." It is a way of working *with* a writer's ideas, in conjunction with someone else's text. As a way of reading, it can take different forms. In the reading and writing assignments that follow the selections in this book, you will sometimes be asked to summarize and paraphrase, to put others' ideas into your terms, to provide your account of what they are saying. This is a way of getting a tentative or provisional hold on a text, its examples and ideas; it allows you a place to begin to work. And sometimes you will be asked to extend a writer's project — to add your examples to someone else's argument, to read your experience through the frame of another's text, to try out the key terms and interpretive schemes in another writer's work. In the assignments that follow Bordo's essay, for example, students are asked both to reproduce her argument and to extend her terms to examples from their own experience.

We have also asked students to read against the grain, to read critically, to turn back, for example, *against* Bordo's project, to ask questions they believe might come as a surprise, to look for the limits of her vision, to provide alternate readings of her examples, to find examples that challenge her argument — to engage her, in other words, in dialogue. Susan Bordo, we say, is quite specific about her age and her experience, her point of view. You are placed at a different moment in time, your experience is different, your schooling and your exposure to images have prepared you differently. Your job, then, is not simply to reproduce Bordo's project in your writing and thinking, but to refine it, to extend it, to put it to the test.

Many of the essays in this book provide examples of writers working against the grain of common sense or everyday language. This is true of John Berger, for example, who redefines the "art museum" against the way it is usually understood. It is true of John Edgar Wideman, who reads against his own text while he writes it—asking questions that disturb the story as it emerges on the page. It is true of Judith Butler, Susan Griffin, and Kwame Anthony Appiah, whose writings show the signs of their efforts to work against the grain of the standard essay, of habitual ways of representing what it means to know something, to be somebody, to speak before others.

/ MANY OF THE ESSAYS IN THIS
BOOK PROVIDE EXAMPLES OF
WRITERS WORKING AGAINST THE
GRAIN OF COMMON SENSE OR
EVERYDAY LANGUAGE.

This, we've found, is the most difficult work for students to do, this working against the grain. For reasons good and bad, students typically define their skill by reproducing, rather than questioning or revising the work of their teachers (or the work of those their teachers ask them to read). It is important to read generously and carefully, and to learn to listen to the projects others have begun. But it is also important to know what you are doing — to understand where this work comes from, whose interests it serves, how and where it is kept together by will rather than desire, and what it might have to do with you. To fail to ask the fundamental questions — Where am I in this? How can I make my mark? Whose interests are represented? What can I learn by reading with or against the grain? — is to mistake skill for understanding, and it is to misunderstand the goals of a liberal education. All of the essays in this book, we would argue, ask to be read, not simply reproduced; they ask to be read and to be read with a difference. Our goal is to make that difference possible.

Reading with and against the grain is one way to think about the work of reading. And even within this metaphor, there are more than two ways of reading. But we might also extend the work of the metaphor. Our students have explored this metaphor and have even come up with metaphors of their own for thinking about what reading is and what it means to do a reading. One student described reading as much like walking to the grocery store — one could take a direct route, focusing on the ultimate goal, perhaps making a list of items as he walked. One could also meander, not worrying about time or what items to purchase, but thinking instead about the sunset or the traffic patterns. Readers can be, in many ways, like walkers — sometimes focused and clear on their goals, sometimes allowing their minds to wander or notice something *other* than getting to the grocery store, sometimes ending up in places they didn't think they were going. Another student likened her reading to looking through a telescope in her astronomy course. For her, reading was like forming constellations, looking at a night sky for those sets of glimmers that might form something familiar, something she could name. A student who was studying civil engineering explained how reading, for him, seemed much like designing a bridge that connects two places. "It can look simple," he writes in an in-class writing activity. "When you drive over a bridge, you don't think about how many tiny details have gone into making the bridge stand. Reading is like that, too. Seems simple, but it's not." You might think of reading in a number of ways. The important part is that you broaden your understanding of what it means to read, that you challenge yourself to read in new ways so that you might then write in new ways as well.

WORKING WITH DIFFICULTY

When we chose the selections for this textbook, we chose them with the understanding that they are difficult to read. And we chose them knowing that students are not their primary audience, that the selections are not speaking directly to you. We chose them, in other words, knowing that we would be asking you to read something you were most likely not prepared to read. But this is what it means to be a student, and it is our goal to take our students seriously. Students have to do things they are not yet ready to do; this is how they learn. Students need to read materials that they are not yet ready to read. This is how they get started; this is where they begin. It is also the case that, in an academic setting, difficulty is not necessarily a problem. If something is hard to read, it is not necessarily the case that the writer is at fault. The work can be hard to read because the writer is thinking beyond the usual ways of thinking. It is hard because it *is* hard, in other words. The text is not saying the same old things in the same old ways.

We believe the best way to work on a difficult text is by *re*reading, and we provide exercises to direct this process ("Questions for a Second Reading"), but you can also work on the difficult text by writing — by taking possession of the work through sentences and paragraphs of your own, through summary, paraphrase, and quotation, by making another writer's work part of your work. The textbook is organized to provide ways for you to work on these difficult selections by writing and rereading. Each of the selections is followed by questions designed to help you get started.

To get a better sense of what we mean by "working with difficulty," it might be useful to look at an example. One of the selections in previous editions of *Ways of Reading* was a chapter from a book titled *Pedagogy of the Oppressed*, by the Brazilian educator Paulo Freire. The chapter is titled "The 'Banking' Concept of Education," and the title summarizes the argument at its most simple level. The standard forms of education, Freire argues, define the teacher as the active agent and the student as the passive agent. The teacher has knowledge and makes deposits from this storehouse into the minds of students, who are expected to receive these deposits completely and without alteration — like moving money from a wallet to the bank vault. And this, he argues, is not a good thing.

One of the writing assignments attached to this selection asked students to think along with Freire and to use his argument to examine a situation from their own experience with schooling. Here is an essay (a very skillful essay) that we received from a freshman in the opening weeks of class. It is relatively short and to the point. It will be familiar. You should have no trouble following it, even without having read the selection by Freire.

The "Banking" Concept of Education

As a high school senior, I took a sociology class that was a perfect example of the "banking" concept of education, as described by Freire. There were approximately thirty students enrolled in the class. Unless each of our brains was computerized for long-term memorization, I don't understand how we were expected to get anything out of the class.

Each class began with the copying of four to five pages of notes, which were already written on the blackboards when we entered the classroom. Fifteen to twenty minutes later, the teacher proceeded to pass out a worksheet, which was to be filled out using only the notes we previously copied as our reference. If a question was raised, her reply was, "It's in the notes."

With approximately ten minutes left in the period, we were instructed to pass our worksheets back one desk. Then, she read the answers to the worksheets and gave a grade according to how many questions we answered correctly.

During the semester, we didn't have any quizzes, and only one test, which consisted of matching and listing-type questions. All test information was taken directly from the daily worksheets, and on no occasion did she give an essay question. This is an example of a test question:

Name three forms of abuse that occur in the family.

1.

2.

3.

In order to pass the class, each piece of information printed on her handouts needed to be memorized. On one occasion, a fellow classmate summed up her technique of teaching perfectly by stating, "This is nothing but education by memorization!"

Anyone who cared at all about his grade in the class did quite well, according to his report card. Not much intelligence is required to memorize vocabulary terms. Needless to say, not too many of us learned much from the class, except that "education by memorization" and the "banking" concept of education, as Freire puts it, are definitely not an interesting or effective system of education.

The essay is confident and tidy and not wrong in its account of the "banking" concept of education. In six short paragraphs, the writer not only "got" Freire but also worked his high school sociology teacher and her teaching methods into the "banking" narrative. We asked the student (as we have asked many students since then): How did you do this? What was the secret? And he was quick to answer, "I read through the Freire essay, and I worked with what I understood and I ignored the rest." And it's true; he did. This is one way to get started. It's OK. You work with what you can.

The difficult sections of Freire's argument (the hard parts, the sections, and the passages our writer ignored) are related to a Marxist analysis of a *system* of education and its interests. Freire does not write just about individuals—a bad teacher and a smart student—although it is certainly easier (and in some ways more comforting) to think that schooling is simply a matter of individual moments and individual actors, good and bad. What is happening in our classrooms, Freire argues, is bigger than the intentions or actions of individuals. He says, for example, "Education as the exercise of domination stimulates the credulity of students, with the ideological intent (often not perceived by educators) of indoctrinating them to adapt to the world of oppression." He writes about how schools "regulate the way the world 'enters into' students." He calls for "problem-posing education": "Problem-posing education is revolutionary futurity." What is at stake, he says, is "humanity." What is required is *conscientização.* He is concerned to promote education in service of "revolution": "A deepened consciousness of their situation leads people to apprehend that situation as an historical reality susceptible of transformation." There is more going on here, in other words, than can be represented simply by a teacher who is lazy or unimaginative.

The student's essay marks a skillful performance. He takes Freire's chapter and makes it consistent with what he knows to say. You hear that in this statement: "'education by memorization' and the 'banking' concept of education, as Freire puts it, are definitely not an interesting or effective system of education." Freire's language becomes consistent with his own (the "banking" concept can be filed away under "education by memorization"), and once this is achieved, the writer's need to do any real work with Freire's text becomes unnecessary— "needless to say." Working with difficult readings often requires a willingness to step outside of what you can conveniently control, and this process often begins with revision. As important as it was for this student to use his essay to get hold of Freire, to open a door or to get a handhold, a place of purchase, a way to begin, it is equally important for a writer to take the next step—and the next step is to revise, particularly where revision is a way of reworking rather than just "fixing" what you have begun.

This was a student of ours, and after talking with him about the first draft, we suggested that he reread "The 'Banking' Concept of Education," this time paying particular attention to the difficult passages, the passages that were hard to understand, those that he had ignored the first time around. We suggested that his revised essay should bring some of those passages into the text. He did just this, and by changing the notion of what he was doing (by working *with* rather than *in spite of* difficulty), he wrote a very different essay. This was real revision, in other words, not just a matter of smoothing out the rough edges. The revision changed the way the writer read, and it changed the way the reader wrote. The revised essay was quite different (and not nearly so confident and skillful—and this was a good thing, a sign of learning). Here is a representative passage:

We never really had to "think" in the class. In fact, we were never permitted to "think," we were merely expected to take in the information and

store it like a computer. Freire calls this act a "violation of [men's] humanity" (p. 85). He states, "Any situation in which some individuals prevent others
from engaging in the process of inquiry is one of violence" (p. 85). I believe
what Freire is speaking of here is . . .

We'll keep his conclusion to ourselves, since the conclusion is not nearly so
important as what has happened to the writer's understanding of what it means
to work on a reading. In this revised paragraph, he brings in phrases from the text,
and the phrases he brings in are not easy to handle; he has to struggle to put
them to use or to make them make sense. The writer is trying to figure out the
urgency in Freire's text. The story of the sociology class was one thing, but how
do you get from there to a statement about a "violation of men's humanity"? The
passage that is quoted is not just dumped in for color; it is there for the writer to
work with, to try to deploy. And that is what comes next:

He states, "Any situation in which some individuals prevent others from
engaging in the process of inquiry is one of violence" (p. 85). I believe
what Freire is speaking of here is . . .

The key moment in writing like this is the moment of translation: "I believe
what Freire is speaking of here is . . ." This is where the writer must step forward
to take responsibility for working inside the terms of Freire's project.

There is much to admire in this revision. It was early in the semester when
writing is always risky, and it took courage and determination for a student to
work with what he couldn't quite understand, couldn't sum up easily, couldn't
command. You can see, even in this brief passage, that the writing has lost some
of the confidence (or arrogance) of the first draft, and as the writer works to think
with Freire about education as a system, the characters of the "student" and the
"teacher" become different in this narrative. And this is good writing. It may not
be as finished as it might need to be later in the semester, but it is writing where
something is happening, where thought is taken seriously.

So, how do you work with a difficult text? You have to get started somewhere
and sometime, and you will almost always find yourself writing before you have
a sense that you have fully comprehended what you have read. You have to
get started somewhere, and then you can go back to work again on what you
have begun by rereading and rewriting. The textbook provides guidelines for
rereading.

When you are looking for help with a particular selection, you can, for example, turn to the "Questions for a Second Reading." Read through *all* of them,
whether they are assigned or not, since they provide several entry points, different ways in, many of them suggested to us by our students in class and in their
essays. You might imagine that these questions and the writing assignments that
follow (and you might read through these writing assignments, too) provide
starting points. Each suggests a different path through the essay. No one can hold
a long and complicated essay in mind all at once. Every reader needs a starting
point, a way in. Having more than one possible starting point allows you to make
choices.

Once you have an entry point, where you have entered and how you have entered will help shape your sense of what is interesting or important in the text. In this sense, you (and not just the author) are organizing the essay or chapter. The text will present its shape in terms of sections or stages. You should look for these road signs—breaks in the text or phrases that indicate intellectual movement, like "on the other hand" or "in conclusion." You can be guided by these, to be sure, but you also give shape to what you read—and you do this most deliberately when you reread. This is where you find (and impose) patterns and connections that are not obvious and not already articulated but that make sense to you and give you a way to describe what you see in what you are reading. In our own teaching, we talk to our students about "scaffolds." The scaffold, we say, represents the way you are organizing the text, the way you are putting it together. A scaffold is made up of lines and passages from the text, the terms you've found that you want to work with, ideas that matter to you, your sense of the progress of the piece.

> IN OUR OWN TEACHING, WE TALK TO OUR STUDENTS ABOUT "SCAFFOLDS." THE SCAFFOLD, WE SAY, REPRESENTS THE WAY YOU ARE ORGANIZING THE TEXT, THE WAY YOU ARE PUTTING IT TOGETHER.

The scaffold can also include the work of others. In groups or in class discussion, take notes on what other students say. This is good advice generally (you can always learn from your colleagues), but it is particularly useful in a class that features reading and writing. Your notes can document the ideas of others, to be sure, but most important, they can give you a sense of where other people are beginning, of where they have entered the text and what they are doing once they have started. You can infer the scaffold they have constructed to make sense of what they read, and this can give highlight and relief, even counterpoint, to your own. And use your teacher's comments and questions, including those on your first drafts, to get a sense of the shape of your work as a reader and a writer. This is not a hunt for ideas, for the right or proper or necessary thing to say about a text. It is a hunt for a method, for a way of making sense of a text without resorting only to summary.

READING AND WRITING: THE QUESTIONS AND ASSIGNMENTS

Active readers, we've said, remake what they have read to serve their own ends, putting things together, figuring out how ideas and examples relate, explaining as best they can material that is difficult or problematic, translating phrases like Richard Rodriguez's "scholarship boy" into their own terms. At these moments, it is hard to distinguish the act of reading from the act of writing. In fact, the connection between reading and writing can be seen as almost a literal one, since the best way you can show your reading of a rich and dense essay like "The Achievement of Desire" is by writing down your thoughts, placing one idea against another, commenting on what you've done, taking examples into account, looking back at where you began, perhaps changing your mind, and moving on.

Readers, however, seldom read a single essay in isolation, as though their only job were to arrive at some sense of what an essay has to say. Although we couldn't begin to provide examples of all the various uses of these ways of reading, it is often the case that readings provide information and direction for investigative projects, whether they are philosophical or scientific in nature. The reading and writing assignments that follow each selection in this book are designed to point you in certain directions, to give you ideas and projects to work with, and to challenge you to see one writer's ideas through another's.

You will find that the questions we have included in our reading and writing assignments often direct you to test what you think an author is saying by measuring it against your own experience. One way for you to develop or test your reading of an essay is to place what the author says in the context of your own experience, searching for examples that are similar to and examples that differ from the author's examples. If the writers in this book are urging you to give strong readings of your common experience, you have access to what they say because they are talking not only to you but about you. You can try out their methods and their terms on examples of your own, continuing their arguments as though you were working together on a common project. Or you can test their arguments as though you want to see not only where and how they will work but also where and how they will not.

Readers, as we have said, seldom read an essay in isolation, as though, having once worked out a reading of Kwame Anthony Appiah's "Racial Identities," they could go on to something else, something unrelated. It is unusual for anyone, at least in an academic setting, to read in so random a fashion. Readers read most often because they have a project in hand — a question they are working on or a problem they are trying to solve. For example, if as a result of reading Appiah's essay you become interested in questions of race and identity, and you begin to notice things you would not have noticed before, then you can read other essays in the book through this frame. If you have a project in mind, that project will help determine how you read these other essays. Sections of an essay that might otherwise seem unimportant suddenly become important — Gloria Anzaldúa's unusual prose style, or John Edgar Wideman's account of his racial politics in Pittsburgh. Appiah may enable you to read Wideman's narrative differently. Wideman may spur you to rethink Appiah. In a sense, you have the chance to become an expert reader, a reader with a project in hand, one who has already done some reading, who has watched others at work, and who has begun to develop a method of analysis and a set of key terms. Imagining yourself operating alongside some of the major figures in contemporary thought can be great fun and heady work — particularly when you have the occasion to speak back to them.

You may find that you have to alter your sense of who a writer is and what a writer does as you work on your own writing. Writers are often told that they need to begin with a clear sense of what they want to do and what they want to say. The writing assignments we've written, we believe, give you a sense of what you want (or need) to do. We define a problem for you to work on, and the problem will frame the task for you. You will have to decide where you will go in the texts you have read to find materials to work with, the primary materials that will give you a place to begin as you work on your essay. It might be best, however, if you did not feel that you need to have a clear sense of what you want to say before you begin. You may begin to develop a sense of what you want to say while you are writing. It may also be the case that the subjects you will be writing about are too big for you to assume that you need to have all the answers or that it is up to you to have the final word or to solve the problems once and for all. When you work on your essays, you should cast yourself in the role of one who is exploring a question, examining what might be said, and speculating on possible rather than certain conclusions. Consider your responses provisional. Think of yourself as a writer intent on opening a subject up rather than closing one down.

> **THINK OF YOURSELF AS A WRITER INTENT ON OPENING A SUBJECT UP RATHER THAN CLOSING ONE DOWN.**

Let us turn briefly now to the three categories of reading and writing assignments you will find in the book.

Questions for a Second Reading

Immediately following each selection are questions designed to guide your second reading. You may, as we've said, prefer to follow your own instincts as you search for the materials to build your understanding of the reading. These questions are meant to assist that process or develop those instincts. Most of the selections in the book are longer and more difficult than those you may be accustomed to reading. They are difficult enough that any reader would have to reread them and work to understand them; these questions are meant to suggest ways of beginning that work.

The second-reading questions characteristically ask you to consider the relations between ideas and examples in what you have read or to test specific statements in the essays against your own experience (so that you can get a sense of the author's habit of mind, his or her way of thinking about subjects that are available to you, too). Some turn your attention to what we take to be key terms or concepts, asking you to define these terms by observing how the writer uses them throughout the essay.

These questions have no simple answers; you will not find a correct answer hidden somewhere in the selection. In short, they are not the sorts of questions asked on SAT or ACT exams. They are real questions. They pose problems for interpretation or indicate sections where, to our minds, there is some interesting work for a reader to do. They are meant to reveal possible ways of reading the text, not to indicate that there is only one correct way, and that we have it.

You may find it useful to take notes as you read through each selection a second time, perhaps in a journal you can keep as a sourcebook for more formal written work. We will often also divide our students into groups, with each group working together with one of the second-reading questions in preparation for a report to the class. There are important advantages for you as a *writer* when you do this kind of close work with the text. Working through a second time, you get a better sense of the argument and of the *shape* of the argument; you get a sense of not only what the author is *saying* but what she is *doing*, and this prepares you to provide not only summary and paraphrase but also a sense of the author and her project. The work of rereading sends you back to the text; the second time through you can locate passages you might very well want to use in your own writing — passages that are particularly interesting to you, or illustrative, or even puzzling and obscure. These become the quotations you can use to bring the author's words into your essay, to bring them in as the object of scrutiny and discussion.

Assignments for Writing

This book actually offers three kinds of writing assignments: assignments that ask you to write about a single essay or story, assignments that ask you to read one selection through the frame of another, and longer sequences of assignments that define a project within which three or four of the selections serve as primary sources. All of these assignments serve a dual purpose. Like the second-reading questions, they suggest a way for you to reconsider the essays; they give you access from a different perspective. The assignments also encourage you to be an engaged reader and actively interpret what you have read. In one way or another, they all invite you to use a reading as a way of framing experience, as a source of terms and methods to enable you to interpret something else — some other text, events and objects around you, or your own memories and experience. The assignment sequences can be found at the end of the book and in *Resources for Teaching Ways of Reading*. The others ("Assignments for Writing" and "Making Connections") come immediately after each selection.

"Assignments for Writing" ask you to write about a single selection. Although some of these assignments call for you to paraphrase or reconstruct difficult passages, most ask you to interpret what you have read with a specific purpose in mind. For most of the essays, one question asks you to interpret a moment from your own experience through the frame of the essay — adapting its method, using its key terms, extending the range of its examples. Other assignments, however, ask you to turn an essay back on itself or to extend the conclusions of the essay by reconsidering the examples the writer has used to make his or her case.

When we talk with teachers and students using *Ways of Reading*, we are often asked about the wording of these assignments. The assignments are long. The wording is often unusual, unexpected. The assignments contain many questions, not simply one. The directions seem indirect, confusing. "Why?" we're asked. "How should we work with these?" When we write assignments, our goal is to point students toward a project, to provide a frame for their reading, a motive for writing, a way of asking certain kinds of questions. In that sense, the assignments should not be read as a set of directions to be followed literally. In fact, they are written to resist that reading, to forestall a writer's desire to simplify, to be efficient, to settle for the first clear line toward the finish. We want to provide a context to suggest how readers and writers might take time, be thoughtful. And we want the projects students work on to become their own. We hope to provoke varied responses, to leave the final decisions to the students. So the assignments try to be open and suggestive rather than narrow and direct. We ask lots of questions, but students don't need to answer them all (or any of them) once they begin to write. Our questions are meant to suggest ways of questioning, starting points. "What do you want?" Our own students ask this question. We want writers to make the most they can of what they read, including our questions and assignments.

So, what's the best way to work with an assignment? The writing assignments we have written will provide a context for writing, even a set of expectations, but the assignments do not provide a set of instructions. The first thing to do, then, is to ask yourself what, within this context, do you want to write about? What is on your mind? What is interesting or pressing for you? What direction can you take that will best allow you to stretch or to challenge yourself or to do something that will be new and interesting? We will often set aside class time to talk through an assignment and what possibilities it might suggest for each student's work. (We don't insist that everyone take the same track.) And we invite students to be in touch with us and with one another outside of class or online. Writers and scholars often rely on their friends and colleagues to help them get an angle, think about where to begin, understand what is new and interesting and what is old and dull. And, then, finally, the moment comes and you just sit down to the keyboard and start writing. There is no magic here, unfortunately. You write out what you can, and then you go back to what you have written to see what you are saying, and to see what comes next, and to think about how to shape it all into an essay to give to readers in the hope that they might call it "eloquent," "persuasive," "beautiful."

Making Connections

The connections questions will have you work with two or more readings at a time. These are not so much questions that ask you to compare or contrast the essays or stories as they are directions on how you might use one text as the context for interpreting another. Mary Louise Pratt, for example, in "Arts of the Contact Zone," looks at the work of a South American native, an Inca named Guaman Poma, writing in the seventeenth century to King Philip III of Spain. His work, she argues, can be read as a moment of contact, one in which different cultures and positions of power come together in a single text—in which a conquered person responds to the ways he is represented in the mind and the language of the conqueror. Pratt's reading of Guaman Poma's letter to King Philip, and the terms she uses to describe the way she reads it, provide a powerful context for a reader looking at essays by other writers, like Gloria Anzaldúa, for whom the "normal" or "standard" language of American culture is difficult, troubling, unsatisfactory, or incomplete. There are, then, assignments that ask you both to extend and to test Pratt's reading through your reading of alternative texts.

Reading one essay through the lens of another becomes a focused form of rereading. To write responses to these assignments, you will need to reread both of the assigned selections. The best way to begin is by taking a quick inventory of what you recall as points of connection. You could do this on your own, with a colleague, or in groups, but it is best to do it with pen and paper (or laptop) in hand. And before you reread, you should come to at least a provisional sense of what you want to do with the assignment. Then you can reread with a project in mind. Be sure to mark passages that you can work with later when you are writing. And look for passages that are interestingly different as well as those that complement each other.

The Assignment Sequences

The assignment sequences are more broad-ranging versions of the "Making Connections" assignments; in the sequences, several reading and writing assignments are linked and directed toward a single goal. They allow you to work on projects that require more time and incorporate more readings than would be possible in a single assignment. And they encourage you to develop your own point of view in concert with those of the professionals who wrote the essays and stories you are reading.

The assignments in a sequence build on one another, each relying on the ones before. A sequence will usually make use of four or five reading selections. The first is used to introduce an area of study or inquiry as well as to establish a frame of reference, a way of thinking about the subject. Subsequent assignments ask you to work through other readings and ideas on the subject.

The sequences allow you to participate in an extended academic project, one in which you take a position, revise it, look at a new example, hear what someone else has to say, revise it again, and see what conclusions you can draw about your subject. These projects always take time—they go through stages and revisions as a writer develops a command over his material, pushing against habitual ways of thinking, learning to examine an issue from different angles, rejecting quick conclusions, seeing the power of understanding that comes from repeated effort, and feeling the pleasure writers take when they find their own place in significant conversations that connect to their lived experience.

> **THE SEQUENCES ALLOW YOU TO PARTICIPATE IN AN EXTENDED ACADEMIC PROJECT.**

THE
Readings

Margaret Randall

GLORIA
Anzaldúa

Gloria Anzaldúa (1942–2004) grew up in southwest Texas, the physical and cultural borderland between the United States and Mexico, an area she called "*una herida abierta*," an open wound, "where the Third World grates against the first and bleeds." Defining herself as lesbian, feminist, Chicana — a representative of the new *mestiza* — she dramatically revised the usual narrative of American autobiography. "I am a border woman," she said. "I grew up between two cultures, the Mexican (with a heavy Indian influence) and the Anglo (as a member of a colonized people in our own territory). I have been straddling that *tejas*-Mexican border, and others, all my life." Cultural, physical, spiritual, sexual, linguistic — the borderlands defined by Anzaldúa extend beyond geography. "In fact," she said, "the Borderlands are present where two or more cultures edge each other, where people of different races occupy the same territory, where under, lower, middle, and upper classes touch, where the space between two individuals shrinks with intimacy." In a sense, her writing argues against the concept of an "authentic," unified, homogeneous culture, the pure "Mexican experience," a nostalgia that underlies much of the current interest in "ethnic" literature.

In the following selection from her book *Borderlands / La Frontera: The New Mestiza* (1987), Anzaldúa mixes genres, moving between poetry and prose, weaving stories with sections that resemble the work of a cultural or political theorist. She tells us a story about her childhood, her culture, and her people that is at once both myth and history. Her prose, too, is mixed, shifting among Anglo-American English, Castilian Spanish, Tex-Mex, Northern Mexican dialect, and Nahuatl (Aztec), speaking to us in the particular mix that represents her linguistic heritage: "Presently this infant language, this bastard language, Chicano Spanish, is not approved by any society. But we Chicanos no longer feel that we need to beg entrance, that we need always to make the first overture — to translate to Anglos, Mexicans, and Latinos, apology blurting out of our mouths with every step. Today we ask to be met halfway. This book is our invitation to you." The book is an invitation, but not always an easy one. The chapter that follows make a variety of demands on the reader. The shifting styles, genres, and languages can be confusing or disturbing, but this is part of the effect of Anzaldúa's prose, part of the experience you are invited to share.

In a chapter from the book that is not included here, Anzaldúa gives this account of her writing:

> In looking at this book that I'm almost finished writing, I see a mosaic pattern (Aztec-like) emerging, a weaving pattern, thin here, thick there. I see a preoccupation with the deep structure, the underlying structure, with the gesso underpainting that is red earth, black earth. . . . This almost finished product seems an assemblage, a montage, a beaded work with several leitmotifs and with a central core, now appearing, now disappearing in a crazy dance. The whole thing has had a mind of its own, escaping me and insisting on putting together the pieces of its own puzzle with minimal direction from my will.

Beyond her prose, she sees the competing values of more traditionally organized narratives, "art typical of Western European cultures, [which] attempts to manage the energies of its own internal system. . . . It is dedicated to the validation of itself. Its task is to move humans by means of achieving mastery in content, technique, feeling. Western art is always whole and always 'in power.'"

Anzaldúa's prose puts you, as a reader, on the borderland; in a way, it re-creates the position of the *mestiza*. As you read, you will need to meet this prose halfway, generously, learning to read a text that announces its difference.

In addition to *Borderlands/La Frontera*, Anzaldúa edited *Haciendo Caras: Making Face/Making Soul* (1990) and coedited an anthology, *This Bridge Called My Back: Writings by Radical Women of Color* (1983). She published a book for children, *Prietita and the Ghost Woman* (1996), which retells traditional Mexican folktales from a feminist perspective. A collection of interviews, *Interviews/Entrevistas*, was published in 2000, and a coedited anthology of multicultural feminist theory titled *This Bridge We Call Home: Radical Visions for Transformation* was published in 2002.

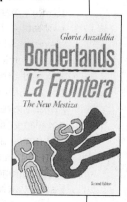

How to Tame a Wild Tongue

"We're going to have to control your tongue," the dentist says, pulling out all the metal from my mouth. Silver bits plop and tinkle into the basin. My mouth is a motherlode.

The dentist is cleaning out my roots. I get a whiff of the stench when I gasp. "I can't cap that tooth yet, you're still draining," he says.

"We're going to have to do something about your tongue," I hear the anger rising in his voice. My tongue keeps pushing out the wads of cotton, pushing back the drills, the long thin needles. "I've never seen anything as strong or as stubborn," he says. And I think, how do you tame a wild tongue, train it to be quiet, how do you bridle and saddle it? How do you make it lie down?

> Who is to say that robbing a people of
> its language is less violent than war?
> —RAY GWYN SMITH[1]

I remember being caught speaking Spanish at recess — that was good for three licks on the knuckles with a sharp ruler. I remember being sent to the corner of the classroom for "talking back" to the Anglo teacher when all I was trying to do was tell her how to pronounce my name. "If you want to be American, speak 'American.' If you don't like it, go back to Mexico where you belong."

"I want you to speak English. *Pa' hallar buen trabajo tienes que saber hablar el inglés bien. Qué vale toda tu educación si todavía hablas inglés con un* 'accent,'" my mother would say, mortified that I spoke English like a Mexican. At Pan American University, I and all Chicano students were required to take two speech classes. Their purpose: to get rid of our accents.

Attacks on one's form of expression with the intent to censor are a violation of the First Amendment. *El Anglo con cara de inocente nos arrancó la lengua.* Wild tongues can't be tamed, they can only be cut out.

OVERCOMING THE TRADITION OF SILENCE

> *Ahogadas, escupimos el oscuro.*
> *Peleando con nuestra propia sombra*
> *el silencio nos sepulta.*

En boca cerrada no entran moscas. "Flies don't enter a closed mouth" is a saying I kept hearing when I was a child. *Ser habladora* was to be a gossip and a liar, to talk too much. *Muchachitas bien criadas*, well-bred girls don't answer back. *Es una falta de respeto* to talk back to one's mother or father. I remember one of the sins I'd recite to the priest in the confession box the few times I went to confession: talking back to my mother, *hablar pa' 'tras, repelar. Hociocona, repelona, chismosa*, having a big mouth, questioning, carrying tales are all signs of being *mal criada*. In my culture they are all words that are derogatory if applied to women — I've never heard them applied to men.

The first time I heard two women, a Puerto Rican and a Cuban, say the word "*nosotras*," I was shocked. I had not known the word existed. Chicanas use *nosotros* whether we're male or female. We are robbed of our female being by the masculine plural. Language is a male discourse.

> And our tongues have become
> dry   the wilderness has
> dried out our tongues   and
> we have forgotten speech.
> — IRENA KLEPFISZ[2]

Even our own people, other Spanish speakers *nos quieren poner candados en la boca*. They would hold us back with their bag of *reglas de academia*.

OYÉ COMO LADRA: EL LENGUAJE DE LA FRONTERA

> *Quien tiene boca se equivoca.*
> — Mexican saying

"*Pocho*, cultural traitor, you're speaking the oppressor's language by speaking English, you're ruining the Spanish language," I have been accused by various Latinos and Latinas. Chicano Spanish is considered by the purist and by most Latinos deficient, a mutilation of Spanish.

But Chicano Spanish is a border tongue which developed naturally. Change, evolución, *enriquecimiento de palabras nuevas por invención o adopción* have created variants of Chicano Spanish, *un nuevo lenguaje. Un lenguaje que corresponde a un modo de vivir*. Chicano Spanish is not incorrect, it is a living language.

For a people who are neither Spanish nor live in a country in which Spanish is the first language; for a people who live in a country in which English is the reigning tongue but who are not Anglo; for a people who cannot entirely identify with either standard (formal, Castilian) Spanish nor standard English, what recourse is left to them but to create their own language? A language which they can connect their identity to, one capable of communicating the realities and values true to themselves — a language with terms that are neither *español ni inglés*, but both. We speak a patois, a forked tongue, a variation of two languages.

WE SPEAK A PATOIS, A FORKED TONGUE, A VARIATION OF TWO LANGUAGES.

Chicano Spanish sprang out of the Chicanos' need to identify ourselves as a distinct people. We needed a language with which we could
communicate with ourselves, a secret language. For some of us, language
is a homeland closer than the Southwest — for many Chicanos today live
in the Midwest and the East. And because we are a complex, heterogeneous
people, we speak many languages. Some of the languages we speak are

1. Standard English
2. Working-class and slang English
3. Standard Spanish
4. Standard Mexican Spanish
5. North Mexican Spanish dialect
6. Chicano Spanish (Texas, New Mexico, Arizona, and California have
   regional variations)
7. Tex-Mex
8. *Pachuco* (called *caló*)

My "home" tongues are the languages I speak with my sister and brothers, with my friends. They are the last five listed, with 6 and 7 being closest
to my heart. From school, the media, and job situations, I've picked up standard and working-class English. From Mamagrande Locha and from reading Spanish and Mexican literature, I've picked up Standard Spanish and
Standard Mexican Spanish. From *los recién llegados*, Mexican immigrants,
and *braceros*, I learned the North Mexican dialect. With Mexicans I'll try
to speak either Standard Mexican Spanish or the North Mexican dialect. From
my parents and Chicanos living in the Valley, I picked up Chicano Texas
Spanish, and I speak it with my mom, younger brother (who married a Mexican and who rarely mixes Spanish with English), aunts, and older relatives.

With Chicanas from *Nuevo México* or *Arizona* I will speak Chicano Spanish a little, but often they don't understand what I'm saying. With most California Chicanas I speak entirely in English (unless I forget). When I first moved
to San Francisco, I'd rattle off something in Spanish, unintentionally embarrassing them. Often it is only with another Chicana *tejano* that I can talk freely.

Words distorted by English are known as anglicisms or *pochismos*. The
pocho is an anglicized Mexican or American of Mexican origin who
speaks Spanish with an accent characteristic of North Americans and
who distorts and reconstructs the language according to the influence
of English.[3] Tex-Mex, or Spanglish, comes most naturally to me. I may
switch back and forth from English to Spanish in the same sentence or
in the same word. With my sister and my brother Nune and with Chicano
tejano contemporaries I speak in Tex-Mex.

From kids and people my own age I picked up *Pachuco*. *Pachuco* (the
language of the zoot suiters) is a language of rebellion, both against Standard Spanish and Standard English. It is a secret language. Adults of the
culture and outsiders cannot understand it. It is made up of slang words
from both English and Spanish. *Ruca* means girl or woman, *vato* means guy
or dude, *chale* means no, *simón* means yes, *churro* is sure, talk is *periquiar*,

pigionear means petting, *que gacho* means how nerdy, *ponte águila* means watch out, death is called *la pelona*. Through lack of practice and not having others who can speak it, I've lost most of the *Pachuco* tongue.

CHICANO SPANISH

Chicanos, after 250 years of Spanish/Anglo colonization, have developed significant differences in the Spanish we speak. We collapse two adjacent vowels into a single syllable and sometimes shift the stress in certain words such as *maíz/maiz, cohete/cuete*. We leave out certain consonants when they appear between vowels: *lado/lao, mojado/mojao*. Chicanos from South Texas pronounce *f* as *j* as in *jue* (*fue*). Chicanos use "archaisms," words that are no longer in the Spanish language, words that have been evolved out. We say *semos, truje, haiga, ansina*, and *naiden*. We retain the "archaic" *j*, as in *jalar*, that derives from an earlier *h* (the French *halar* or the Germanic *halon* which was lost to standard Spanish in the sixteenth century), but which is still found in several regional dialects such as the one spoken in South Texas. (Due to geography, Chicanos from the Valley of South Texas were cut off linguistically from other Spanish speakers. We tend to use words that the Spaniards brought over from Medieval Spain. The majority of the Spanish colonizers in Mexico and the Southwest came from Extremadura — Hernán Cortés was one of them — and Andalucía. Andalucians pronounce *ll* like a *y*, and their *d*'s tend to be absorbed by adjacent vowels: *tirado* becomes *tirao*. They brought *el lenguaje popular, dialectos, y regionalismos*.)[4]

Chicanos and other Spanish speakers also shift *ll* to *y* and *z* to *s*.[5] We leave out initial syllables, saying *tar* for *estar*, *toy* for *estoy*, *hora* for *ahora* (*cubanos* and *puertorriqueños* also leave out initial letters of some words). We also leave out the final syllable such as *pa* for *para*. The intervocalic *y*, the *ll* as in *tortilla, ella, botella*, gets replaced by *tortia* or *toriya, ea, botea*. We add an additional syllable at the beginning of certain words: *atocar* for *tocar, agastar* for *gastar*. Sometimes we'll say *lavaste las vacijas*, other times *lavates* (substituting the *ates* verb endings for the *aste*).

We use anglicisms, words borrowed from English: *bola* from ball, *carpeta* from carpet, *máchina de lavar* (instead of *lavadora*) from washing machine. Tex-Mex argot, created by adding a Spanish sound at the beginning or end of an English word such as *cookiar* for cook, *watchar* for watch, *parkiar* for park, and *rapiar* for rape, is the result of the pressures on Spanish speakers to adapt to English.

We don't use the word *vosotros/as* or its accompanying verb form. We don't say *claro* (to mean yes), *imagínate*, or *me emociona*, unless we picked up Spanish from Latinas, out of a book, or in a classroom. Other Spanish-speaking groups are going through the same, or similar, development in their Spanish.

LINGUISTIC TERRORISM

Deslenguadas. Somos los del español deficiente. We are your linguistic nightmare, your linguistic aberration, your linguistic *mestizaje*,

the subject of your *burla*. Because we speak with tongues of fire
we are culturally crucified. Racially, culturally, and linguistically
somos huérfanos — we speak an orphan tongue.

Chicanas who grew up speaking Chicano Spanish have internalized the
belief that we speak poor Spanish. It is illegitimate, a bastard language.
And because we internalize how our language has been used against us by
the dominant culture, we use our language differences against each other.

Chicana feminists often skirt around each other with suspicion and
hesitation. For the longest time I couldn't figure it out. Then it dawned on me.
To be close to another Chicana is like looking into the mirror. We are afraid
of what we'll see there. *Pena*. Shame. Low estimation of self. In childhood we
are told that our language is wrong. Repeated attacks on our native tongue
diminish our sense of self. The attacks continue throughout our lives.

Chicanas feel uncomfortable talking in Spanish to Latinas, afraid of
their censure. Their language was not outlawed in their countries. They
had a whole lifetime of being immersed in their native tongue; generations, centuries in which Spanish was a first language, taught in school,
heard on radio and TV, and read in the newspaper.

If a person, Chicana or Latina, has a low estimation of my native
tongue, she also has a low estimation of me. Often with *mexicanas y latinas*
we'll speak English as a neutral language. Even among Chicanas we tend
to speak English at parties or conferences. Yet, at the same time, we're
afraid the other will think we're *agringadas* because we don't speak
Chicano Spanish. We oppress each other trying to out-Chicano each other,
vying to be the "real" Chicanas, to speak like Chicanos. There is no one
Chicano language just as there is no one Chicano experience. A monolingual Chicana whose first language is English or Spanish is just as much
a Chicana as one who speaks several variants of Spanish. A Chicana from
Michigan or Chicago or Detroit is just as much a Chicana as one from the
Southwest. Chicano Spanish is as diverse linguistically as it is regionally.

By the end of this [the twentieth] century, Spanish speakers will
comprise the biggest minority group in the United States, a country where
students in high schools and colleges are encouraged to take French
classes because French is considered more "cultured." But for a language
to remain alive it must be used.[6] By the end of this century English, and
not Spanish, will be the mother tongue of most Chicanos and Latinos.

So, if you want to really hurt me, talk badly about my language. Ethnic identity is twin skin to linguistic identity — I am my language. Until I can take
pride in my language, I cannot take pride in myself. Until I can accept as
legitimate Chicano Texas Spanish, Tex-Mex, and all the other languages I
speak, I cannot accept the legitimacy of myself. Until I am free to write bilingually and to switch codes without having always to translate, while I still
have to speak English or Spanish when I would rather speak Spanglish,
and as long as I have to accommodate the English speaker rather than having them accommodate me, my tongue will be illegitimate.

I will no longer be made to feel ashamed of existing. I will have my voice: Indian, Spanish, white. I will have my serpent's tongue — my woman's voice, my sexual voice, my poet's voice. I will overcome the tradition of silence.

> My fingers
> move sly against your palm
> Like women everywhere, we speak in code. . . .
> — MELANIE KAYE / KANTROWITZ[7]

"VISTAS," CORRIDOS, Y COMIDA:
MY NATIVE TONGUE

In the 1960s, I read my first Chicano novel. It was *City of Night* by John Rechy, a gay Texan, son of a Scottish father and a Mexican mother. For days I walked around in stunned amazement that a Chicano could write and could get published. When I read *I Am Joaquín*[8] I was surprised to see a bilingual book by a Chicano in print. When I saw poetry written in Tex-Mex for the first time, a feeling of pure joy flashed through me. I felt like we really existed as a people. In 1971, when I started teaching High School English to Chicano students, I tried to supplement the required texts with works by Chicanos, only to be reprimanded and forbidden to do so by the principal. He claimed that I was supposed to teach "American" and English literature. At the risk of being fired, I swore my students to secrecy and slipped in Chicano short stories, poems, a play. In graduate school, while working toward a Ph.D., I had to "argue" with one adviser after the other, semester after semester, before I was allowed to make Chicano literature an area of focus.

Even before I read books by Chicanos or Mexicans, it was the Mexican movies I saw at the drive-in — the Thursday night special of $1.00 a carload — that gave me a sense of belonging. "*Vámonos a las vistas,*" my mother would call out and we'd all — grandmother, brothers, sister, and cousins — squeeze into the car. We'd wolf down cheese and bologna white bread sandwiches while watching Pedro Infante in melodramatic tear-jerkers like *Nosotros los pobres,* the first "real" Mexican movie (that was not an imitation of European movies). I remember seeing *Cuando los hijos se van* and surmising that all Mexican movies played up the love a mother has for her children and what ungrateful sons and daughters suffer when they are not devoted to their mothers. I remember the singing-type "westerns" of Jorge Negrete and Miguel Aceves Mejía. When watching Mexican movies, I felt a sense of homecoming as well as alienation. People who were to amount to something didn't go to Mexican movies, or *bailes*, or tune their radios to *bolero, rancherita,* and *corrido* music.

The whole time I was growing up, there was *norteño* music sometimes called North Mexican border music, or Tex-Mex music, or Chicano music, or *cantina* (bar) music. I grew up listening to *conjuntos,* three- or four-piece bands made up of folk musicians playing guitar, *bajo sexto,* drums, and button accordion, which Chicanos had borrowed from the German immigrants who had come to Central Texas and Mexico to farm and build breweries. In the Rio Grande Valley, Steven Jordan and Little Joe Hernández were popular, and Flaco Jiménez was the accordion king. The rhythms of Tex-Mex music are those of the polka, also adapted from the Germans, who in turn had borrowed the polka from the Czechs and Bohemians.

I remember the hot, sultry evenings when *corridos* — songs of love and death on the Texas-Mexican borderlands — reverberated out of cheap amplifiers from the local *cantinas* and wafted in through my bedroom window.

Corridos first became widely used along the South Texas/Mexican border during the early conflict between Chicanos and Anglos. The *corridos* are usually about Mexican heroes who do valiant deeds against the Anglo oppressors. Pancho Villa's song, "*La cucaracha*," is the most famous one. *Corridos* of John F. Kennedy and his death are still very popular in the Valley. Older Chicanos remember Lydia Mendoza, one of the great border *corrido* singers who was called *la Gloria de Tejas*. Her "*El tango negro*," sung during the Great Depression, made her a singer of the people. The ever-present *corridos* narrated one hundred years of border history, bringing news of events as well as entertaining. These folk musicians and folk songs are our chief cultural mythmakers, and they made our hard lives seem bearable.

I grew up feeling ambivalent about our music. Country-western and rock-and-roll had more status. In the fifties and sixties, for the slightly educated and *agringado* Chicanos, there existed a sense of shame at being caught listening to our music. Yet I couldn't stop my feet from thumping to the music, could not stop humming the words, nor hide from myself the exhilaration I felt when I heard it.

There are more subtle ways that we internalize identification, especially in the forms of images and emotions. For me food and certain smells are tied to my identity, to my homeland. Woodsmoke curling up to an immense blue sky; woodsmoke perfuming my grandmother's clothes, her skin. The stench of cow manure and the yellow patches on the ground; the crack of a .22 rifle and the reek of cordite. Homemade white cheese sizzling in a pan, melting inside a folded *tortilla*. My sister Hilda's hot, spicy *menudo*, *chile colorado* making it deep red, pieces of *panza* and hominy floating on top. My brother Carito barbequing *fajitas* in the backyard. Even now and 3,000 miles away, I can see my mother spicing the ground beef, pork, and venison with *chile*. My mouth salivates at the thought of the hot steaming *tamales* I would be eating if I were home.

SI LE PREGUNTAS A MI MAMÁ, "¿QUÉ ERES?"

> Identity is the essential core of who
> we are as individuals, the conscious
> experience of the self inside.
> — GERSHEN KAUFMAN [9]

Nosotros los Chicanos straddle the borderlands. On one side of us, we are constantly exposed to the Spanish of the Mexicans, on the other side we hear the Anglos' incessant clamoring so that we forget our language. Among ourselves we don't say *nosotros los americanos, o nosotros los españoles, o nosotros los hispanos.* We say *nosotros los mexicanos* (by *mexicanos* we do not mean citizens of Mexico; we do not mean a national identity, but a racial one). We distinguish between *mexicanos del otro lado* and *mexicanos de este lado.* Deep in our hearts we believe that being Mexican has nothing to do with which country one lives in. Being Mexican is a state of soul — not one of mind, not one of citizenship. Neither eagle nor serpent, but both. And like the ocean, neither animal respects borders.

> *Dime con quien andas y te diré quien eres.*
> (Tell me who your friends are and I'll tell you who you are.)
> — Mexican saying

Si le preguntas a mi mamá, "¿Qué eres?" te dirá, "Soy mexicana." My brothers and sister say the same. I sometimes will answer *"soy mexicana"* and at others will say *"soy Chicana" o "soy tejana."* But I identified as *"Raza"* before I ever identified as *"mexicana"* or "Chicana."

As a culture, we call ourselves Spanish when referring to ourselves as a linguistic group and when copping out. It is then that we forget our predominant Indian genes. We are 70–80 percent Indian.[10] We call ourselves Hispanic[11] or Spanish-American or Latin American or Latin when linking ourselves to other Spanish-speaking peoples of the Western hemisphere and when copping out. We call ourselves Mexican-American[12] to signify we are neither Mexican nor American, but more the noun "American" than the adjective "Mexican" (and when copping out).

> *SI LE PREGUNTAS A MI MAMÁ, "¿QUÉ ERES?" TE DIRÁ, "SOY MEXICANA."*

Chicanos and other people of color suffer economically for not acculturating. This voluntary (yet forced) alienation makes for psychological conflict, a kind of dual identity — we don't identify with the Anglo-American cultural values and we don't totally identify with the Mexican cultural values. We are a synergy of two cultures with various degrees of Mexicanness or Angloness. I have so internalized the borderland conflict that sometimes I feel like one cancels out the other and we are zero, nothing, no one. *A veces no soy nada ni nadie. Pero hasta cuando no lo soy, lo soy.*

When not copping out, when we know we are more than nothing, we call ourselves Mexican, referring to race and ancestry; *mestizo* when affirming both our Indian and Spanish (but we hardly ever own our Black) ancestry; Chicano when referring to a politically aware people born and/or raised in the United States; *Raza* when referring to Chicanos; *tejanos* when we are Chicanos from Texas.

Chicanos did not know we were a people until 1965 when Cesar Chavez and the farmworkers united and *I Am Joaquín* was published and *la Raza Unida* party was formed in Texas. With that recognition, we became a distinct people. Something momentous happened to the Chicano soul — we became aware of our reality and acquired a name and a language

(Chicano Spanish) that reflected that reality. Now that we had a name, some of the fragmented pieces began to fall together — who we were, what we were, how we had evolved. We began to get glimpses of what we might eventually become.

Yet the struggle of identities continues, the struggle of borders is our reality still. One day the inner struggle will cease and a true integration take place. In the meantime, *tenémos que hacer la lucha. ¿Quién está protegiendo los ranchos de mi gente? ¿Quién está tratando de cerrar la fisura entre la india y el blanco en nuestra sangre? El Chicano, si, el Chicano que anda como un ladrón en su propia casa.*

Los Chicanos, how patient we seem, how very patient. There is the quiet of the Indian about us.[13] We know how to survive. When other races have given up their tongue we've kept ours. We know what it is to live under the hammer blow of the dominant *norteamericano* culture. But more than we count the blows, we count the days the weeks the years the centuries the aeons until the white laws and commerce and customs will rot in the deserts they've created, lie bleached. *Humildes* yet proud, *quietos* yet wild, *nosotros los mexicanos-Chicanos* will walk by the crumbling ashes as we go about our business. Stubborn, persevering, impenetrable as stone, yet possessing a malleability that renders us unbreakable, we, the *mestizas* and *mestizos*, will remain.

NOTES

[1] Ray Gwyn Smith, *Moorland Is Cold Country*, unpublished book. [All notes are Anzaldúa's.]

[2] Irena Klepfisz, "*Di rayze aheym*/The Journey Home," in *The Tribe of Dina: A Jewish Women's Anthology*, Melanie Kaye/Kantrowitz and Irena Klepfisz, eds. (Montpelier, VT: Sinister Wisdom Books, 1986), 49.

[3] R. C. Ortega, *Dialectología Del Barrio*, trans. Hortencia S. Alwan (Los Angeles, CA: R. C. Ortega Publisher & Bookseller, 1977), 132.

[4] Eduardo Hernandéz-Chávez, Andrew D. Cohen, and Anthony F. Beltramo, *El Lenguaje de los Chicanos: Regional and Social Characteristics of Language Used by Mexican Americans* (Arlington, VA: Center for Applied Linguistics, 1975), 39.

[5] Hernandéz-Chávez, xvii.

[6] Irena Klepfisz, "Secular Jewish Identity: Yidishkayt in America," in *The Tribe of Dina*, Kaye/Kantrowitz and Klepfisz, eds., 43.

[7] Melanie Kaye/Kantrowitz, "Sign," in *We Speak in Code: Poems and Other Writings* (Pittsburgh, PA: Motheroot Publications, Inc., 1980), 85.

[8] Rodolfo Gonzales, *I Am Joaquín/Yo Soy Joaquín* (New York, NY: Bantam Books, 1972). It was first published in 1967.

[9] Gershen Kaufman, *Shame: The Power of Caring* (Cambridge, MA: Schenkman Books, Inc., 1980), 68.

[10] John R. Chávez, *The Lost Land: The Chicano Images of the Southwest* (Albuquerque, NM: University of New Mexico Press, 1984), 88–90.

[11] "Hispanic" is derived from *Hispanis* (*España*, a name given to the Iberian Peninsula in ancient times when it was a part of the Roman Empire) and is a term designated by the U.S. government to make it easier to handle us on paper.

[12] The Treaty of Guadalupe Hidalgo created the Mexican-American in 1848.

[13] Anglos, in order to alleviate their guilt for dispossessing the Chicano, stressed the Spanish part of us and perpetrated the myth of the Spanish Southwest. We have accepted the fiction that we are Hispanic, that is Spanish, in order to accommodate ourselves to the dominant culture and its abhorrence of Indians. Chávez, 88–91.

QUESTIONS FOR A SECOND READING

1. The most immediate challenge to many readers of this chapter will be the sections that are written in Spanish. Part of the point of a text that mixes languages is to give non-Spanish-speaking readers the feeling of being lost, excluded, left out. What is a reader to do with this prose? One could learn Spanish and come back to reread, but this is not a quick solution and, according to Anzaldúa, not even a completely satisfactory one, since some of her Spanish is drawn from communities of speakers not represented in textbooks and classes.

   So how do you read this text if you don't read Spanish? Do you ignore the words? sound them out? improvise? Anzaldúa gives translations of some words or phrases, but not all. Which ones does she translate? Why? Reread these chapters with the goal of explaining how you handled Anzaldúa's polyglot style.

2. This chapter is made up of shorter sections written in a variety of styles (some as prose poems, some with endnotes, some as stories). And while the sections are obviously ordered, the order is not a conventional argumentative one. The text is, as Anzaldúa says elsewhere in her book, "an assemblage, a montage, a beaded work, . . . a crazy dance":

   > In looking at this book that I'm almost finished writing, I see a mosaic pattern (Aztec-like) emerging, a weaving pattern, thin here, thick there. . . . This almost finished product seems an assemblage, a montage, a beaded work with several leitmotifs and with a central core, now appearing, now disappearing in a crazy dance. The whole thing has had a mind of its own, escaping me and insisting on putting together the pieces of its own puzzle with minimal direction from my will. It is a rebellious, willful entity, a precocious girl-child forced to grow up too quickly, rough, unyielding, with pieces of feather sticking out here and there, fur, twigs, clay. My child, but not for much longer. This female being is angry, sad, joyful, is Coatlicue, dove, horse, serpent, cactus. Though it is a flawed thing — clumsy, complex, groping, blind thing, for me it is alive, infused with spirit. I talk to it; it talks to me.

   This is not, in other words, a conventional text; it makes unexpected demands on a reader. As you reread, mark sections you could use to talk about how, through the text, Anzaldúa invents a reader and/or a way of reading. Who is Anzaldúa's ideal reader? What does he or she need to be able to do?

3. Although Anzaldúa's text is not a conventional one, it makes an argument and proposes terms and examples for its readers to negotiate. How might you summarize Anzaldúa's argument in this chapter? How does the chapter mark stages or parts of her argument? As you reread this selection, mark those passages where Anzaldúa seems to you to be creating a case or an argument. What are its key terms? its key examples? its conclusions?

• • • ● • •

ASSIGNMENTS FOR WRITING

1. Anzaldúa has described her text as a kind of crazy dance (see the second "Question for a Second Reading"); it is, she says, a text with a mind of its own, "putting together the pieces of its own puzzle with minimal direction from my will." Hers is a prose full of variety and seeming contradictions; it is a writing that could be said to represent the cultural "crossroads" which is her experience / sensibility.

    As an experiment whose goal is the development of an alternate (in Anzaldúa's terms, a mixed or *mestiza*) understanding, write an autobiographical text whose shape and motives could be described in her terms: a mosaic, woven, with numerous overlays; a montage, a beaded work, a crazy dance, drawing on the various ways of thinking, speaking, understanding that might be said to be part of your own mixed cultural position, your own mixed sensibility.

    To prepare for this essay, think about the different positions you could be said to occupy, the different voices that are part of your background or present, the competing ways of thinking that make up your points of view. Imagine that your goal is to present your world and your experience to those who are not necessarily prepared to be sympathetic or to understand. And, following Anzaldúa, you should work to construct a mixed text, not a single unified one. This will be hard, since you will be writing what might be called a "forbidden" text, one you have not been prepared to write.

2. In *"La Conciencia de la Mestiza / Towards a New Consciousness,"* the last essaylike chapter in her book (the remaining chapters are made up of poems), Anzaldúa steps forward to define her role as writer and yours as reader. She says, among other things,

    > Many women and men of color do not want to have any dealings with white people. . . . Many feel that whites should help their own people rid themselves of race hatred and fear first. I, for one, choose to use some of my energy to serve as mediator. I think we need to allow whites to be our allies. Through our literature, art, *corridos*, and folktales we must share our history with them so when they set up committees to help Big Mountain Navajos or the Chicano farmworkers or los *Nicaragüenses* they won't turn people away because of their racial fears and ignorances. They will come to see that they are not helping us but following our lead.
    >
    > Individually, but also as a racial entity, we need to voice our needs. We need to say to white society: We need you to accept the fact that Chicanos are different, to acknowledge your rejection and negation of us. We need you to own the fact that you looked upon us as less than human, that you stole our lands, our personhood, our self-respect. We need you to make public restitution: to say that, to

compensate for your own sense of defectiveness, you strive for power over us, you erase our history and our experience because it makes you feel guilty — you'd rather forget your brutish acts. To say you've split yourself from minority groups, that you disown us, that your dual consciousness splits off parts of yourself, transferring the "negative" parts onto us. . . . To say that you are afraid of us, that to put distance between us, you wear the mask of contempt. Admit that Mexico is your double, that she exists in the shadow of this country, that we are irrevocably tied to her. Gringo, accept the doppelganger in your psyche. By taking back your collective shadow the intracultural split will heal. And finally, tell us what you need from us.

This is only a part of the text — one of the ways it defines the roles of reader and writer — but it is one that asks to be taken account of, with its insistent list of what a white reader must do and say. (Of course not every reader is white, and not all white readers are the same. What Anzaldúa is defining here is a "white" way of reading.)

Write an essay in which you tell a story of reading, the story of your work with the chapter of *Borderlands/La Frontera* reprinted here. Think about where you felt at home with the text and where you felt lost, where you knew what you were doing and where you needed help; think about the position (or positions) you have taken as a reader and how it measures up against the ways Anzaldúa has figured you in the text, the ways she has anticipated a response, imagined who you are and how you habitually think and read.

3. In "How to Tame a Wild Tongue," Anzaldúa says, "I will no longer be made to feel ashamed of existing. I will have my voice: Indian, Spanish, white. I will have my serpent's tongue — my woman's voice, my sexual voice, my poet's voice" (p. 31). Anzaldúa speaks about "having her voice," not a single, "authentic" voice, but one she names in these terms: Indian, Spanish, white; woman, lesbian, poet. What is "voice" as defined by this chapter? Where does it come from? What does it have to do with the act of writing or the writer?

As you reread this chapter, mark those passages that you think best represent Anzaldúa's voices. Using these passages as examples, write an essay in which you discuss how these voices are different — both different from one another and different from a "standard" voice (as a "standard" voice is imagined by Anzaldúa). What do these voices represent? How do they figure in your reading? in her writing?

4. Anzaldúa's writing is difficult to categorize as an essay or a story or a poem; it has all of these within it. The writing may appear to have been just put together, but it is more likely that it was carefully crafted to represent the various voices Anzaldúa understands to be a part of her. She speaks directly about her voices — her woman's voice, her sexual voice, her poet's voice; her Indian, Spanish, and white voices on page 31 of "How to Tame a Wild Tongue."

Following Anzaldúa, write an argument of your own, one that requires you to use a variety of voices, in which you carefully present the various voices that you feel are a part of you or a part of the argument.

When you have completed this assignment, write a two-page essay in which you explain why the argument you made might be worth a reader's attention.

• • • ● • • •

MAKING CONNECTIONS

1. In "Arts of the Contact Zone" (p. 512), Mary Louise Pratt talks about the "auto-ethnographic" text, "a text in which people undertake to describe themselves in ways that engage with representations others have made of them," and about "transculturation," the "processes whereby members of subordinated or marginal groups select and invent from materials transmitted by a dominant or metropolitan culture."

   Write an essay in which you present a reading of this chapter as an example of an autoethnographic and/or transcultural text. You should imagine that you are writing to someone who is not familiar with either Pratt's argument or Anzaldúa's book. Part of your work, then, is to present Anzaldúa's text to readers who don't have it in front of them. You have the example of Pratt's reading of Guaman Poma's *New Chronicle and Good Government*. And you have her discussion of the "literate arts of the contact zone." Think about how Anzaldúa's text might be similarly read, and about how her text does and doesn't fit Pratt's description. Your goal should be to add an example to Pratt's discussion and to qualify it, to give her discussion a new twist or spin now that you have had a chance to look at an additional example.

2. Writers often layer their essays with metaphors or, in Anzaldúa's case, with narratives that serve as kinds of metaphor. One way to identify moments of metaphor that layer a piece of writing is to notice when particular sentences or images seem to carry more than one meaning. For example, when Anzaldúa tells us what the dentist says ("We're going to have to do something about your tongue"), we might notice that the dentist's statement has more than one meaning, that what he literally says is meant to signal something else, something larger and more complex than this specific moment. Many of the writers in this collection make use of metaphor in their work, inviting readers to see multiple meanings in a single moment.

   Reread Anzaldúa, looking for those metaphorical moments, marking sentences that seem to point to something larger. Then reread Susan Griffin's "Our Secret" (p. 381), looking for similar moments. Write an essay in which you guide your own reader through these authors' use of metaphor, choosing some specific examples from each essay. Consider the following questions: How do these passages point to something larger than themselves? How are you, as a reader, affected by the use of the metaphor, and how does the metaphor serve to layer the essay—to complicate or illuminate its subject matter? Why do writers rely on metaphors?

3. Anzaldúa writes, "So, if you want to really hurt me, talk badly about my language. Ethnic identity is twin skin to linguistic identity—I am my language" (p. 30). In "How to Tame a Wild Tongue," Anzaldúa seems to suggest that our language(s) are essential to our identities, perhaps even essential to our humanity, or to what Judith Butler calls "a livable life." Both Butler and Anzaldúa seem concerned with, as Butler puts it, the ways "life itself becomes foreclosed when the right way is decided in advance, when we impose what is right for everyone and without finding a way to enter into community, and to discover there the 'right' in the midst of cultural translation" (p. 255). Butler wrote "Beside Oneself: On the Limits of Sexual Autonomy" about twenty years after Anzaldúa first published "How to Tame a Wild Tongue," and while Butler's piece does not specifically address the linguistic particularities of Anzaldúa's piece, their work is certainly in conversation—raising some similar questions and offering some alternative ways of thinking about culture, identity, and language.

Write an essay in which you enact some inquiry into a specific question (likely an unanswerable one) that you think is key for *both* Butler and Anzaldúa. You might begin with the question: what seems to be the central questions for each writer, and how do those central questions overlap? Once you've brainstormed a bit (perhaps even with classmates) about these central questions, choose one that is particularly interesting to you. In your essay, you'll want to both argue for the importance of asking this question in the first place *and* discuss the ways Butler and Anzaldúa offer you answers or approaches to this central question.

KWAME ANTHONY
Appiah

Kwame Anthony Appiah (pronounced AP-eea, with the accent on the first syllable) was born in London; he grew up in Ghana, in the town of Asante; he took his MA and PhD degrees from Cambridge University in England; he is now a citizen of the United States. He has taught at Yale, Cornell, Duke, Harvard, and, most recently, Princeton, where he is the Laurence S. Rockefeller University Professor of Philosophy and a member of the University Center for Human Values. Appiah's father was Ghanaian and a leader in the struggle for Pan-Africanism and Ghanaian independence from Britain; his mother, originally Peggy Cripps, was British and the daughter of a leading figure in the Labour government. Appiah's work circulates widely and has won numerous awards. He was elected to the American Academy of Arts and Sciences and the American Philosophical Society and was inducted in 2008 into the American Academy of Arts and Letters. In 2012, he was awarded the National Humanities Medal.

Appiah's life illustrates the virtues of a "rooted cosmopolitanism," a term he offers to describe a desired way of living in the world, and it illustrates the difficulties we face in naming someone as black or white or African or American. In the preface to his book *The Ethics of Identity* (2004), he says,

> What has proved especially vexatious, though, is the effort to take account of those social forms we now call identities: genders and sexual orientations, ethnicities and nationalities, professions and vocations. Identities make ethical claims because — and this is just a fact about the world we human beings have created — we make our lives as men and as women, as gay and as straight people, as Ghanaians and as Americans, as blacks and as whites. Immediately, conundrums start to assemble. Do identities represent a curb on autonomy, or do they provide its contours: What claims, if any, can identity groups as such justly make upon the state? These are concerns that have gained a certain measure of salience in recent political philosophy, but, as I hope to show, they are anything but newfangled. What's modern is that we conceptualize identity in particular ways. What's age-old is that when we are asked — and ask ourselves — who we are, we are being asked what we are as well. (p. xiv)

Appiah is an award-winning and prolific writer. His books include *Assertion and Conditionals* (1985); *For Truth in Semantics* (1986); *In My Father's House: Africa in the Philosophy of Culture* (1992); *The Ethics of Identity* (2005); *Cosmopolitanism: Ethics in a World of Strangers* (2007); *The Honor Code: How Moral Revolutions Happen* (2010); and *Lines of Descent: W. E. B. Du Bois and the Emergence of Identity* (2014). He is also the author of three mystery novels, *Avenging Angel* (1991), *Nobody Likes Letitia* (1994), and *Another Death in Venice* (1995); a textbook, *Thinking It Through: An Introduction to Contemporary Philosophy* (2003); and, with Henry Louis Gates Jr., edited the *Encarta Africana* CD-ROM encyclopedia. The selection that follows was taken from a book coauthored with Amy Gutmann, *Color Conscious: The Political Morality of Race* (1996), winner of the 1997 Ralph J. Bunche award from the American Political Science Association. *Color Conscious* is drawn from the lectures Appiah and Gutmann gave as the Tanner Lectures on Human Values at the University of California, San Diego. We've included one section from Appiah's half of the exchange, so at times you will hear him allude to things he said earlier in that chapter. The section we've provided can, however, easily stand alone and be read as a single, coherent essay.

As you read "Racial Identities," it will help to pay particular attention to *voice*—to the way the writer locates himself within available ways of speaking and thinking. Appiah writes as a philosopher. That is, he writes from within ideas, from within trains of thought. He is not necessarily endorsing these ways of thinking. They are not necessarily his thought processes, or ones he would endorse. He is trying them on, testing their consequences or limits, showing where they might lead.

You can't, in other words, quickly assume that an affirmative sentence expresses Appiah's own thoughts or beliefs. This is tricky. For example, listen to these sentences. Where might you locate Appiah?

> I have insisted that African-Americans do not have a single culture, in the sense of shared language, values, practices, and meanings. But many people who think of races as groups defined by shared cultures, conceive that sharing in a different way. They understand black people as sharing black culture by *definition*: jazz or hip-hop belongs to an African-American, whether she likes it or knows anything about it, because it is culturally marked as black. Jazz belongs to a black person who knows nothing about it more fully or naturally than it does to a white jazzman. (p. 52)

Appiah is not saying that he believes jazz belongs to a black person more fully or naturally than it does to a white person. He is saying that "many people" have a way of thinking about race and culture that will lead them to such statements or beliefs.

Learning to read along with a philosopher, with a writer who is thinking about ways of thinking, is challenging. As you read, keep an ear cocked for moments when Appiah gives voice to others, and be alert for those moments (and they are fewer) when he speaks for himself.

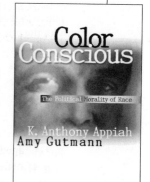

Racial Identities

"SPEAKING OF CIVILIZATIONS"

In 1911, responding to what was already clear evidence that race was not doing well as a biological concept, W.E.B. Du Bois, the African-American sociologist, historian, and activist, wrote in *The Crisis,* the magazine of the NAACP, which he edited:

> The leading scientists of the world have come forward ... and laid down in categorical terms a series of propositions[1] which may be summarized as follows:
>
> 1. (a) It is not legitimate to argue from differences in physical characteristics to differences in mental characteristics ...
>
> 2. The civilization of a ... race at any particular moment of time offers no index to its innate or inherited capacities ...[2]

And he concluded: "So far at least as intellectual and moral aptitudes are concerned we ought to speak of civilizations where we now speak of races."[3] I have argued before that Du Bois's proposal to "speak of civilizations" turns out not to replace a biological notion but simply to hide it from view.[4] I think there are various difficulties with the way that argument proceeded, and I should like to do better. So let me try to reconstruct a sociohistorical view that has more merit than I have previously conceded.

Among the most moving of Du Bois's statements of the meaning of "race" conceived in sociohistorical terms is the one in *Dusk of Dawn,* the "autobiography of a race concept," as he called it, which he published in 1940. Du Bois wrote:

> The actual ties of heritage between the individuals of this group, vary with the ancestors that they have in common with many others: Europeans and Semites, perhaps Mongolians, certainly American Indians. But the physical bond is least and the badge of color relatively unimportant save as a badge; the real essence of this kinship is its social heritage of slavery; the discrimination and insult; and this heritage binds together not simply the children of Africa, but extends through yellow Asia and into the South Seas. It is this unity that draws me to Africa.[5]

For reasons I shall be able to make clear only when I have given my account, Du Bois's own approach is somewhat misleading. So instead of proceeding with exegesis of Du Bois, I must turn next to the task of shaping a sociohistorical account of racial identity. Still, as it turns out, it is helpful to start from Du Bois's idea of the "badge of color."

RACIAL IDENTITY AND RACIAL IDENTIFICATION[6]

I have argued that Jefferson and Arnold thought that when they applied a racial label they were identifying people with a shared essence. I have argued, also, that they were wrong — and, I insist, not slightly but wildly wrong. Earlier in American history the label "African" was applied to many of those who would later be thought of as Negroes, by people who may have been under the impression that Africans had more in common culturally, socially, intellectually, and religiously than they actually did. Neither of these kinds of errors, however, stopped the labeling from having its effects. As slavery in North America became racialized in the colonial period, being identified as an African, or, later, as a Negro, carrying the "badge of color," had those predictable negative consequences, which Du Bois so memorably captured in the phrase "the social heritage of slavery; the discrimination and insult."

If we follow the badge of color from "African" to "Negro" to "colored race" to "black" to "Afro-American" (and this ignores such fascinating detours as the route by way of "Afro-Saxon") we are thus tracing the history not only of a signifier, a label, but also a history of its effects. At any time in this history there was, within the American colonies and the United States that succeeded them, a massive consensus, both among those labeled black and among those labeled white, as to who, in their own communities, fell under which labels. (As immigration from China and other parts of the "Far East" occurred, an Oriental label came to have equal stability.) There was, no doubt, some "passing"; but the very concept of passing implies that, if the relevant fact about the ancestry of these individuals had become known, most people would have taken them to be traveling under the wrong badge.

The major North American exception was in southern Louisiana, where a different system in which an intermediary Creole group, neither white nor black, had social recognition; but *Plessy v. Ferguson* reflected the extent to which the Louisiana Purchase effectively brought even that state gradually into the American mainstream of racial classification. For in that case Homer Adolph Plessy — a Creole gentleman who could certainly have passed in most places for white — discovered in 1896, after a long process of appeal, that the Supreme Court of the United States proposed to treat him as a Negro and therefore recognize the State of Louisiana's right to keep him and his white fellow citizens "separate but equal."

The result is that there are at least three sociocultural objects in America — blacks, whites and Orientals — whose membership at any time is relatively, and increasingly, determinate. These objects are historical in this sense: to identify all the members of these American races over time, you cannot seek a single criterion that applies equally always; you can find the starting point for the race — the subcontinental source of the population of individuals that defines its initial membership — and then apply at each historical moment the criteria of intertemporal continuity that apply at that moment to decide which individuals in the next generation count as belonging to the group. There is from the very beginning until the present, at the heart of the system, a simple rule that very few would dispute even today: where both parents are of a single race, the child is of the same race as the parents.

The criteria applicable at any time may leave vague boundaries. They certainly change, as the varying decisions about what proportion of African ancestry made one black or the current uncertainty as to how to assign the children of white-yellow "miscegenation" demonstrate. But they always definitely assign some people to the group and definitely rule out others; and for most of America's history the class of people about whom there was uncertainty (are the Florida Seminoles black or Indian?) was relatively small.[7]

Once the racial label is applied to people, ideas about what it refers to, ideas that may be much less consensual than the application of the label, come to have their social effects. But they have not only social effects but psychological ones as well; and they shape the ways people conceive of themselves and their projects. In particular, the labels can operate to shape what I want to call "identification": the process through which an individual intentionally shapes her projects — including her plans for her own life and her conception of the good — by reference to available labels, available identities.

Identification is central to what Ian Hacking has called "making up people."[8] Drawing on a number of examples, but centrally homosexuality and multiple personality syndrome, he defends what he calls a "dynamic nominalism," which argues that "numerous kinds of human beings and human acts come into being hand in hand with our invention of the categories labeling them."[9] I have just articulated a dynamic nominalism about a kind of person that is currently usually called "African-American."

Hacking reminds us of the philosophical truism, whose most influential formulation is in Elizabeth Anscombe's work on intention, that in intentional action people act "under descriptions"; that their actions are conceptually shaped. It follows, of course, that what people can do depends on what concepts they have available to them; and among the concepts that may shape one's action is the concept of a certain kind of person and the behavior appropriate to that kind.

Hacking offers as an example Sartre's brilliant evocation, in *Being and Nothingness*, of the Parisian *garçon de café*: "His movement is quick and forward, a little too precise, a little too rapid. He comes toward the patrons with a step a little too quick. He bends forward a little too eagerly, his eyes express an interest too solicitous for the order of the customer."[10] Hacking comments:

> Sartre's antihero chose to be a waiter. Evidently that was not a possible choice in other places, other times. There are servile people in most societies, and servants in many, but a waiter is something specific, and a *garçon de café* more specific. . . .

As with almost every way in which it is possible to be a person, it is possible to be a *garçon de café* only at a certain time, in a certain place, in a certain social setting. The feudal serf putting food on my lady's table can no more choose to be a *garçon de café* than he can choose to be lord of the manor. But the impossibility is evidently of a different kind.[11]

The idea of the *garçon de café* lacks, so far as I can see, the sort of theoretical commitments that are trailed by the idea of the black and the white, the homosexual and the heterosexual. So it makes no sense to ask of someone who has a job as a *garçon de café* whether that is what he really is. The point is not that we do not have expectations of the *garçon de café*: that is why it is a recognizable identity. It is rather that those expectations are about the performance of the role; they depend on our assumption of intentional conformity to those expectations. As I spent some time arguing earlier, we *can* ask whether someone is really of a black race, because the constitution of this identity is generally theoretically committed: we expect people of a certain race to behave a certain way not simply because they are conforming to the script for that identity, performing that role, but because they have certain antecedent properties that are consequences of the label's properly applying to them. It is because ascription of racial identities — the process of applying the label to people, including ourselves — is based on more than intentional identification that there can be a gap between what a person ascriptively is and the racial identity he performs: it is this gap that makes passing possible.

Race is, in this way, like all the major forms of identification that are central to contemporary identity politics: female and male; gay, lesbian, and straight; black, white, yellow, red, and brown; Jewish-, Italian-, Japanese-, and Korean-American; even that most neglected of American identities, class. There is, in all of them, a set of theoretically committed criteria for ascription, not all of which are held by everybody, and which may not be consistent with one another even in the ascriptions of a single person; and there is then a process of identification in which the label shapes the intentional acts of (some of) those who fall under it.

It does not follow from the fact that identification shapes action, shapes life plans, that the identification itself must be thought of as voluntary. I don't recall ever choosing to identify as a male;[12] but being male has shaped many of my plans and actions. In fact, where my ascriptive identity is one on which almost all my fellow citizens agree, I am likely to have little sense of choice about whether the identity is mine; though I *can* choose how central my identification with it will be — choose, that is, how much I will organize my life around that identity. Thus if I am among those (like the unhappily labeled "straight-acting gay men," or most American Jews) who are able, if they choose, to escape

> I DON'T RECALL EVER CHOOSING TO IDENTIFY AS A MALE, BUT BEING MALE HAS SHAPED MANY OF MY PLANS AND ACTIONS.

ascription, I may choose not to take up a gay or a Jewish identity; though this will require concealing facts about myself or my ancestry from others.

If, on the other hand, I fall into the class of those for whom the consensus on ascription is not clear — as among contemporary so-called biracials, or bisexuals, or those many white Americans of multiple identifiable ethnic heritages[13] — I may have a sense of identity options: but one way I may exercise them is by marking myself ethnically (as when someone chooses to wear an Irish pin) so that others will then be more likely to ascribe that identity to me.

DIFFERENCES AMONG DIFFERENCES

Collective identities differ, of course, in lots of ways; the body is central to race, gender, and sexuality but not so central to class and ethnicity. And, to repeat an important point, racial identification is simply harder to resist than ethnic identification. The reason is twofold. First, racial ascription is more socially salient: unless you are morphologically atypical for your racial group, strangers, friends, officials are always aware of it in public and private contexts, always notice it, almost never let it slip from view. Second — and again both in intimate settings and in public space — race is taken by so many more people to be the basis for treating people differentially. (In this respect, Jewish identity in America strikes me as being a long way along a line toward African-American identity: there are ways of speaking and acting and looking — and it matters very little whether they are "really" mostly cultural or mostly genetic — that are associated with being Jewish; and there are many people, white and black, Jewish and Gentile, for whom this identity is a central force in shaping their responses to others.)

This much about identification said, we can see that Du Bois's analytical problem was, in effect, that he believed that for racial labeling of this sort to have the obvious real effects that it did have — among them, crucially, his own identification with other black people and with Africa — there must be some real essence that held the race together. Our account of the history of the label reveals that this is a mistake: once we focus, as Du Bois almost saw, on the racial badge — the signifier rather than the signified, the word rather than the concept — we see both that the effects of the labeling are powerful and real and that false ideas, muddle and mistake and mischief, played a central role in determining both how the label was applied and to what purposes.

This, I believe, is why Du Bois so often found himself reduced, in his attempts to define race, to occult forces: if you look for a shared essence you won't get anything, so you'll come to believe you've missed it, because it is super-subtle, difficult to experience or identify: in short, mysterious. But if, as I say, you understand the sociohistorical process of construction of the race, you'll see that the label works despite the absence of an essence.

Perhaps, then, we can allow that what Du Bois was after was the idea of racial identity, which I shall roughly define as a label, R, associated with *ascriptions* by most people (where ascription involves descriptive criteria for applying the label); and *identifications* by those that fall under it (where identification implies a shaping role for the label in the intentional acts of the possessors, so that they sometimes act *as an* R), where there is a history of associating possessors of the label with an inherited racial essence (even if some who use the label no longer believe in racial essences).

In fact, we might argue that racial identities could persist even if nobody believed in racial essences, provided both ascription and identification continue.

There will be some who will object to my account that it does not give racism a central place in defining racial identity: it is obvious, I think, from the history I have explored, that racism has been central to the development of race theory. In that sense racism has been part of the story all along. But you might give an account of racial identity in which you counted nothing as a racial essence unless it implied a hierarchy among the races;[14] or unless the label played a role in racist practices. I have some sympathy with the former strategy; it would fit easily into my basic picture. To the latter strategy, however, I make the philosopher's objection that it confuses logical and causal priority: I have no doubt that racial theories grew up, in part, as rationalizations for mistreating blacks, Jews, Chinese, and various others. But I think it is useful to reserve the concept of racism, as opposed to ethnocentrism or simply inhumanity, for practices in which a race concept plays a central role. And I doubt you can explain racism without first explaining the race concept.

I *am* in sympathy, however, with an animating impulse behind such proposals, which is to make sure that here in America we do not have discussions of race in which racism disappears from view. As I pointed out, racial identification is hard to resist in part because racial ascription by others is so insistent; and its effects — especially, but by no means exclusively, the racist ones — are so hard to escape. It is obvious, I think, that the persistence of racism means that racial ascriptions have negative consequences for some and positive consequences for others — creating, in particular, the white-skin privilege that it is so easy for people who have it to forget; and it is clear, too, that for those who suffer from the negative consequences, racial identification is a predictable response, especially where the project it suggests is that the victims of racism should join together to resist it. I shall return later to some of the important moral consequences of present racism and the legacy of racisms of the past.

But before I do, I want to offer some grounds for preferring the account of racial identity I have proposed, which places racial essences at its heart, over some newer accounts that see racial identity as a species of cultural identity.

CULTURAL IDENTITY IN AN AGE OF MULTICULTURALISM

Most contemporary racial identification — whether it occurs in such obviously regressive forms as the white nationalism of the Aryan Nation or in an Afrocentrism about which, I believe, a more nuanced position is appropriate — most naturally expresses itself in forms that adhere to modified (and sometimes unreconstructed) versions of the old racial essences. But the legacy of the Holocaust and the old racist biology has led many to be wary of racial essences and to replace them with cultural essences. Before I turn to my final cautionary words about racial identifications, I want to explore, for a moment, the substitution of cultures for races that has occurred in the movement for multiculturalism.

In my dictionary I find as a definition for "culture" "the totality of socially transmitted behavior patterns, arts, beliefs, institutions, and all other products of human work and thought."[15] Like most dictionary definitions, this is, no doubt, a proposal on which one could improve. But it surely picks out a familiar constellation of ideas. That is, in fact, the sense in which anthropologists largely use the term nowadays. The culture of the Asante or the Zuni, for the anthropologist, includes every object they make — material culture — and everything they think and do.

The dictionary definition could have stopped there, leaving out the talk of "socially transmitted behavior patterns, arts, beliefs, institutions" because these *are* all products of human work and thought. They are mentioned because they are the residue of an older idea of culture than the anthropological one; something more like the idea we might now express with the word "civilization": the "socially transmitted behavior patterns" of ritual, etiquette, religion, games, arts; the values that they engender and reflect; and the institutions — family, school, church, state — that shape and are shaped by them.[16] The habit of shaking hands at meetings belongs to culture in the anthropologist's sense; the works of Sandro Botticelli and Martin Buber and Count Basie belong to culture also, but they belong to civilization as well.

There are tensions between the concepts of culture and of civilization. There is nothing, for example, that requires that an American culture should be a totality in any stronger sense than being the sum of all the things we make and do.

American civilization, on the other hand, would have to have a certain coherence. Some of what is done in America by Americans would not belong to American civilization because it was too individual (the particular bedtime rituals of a particular American family); some would not belong because it was not properly American, because (like a Hindi sentence, spoken in America) it does not properly cohere with the rest.

The second, connected, difference between culture and civilization is that the latter takes values to be more central to the enterprise, in two ways. First, civilization is centrally defined by moral and aesthetic values: and the coherence of a civilization is, primarily, the coherence of those values with each other and, then, of the group's behavior and institutions with its values. Second, civilizations are essentially to be evaluated: they can be better and worse, richer and poorer, more and less interesting. Anthropologists, on the whole, tend now to avoid the relative evaluation of cultures, adopting a sort of cultural relativism, whose coherence philosophers have tended to doubt. And they do not take values as more central to culture than, for example, beliefs, ideas, and practices.

The move from "civilization" to "culture" was the result of arguments. The move away from evaluation came first, once people recognized that much evaluation of other cultures by the Europeans and Americans who invented anthropology had been both ignorant and biased. Earlier criticisms of "lower" peoples turned out to involve crucial misunderstandings of their ideas; and it eventually seemed clear enough, too, that nothing more than differences of upbringing underlay the distaste of some Westerners for unfamiliar habits. It is a poor move from recognizing certain evaluations as mistaken to giving up evaluation altogether, and anthropologists who adopt cultural relativism often preach more than practice it. Still, this cultural relativism was a response to real errors. That it is the wrong response doesn't make the errors any less erroneous.

The arguments against "civilization" were in place well before the midcentury. More recently, anthropologists began to see that the idea of the coherence of a civilization got in the way of understanding important facts about other societies (and, in the end, about our own). For even in some of the "simplest" societies, there are different values and practices and beliefs and interests associated with different social groups (for example, women as opposed to men). To think of a civilization as coherent was to miss the fact that these different values and beliefs were not merely different but actually opposed. Worse, what had been presented as the coherent unified worldview of a tribal people often turned out, on later inspection, to be merely the ideology of a dominant group or interest.

But the very idea of a coherent structure of beliefs and values and practices depends on a model of culture that does not fit our times — as we can see if we explore, for a moment, the ideal type of a culture where it might seem to be appropriate.

A COMMON CULTURE

There is an ideal — and thus to a certain extent imaginary — type of small-scale, technologically uncomplicated, face-to-face society, where most interactions are with people whom you know, that we call "traditional." In such a society every adult who is not mentally disabled speaks the same language. All share a vocabulary and a grammar and an accent. While there will be some words in the language that are not known by everybody — the names of medicinal herbs, the language of some religious rituals — most are known to all normal adults. To share a language is to participate in a complex set of mutual expectations and understandings: but in such a society it is not only linguistic behavior that is coordinated through universally known expectations and understandings. People will share an understanding of many practices — marriages, funerals, other rites of passage — and will largely share their views about the general workings not only of the social but also of the natural world. Even those who are skeptical about particular elements of belief will nevertheless know what everyone is supposed to believe, and they will know it in enough detail to behave very often as if they believed it, too.

A similar point applies to many of the values of such societies. It may well be that some people, even some groups, do not share the values that are enunciated in public and taught to children. But, once more, the standard values are universally known, and even those who do not share them know what it would be to act in conformity with them and probably do so much of the time.

In such a traditional society we may speak of these shared beliefs, values, signs, and symbols as the common culture; not, to insist on a crucial point, in the sense that everyone in the group actually holds the beliefs and values but in the sense that everybody knows what they are and everybody knows that they are widely held in the society.

Now, the citizens of one of those large "imagined communities" of modernity we call "nations" need not have, in this sense, a common culture. There is no single shared body of ideas and practices in India, or, to take another example, in most contemporary African states. And there is not now and there has never been a common culture in the United States, either. The reason is simple: the United States has always been multilingual, and has always had minorities who did not speak or understand English. It has always had a plurality of religious traditions; beginning with American Indian religions and Puritans and Catholics and Jews and including now many varieties of Islam, Buddhism, Jainism, Taoism, Bahai, and so on. And many of these religious traditions have been quite unknown to one another. More than this, Americans have also always differed significantly even among those who do speak English, from North to South and East to West, and from country to city, in customs of greeting, notions of civility, and a whole host of other ways. The notion that what has held the United States together historically over its great geographical range is a common culture, like the common culture of my traditional society, is — to put it politely — not sociologically plausible.

> **THERE IS NOT NOW AND THERE HAS NEVER BEEN A COMMON CULTURE IN THE UNITED STATES.**

The observation that there is no common American national culture will come as a surprise to many: observations about American culture, taken as a whole, are common. It is, for example, held to be individualist, litigious, racially obsessed. I think each of these claims is actually true, because what I mean when I say there is no common culture of the United States is not what is denied by someone who says that there is an American culture.

Such a person is describing large-scale tendencies within American life that are not necessarily participated in by all Americans. I do not mean to deny that these exist. But for such a tendency to be part of what I am calling the *common culture* they would have to derive from beliefs and values and practices (almost) universally shared and known to be so. And *that* they are not.

At the same time, it has also always been true that there was a dominant culture in these United States. It was Christian, it spoke English, and it identified with the high cultural traditions of Europe and, more particularly, of England. This dominant culture included much of the common culture of the dominant classes — the government and business and cultural elites — but it was familiar to many others who were subordinate to them. And it was not merely an effect but also an instrument of their domination.

The United States of America, then, has always been a society of many common cultures, which I will call, for convenience, sub-cultures, (noting, for the record, that this is not the way the word is used in sociology).

It would be natural, in the current climate, with its talk of multiculturalism, to assume that the primary subgroups to which these subcultures are attached will be ethnic and racial groups (with religious denominations conceived of as a species of ethnic group). It would be natural, too, to think that the characteristic difficulties of a multicultural society arise largely from the cultural differences between ethnic groups. I think this easy assimilation of ethnic and racial subgroups to subcultures is to be resisted.

First of all, it needs to be argued, and not simply assumed, that black Americans, say, taken as a group, *have* a common culture: values and beliefs and practices that they share and that they do not share with others. This is equally true for, say, Chinese-Americans; and it is a fortiori true of white Americans. What seems clear enough is that being an African-American or an Asian-American or white is an important social identity in the United States. Whether these are important social identities because these groups have shared common cultures is, on the other hand, quite doubtful, not least because it is doubtful whether they *have* common cultures at all.

The issue is important because an analysis of America's struggle with difference as a struggle among cultures suggests a mistaken analysis of how the problems of diversity arise. With differing cultures, we might expect misunderstandings arising out of ignorance of each others' values, practices, and beliefs; we might even expect conflicts because of differing values or beliefs. The paradigms of difficulty in a society of many cultures are misunderstandings of a word or a gesture; conflicts over who should take custody of the children after a divorce; whether to go the doctor or to the priest for healing.

Once we move from talking of cultures to identities whole new kinds of problems come into view. Racial and ethnic identities are, for example, essentially contrastive and relate centrally to social and political power; in this way they are like genders and sexualities.

Now, it is crucial to understanding gender and sexuality that women and men and gay and straight people grow up together in families, communities, denominations. Insofar as a common culture means common beliefs, values, and practices, gay people and straight people in most places have a common culture: and while there are societies in which the socialization of children is so structured by gender that women and men have seriously distinct cultures, this is not a feature of most "modern" societies. And it is perfectly possible for a black and a white American to grow up together in a shared adoptive family — with the same knowledge and values — and still grow into separate racial identities, in part because their experience outside the family, in public space, is bound to be racially differentiated.

I have insisted that we should distinguish between cultures and identities; but ethnic identities characteristically have cultural distinctions as one of their primary marks. That is why it is so easy to conflate them. Ethnic identities are created in family and community life. These — along with mass-mediated culture, the school, and the college — are, for most of us, the central sites of the social transmission of culture. Distinct practices, ideas, norms go with each ethnicity in part because people *want* to be ethnically distinct: because many people want the sense of solidarity that comes from being unlike others. With ethnicity in modern society, it is often the distinct identity that comes first, and the cultural distinction that is created and maintained because of it — not the other way around. The distinctive common cultures of ethnic and religious identities matter not simply because of their contents but also as markers of those identities.

> **I HAVE INSISTED THAT WE SHOULD DISTINGUISH BETWEEN CULTURES AND IDENTITIES.**

In the United States, not only ethnic but also racial boundaries are culturally marked. In *White Women, Race Matters: The Social Construction of Whiteness*,[17] Ruth Frankenberg records the anxiety of many white women who do not see themselves as white "ethnics" and worry, therefore, that they have no culture.[18] This is somewhat puzzling in people who live, as every normal human being does, in rich structures of knowledge, experience, value and meaning; through tastes and practices: it is perplexing, in short, in people with normal human lives. But the reason these women do not recognize that they have a culture is because none of these things that actually make up their cultural lives are marked as white, as belonging specially to them: and the things that *are* marked as white (racism, white privilege) are things they want to repudiate. Many African-Americans, on the other hand, have cultural lives in which the ways they eat, the churches they go to, the music they listen to, and the ways they speak *are* marked as black: their identities are marked by cultural differences.

I have insisted that African-Americans do not have a single culture, in the sense of shared language, values, practices, and meanings. But many people who think of races as groups defined by shared cultures, conceive that sharing in a different way. They understand black people as sharing black culture *by definition*: jazz or hip-hop belongs to an African-American, whether she likes it or knows anything about it, because it is culturally marked as black. Jazz belongs to a black person who knows nothing about it more fully or naturally than it does to a white jazzman.

WHAT MATTERS ABOUT CULTURE:
ARNOLD AGAIN

This view is an instance of what my friend Skip Gates has called "cultural geneticism."[19] It has, in Bertrand Russell's wicked phrase, "the virtues of theft over honest toil." On this view, you earn rights to culture that is marked with the mark of your race — or your nation — simply by having a racial identity. For the old racialists, as we saw, your racial character was something that came with your essence; this new view recognizes that race does not bring culture, and generously offers, by the wave of a wand, to correct Nature's omission. It is as generous to whites as it is to blacks. Because Homer and Shakespeare are products of Western culture, they are awarded to white children who have never studied a word of them, never heard their names. And in this generous spirit the fact is forgotten that cultural geneticism deprives white people of jazz and black people of Shakespeare. This is a bad deal — as Du Bois would have insisted. "I sit with Shakespeare," the Bard of Great Barrington wrote, "and he winces not."

There is nothing in cultural geneticism of the ambition or the rigor of Matthew Arnold's conception, where culture is, as he says in *Culture and Anarchy,* "the disinterested and active use of reading, reflection and observation,"[20] and what is most valuable to us in culture, in the anthropological sense, is earned by intellectual labor, by self-cultivation. For Arnold, true culture is a process "which consists in becoming something rather than in having something, in an inward condition of the mind and spirit";[21] whose aim is a "perfection in which characters of beauty and intelligence are both present, which unites, 'the two noblest of things,' — as Swift, who of one of the two, at any rate, had himself all too little, most happily calls them in his *Battle of the Books,* — 'the two noblest of things, sweetness and light.'"[22]

Arnold's aim is not, in the proper sense, an elitist one: he believes that this cultivation is the proper aim of us all.

> This is the *social idea*; and the men of culture are the true apostles of equality. The great men of culture are those who have had a passion for diffusing, for making prevail, for carrying from one end of society to the other, the best knowledge, the best ideas of their time; who have laboured to divest knowledge of all that was harsh, uncouth, difficult, abstract, professional, exclusive; to humanise it, to make it efficient outside the clique of the cultivated and learned, yet still remaining the *best* knowledge and thought of the time, and a true source, therefore, of sweetness and light.[23]

If you have this view of culture, you will think of cultural geneticism as the doctrine of the ignorant or the lazy, or at least of those who pander to them. And it is a view of culture whose adoption would diminish any society that seriously adopted it.

Not only is the conflation of identities and cultures mistaken, the view of cultural possession that underlies that error is the view of the Philistine, who, in Arnold's translation of Epictetus, makes "a great fuss about exercise, a great fuss about eating, a great fuss about drinking, a great fuss about walking, a great fuss about riding. All these things ought to be done merely *by the way*: the formation of the spirit and character must be our real concern."[24]

IDENTITIES AND NORMS

I have been exploring these questions about culture in order to show how unsatisfactory an account of the significance of race that mistakes identity for culture can be. But if this is the wrong route from identity to moral and political concerns, is there a better way?

We need to go back to the analysis of racial identities. While the theories on which ascription is based need not themselves be normative, these identities come with normative as well as descriptive expectations; about which, once more, there may be both inconsistency in the thinking of individuals and fairly widespread disagreement among them. There is, for example, a very wide range of opinions among American Jews as to what their being Jewish commits them to; and while most Gentiles probably don't think about the matter very much, people often make remarks that suggest they admire the way in which, as they believe, Jews have "stuck together," an admiration that seems to presuppose the moral idea that it is, if not morally obligatory, then at least morally desirable, for those who share identities to take responsibility for each other. (Similar comments have been made increasingly often about Korean-Americans.)

We need, in short, to be clear that the relation between identities and moral life are complex. In the liberal tradition, to which I adhere, we see public morality as engaging each of us as individuals with our individual "identities": and we have the notion, which comes (as Charles Taylor has rightly argued)[25] from the ethics of authenticity, that, other things being equal, people have the right to be acknowledged publicly as what they already really are. It is because someone is already authentically Jewish or gay that we deny them something in requiring them to hide this fact, to "pass," as we say, for something that they are not. Charles Taylor has suggested that we call the political issues raised by this fact the politics of recognition: a politics that asks us to acknowledge socially and politically the authentic identities of others.

> CHARLES TAYLOR HAS SUGGESTED THAT WE CALL THE POLITICAL ISSUES RAISED BY THIS FACT THE POLITICS OF RECOGNITION: A POLITICS THAT ASKS US TO ACKNOWLEDGE SOCIALLY AND POLITICALLY THE AUTHENTIC IDENTITIES OF OTHERS.

As has often been pointed out, however, the way much discussion of recognition proceeds is strangely at odds with the individualist thrust of talk of authenticity and identity. If what matters about me is my individual and authentic self, why is so much contemporary talk of identity about large categories — race, gender, ethnicity, nationality, sexuality — that seem so far from individual? What is the relation between this collective language and the individualist thrust of the modern notion of the self? How has social life come to be so bound up with an idea of identity that has deep roots in romanticism with its celebration of the individual over against society?[26]

The connection between individual identity, on the one hand, and race and other collective identities, on the other, seems to be something like this: each person's individual identity is seen as having two major dimensions. There is a collective dimension, the intersection of her collective identities; and there is what I will call a personal dimension, consisting of other socially or morally important features of the person — intelligence, charm, wit, cupidity — that are not themselves the basis of forms of collective identity.

The distinction between these two dimensions of identity is, so to speak, a sociological rather than a logical distinction. In each dimension we are talking about properties that are important for social life. But only the collective identities count as social categories, kinds of person. There is a logical category but no social category of the witty, or the clever, or the charming, or the greedy: people who share these properties do not constitute a social group, in the relevant sense. The concept of authenticity is central to the connection between these two dimensions; and there is a problem in many current understandings of that relationship, a misunderstanding one can find, for example, in Charles Taylor's recent (brilliant) essay *Multiculturalism and the Politics of Recognition.*

AUTHENTICITY

Taylor captures the ideal of authenticity in a few elegant sentences: "There is a certain way of being that is *my* way. I am called upon to live my life in this way. . . . If I am not [true to myself], I miss the point of my life."[27] To elicit the problem, here, let me start with a point Taylor makes in passing about Herder: "I should note here that Herder applied his concept of originality at two levels, not only to the individual person among other persons, but also to the culture-bearing people among other peoples. Just like individuals, a Volk should be true to itself, that is, its own culture."[28] It seems to me that in this way of framing the issue less attention than necessary is paid to the connection between the originality of persons and of nations. After all, in many places nowadays, the individual identity, whose authenticity screams out for recognition, is likely to have an ethnic identity (which Herder would have seen as a national identity) as a component of its collective dimension. It is, among other things, my being, say, an African-American that shapes the authentic self that I seek to express.[29] And it is, in part, because I seek to express my self that I seek recognition of an African-American identity. This is the fact that makes problems: for recognition as an African-American means social acknowledgment of that collective identity, which requires not just recognizing its existence but actually demonstrating respect for it. If, in understanding myself as African-American, I see myself as resisting white norms, mainstream

American conventions, the racism (and, perhaps, the materialism or the individualism) of "white culture," why should I at the same time seek recognition from these white others?

There is, in other words, at least an irony in the way in which an ideal — you will recognize it if I call it the bohemian ideal — in which authenticity requires us to reject much that is conventional in our society is turned around and made the basis of a "politics of recognition."

Irony is not the bohemian's only problem. It seems to me that this notion of authenticity has built into it a series of errors of philosophical anthropology. It is, first of all, wrong in failing to see what Taylor so clearly recognizes, namely the way in which the self is, as he says, dialogically constituted. The rhetoric of authenticity proposes not only that I have a way of being that is all my own but that in developing it I must fight against the family, organized religion, society, the school, the state — all the forces of convention. This is wrong, however, not only because it is in dialogue with other people's understandings of who I am that I develop a conception of my own identity (Charles Taylor's point) but also because my identity is crucially constituted through concepts (and practices) made available to me by religion, society, school, and state, and mediated to varying degrees by the family (Hacking's point about "making up people"). Dialogue shapes the identity I develop as I grow up: but the very material out of which I form it is provided, in part, by my society, by what Taylor calls its language in "a broad sense."[30] I shall borrow and extend Taylor's term "monological" here to describe views of authenticity that make these connected errors.

I used the example of African-Americans just now, and it might seem that this complaint cannot be lodged against an American black nationalism: African-American identity, it might be said, is shaped by African-American society, culture, and religion. "It is dialogue with these black others that shapes the black self; it is from these black contexts that the concepts through which African-Americans shape themselves are derived. The white society, the white culture, over against which an African-American nationalism of the counterconventional kind poses itself, is therefore not part of what shapes the collective dimension of the individual identities of black people in the United States."

This claim is simply wrong. And what shows it is wrong is the fact that it is in part a recognition of a black identity by "white society" that is demanded by nationalism of this form. And "recognition" here means what Taylor means by it, not mere acknowledgment of one's existence. African-American identity, as I have argued, is centrally shaped by American society and institutions: it cannot be seen as constructed solely within African-American communities. African-American culture, if this means shared beliefs, values, practices, does not exist: what exists are African-American cultures, and though these are created and sustained in large measure by African-Americans, they cannot be understood without reference to the bearers of other American racial identities.

There is, I think, another error in the standard framing of authenticity as an ideal, and that is the philosophical realism (which is nowadays usually called "essentialism") that seems inherent in the way questions of authenticity are normally posed. Authenticity speaks of the real self buried in there, the self one has to dig out and express. It is only later, after romanticism, that the idea develops that one's self is something that one creates, makes up, so that every life should be an artwork whose creator is, in some sense, his or her own greatest creation. (This is, I suppose, an idea one of whose sources is Oscar Wilde; but it is surely very close to the self-cultivation that Arnold called "culture.")

Of course, neither the picture in which there is just an authentic nugget of selfhood, the core that is distinctively me, waiting to be dug out, nor the notion that I can simply make up any self I choose, should tempt us. We make up selves from a tool kit of options made available by our culture and society — in ways that I pointed out earlier. We do make choices, but we don't determine the options among which we choose.[31]

> WE MAKE UP SELVES FROM A TOOL KIT OF OPTIONS MADE AVAILABLE BY OUR CULTURE AND SOCIETY. . . . WE DO MAKE CHOICES, BUT WE DON'T DETERMINE THE OPTIONS AMONG WHICH WE CHOOSE.

If you agree with this, you will wonder how much of authenticity we should acknowledge in our political morality: and that will depend, I suppose, on whether an account of it can be developed that is neither essentialist nor monological.

It would be too large a claim that the identities that claim recognition in the multicultural chorus *must* be essentialist and monological. But it seems to me that one reasonable ground for suspicion of much contemporary multicultural talk is that the conceptions of collective identity they presuppose are indeed remarkably unsubtle in their understandings of the processes by which identities, both individual and collective, develop. The story I have told for African-American identity has a parallel for other collective identities: in all of them, I would argue, false theories play a central role in the application of the labels; in all of them the story is complex, involves "making up people," and cannot be explained by an appeal to an essence.

BEYOND IDENTITY

The large collective identities that call for recognition come with notions of how a proper person of that kind behaves: it is not that there is *one* way that blacks should behave, but that there are proper black modes of behavior. These notions provide loose norms or models, which play a role in shaping the life plans of those who make these collective identities central to their individual identities; of the identifications of those who fly under these banners.[32] Collective identities, in short, provide what we might call scripts: narratives that people can use in shaping their life plans and in telling their life stories. In our society (though not, perhaps, in the England of Addison and Steele) being witty does not in this way suggest the life script of "the wit." And that is why what I called the personal dimensions of identity work differently from the collective ones.

This is not just a point about modern Westerners: cross-culturally it matters to people that their lives have a certain narrative unity; they want to be able to tell a story of their lives that makes sense. The story — my story — should cohere in the way appropriate by the standards made available in my culture to a person of my identity. In telling that story, how I fit into the wider story of various collectivities is, for most of us, important. It is not just gender identities that give shape (through, for example, rites of passage into woman- or manhood) to one's life: ethnic and national identities too fit each individual story into a larger narrative. And some of the most "individualist" of individuals value such things. Hobbes spoke of the desire for glory as one of the dominating impulses of human beings, one that was bound to make trouble for social life. But glory can consist in fitting and being seen to fit into a collective history: and so, in the name of glory, one can end up doing the most social things of all.

> **CROSS-CULTURALLY IT MATTERS TO PEOPLE THAT THEIR LIVES HAVE A CERTAIN NARRATIVE UNITY; THEY WANT TO BE ABLE TO TELL A STORY OF THEIR LIVES THAT MAKES SENSE.**

How does this general idea apply to our current situation in the multicultural West? We live in societies in which certain individuals have not been treated with equal dignity because they were, for example, women, homosexuals, blacks, Catholics. Because, as Taylor so persuasively argues, our identities are dialogically shaped, people who have these characteristics find them central — often, negatively central — to their identities. Nowadays there is a widespread agreement that the insults to their dignity and the limitations of their autonomy imposed in the name of these collective identities are seriously wrong. One form of healing of the self that those who have these identities participate in is learning to see these collective identities not as sources of limitation and insult but as a valuable part of what they centrally are. Because the ethics of authenticity requires us to express what we centrally are in our lives, they move next to the demand that they be recognized in social life as women, homosexuals, blacks, Catholics. Because there was no good reason to treat people of these sorts badly, and because the culture continues to provide degrading images of them nevertheless, they demand that we do cultural work to resist the stereotypes, to challenge the insults, to lift the restrictions.

These old restrictions suggested life scripts for the bearers of these identities, but they were negative ones. In order to construct a life with dignity, it seems natural to take the collective identity and construct positive life scripts instead.

An African-American after the Black Power movement takes the old script of self-hatred, the script in which he or she is a nigger, and works, in community with others, to construct a series of positive black life scripts. In these life scripts, being a Negro is recoded as being black: and this requires, among other things, refusing to assimilate to white norms of speech and behavior. And if one is to be black in a society that is racist then one has constantly to deal with assaults on one's dignity. In this context, insisting on the right to live a dignified life will not be enough. It will not even be enough to require that one be treated with equal dignity despite being black: for that will require a concession that being black counts naturally or to some degree against one's dignity. And so one will end up asking to be respected *as a black*.

I hope I seem sympathetic to this story. I *am* sympathetic. I see how the story goes. It may even be historically, strategically necessary for the story to go this way.[33] But I think we need to go on to the next necessary step, which is to ask whether the identities constructed in this way are ones we can all be happy with in the longer run. What demanding respect for people *as blacks* or *as gays* requires is that there be some scripts that go with being an African-American or having same-sex desires. There will be proper ways of being black and gay: there will be expectations to be met; demands will be made. It is at this point that someone who takes autonomy seriously will want to ask whether we have not replaced one kind of tyranny with another. If I had to choose between Uncle Tom and Black Power, I would, of course, choose the latter. But I would like not to have to choose. I would like other options. The politics of recognition requires that one's skin color, one's sexual body, should be politically acknowledged in ways that make it hard for those who want to treat their skin and their sexual body as personal dimensions of the self. And "personal" doesn't mean "secret" but "not too tightly scripted," "not too constrained by the demands and expectations of others."

> IF I HAD TO CHOOSE BETWEEN UNCLE TOM AND BLACK POWER, I WOULD, OF COURSE, CHOOSE THE LATTER. BUT I WOULD LIKE NOT TO HAVE TO CHOOSE. I WOULD LIKE OTHER OPTIONS.

In short, so it seems to me, those who see potential for conflict between individual freedom and the politics of identity are right.

WHY DIFFERENCES BETWEEN GROUPS MATTER

But there is a different kind of worry about racial identities; one that has not to do with their being too tightly scripted but with a consequence of their very existence for social life. We can approach the problem by asking why differences between groups matter.

This is, I think, by no means obvious. If some minority groups — Korean-Americans, say — do especially well, most people feel, "More power to them." We worry, then, about the minorities that fail. And the main reason why people currently worry about minorities that fail is that group failure may be evidence of injustice to individuals. That is the respectable reason why there is so much interest in hypotheses, like those of Murray and Herrnstein, that suggest a different diagnosis. But let us suppose that we can get rid of what we might call Sowellian discrimination: discrimination, that is, as understood by Thomas Sowell, which is differential treatment based on false (or perhaps merely unwarranted) beliefs about the different average capacities of racial groups.[34]

Even without Sowellian discrimination socioeconomic disparities between groups threaten the fairness of our social arrangements. This issue can be kept clear only if we look at the matter from the point of view of an individual. Suppose I live in a society with two groups, blacks and whites. Suppose that, for whatever reason, the black group to which I obviously belong scores averagely low on a test that is genuinely predictive of job performance. Suppose the test is expensive. And suppose I would have, in fact, a high score on this test and that I would, in fact, perform well.[35] In these circumstances it may well be economically rational for an employer, knowing what group I belong to, simply not to give me the test, and thus not to hire me.[36] The employer has acted in a rational fashion; there is no Sowellian discrimination here. But most people will understand me if I say that I feel that this outcome is unfair. One way of putting the unfairness is to say, "What I can do and be with my talents is being held back because others, over whose failings I have no control, happen to have the characteristics they do."

Capitalism — like life — is full of such unfairness: luck — from lotteries to hurricanes — affects profit. And we can't get rid of all unfairness; for if we had perfect insurance, zero risk, there'd be no role for entrepreneurship, no markets, no capitalism. But we do think it proper to mitigate some risks. We think, for example, that we should do something about bad luck when it has large negative effects on individual people, or if it forces them below some socioeconomic baseline — we insure for car accidents, death, loss of home; the government helps those ruined by large-scale acts of God. We don't worry much about the chance production of small negative effects on individuals, even large numbers of individuals.

It is at least arguable that in our society the cost to competent, well-behaved individual blacks and Hispanics[37] of being constantly treated as if they have to measure up — the cost in stress, in anger, in lost opportunities — is pretty high.[38] It would be consistent with a general attitude of wanting to mitigate risks with large negative consequences for individuals to try to do something about it.[39]

This specific sort of unfairness — where a person is atypically competent in a group that is averagely less competent — is the result, among other things, of the fact that jobs are allocated by a profit-driven economy and the fact that I was born into a group in which I am atypical. The latter fact may or may not be the consequence of policies adopted by this society. Let's suppose it isn't: so society isn't, so to speak, causally responsible. According to some — for example, Thomas Sowell, again — that means it isn't morally responsible, either: you don't have to fix what you didn't break.

I'm not so sure. First, we can take collective responsibility, "as a society," for harms we didn't cause; as is recognized in the Americans with Disabilities Act. But second, the labor market is, after all, an institution: in a modern society it is kept in place by such arrangements as the laws of contract, the institution of money, laws creating and protecting private property, health and safety at work, and equal employment laws. Sowell may disapprove of some of these, but he can't disapprove of all of them; without all of them, there'd be no capitalism. So the outcome is the result not only of my bad luck but of its interaction with social arrangements, which could be different.

Thus once we grasp the unfairness of this situation, people might feel that something should be done about it. One possible thing would be to try to make sure there were no ethnic minorities significantly below norm in valuable skills. If the explanation for most significant differences between groups is not hereditary, this could be done, in part, by adopting policies that discouraged significant ethnic differentiation, which would gradually produce assimilation to a single cultural norm. Or it could be done by devoting resources most actively to the training of members of disadvantaged groups.

Another — more modest — move would be to pay special attention to finding talented members of minority groups who would not be found when employers were guided purely by profit.

A third — granted once more that the differences in question are not largely hereditary — would be to explore why there are such differences and to make known to people ways of giving themselves or their children whatever aptitudes will maximize their life chances, given their hereditary endowments.

Fourth, and finally, for those differences that were hereditary it would be possible to do research to seek to remedy the initial distribution by the genetic lottery — as we have done in making it possible for those without natural resistance to live in areas where malaria and yellow fever are endemic.

Each of these strategies would cost something, and the costs would be not only financial. Many people believe that the global homogenization of culture impoverishes the cultural fabric of our lives. It is a sentiment, indeed, we find in Arnold: "My brother Saxons have, as is well known, a terrible way with them of wanting to improve everything but themselves off the face of the earth; I have no passion for finding nothing but myself everywhere; I like variety to exist and to show itself to me, and I would not for the world have the lineaments of the Celtic genius lost."[40] The first strategy — of cultural assimilation — would undoubtedly escalate that process. And all these strategies would require more knowledge than we now have to apply in actual cases so as to guarantee their success. Anyone who shares my sense that there is an unfairness here to be met, an unfairness that has something to do with the idea that what matters is individual merit, should be interested in developing that kind of knowledge.

But I want to focus for a moment on a general effect of these four strategies. They would all produce a population less various in some of the respects that make a difference to major socioeconomic indicators. This would not mean that everybody would be the same as everybody else — but it could lead to a more recreational conception of racial identity. It would make African-American identity more like Irish-American identity is for most of those who care to keep the label. And that would allow us to resist one persistent feature of ethnoracial identities: that they risk becoming the obsessive focus, the be-all and end-all, of the lives of those who identify with them. They lead people to forget that their individual identities are complex and multifarious — that they have enthusiasms that do not flow from their race or ethnicity, interests and tastes that cross ethnoracial boundaries, that they have occupations or professions, are fans of clubs and groups. And they then lead them, in obliterating the identities they share with people outside their race or ethnicity, away from the possibility of identification with Others. Collective identities have a tendency, if I may coin a phrase, to "go imperial," dominating not only people of other identities, but the other identities, whose shape is exactly what makes each of us what we individually and distinctively are.

COLLECTIVE IDENTITIES HAVE A TENDENCY, IF I MAY COIN A PHRASE, TO "GO IMPERIAL."

In policing this imperialism of identity — an imperialism as visible in racial identities as anywhere else — it is crucial to remember always that we are not simply black or white or yellow or brown, gay or straight or bisexual, Jewish, Christian, Moslem, Buddhist, or Confucian but that we are also brothers and sisters; parents and children; liberals, conservatives, and leftists; teachers and lawyers and auto-makers and gardeners; fans of the Padres and the Bruins; amateurs of grunge rock and lovers of Wagner; movie buffs; MTV-holics, mystery-readers; surfers and singers; poets and pet-lovers; students and teachers; friends and lovers. Racial identity can be the basis of resistance to racism; but even as we struggle against racism — and though we have made great progress, we have further still to go — let us not let our racial identities subject us to new tyrannies.

IN CONCLUSION

Much of what I have had to say in this essay will, no doubt, seem negative. It is true that I have defended an analytical notion of racial identity, but I have gone to worry about too hearty an endorsement of racial identification. Let me quote Matthew Arnold again, for the last time: "I thought, and I still think, that in this [Celtic] controversy, as in other controversies, it is most desirable both to believe and to profess that the work of construction is the fruitful and important work, and that we are demolishing only to prepare for it."[41] So here are my positive proposals: live with fractured identities; engage in identity play; find solidarity, yes, but recognize contingency, and, above all, practice irony.[42] In short I have only the proposals of a banal "postmodernism." And there is a regular response to these ideas from those who speak for the identities that now demand recognition, identities toward which so many people have struggled in dealing with the obstacles created by sexism, racism, homophobia. "It's all very well for you. You academics live a privileged life; you have steady jobs; solid incomes; status from your place in maintaining cultural capital. Trifle with your own identities, if you like; but leave mine alone."

To which I answer only: my job as an intellectual is to call it as I see it. I owe my fellow citizens respect, certainly, but not a feigned acquiescence. I have a duty to reflect on the probable consequences of what I say; and then, if I still think it worth saying, to accept responsibility for them. If I am wrong, I say, you do not need to plead that I should tolerate error for the sake of human liberation; you need only correct me. But if I am right, so it seems to me, there is a work of the imagination that we need to begin.

And so I look forward to taking up, along with others, the fruitful imaginative work of constructing collective identities for a democratic nation in a world of democratic nations; work that must go hand in hand with cultivating democracy here and encouraging it everywhere else. About the identities that will be useful in this project, let me say only this: the identities we need will have to recognize *both* the centrality of difference within human identity *and* the fundamental moral unity of humanity.

NOTES

[1] This claim was prompted by G. Spiller, ed., *Papers in Inter-Racial Problems Communicated to the First Universal Races Congress Held at the University of London, July 26–29, 1911* (London: P. S. King and Son, 1911). Republished with an introduction by H. Aptheker (Secaucus, N.J.: Citadel Press, 1970). [All notes are Appiah's.]

[2] W.E.B. Du Bois, "Races," in *Writings in Periodicals Edited by W.E.B. Du Bois, Vol. 1, 1911–1925,* compiled and edited by Herbert Aptheker (Milwood, N.Y.: Kraus-Thomson Organization Limited, 1983), p. 13.

[3] Ibid., p. 14.

[4] "The Uncompleted Argument: Du Bois and the Illusion of Race," reprinted from *Critical Inquiry* 12 (Autumn 1985). In *"Race," Writing and Difference,* ed. Henry Louis Gates, Jr. (Chicago: University of Chicago Press, 1986), pp. 21–37. Lucius Outlaw has remonstrated with me about this in the past; these rethinkings are prompted largely by discussion with him.

[5] Du Bois, *Dusk of Dawn: An Essay toward an Autobiography of a Race Concept* (New York: Harcourt, Brace, 1940). Reprinted with introduction by Herbert Aptheker (Milwood, N.Y.: Kraus-Thomson Organization Limited, 1975), pp. 116–17.

[6] I am conscious here of having been pushed to rethink my views by Stuart Hall's Du Bois lectures at Harvard in the spring of 1994, which began with a nuanced critique of my earlier work on Du Bois's views.

[7] See Kevin Mulroy, *Freedom on the Border: The Seminole Maroons in Florida, the Indian Territory, Coahuila, and Texas* (Lubbock, Tex.: Texas Tech University Press, 1993).

[8] Ian Hacking, "Making Up People" reprinted from *Reconstructing Individualism: Autonomy, Individuality and the Self in Western Thought,* ed. Thomas Heller, Morton Sousa, and David Wellbery (Stanford: Stanford University Press, 1986), in *Forms of Desire: Sexual Orientation and the Social Constructionist Controversy,* ed. Edward Stein (New York: Routledge, 1992), pp. 69–88 (page references are to this version).

[9] Hacking, "Making Up People," p. 87.

[10] Cited in ibid., p. 81.

[11] Ibid., p. 82.

[12] That I don't recall it doesn't *prove* that I didn't, of course.

[13] See Mary C. Waters, *Ethnic Options: Choosing Identities in America* (Berkeley and Los Angeles: University of California Press, 1990).

[14] This is the proposal of a paper on metaphysical racism by Berel Lang at the New School for Social Research seminar "Race and Philosophy" in October 1994, from which I learned much.

[15] *American Heritage Dictionary III for DOS* (3d ed.) (Novato, Calif.: Word-star International Incorporated, 1993).

[16] The distinction between culture and civilization I am marking is not one that would have been thus marked in nineteenth-century ethnography or (as we would now say) social anthropology: culture and civilization were basically synonyms, and they were both primarily used in the singular. The distinctions I am making draw on what I take to be the contemporary resonances of these two words. If I had more time, I would explore the history of the culture concept the sort of way we have explored "race."

[17] Ruth Frankenberg, *White Women, Race Matters: The Social Construction of Whiteness* (Minneapolis: University of Minnesota Press, 1993).

[18] The discussion of this work is shaped by conversation with Larry Blum, Martha Minow, David Wilkins, and David Wong.

[19] Gates means the notion to cover thinking in terms of cultural patrimony quite generally, not just in the case of race. See Henry Louis Gates, Jr., *Loose Canons* (New York: Oxford University Press, 1993).

[20] Matthew Arnold, *Culture and Anarchy*, ed. Samuel Lipman (New Haven: Yale University Press, 1994), p. 119.

[21] Ibid., p. 33.

[22] Ibid., p.37.

[23] Ibid., p. 48. The phrase "sweetness and light" is from Jonathan Swift's *Battle of the Books* (1697). The contest between the ancients (represented there by the bee) and the moderns (represented by the spider) is won by the ancients, who provide, like the bee, both honey and wax — sweetness and light. Sweetness is, then, aesthetic, and light intellectual, perfection.

[24] Arnold, *Culture and Anarchy*, p. 36.

[25] Charles Taylor, *Multiculturalism and "The Politics of Recognition."* With commentary by Amy Gutmann, ed., K. Anthony Appiah, Jürgen Habermas, Steven C. Rockefeller, Michael Walzer, and Susan Wolf (Princeton: Princeton University Press, 1994).

[26] Taylor reminds us rightly of Trilling's profound contributions to our understanding of this history. I discuss Trilling's work in chap. 4 of *In My Father's House.*

[27] Taylor, *Multiculturalism*, p. 30.

[28] Ibid., p. 31.

[29] And, for Herder, this would be a paradigmatic national identity.

[30] The broad sense "cover[s] not only the words we speak, but also other modes of expression whereby we define ourselves, including the 'languages' of art, of gesture, of love, and the like" (p. 32).

[31] This is too simple, too, for reasons captured in Anthony Giddens's many discussions of "duality of structure."

[32] I say "make" here not because I think there is always conscious attention to the shaping of life plans or a substantial experience of choice but because I want to stress the antiessentialist point that there are choices that can be made.

[33] Compare what Sartre wrote in his "Orphée Noir," in *Anthologie de la Nouvelle Poésie Nègre et Malagache de Langue Francaise*, ed. L. S. Senghor, p. xiv. Sartre argued, in effect, that this move is a necessary step in a dialectical progression. In this passage he explicitly argues that what he calls an "antiracist racism" is a path to the "final unity . . . the abolition of differences of race."

[34] "Once the possibility of economic performance differences between groups is admitted, then differences in income, occupational 'representation,' and the like do not, in themselves, imply that decision-makers took race or ethnicity into account. However, in other cases, group membership may in fact be used as a proxy for economically meaningful variables, rather than reflecting either mistaken prejudices or even subjective affinities and animosities." Thomas Sowell, *Race and Culture: A World View* (New York: Basic Books, 1994), p. 114.

[35] You need both these conditions, because a high score on a test that correlates well for some skill doesn't necessarily mean you will perform well. And, in fact, Sowell discusses the fact that the same IQ score predicts different levels of economic success for different ethnic groups; ibid., pp. 173, 182.

[36] Knowing this, I might offer to pay myself, if I had the money: but that makes the job worth less to me than to members of the other groups. So I lose out again.

[37] Let me explicitly point out that many of these people are not middle-class.

[38] I actually think that there is still rather more Sowellian discrimination than Sowell generally acknowledges; but that is another matter.

[39] It will seem to some that I've avoided an obvious argument here, which is that the inequalities in resources that result from differences in talents under capitalism need addressing. I agree. But the argument I am making here is meant to appeal to only extremely unradical individualist ideas; it's designed not to rely on arguing for egalitarian outcomes directly.

[40] Matthew Arnold, *On the Study of Celtic Literature and on Translating Homer* (New York: MacMillan, 1883), p. 11.

[41] Ibid., p. ix.

[42] See, for example, Richard Rorty, *Contingency, Irony and Solidarity* (New York: Cambridge University Press, 1989), and my review of it: "Metaphys. Ed.," *Village Voice*, September 19, 1989, p. 55.

· · • • • · ·

QUESTIONS FOR A SECOND READING

1. Appiah's essay is a reader-friendly one — that is, it goes out of its way to address, engage, anticipate, and assist its readers. This engagement is a *technical* feat; it is a strategy. It is the result of something Appiah *does* as a writer. His work suggests strategies that you, too, could adopt and use.

    Take note, for example, of the ways in which Appiah punctuates the text. Punctuation is often discussed in relation to the sentence. Writers use marks of punctuation (commas, dashes, colons, semicolons, parentheses) to organize sentences and to help readers locate themselves in relation to what they are reading. Writers also punctuate longer units of text, such as essays or chapters. Appiah's text provides an excellent model of this practice. You can notice immediately how he uses white space and subheadings to organize the essay into sections.

    There are also, however, many moments when Appiah speaks as a writer about the text he is writing (and that you are reading). He does this to remind you (and perhaps himself) where you have been and where you are going in relation to this long piece of writing. Here are some examples:

    > For reasons I shall be able to make clear only when I have given my account, Du Bois's own approach is somewhat misleading. So instead of proceeding with exegesis of Du Bois, I must turn next to the task of shaping a sociohistorical account of racial identity. (p. 42)

    > There will be some who will object to my account that it does not give racism a central place in defining racial identity. (p. 47)

    > I shall return later to some of the important moral consequences of present racism and the legacy of racisms of the past. (p. 47)

    > But before I do, I want to offer some grounds for preferring the account of racial identity I have proposed, which places racial essences at its heart, over some newer accounts that see racial identity as a species of cultural identity. (p. 47)

    > I have been exploring these questions about culture in order to show how unsatisfactory an account of the significance of race that mistakes identity for culture can be. But if this is the wrong route from identity to moral and political concerns, is there a better way? (p. 54)

    As you reread the text, take note of the places where Appiah is punctuating his essay — places where Appiah, as a writer, seems to have you, his reader, in mind.

2. Although this is a reader-friendly text, it is also a learned text. It contains casual references to writers and scholars whom you may not recognize:

W. E. B. Du Bois, Ian Hacking, Matthew Arnold, Charles Taylor, Thomas Sowell — to list just a few. Using the Internet as well as the library (so that you can put your hands on books and scholarly journals) and perhaps working in a group, create brief glosses on some of these writers and their work. Who are they? What are their concerns? And why might they be useful or interesting or important to Appiah?

3. We asked that you pay special attention to voice during your first reading of this essay. Remember that Appiah does not necessarily agree with all of the affirmative statements he makes — in many instances, he is instead exploring the potential consequences of a particular thought process or contention. In other instances, though, Appiah shifts back into his own voice and speaks for himself.

    Here, for example, is a moment when Appiah acknowledges the twist and turns of his methods. He has come to this position: "The notion that what has held the United States together historically over its great geographical range is a common culture . . . is — to put it politely — not sociologically plausible." He goes on:

    > The observation that there is no common American national culture will come as a surprise to many: observations about American culture, taken as a whole, are common. It is, for example, held to be individualist, litigious, racially obsessed. I think each of these claims is actually true, because what I mean when I say there is no common culture of the United States is not what is denied by someone who says that there is an American culture. (p. 50)

    As you reread, chart the moments when Appiah takes on (speaks from within) someone else's way of thinking and speaking. Also chart the moments when you feel he is finally speaking for himself. How do you know? When and where is Appiah most likely to come forward and to speak for himself?

4. In each section of his essay, Appiah works with key terms. He is the sort of philosopher who believes that in order to think better, we need to have a better command of our words, of the language we use to articulate what we know. Here are some clusters of terms from the essay: *identity, identification, racial identity, racial identification, collective identities; culture, common culture, multiculturalism, civilization; narratives, scripts, life stories, authenticity; the politics of recognition, the politics of identity; freedom, tyranny, democracy.*

    As you reread, take a particular term (or cluster of terms) that seems interesting, important, or compelling, and follow Appiah's use of this term (or cluster) through one of the subsections of the essay. Then, write a brief paragraph of translation. It could begin something like this: "In the section titled 'Cultural Identity in an Age of Multiculturalism,' Appiah talks about culture and civilization, and this is what I think he is trying to say . . ." You might conclude: "This is important to him because . . ."

5.   As he prepares for the final section of his essay, Appiah offers a surprising list:

> In policing this imperialism of identity — an imperialism as visible in racial identities as anywhere else — it is crucial to remember always that we are not simply black or white or yellow or brown, gay or straight or bisexual, Jewish, Christian, Moslem, Buddhist, or Confucian but that we are also brothers and sisters; parents and children; liberals, conservatives and leftists; teachers and lawyers and automakers and gardeners; fans of the Padres and the Bruins; amateurs of grunge rock and lovers of Wagner; movie buffs; MTV-holics; mystery-readers; surfers and singers; poets and pet-lovers; students and teachers; friends and lovers. Racial identity can be the basis of resistance to racism; but even as we struggle against racism — and though we have made great progress, we have further still to go — let us not let our racial identities subject us to new tyrannies. (p. 62)

A list like that is a generous gesture. It invites additions; it invites *you* to join in. It is also a leveling gesture — Jewish or Christian, gay or straight, poets and pet-lovers, Padres and Bruins: all of these identity markers have equal status.

This long list is an invitation to, as Appiah advises, "engage in identity play." Retype the first part of the sentence, the words up to the "but" clause ("but that we are also . . ."), and then prepare your list. Your list should be a distinctive one that represents the range of identifications you might offer as working terms of identity. Think of the list as something you would present to the rest of the class.

When you are done with that sentence, take a minute to think about what your list represents — what it represents as an act, as a way of enacting as well as thinking about the "fruitful imaginative work of constructing collective identities for a democratic nation" (p. 63). Write out a short paragraph that you might offer as a response to Appiah's conclusion.

· · · ● · · ·

ASSIGNMENTS FOR WRITING

1.   What might be the consequences of Appiah's argument? If, as a mental exercise (or because you are convinced), you follow Appiah's line of thought, what effects might this have on the ways you (or "we") think, act, speak, and write? What might change? How?

These questions offer a way to begin thinking about an essay. If you choose to write this essay, here is one approach to writing it.

Choose one or two of the essay's subsections and let them represent a line of argument. (Because the essay is long and complicated, it is difficult to work with in its entirety.) You'll need to bring this argument to your readers — smart people, but people who have not yet read "Racial Identities." To present Appiah's line of thinking, use a combination of summary, paraphrase, and block quotation. If you want to make reference to the shape of the entire essay, do so only in two or three sentences. Focus on the details in the subsection (or subsections) you have chosen as your point of focus.

Then, to make this project *your* project, and to make it an intellectual project (and not just a rehearsal of received opinion or an "I have a dream" speech), you will need to think carefully about something (an example, most likely) that you can bring to the discussion, something you can bring into conversation with the examples provided by Appiah. Think about this. The choice is important. For ideas, look to your reading (or viewing or listening), to your immediate experience, to the current institutional, political, or cultural scenes where you are or have been a player—look to situations that you know well.

Your account of Appiah's thinking will certainly be important to what you write, but equally important will be the example you provide. Your example will allow you to focus your attention to racial thinking as it is (or has been) most crucially and most interestingly present to you and to your generation or cohorts, to the people for whom you feel authorized to speak.

2. Consider this passage from "Racial Identities":

> Collective identities, in short, provide what we might call scripts: narratives that people can use in shaping their life plans and in telling their life stories. In our society (though not, perhaps, in the England of Addison and Steele) being witty does not in this way suggest the life script of "the wit." And that is why what I called the personal dimensions of identity work differently from the collective ones.
>
> This is not just a point about modern Westerners: cross-culturally it matters to people that their lives have a certain narrative unity; they want to be able to tell a story of their lives that makes sense. The story — my story — should cohere in the way appropriate by the standards made available in my culture to a person of my identity. In telling that story, how I fit into the wider story of various collectivities is, for most of us, important. (pp. 57–58)

Your project in this assignment is to consider the terms, the stages, the conclusions, and the consequences of Appiah's argument in his essay "Racial Identities." If, as a mental exercise (or because you are convinced), you accept Appiah's notion that "[c]ollective identities, in short, provide what we might call scripts: narratives that people can use in shaping their life plans and in telling their life stories" (pp. 57–58), how might you tell a story that places yourself in relation to the available scripts, to the life stories available to a person like you—a person of your culture (or collectivity), a person of your age, now, in the second decade of the twenty-first century?

You are not required to write in the genre of the memoir (as though you were writing a chapter of your autobiography), but many find that doing so is an inviting way to begin. What a reader wants is a view of you and your world, not in the pen-pal sense of what you look like or what you prefer in music, but with the goal of understanding something more general, something about people like you, something about what it is that shapes and defines a person or an identity in this place and at this point in time. In Appiah's terms, your writing will negotiate the competing demands of a life and a "script," of the personal and the collective, of individual freedom and the politics of identity.

We are trying to avoid the word "essay" in describing this project, since that word carries certain generic restrictions. Our advice is for you to begin not with a generalization but with some specific scene or scenes. Begin with a story (or stories) rather than with an argument. If people are speaking, you may choose to let them speak as characters speak in fiction. You may write in the first person if you find it helpful to do so.

3. In the final section of his essay, "In Conclusion," Appiah says, "So here are my positive proposals: live with fractured identities; engage in identity play; find solidarity, yes, but recognize contingency, and, above all, practice irony" (p. 62).

What might it mean to live a life in these terms? Write an essay in which you present Appiah's conclusion to readers (smart readers, interested readers) who have not yet read Appiah's essay. Where do these positive proposals come from? What is at stake in putting them into play? Why does Appiah express them with such urgency?

Write an essay in which you present Appiah's conclusion but where you also extend those conclusions to consider the contexts within which you hear and receive these proposals. Who else is telling you how to live your life? What advice is being provided to you? Where and by whom? What examples of appropriate conduct are offered to you by the culture — in books or movies, in magazines, or online? What forms of advice do you listen to or seek out? What uses or contexts can you imagine for words or phrases like "fractured identities," "identity play," "contingency," and "irony"?

Appiah says, "If I am wrong, . . . you need only correct me. But if I am right, so it seems to me, there is a work of the imagination that we need to begin" (p. 63). With some particular examples in mind, what might you say in turn?

· • • ● • • ·

MAKING CONNECTIONS

1. Both John Edgar Wideman's "Our Time" (p. 622) and Kwame Anthony Appiah's "Racial Identities" call attention to the difficulties of representing and understanding the experience of those whom we call "African Americans"—the difficulty of telling their story, of getting it right, of recovering experience from the representations of others.

Write an essay in which you represent these two texts as examples of writers working on a problem that has a particular urgency for all Americans, not just black Americans. How might you name this problem? What do you find compelling in each of these approaches to the problem? And what might this problem have to do with you — as a writer, a thinker, a person, and a citizen?

2. Both Kwame Anthony Appiah's "Racial Identities" and Ruth Behar's "The Vulnerable Observer" (p. 113) have distinctive styles, voices, and methods. A character emerges in each essay, a figure representing one version of a well-schooled, learned, and articulate adult, an intellectual — someone who reads widely and thinks closely, freshly, and methodically about big questions; someone with ideas and with style; someone who is defined in relation to sources, to books, and other writers; and someone who takes pains to engage his or her readers. This is an intellectual, then, who has a desire to reach others, to address them, to bring them into his or her point of view.

Write an essay in which you discuss the figure of the intellectual represented in these two essays. You'll need to work closely with a few key and representative moments in the texts. Your essay should assess this figure in relation to your own education — better yet, in relation to the kind of figure you intend to cut as a well-schooled adult, as an intellectual, as a person with ideas and knowledge and something to say.

3. As he prepares for the final section of his essay, Kwame Anthony Appiah offers a surprising list to counter what he refers to as the "imperialism of identity":

> In policing this imperialism of identity — an imperialism as visible in racial identities as anywhere else — it is crucial to remember always that we are not simply black or white or yellow or brown, gay or straight or bisexual, Jewish, Christian, Moslem, Buddhist, or Confucian but that we are also brothers and sisters; parents and children; liberals, conservatives, and leftists; teachers and lawyers and auto-makers and gardeners; fans of the Padres and the Bruins; amateurs of grunge rock and lovers of Wagner; movie buffs; MTV-holics, mystery-readers; surfers and singers; poets and pet-lovers; students and teachers; friends and lovers. Racial identity can be the basis of resistance to racism; but even as we struggle against racism — and though we have made great progress, we have further still to go — let us not let our racial identities subject us to new tyrannies. (p. 62)

Both Edward Said's chapter "States" (p. 599) and Ta-Nehisi Coates's "Between the World and Me" (p. 277) examine questions of identity. Choose one of these two selections, and then choose one section of that excerpt—a section that speaks to you, that seems particularly compelling for how it represents identity as both a problem and a possibility—and use it as an example to test and question Appiah's argument. Where and how might Said or Coates use a term like *imperialism*? Appiah celebrates "fractured identities," "identity play," "contingency," and "irony." How might you understand Said's or Coates's argument in relation to these terms?

Write an essay that considers two of these writers and their arguments concerning identity.

ON THE WHOLE, IT WENT AS WELL AS I COULD HAVE HOPED. MOM'S BOYFRIEND, BOB, CAME OVER FOR DINNER THAT NIGHT.

SHE SAYS IT'S SOMETHING SHE HAS TO DO.

AND YOU'RE OKAY WITH IT?

I FEEL RECKLESS. TELL EVERYONE.

I'M GONNA GO DO MY PUZZLE.

BOB IS A RETIRED PSYCHIATRIST. HE HAD SOME INSIGHT INTO MY BROOK DREAM.

WATER IS USUALLY ABOUT CREATIVITY. THAT SEEMS AUSPICIOUS FOR YOUR PROJECT.

I JUST HOPE IT WON'T BE ALL ANGRY, ALL ABOUT HOW AWFUL YOUR FATHER WAS.

THIS IS ONE OF MY DIFFICULTIES NOW...

...MY FEAR THAT MOM WILL FIND THIS MEMOIR ABOUT HER "ANGRY." ANOTHER DIFFICULTY IS THE FACT THAT THE STORY OF MY MOTHER AND ME IS UNFOLDING EVEN AS I WRITE IT.

DID YOU SEE DANIEL MENDELSOHN'S ARTICLE ON MEMOIR IN *THE NEW YORKER*?

IT'S GOOD. ISN'T HE THE ONE WHO BEAT YOU FOR THAT PRIZE?

UH...NO.

UH... YEAH.

YET ANOTHER DIFFICULTY IS THE FACT THAT MY MOTHER CONSIDERS MEMOIR A SUSPECT GENRE. THIS ADDS A CONFUSING OBSERVER EFFECT TO THE WHOLE PROCESS.

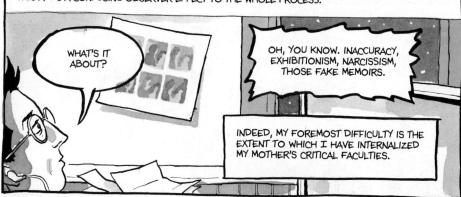

WHAT'S IT ABOUT?

OH, YOU KNOW. INACCURACY, EXHIBITIONISM, NARCISSISM, THOSE FAKE MEMOIRS.

INDEED, MY FOREMOST DIFFICULTY IS THE EXTENT TO WHICH I HAVE INTERNALIZED MY MOTHER'S CRITICAL FACULTIES.

AS OF THIS MOMENT, I'VE BEEN STRUGGLING FOR FOUR YEARS WITH THE WRITING OF THIS BOOK, THIS MEMOIR ABOUT MY MOTHER.

DID I TELL YOU I'M ORDERING THAT CHLORINE-RESISTANT SWIMSUIT?

I TALK TO MY MOTHER ALMOST EVERY DAY. THAT IS, I CALL, SHE TALKS, I LISTEN. THAT'S OUR PATTERN.

IT COSTS A HUNDRED DOLLARS, BUT I GO THROUGH SEVERAL SPEEDOS A YEAR.

I MUST CONFESS THAT I HAVE TAKEN TO TRANSCRIBING WHAT SHE SAYS. I DON'T THINK SHE KNOWS I'M DOING IT, WHICH MAKES IT A BIT UNETHICAL.

1/29/2010, 4:15pm
article in New Yorker on memoir
Isn't daniel mendelsohn the one who be

A new chlorine-resistant swimsuit, for $1
Maybe I'll decide to spring for it. I go th
not sure about size. Sizes don't mean anything any more?

THE ARCHITECTURAL REVIEW BOARD SAID SHE COULDN'T PUT UP VINYL SID-ING, BUT THE TOWN OVERRULED THEM BECAUSE SHE'S A POOR WIDOW.

Siz

somebody bought that house down the street when it was up for auction, and th
flipped it. They covered up the original painted brick and slapped on vinyl siding
They ruined it. You know how it was when I moved up here. A woman wanted to
up vinyl siding and the arch. review board said no, but the town overruled them

BUT I WANT TO CAPTURE HER VOICE, HER PRECISE WORDING, HER DEADPAN HUMOR. I DON'T THINK I COULD POSSIBLY RE-CREATE IT ON MY OWN.

WELL, I'M A POOR WIDOW, TOO, AND I DON'T WANT TO LOOK AT VINYL SIDING!

I'M TRYING SO HARD TO GET DOWN WHAT SHE'S SAYING THAT I'M NOT REALLY LISTENING PROPERLY.

UH HUH...

I WOULD HAVE MORE SCRUPLES ABOUT THIS, I LIKE TO THINK, IF I DIDN'T SUSPECT THAT SHE WAS NOT SO MUCH TALKING TO ME AS DRAFTING HER OWN DAILY JOURNAL ENTRY OUT LOUD.

MY MOTHER HAS ALWAYS KEPT A JOURNAL. SHE INSISTS THIS IS JUST A RECORD OF THINGS SHE'S DONE. OF EXTERNAL, AS OPPOSED TO INTERNAL, EXPERIENCE.

I SHARE THIS COMPULSION FOR KEEPING TRACK OF LIFE.

MY MOTHER LOGS HER DAILY ACTIVITIES IN HER JOURNAL. AND EVERY DAY SHE READS ANOTHER JOURNAL--THE *NEW YORK TIMES*.

IF YOU'RE GOING OUT, CAN YOU GET ME A COPY OF TO-DAY'S PAPER?

NOT ONLINE. THE NEWSPRINT, THE THING ITSELF.

THE TRUCK DIDN'T GET HERE BECAUSE OF THE BLIZZARD, SO NO ONE HAS IT.

YOU WANT ME TO MAIL TODAY'S *NEW YORK TIMES* FROM VERMONT TO PENNSYLVANIA?

I KNOW! IT'S MY OCD. BUT I HATE MISSING ANY NEWS. AND THE PUZZLE.

I OFTEN THINK OF THIS PASSAGE FROM VIRGINIA WOOLF'S DIARY: "WHAT A DISGRACEFUL LAPSE! NOTHING ADDED TO MY DISQUISITION, & LIFE ALLOWED TO WASTE LIKE A TAP LEFT RUNNING. ELEVEN DAYS UNRECORDED."

I STARTED MY OWN DIARY AS A CHILD. AND WHEN A SPELL OF OBSESSIVE-COMPULSIVE DISORDER MADE MY ENTRIES TOO TIME-CONSUMING, MY MOTHER SAT ON MY BED AND TOOK DICTATION.

MOTHER WENT TO SCHOOL TO SUBSTITUTE TEACH. MARY-JO BROUGHT IN A LOVE TEST THAT WE DID ON THE BUS.

GETTING HER UNDIVIDED ATTENTION WAS A RARE TREAT. IT FELT MIRACULOUS, ACTUALLY--LIKE PERSUADING A HUMMINGBIRD TO PERCH ON YOUR FINGER.

I DIDN'T GET MUCH DONE. I WENT TO MY PIANO LESSON. I GOT BACH'S MINUET.

SHE WAS LISTENING TO ME. WHAT-EVER I SAID, SHE WROTE DOWN.

I FOUND THIS CALMING. COMPOSING.

MY MOTHER COMPOSED ME AS I NOW COMPOSE HER.

SHE LIKES TO USE SCRUBBING BUBBLES, BUT I TOLD HER TO USE THE COMET.

THE RUNNING TAP OF HER LIFE FLOWS THROUGH MY FINGERS.

FLICKATICKA TACKATICKA TIC

SOMETIMES THERE WILL BE A LULL AND MY MOTHER WILL ASK ME THIS QUESTION:

HOW ARE YOU DOING?

MY CONSIDERABLE VERBAL APTITUDE OFTEN FAILS ME COMPLETELY WHEN I'M TALKING TO MY MOTHER.

When she cleans the bathroo
to use the comet.

She asks how I'm doing.|

THROUGHOUT MY TWENTIES AND THIRTIES, SHE NEVER ASKED ME ABOUT MY LIFE.

EVEN NOW, WHEN SHE POSES THE QUESTION POINT-BLANK, I KNOW HER ATTENTION FOR MY ANSWER IS LIMITED.

UHH...

THE PRESSURE TO BE CONCISE, ENTERTAINING, AND APPOSITE IN THIS SMALL WINDOW IS FIERCE. MORE OFTEN THAN NOT, I PASS WITH A "FINE. NOTHING NEW TO REPORT."

I...

BUT I KNOW I CAN'T BLAME HER FOR DOMINATING OUR CONVERSATIONS IF I REFUSE TO PARTICIPATE. SO SOMETIMES, LIKE TODAY, I DIVULGE SOMETHING.

I HAVE TO REWRITE MY BOOK.

WHAT?!

I HAVE TO START OVER. I...I FEEL LIKE I'M WRITING AROUND SOMETHING.

HA!

SHE'S LAUGHING IN WHAT SEEMS LIKE AN UNDERSTANDING WAY. SHE DOESN'T ASK ME WHAT IT IS THAT I'M WRITING AROUND.

YOU HAVE TOO MANY STRANDS!

SHE KNOWS THIS BOOK IS ABOUT MY RELATIONSHIP WITH HER, AND SHE SEEMS TO FEEL ABOUT IT ROUGHLY THE WAY SHE FELT ABOUT THE BOOK ON MY FATHER--RESIGNED.

WELL, I READ IT IN THE WRONG ORDER. I COULDN'T FIGURE OUT THE PAGINATION. I'LL HAVE TO LOOK AT IT AGAIN.

I HAD RECENTLY SENT HER WHAT I THOUGHT WAS THE FIRST CHAPTER. WE DISCUSSED IT, FOR ABOUT THREE MINUTES, DURING MY CHRISTMAS VISIT.

THE CHAPTER HAD BEEN A TURGID ABSTRACTION ABOUT THE SELF AND DESIRE THAT BARELY MENTIONED MY MOTHER.

ALISON, YOU SHOULD JUST WRITE WHATEVER YOU WANT TO WRITE.

HER TONE WAS WEARY BUT NOT UNKIND. SHE SEEMED TO BE SAYING, "WRITE ABOUT ME IF YOU MUST, BUT DON'T ASK ME TO APPROVE IT."

WELL... THANK YOU.

TWO NIGHTS AFTER RECEIVING THIS MIXED BLESSING, I HAD AN ECHO OF THE BROOK DREAM I'D HAD TEN YEARS EARLIER. I WAS SOMEWHAT BETTER EQUIPPED THIS TIME.

I WAS INSIDE A CAVE, ON AN UNDERGROUND LAKE.

THE ONLY WAY OUT WAS TO DIVE INTO THE WATER AND SWIM UNDERNEATH THE ROCK LEDGE. IF I DID THIS, I'D COME UP ON THE OTHER SIDE, UNDER THE OPEN SKY.

I KNEW I COULD MAKE IT, BUT AT THE SAME TIME I WAS TERRIFIED OF GETTING STUCK DOWN THERE. I STALLED, FUSSING WITH MY MASK TO GET A GOOD SEAL.

FINALLY, I HAD DETERMINED TO JUMP...

...WHEN I WOKE UP.

I TOOK THIS DREAM, LIKE THE EARLIER ONE, AS A GOOD SIGN, AN INDICATION THAT I WAS GETTING SOMEWHERE WITH MY WRITING.

BUT WITHIN A FEW DAYS, IT BECAME CLEAR THAT "GETTING SOME-WHERE" MEANT STARTING OVER. THIS FELT ODDLY ENCOURAGING.

Thursday, January 28
week 4 of 2010

173 days

8AM Write

IT HAD BEEN FIVE MONTHS SINCE THIS BOOK WAS DUE, AND SIX SINCE MY LAST PERIOD.

LIKE MY MOTHER, I KEEP A LOG OF THE EVENTS OF DAILY, EXTERNAL LIFE. BUT UNLIKE HER, I ALSO RECORD A GREAT DEAL OF INFOR-MATION ABOUT MY INTERNAL LIFE.

ALTHOUGH I'M OFTEN CONFUSED ABOUT PRECISELY WHERE THE DEMARCATION LIES.

VIRGINIA WOOLF SEEMS TO HAVE CONSIDERED HER OWN DIARY TO BE MORE OF AN EXTERNAL RECORD, AN ACCOUNT OF "LIFE" RATHER THAN "THE SOUL."

Monday 19 February

How it would interest me if this diary were ever to become a real diary: something in which I could see changes, trace moods developing; but then I should have to speak of the soul, & did I not banish the soul when I began? What happens is, as usual, that I'm going to write about the soul, & life breaks in. Talking of diaries sets me thinking of old Kate, in the dining room at 4 Rosary Gardens; & how she opened the cabinet (wh. I remember) & there in a row on a shelf were her diaries from Jan 1 1877.[13] Some were brown; others red; all the same to a t. And I made her read an entry; one of many thousand days, like pebbles

WOOLF'S DISMISSAL OF "THE SOUL" REMINDS ME A BIT OF MY MOTHER'S INSISTENCE THAT HER OWN JOURNAL IS LITTLE MORE THAN A COMPLETED TO-DO LIST, THAT SHE NEVER RE-READS IT...

...THAT IN FACT SHE'S THROWN WHOLE CHUNKS OF IT AWAY.

To the Lighthouse Virginia Woolf

MOMENTS of BEING

AUTOBIOGRAPHICAL WRITING

Virginia Woolf

THE DIARY of Virginia Woolf

VOLUME TWO 1920-1924

2002

I'M SURE THESE THINGS ARE TRUE.

BUT THE WAY SHE SAYS THEM FEELS LIKE AN IMPLIED CRITICISM. AS IF SHE'S COMPARING HER OWN SELFLESS-NESS TO MY SELF-ABSORPTION.

BUT OF COURSE THAT'S JUST EVIDENCE OF MY SELF-ABSORPTION. MY MOTHER IS PROBABLY NOT THINKING ANYTHING LIKE THIS.

IN FACT, MY DESIRE TO THINK THAT SHE'S THINKING OF ME AT ALL IS A BIT PATHETIC.

SHE LOOMS MUCH LARGER IN MY PSYCHE THAN I LOOM IN HERS. WOOLF SAYS THAT HER OWN MOTHER, WHO DIED WHEN VIRGINIA WAS THIRTEEN, OBSESSED HER UNTIL SHE WAS FORTY-FOUR.

> when I was thirteen, until I was forty-four. Then one day walking round Tavistock Square I made up, as I sometimes make up my books, *To the Lighthouse*; in a great, apparently involuntary, rush. One thing burst into another. Blowing bubbles out of a pipe

LET'S LEAVE ASIDE THE ANNOYING RAPIDITY WITH WHICH SHE DISPATCHED THIS MASTERPIECE. THE POINT IS, WHAT HAPPENED AFTERWARD.

> when it was written, I ceased to be obsessed by my mother. I no longer hear her voice; I do not see her. I suppose that I did for myself what psycho-analysts do for their patients. I expressed some very long felt and deeply felt emotion. And in expressing it I explained it and then laid it to rest. But what is

I'VE BEEN IN THERAPY FOR NEARLY MY ENTIRE ADULT LIFE AND HAVE NOT LAID MY DEEPLY FELT EMOTIONS ABOUT MY MOTHER TO REST.

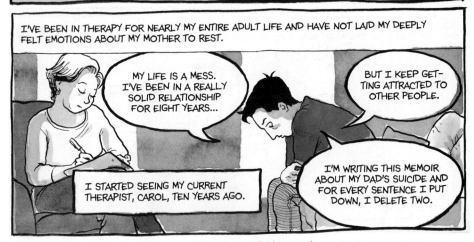

MY LIFE IS A MESS. I'VE BEEN IN A REALLY SOLID RELATIONSHIP FOR EIGHT YEARS...

BUT I KEEP GET-TING ATTRACTED TO OTHER PEOPLE.

I STARTED SEEING MY CURRENT THERAPIST, CAROL, TEN YEARS AGO.

I'M WRITING THIS MEMOIR ABOUT MY DAD'S SUICIDE AND FOR EVERY SENTENCE I PUT DOWN, I DELETE TWO.

I'D PRETEND I WAS A "CRIPPLED" CHILD, AND MOM WOULD PLAY ALONG WITH IT.

YOU'LL NEED THESE CRUTCHES.

IT WAS SO FUN. WHER-EVER I WENT WITH THE FANTASY, SHE WAS RIGHT THERE.

FOR MY FIRST TWO YEARS WITH CAROL, I JUST SAT ON THE COUCH. BUT THEN I BEGAN LYING DOWN ON IT. IN THE TIME I'VE BEEN SEEING HER, SHE HAS BECOME A PSYCHOANALYST.

WHY AM I LYING HERE?

ANALYSIS AND THERAPY ARE DIFFERENT IN MANY WAYS, BUT THE SEATING ARRANGE-MENT IS A BIG ONE.

I SHOULD BE WORKING.

IN THIS POSITION THE PATIENT CAN'T SEE THE ANALYST. AND LYING DOWN, IN THEORY, ALLOWS MORE READY ACCESS TO THE UNCONSCIOUS.

I'M NEVER GONNA GET THIS FUCKING BOOK DONE.

ANALYSIS IS IN NO HURRY TO GET TO THE BOTTOM OF THINGS. THERAPY IS USUALLY A SHORTER-TERM PROPOSITION, MORE FOCUSED ON SYMPTOM RELIEF.

I CAN'T TELL WHETHER IT'S NORMAL CREATIVE STRIFE OR MENOPAUSAL INSANITY.

ALSO, A PSYCHOANALYST MUST UNDERGO A TRAINING ANALYSIS OF THEIR OWN.

ONE REASON THIS MEMOIR IS TAKING ME SO LONG IS THAT I'M TRYING TO FIGURE OUT--FROM BOTH SIDES OF THE COUCH--JUST WHAT IT IS THAT PSYCHO-ANALYSTS DO FOR THEIR PATIENTS.

IN PARTICULAR, I HAVE BEEN STUDYING THE WORK OF THE BRITISH PSYCHOANALYST AND PEDIATRICIAN DONALD WINNICOTT.

PLUS I STILL CAN'T FIGURE OUT HOW TO FIT WINNICOTT IN.

IT HAS TAKEN ME SEVERAL YEARS TO FEEL AS IF I HAVE EVEN A SLENDER GRASP OF HIS CURIOUSLY COMPELLING IDEAS.

WHAT IS IT ABOUT HIM THAT YOU'RE SO DRAWN TO?

I WANT HIM TO BE MY MOTHER.

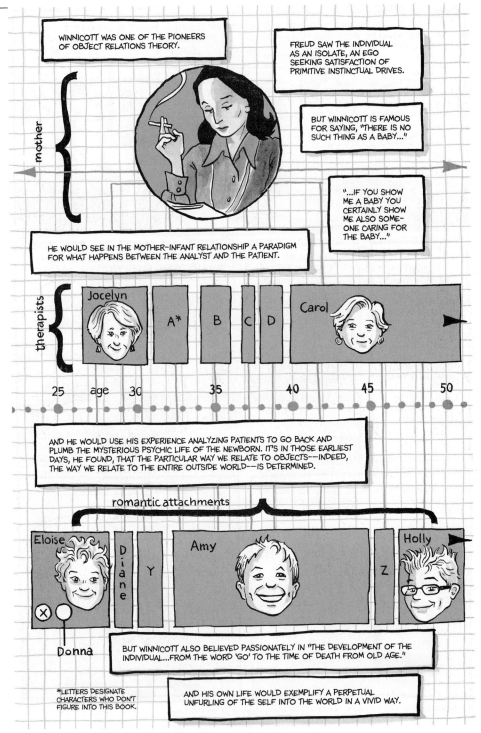

WINNICOTT WAS ONE OF THE PIONEERS OF OBJECT RELATIONS THEORY.

FREUD SAW THE INDIVIDUAL AS AN ISOLATE, AN EGO SEEKING SATISFACTION OF PRIMITIVE INSTINCTUAL DRIVES.

BUT WINNICOTT IS FAMOUS FOR SAYING, "THERE IS NO SUCH THING AS A BABY..."

"...IF YOU SHOW ME A BABY YOU CERTAINLY SHOW ME ALSO SOMEONE CARING FOR THE BABY..."

mother

HE WOULD SEE IN THE MOTHER–INFANT RELATIONSHIP A PARADIGM FOR WHAT HAPPENS BETWEEN THE ANALYST AND THE PATIENT.

therapists

Jocelyn   A*   B   C   D   Carol

25   age   30   35   40   45   50

AND HE WOULD USE HIS EXPERIENCE ANALYZING PATIENTS TO GO BACK AND PLUMB THE MYSTERIOUS PSYCHIC LIFE OF THE NEWBORN. IT'S IN THOSE EARLIEST DAYS, HE FOUND, THAT THE PARTICULAR WAY WE RELATE TO OBJECTS––INDEED, THE WAY WE RELATE TO THE ENTIRE OUTSIDE WORLD––IS DETERMINED.

romantic attachments

Eloise   Diane   Y   Amy   Z   Holly

⊗ ○

Donna

BUT WINNICOTT ALSO BELIEVED PASSIONATELY IN "THE DEVELOPMENT OF THE INDIVIDUAL...FROM THE WORD 'GO' TO THE TIME OF DEATH FROM OLD AGE."

*LETTERS DESIGNATE CHARACTERS WHO DON'T FIGURE INTO THIS BOOK.

AND HIS OWN LIFE WOULD EXEMPLIFY A PERPETUAL UNFURLING OF THE SELF INTO THE WORLD IN A VIVID WAY.

WHY DO YOU WANT HIM TO BE YOUR MOTHER?

I DUNNO.

BUT I KNOW THAT IF HE HAD BEEN MY MOTHER, I WOULDN'T BE SUFFERING OVER THIS BOOK.

I'D BE DOING SOMETHING USEFUL.

THE THING IS, I CAN'T WRITE THIS BOOK UNTIL I GET HER OUT OF MY HEAD.

BUT THE ONLY WAY TO GET HER OUT OF MY HEAD IS BY WRITING THE BOOK!

IT'S A PARADOX.

MY MOTHER'S EDITORIAL VOICE--PRECISIAN, DISPASSIONATE, ELEGANT, ADVERBLESS--IS LODGED DEEP IN MY TEMPORAL LOBES.

OR A DILEMMA OR SOMETHING.

I DON'T KNOW.

I DON'T KNOW ANYTHING.

HOW I ENVY THE INVOLUNTARY TORRENT OF WORDS AND IMAGES THAT CAME TO VIRGINIA WOOLF THAT DAY IN TAVISTOCK SQUARE.

IT WAS SOMETIME BETWEEN OCTOBER 1924 AND THE FOLLOWING SPRING.

WOOLF NEVER UNDERWENT PSYCHOANALYSIS. HER BROTHER ADRIAN DID, THOUGH.

VIRGINIA WROTE RATHER SNIDELY TO HER SISTER, "I GATHER THAT HIS TRAGEDY--AS THE DR. CALLS IT--IS ALL OUR DOING. HE WAS SUPPRESSED AS A CHILD."

WOOLF WOULDN'T REALLY READ FREUD FOR ANOTHER TEN YEARS OR SO...

...THOUGH THE HOGARTH PRESS, WHICH SHE FOUNDED WITH HER HUSBAND, LEONARD, HAD JUST PUBLISHED HIS COLLECTED PAPERS.

THESE HAD BEEN TRANSLATED BY JAMES AND ALIX STRACHEY, THE BROTHER AND SISTER-IN-LAW OF VIRGINIA'S CLOSE FRIEND LYTTON.

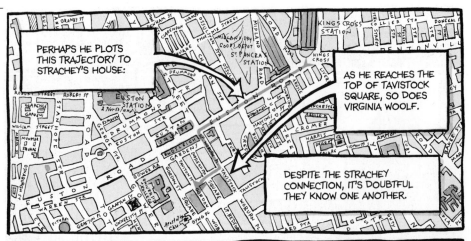

IN A FEW MINUTES, BOTH OF THEM HAVE LEFT THE OUTSIDE WORLD.

DONALD IS ON STRACHEY'S COUCH AT 41 GORDON SQUARE.

AND VIRGINIA IS INSIDE 52 TAVISTOCK SQUARE, PERHAPS CONTINUING TO THINK ABOUT THIS NEW NOVEL, THE ONE THAT WILL LAY HER MOTHER TO REST.

DONALD IS VERY POSSIBLY THINKING ABOUT HIS MOTHER, TOO. SHE HAS EITHER JUST DIED, OR WILL DIE BEFORE 1925 IS OUT. I CAN'T FIND THE EXACT DATE.

MY MOTHER WAS DISGUISED IN A BEARSKIN. THEN HER PENIS POPPED OUT AND CASTRATED ME.

THIS WAS AN ACTUAL DREAM OF WINNICOTT'S. ALTHOUGH I AM ENJOYING THIS LITTLE FORAY INTO FICTION, I FEEL THE NECESSITY OF "CLINGING AS TIGHT TO FACTS AS I CAN," AS WOOLF WROTE IN HER 1923 DIARY ABOUT HER PROGRESS ON *MRS. DALLOWAY.*

BUT I AM NOT ULTIMATELY INTERESTED IN WRITING FICTION. I CAN'T MAKE THINGS UP. OR RATHER, I CAN ONLY MAKE THINGS UP ABOUT THINGS THAT HAVE ALREADY HAPPENED.

I HAVE TO REWRITE MY BOOK.

WHAT?!

I HAVE TO START OVER.

ONCE MY MOTHER TOLD ME SHE WISHED I HAD WRITTEN THE BOOK ABOUT MY FATHER AS FICTION.

ON THE THEORY THAT IT WOULD NOT HAVE EXPOSED OUR FAMILY IN THE WAY MEMOIR DID.

I EXPLAINED THAT THE WHOLE POINT OF THE BOOK WAS THAT IT WAS TRUE, AND THAT EVEN IF I HAD FICTIONALIZED IT, PEOPLE WOULD ASSUME IT WAS AUTOBIOGRAPHICAL.

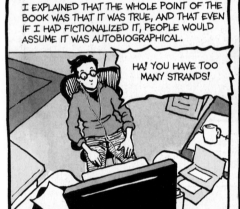

HA! YOU HAVE TOO MANY STRANDS!

THIS HAD NOT SWAYED HER. *TO THE LIGHTHOUSE* IS FICTION, OF COURSE, BUT HEAVILY AUTOBIOGRAPHICAL.

I DO. I JUST NEED TO TELL A STORY.

IN THE SAME WAY VIRGINIA WOOLF DISTINGUISHES BETWEEN "LIFE" AND "THE SOUL" IN HER DIARY, SHE DISTINGUISHES BETWEEN "TWO KINDS OF TRUTH" IN WRITING BIOGRAPHY.

YES. NARRATIVE IS WHAT THEY WANT.

BUT IT'S HARD TO FIGURE OUT WHAT THE STORY IS.

"LET THE BIOGRAPHER PRINT FULLY, COMPLETELY, ACCURATELY, THE KNOWN FACTS WITHOUT COMMENT; THEN LET HIM WRITE THE LIFE AS FICTION."

IN *TO THE LIGHTHOUSE*, THE CHARACTER LILY BRISCOE HAS A BRIEF VISION AS SHE WATCHES MR. AND MRS. RAMSAY PLAYING CATCH WITH THEIR CHILDREN.

ing catches. And suddenly the meaning which, for no reason at all, as perhaps they are stepping out of the Tube or ringing a doorbell, descends on people, making them symbolical, making them representative, came upon them, and made them in the dusk standing, look-ing, the symbols of marriage, husband and wife. Then, after an instant, the symbolical outline which tran-scended the real figures sank down again, and they became, as they met them, Mr. and Mrs. Ramsay watch-ing the children throwing catches. But still for a mo-

THIS "SYMBOLI-CAL" QUAL-ITY THAT TRANSCENDS MERE "REAL FIGURES" SEEMS TO BE WHAT FICTION ACHIEVES FOR WOOLF--A DEEPER TRUTH THAN FACTS.

PERHAPS THAT'S WHY SHE FOUND IT "DIFFICULT TO GIVE ANY CLEAR DESCRIPTION" OF HER ACTUAL, NONFICTIONAL MOTHER. SHE WAS "ASTONISHINGLY BEAUTIFUL..."

But apart from her beauty, if the two can be separated, what was she herself like? Very quick; very direct; practical; and amusing. I say at once offhand. She could be sharp, she disliked affectation. "If

ALL THESE THINGS WILL DO VERY WELL TO DESCRIBE MY MOTHER, TOO.

BUT IT'S HARD TO FIGURE OUT WHAT THE STORY IS.

I'M READING SYLVIA PLATH'S DIARIES. *SHE* PUT HER *HEAD* IN THE OVEN.

ALISON BECHDEL

MOM MEANS THIS KINDLY, COMMISERATINGLY. "OH, THE WRITER'S LIFE." STILL, I THINK OF MY OWN OVEN AND AM GLAD IT'S ELECTRIC.

OH! I FOUND MY LOST POEM!

GREAT! I WAS GONNA TELL YOU HOW TO SEARCH THE COMPUTER.

I FIGURED IT OUT MYSELF!

MOM STARTED WRITING POETRY IN HER YOUTH, STOPPED FOR ALL THE YEARS OF MARRIAGE, CHILDREN, AND HER CAREER TEACHING HIGH SCHOOL. NOW SHE'S TAKEN IT UP AGAIN.

OH, THE JEHOVAH'S WITNESS LADY IS AT THE DOOR. I HAVE TO GO.

UH...OKAY.

SHE INSISTS THAT SHE'S NOT A POET.

BYE.

I HAVE NEVER READ SYLVIA PLATH. MY MOTHER HAS NEVER READ VIRGINIA WOOLF. IN GENERAL, WE HAVE STAYED OUT OF ONE ANOTHER'S WAY LIKE THIS.

WHEN SHE WAS EXACTLY THE AGE I AM NOW, AND I WAS IN MY EARLY TWENTIES, MOM RESPONDED TO A LETTER I'D WRITTEN TO HER ABOUT A DREAM I'D HAD.

will probably hear from him since he wants to stay over with you on his way home.

I have puzzled over your dream. I don't know what it means. I dream about brain tumors and babies. I am staring out my dirty windows at the lilac buds. Now I am trying to analyze why I put those two things together. <u>Why do you and I do that?</u> Patterns are my existence. Everything has significance. Everything must fit. It's enough to drive you crazy.

Today I gave one class a list of wo
your enemy. Sycophant, philandere
little rash, but I didn't have tim

BRAIN TUMORS AND BABIES.
DIRTY WINDOWS AND LILAC BUDS.

THIS SEARCH FOR MEANINGFUL PATTERNS MAY VERY WELL BE CRAZY, BUT TO BE ENLISTED WITH HER IN IT THRILLS ME. "WHY DO YOU AND I DO THAT?"

I AM CARRYING ON HER MISSION.

I'VE ALWAYS BEEN FASCINATED BY THIS SNAPSHOT OF THE TWO OF US.

BUT I DIDN'T REALIZE UNTIL RELATIVELY RECENTLY THAT IT WAS ONE OF A SEQUENCE.

FIVE OTHER SHOTS HAD BEEN SCATTERED ABOUT IN DIFFERENT ALBUMS AND BOXES.

I CALLED MOM A FEW DAYS AFTER THE HEAD-IN-THE-OVEN CONVERSATION.

HEY, MOM. JUST CHECKING IN. WHERE ARE YA? CALL ME.

I DON'T HAVE THE NEGATIVES, SO THERE'S NO WAY TO KNOW THEIR CHRONOLOGICAL ORDER. BUT I'VE ARRANGED THEM ACCORDING TO MY OWN NARRATIVE.

MOM IS MAKING FACES AND PRESUMABLY SOUNDS AT ME. IN EACH SHOT, I REFLECT HER EXPRESSION AND THE SHAPE OF HER MOUTH WITH UNCANNY PRECISION.

BUT "THERE IS NOTHING MYSTICAL ABOUT THIS," SAYS DONALD WINNICOTT, IN *THE ORDINARY DEVOTED MOTHER.*

agrees, that *ordinarily* the woman enters into a phase, a phase from which she *ordinarily* recovers in the weeks and months after the baby's birth, in which to a large extent she is the baby and the baby is her. There is nothing mystical about

FOR A LONG TIME I RESISTED INCLUDING MY PRESENT-DAY INTERACTIONS WITH MOM IN THIS BOOK PRECISELY BECAUSE THEY'RE SO "ORDINARY."

DRRINNG!

MOM!

HI. I WAS AT THE GYM. HAD TO GET MY LAPS IN.

THE PHOTOS WERE TAKEN RIGHT ABOUT THE TIME MOM REALIZED THAT SHE WAS PREGNANT AGAIN.

SHE'S A SNOB, TOO. A SNOB AND A BRAT.

I THOUGHT YOU LIKED HER.

THERE ARE THREE MAIN REASONS, WINNICOTT SAYS, WHY A MOTHER MIGHT NOT BE ABLE TO "GIVE HERSELF OVER TO THIS PREOCCUPATION WITH THE CARE OF HER INFANT."

SHE'S ALWAYS ASKING HER THERAPIST FOR PERMISSION TO HATE HER MOTHER.

ONE, SHE DIES. TWO, SHE "STARTS UP A NEW PREGNANCY BEFORE THE TIME THAT SHE HAD THOUGHT OUT AS APPROPRIATE." THREE...

"AM I ALLOWED TO HATE MY MOTHER?"

"NO!"

THE ORDINARY DEVOTED MOTHER

ing. Or a mother becomes depressed and she can feel herself depriving her child of what the child needs, but she cannot help the onset of a mood swing, which may quite easily be reactive to something that has impinged in her private life. Here she is causing trouble, but no one would blame her.

In other words there are all manner of reasons why some children do get let down before they are able to avoid being wounded or maimed in personality by the fact.

Here I must go back to the idea of blame. It is necessary for us to be able to look at human growth and development, with all its complexities that are internal or personal to the child, and we must be able to say: here the ordinary devoted mother factor failed, without blaming anyone. For my part I have no interest whatever in apportioning blame. Mothers

OH, SERENA'S GRANDDAUGHTER JUST GOT HER PERIOD. SHE'S ONLY TWELVE. THAT'S SO SAD. TWELVE IS TOO YOUNG.

UHH...I THINK TWELVE IS KINDA NORMAL.

I HAVE NOT BEEN MAIMED, ONLY WOUNDED, AND PERHAPS NOT IRREPARABLY.

her baby and in his or her care. At three or four months after being born the baby may be able to show that he or she knows what it is like to be a mother, that is a mother in her state of being devoted to something that is not in fact herself.

THE PICTURE OF ME LOOKING AT THE CAMERA FEELS LIKE A PICTURE OF THE END OF MY CHILDHOOD.

WELL, I'M HEARTBROKEN. SHE WON'T BE A CHILD ANYMORE.

"SHE IS THE BABY AND THE BABY IS HER." I DISAGREE THAT THERE IS NOTHING MYSTICAL ABOUT THIS.

No! (mom, as if she's SP's therapi
Serena's granddaughter just got h
is too young....
Well I'm heartbroken.
She won't be a child anymo

FOR TWO SEPARATE BEINGS TO
BE IDENTICAL--TO BE ONE...

oung....

heartbroken

n't be a child

Humanism

Images were first made to conjure up the appearance of something that was absent. Gradually it became evident that an image could outlast what it represented; it then showed how something or somebody had once looked — and thus by implication how the subject had once been seen by other people. Later still the specific vision of the image-maker was also recognized as part of the record. An image became a record of how X had seen Y. This was the result of an increasing consciousness of individuality, accompanying an increasing awareness of history. It would be rash to try to date this last development precisely. But certainly in Europe such consciousness has existed since the beginning of the Renaissance.

No other kind of relic or text from the past can offer such a direct testimony about the world which surrounded other people at other times. In this respect images are more precise and richer than literature. To say this is not to deny the expressive or imaginative quality of art, treating it as mere documentary evidence; the more imaginative the work, the more profoundly it allows us to share the artist's experience of the visible.

Yet when an image is presented as a work of art, the way people look at it is affected by a whole series of learned assumptions about art. Assumptions concerning:

> Beauty
> Truth
> Genius
> Civilization
> Form
> Status
> Taste, etc.

Many of these assumptions no longer accord with the world as it is. (The world-as-it-is is more than pure objective fact, it includes consciousness.) Out of true with the present, these assumptions obscure the past. They

Frans Hals Museum, Haarlem, The Netherlands/Peter Willi/The Bridgeman Art Library

Regents of the Old Men's Alms House by Hals [1580–1666].

Frans Hals Museum, Haarlem, The Netherlands.
Album/Art Resource, NY

Regentesses of the Old Men's Alms House by Hals [1580–1666].

mystify rather than clarify. The past is never there waiting to be discovered, to be recognized for exactly what it is. History always constitutes the relation between a present and its past. Consequently fear of the present leads to mystification of the past. The past is not for living in; it is a well of conclusions from which we draw in order to act. Cultural mystification of the past entails a double loss. Works of art are made unnecessarily remote. And the past offers us fewer conclusions to complete in action.

When we "see" a landscape, we situate ourselves in it. If we "saw" the art of the past, we would situate ourselves in history. When we are prevented from seeing it, we are being deprived of the history which belongs to us. Who benefits from this deprivation? In the end, the art of the past is being mystified because a privileged minority is striving to invent a history which can retrospectively justify the role of the ruling classes, and such a justification can no longer make sense in modern terms. And so, inevitably, it mystifies.

Let us consider a typical example of such mystification. A two-volume study was recently published on Frans Hals.[1] It is the authoritative work to date on this painter. As a book of specialized art history it is no better and no worse than the average.

The last two great paintings by Frans Hals portray the Governors and the Governesses of an Alms House for old paupers in the Dutch seventeenth-century city of Haarlem. They were officially commissioned portraits. Hals, an old man of over eighty, was destitute. Most of his life he had been in debt. During the winter of 1664, the year he began painting these pictures, he obtained three loads of peat on public charity, otherwise he would have frozen to death. Those who now sat for him were administrators of such public charity.

The author records these facts and then explicitly says that it would be incorrect to read into the paintings any criticism of the sitters. There is no evidence, he says, that Hals painted them in a spirit of bitterness. The author considers them, however, remarkable works of art and explains why. Here he writes of the Regentesses:

> Each woman speaks to us of the human condition with equal importance. Each woman stands out with equal clarity against the *enormous* dark surface, yet they are linked by a firm rhythmical arrangement and the subdued diagonal pattern formed by their heads and hands. Subtle modulations of the *deep*, glowing blacks contribute to the *harmonious fusion* of the whole and form an *unforgettable contrast* with the *powerful* whites and vivid flesh tones where the detached strokes reach *a peak of breadth and strength*. [Berger's italics]

The compositional unity of a painting contributes fundamentally to the power of its image. It is reasonable to consider a painting's composition. But here the composition is written about as though it were in itself the emotional charge of the painting. Terms like *harmonious fusion, unforgettable contrast*, reaching *a peak of breadth and strength* transfer the emotion provoked by the image from the plane of lived experience, to that of disinterested "art appreciation." All conflict disappears. One is left with the unchanging "human condition," and the painting considered as a marvellously made object.

Very little is known about Hals or the Regents who commissioned him. It is not possible to produce circumstantial evidence to establish what their relations were. But there is the evidence of the paintings themselves: the evidence of a group of men and a group of women as seen by another man, the painter. Study this evidence and judge for yourself.

The art historian fears such direct judgment:

> As in so many other pictures by Hals, the penetrating characterizations almost seduce us into believing that we know the personality traits and even the habits of the men and women portrayed.

Hals gives each individual a personality

Both images: Frans Hals Museum, Haarlem, The Netherlands. Album/Art Resource, NY.

What is this "seduction" he writes of? It is nothing less than the paintings working upon us. They work upon us because we accept the way Hals saw his sitters. We do not accept this innocently. We accept it in so far as it corresponds to our own observation of people, gestures, faces, institutions. This is possible because we still live in a society of comparable social relations and moral values. And it is precisely this which gives the paintings their psychological and social urgency. It is this — not the painter's skill as a "seducer" — which convinces us that we *can* know the people portrayed.

[handwritten: It is our ideas of society that give us the idea notion that we know these people]

The author continues:

> In the case of some critics the seduction has been a total success. It has, for example, been asserted that the Regent in the tipped slouch hat, which hardly covers any of his long, lank hair, and whose curiously set eyes do not focus, was shown in a drunken state. [below]

This, he suggests, is a libel. He argues that it was a fashion at that time to wear hats on the side of the head. He cites medical opinion to prove that the Regent's expression could well be the result of a facial paralysis. He insists that the painting would have been unacceptable to the Regents if one of them had been portrayed drunk. One might go on discussing each of these points for pages. (Men in seventeenth-century Holland wore their hats on the side of their heads in order to be thought of as adventurous and pleasure-loving. Heavy drinking was an approved practice. Etcetera.) But such a discussion would take us even farther away from the only confrontation which matters and which the author is determined to evade.

[handwritten: poor]

In this confrontation the Regents and Regentesses stare at Hals, a destitute old painter who has lost his reputation and lives off public charity; he examines them through the eyes of a pauper who must nevertheless try to be objective; i.e., must try to surmount the way he sees as a pauper. This is the drama of these paintings. A drama of an "unforgettable contrast."

Frans Hals Museum, Haarlem, The Netherlands / Peter Willi/The Bridgeman Art Library

Mystification has little to do with the vocabulary used. Mystification is the process of explaining away what might otherwise be evident. Hals was the first portraitist to paint the new characters and expressions created by capitalism. He did in pictorial terms what Balzac did two centuries later in literature. Yet the author of the authoritative work on these paintings sums up the artist's achievement by referring to

> Hals's unwavering commitment to his personal vision, which enriches our consciousness of our fellow men and heightens our awe for the ever-increasing power of the mighty impulses that enabled him to give us a close view of life's vital forces.

[handwritten: Painting the rich]

That is mystification.

In order to avoid mystifying the past (which can equally well suffer pseudo-Marxist mystification) let us now examine the particular relation which now exists, so far as pictorial images are concerned, between the present and the past. If we can see the present clearly enough, we shall ask the right questions of the past.

Today we see the art of the past as nobody saw it before. We actually perceive it in a different way.

This difference can be illustrated in terms of what was thought of as perspective. The convention of perspective, which is unique to European art and which was first established in the early Renaissance, centers everything on the eye of the beholder. It is like a beam from a lighthouse — only instead of light traveling outwards, appearances travel in. The conventions called those appearances *reality*. Perspective makes the single eye the center of the visible world. Everything converges on to the eye as to the vanishing point of infinity. The visible world is arranged for the spectator as the universe was once thought to be arranged for God.

Your eyes are the center of the universe

According to the convention of perspective there is no visual reciprocity. There is no need for God to situate himself in relation to others: he is himself the situation. The inherent contradiction in perspective was that it structured all images of reality to address a single spectator who, unlike God, could only be in one place at a time.

After the invention of the camera this contradiction gradually became apparent.

I'm an eye. A mechanical eye. I, the machine, show you a world the way only I can see it. I free myself for today and forever from human immobility. I'm in constant movement. I approach and pull away from objects. I creep under them. I move alongside a running horse's mouth. I fall and rise with the falling and rising bodies. This is I, the machine, maneuvring in the chaotic movements, recording one movement after another in the most complex combinations.

Still from *Man with a Movie Camera* by Vertov [1895–1954].

Freed from the boundaries of time and space, I coordinate any and all points of the universe, wherever I want them to be. My way leads towards the creation of a fresh perception of the world. Thus I explain in a new way the world unknown to you.[2]

The camera isolated momentary appearances and in so doing destroyed the idea that images were timeless. Or, to put it another way, the camera showed that the notion of time passing was inseparable from the experience of the visual (except in paintings). What you saw depended upon where you were when. What you saw was relative to your position in time and space. It was no longer possible to imagine everything converging on the human eye as on the vanishing point of infinity.

This is not to say that before the invention of the camera men believed that everyone could see everything. But perspective organized the visual field as though that were indeed the ideal. Every drawing or painting that used perspective proposed to the spectator that he was the unique center of the world. The camera — and more particularly the movie camera — demonstrated that there was no center.

The invention of the camera changed the way men saw. The visible came to mean something different to them. This was immediately reflected in painting.

THE INVENTION OF THE CAMERA CHANGED THE WAY MEN SAW.

For the Impressionists the visible no longer presented itself to man in order to be seen. On the contrary, the visible, in continual flux, became fugitive. For the Cubists the visible was no longer what confronted the single eye, but the totality of possible views taken from points all round the object (or person) being depicted [below].

The invention of the camera also changed the way in which men saw paintings painted long before the camera was invented. Originally paintings were an integral part of the building for which they were designed. Sometimes in an early Renaissance church or chapel one has the feeling that the images on the wall are records of the building's interior life, that

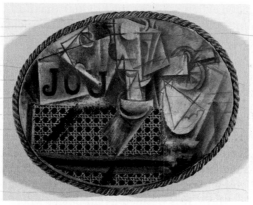

Still Life with Wicker Chair by Picasso [1881–1973].

Church of St. Francis at Assisi.

together they make up the building's memory — so much are they part of the particularity of the building [at left].

The uniqueness of every painting was once part of the uniqueness of the place where it resided. Sometimes the painting was transportable. But it could never be seen in two places at the same time. When the camera reproduces a painting, it destroys the uniqueness of its image. As a result its meaning changes. Or, more exactly, its meaning multiplies and fragments into many meanings.

This is vividly illustrated by what happens when a painting is shown on a television screen. The painting enters each viewer's house. There it is surrounded by his wallpaper, his furniture, his mementos. It enters the atmosphere of his family. It becomes their talking point. It lends its meaning to their meaning. At the same time it enters a million other houses and, in each of them, is seen in a different context. Because of the camera, the painting now travels to the spectator rather than the spectator to the painting. In its travels, its meaning is diversified.

One might argue that all reproductions more or less distort, and that therefore the original painting is still in a sense unique. Here [on the next page] is a reproduction of the *Virgin of the Rocks* by Leonardo da Vinci.

Having seen this reproduction, one can go to the National Gallery to look at the original and there discover what the reproduction lacks. Alternatively one can forget about the quality of the reproduction and simply be reminded, when one sees the original, that it is a famous painting of which somewhere one has already seen a reproduction. But in either case the uniqueness of the original now lies in it being *the original of a reproduction.* It is no longer what its image shows that strikes one as unique; its first meaning is no longer to be found in what it says, but in what it is.

This new status of the original work is the perfectly rational consequence of the new means of reproduction. But it is at this point that a process of mystification again enters. The meaning of the original work no longer lies in what it uniquely says but in what it uniquely is. How is its unique existence evaluated and defined in our present culture? It is defined as an object whose value depends

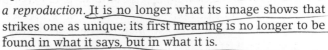

Handwritten margin note: Camera took away painting uniqueness and gave it multiple meanings

upon its rarity. This market is affirmed and gauged by the price it fetches on the market. But because it is nevertheless "a work of art" — and art is thought to be greater than commerce — its market price is said to be a reflection of its spiritual value. Yet the spiritual value of an object, as distinct from a message or an example, can only be explained in terms of magic or religion. And since in modern society neither of these is a living force, the art object, the "work of art," is enveloped in an atmosphere of entirely bogus religiosity. Works of art are discussed and presented as though they were holy relics: relics which are first and foremost evidence of their own survival. The past in which they originated is studied in order to prove their survival genuine. They are declared art when their line of descent can be certified.

© National Gallery, London/Art Resource, NY

Virgin of the Rocks by Leonardo da Vinci [1452–1519].

Before the *Virgin of the Rocks* the visitor to the National Gallery would be encouraged by nearly everything he might have heard and read about the painting to feel something like this: "I am in front of it. I can see it. This painting by Leonardo is unlike any other in the world. The National Gallery has the real one. If I look at this painting hard enough, I should somehow be able to feel its authenticity. The *Virgin of the Rocks* by Leonardo da Vinci: it is authentic and therefore it is beautiful."

To dismiss such feelings as naive would be quite wrong. They accord perfectly with the sophisticated culture of art experts for whom the National Gallery catalogue is written. The entry on the *Virgin of the Rocks* is one of the longest entries. It consists of fourteen closely printed pages. They do not deal with the meaning of the image. They deal with who commissioned the painting, legal squabbles, who owned it, its likely date, the families of its owners. Behind this information lie years of research. The aim of the research is to prove beyond any shadow of doubt that the painting is a genuine Leonardo. The secondary aim is to prove that an almost identical painting in the Louvre is a replica of the National Gallery version.

French art historians try to prove the opposite.

The National Gallery sells more reproductions of Leonardo's cartoon of *The Virgin and Child with St. Anne and St. John the Baptist* [on the next page] than any other picture in their collection. A few years ago it was known only to scholars. It became famous because an American wanted to buy it for two and a half million pounds.

Now it hangs in a room by itself. The room is like a chapel. The drawing is behind bullet-proof perspex. It has acquired a new kind of impressiveness.

National
Gallery

Virgin of the Rocks by Leonardo da Vinci
[1452–1519]. Louvre Museum.

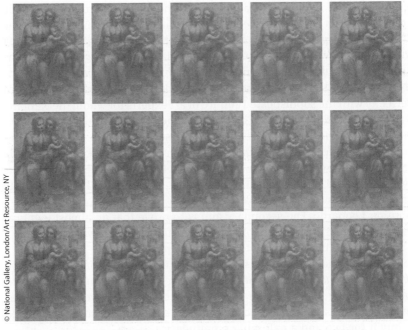

The Virgin and Child with St. Anne and St. John the Baptist by Leonardo da Vinci
[1452–1519].

Not because of what it shows — not because of the meaning of its image. It has become impressive, mysterious, because of its market value.

The bogus religiosity which now surrounds original works of art, and which is ultimately dependent upon their market value, has become the substitute for what paintings lost when the camera made them reproducible. Its function is nostalgic. It is the final empty claim for the continuing values of an oligarchic, undemocratic culture. If the image is no longer unique and exclusive, the art object, the thing, must be made mysteriously so.

The majority of the population do not visit art museums. The following table shows how closely an interest in art is related to privileged education.

National proportion of art museum visitors according to level of education: Percentage of each educational category who visit art museums

	Greece	Poland	France	Holland		Greece	Poland	France	Holland
With no educational qualification	0.02	0.12	0.15	—	Only secondary education	10.5	10.4	10	20
Only primary education	0.30	1.50	0.45	0.50	Further and higher education	11.5	11.7	12.5	17.3

Source: Pierre Bourdieu and Alain Darbel, *L'Amour de l'art*, Editions de Minuit, Paris 1969, Appendix 5, table 4.

The majority take it as axiomatic that the museums are full of holy relics which refer to a mystery which excludes them: the mystery of unaccountable wealth. Or, to put this another way, they believe that original masterpieces belong to the preserve (both materially and spiritually) of

Of the places listed below which does a museum remind you of most?

	Manual workers	Skilled and white collar workers	Professional and upper managerial
	%	%	%
Church	66	45	30.5
Library	9	34	28
Lecture hall	—	4	4.5
Department store or entrance hall in public building	—	7	2
Church and library	9	2	4.5
Church and lecture hall	4	2	—
Library and lecture hall	—	—	2
None of these	4	2	19.5
No reply	8	4	9
	100 (n = 53)	100 (n = 98)	100 (n = 99)

Source: as above, Appendix 4, table 8.

the rich. Another table indicates what the idea of an art gallery suggests to each social class.

In the age of pictorial reproduction the meaning of paintings is no longer attached to them; their meaning becomes transmittable: that is to say it becomes information of a sort, and, like all information, it is either put to use or ignored; information carries no special authority within itself. When a painting is put to use, its meaning is either modified or totally changed. One should be quite clear about what this involves. It is not a question of reproduction failing to reproduce certain aspects of an image faithfully; it is a question of reproduction making it possible, even inevitable, that an image will be used for many different purposes and that the reproduced image, unlike an original work, can lend itself to them all. Let us examine some of the ways in which the reproduced image lends itself to such usage.

Reproduction isolates a detail of a painting from the whole. The detail is transformed. An allegorical figure becomes a portrait of a girl.

Venus and Mars by Botticelli [1445–1510].

film takes time to explain, while a painting doesn't

When a painting is reproduced by a film camera it inevitably becomes material for the film-maker's argument.

A film which reproduces images of a painting leads the spectator, through the painting, to the film-maker's own conclusions. The painting lends authority to the film-maker. This is because a film unfolds in time and a painting does not. In a film the way one image follows another, their succession, constructs an argument which becomes irreversible. In a painting all its elements are there to be seen simultaneously. The spectator may need time to examine each element of the painting but whenever he reaches a conclusion, the simultaneity of the whole painting is there to reverse or qualify his conclusion. The painting maintains its own authority [below]. Paintings are often reproduced with words around them.

Erich Lessing/Art Resource, NY

Procession to Calvary by Breughel [1525–1569].

Erich Lessing /Art Resource, NY

[handwritten annotation in left margin: acknowing that Van gogh killed himself after painting this makes it dark]

This is a landscape of a cornfield with birds flying out of it. Look at it for a moment [below]. Then turn the page. [See page 157].

It is hard to define exactly how the words have changed the image but undoubtedly they have. The image now illustrates the sentence.

In this essay each image reproduced has become part of an argument which has little or nothing to do with the painting's original independent meaning. The words have quoted the paintings to confirm their own verbal authority. . . .

Reproduced paintings, like all information, have to hold their own against all the other information being continually transmitted.

Consequently a reproduction, as well as making its own references to the image of its original, becomes itself the reference point for other images. The meaning of an image is changed according to what one sees

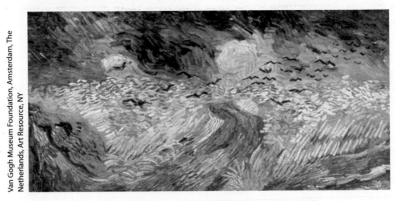

Wheatfield with Crows by Van Gogh [1853–1890].

Van Gogh Museum Foundation, Amsterdam, The Netherlands, Art Resource, NY

Van Gogh Museum Foundation, Amsterdam, The
Netherlands, Art Resource, NY

*This is the last picture that Van Gogh painted
before he killed himself.*

immediately beside it or what comes immediately after it. Such authority
as it retains, is distributed over the whole context in which it appears.

Because works of art are reproducible, they can, theoretically, be used
by anybody. Yet mostly — in art books, magazines, films, or within gilt frames
in living-rooms — reproductions are still used to bolster the illusion that
nothing has changed, that art, with its unique undiminished authority, jus-
tifies most other forms of authority, that art makes inequality seem noble
and hierarchies seem thrilling. For example, the whole concept of the National Cultural Heritage exploits the authority of art to glorify the present
social system and its priorities.

The means of reproduction are used politically and commercially to
disguise or deny what their existence makes possible. But sometimes
individuals use them differently [See page 158].

Adults and children sometimes have boards in their bedrooms or
living-rooms on which they pin pieces of paper: letters, snapshots, reproductions of paintings, newspaper cuttings, original drawings, postcards.
On each board all the images belong to the same language and all are
more or less equal within it, because they have been chosen in a highly
personal way to match and express the experience of the room's inhabitant. Logically, these boards should replace museums.

What are we saying by that? Let us first be sure about what we are
not saying.

We are not saying that there is nothing left to experience before original works of art except a sense of awe because they have survived. The
way original works of art are usually approached — through museum catalogues, guides, hired cassettes, etc. — is not the only way they might be
approached. When the art of the past ceases to be viewed nostalgically, the
works will cease to be holy relics — although they will never re-become
what they were before the age of reproduction. We are not saying original
works of art are now useless.

Original paintings are silent and still in a sense that information never is. Even a reproduction hung on a wall is not comparable in this respect for in the original the silence and stillness permeate the actual material, the paint, in which one follows the traces of the painter's immediate gestures.

ORIGINAL PAINTINGS ARE SILENT AND STILL IN A SENSE THAT INFORMATION NEVER IS.

This has the effect of closing the distance in time between the painting of the picture and one's own act of looking at it. In this special sense all paintings are contemporary. Hence the immediacy of their testimony. Their historical moment is literally there before our eyes. Cézanne made a similar observation from the painter's point of view. "A minute in the world's life passes! To paint it in its reality, and forget everything for that! To become that minute, to be the sensitive plate . . . give the image of what we see, forgetting everything that has appeared before our time. . . ." What we make of that painted moment when it is before our eyes depends upon what we expect of art, and that in turn depends today upon how we have already experienced the meaning of paintings through reproductions.

Nor are we saying that all art can be understood spontaneously. We are not claiming that to cut out a magazine reproduction of an archaic Greek head, because it is reminiscent of some personal experience, and to pin it to a board beside other disparate images, is to come to terms with the full meaning of that head.

The idea of innocence faces two ways. By refusing to enter a conspiracy, one remains innocent of that conspiracy. But to remain innocent may also be to remain ignorant. The issue is not between innocence and knowledge (or between the natural and the cultural) but between a total approach to art which attempts to relate it to every aspect of experience and the esoteric approach of a few specialized experts who are the clerks of the nostalgia of a ruling class in decline. (In decline, not before the proletariat, but before the new power of the corporation and the state.) The real question is: to whom does the meaning of the art of the past properly belong? to those who can apply it to their own lives, or to a cultural hierarchy of relic specialists?

The visual arts have always existed within a certain preserve; originally this preserve was magical or sacred. But it was also physical: it was the place, the cave, the building, in which, or for which, the work was made. The experience of art, which at first was the experience of ritual, was set apart from the rest of life — precisely in order to be able to exercise power over it. Later the preserve of art became a social one. It entered the culture of the ruling class, while physically it was set apart and isolated in their palaces and houses. During all this history the authority of art was inseparable from the particular authority of the preserve.

What the modern means of reproduction have done is to destroy the authority of art and to remove it — or, rather, to remove its images which they reproduce — from any preserve. For the first time ever, images of art have become ephemeral, ubiquitous, insubstantial, available, valueless, free. They surround us in the same way as a language surrounds us. They have entered the mainstream of life over which they no longer, in themselves, have power.

Woman Pouring Milk by Vermeer [1632–1675].

Erich Lessing/Art Resource, NY

Yet very few people are aware of what has happened because the means of reproduction are used nearly all the time to promote the illusion that nothing has changed except that the masses, thanks to reproductions, can now begin to appreciate art as the cultured minority once did. Understandably, the masses remain uninterested and skeptical.

If the new language of images were used differently, it would, through its use, confer a new kind of power. Within it we could begin to define our experiences more precisely in areas where words are inadequate. (Seeing comes before words.) Not only personal experience, but also the essential historical experience of our relation to the past: that is to say the experience of seeking to give meaning to our lives, of trying to understand the history of which we can become the active agents.

The art of the past no longer exists as it once did. Its authority is lost. In its place there is a language of images. What matters now is who uses that language for what purpose. This touches upon questions of copyright for reproduction, the ownership of art presses and publishers, the total policy of public art galleries and museums. As usually presented, these are narrow professional matters. One of the aims of this essay has been to show that what is really at stake is much larger. A people or a class which is cut off from its own past is far less free to choose and to act as a people or class than one that has been able to situate itself in history. This is why — and this is the only reason why — the entire art of the past has now become a political issue.

• • • • •

J. LL. Banús/Age Fotostock

Walter Benjamin

Many of the ideas in the preceding essay have been taken from another, written over forty years ago by the German critic and philosopher Walter Benjamin.

His essay was entitled The Work of Art in the Age of Mechanical Reproduction. *This essay is available in English in a collection called* Illuminations *(Cape, London, 1970).*

NOTES

[1] Seymour Slive, *Frans Hals* (Phaidon, London). [All notes are Berger's.]

[2] This quotation is from an article written in 1923 by Dziga Vertov, the revolutionary Soviet film director.

We were unable to reproduce all of the images from the original text of "Ways of Seeing." If you would like to track them down, you might look for a copy of Berger's book *Ways of Seeing* in your college or university library. You'll find them there. —Eds.

On Rembrandt's
Woman in Bed

It is strange how art historians sometimes pay so much attention, when trying to date certain paintings, to "style," inventories, bills, auction lists, and so little to the painted evidence concerning the model's age. It is as if they do not trust the painter on this point. For example, when they try to date and arrange in chronological order Rembrandt's paintings of Hendrickje Stoffels. No painter was a greater expert about the process of aging, and no painter has left us a more intimate record of the great love of his life. Whatever the documentary conjectures may allow, the paintings make it clear that the love between Hendrickje and the painter lasted for about twenty years, until her death, six years before his.

Woman in Bed by Rembrandt.

She was ten or twelve years younger than he. When she died she was, on the evidence of the paintings, at the very least forty-five, and when he first painted her she could certainly not have been older than twenty-seven. Their daughter, Cornelia, was baptized in 1654. This means that Hendrickje gave birth to their child when she was in her mid-thirties.

The *Woman in Bed* (from Edinburgh) was painted, by my reckoning, a little before or a little after the birth of Cornelia. The historians suggest that it may be a fragment taken from a larger work representing the wedding night of Sarah and Tobias. A biblical subject for Rembrandt was always contemporary. If it is a fragment, it is certain that Rembrandt finished it, and bequeathed it finally to the spectator, as his most intimate painting of the woman he loved.

There are other paintings of Hendrickje. Before the *Bathsheba* in the Louvre, or the *Woman Bathing* in the National Gallery (London), I am wordless. Not because their genius inhibits me, but because the experience from which they derive and which they express — desire experiencing itself as something as old as the known world, tenderness experiencing itself as the end of the world, the eyes' endless rediscovery, as if for the first time, of their love of a familiar body — all this comes before and goes beyond words. No other paintings lead so deftly and powerfully to silence. Yet, in both, Hendrickje is absorbed in her own actions. In the painter's vision of her there is the greatest intimacy, but there is no mutual intimacy between them. They are paintings which speak of his love, not of hers.

In the painting of the *Woman in Bed* there is a complicity between the woman and the painter. This complicity includes both reticence and abandon, day and night. The curtain of the bed, which Hendrickje lifts up with her hand, marks the threshold between daytime and nighttime.

In two years, by daylight, Van Rijn will be declared bankrupt. Ten years before, by daylight, Hendrickje came to work in Van Rijn's house as a nurse for his baby son. In the light of Dutch seventeenth-century accountability and Calvinism, the housekeeper and the painter have distinct and separate responsibilities. Hence their reticence.

At night, they leave their century.

> A necklace hangs loose across her breasts,
> And between them lingers —
> yet is it a lingering
> and not an incessant arrival? —
> the perfume of forever.
> A perfume as old as sleep,
> as familiar to the living as to the dead.

Leaning forward from her pillows, she lifts up the curtain with the back of her hand, for its palm, its face, is already welcoming, already making a gesture which is preparatory to the act of touching his head.

She has not yet slept. Her gaze follows him as he approaches. In her face the two of them are reunited. Impossible now to separate the two images: his image of her in bed, as he remembers her: her image of him as she sees him approaching their bed. It is nighttime.

On Caravaggio's *The Calling of St. Matthew*

One night in bed you asked me who was my favorite painter. I hesitated, searching for the least knowing, most truthful answer. Caravaggio. My own reply surprised me. There are nobler painters and painters of greater breadth of vision. There are painters I admire more and who are more admirable. But there is none, so it seems — for the answer came unpremeditated — to whom I feel closer.

The few canvases from my own incomparably modest life as a painter, which I would like to see again, are those I painted in the late 1940s of the streets of Livorno. This city was then war-scarred and poor, and it was there that I first began to learn something about the ingenuity of the dispossessed. It was there too that I discovered that I wanted as little as possible to do in this world with those who wield power. This has turned out to be a lifelong aversion.

The Calling of St. Matthew by Caravaggio.

The complicity I feel with Caravaggio began, I think, during that time in Livorno. He was the first painter of life as experienced by the popolaccio, the people of the backstreets, les sans-culottes, the lumpenproletariat, the lower orders, those of the lower depths, the underworld. There is no word in any traditional European language which does not either denigrate or patronize the urban poor it is naming. That is power.

Following Caravaggio up to the present day, other painters — Brower, Ostade, Hogarth, Goya, Géricault, Guttuso — have painted pictures of the same social milieu. But all of them — however great — were genre pictures, painted in order to show others how the less fortunate or the more dangerous lived. With Caravaggio, however, it was not a question of presenting scenes but of seeing itself. He does not depict the underworld for others: his vision is one that he shares with it.

In art-historical books Caravaggio is listed as one of the great innovating masters of chiaroscuro and a forerunner of the light and shade later used by Rembrandt and others. His vision can of course be considered art-historically as a step in the evolution of European art. Within such a perspective *a* Caravaggio was almost inevitable, as a link between the high art of the Counter Reformation and the domestic art of the emerging Dutch bourgeoisie, the form of this link being that of a new kind of space, defined by darkness as well as by light. (For Rome and for Amsterdam damnation had become an everyday affair.)

IN ART-HISTORICAL BOOKS CARAVAGGIO IS LISTED AS ONE OF THE GREAT INNOVATING MASTERS OF CHIAROSCURO.

For the Caravaggio who actually existed — for the boy called Michelangelo born in a village near Bergamo, not far from where my friends, the Italian woodcutters, come — light and shade, as he imagined and saw them, had a deeply personal meaning, inextricably entwined with his desires and his instinct for survival. And it is by this, not by any art-historical logic, that his art is linked with the underworld.

His chiaroscuro allowed him to banish daylight. Shadows, he felt, offered shelter as can four walls and a roof. Whatever and wherever he painted he really painted interiors. Sometimes — for *The Flight into Egypt* or one of his beloved John the Baptists — he was obliged to include a landscape in the background. But these landscapes are like rugs or drapes hung up on a line across an inner courtyard. He only felt at home — no, that he felt nowhere — he only felt relatively at ease *inside*.

His darkness smells of candles, overripe melons, damp washing waiting to be hung out the next day: it is the darkness of stairwells, gambling corners, cheap lodgings, sudden encounters. And the promise is not in what will flare against it, but in the darkness itself. The shelter it offers is only relative, for the chiaroscuro reveals violence, suffering, longing, mortality, but at least it reveals them intimately. What has been banished, along with the daylight, are distance and solitude — and both these are feared by the underworld.

Those who live precariously and are habitually crowded together develop a phobia about open spaces which transforms their frustrating lack of space and privacy into something reassuring. He shared those fears.

The Calling of St. Matthew depicts five men sitting round their usual table, telling stories, gossiping, boasting of what one day they will do, counting money. The room is dimly lit. Suddenly the door is flung open. The two figures who enter are still part of the violent noise and light of the invasion. (Berenson wrote that Christ, who is one of the figures, comes in like a police inspector to make an arrest.)

Two of Matthew's colleagues refuse to look up, the other two younger ones stare at the strangers with a mixture of curiosity and condescension. Why is he proposing something so mad? Who's protecting him, the thin one who does all the talking? And Matthew, the tax-collector with a shifty conscience which has made him more unreasonable than most of his colleagues, points at himself and asks: Is it really I who must go? Is it really I who must follow you?

How many thousands of decisions to leave have resembled Christ's hand here! The hand is held out towards the one who has to decide, yet it is ungraspable because so fluid. It orders the way, yet offers no direct support. Matthew will get up and follow the thin stranger from the room, down the narrow streets, out of the district. He will write his gospel, he will travel to Ethiopia and the South Caspian and Persia. Probably he will be murdered.

And behind the drama of this moment of decision in the room at the top of the stairs, there is a window, giving onto the outside world. Traditionally in painting, windows were treated either as sources of light or as frames framing nature or framing an exemplary event outside. Not so this window. No light enters by it. The window is opaque. We see nothing. Mercifully we see nothing because what is outside is bound to be threatening. It is a window through which only the worst news can come.

· · · ● · · ·

QUESTIONS FOR A SECOND READING

1. Berger says, "The past is never there waiting to be discovered, to be recognized for exactly what it is. History always constitutes the relation between a present and its past" (p. 145). And he says, "If we 'saw' the art of the past, we would situate ourselves in history. When we are prevented from seeing it, we are being deprived of the history which belongs to us" (p. 145). As you reread this essay, pay particular attention to Berger's uses of the word "history." What does it stand for? What does it have to do with looking at pictures? How might you define the term if your definition were based on its use in this essay?

    You might take Berger's discussion of the Hals paintings as a case in point. What is the relation Berger establishes between the past and the present? If he has not "discovered" the past or recognized it for exactly what it is, what has Berger done in writing about these paintings? What might it mean to say that he has "situated" us in history or has returned a history that belongs to us? And in what way might this be said to be a political act?

2. Berger argues forcefully that the account of the Hals painting offered by the unnamed art historian is a case of "mystification." How would you characterize Berger's account of that same painting? Would you say that he sees what is "really" there? If so, why wasn't it self-evident? Why does it take an expert to see "clearly"? As you read back over the essay, look for passages you could use to characterize the way Berger looks at images or paintings. If, as he says, "The way we see things is affected by what we know or what we believe," what does he know and what does he believe?

· · · ● · · ·

ASSIGNMENTS FOR WRITING

1. We are not saying that there is nothing left to experience before original works of art except a sense of awe because they have survived. The way original works of art are usually approached — through museum catalogues, guides, hired cassettes, etc. — is not the only way they might be approached. When the art of the past ceases to be viewed nostalgically, the works will cease to be holy relics — although they will never re-become what they were before the age of reproduction. We are not saying original works of art are now useless. (p. 157)

    Berger argues that there are barriers to vision, problems in the ways we see or don't see original works of art, problems that can be located in and overcome by strategies of approach.

    For Berger, what we lose if we fail to see properly is history: "If we 'saw' the art of the past, we would situate ourselves in history. When we are prevented from seeing it, we are being deprived of the history which belongs to us" (p. 145). It is not hard to figure out who, according to Berger, prevents us from seeing the art of the past. He says it is the ruling class. It is difficult, however, to figure out what he believes gets in the way and what all this has to do with history.

For this assignment, write an essay explaining what, as you read Berger, it is that gets in the way when we look at paintings, and what it is that we might do to overcome the barriers to vision (and to history). You should imagine that you are writing for someone who is interested in art, and is perhaps preparing to go to a museum, but has not read Berger's essay. You will, that is, need to be careful in summary and paraphrase.

2. Berger says that the real question is this: "To whom does the meaning of the art of the past properly belong?" Let's say, in Berger's spirit, that it belongs to you. Look again at the painting by Vermeer, *Woman Pouring Milk*, that is included in "Ways of Seeing" (p. 159). Berger includes the painting but without much discussion, as though he were, in fact, leaving it for you. Write an essay that shows others how they might best understand that painting. You should offer this lesson in the spirit of John Berger. Imagine that you are doing this work for him, perhaps as his apprentice.

3.   Original paintings are silent and still in a sense that information never is. "Even a reproduction hung on a wall is not comparable in this respect for in the original the silence and stillness permeate the actual material, the paint, in which one follows the traces of the painter's immediate gestures. "This has the effect of closing the distance in time between the painting of the picture and one's own act of looking at it. . . . What we make of that painted moment when it is before our eyes depends upon what we expect of art, and that in turn depends today upon how we have already experienced the meaning of paintings through reproductions. (p. 158)

While Berger describes original paintings as silent in this passage, it is clear that these paintings begin to speak if one approaches them properly, if one learns to ask "the right questions of the past." Berger demonstrates one route of approach, for example, in his reading of the Hals paintings, where he asks questions about the people and objects and their relationships to the painter and the viewer. What the paintings might be made to say, however, depends on the viewer's expectations, his sense of the questions that seem appropriate or possible. Berger argues that, because of the way art is currently displayed, discussed, and reproduced, the viewer expects only to be mystified.

For this paper, imagine that you are working against the silence and mystification Berger describes. Go to a museum—or, if that is not possible, to a large-format book of reproductions in the library (or, if that is not possible, to the reproductions on the web)—and select a painting that seems silent and still, yet invites conversation. Your job is to figure out what sorts of questions to ask, to interrogate the painting, to get it to speak, to engage with the past in some form of dialogue. Write an essay in which you record this process and what you have learned from it. Somewhere in your paper, perhaps at the end, turn back to Berger's essay and speak to it about how this process has or hasn't confirmed what you take to be Berger's expectations.

Note: If possible, include with your essay a reproduction of the painting you select. (Check the postcards at the museum gift shop.) In any event, you want to make sure that you describe the painting in sufficient detail for your readers to follow what you say.

4. In "Ways of Seeing," Berger says,

> If the new language of images were used differently, it would, through its use, confer a new kind of power. Within it we could begin to define our experiences more precisely in areas where words are inadequate.... Not only personal experience, but also the essential historical experience of our relation to the past: that is to say the experience of seeking to give meaning to our lives, of trying to understand the history of which we can become the active agents. (p. 160)

As a writer, Berger is someone who uses images (including some of the great paintings of the Western tradition) "to define [experience] more precisely in areas where words are inadequate." In *And Our Faces, My Heart, Brief as Photos*, a wonderful book that is both a meditation on time and space and a long love letter, Berger writes about paintings in order to say what he wants to say to his lover. We have included two examples, descriptions of Rembrandt's *Woman in Bed* and Caravaggio's *The Calling of St. Matthew*.

Read these as examples, as lessons in how and why to look at, to value, to think with, to write about paintings. Then use one or both as a way of thinking about the concluding section of "Ways of Seeing." You can assume that your readers have read Berger's essay but have difficulty grasping what he is saying in that final section, particularly since it is a section that seems to call for action, asking the reader to do something. Of what use might Berger's example be in trying to understand what we might do with and because of paintings?

· · ● · · ·

MAKING CONNECTIONS

1. Walker Percy in "The Loss of the Creature" (p. 472), like John Berger in "Ways of Seeing," talks about the problems people have seeing things. "How can the sightseer recover the Grand Canyon?" Percy asks. "He can recover it in any number of ways, all sharing in common the stratagem of avoiding the approved confrontation of the tour and the Park Service" (p. 473). There is a way in which Berger also tells a story about tourists — tourists going to a museum to see paintings, to buy postcards, gallery guides, reprints, and T-shirts featuring the image of the Mona Lisa. "The way original works of art are usually approached — through museum catalogues, guides, hired cassettes, etc. — is not the only way they might be approached. When the art of the

past ceases to be viewed nostalgically, the works will cease to be holy relics—although they will never re-become what they were before the age of reproduction" (p. 157).

Write an essay in which you describe possible "approaches" to a painting in a museum, approaches that could provide for a better understanding or a more complete "recovery" of that painting than would be possible to a casual viewer, to someone who just wandered in, for example, with no strategy in mind. You should think of your essay as providing real advice to a real person. (You might, if you can, work with a particular painting in a particular museum.) What should that person do? How should that person prepare? What would the consequences be?

At least one of your approaches should reflect Percy's best advice to a viewer who wanted to develop a successful strategy, and at least one should represent the best you feel Berger would have to offer. When you've finished explaining these approaches, go on in your essay to examine the differences between those you associate with Percy and those you associate with Berger. What are the key differences? And what do they say about the different ways these two thinkers approach the problem of why we do or do not see that which lies before us?

2. Both John Berger in "Ways of Seeing" and Michel Foucault in "Panopticism" (p. 328) discuss what Foucault calls "power relations." Berger claims that "the entire art of the past has now become a political issue," and he makes a case for the evolution of a "new language of images" that could "confer a new kind of power" if people were to understand history in art. Foucault argues that the Panopticon signals an "inspired" change in power relations. "It is," he says, "an important mechanism, for it automatizes and disindividualizes power. Power has its principle not so much in a person as in a certain concerted distribution of bodies, surfaces, lights, gazes; in an arrangement whose internal mechanisms produce the relation in which individuals are caught up" (p. 334).

Both Berger and Foucault create arguments about power and its methods and goals. As you read through their essays, mark passages you might use to explain how each author thinks about power—where it comes from, who has it, how it works, where you look for it, how you know it when you see it, what it does, where it goes. You should reread the essays as a pair, as part of a single project in which you are seeking to explain theories of power.

Write an essay in which you present and explain "Ways of Seeing" and "Panopticism" as examples of Berger's and Foucault's theories of power and vision. Both Berger and Foucault are arguing against usual understandings of power and knowledge and history. In this sense, their projects are similar. Of course, there may be notable and interesting differences in their projects as well, and these might also be worth exploring.

3. In "Beauty (Re)discovers the Male Body" (p. 186), Susan Bordo refers to John Berger and his work in *Ways of Seeing*, although she refers to a different chapter from the one included here. In general, however, both Berger and Bordo

are concerned with how we see and read images; both seek to correct the ways images are used and read; both trace the ways images serve the interests of money and power; both texts are written to teach readers how and why they should pay a different kind of attention to the images around them.

For this assignment, use Bordo's work to reconsider Berger's. Write an essay in which you consider the two chapters as examples of an ongoing project. Berger's essay precedes Bordo's by about a quarter of a century. If you look closely at one or two of their examples, and if you look at the larger concerns of their arguments, are they saying the same things? doing the same work? If so, how? And why is such work still necessary? If not, how do their projects differ? And how might you explain those differences?

GLORIA
Bird

Gloria Bird was born in 1951 in Washington State. She attended Portland Community College and in 1990 received her BA in English from Lewis & Clark College, both in Portland, Oregon. She received her MA in English in 1992 from the University of Arizona in Tucson. She taught literature and creative writing at the Institute of American Indian Arts for five years, and currently teaches at the Wellpinit, Washington, campus of Salish Kootenei College. Bird has been a recipient of the Oregon Institute of Literary Arts' Oregon Writer's Grant (1988) and the Witter Bynner Foundation grant (1993). She is also a founding member of the Northwest Native American Writers Association and an associate editor for the *Wicazo Sa Review*, and was a contributing editor for *Indian Artist Magazine*.

Bird is a member of the Spokane Tribe of Washington State and works for the Spokane Tribe of Indians in Wellpinit, Washington, in addition to teaching and writing. Her poetry and criticism focus on Native American identity and colonialism. She has published two books of her own poetry: *Full Moon on the Reservation* (1993), for which she won the Diane Decorah Memorial Award, and *The River of History* (1997). Along with Joy Harjo, Bird edited the anthology *Reinventing the Enemy's Language: Contemporary Native Women's Writing of North America* (1997). Bird also coauthored *A Filmography for Native American Education* (1973) with Carroll Warner Williams. She is currently working on a large ongoing project started in 1988: a poetry collection focusing on the Nez Perce retreat of 1877.

In the following essay from the anthology *Here First: Autobiographical Essays by Native American Writers* (2000), Bird grapples with the "misrepresentations of 'Indian' that are legitimized in academia and pop culture about Native peoples" and her own scholarly orientation and methods. She cites African American feminist literature as an influence that led her to study the internalization of colonial attitudes by colonized peoples. A passion and drive for seeking justice permeates her work. In "Breaking the Silence: Writing as 'Witness,'" published in *Speaking for the Generations: Native Writers on Writing* in 1998 by the University of Arizona Press, Bird expounds upon the ethical imperative inherent in the kind of work she does. She explains that stories and memoirs provide strength to marginalized peoples through the processes of witnessing and testimony. These processes, she writes, are "viable tools that

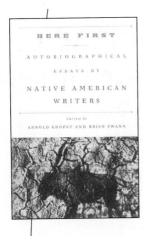

HERE FIRST

AUTOBIOGRAPHICAL

ESSAYS BY

NATIVE AMERICAN
WRITERS

EDITED BY
ARNOLD KRUPAT AND BRIAN SWANN

serve the purposes of decolonization by providing details of individual processing of the complexities of inheritance that living in the aftermath of colonization provides" (*Speaking for the Generations*, p. 29).

Autobiography as Spectacle: An Act of Liberation or the Illusion of Liberation?

> Between colonizer and colonized there is room only for forced labor, intimidation, pressure, the police, taxation, theft, rape, compulsory crops, contempt, mistrust, arrogance, self-complacency, swinishness, brainless elites, degraded masses. No human contact, but relations of domination and submission which turn the colonizing man into a classroom monitor, an army sergeant, a prison guard, a slave driver, and the indigenous man into an instrument of production.
>
> My turn to state an equation: colonization = "thingification. . . ."
>
> I hear the storm. They talk to me about progress, about "achievements," diseases cured, improved standards of living. *I* am talking about societies drained of their essence, cultures trampled underfoot, institutions smashed, magnificent artistic creations destroyed, extraordinary *possibilities* wiped out. . . . I am talking about millions of men torn from their gods, their land, their habits, their life — from life, from the dance, from wisdom.
>
> — AIMÉ CÉSAIRE, *Discourse on Colonialism* (21–22)

I begin with Césaire as a springboard into my discussion of being Native in America because it is good for perspective. (Who knows the tactics of colonialism better than the colonized?) Also, as a Native writer I am intimately involved in evaluating the aftermath of colonization and its impact that cannot help but shape my life and my own perceptions of the world. The competing stories of the indigenous peoples' sense of tribal histories and the privileged, legitimized perspectives on national history are on a collision course. It is from this place that I write, digesting, and ultimately attempt to undo the damage that colonization has wrought. From the Third World, the war dance in the blood has been reawakened.

Placing my story on public display is not something I have undertaken lightly. I enter this discourse hesitantly, knowing that my story, my life, my words are all a part of a spectacle, a peering into Indian life and thought that is in a sense intrusive. I have agreed because of the opportunity this offers to counter some of the misrepresentations of "Indian" that are legitimized in academia and pop culture about Native peoples. To this end, I would like to place my story against the backdrop of colonial context to address some of the misperceptions about Native people that

I ENTER THIS DISCOURSE HESITANTLY, KNOWING THAT MY STORY, MY LIFE, MY WORDS ARE ALL PART OF A SPECTACLE, A PEERING INTO INDIAN LIFE AND THOUGHT THAT IS IN A SENSE INTRUSIVE.

compose the construct of "Indian" in the mainstream. I understand that the Native Other when viewed up close should pose no threat in a system where all transferable signs mirror the image of *all that I am not*. And so I begin with the paradox of constructing an idea of "self" in terms that presuppose a colonial mental bondage.

How I have come to know myself as Indian is contradicted continually in mainstream pop culture, in commercials, in ads in magazines, and in film. I recognize that outside of my immediate Native community, images of Indians are not held up as either the ideal or a template for "beauty." From my perspective, then, I am continually forced to negotiate between *what I know* and what I am told about myself as an Indian. Neither do I believe that my dilemma in this case or my particular experience is unique to me. As an example, I recall a day when my oldest daughter, who was four years old, came home crying. She had been next door playing with a neighbor's child. They had been watching an old black-and-white western on TV. The neighbor boy pointed to the screen laughing at the hooting Indians being chased by cavalry and told her that she was an "Indian." I hugged my heartbroken daughter and said, "But you *are* an Indian." She told me right back, "But I'm not *that* kind of Indian." None of us are.

I attended one year at public school (one out of two years spent outside of the Bureau of Indian Affairs Indian boarding school system). In the Washington State history text, the history of Northwest Native peoples was given in one full paragraph that highlighted Chief Sealth, for whom the city of Seattle was named. Not only did it appear that we Natives of Washington State did not exist, but we also had not apparently made a contribution worth mentioning.

Having lived on reservations during the early part of my life, the areas of Native history and shared cultural knowledge were often assisted by *place*. With our grandparents, we, my younger sister and I, traveled to the reservation to picnic, to sit under the trees on blankets and listen to our grandparents talking. We often found ourselves above Tshimakain Creek, where the land sloped down into a brush-filled ravine surrounded by pine trees, a favorite spot of my grandfather. On the rise above where we sat to eat stood a pine tree that formed a huge Y. In the center of its branches, where the two arms met the trunk of the tree, a cradleboard lay on its side, the tree growing up and around it. It looked as though a great hand had forced the cradleboard straight down into the heart of the tree, the headrest jutting from one side and the footrest from the other.

The story is a simple one: *The people were running from cavalry, and a young mother placed her baby in the cradleboard in the Y of the tree to save it, running, leading the cavalry in another direction from her child. She never returned.*

Later, the story of Colonel Steptoe, defeated at the butte named for his humiliation, unfolds. In retaliation, the army killed the Indians' horses, approximately seven hundred animals belonging to the Spokanes. Though these two events may not be directly connected they are to my mind a reminder of our history, filled with violence and oppression. The Spokane were considered "hostile" as were all tribal groups who refused to sign treaties, an act of resistance that would inevitably lead to reduced land-holdings and confine them to a reservation.

My grandparents would have been too young to have lived through those times. But maybe my great-grandmother, my *tu pi ya*? While we sat contemplating fried chicken and potato salad, swatting the ants from the blanket, my mind rushed forward to the conclusion of the story of the baby tied into the cradleboard, who cried into the night, rocking in the arms of the sleepless tree.

Once, on returning home, I went in search of this picnic spot, driving in circles and following dead-end dirt roads to rediscover the place rooted in my memories as cradling tribal and family history. The site was not to be found. I was told later that some young men out on a drinking/shooting spree had shot the cradleboard into nothing. How well we Indians have learned from the colonizer to devalue our history.

Take, for instance, then President Ronald Reagan speaking in Moscow in 1988:

> Let me tell you just a little something about the American Indian in our land. We have provided millions of acres of land for what are called "preservations" — or, "reservations," I should say. They, from the beginning, announced that they wanted to maintain their way of life as they had always lived, there on the plains and the desert, and so forth. And we set up these reservations so they could. And we have a Bureau of Indian Affairs to help take care of them. At the same time, we provide education for them — schools on the reservations. And they are free also to leave the reservations and be American citizens among the rest of us — and many do. Some still prefer, however, that early way of life. And we have done everything we can to meet their demands as to what and how they want to live. Maybe we made a mistake; maybe we should not have humored them in that wanting to stay in that primitive lifestyle. Maybe we should have said, no, come join us, be citizens.[1]

That the then president of the United States could be as publicly oblivious to Native peoples to the extent that our citizenship was in question, and that our livelihood was perceived as "primitive"; to deny the United States' obligation to uphold Indian treaties; to offhandedly refer to Indian reservations as "preservations"; to suggest that it was a "mistake" to set aside these lands (conveniently forgetting that this was done in exchange for Indians' ceding larger tracts of land); to suggest that this was a pacification move on the part of the United States, "to humor them," meaning us, is an outrage. I view Reagan's ignorance of Indian history, and consequently American history, as a mirror of America's basic lack of knowledge about us.

Only last year, my thirteen-year-old son came home from school with homework in social studies in which one of his questions required his answering that *wampum belts = money*. Commodification of Native systems of documenting agreements is a gross misinterpretation. Though it is not surprising that the historical significance of tribal agreements are mediated through Euro-American standards based upon exchange value.

The commodification of "Indian" has also reached the dialogue of Native peoples themselves, exemplifying, at least to this writer, the extent of the colonization. That my tribal ID has currency value and that tribes are now in the business of selling memberships clouds further the issue of legitimate claim. There is an irony to the *buying into* the effects of colonization, such as oppression, dispossession, the inherited guilt and shame many of us have been made to associate with our being Indian. The commodity gain, the immediate profit, is an assumed access to Native spiritual and cultural knowledge, which I read as the paraphernalia of romanticism of Native peoples. This phenomenon *does* have an exchange value in a corrupt system.

> **THE DIFFICULTY OF COMMUNICATING IS NOT SO MUCH A QUESTION OF SPEAKING ACROSS CULTURES SO MUCH AS IT IS A PROBLEM OF SPEAKING ACROSS REALITIES THAT ARE CULTURE BOUND.**

I understand that the way I have come to know myself as Indian has been a process of socialization which includes a way of perceiving the world that is unique to the people from whom I am descended. This apprehension of the world is culture bound and serves as an axiom of how my perception differs from *the Other*'s perception or *reality* of the world. As I see it, the difficulty of communicating is not so much a question of speaking across cultures so much as it is a problem of speaking across realities that are culture bound. It's always easier to move through the world oblivious. By that I mean that it is easier to rely solely on what can be seen, touched, and proven. The extreme of that seems to be manipulating those who live obliviously by becoming an Indian-on-call, where one can always claim to have had a vision or a shamanic ancestor, for example. It appears that the quickest way to "Indianness" is the path of least resistance.

For Native peoples reared in Native communities, it is easy to spot the impostors, whose claim to "Indianness" as a solid, unbending reality reeks of self-centeredness and currency. Neither does a brown face automatically assure "Indianness," only a shared marginalization. I hear the storm, and in that the outcry at "essentialism." Still, I believe it is easier on the reservation to talk about *being* Indian. As my mother says, "If you have to claim to be a medicine man, then you aren't."

There is a comic scene, for instance, in the movie *Thunderheart* where the tribal policeman (Graham Greene) informs the FBI agent (Val Kilmer) that he, Kilmer, has had a *vision*. Incredulous, Greene tells Kilmer how he's lived on the reservation all his life and has never had a vision. This seemingly harmless, near throwaway scene points to one of the conflicting representations of "Indian," and exemplifies the contradictions at work in mainstream consciousness about "Indianness." Which is that anything Indian is public domain property and that sacredness is not respected or is applied superficially and arbitrarily to everything. But, hey, we're supposed to be entertained.

The basic premise for the movie relies upon our buying into the idea that a young man of Indian descent who has been reared far from his origins — and who has learned early to be ashamed of his Indian father — begins having visions. The plot is to take, for all practical purposes, this white guy, a descendant of Indian heritage, place him on an Indian reservation where he begins *seeing* things, namely, the massacre of Wounded Knee, his people being chased by cavalry and shot down, and remnants of the people dancing the Ghost Dance. We witness his transformation from anti-Indian white who disclaims the people who live in Third World conditions in the middle of the United States ("These are not my people") in the beginning, to pro-Indian red in the end, befriending along the way the tribal policeman and a medicine man — who tells him that "Mr. Magoo is not to be trusted."

The backdrop to the plot are the issues surrounding American Indian Movement (AIM, aka ARM in the movie) activity on the Pine Ridge Reservation, and the death of Anna Mae Aquash, though all of the details surrounding these issues have been fictionalized. But perhaps the saving grace of this movie is that the FBI are not the good guys — and, in fact, are the criminals. The uncomfortable truth of this film, if there is one to be found, is the representation of Indians oppressing other Indians. The usefulness of this last configuration should not be underestimated nor the impact upon Native communities overlooked. I will return to this idea later, but I would like to digress to comment upon why I find the critique of Native representation useful.

I began writing as a poet, but received my degree in literature. Along the way, I have been influenced by the personal narrative writing styles of African American feminist writers, and began writing criticism that attempted to *read* Native American literatures as a product of colonization, looking at ways that Native peoples have internalized colonial attitudes and beliefs about themselves that appear in their creative work. Early on, I questioned the usefulness of this type of criticism and wondered whether or not it was self-defeating to criticize other Native writers. That process could be thought of as playing into the hands of the colonizer. I am still struggling with the moral dilemma this poses for me; aggressive criticism goes against the way I have been raised. I suspect this has a bearing on why there are few Native writers who write literary criticism.

My alternative was to practice what I preached in my own creative endeavors. I began writing prose poems in which I incorporate criticism of Native representation — knowing full well that there would be critics of both the form and content. It is not my intention here to argue poetic strategies. If anyone has the need to engage in that discussion, they may.

The issues of representation overlap with and are as complex as issues of identity. We are often caught between the crossfire of realism and perpetuating stereotypes, especially when it comes to sensitive subjects. For instance, in how we represent the problem of alcoholism in our work or, simply, in how we discuss individual family/tribal history. For me, being Indian in the United States is filled with innumerable complexities and mixed feelings, but ultimately I have to attend to the business of interrogating damaging stereotypes and representations of Indians for the sake of my children. I take this as my duty, which it certainly is, not only for my own children, but the children who are entrusted to me throughout the school year.

I relate my story to that of my family and the people I am descended from, and it goes without saying that I cannot separate my story from theirs. We are a rural, reservation people and nothing in my memory is sparked by a single artistic influence. But I should qualify that statement. The women of my family have all been beadworkers, including myself, although this is not out of the ordinary where I come from. I have always felt that my family's lives and stories, and therefore my own, are uninteresting, and that we are an ordinary people. I've taken a lot for granted, and it is only through time that I have been able to recognize and distinguish our particular difference.

My grandmother, aunts, uncles, my mother, my sisters, and our combined children are enrolled members of the Spokane tribe of Indians. My ancestors are the *slawtews*, or Chewelah, a band of the Flathead. Among the immediate family (mother, sisters, and our combined children), we represent an amalgamation of tribal groups, including: Flathead, Spokane, Sonoran Mexican Indian, Hopi, Laguna Pueblo, Santo Domingo Pueblo, Thompson (Canadian Native), Haida/Lummi, and Nez Perce. We, my family, are the products of the ongoing process of colonization by virtue of intertribal marriage.

In Chewelah, the night sky mirrored the bowl of the valley held between the dark, lush mountains. In summer, my sisters and I would camp out in our grandparents' yard, making our beds of blankets and sleeping bags in the soft grass. In the fifties, my older sister was in her early teens. She taught us to distinguish the Big Dipper and Little Dipper in the sky — empowering knowledge for the minds of young Indian girls, that. We were comforted and smug in familiar surroundings. Life was so simple. And as we lay beneath the stars, she taught us sappy love songs that she'd learned from the radio, and it didn't take much coaxing on her part. We sang loudly, wildly up to the stars: "Will I be pretty, will I be rich?/*Que sera, sera*, whatever will be, will be." In the morning we shook the earwigs loose that clung to the bottom of our damp blankets and watched them scurry from the sunlight back into the deep grass.

I look back on our lives, which from that early age were instilled with the conflicting values of the world we lived in. On the one hand we learned to appreciate the stories of tribal history and the landbase, to read the sky, to find food in the woods. But then again, we were not encouraged as women to aspire to more than becoming someone's wife, all three of us marrying badly. *Que sera, sera*.

From my family, I have been informed by two conflicting narratives. There is a story my older sister told me about a woman who was captured by "stick Indians" and taken to the woods, where she lived with them for years. One day, she walked out of the woods and back to her people. It doesn't matter if the story is true or not. The point is that the story became family mythology that touched my life.

My father also tells a story of his ancestors, who came into this country from Mexico. This story, too, may not be true. He tells of an ancestor who was the daughter of a wealthy man who did not want his daughter marrying a poor man with whom she had fallen in love. He sent her away by stagecoach, and en route the stagecoach was robbed of its wealth and of the daughter by the man the daughter was forbidden to marry. Both disappeared together. Regardless of the validity of the story, it informs me of that part of myself that I have inherited from my father. What I "read" in my father's story is the internalization of class distinctions that are made by non-Native peoples. It is the inverted story of the Indian princess all over again — everyone, my father included, wanting to believe themselves descended from royalty, or if not royalty, the next best thing, the monied. I can only speculate as to the source of that wealth in a land notorious for the exploitation of its indigenous people, and would not pride myself for having descended from death-mongers.

Though both my grandparents on my father's side were very dark-complected people, my father claims he is "Spanish, not Mexican." At other times, he has claimed that we are descended from the Aztec. In the former, he has learned to deny himself and the part of him that is indigenous, a complete contradiction of how he lives his life as an "Indian" (going to powwows, serving on the Indian PTA, fathering Indian children, and collecting powwow music). How his contradictory attitude impacts on my perception as his offspring is that I choose to accept his parents, whom I never knew, as Native Mexican peoples. As Indian.

These stories that have informed my life have also informed my dreamscape: where stick Indians live, and a former life where I was also captive of a Mexican husband, but ran off from the hacienda with the gardener. I have no doubt that stick Indians *do* live, and that the gardener in my dream of my former life explains the connection to the father of my older daughters, a Pueblo.

In my mind, I am not any more Aztec than I am "Spanish." In my reality, my father is descended from Mexican itinerant workers: Mexican Indians. In an old photograph of his parents, they are a dark-skinned people: his mother is very round, her body like a mountain, as solid; his father is a sinewy-bodied man, the product of hard work. By heredity, it could be possible to call myself chicana, though I have been socialized as Indian. This is how I know myself.

To return to the subject of Indians oppressing other Indians, as mentioned earlier, and how this has affected my life, I offer another story. On the reservation, tribal politics are not all that different from mainstream politics — which are bound to issues of power, how it corrupts, how it is wielded unethically. Back home several years ago, one member of the Tribal Council had pushed a law through that allowed the enrollment of children who had one parent of Canadian Native descent in order to enroll his grandchildren. Ironically, Canadian Natives are not considered Indian, in spite of the fact that several of the northern-border tribal groups have families on both sides. Take, for example, the Okanogan band of the Colville, the Blackfeet, the Cree, and Iroquoian peoples.

Enrollments are part of the public record and are published in the tribal newsletter. When my mother saw the announcement of the enrollment of this man's grandchildren, she began the process of application for enrollment for my children whose father is of Canadian Native descent. She filed the necessary paperwork, and was soon notified that the law had been rescinded. My children were enrolled two years later, only after she spoke directly to Tribal Council members, demonstrating through oral repetition of family genealogy how that particular tribal councilman's great-grandfather and ours were blood brothers and how we are related.

There are two parts of my life: growing up on the reservation and then my experience in the educational system, which has separated me from that earlier life. To be eligible to attend BIA boarding schools, you have to be an enrolled member of an Indian tribe. Maybe more to the point is that students come from reservations. Why so few "Native" writers have been educated in that system — uprooted from their homelands, people, and lifestyles — has never, to my knowledge, been raised. It brings up, for me, other related issues. For instance, that the inferior education of Indian children has never become an issue, and that issues of class are not acknowledged. Yet I ask those self-evaluating questions of myself. I look at my participation in the process of undoing the damage that colonization has wrought, and do not hesitate to question, "Am I the product of my own assimilation, the mnemonic device of hegemonic order?" in poem.

What have not been adequately addressed are the many differences between the People and ourselves, meaning Native writers, and these *are* issues of class. I have been educated in a system that is designed to deny us on many levels; but as a participant in that system, which has earned me a "site of privilege" from which to speak, however marginally, what have I become? And if the answer to that question remains continually out of reach, it does not keep me from asking of myself, because I *say* as I please, is this an act of liberation or the illusion of liberation?

> I HAVE BEEN EDUCATED IN A SYSTEM THAT IS DESIGNED TO DENY US ON MANY LEVELS; BUT AS A PARTICIPANT IN THAT SYSTEM, WHICH HAS EARNED ME A "SITE OF PRIVILEGE" FROM WHICH TO SPEAK, HOWEVER MARGINALLY, WHAT HAVE I BECOME?

In the United States, the existence of the BIA boarding school system is not common knowledge. In an undergraduate course on the Brontë sisters, we were discussing the repressed atmosphere of early English boarding schools. The instructor blithely commented on how that system was in the historical past, and assured the class that there weren't such types of schools anymore. I offered that, yes, there were, and in fact, in this country. I mentioned how I'd spent most of my life before and throughout high school in boarding schools that were very much parallel to the oppressive atmosphere of those we were reading about. I was a scholarship student and, needless to say, my comments were not well received in the posh, private school among the bright-eyed eighteen-year-old children of the upper classes, and earned me thereafter the contempt of my instructor.

To return again to the words of Aimé Césaire with which I began, I would like to point out that as a Native person, Césaire addresses the same underlying issues of colonization to which Native people often refer. Although I feel that this is, or should be, a beginning place only, a recognition of the submerged pain that we have inherited. Because in that recognition, perhaps healing can follow. I frequently come in contact with outside perceptions of Native peoples, and cannot help but notice how, in general, there is an unwillingness to interrogate the site of privilege as it filters down through the strata of Native lives in the process of colonization. It is not either bitterness or conflict that motivates my work, though I am sure that some will perceive the material as conflict-motivated. There is a correlation I would like to make between qualitative lived experience and quantitative learned experience that from a Native perspective I feel is missing in our, meaning Native writers', discussions. This requires a willingness to uncover the layering of stereotypes and romanticisms of the public "Indian." For me, what has worked is that through a discussion of where the personal, the public, and political arenas intersect in my life, I can make sense of what "it" means to me. The "it," the dance through the sawing jaws of colonization.

NOTE

[1] From "President Reagan's Remarks and a Question-and-Answer Session with the Students and Faculty at Moscow State University, May 31, 1988," in *Ronald Reagan: The Great Communicator,* Internet (p. 10 of 12), March 10, 1998. [Note is Bird's.]

• • ● • • -

QUESTIONS FOR A SECOND READING

1. As you reread Bird's essay, on each page circle three to four words that seem to you to be central to Bird's questions and arguments. Make a list of these words. Why do these particular terms seem central to you? How do you understand them in the context of Bird's essay and also in the context of your own experience? Be prepared to discuss these questions in a small group.

2. Spend some time rereading the epigraph to Bird's essay, which comes from Aimé Césaire's essay *Discourse on Colonialism* (1950). Make it your project to study this epigraph. Do some research online: Who was Aimé Césaire? What can you learn about the essay this passage comes from? Finally, make some notes for yourself about what you think this passage suggests. In thinking about Bird's essay, what seems most significant about the epigraph?

3. Consider the full title of Bird's essay, "Autobiography as Spectacle: An Act of Liberation or the Illusion of Liberation?" Why do you think Bird chooses the word "spectacle"? And how do you think Bird answers this question of whether telling one's story is liberating or not? How does her essay complicate your own previous understandings about autobiography?

· · ● · · —

ASSIGNMENTS FOR WRITING

1. In the third "Question for a Second Reading," we invite you to think about Bird's title, "Autobiography as Spectacle: An Act of Liberation or the Illusion of Liberation?" After you've taken notes and done some thinking about the questions raised in that prompt, write an essay in which you engage critically with both Bird's arguments and her questions about autobiography.

What are Bird's assertions and questions about autobiography? Where does she seem to make an argument, and where does she seem to raise questions? How can you tell whether an author is making a claim about what is true or whether the author is uncertain? How might Bird's moments of uncertainty be imagined as productive, or as part of the point of the essay? What is your position on both Bird's arguments and her questions? Do you have new questions of your own about "autobiography as spectacle"?

2. Bird provides us with an extensive discussion of and excerpt from Ronald Reagan's comments on Native Americans from 1988. Additionally, she provides examples of representations of Native Americans in film. She offers readings of her examples, providing her interpretations and perspective on what she hears and sees in these examples. We might think of Bird, in these moments, as "reading culture," as looking closely at how the subject at hand (Native Americans) is discussed, represented, and understood by others.

Bird worked on this essay in the late 1990s; one question worth thinking about is what Bird might notice about our current moment in history. Do some research in which you try to look for current examples of how Native Americans are discussed, represented, and understood by others. To help you get started, you might consider looking at discussions of professional sports logos or the problematic town seal of Whitesboro, New York. These are just two examples of when and how Native Americans have been discussed, represented, and understood by those outside their communities.

Write an essay in which you choose two to three examples you find in the media. What might Bird say about these examples? How does her essay help you "read culture" so that you can provide the readers of your essay with interpretations and critiques of what you find? You should quote both from the representations you find and from Bird's essay as a way of giving your readers both a window into Bird's essay and a sense of how Bird's essay might help us "read culture."

3. One of Bird's central terms in this essay is *colonialism*. What do you know about this term? You might want to do some research about the term itself and how it is used and circulated. What histories or current events is Bird

drawing to our attention by using this term, which appears both in her essay and in the epigraph to the essay?

Write an essay in which you explain to another person how Bird's essay relates to colonialism. You might start by helping your reader understand what colonialism means, what Bird's essay is about, and how these two elements are related. Then, in your essay itself, you'll want to explain the relationship between colonialism and autobiography, and between colonialism and representations of Native Americans.

You might end by explaining to this imagined person how this discussion is relevant to some current events that might be happening around you right now. Why is the term *colonialism* significant? And how does thinking about this concept further our thinking about social justice, identity, or history?

• • ● • • •

MAKING CONNECTIONS

1. Many of the essays in this collection make use of or raise questions about autobiography as a way of thinking about social justice, political questions, and cultural representation. For example, we might understand writers like John Edgar Wideman, Joy Castro, Richard Rodriguez, Susan Griffin, Edward Said, Richard E. Miller, Alison Bechdel, and, of course, Gloria Bird, as addressing questions about autobiography.

   Choose two or three of these writers and begin to develop your own theory of autobiography, using specific passages from each writer's work to interrogate, develop, and support your own claims about autobiography. Your essay could consider questions such as the following: What does it mean to do the work of autobiography? How do you understand the relationship between personal experience and intellectual ideas? What work can autobiography do for the writer and/or readers? What does your own experience writing about your own life tell you about these questions? And, finally, what are the difficulties and rewards of writing autobiographical essays?

2. Bird writes of her son that he "came home from school with homework in social studies in which one of his questions required his answering that *wampum belts = money.* Commodification of Native systems of documenting agreements is a gross misinterpretation" (p. 175).

   Bird may be pointing out that Euro-American "readers" see Native American traditions and communities through the lens of their own understanding of the world—thus, the Euro-American lens fails to see or understand at all.

   Ruth Behar, in "The Vulnerable Observer," also has some interesting ideas about this question of who is looking at whom, and what they see. What do you imagine Behar might say about Bird's essay? How might Behar extend, complicate, or understand Bird's questions and claims? How do these two writers together offer a way of understanding what it means to see others, to talk about others, and to represent others? And, finally, how do these two writers together offer a way of understanding what it means to see ourselves as well?

SUSAN
Bordo

Susan Bordo (b. 1947) is the Otis A. Singletary Chair of Humanities at the University of Kentucky. Bordo is a philosopher, and while her work has touched on figures and subjects traditional to the study of philosophy (René Descartes, for example), she brings her training to the study of culture, including popular culture and its representations of the body. In other words, she is a philosopher who writes not only about Plato but also about Madonna and John Travolta.

In *Unbearable Weight: Feminism, Western Culture, and the Body* (1993), Bordo looks at the complicated cultural forces that have produced our ways of understanding and valuing a woman's body. These powerful forces have shaped not only attitudes and lives but, through dieting, training, and cosmetic surgery, the physical body itself. *Unbearable Weight* was nominated for the 1993 Pulitzer Prize; it won the Association for Women in Psychology's Distinguished Publication Award and was named by the *New York Times* as one of the Notable Books of 1993. The book had a broad audience and made a significant contribution to the academic study of gender and the body. In fact, Bordo's work (in this book and those that followed) has been central to the newly evolving field of "body studies." Bordo is also the author of *The Flight to Objectivity: Essays on Cartesianism and Culture* (1987); *Twilight Zones: The Hidden Life of Cultural Images from Plato to O.J.* (1997); and *The Creation of Anne Boleyn: A New Look at England's Most Notorious Queen* (2013). She is coeditor (with Alison Jaggar) of *Gender/Body/Knowledge: Feminist Reconstruction of Being and Knowing* (1989) and editor of *Feminist Interpretations of Descartes* (1999).

In 1992, Bordo says, as she was finishing work on *Unbearable Weight*, she received a letter from Laurence Goldstein, editor of *Michigan Quarterly Review*, asking her to write a review article on a surprising series of recently published books concerning men and masculinity. It was as though the feminist work on women as figures of thought and commerce had made the category of the "male" equally available for study and debate. She said,

> It was as if Larry had read my mind. . . . I had known for a long time that I wanted to write about men and their bodies; it seemed the logical, natural, almost inevitable next step. I just wasn't expecting to begin quite so soon. But I couldn't resist the opportunity. . . .

The review essay was the beginning of what became her next major publication, *The Male Body: A New Look at Men in Public and Private* (1999), from which the following selection is drawn. As was the case with *Unbearable Weight, The Male Body* has been read with great interest and care by a wide audience, and it received favorable reviews in the *New York Times, Elle,* and *Vanity Fair*. In *The Male Body*, Bordo writes about her father, about the 1950s, about gay men and straight men, about movies, and about sex manuals. The chapter we have chosen, "Beauty (Re)discovers the Male Body," comes from a section titled "Public Images" and looks specifically at the use of men in advertising, where men's bodies (rather than women's, as in the usual case) are presented as objects of pleasure and instances of commerce. There is a powerful argument here about gender, identity, and the media (about how we come to see and value our physical selves). The writing is witty, committed, and engaging — moving from personal history to cultural history, deftly bringing in key concepts from contemporary literary and media theory, like the concept of the "gaze." In this chapter, Bordo provides a compelling example of what it means to read closely, to read images as well as words, and to write those close readings into an extended argument. She brings the concerns of a philosopher to the materials of everyday life.

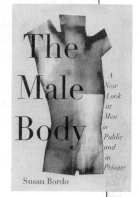

Beauty (Re)discovers the Male Body

MEN ON DISPLAY

Putting classical art to the side for the moment, the naked and near-naked female body became an object of mainstream consumption first in *Playboy* and its imitators, then in movies, and only then in fashion photographs. With the male body, the trajectory has been different. Fashion has taken the lead, the movies have followed. Hollywood may have been a chest-fest in the fifties, but it was male clothing designers who went south and violated the really powerful taboos — not just against the explicit depiction of penises and male bottoms but against the admission of all sorts of forbidden "feminine" qualities into mainstream conceptions of manliness.

It was the spring of 1995, and I was sipping my first cup of morning coffee, not yet fully awake, flipping through *The New York Times Magazine*, when I had my first real taste of what it's like to inhabit this visual culture as a man. It was both thrilling and disconcerting. It was the first time in my experience that I had encountered a commercial representation of a male body that seemed to deliberately invite me to linger over it. Let me make that stronger — that seemed to reach out to me, interrupting my mundane but peaceful Sunday morning, and provoke me into erotic consciousness, whether or not I wanted it. Women — both straight and gay — have always gazed covertly, of course, squeezing our illicit little titillations out of representations designed for — or pretending to — other purposes than to turn us on. *This* ad made no such pretense. It caused me to knock over my coffee cup, ruining the more cerebral pleasures of the *Book Review*. Later, when I had regained my equilibrium, I made a screensaver out of him, so I could gaze at my leisure.

I'm sure that many gay men were as taken as I was, and perhaps some gay women too. The erotic charge of various sexual styles is not neatly mapped onto sexual orientation (let alone biological sex). Brad Pitt's baby-butch looks are a turn-on to many lesbians, while I — regarded by most of my gay friends as a pretty hard-core heterosexual — have always found Anne Heche irresistible (even before Ellen did). A lesbian friend of mine, reading a draft of my section on biblical S&M, said the same movies influenced her later attraction to butch *women*. Despite such complications, until recently only heterosexual men have continually been inundated by popular cultural images *designed* with their sexual responses (or, at least, what those sexual responses are imagined to be) in mind. It's not entirely a gift. On the minus side is having one's composure continually challenged by what Timothy Beneke has aptly described as a culture of "intrusive images," eliciting fantasies, emotions, and erections at times and

Calvin Klein

in places where they might not be appropriate. On the plus side is the cultural permission to be a voyeur.

Some psychologists say that the circuit from eyes to brain to genitals is a quicker trip for men than for women. "There's some strong evidence," popular science writer Deborah Blum reports, citing studies of men's responses to pictures of naked women, "that testosterone is wired for visual response." Maybe. But who is the electrician here? God? Mother Nature? Or Hugh Hefner? Practice makes perfect. And women have had little practice. The Calvin Klein ad made me feel like an adolescent again, brought me back to that day when I saw Barry Resnick on the basketball court of Weequahic High and realized that men's legs could make me weak in the knees. Men's legs? I knew that *women's* legs were supposed to be sexy. I had learned that from all those hose-straightening scenes in the movies. But men's legs? Who had ever seen a woman gaga over some guy's legs in the movies? Or even read about it in a book? Yet the muscular grace of Barry's legs took my breath away. Maybe something was wrong with me. Maybe my sex drive was too strong, too much like a man's. By the time I came across that Calvin Klein ad, several decades of feminism and life experience had left me a little less worried about my sex drive. Still, the sight of that model's body made me feel that my sexual education was still far from complete.

I brought the ad to classes and lectures, asking women what they thought of him. Most began to sweat the moment I unfolded the picture, then got their bearings and tried to explore the bewitching stew of sexual elements the picture has to offer. The model — a young Jackson Browne look-alike — stands there in his form-fitting and rip-speckled Calvin Klein briefs, head lowered, dark hair loosely falling over his eyes. His body projects strength, solidity; he's no male waif. But his finely muscled chest is not so overdeveloped as to suggest a sexuality immobilized by the thick matter of the body. Gay theorist Ron Long, describing contemporary gay sexual aesthetics — lean, taut, sinuous muscles rather than Schwarzenegger bulk — points to a "dynamic tension" that the incredible hulks lack. Stiff, engorged Schwarzenegger bodies, he says, seem to *be* surrogate penises — with nowhere to go and nothing to do but stand there looking massive — whereas muscles like this young man's seem designed for movement, for sex. His body isn't a stand-in phallus; rather, he *has* a penis — the real thing, not a symbol, and a fairly breathtaking one, clearly outlined through the soft jersey fabric of the briefs. It seems slightly erect, or perhaps that's his nonerect size; either way, there's a substantial presence there that's palpable (it looks so touchable, you want to cup your hand over it) and very, very male.

> AT THE SAME TIME, HOWEVER, MY GAZE IS INVITED BY SOMETHING "FEMININE" ABOUT THE YOUNG MAN.

At the same time, however, my gaze is invited by something "feminine" about the young man. His underwear may be ripped, but ever so slightly, subtly; unlike the original ripped-underwear poster boy Kowalski, he's hardly a thug. He doesn't stare at the viewer challengingly, belligerently, as do so many models in other ads for male underwear, facing off like a street tough passing a member of the rival gang on the street. ("Yeah, this is an underwear ad and I'm half naked. But I'm still the one in charge here. Who's gonna look away first?") No, this model's languid body posture, his averted look are classic signals, both in the "natural" and the "cultural" world, of willing subordination. He offers himself nonaggressively to the gaze of another. Hip cocked in the snaky S-curve usually reserved for depictions of women's bodies, eyes downcast but not closed, he gives off a sultry, moody, subtle but undeniably seductive consciousness of his erotic allure. Feast on me, I'm here to be looked at, my body is for your eyes. Oh my.

Such an attitude of male sexual supplication, although it has (as we'll see) classical antecedents, is very new to contemporary mainstream representations. Homophobia is at work in this taboo, but so are attitudes about gender that cut across sexual orientation. For many men, both gay and straight, to be so passively dependent on the gaze of another person for one's sense of self-worth is incompatible with being a real man. As we'll see, such notions about manliness are embedded in Greek culture, in contemporary visual representation, and even (in disguised form) in existentialist philosophy. "For the woman," as philosopher Simone de Beauvoir writes, ". . . the absence of her lover is always torture; he is an eye, a judge . . . away from him, she is dispossessed, at once of herself and of the world." For Beauvoir's sometime lover and lifelong soul mate Jean-Paul Sartre, on the other hand, the gaze (or the Look, as he called it) of another person — including the gaze of one's lover — is the "hell" that other people represent. If we were alone in the world, he argues, we would be utterly free — within physical constraints — to be whomever we wanted to be, to be the creatures of our own self-fantasies, to define our behavior however we like. Other people intrude on this solipsism, and have the audacity to see us from their own perspective rather than ours. The result is what Sartre calls primordial Shame under the eyes of the Other, and a fierce desire to reassert one's freedom. The other person has stolen "the secret" of who I am. I must fight back, resist their attempts to define me.

I understand, of course, what Sartre is talking about here. We've all, male and female alike, felt the shame that another pair of eyes can bring. Sartre's own classic example is of being caught peeking through a keyhole by another person. It isn't until those other eyes are upon you that you truly feel not just the "wrongness" of what you are doing, but — Sartre would argue — the very fact that you are doing it. Until the eyes of another are upon us, "catching us" in the act, we can deceive ourselves, pretend. Getting caught in moments of fantasy or vanity may be especially shameful. When I was an adolescent, I loved to pretend I was a radio personality, and talking into an empty coffee can created just the right sound. One day, my mother caught me speaking in the smooth and slightly sultry tones that radio personalities had even in those days. The way I felt is what Sartre means when he describes the Look of another person as the fulcrum of shame-making. My face got hot, and suddenly I saw how ridiculous I must have seemed, my head in the Chock Full O' Nuts, my narcissistic fantasies on full display. I was caught, I wanted to run.

The disjunction between self-conception and external judgment can be especially harsh when the external definitions carry racial and gender stereotypes with them. Sartre doesn't present such examples — he's interested in capturing the contours of an existential situation shared by all rather than in analyzing the cultural differences that affect that situation — but they are surely relevant to understanding the meaning of the Look of the Other. A black man jogs down the street in sweat clothes, thinking of the class he is going to teach later that day; a white woman passes him, clutches her handbag more tightly, quickens her step; in her eyes, the teacher is a potentially dangerous animal. A Latin American student arrives early the first day of college; an administrator, seeing him in the still-deserted hall, asks him if he is the new janitor. The aspiring student has had his emerging identity erased, a stereotype put in its place by another pair of eyes. When women are transformed from professionals to "pussies" by the comments of men on the street, it's humiliating, not so much because we're puritans as because we sense the hostility in the hoots, the desire to bring an uppity woman down to size by reminding her that she's just "the sex" (as Beauvoir put it).

We may all have felt shame, but — as the different attitudes of Beauvoir and Sartre suggest — men and women are socially sanctioned to deal with the gaze of the Other in different ways. Women learn to anticipate, even play to the sexualizing gaze, trying to become what will please, captivate, turn shame into pride. (In the process, we also learn how sexy being gazed at can feel — perhaps precisely because it walks the fine edge of shame.) Many of us, truth be told, get somewhat addicted to the experience. I'm renting a video, feeling a bit low, a bit tired. The young man at the counter, unsolicited, tells me I'm "looking good." It alters everything, I feel fine, alive; it seems to go right down to my cells. I leave the store feeling younger, stronger, more awake. When women sense that they are not being assessed sexually — for example, as we age, or if we are disabled — it may feel like we no longer exist.

Women may dread being surveyed harshly — being seen as too old, too fat, too flat-chested — but men are not supposed to enjoy being surveyed *period*. It's feminine to be on display. Men are thus taught — as my uncle Leon used to say — to be a moving target. Get out of range of those eyes, don't let them catch you — even as the object of their fantasies (or, as Sartre would put it, don't let them "possess," "steal" your freedom). This phobia has even distorted scientific research.... Evolutionary theorists have long acknowledged display as an important feature of courting behavior among primates — except when it comes to *our* closest ancestors. With descriptions of hominid behavior, male display behavior "suddenly drops out of the primate evolutionary picture" (Sheets-Johnstone) and is replaced by the concept of year-round female sexual receptivity. It seems that it has been intolerable, unthinkable for male evolutionary theorists to imagine the bodies of their male ancestors being on display, sized up, dependent on selection (or rejection) by female hominids.

Scientists and "ordinary guys" are totally in synch here, as is humorously illustrated in Peter Cattaneo's popular 1997 British film *The Full Monty*. In the film, a group of unemployed metalworkers in Sheffield, England, watch a Chippendale's show and hatch the money-making scheme of presenting their own male strip show in which they will go right down to the "full Monty." At the start of the film, the heroes are hardly pillars of successful manliness (Gaz, their leader, refers to them as "scrap"). Yet even they have been sheltered by their guyhood, as they learn while putting the show together. One gets a penis pump. Another borrows his wife's face cream. They run, they wrap their bellies in plastic, they do jumping jacks, they get artificial tans. The most overweight one among them (temporarily) pulls out of the show. Before, these guys hadn't lived their lives under physical scrutiny, but in male action mode, in which men are judged by their accomplishments. Now, anticipating being on display to a roomful of spectators, they suddenly realize how it feels to be judged as women routinely are, sized up by another pair of eyes. "I pray that they'll be a bit more understanding about us" than they've been with women, David (the fat one) murmurs.

They get past their discomfort, in the end, and their show is greeted with wild enthusiasm by the audience. The movie leaves us with this feel-good ending, not raising the question obvious to every woman watching the film: would a troupe of out-of-shape women be received as warmly, as affectionately? The climactic moment when the men throw off their little pouches is demurely shot from the rear, moreover, so we — the audience — don't get "the full Monty." Nonetheless, the film gently and humorously makes an important point: for a heterosexual man to offer himself up to a sexually evaluating gaze is for him to make a large, scary leap — and not just because of the anxieties about size . . . (the guy who drops out of the show, remember, is embarrassed by his fat, not his penis). The "full Monty" — the naked penis — is not merely a body part in the movie (hence it doesn't really matter that the film doesn't show it). It's a symbol for male exposure, vulnerability to an evaluation and judgment that women — clothed or naked — experience all the time.

I had to laugh out loud at a 1997 *New York Times Magazine* "Style" column, entitled "Overexposure," which complained of the "contagion" of nudity spreading through celebrity culture. "Stars no longer have private parts," the author observed, and fretted that civilians would soon also be measured by the beauty of their buns. I share this author's concern about our body-obsessed culture. But, pardon me, he's just noticing this now??? Actresses have been baring their breasts, their butts, even their bushes, for some time, and ordinary women have been tromping off to the gym in pursuit of comparably perfect bodies. What's got the author suddenly crying "overkill," it turns out, is Sly Stallone's "surreally fat-free" appearance on the cover of *Vanity Fair*, and Rupert Everett's "dimpled behind" in a Karl Lagerfeld fashion spread. Now that *men* are taking off their clothes, the culture is suddenly going too far. Could it be that the author doesn't even "read" all those naked female bodies as "overexposed"? Does he protest a bit too much when he declares in the first sentence of the piece that he found it "a yawn" when Dirk Diggler unsheathed his "prosthetic shillelagh" ("penis" is still a word to be avoided whenever possible) at the end of *Boogie Nights*? A yawn? My friend's palms were sweating profusely, and I was not about to drop off to sleep either.

As for dimpled behinds, my second choice for male pinup of the decade is the Gucci series of two ads in which a beautiful young man, shot from the rear, puts on a pair of briefs. In the first ad, he's holding them in his hands, contemplating them. Is he checking out the correct washing-machine temp? It's odd, surely, to stand there looking at your underwear,

but never mind. The point is: his underwear is in his hands, not on his butt. *It* — his bottom, that is — is gorgeously, completely naked — a motif so new to mainstream advertising (but since then catching on rapidly) that several of my friends, knowing I was writing about the male body, e-mailed me immediately when they saw the ad. In the second ad, he's put the underwear on, and is adjusting it to fit. Luckily for us, he hasn't succeeded yet, so his buns are peeking out the bottom of the underwear, looking biteable. For the *Times* writer, those buns may be an indecent exposure of parts that should be kept private (or they're a boring yawn, I'm afraid he can't have it both ways), but for me — and for thousands of gay men across the country — this was a moment of political magnitude, and a delicious one. The body parts that *we* love to squeeze (those plastic breasts, they're the real yawn for me) had come out of the closet and into mainstream culture, where *we* can enjoy them without a trip to a specialty store.

But all this is very new. Women aren't used to seeing naked men frankly portrayed as "objects" of a sexual gaze (and neither are heterosexual men, as that *Times* writer makes clear). So pardon me if I'm skeptical when I read arguments about men's greater "biological" responsiveness to visual stimuli. These "findings," besides being ethnocentric (no one thinks to poll Trobriand Islanders), display little awareness of the impact of changes in cultural representations on our capacities for sexual response. Popular science writer Deborah Blum, for example, cites a study from the Kinsey Institute which showed a group of men and women a series of photos and drawings of nudes, both male and female:

> Fifty-four percent of the men were erotically aroused versus 12 percent of the women — in other words, more than four times as many men. The same gap exists, on a much larger scale, in the business of pornography, a $500-million-plus industry in the U.S. which caters almost exclusively to men. In the first flush of 1970s feminism, two magazines — *Playgirl* and *Viva* — began publishing male centerfolds. *Viva* dropped the nude photos after surveys showed their readers didn't care for them; the editor herself admitted to finding them slightly disgusting.

Blum presents these findings as suggestive of a hard-wired difference between men and women. I'd be cautious about accepting that conclusion. First of all, there's the question of which physiological responses count as "erotic arousal" and whether they couldn't be evidence of other states. Clearly, too, we can *learn* to have certain physiological responses — and to suppress them — so nothing biologically definitive is proved by the presence or absence of physical arousal.

Studies that rely on viewers' *own* reports need to be carefully interpreted too. I know, from talking to women students, that they sometimes aren't all that clear about *what* they feel in the presence of erotic stimuli, and even when they are, they may not be all that comfortable admitting what they feel. Hell, not just my students! Once, a lover asked me, as we were about to part for the evening, if there was anything that we hadn't done that I'd really like to do. I knew immediately what that was: I wanted him to undress, very slowly, while I sat on the floor and just watched. But I couldn't tell him. I was too embarrassed. Later, alone in my compartment on the train, I sorely regretted my cowardice. The fact is that I love to watch a man getting undressed, and I especially like it if he is conscious of being looked at. But there is a long legacy of shame to be overcome here, for both sexes, and the cultural models are only now just emerging which might help us move beyond it.

Perhaps, then, we should wait a bit longer, do a few more studies, before we come to any biological conclusions about women's failure to get aroused by naked pictures. A newer (1994) University of Chicago study found that 30 percent of women ages eighteen to forty-four and 19 percent of women ages forty-five to fifty-nine said they found "watching a partner undress" to be "very appealing." ("Not a bad percentage," Nancy Friday comments, "given that Nice Girls didn't look.") There's still a gender gap — the respective figures for men of the same age groups were 50 percent and 40 percent. We're just learning, after all, to be voyeuses. Perhaps, too, heterosexual men could learn to be less uncomfortable offering themselves as "sexual objects" if they realized the pleasure women get from it. Getting what you have been most deprived of is the best gift, the most healing gift, the most potentially transforming gift — because it has the capacity to make one more whole. Women have been deprived not so much of the *sight* of beautiful male bodies as the experience of having the male body *offered* to us, handed to us on a silver platter, the way female bodies — in the ads, in the movies — are handed to men. Getting this from her partner is the erotic equivalent of a woman's coming home from work to find a meal prepared and ready for her. Delicious — even if it's just franks and beans.

THANKS, CALVIN!

Despite their bisexual appeal, the cultural genealogy of the ads I've been discussing and others like them is to be traced largely through gay male aesthetics, rather than a sudden blossoming of appreciation for the fact that women might enjoy looking at sexy, well-hung young men who don't appear to be about to rape them. Feminists might like to imagine that Madison Avenue heard our pleas for sexual equality and finally gave us "men as sex objects." But what's really happened is that women have been the beneficiaries of what might be described as a triumph of pure consumerism — and with it, a burgeoning male fitness and beauty culture — over homophobia and the taboos against male vanity, male "femininity," and erotic display of the male body that have gone along with it.

Throughout [the twentieth] century, gay photographers have created a rich, sensuous, and dramatic tradition which is unabashed in eroticizing the male body, male sensuousness, and male potency, including penises. But until recently, such representations have been kept largely in the closet. Mainstream responses to several important exhibits which opened in the seventies — featuring the groundbreaking early work of Wilhelm von Gloeden, George Dureau, and George Platt Lynes as well as then-contemporary artists such as Robert Mapplethorpe, Peter Hujar, and Arthur Tress — would today probably embarrass the critics who wrote about them when they opened. John Ashbery, in *New York* magazine, dismissed the entire genre of male nude photography with the same sexist tautology that covertly underlies that *Times* piece on cultural "overexposure": "Nude women seem to be in their natural state; men, for some reason, merely look undressed. . . . When is a nude not a nude? When it is male." (Substitute "blacks" and "whites" for "women" and "men" and you'll see how offensive the statement is.)

For other reviewers, the naked male, far from seeming "merely undressed," was unnervingly sexual. *New York Times* critic Gene Thompson wrote that "there is something disconcerting about the sight of a man's naked body being presented as a sexual object"; he went on to describe the world of homoerotic photography as one "closed to most of us, fortunately." Vicki Goldberg, writing for the *Saturday Review*, was more appreciative of the "beauty and dignity" of the nude male body, but concluded that so long as its depiction was erotic in emphasis, it will "remain half-private, slightly awkward, an art form cast from its traditions and in search of some niche to call its home."

Goldberg needed a course in art history. It's true that in classical art, the naked human body was often presented as a messenger of spiritual themes, and received as such. But the male bodies sculpted by the Greeks and Michelangelo were not exactly nonerotic. It might be more accurate to say that in modernity, with the spiritual interpretation of the nude body no longer a convention, the contemporary homophobic psyche is not screened from the sexual charge of the nude male body. Goldberg was dead wrong about something else too. Whatever its historical lineage, the frankly sexual representation of the male body was to find, in the next twenty years, a far from private "niche to call its home": consumer culture discovered its commercial potency.

> **THE MALE BODIES SCULPTED BY THE GREEKS AND MICHELANGELO WERE NOT EXACTLY NONEROTIC.**

Calvin Klein had his epiphany, according to one biography, one night in 1974 in New York's gay Flamingo bar:

> As Calvin wandered through the crowd at the Flamingo, the body heat rushed through him like a revelation; this was the cutting edge. . . . [The] men! The men at the Flamingo had less to do about sex for him than the notion of portraying men as gods. He realized that what he was watching was the freedom of a new generation, unashamed, in-the-flesh embodiments of Calvin's ideals: straight-looking, masculine men, with chiseled bodies, young Greek gods come to life. The vision of shirtless young men with hardened torsos, all in blue jeans, top button opened, a whisper of hair from the belly button disappearing into the denim pants, would inspire and inform the next ten years of Calvin Klein's print and television advertisements.

Klein's genius was that of a cultural Geiger counter; his own bisexuality enabled him to see that the phallic body, as much as any female figure, is an enduring sex object within Western culture. In America in 1974, however, that ideal was still largely closeted. Only gay culture unashamedly sexualized the lean, fit body that virtually everyone, gay and straight, now aspires to. Sex, as Calvin Klein knew, sells. He also knew that gay sex wouldn't sell to straight men. But the rock-hard, athletic gay male bodies that Klein admired at the Flamingo did not advertise their sexual preference through the feminine codes—limp wrists, raised pinkie finger, swishy walk—which the straight world then identified with homosexuality. Rather, they embodied a highly masculine aesthetic that—although definitely exciting for gay men — would scream "heterosexual" to (clueless) straights. Klein knew just the kind of clothing to show that body off in too. As Steven Gaines and Sharon Churcher tell it:

> He had watched enough attractive young people with good bodies in tight jeans dancing at the Flamingo and Studio 54 to know that the "basket" and the behind was what gave jeans sex appeal. Calvin sent his assistants out for several pairs of jeans, including the classic five-button Levi's, and cut them apart to see how they were made. Then he cut the "rise," or area from the waistband to under the groin, much shorter to accentuate the crotch and pull the seam up between the buttocks, giving the behind more shape and prominence. The result was instant sex appeal — and a look that somehow Calvin just *knew* was going to sell.

So we come to the mainstream commercialization of the aesthetic legacy of Stanley Kowalski and those inspired innovations of Brando's costumer in *A Streetcar Named Desire*. When I was growing up, jeans were "dungarees" — suitable for little kids, hayseeds, and juvenile delinquents, but not for anyone to wear on a date. Klein transformed jeans from utilitarian garments to erotic second skins. Next, Klein went for underwear. He wasn't the first, but he was the most daring. In 1981, Jockey International had broken ground by photographing Baltimore Oriole pitcher Jim Palmer in a pair of briefs (airbrushed) in one of its ads — selling $100 million worth of underwear by year's end. Inspired by Jockey's success, in 1983 Calvin Klein put a forty-by-fifty-foot Bruce Weber photograph of Olympic pole vaulter Tom Hintnaus in Times Square, Hintnaus's large penis clearly discernible through his briefs. The Hintnaus ad, unlike the Palmer ad, did not employ any of the usual fictional rationales for a man's being in his underwear — for example, the pretense that the man is in the process of getting dressed — but blatantly put Hintnaus's body on display, sunbathing on a rooftop, his skin glistening. The line of shorts "flew off the shelves" at Bloomingdale's and when Klein papered bus shelters in Manhattan with poster versions of the ad they were all stolen overnight.

Images of masculinity that will do double (or triple or quadruple) duty with a variety of consumers, straight and gay, male and female, are not difficult to create in a culture like ours, in which the muscular male body has a long and glorious aesthetic history. That's precisely what Calvin Klein was the first to recognize and exploit — the possibility and profitability of what is known in the trade as a "dual marketing" approach. Since then, many advertisers have taken advantage of Klein's insight. A recent Abercrombie & Fitch ad, for example, depicts a locker room full of young, half-clothed football players getting a postmortem from their coach after a game. Beautiful, undressed male bodies doing what real men are "supposed to do." Dirty uniforms and smudged faces, wounded players, helmets. What could be more straight? But as iconography depicting a culture of exclusively male bodies, young, gorgeous, and well-hung, what could be more "gay"?

Bronzed and beautiful Tom Hintnaus: a breakthrough ad for Calvin Klein — and the beginning of a new era for the unabashed erotic display of the male body.

It required a Calvin Klein to give the new vision cultural form. But the fact is that if we've entered a brave, new world of male bodies it is largely because of a more "material" kind of epiphany — a dawning recognition among advertisers of the buying power of gay men. For a long time prejudice had triumphed over the profit motive, blinding marketers to just how sizable — and well-heeled — a consumer group gay men represent. (This has been the case with other "minorities" too. Hollywood producers, never bothering to do any demographics on middle-class and professional African American women — or the issues that they share with women of other races and classes in this culture — were shocked at the tremendous box office success of *Waiting to Exhale*. They won't make that particular mistake again.) It took a survey conducted by *The Advocate* to jolt corporate America awake about gay consumers. The survey, done between 1977 and 1980, showed that 70 percent of its readers aged twenty to forty earned incomes well above the national median. Soon, articles were appearing on the business pages of newspapers, like one in 1982 in *The New York Times Magazine*, which described advertisers as newly interested in "wooing . . . the white, single, well-educated, well-paid man who happens to be homosexual."

"Happens to be homosexual": the phrasing — suggesting that sexual identity is peripheral, even accidental — is telling. Because of homophobia, dual marketing used to require a delicate balancing act, as advertisers tried to speak to gays "in a way that the straight consumer will not notice." Often, that's been accomplished through the use of play and parody, as in Versace's droll portraits of men being groomed and tended by male servants, and Diesel's overtly narcissistic gay posers. "Thanks, Diesel, for making us so very beautiful," they gush. Or take the ad below, with its gorgeous, mechanically inept model admitting that he's "known more for my superb bone construction and soft, supple hair than my keen intellect." The playful tone reassures heterosexual consumers that the vanity

"I'm known more for my superb bone construction and soft, supple hair than my keen intellect. But even I can hook up Kenwood's Centerstage Home Theater System in a few minutes."

(and mechanical incompetence) of the man selling the product is "just a joke." For gay consumers, on the other hand, this reassurance is *itself* the "joke"; they read the humor in the ad as an insider wink, which says, "This is for *you*, guys." The joke is further layered by the fact that they know the model in the ad is very likely to be gay.

Contrast this ad to the ostentatious heterosexual protest of a Perry Ellis ad which appeared in the early 1990s (and no, it's not a parody):

> I hate this job. I'm not just an empty suit who stands in front of a camera, collects the money and flies off to St. Maarten for the weekend.
>
> I may model for a living, but I hate being treated like a piece of meat. I once had a loud-mouthed art director say "Stand there and pretend you're a human." I wanted to punch him, but I needed the job.
>
> What am I all about? Well, I know I'm very good-looking, and there are days when that is enough. Some nights, when I'm alone, it's not.
>
> I like women — all kinds.
>
> I like music — all kinds.
>
> I like myself so I don't do drugs.
>
> Oh yeah, about this fragrance. It's good. Very good.
>
> When I posed for this picture, the art director insisted that I wear it while the pictures were being taken. I thought it was silly, but I said "What the hell? It's their money."
>
> After a while, I realized I like this fragrance a lot. When the photo shoot was over, I walked right over, picked up the bottle, put it in my pocket and said "If you don't mind, I'd like to take this as a souvenir." Then I smiled my best f — you smile and walked out.
>
> Next time, I'll pay for it.
>
> It's that good.

Today, good-looking straight guys are flocking to the modeling agencies, much less concerned about any homosexual taint that will cleave to them. It's no longer necessary for an ad to plant its tongue firmly in cheek when lavishing erotic attention on the male body — or to pepper the ad with proofs of heterosexuality. It used to be, if an advertisement aimed at straight men dared to show a man fussing over his looks with seemingly romantic plans in mind, there had better be a woman in the picture, making it clear just *whom* the boy was getting pretty for. To sell a muscle-building product to heterosexuals, of course, you had to link it to virility and the ability to attract women on the beach. Today, muscles are openly sold for their looks; Chroma Lean nutritional supplement unabashedly compares the well-sculpted male body to a work of art (and a gay male icon, to boot) — Michelangelo's "David." Many ads display the naked male body without shame or plot excuse, and often exploit rather than resolve the sexual ambiguity that is generated.

Today, too, the athletic, muscular male body that Calvin plastered all over buildings, magazines, and subway stops has become an aesthetic norm, for straights as well as gays. "No pecs, no sex," is how the trendy David Barton gym sells itself: "My motto is not 'Be healthy'; it's 'Look better naked,'" Barton says. The notion has even made its way into that most determinedly heterosexual of contexts, a Rob Reiner film. In *Sleepless in Seattle*, Tom Hanks's character, who hasn't been on a date in fifteen years, asks his friend (played by Rob) what women are looking for nowadays. "Pecs and a cute butt," his friend replied without hesitation. "You can't even turn on the news nowadays without hearing about how some babe thought some guy's butt was cute. Who the first woman to say this was I don't know, but somehow it caught on." Should we tell Rob that it wasn't a woman who started the craze for men's butts?

ROCKS AND LEANERS

We "nouvelles voyeuses" thus owe a big measure of thanks to gay male designers and consumers, and to the aesthetic and erotic overlap — not uniform or total, but significant — in what makes our hearts go thump. But although I've been using the term for convenience, I don't think it's correct to say that these ads depict men as "sex objects." Actually, I find that whole notion misleading, whether applied to men or women, because it seems to suggest that what these representations offer is a body that is inert, depersonalized, flat, a mere thing. In fact, advertisers put a huge amount of time, money, and creativity into figuring out how to create images of beautiful bodies that are heavy on attitude, style, associations with pleasure, success, happiness. The most compelling images are suffused with "subjectivity" — they *speak* to us, they seduce us. Unlike other kinds of "objects" (chairs and tables, for example), they don't let us use them in any way we like. In fact, they exert considerable power over us — over our psyches, our desires, our self-image.

How do male bodies in the ads speak to us nowadays? In a variety of ways. Sometimes the message is challenging, aggressive. Many models stare coldly at the viewer, defying the observer to view them in any way other than how they have chosen to present themselves: as powerful, armored, emotionally impenetrable. "I am a rock," their bodies (and sometimes their genitals) seem to proclaim. Often, as in the Jackson Browne look-alike ad, the penis is prominent, but *unlike* the penis in that ad, its presence is martial rather than sensual. Overall, these ads depict what I would describe as "face-off masculinity," in which victory goes to the dominant contestant in a game of will against will. Who can stare the other man down? Who will avert his eyes first? Whose gaze will be triumphant? Such moments — "facing up," "facing off," "staring down" — as anthropologist David Gilmore has documented, are a test of macho in many cultures, including our own. "Don't eyeball me!" barks the sergeant to his cadets in training in *An Officer and a Gentleman*; the authority of the stare is a prize to be won only with full manhood. Before then, it is a mark of insolence — or stupidity, failure to understand the codes of masculine rank. In *Get Shorty*, an unsuspecting film director challenges a mob boss to look him in the eye; in return, he is hurled across the room and has his fingers broken.

Face-off masculinity.

"Face-off" ads, except for their innovations in the amount of skin exposed, are pretty traditional — one might even say primal — in their conception of masculinity. Many other species use staring to establish dominance, and not only our close primate relatives. It's how my Jack Russell terrier intimidates my male collie, who weighs over four times as much as the little guy but cowers under the authority of the terrier's macho stare. In the doggie world, size doesn't matter; it's the power of the gaze — which indicates the power to stand one's ground — that counts. My little terrier's dominance, in other words, is based on a convincing acting job — and it's one that is very similar, according to William Pollack, to the kind of performance that young boys in our culture must learn to master. Pollack's studies of boys suggest that a set of rules — which he calls "The Boy Code" — govern their behavior with each other. The first imperative of the code — "Be a sturdy oak" — represents the emotional equivalent of "face-off masculinity": Never reveal weakness. Pretend to be confident even though you may be scared. Act like a rock even when you feel shaky. Dare others to challenge your position.

The face-off is not the only available posture for male bodies in ads today. Another possibility is what I call "the lean" — because these bodies are almost always reclining, leaning against, or propped up against something in the fashion typical of women's bodies. James Dean was probably our first pop-culture "leaner"; he made it stylish for teenagers to slouch. Dean, however, never posed as languidly or was as openly seductive as some of the high-fashion leaners are today. A recent Calvin Klein "Escape" ad depicts a young, sensuous-looking man leaning against a wall, arm raised, dark underarm hair exposed. His eyes seek out the imagined viewer, soberly but flirtatiously. "*Take Me*," the copy reads.

Languid leaners have actually been around for a long time. Statues of sleeping fauns, their bodies draped languorously, exist in classical art alongside more heroic models of male beauty. I find it interesting, though, that Klein has chosen Mr. Take Me to advertise a perfume called "Escape." Klein's "Eternity" ads usually depict happy, heterosexual couples, often with a child. "Obsession" has always been cutting-edge, sexually ambiguous erotica. This ad, featuring a man offering himself up seductively, invitingly to the observer, promises "escape." From what? *To* what? Men have complained, justly, about the burden of always having to be the sexual initiator, the pursuer, the one of whom sexual "performance" is expected. Perhaps the escape is from these burdens, and toward the freedom to indulge in some of the more receptive pleasures traditionally reserved for women. The pleasures, not of staring someone down but of feeling one's body caressed by another's eyes, of being the one who receives the awaited call rather than the one who must build up the nerve to make the call, the one who doesn't have to hump and pump, but is permitted to lie quietly, engrossed in reverie and sensation.

> NEVER REVEAL WEAKNESS. PRETEND TO BE CONFIDENT EVEN THOUGH YOU MAY BE SCARED.

Some people describe these receptive pleasures as "passive" — which gives them a bad press with men, and is just plain inaccurate too. "Passive" hardly describes what's going on when one person offers himself or herself to another. Inviting, receiving, responding — these are active behaviors too, and rather thrilling ones. It's a macho bias to view the only *real* activity as that which takes, invades, aggresses. It's a bias, however, that's been with us for a long time, in both straight and gay cultures. In many

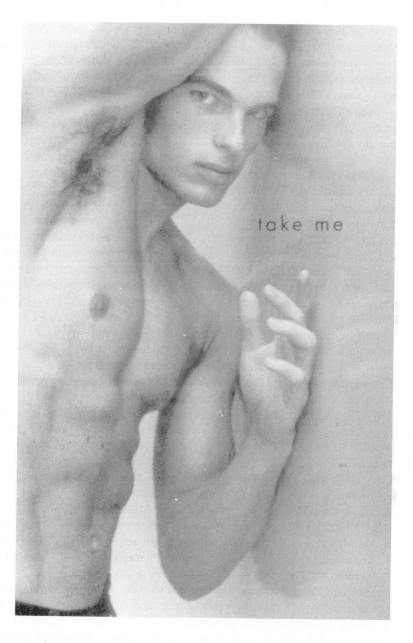

take me

Latin cultures, it's not a disgrace to sleep with other men, so long as one
is *activo* (or *machista*) — the penetrator rather than the penetratee. To be
a *pasivo*, on the other hand, is to be socially stigmatized. It's that way in
prison cultures too — a good indication of the power hierarchies involved.
These hierarchies date back to the ancient Greeks, who believed that passivity, receptivity, penetrability were marks of inferior feminine being. The
qualities were inherent in women; it was our nature to be passively controlled by our sexual needs. (Unlike us, the Greeks viewed women — not

men — as the animalistic ones.) Real Men, who unlike women had the necessary rationality and will, were expected to be judicious in the exercise of their desires. But being judicious and being "active" — deciding when to pursue, whom to pursue, making advances, pleading one's case — went hand in hand.

Allowing oneself to be pursued, flirting, accepting the advances of another, offering one's body — these behaviors were permitted also (but only on a temporary basis) to still-developing, younger men. These young men — not little boys, as is sometimes incorrectly believed — were the true "sex objects" of elite Greek culture. Full-fledged male citizens, on the other hand, were expected to be "active," initiators, the penetrators not the penetratees, masters of their own desires rather than the objects of another's. Plato's *Symposium* is full of speeches on the different sexual behaviors appropriate to adult men with full beards and established professions and glamorous young men still revered more for their beauty than their minds. But even youth could not make it okay for a man to behave *too much* like a woman. The admirable youth was the one who — unlike a woman — was able to remain sexually "cool" and remote, to keep his wits about him. "Letting go" was not seemly.

Where does our culture stand today with respect to these ideas about men's sexuality? Well, to begin with, consider how rarely male actors are shown — on their faces, in their utterances, and not merely in the movements of their bodies — having orgasms. In sex scenes, the moanings and writhings of the female partner have become the conventional cinematic code for heterosexual ecstasy and climax. The male's participation is largely represented by caressing hands, humping buttocks, and — on rare occasions — a facial expression of intense concentration. She's transported to another world; he's the pilot of the ship that takes her there. When men are shown being transported themselves, it's usually been played for comedy (as in Al Pacino's shrieks in *Frankie and Johnny*, Eddie Murphy's moanings in *Boomerang*, Kevin Kline's contortions in *A Fish Called Wanda*), or it's coded to suggest that something is not quite normal about the man — he's sexually enslaved, for example (as with Jeremy Irons in *Damage*). Mostly, men's bodies are presented like action-hero toys — wind them up and watch them perform.

Hollywood — still an overwhelmingly straight-male-dominated industry — is clearly not yet ready to show us a man "passively" giving himself over to another, at least not when the actors in question are our cultural icons. Too feminine. Too suggestive, metaphorically speaking, of penetration by another. But perhaps fashion ads are less uptight? I decided to perform an experiment. I grouped ads that I had collected over recent years into a pile of "rocks" and a pile of "leaners" and found, not surprisingly, that both race and age played a role. African American models, whether in *Esquire* or *Vibe*, are almost always posed facing-off. And leaners tend to be younger than rocks. Both in gay publications and straight ones, the more languid, come-hither poses in advertisements are of boys and very young men. Once a certain maturity line is crossed, the challenging stares, the "face-off" postures are the norm. What does one learn from these ads? Well, I wouldn't want to claim too much. It used to be that one could tell a lot about gender and race from looking at ads. Racial stereotypes were transparent, the established formulas for representing men and women were pretty clear (sociologist Erving Goffman even called ads "gender advertisements"), and when the conventions were defied it was usually because advertisers sensed (or discovered in their polls) that social shifts had made consumers ready to receive new images. In this "post-modern" age, it's more of a free-for-all, and images are often more reactive to each other than to social change. It's the viewers' jaded eye, not their social prejudices,

A youthful, androgynous "leaner" — appropriately enough, advertising [CK One] fragrance "for a man or a woman."

that is the prime consideration of every ad campaign, and advertisers are quick to tap into taboos, to defy expectations, simply in order to produce new and arresting images. So it wouldn't surprise me if we soon find languid black men and hairy-chested leaners in the pages of *Gentlemen's Quarterly*.

But I haven't seen any yet. At the very least, the current scene suggests that even in this era of postmodern pastiche racial clichés and gender taboos persist; among them, we don't want grown men to appear too much the "passive" objects of another's sexual gaze, another's desires. We appear, still, to have somewhat different rules for boys and men. As in ancient Greece, boys are permitted to be seductive, playful, to flirt with being "taken." *Men* must still be in command. Leonardo DiCaprio, watch out. Your days may be numbered.

"HONEY, WHAT DO I WANT TO WEAR?"

Just as fifties masculinity was fought over (metaphorically speaking) by Stanley Kowalski and Stanley Banks, the male fashion scene of the nineties involves a kind of contest for the souls of men too. Calvin Klein, Versace, Gucci, Abercrombie & Fitch have not only brought naked bottoms and bulging briefs onto the commercial scene, they present underwear, jeans, shirts, and suits as items for enhancing a man's appearance and sexual appeal. They suggest

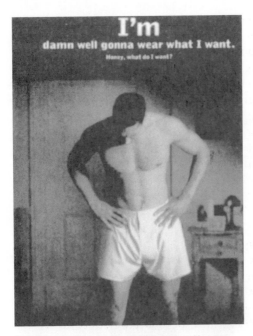

I'm
damn well gonna wear what I want.
Honey, what do I want?

"I'm damn well gonna wear what I want. Honey, what do I want?"

it's fine for a man to care about how he looks and to cultivate an openly erotic style. In response, aggressively heterosexual Dockers and Haggar ads compete — for the buying dollar of men, but in the process for their gender consciousness too — by stressing the no-nonsense utility of khakis. Consider the Haggar casuals advertisement on this page, and what it says about how "real men" should feel about their clothes:

"I'm damn well gonna wear what I want. . . . Honey, what do I want?"

Looked at in one light, the man in the advertisement is being made fun of, as a self-deceived blusterer who asserts his independence "like a man" and in the next breath reveals that he is actually a helpless little boy who needs his mommy to pick out his clothes for him. But fashion incompetence is a species of helplessness that many men feel quite comfortable with, even proud of. Recognizing this, Haggar and Dockers are among those manufacturers who have put a great deal of effort into marketing "nonfashion-guy fashion" to a niche of straight men — working-class and yuppie — who, they presume, would be scared off by even a whiff of "feminine" clothes-consciousness. Here's another one from Haggar's:

"In the female *the ability to match colors comes at an early age. In the* male *it comes when he marries a female."*

The juxtaposition of inept male / fashion-conscious female, which with one stroke establishes the masculinity *and* the heterosexuality of the depicted man, is a staple of virtually every Haggar ad. In a Haggar television spot with voice-over by John Goodman (Roseanne's beefy former television husband), a man wakes up, sleepily pulls on a pair of khakis, and goes outside to get the paper:

"I am not what I wear. I'm not a pair of pants, or a shirt." (He then walks by his wife, handing her the front section of the paper.) *"I'm not in touch with my inner child. I don't read poetry, and I'm not politically correct."* (He goes down a hall, and his kid snatches the comics from him.) *"I'm just a guy, and I don't have time to think about what I wear, because I've got a lot of important guy things to do."* (Left with only the sports section of the paper, he heads for the bathroom.) *"One-hundred-per-cent-cotton-wrinkle-free khaki pants that don't require a lot of thought. Haggar. Stuff you can wear."*

Yes, it's a bit of a parody, but that only allows Haggar to double its point that real guys have better things to do than think about what they are going to wear or how they appear to others. The guy who would be so worried about his image that he couldn't poke fun at himself wouldn't be a real guy at all. Real guys don't take themselves so seriously! That's for wimps who favor poetry, self-help psychology, and bleeding-heart politics. That's for girls, and for the men who are pussy-whipped by them.

In Haggar's world, real guys don't choose clothing that will enhance the appearance of their bodies or display a sense of style; real guys just put on some "stuff" to wear because they have to, it's socially required. The less decorative, the better. "We would never do anything with our pants that would frighten anyone away," says Dockers designer Gareth Morris as reported in a 1997 piece in *The New Yorker*. "We'd never do too many belt loops, or an unusual base cloth ... [or] zips or a lot of pocket flaps and details on the back." Pocket flaps, the ultimate signifier of suspect sexuality! In such ads, male naiveté about the sexual potency of clothes, as agency maven David Altschiller claims, is critical. "In women's advertising," he points out, "self-confidence is sexy. But if a man is self-confident — if he knows he is attractive and is beautifully dressed — then he's not a man anymore. He's a fop. He's effeminate." In Dockers' "Nice Pants" television ads, for example, it's crucial that the guy not *know* his pants are "nice" until a gorgeous woman points it out to him.

It's no accident that the pants are described via the low-key understatement "nice" (rather than "great," for example, which would suggest that the guy was actually *trying* to look good). For the real man (according to Dockers), the mirror is a tool, not a captivating pool; if he could, he'd look the other way while he shaves. Many other advertisers capitalize on such notions, encouraging men to take care of their looks, but reassuring them that it's for utilitarian or instrumental purposes. Cosmetic surgeons emphasize the corporate advantage that a face-lift or tummy tuck will give the aging executive: "A youthful look," as one says, "gives the appearance of a more dynamic, charging individual who will go out and get the business." Male grooming products too are often marketed by way of "action hero" euphemisms which obscure their relation to feminine versions of the same product (a male girdle marketed by BodySlimmers is called the Double Agent Boxer) and the fact that their function is to enhance a man's appearance: hair spray as "hair control," exfoliating liquid as "scruffing lotion," astringents as "scrubs," moisturizers and fragrances as "after" or "pre" accompaniments to that most manly of rituals, the shave. They often have names like Safari and Chaps and Lab Series, and come in containers shaped like spaceships and other forms a girl could have some fun with.

The notions about gender that are maintained in this marketing run deeper than a refusal to use the word "perfume" for products designed to make men smell good. In the late seventies, coincident with the development of feminist consciousness about these matters, art historian John Berger discovered what he argued were a set of implicit cultural paradigms

First of all, for most of human history, there haven't been radically different "masculine" and "feminine" attitudes toward beauty and decorativeness. On farms, frontiers, and feudal estates, women were needed to work alongside men and beauty was hardly a priority for either. Among aristocrats, it was most important to maintain class privilege (rather than gender difference), and standards of elegance for both sexes (as Anne Hollander's fascinating *Sex and Suits* documents) were largely the same: elaborate headwear, cosmetics, nonutilitarian adornments, and accessories. Attention to beauty was associated not with femininity but with a life that was both privileged and governed by exacting standards. The constrictions, precarious adornments, elaborate fastenings reminded the elite that they were highly civilized beings, not simple peasant "animals." At the same time, decorativeness was a mode of royal and aristocratic competition, as households and courts would try to out-glam each other with jewels and furs. Hollander describes a sixteenth-century summit meeting between Francis I and Henry VIII, in which everyone wore "silver covered with diamonds, except when they were in cloth of gold and covered with rubies. Everything was lined with ermine and everything was 20 yards long, and there were plumes on everybody." Everybody — male or female — had to be as gorgeous as possible. It was a mode of power competition.

Until roughly the fourteenth century, men and women didn't even dress very differently. (Think of the Greeks and Romans and their unisex robes and togas.) Clear differences started to emerge only in the late Middle Ages and early Renaissance: women's breasts began to be exposed and emphasized in tight bodices, while their legs were covered with long skirts. Men's legs — and sometimes their genitals as well — were "fully articulated" and visible through pantaloons (what we call "tights"), with body armor covering the chest. While to our sensibilities, the shapely legs and genitals of men in tights (unless required by a ballet or historical drama) are either to be laughed at or drooled over, Hollander argues that in the Renaissance, to outline the male body was to make it more "real" and "natural," less a template for sexual fantasy (as women's bodies were becoming). This trend continued, with men's clothing getting progressively more unrestrictive, tailored, simple and women's more stiff, tightly fitted, decorative. Still, into the seventeenth century, fashionable gentlemen continued to wear lace and silk, and to don powder and wigs before appearing in public. Hollander regards the nineteenth century as a "great divide," after which not only the styles of men's and women's clothing (trousers for men, increasingly romantic froufrou for women) would become radically different, but ideas about them as well. Men's clothing must now be "honest, comfortable, and utilitarian," while women's begins to develop a reputation for being "frivolous" and "deceptive." The script for "men act and women appear" was being written — right onto male and female clothing.

Looking beyond fashion to the social world (something Hollander refuses to do, but I'll venture), it's hard not to speculate that these changes anticipate the emergence of the middle class and the nineteenth-century development of distinctively separate spheres for men and women within it. In the industrial era, men's sphere — increasingly the world of manufacturing, buying, selling, power brokering — was performance-oriented, and demanded "no nonsense." Women, for their part, were expected not only to provide a comfortable, well-ordered home for men to return to but to offer beauty, fantasy, and charm for a man to "escape" to and restore himself with after the grim grind of the working day. As this division of labor developed, strong dualistic notions about "masculinity" and "femininity" began to emerge, with sanctions against the man or woman who dared to cross over to the side of the divide where they did not belong "by nature."

By the end of the nineteenth century, older notions of manliness premised on altruism, self-restraint, and moral integrity — qualities that women could have too — began to be understood as vaguely "feminine." Writers and politicians (like Teddy Roosevelt) began to complain loudly about the emasculating effects of civilization and the excessive role played by women teachers in stifling the development of male nature. New words like "pussyfoot" and "stuffed shirt" — and, most deadly, "sissy" — came into parlance, and the "homosexual" came to be classified as a perverse personality type which the normal, heterosexual male had to prove himself distinct from. (Before, men's relations with each other had been considerably more fluid, and even the heterosexual male was allowed a certain degree of physical intimacy and emotional connection — indeed, "heterosexuality" as such was a notion that hardly made sense at the time.) A new vogue for body-building emerged. "Women pity weakly men," O. S. Fowler warned, but they love and admire "right hearty feeders, not dainty; sprightly, not tottering; more muscular than exquisite, and more powerful than effeminate, in mind and body." To be "exquisite," to be decorative, to be on display, was now fully woman's business, and the man who crossed that line was a "fop."

From that time on, male "vanity" went into hiding, and when cosmetic products for men began to be marketed (for men *did* use them, albeit in secret), they had to justify themselves, as Kathy Piess documents, through the manly rhetoric of efficiency, rugged individualism, competitive advantage, autonomy. While Pompeian cream promises to "beautify and youthify" women, the same product for men will help them "win success" and "make promotion easier" on the job. Even that most manly of rituals (from our perspective), shaving, required special rhetoric when home shaving was first introduced early in the twentieth century. "The Gillette is typical of the American spirit," claimed a 1910 ad. "Its use starts habits of energy — of initiative. And men who *do* for themselves are men who *think* for themselves." Curley's Easy-Shaving Safety Razor claimed that "the first Roman to shave every day was no fop, but Scipio, conqueror of Africa." When it came to products used also by women — like scents and creams — manufacturers went out of their way to reassure prospective customers of their no-nonsense "difference," through action names (Brisk,

Dash, Vim, Keen, Zest) and other means. When Florian, a line of men's toiletries, was introduced in 1929, its creator, Carl Weeks, advised druggists to locate the products near cigar (again!) counters, using displays featuring manly accouterments like boxing gloves, pipes, footballs. This, he argued, "will put over the idea that the mascu-*line* is all *stag*. It's for he-men with no women welcome nohow."

This isn't to say that from the turn of the nineteenth century on, the drive to separate "masculine" and "feminine" attitudes toward self-beautification pushed forward relentlessly. For one thing, culture is never of one piece; it has its dominant images, but also its marginal, recessive, and countercultural images. For another, the history of gender ideology didn't end with the nineteenth century, as dramatic as its changes were. A century of mutations and permutations followed, as demanded by social, economic, and political conditions. Older ideals lingered too and were revived when needed. The Depression, for example, brought a love affair with (a fantasy of) aristocratic "class" to popular culture, and a world of Hollywood representations . . . in which sexual difference was largely irrelevant, the heroes and heroines of screwball comedy a matched set of glamorously attired cutups. In these films, the appeal of actors like Cary Grant, Fred Astaire, and William Powell was largely premised not on assertions of masculine performance but on their elegance, wit, and charm. Their maleness wasn't thrown into question by the cut of their suits. Rather, being fashionable signified that they led an enviable life of pleasure and play. Such associations still persist today. Fashion advertisements for Ralph Lauren, Valentino, Hugo Boss, and many others are crafted to appeal to the class consciousness of consumers; in that universe, one can never be too beautiful or too vain, whatever one's sex.

In the screwball comedies, it didn't matter whether you were a man or a woman, everyone's clothes sparkled and shone. Following the lead of the movies, many advertisements of the thirties promoted a kind of androgynous elegance. But others tried to have their cake and eat it too, as in a 1934 ad for Fougère Royale aftershave, which depicts a group of tony men in tuxedos, hair slicked back, one even wearing a pince-nez, but with the caption "Let's *not* join the ladies!" We may be glamorous, even foppish — but *puh-lease! Ladies* we're not! I should note, too, that while the symbols of "class" can function to highlight equality between men and women, they can also be used to emphasize man's superiority over women — as in a contemporary Cutty Sark ad in which a glamorously attired woman relaxes, dreamily stroking a dog, while the tuxedo-clad men standing around her engage in serious conversation (about stocks, I imagine); these guys don't need to go off into the drawing room in order to escape the ladies; they can keep one around for a bit of decorativeness and sensual pleasure while she remains in her own, more languorous world within their own.

During World War II, movies and magazines continued to celebrate independent, adventurous women, to whom men were drawn "as much for their spirit and character as for their looks."[1] But when the fighting men returned, the old Victorian division of labor was revived with a new commercial avidity, and the world became one in which "men act" (read: *work*) and "women appear" (read: *decorate* — both themselves and their houses) — with a vengeance. Would Barbie get on a horse without the proper accessories? Would the Marlboro Man carry a mirror with him on the trail? By the late fifties and early sixties, the sexy, wisecracking, independent-minded heroine had morphed into a perky little ingenue. Popular actresses Annette Funicello, Connie Stevens, and Sandra Dee were living Barbie dolls, their femininity blatantly advertised on their shirt-waisted bodies. They had perfectly tended bouffant hairdos (which I achieved for myself by sleeping on the cardboard cylinders from toilet tissue rolls) and wore high heels even when washing dishes (I drew the line at that). And what about the dashing, cosmopolitan male figure in fashionable clothes? He now was usually played as a sissy or a heel — as for example Lester (Bob Evans), the slick playboy of *The Best of Everything*, who seduces gullible April (Diane Baker) with his big-city charm, then behaves like a cad when she gets pregnant.

There have always been ways to market male clothes consciousness, however. Emphasizing neatness is one. Our very own Ronnie Reagan (when he was still a B-movie star) advertised Van Heusen shirts as "the neatest Christmas gift of all" because they "won't wrinkle . . . ever!!" Joining elegance with violence is another. James Bond could get away with wearing beautiful suits because he was ruthless when it came to killing and bedding. (A men's cologne, called 007, was advertised in the sixties with clips from *Thunderball*, the voice-over recommending: "When you use 007, be kind" because "it's loaded" and "licensed to kill . . . women.") The elegant male who is capable of killing is like the highly efficient secretary who takes off her glasses to reveal a passionate, gorgeous babe underneath: a species of tantalizing, sexy disguise.

When elegance marks one man's superior class status over another it gives him a competitive edge (as was the dominant function of elegance before the eighteenth century) rather than turning him into a fop. "We have our caste marks, too" ran a 1928 ad for Aqua Velva, which featured a clean-shaven, top-hatted young man, alongside a turbaned, bejeweled, elite Indian man. This ad, however, proved to be problematic, as Kathy Piess points out. American men didn't like being compared with dark-skinned foreigners, even aristocratic ones. The more dominant tradition — among Europeans as well as Americans — has been to portray an order in which the clean, well-shaven white man is being served or serviced by the dark ones, as in a 1935 American ad for Arrow Shirts in which the black maid is so fashion-clueless that she doesn't even know what a manufacturer's label is, or in a German ad for shaving soap depicting the "appropriate" relation between the master race and the Others.

Such codes were clearly being poked fun at — how successfully I'm not sure — when a 1995 Arrid Extra-Dry commercial depicted African American pro basketball player Charles Barkley dressed up as a nineteenth-century British colonial, declaring that anything less than

Arrid "would be uncivilized." The commercial, however, is not just (argu-ably) a poke at the racist equation of civilization and whiteness. It's also, more subtly, a playful assertion of some distinctive African American atti-tudes toward male display. "Primordial perspiration," Barkley says in the commercial, "shouldn't mess with your style." And "style" is a concept whose history and cultural meanings are very different for blacks and whites in this country. Among many young African American men, appear-ing in high style, "cleaned up" and festooned with sparkling jewelry, is not a sign of effeminacy, but potency and social standing. Consider the follow-ing description, from journalist Playthell Benjamin's 1994 memoir, *Lush Life* (while you're reading it, you might also recall Anne Hollander's description of Henry VIII's summit meeting):

[Fast Black] was dressed in a pair of white pants, white buck shoes, and a long-sleeve white silk shirt — which was open to his navel and revealed a 24-karat gold chain from which hung a gold medallion set with precious stones: diamonds, rubies, and emeralds. His massively muscled body was strikingly displayed in a white see-through silk shirt, and the trousers strained to contain his linebacker thighs. His eyes were bloodshot and his skin was tight against his face, giving it the look of an ebony mask. He struck me right off as a real dangerous muthafucka; mean enough to kill a rock.

A "real dangerous muthafucka" in a white see-through silk shirt? For the white boys to whom the Dockers and Haggar ads are largely addressed, see-through silk is for girls, and showing off one's body — particularly with sensuous fabrics — is a "fag" thing. Thus, while a Haggar ad may play up the sensual appeal of soft fabrics — *"These clothes are very soft and they'll never wrinkle"* — it makes sure to include a parenthetical (and sexist) reference to a dreamed-of wife: *"Too bad you can't marry them."* But sartorial sensuality and decorativeness, as I've learned, do not necessarily mean "femininity" for African American men.

When I first saw the Charles Barkley commercial, the word "style" slipped by me unnoticed, because I knew very little about the history of African American aesthetics. An early paper of mine dealing with Berger's equation was utterly oblivious to racial differences that might confound the formula "men act and women appear." Luckily, an African American male colleague of mine gently straightened me out, urging me to think about Mike Tyson's gold front tooth as something other than willful masculine defiance of the tyranny of appearance. Unfortunately, at that time not much of a systematic nature had been written about African American aesthetics; I had to find illuminating nuggets here and there. Then, just this year, Shane White and Graham White's *Stylin'* appeared. It's a fascinating account of how the distinctive legacy of African aesthetics was maintained and creatively, sometimes challengingly, incorporated into the fashion practices of American blacks, providing a vibrant (and frequently subversive) way for blacks to "write themselves into the American story."

Under slavery, white ownership of blacks was asserted in the most concrete, humiliating way around the display of the body on the auction block. Slaves were often stripped naked and instructed to show their teeth like horses being examined for purchase. Women might have their hair cut off. Everyone's skin would be polished to shine, as apples are polished in grocery stores today. As a former slave described it:

"The first thing they had to do was wash up and clean up real good and take a fat greasy meat skin and run over their hands, face and also their feet, or in other words, every place that showed about their body so that they would look real fat and shiny. Then they would trot them out before their would-be buyers and let them look over us real good, just like you would a bunch of fat cows that you were going to sell on the market and try to get all you could for them."

It makes perfect sense that with the body so intimately and degradingly under the control of the slave owner, opportunities to "take back" one's own body and assert one's own cultural meanings with it would have a special significance. On Sundays, slaves would dress up for church in the most colorful, vibrant clothes they could put together — a temporary escape from and an active repudiation of the subservience their bodies were forced into during the week. Their outfits, to white eyes, seemed "clashing" and mismatched. But putting together unusual combinations of color, texture, and pattern was an essential ingredient of West African textile traditions, handed down and adapted by African American women. Color and shape "coordination" — the tyranny of European American fashion until pretty recently — were not the ruling principles of style. "Visual aliveness," *Stylin'* reports, was. The visual aliveness of the slaves' Sunday best, so jangling to white sensibilities, was thus the child both of necessity — they were forced to construct their outfits through a process of bricolage, putting them together from whatever items of clothing were available — and aesthetic tradition.

From the start, whites perceived there was something insubordinate going on when blacks dressed up — and they were not entirely wrong. "Slaves were only too keen to display, even to flaunt, their finery both to slaves and to whites"; the Sunday procession was, as I've noted, a time to reclaim the body as one's own. But at the same time, blacks were not just "flaunting," but preserving and improvising on vibrant African elements of style whose "flashiness" and "insolence" were largely in the eye of the white beholder, used to a very different aesthetic. The cultural resistance going on here was therefore much deeper than offended whites (and probably most blacks too) realized at the time. It wasn't simply a matter of refusal to behave like Stepin Fetchit, with head lowered and eyes down. A new culture of unpredictable, playfully decorative, visually bold fashion was being created — and it would ultimately (although not for some time) transform the world of mainstream fashion as much as Klein's deliberately erotic underwear and jeans.

THE MOST DAZZLINGLY DRESSED MEN, OFTEN JAZZ MUSICIANS, WERE KNOWN AS "SPORTS."

After "emancipation," funeral marches and celebratory promenades were a regular feature of black city life, in which marchers, male and female alike, were "emblazoned in colorful, expensive clothes," the men in "flashy sports outfits: fancy expensive silk shirts, new pants, hats, ties, socks," "yellow trousers and yellow silk shirts," and "bedecked with silk-and-satin-ribboned streamers, badges." Apart from formal processions, streets like Memphis's Beale Street and New Orleans's Decatur Street were ongoing informal sites for "strolling" and display. The most dazzlingly dressed men, often jazz musicians, were known as "sports." As "Jelly Roll" Morton describes it, each "sport" had to have a Sunday suit, with coat and pants that did not match, and crisply pressed trousers as tight as sausage skins. Suspenders were essential and had to be "very loud," with one strap left provocatively "hanging down." These guys knew how to "use their walk" too. The sport would walk down the street in a "very mosey" style: "Your hands is at your sides with your index fingers stuck out and you kind of struts with it." Morton — by all accounts a particularly flashy sport — had gold on his teeth and a diamond in one of them. "Those days," he recalled, "I thought I would die unless I had a hat with the emblem Stetson in it and some Edwin Clapp shoes." Shades of Tony Manero. Or King Henry VIII.

In fact, the flashiest African American male styles have partaken both of the African legacy and European notions of "class." Although the origin of the zoot suit — broad shoulders, long coats, ballooning, peg-legged trousers, usually worn with a wide-brimmed hat — is debated, one widely believed account says it was based on a style of suit worn by the Duke of Windsor. Another claims Rhett Butler in *Gone With the Wind* was the inspiration for the zoot suit (if so, it is a "deep irony," as the authors of *Stylin'* comment). But whatever its origins, the zoot suit, worn during the forties when cloth conservation orders ruled the use of that much fabric illegal, was a highly visible and dramatic statement in *disunity* and defiance of "American Democracy," a refusal to accede to the requirements of patriotism. Even more so than the slave's Sunday promenade, the zoot-suiter used "style" aggressively to assert opposition to the culture that had made him marginal to begin with — without his assent.

The use of high style for conspicuous display or defiance is still a big part of male street culture, as sociologist Richard Majors notes: "Whether it's your car, your clothes, your young body, your new hairdo, your jewelry, you style it. The word 'style' in [African American] vernacular usage means to show off what you've got. And for teenagers with little money and few actual possessions, showing off what you do have takes on increased importance. As one youth puts it, 'It's identity. It's a big ego trip.'"

What's changed since Majors wrote these words in the early nineties is the increasing commercial popularity of hip-hop music and culture, which has turned the rebellious stylings of street youth into an empire of images and products, often promoted (and sometimes designed) by big-name stars. With postmodern sensibilities (grab what you like) ruling the fashion world, moreover, what once were signature elements of black street style have been incorporated — as gay styles have also been incorporated — in the fashions of other worlds, both "high" (designer clothing) and "low" (white high school boys with their pants slung low, trying to look so cool).

Despite the aggressive visibility of hip-hop culture, "showing off what you've got" has not been the only influential definition of style among African Americans. In the late nineteenth and early twentieth century, several etiquette books were published, written by middle-class blacks, promoting a very different fashion ideal. The *National Capital Code of Etiquette*, published in 1889, warned young men to "avoid colors that do not blend with the remainder of your wearing apparel, and above all things shun the so-called 'loud' ties with colors that fairly shriek unto Heaven. . . ." The young black men should also avoid "bright reds, yellows and light greens as you would the plague" and never, ever strut or swagger.

Two versions of "style": "Style point" and "life, unity, peace."

Hortense Powdermaker, who studied black life in Indianola, Mississippi, in the late 1930s, noted that better-off African Americans "deliberately avoided bright colors" and were offended when clerks, on the basis of "the Negroe's reputation for wearing gaudy clothes," assumed they wanted something "loud." Those who advocated a less ostentatious style were dismayed by the lower-class practice of adorning healthy front teeth with gold, while leaving bad back teeth unattended.

A recent *Essence* list of fashion "do's and don'ts" emphasizes this deliberately understated — and in today's world, "professional" — conception of black male style. "Yes" to well-groomed hands, well-fitting suit and a "definite sense of self." "No" to "glossy polished nails," "cologne that arrives before he does," "Mr. T jewelry (the T stands for tacky)," and "saggy jeans on anyone old enough to remember when 'Killing Me Softly' was *first* released." Even in their most muted variations, African American styles have done a great deal to add color, playfulness, and unexpected, sexy little fillips to "tasteful," professional male clothing: whimsical ties, internationally inspired shirts and sweaters, and, in general, permission to be slightly dramatic, flirtatious, and ironic with one's clothes. The rule of always matching patterns, too, no longer holds in the world of high fashion, the result of a collaboration (not necessarily conscious, of course) between postmodern sensibilities and the slave legacy of bricolage.

Superstar Michael Jordan (his masculine credentials impeccable, his reputation as a family man solidly established over the years), a very effective spokesperson for style, has done a great deal to make fashionableness, even "feminine" decorativeness, congruous with masculinity. This year, he was named *GQ*'s "Most Stylish Man." "How stylish is Michael

Jordan?" *GQ* asks. "Answer: So stylish he can get away with wearing five rings!" Of course, the fact that Jordan can "get away" with wearing five rings reveals *GQ*'s cultural biases. For the magazine, Jordan's stylishness resides in the "drape of his suits, in the plain gold hoop in his left ear, in the tempered, toned-down body language of his late career." For *GQ*, subtlety equals style. For Jordan too. But of course that plain gold hoop would not have been viewed as so tastefully subtle had Jordan not made it an acceptable item of male decorativeness.

Jordan, God bless him, is also unabashed in admitting that he shops more than his wife, and that he gets his inspiration from women's magazines. The night before he goes on the road, he tries on every outfit he's going to wear. He describes himself as a "petite-type person" who tries to

hide this with oversize clothes and fabrics that drape. When questioned about the contradiction between the "manliness" of sports and his "feminine" love of fashion, Jordan replies that "that's the fun part — I can get away from the stigma of being an athlete." Saved by fashion from the "stigma" of being a sweaty brute — that's something, probably, that only an African American man can fully appreciate. The fact that it's being an athlete and not "femininity" that's the "stigma" to be avoided by Jordan — that's something a woman's got to love.

The ultimate affront to Dockers masculinity, however, is undoubtedly the Rockport ad [on page 221], with drag superstar RuPaul in a beautifully tailored suit. His feet and his stare are planted — virtually identically to Michael Jordan's posture in the feature I've just discussed — in that unmistakable (and here, ironic) grammar of face-off ad masculinity. "I'm comfortable being a MAN," declares RuPaul. "I'm comfortable being a woman too," of course, is the unwritten subtext. Man, woman, what's the difference so long as one is "uncompromising" about style?

MY WORLD . . . AND WELCOME TO IT?

Despite everything I've said thus far, I feel decidedly ambivalent about consumer culture's inroads into the male body. I *do* find it wonderful — as I've made abundantly clear — that the male form, both clothed and unclothed, is being made so widely available for sexual fantasy and aesthetic admiration. I like the fact that more and more heterosexual white guys are feeling permission to play with fashion, self-decoration, sensual presentation of the self. Even Dockers has become a little less "me a guy . . . duh!" in its ads and spreads for khakis, which now include spaced-out women as well as men.

But I also know what it's like to be on the other side of the gaze. I know its pleasures, and I know its agonies — intimately. Even in the second half of the twentieth century, beauty remains a prerequisite for female success. In fact, in an era characterized by some as "postfeminist," beauty seems to count more than it ever did before, and the standards for achieving it have become more stringent, more rigorous, than ever. We live in an empire ruled not by kings or even presidents, but by images. The tight buns, the perfect skin, the firm breasts, the long, muscled legs, the bulge-less, sagless bodies are everywhere. Beautiful women, everywhere, telling the rest of us how to stand, how to swing our hair, how slim we must be.

Actually, all this flawless beauty is the product of illusion, generated with body doubles, computers, artful retouching. "Steal this look!" the lifestyles magazines urge women; it's clear from the photo that great new haircut of Sharon Stone's could change a woman's life. But in this era of digital retouching not even Sharon Stone looks like Sharon Stone. (Isabella Rossellini, who used to be the Lancôme girl before she got too old, has said that her photos are so enhanced that when people meet her they tell her, "Your sister is so beautiful.") Still, we try to accomplish the impossible, and often get into trouble. Illusions set the standard for real women, and they spawn special disorders and addictions: in trying to become as fat-free and poreless as the ads, one's fleshly body is pushed to achieve the impossible.

I had a student who admitted to me in her journal that she had a makeup addiction. This young woman was unable to leave the house — not even to walk down to the corner mailbox — without a full face and body cover-up that took her over an hour and a half to apply. In her journal, she described having escalated over a year or so from minimal "touching-up" to a virtual mask of foundation, powder, eyebrow pencil, eye shadow, eye-liner, mascara, lip liner, lipstick — a mask so thorough, so successful in its illusionary reality that her own naked face now looked grotesque to her, mottled, pasty, featureless. She dreaded having sex with her boyfriend, for fear some of the mask might come off and he would see what she looked like underneath. As soon as they were done, she would race to the bath-room to reapply; when he stayed over, she would make sure to sleep lightly, in order to wake up earlier than he. It's funny — and not really funny. My student's disorder may be one generated by a superficial, even insane cul-ture, a disorder befitting the Oprah show rather than a PBS documentary. But a disorder nonetheless. Real. Painful. Deforming of her life.

So, too, for the eating disorders that run rampant among girls and women. In much of my writing on the female body, I've chronicled how these disorders have spread across race, class, and ethnic differences in this culture. Today, serious problems with food, weight, and body image are no longer (if they ever were) the province of pampered, narcissistic, heterosexual white girls. To imagine that they are is to view black, Asian, Latin, lesbian, and working-class women as outside the loop of the domi-nant culture and untouched by its messages about what is beautiful — a mistake that has left many women feeling abandoned and alone with a disorder they weren't "supposed" to have. Today, eating problems are vir-tually the norm among high school and college women — and even younger girls. Yes, of course there are far greater tragedies in life than gaining five pounds. But try to reassure a fifteen-year-old girl that her success in life doesn't require a slender body, and she will think you dropped from another planet. *She* knows what's demanded; she's learned it from the movies, the magazines, the soap operas.

There, the "progressive" message conveyed by giving the girls and women depicted great careers or exciting adventures is overpowered, I think, by the more potent example of their perfect bodies. The plots may say: "The world is yours." The bodies caution: "But only if you aren't fat." What counts as "fat" today? Well, Alicia Silverstone was taunted by the press when she appeared at the Academy Awards barely ten pounds heavier than her (extremely) svelte self in *Clueless*. Janeane Garofalo was the "fat one" in *The Truth About Cats and Dogs*. Reviews of *Titanic* described Kate Winslett as plump, overripe, much too hefty for ethereal Leonardo DiCaprio. Any anger you detect here is personal too. I ironed my hair in the sixties, have dieted all my life, continue to be deeply ashamed of those parts of my body — like my peasant legs and zaftig behind — that our culture has coded as ethnic excess. I suspect it's only an accident of generational timing or a slight warp in the fabric of my cultural environment that prevented me from developing an eating disorder. I'm not a makeup junky like my student, but I am becoming somewhat addicted nowadays to alpha-hydroxies, skin drenchers, quenchers, and other "age-defying" potions.

No, I don't think the business of beauty is without its pleasures. It offers a daily ritual of transformation, renewal. Of "putting oneself together" and walking out into the world, more confident than you were, anticipating attraction, flirtation, sexual play. I love shopping for makeup with my friends. (Despite what Rush Limbaugh tells you, feminism — certainly not feminism in the nineties — is not synonymous with unshaved legs.) Women bond over shared makeup, shared beauty tips. It's fun. Too often, though, our bond is over shared pain — over "bad" skin, "bad" hair, "bad" legs. There's always that constant judgment and evaluation — not only by actual, living men but by an ever-present, watchful cultural gaze which always has its eye on our thighs — no matter how much else we accomplish. We judge each other that way too, sometimes much more nastily than men. Some of the bitchiest comments about Marcia Clark's hair and Hillary Clinton's calves have come from women. But if we are sometimes our "own worst enemies," it's usually because we see in each other not so much competition as a reflection of our fears and anxieties about ourselves. In this culture, all women suffer over their bodies. A demon is loose in our consciousness and can't easily be controlled. We see the devil, fat calves, living on Hillary's body. We point our fingers, like the accusers at Salem. Root him out, kill *her*!

And now men are suddenly finding that devil living in their flesh. If someone had told me in 1977 that in 1997 *men* would comprise over a quarter of cosmetic-surgery patients, I would have been astounded. I never dreamed that "equality" would move in the direction of men worrying *more* about their looks rather than women worrying less. I first suspected that something major was going on when the guys in my gender classes stopped yawning and passing snide notes when we discussed body issues, and instead began to protest when the women talked as though they were the only ones "oppressed" by standards of beauty. After my book *Unbearable Weight* appeared, I received several letters from male anorexics, reminding me that the incidence of such disorders among men was on the rise. Today, as many as a million men — and eight million women — have an eating disorder.

> I NEVER DREAMED THAT "EQUALITY" WOULD MOVE IN THE DIRECTION OF MEN WORRYING *MORE* ABOUT THEIR LOOKS RATHER THAN WOMEN WORRYING LESS.

Then I began noticing all the new men's "health" magazines on the newsstands, dispensing diet and exercise advice ("A Better Body in Half the Time," "50 Snacks That Won't Make You Fat") in the same cheerleaderish mode that Betty Friedan had once chastised the women's magazines for: "It's Chinese New Year, so make a resolution to custom-order your next takeout. Ask that they substitute wonton soup for oil. Try the soba noodles instead of plain noodles. They're richer in nutrients and contain much less fat." I guess the world doesn't belong to the meat-eaters anymore, Mr. Ben Quick.

It used to be a truism among those of us familiar with the research on body-image problems that most men (that is, most straight men, on whom the studies were based) were largely immune. Women, research showed, were chronically dissatisfied with themselves. But men tended, if anything, to see themselves as better-looking than they (perhaps) actually were. Peter Richmond, in a 1987 piece in *Glamour*, describes his "wonderful male trick" for seeing what he wants to see when he looks in the mirror:

> I edit out the flaws. Recently, under the influence of too many Heinekens in a strange hotel room, I stood in front of a wrap-around full-length mirror and saw, in a moment of nauseous clarity, how unshapely my stomach and butt have become. The next morning, looking again in the same mirror, ready to begin another business day, I simply didn't see these offending areas.

Notice all the codes for male "action" that Richmond has decorated his self-revelation with. "Too many Heinekens," "another business day"—all reassurances that other things matter more to him than his appearance. But a decade later, it's no longer so easy for men to perform these little tricks. Getting ready for the business day is apt to exacerbate rather than divert male anxieties about the body, as men compete with fitter, younger men and fitter, more self-sufficient women. In a 1994 survey, 6,000 men ages eighteen to fifty-five were asked how they would like to see themselves. Three of men's top six answers were about looks: attractive to women, sexy, good-looking. Male "action" qualities — assertiveness, decisiveness — trailed at numbers eight and nine.

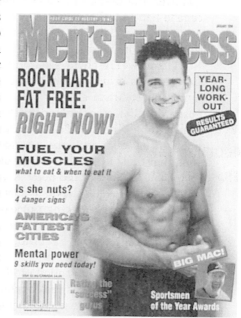

"Back when bad bodies were the norm," claims *Fortune* writer Alan Farnham (again, operating with the presumption of heterosexuality), "money distinguished male from male. Now muscles have devalued money," and the market for products and procedures "catering to male vanity" (as *Fortune* puts it) is $9.5 billion or so a year. "It's a Face-Lifted,

Tummy-Tucked Jungle Out There," reports *The New York Times*. To compete, a man

> could buy Rogaine to thicken his hair. He could invest in Body-Slimmers
> underwear for men, by the designer Nancy Ganz, with built-in support to
> suck in the waist. Or he could skip the aloe skin cream and go on to a
> more drastic measure, new to the male market: alpha-hydroxy products
> that slough off dead skin. Or he could rub on some belly- and thigh-
> shrinking creams. . . . If rubbing cream seems too strenuous, [he] can just
> don an undershirt from Mountainville House, to "shape up and pull in
> loose stomachs and sagging chests," with a diamond-shaped insert at the
> gut for "extra control." . . . Plastic surgery offers pectoral implants to make
> the chest appear more muscular, and calf muscle implants to give the leg
> a bodybuilder shape. There is liposuction to counter thickening middles
> and accumulating breast and fatty tissue in the chest . . . and a half-dozen
> surgical methods for tightening skin.

Some writers blame all this on sexual equality in the workplace. Anthropologist Lionel Tiger offers this explanation: "Once," he says, "men could fairly well control their destiny through providing resources to women, but now that the female is obliged to earn a living, he himself becomes a resource. He becomes his own product: Is he good-looking? Does he smell good? Before, when he had to provide for the female, he could have a potbelly. Now he has to appear attractive in the way the female had to be." Some evidence does support this. A *Psychology Today* survey found that the more financially secure the woman, the more important a man's looks were to her.

I, however, tend to see consumer capitalism rather than women's expectations or proclivities as the true motor driving male concern with appearance. Calvin gave us those muscled men in underwear. Then the cosmetics, diet, exercise, and surgery industries elbowed in, providing the means for everyone to develop that great Soloflex body. After all, why should they restrict themselves to female markets if they can convince men that their looks need constant improvement too? The management and enhancement of the body is a gold mine for consumerism, and one whose treasures are inexhaustible, as women know. Dieting and staving off aging are never-ending processes. Ideals of beauty can be endlessly tinkered with by fashion designers and cosmetic manufacturers, remaining continually elusive, requiring constant new purchases, new kinds of work on the body.

John Berger's opposition of "acting" and "appearing," this body work reveals, is something of a false duality — and always has been. "Feminine" attention to appearance is hardly the absence of activity, as men are learning. It takes time, energy, creativity, dedication. It can *hurt*. Nowadays, the "act/appear" duality is even less meaningful, as the cultivation of the suitably fit appearance has become not just a matter of sexual allure but also a demonstration that one has the "right stuff": will, discipline, the ability to stop whining and "just do it." When I was growing up in the sixties, a muscular male body meant beefy but dumb jock; a middle-class girl could drool over him but probably wouldn't want to marry him. Today, with a booming "gymnasium culture" existing (as in ancient Greece) for professional men and with it a revival of the Greek idea that a good mind and a good body are not mutually exclusive, even Jeff Goldblum has got muscles, and the only type of jock he plays is a computer jock.

All of this, as physicians have begun to note, is landing more and more men straight into the formerly female territory of body-image dysfunction, eating disorders, and exercise compulsions. Last year, I read a survey that reported that 90 percent of male undergraduates believe that they are not muscular enough. That sent warning bells clanging in my mind, and sure enough, there's now a medical category for "muscle dysmorphia" (or "bigorexia," as it's actually sometimes called!), a kind of reverse anorexia in which the sufferer sees his muscles as never massive enough. Researchers are "explaining" bigorexia in the same dumb way they've tended to approach women's disorders — as a combination of bad biochemistry and "triggering events," such as being picked on. They just don't seem to fully appreciate the fact that bigorexia — like anorexia — only blooms in a very particular cultural soil. Not even the ancient Greeks — who revered athletic bodies and scorned weaklings, but also advised moderation in all things — produced "muscle dysmorphics." (Or at least, none of the available medical texts mention anything like it.) Anorexia and bigorexia, like so many contemporary disorders, are diseases of a culture that doesn't know when to stop.

Those beautiful bodies of Greek statues may be the historical inspiration for the muscled men in underwear of the Calvin Klein ads. But the fact is that studying the ancient Greeks reveals a different set of attitudes toward beauty and the body than our contemporary ideals, both homosexual and heterosexual. As is well known by now (although undiscussed when I studied philosophy as an undergraduate), Plato was not above appreciating a beautiful young body. In *Symposium*, he describes the beauty of the body as evidence of the presence of the divine on earth, and the original spur to all "higher" human endeavors (as well as earthly, sexual love). We see someone dazzling, and he or she awakens the soul to its natural hunger to be lifted above the mundane, transitory, mortal world. Some people seek that transcendence through ordinary human intercourse, and achieve the only immortality they will know through the begetting of human offspring and the continuation of the human race. For others, the beautiful body of another becomes the inspiration for a life-long search for beauty in all its forms, the creation of beautiful art, beautiful words, beautiful ideals, beautiful cities. They will achieve their immortality through communion with something beyond the body — the idea of Beauty itself.

So human beauty is a pretty far-ranging and powerful thing for Plato, capable of evoking worlds beyond itself, even recalling a previous life when we dwelt among timeless, perfect forms. But human beauty, significantly (in fact, all earthly beauty), can only offer a glimpse of heavenly perfection. It's our nature to be imperfect, after all, and anyone who tries to overcome that limitation on earth is guilty of hubris — according to the Greeks. Our own culture, in contrast, is one without "limits" (a frequent theme of advertisements and commercials) and seemingly without any fear of hubris. Not only do we expect perfection in the bodies of others (just take a gander at some personal ads), we are constantly encouraged to achieve it ourselves, with the help of science and technology and the products and services they make available to us. "This body could be yours," the chiseled Greek statue in the Soloflex commercial tells us (and for only twenty minutes three times a week — give me a break!). "Timeless Beauty Is Within Your Reach," reads an ad for cosmetic surgery. Plato is rolling over in his grave.

For Plato (unlike Descartes) there are no "mere" physical bodies; bodies are lit with meaning, with memory. Our culture is more Cartesian; we like to think of our bodies as so much stuff, which can be tinkered with without any consequences for our soul. We bob our "family noses," lift our aging faces, suction extra fat, remove minor "flaws" with seemingly little concern for any "deep" meaning that our bodies might have, as repositories of our histories, our ethnic and racial and family lineage, our personalities. Actually, much of the time our intentions are to deliberately shed those meanings: to get rid of that Jewish nose, to erase the years from our faces. Unlike the Platonic philosopher, we aren't content to experience timelessness in philosophy, art, or even the beautiful bodies of others; we want to stop time on our own bodies too. In the process, we substitute individualized beauty — the distinctive faces of the generation of beautiful actresses of my own age, for example — for generic, very often racialized, reproducible codes of youth.

The fact is that we're not only Cartesian but Puritan in our attitudes toward the body. The Greeks went for muscles, sure, but they would have regarded our exercise compulsions as evidence of a system out of control. They thought it unseemly — and a failure of will — to get too self-obsessed with *anything*. They were into the judicious "management" of the body (as French philosopher Michel Foucault has put it), not its utter subjugation. We, on the other hand, can become what our culture considers to be sexually alluring only if we're willing to regard our flesh as recalcitrant metal, to be pummeled, burned, and tempered into steel, day in and day out. No pain, no gain. Obsessively pursuing these ideals has deprived both men *and* women of the playful eros of beauty, turned it all into constant, hard work. I love gay and black body cultures for their flirtatiousness, their tongue-in-cheekness, their irony, their "let's dress up and have some fun" attitudes. Consumer culture, unfortunately, can even grind playfulness into a commodity, a required item for this year's wardrobe.

For all its idealization of the beauty of the body, Greek culture also understood that beauty could be "inner." In the *Symposium*, a group of elite Greeks discourse on the nature of love. Everyone except for Socrates and Aristophanes is in love with someone else at the party, and they're madly flirting, advancing their own romantic agendas through their speeches. Among the participants are the most beautiful young men of their crowd. Socrates himself is over fifty at the time, and not a pretty man to look at (to put it generously). Yet as we're told at the beginning (and this seems to have been historically true), nearly everyone has at one time or another been "obsessed" with him, "transported, completely possessed" — by his cleverness, his irony, his ability to weave a spell with words and ideas. Even the most dazzling Athenian of them all — soldier superhero Alcibiades, generally regarded as one of the sexiest, handsomest men in town, who joins the party late (and drunk) with a beautiful wreath of violets and ivy and ribbons in his hair — is totally, madly smitten with Socrates.

Alcibiades' love for Socrates is *not* "Platonic" in the sense in which we have come to understand that term. In fact, Alcibiades is insulted because Socrates has refused to have sex with him. "The moment he starts to speak," he tells the crowd of his feelings for Socrates, "I am beside myself: my heart starts leaping in my chest, the tears come streaming down my face." This is not the way it usually goes. In the more normal Greek scheme of things, it's the beautiful young man — like Alcibiades — who is supposed to start the heart of the older man thumping, and who flirtatiously withholds his favors while the older lover does his best to win him. Alcibiades is in a state about this role reversal, but he understands why it has happened. He compares Socrates to a popular kind of satyr statue, which (like the little lacquered Russian dolls we're more familiar with) could be opened to reveal another figure within. Socrates may be ugly as a satyr on the outside, but "once I had a glimpse of the figures within — they were so godlike, so bright and beautiful, so utterly amazing, that I no longer had a choice — I just had to do whatever he told me."

We pay constant lip service to beauty that is more than skin-deep. The talk shows frequently parade extreme May-December matings for our ogling too. But the fact is that the idea of a glamorous young man being romantically, *sexually* obsessed with someone old and "ugly" — same-sex or other-sex and no matter what other sterling qualities he or she may have — is pretty much beyond us. Historically, men have benefited from a double standard which culturally codes their gray hair, middle-age paunches, facial lines, as signs of wisdom and experience rather than advancing decrepitude. My older gay male friends lament that those days are over for them. And if those new polls about women's attitudes are to be believed, the clock is ticking on that double standard for heterosexual men, too — no matter how hard Hollywood tries to preserve it. With more and more expectation that men be as physically well-tended as women, those celluloid pairings of Woody Allen and women half as old and forty-six times as good-looking are becoming more of a hoot every day.

There is something anti-sensual to me about current aesthetics. There's so much that my younger friends go "uggh" over. Fat — yecch! Wrinkles — yuck! They live in a constant state of squeamishness about the flesh. I find that finely muscled young Calvin Klein model beautiful and sexy, sure. But I also was moved by Clint Eastwood's aging chest in *The Bridges of Madison County*. Deflated, skin loose around the waistband of his pants, not a washboard ridge in sight — for me, they signaled that East-wood (at least for this role) had put Dirty Harry away for good, become a real, warm, penetrable, vulnerable human being instead of a make-my-day machine. Call me old-fashioned, but I find that very sexy. For a culture obsessed with youth and fitness, in contrast, sagging flesh is almost the ultimate signifier of decay and disorder. We prefer the clean machine — and are given it, in spades. Purified of "flaws," all loose skin tightened, armored with implants, digitally enhanced, the bodies of most movie stars and models are fully dressed even when naked.

In *Saturday Night Fever*, John Travolta had been trim, but (by con-temporary standards) a bit "soft." Six years later, Travolta re-created Tony Manero in the sequel, *Staying Alive*. This time, however, the film was directed by Sylvester Stallone, who showed Travolta a statue of a discus thrower and asked, "How would you like to look like that?" "Terrific," Travolta replied, and embarked on a seven-month program of fitness training that literally redesigned his body into a carbon copy of Sly's. In the film, his body was "perfect": gleaming and muscular, without an ounce of fat. He was nice to look at. But if I had to choose between the Tony Manero of *Fever* and the Tony Manero of *Staying Alive*, it'd be no contest. I'd rather spend time (and have sex) with a dancing man with love handles than with a Greek statue who gets in a nasty mood if he misses a workout.

NOTE

1 Not that women's beauty was dispensable. Concern for her looks symbolized that although she worked as hard as a man, a woman's mind was still on the *real* men who were fighting for her freedom. (An ad for Tangee lipstick describes "a woman's lipstick [as] an instrument of personal morale that helps her to conceal heartbreak or sorrow; gives her self-confidence when it's badly needed. . . . It symbolizes one of the reasons why we are fighting . . . the precious right of women to be feminine and lovely — under any circumstances.") The woman of this period was a creature of both "appearance" *and* "action" — a kind of forerunner to today's superwoman. [Note is Bordo's.]

BIBLIOGRAPHY

Beauvoir, Simone de. (1952). *The Second Sex*. New York: Vintage Books.
Berger, John. (1972). *Ways of Seeing*. Great Britain: Penguin Books.
Blum, Deborah. (1997). *Sex on the Brain: The Biological Differences Between Men and Women*. New York: Viking Penguin.
Boyd, Herbert, and Robert Allen (eds.). (1995). *Brotherman*. New York: Ballantine.
Clark, Danae. (1995). "Commodity Lesbianism." In Kate Meuhuron and Gary Persecute (eds.). *Free Spirits*. Englewood Cliffs, NJ: Prentice Hall, pp. 82–94.
Clarkson, Wensley. (1997). *John Travolta: Back in Character*. Woodstock: Overlook Press.
Ellenzweig, Allen. (1992). *The Homoerotic Photograph*. New York: Columbia University Press.
Farnham, Alan. (1996). "You're So Vain," *Fortune*, September 9, pp. 66–82.
Foucault, Michel. (1985). *The Use of Pleasure*. New York: Vintage Books.
Friday, Nancy. (1996). *The Power of Beauty*. New York: HarperCollins.
Gaines, Steven, and Sharon Churcher. (1994). *Obsession: The Lives and Times of Calvin Klein*. New York: Avon Books.
Gilmore, David. (1990). *Manhood in the Making*. New Haven: Yale University Press.
Gladwell, Malcolm. (1997). "Listening to Khakis," *The New Yorker*, July 28, pp. 54–58.
Hollander, Anne. (1994). *Sex and Suits: The Evolution of Modern Dress*. New York: Kodansha International.

Long, Ron. (1997). "The Fitness of the Gym," *Harvard Gay and Lesbian Review*, Vol. IV, No. 3, Summer, pp. 20–22.

Majors, Richard, and Janet Mancini Billson. (1992). *Cool Pose: The Dilemmas of Black Manhood in America*. New York: Lexington Books.

Piess, Kathy. (1998). *Hope in a Jar: The Making of America's Beauty Culture*. New York: Metropolitan Books.

Pieterse, Jan Nederveen. (1990). *White on Black: Images of Africa and Blacks in Western Popular Culture*. New Haven: Yale University Press.

Plato. (1989). *Symposium*. Trans. Alexander Nehama. Indianapolis: Hackett Publishing.

Richmond, Peter. (1987). "How Do Men Feel About Their Bodies?" *Glamour*, April, pp. 312–13, 369–72.

Rotundo, E. Anthony. (1993). *American Manhood: Transformations in Masculinity from the Revolution to the Modern Era*. New York: Basic Books.

Sartre, Jean-Paul. (1966). *Being and Nothingness*. New York: Washington Square Press.

Shaw, Dan. (1994). "Mirror, Mirror," *New York Times*, May 29, Section 9, pp. 1, 6.

Sheets-Johnstone, Maxine. (1994). *The Roots of Power: Animate Form and Gendered Bodies*. Chicago: Open Court.

Spindler, Amy. (1996). "It's a Face-Lifted, Tummy-Tucked Jungle Out There," *New York Times*, June 9.

Taylor, John. (1995). "The Long Hard Days of Dr. Dick," *Esquire*, September, pp. 120–30.

White, Shane, and Graham White. (1998). *Stylin'*. Ithaca: Cornell University Press.

· · ● ● ● · · ·

QUESTIONS FOR A SECOND READING

1. This is a long essay. The writing operates under a set of expectations that does not value efficiency. The writing says, "It is better to take time with this, better to take time rather than hurry, rather than rushing to say what must be said, rather than pushing to be done. Slow down, relax, take your time. This can be fun." While there is attention to a "thesis," the organizing principle of this essay is such that the real work and the real pleasure lie elsewhere. Work and pleasure. As you reread, pay particular attention to how Bordo controls the pace and direction of the essay, where she prolongs the discussion and where and when she shifts direction. Think of this as a way for her (and you) to get work done. And think about it as a way of organizing the pleasure of the text. Be prepared to describe how she does this and whether it works for you (or doesn't). And be prepared to talk about the possibilities of adapting this strategy (a strategy of more rather than less) in your own writing.

2. This is a long essay divided into subsections. The subsections mark stages in the presentation. The subsections allow you to think about form in relation to units larger than the paragraph but smaller than the essay. As you reread, pay attention to these sections. How are they organized internally? How are they arranged? How do they determine the pace or rhythm of your reading, the tonality or phrasing of the text? Which is the slowest, for example? Which is the loudest? And why? And where are they placed? What do they do to the argument?

3. Bordo is a distinctive and stylish writer. She is also one of many writers who are thinking about visual culture and popular culture (about movies, TV, and advertisements) in relation to (what Bordo refers to as) "consumer capitalism."

For those who know this work, she makes use of some terms and strategies common to cultural studies. One is to think about "subject position." Bordo says that when she saw the Calvin Klein ad, she had her "first real taste of what it's like to inhabit this visual culture as a man" (p. 186). Another related strategy is to think about how and where one is positioned, as subject or object, in the moment of vision, a moment of looking, when you are defined by the "gaze" of another or when your "gaze" is the source of definition. She says, for example, "For many men, both gay and straight, to be so passively dependent on the gaze of another person for one's sense of self-worth is incompatible with being a real man." She works this out in the section where she talks about Jean-Paul Sartre and Simone de Beauvoir (pp. 189–90). As you reread the chapter, pay particular attention to where and how Bordo invokes and/or inhabits the "subject position" of people different from herself. How are these differences defined? (You might make a list.) Where is she most convincing? least convincing? And, finally, be prepared to speak back to the text from what you take to be your own "subject position." How does it look to you?

4. At one point, Bordo speaks directly to you and invites you into her project: "So the next time you see a Dockers or Haggar ad, think of it not only as an advertisement for khakis but also as an advertisement for a certain notion of what it means to be a man" (p. 211). You don't have to be limited to Dockers, Haggar, or khaki, but as you reread the essay, keep your eye out for advertisements that come your way, advertisements that seem perfect for thinking along with Bordo, for thinking her thoughts but also for thinking about how things have changed or might be seen differently. Clip these or copy them and bring them to class.

• • • ● • • •

ASSIGNMENTS FOR WRITING

1. Bordo looks back to the history of advertising (the "cultural genealogy of the ads I've been discussing"), and she works directly with the ads that prompted and served this chapter in her book. These images are a key part of the writing.

    Bordo also speaks directly to you and invites you into her project: "So the next time you see a Dockers or Haggar ad, think of it not only as an advertisement for khakis but also as an advertisement for a certain notion of what it means to be a man" (p. 211). You don't have to be limited to Dockers, Haggar, or khaki, but as you reread the essay and prepare for this writing assignment, keep your eye out for advertisements that come your way, advertisements that seem perfect for thinking along with Bordo (or advertisements that seem like interesting counterexamples). Clip these or copy them so that you can use them, as she does, as material for writing.

    Write an essay in which you take up Bordo's invitation. You should assume an audience that has not read Bordo (or not read her work recently), so you will need to take time to present the terms and direction of her argument. Your goal, however, is to extend her project to your moment in time, when advertising may very well have moved on to different images of men and strategies of presentation. Bordo is quite specific about her age and experience, her point of view. You should be equally specific. You, too, should establish your point of view. You are placed at a different moment in time, your experience is different, and your exposure to images has prepared you differently. You write from a different subject position. Your job, then, is not simply to reproduce Bordo's project but to extend it, to refine it, to put it to the test.

2. The first two second-reading questions point attention to the length of the essay and to its organization. Here, in effect, is what they say:

> "Beauty (Re)discovers the Male Body" is a long essay. The writing operates under a set of expectations that does not value efficiency. The writing says, "It is better to take time with this, better to take time rather than hurry, rather than rushing to say what must be said, rather than pushing to be done. Slow down, relax, take your time. This can be fun." While there is attention to a "thesis," the organizing principle of this essay is such that the real work and the real pleasure lie elsewhere. Work and pleasure. As you reread, pay particular attention to how Bordo controls the pace and direction of the essay, where she prolongs the discussion and where and when she shifts direction. Think of this as a way for her (and you) to get work done. And think about it as a way of organizing the pleasure of the text.
>
> This is a long essay divided into subsections. The subsections mark stages in the presentation. The subsections allow you to think about form in relation to units larger than the paragraph but smaller than the essay. As you reread, pay attention to these sections. How are they organized internally? How are they arranged? How do they determine the pace or rhythm of your reading, the tonality or phrasing of the text? Which is the slowest, for example? Which is the loudest? And why? And where are they placed? What do they do to the argument?

Take time to reread and to think these questions through. It has become common for scholars and teachers to think about the pleasure, even the "erotics" of the text. This is not, to be sure, the usual language of the composition classroom. Write an essay in which you describe the pleasures (and, if you choose, the problems) of Bordo's writing. Describe how it is organized, and how it organizes your time and attention. Describe how it works (or doesn't) for you as a reader, how it works (or doesn't) for her as a writer and thinker. You can, to be sure, make reference to other things you are reading or have read or to the writing you are doing (and have done) in school.

3. Bordo assumes, always, that the representations of men's bodies are generally read (or viewed) in the context of the similar use of women's bodies — in art, in advertising, in visual popular culture (including film and

television). For this assignment, choose two sources—one ad directed, you feel, primarily to men and another ad directed primarily to women—or you might look more generally at all of the ads in two magazines, one directed (you feel) primarily to men and another to women. Write an essay in which you use Bordo's essay, and its claims, to think through your examples. You will need to take time to present your examples (including, ideally, the images) and Bordo's understanding of the role of gender in the ways images of the body are designed, presented, and read. How can you both present *and* extend Bordo's work on gender and advertising?

4. Bordo says that when she saw the Calvin Klein ad, she had her "first real taste of what it's like to inhabit this visual culture as a man" (p. 186). Throughout the essay she makes reference to her "subject position" and to the subject position of other viewers, both real and imagined—viewers younger or older, viewers of another race or ethnicity, men, viewers who are gay rather than straight. As you prepare to write this essay, reread the chapter (see the "Questions for a Second Reading"), and pay particular attention to those moments when Bordo speaks to the effects of particular ads, and when she speaks from her or from another subject position. Think carefully about how she is "reading" and responding to these images. Think with equal care about what you see and how you respond; think, that is, about how you might articulate the reactions from your "subject position" or from those that Bordo has not yet been able to imagine. Choose one or two of her examples and write about them as she sees and understands them, but also as you see or understand them. How do these images look to you and at you? How might you speak back to Bordo? Make sure to develop both positions with care and detail. And, at the end, think about how you might best explain the differences.

· · ● · · ·

MAKING CONNECTIONS

1. In "Beauty (Re)discovers the Male Body," Susan Bordo refers to John Berger and his work in *Ways of Seeing*, although she refers to a different chapter from the one included here (p. 142). In general, however, both Berger and Bordo are concerned with how we see and read images; both seek to correct the ways images are used and read; both trace the ways images serve the interests of money and power; both texts are written to teach readers how and why they should pay a different kind of attention to the images around them.

For this assignment, use Bordo's work to reconsider Berger's. Write an essay in which you consider the two chapters as examples of an ongoing project. Berger's essay precedes Bordo's by about a quarter of a century. If you look closely at one or two of their examples, and if you look at the larger concerns of their arguments, are they saying the same things? doing the same work? If so, how? And why is such work still necessary? If not, how do their projects differ? And how might you explain those differences?

2. Like Susan Bordo, Susan Griffin in "Our Secret" (p. 381) is working as a feminist social historian. She takes familiar social practices (advertising, representations of the past and of the self) and attempts to help readers see them differently, not as simply natural or arbitrary but as practices that have important social and political consequences. Read this text alongside Bordo's. Write an essay in which you explore and describe the reading and writing strategies employed by these two writers. As researchers, how do they gather their materials, weigh them, think them through? What do they notice, and what do they do with what they notice? What makes each project historical? What makes it feminist? How might the two texts speak to each other? Looking at characteristic examples drawn from both writers, what might you conclude about the relative value — to you and to history — of each writer's project?

© Markus Kirchgessner/laif/Redux

JUDITH
Butler

Judith Butler is the Maxine Elliot Professor in the departments of rhetoric and comparative literature at the University of California at Berkeley. She is also the Hannah Arendt Professor of Philosophy at the European Graduate School in Saas-Fee, Switzerland, where she teaches an intensive summer seminar. She was an undergraduate at Bennington College and then Yale University; she received her PhD in philosophy from Yale in 1984. Her first training as a philosopher, she said, was at the synagogue in her hometown, Cleveland.

Butler is a prolific and controversial writer whose topics range from gender to sexuality to war. Her books include *Subjects of Desire: Hegelian Reflections in Twentieth-Century France* (1987); *Gender Trouble: Feminism and the Subversion of Identity* (1990); *Bodies That Matter: On the Discursive Limits of "Sex"* (1993); *Excitable Speech: A Politics of the Performative* (1997); *Precarious Life: Powers of Violence and Mourning* (2004); and *Undoing Gender* (2004), a collection of essays, including the selection that follows. More recently she has published *Parting Ways: Jewishness and the Critique of Zionism* (2012); *Dispossession: The Performative in the Political* (2013, with Athena Athanasiou); *Senses of the Subject* (2015); and *Notes toward a Performative Theory of Assembly* (2015).

Butler's second book, *Gender Trouble*, was extraordinarily successful — that is, it was widely read around the world, translated into several languages, taught in graduate and undergraduate seminars, and referenced in thousands of books and essays. It is, perhaps, one of the most important books of its time; it remains profoundly influential. The argument calls into question the commonplace and controlling assumption that human beings are divided into two clear-cut groups, men and women. Butler challenges this binary, demonstrating that much that is taken for granted about gender is problematic, even illogical. Whatever the individual body, gender identity is more complicated, more diverse, more flexible than assumed by a simple binary, male and female. Gender identity, she argues, is "performative"; it is not the natural result of who we are biologically; it is a product, rather, of how we think, act, imagine, and desire, and these performances are subject to change.

> There is no gender identity behind the expressions of gender; . . . identity is performatively constituted by the very "expressions" that are said to be its results. (*Gender Trouble*, p. 25)

This was the compelling and difficult conclusion: although gender identity is shaped by cultural norms and conventions, and although bodies and biology matter, gender identity is mutable, available to change. It is open to revision, resistance, subversion, and improvisation—sometimes willed, sometimes not. This thought was terrifying for some and liberating for others.

Butler is known for the difficulty of her prose. In fact, the difficulty could be said to be exemplary. In 1998, she was announced as the "winner" of a Bad Writing Contest sponsored by the journal *Philosophy and Literature*, where her prose was singled out for its "anxiety-inducing obscurity." The incident garnered substantial attention in the academic and popular press and became an important point of reference as the nation tried to sort out its relation to the academy, to intellectuals, and to their attempts to bring critical theory to bear on matters of daily life and common concern. In her response to the award, Butler pointed out that the "winners" tended to be people who were writing against common-sense understandings of gender, race, class, and nation. She argued that prose is easy to read when it says what we already know and believe, but that it is harder to read (and to write) a prose that is struggling against the usual ways of thinking and speaking.

UNDOING GENDER
JUDITH BUTLER

> There is a lot in ordinary language and in received grammar that constrains our thinking. . . . I'm not sure we're going to be able to struggle effectively against those constraints or work within them in a productive way unless we see the ways in which grammar is both producing and constraining our sense of what the world is. (*Excitable Speech: A Politics of the Performative,* pp. 732–33)

Anxiety, perhaps, is the necessary effect of such a project, an alternative to complacency. And so, she concluded in a *New York Times* op-ed article, the controversy was not so much about her prose as about what was appropriate in the classroom and in academic life. "We have an intellectual disagreement about what kind of world we want to live in, and what intellectual resources we must preserve as we make our way toward the politically new."

The other side of the argument is easier to grasp and easier to represent—that such prose is self-indulgent, divisive, posturing, disrespectful of its audience. One thing is certain, however. Butler is widely read and widely cited and is one of the most important, controversial, and influential theorists of our time. Her writing has changed the ways we think, speak, and write about sexuality, gender, and desire. The selection that follows thinks about gender identity in relation to the question of what "constitutes the human," who is granted this recognition and who is not. Butler raises this as a philosophical question, but she is also very interested in the political, in the actual human beings whose lives bear the consequence of being understood as impossible, illegible, and thereby alien, located outside the common understandings of what it means to be a person.

Beside Oneself: On the Limits of Sexual Autonomy

What makes for a livable world is no idle question. It is not merely a question for philosophers. It is posed in various idioms all the time by people in various walks of life. If that makes them all philosophers, then that is a conclusion I am happy to embrace. It becomes a question for ethics, I think, not only when we ask the personal question, what makes my own life bearable, but when we ask, from a position of power, and from the point of view of distributive justice, what makes, or ought to make, the lives of others bearable? Somewhere in the answer we find ourselves not only committed to a certain view of what life is, and what it should be, but also of what constitutes the human, the distinctively human life, and what does not. There is always a risk of anthropocentrism here if one assumes that the distinctively human life is valuable — or most valuable — or is the only way to think the problem of value. But perhaps to counter that tendency it is necessary to ask both the question of life and the question of the human, and not to let them fully collapse into one another.

WE ARE CONSTITUTED POLITICALLY IN PART BY VIRTUE OF THE SOCIAL VULNERABILITY OF OUR BODIES; WE ARE CONSTITUTED AS FIELDS OF DESIRE AND PHYSICAL VULNERABILITY, AT ONCE PUBLICLY ASSERTIVE AND VULNERABLE.

I would like to start, and to end, with the question of the human, of who counts as the human, and the related question of whose lives count as lives, and with a question that has preoccupied many of us for years: what makes for a grievable life? I believe that whatever differences exist within the international gay and lesbian community, and there are many, we all have some notion of what it is to have lost somebody. And if we've lost, then it seems to follow that we have had, that we have desired and loved, and struggled to find the conditions for our desire. We have all lost someone in recent decades from AIDS, but there are other losses that inflict us, other diseases; moreover, we are, as a community, subjected to violence, even if some of us individually have not been. And this means that we are constituted politically in part by virtue of the social vulnerability of our bodies; we are constituted as fields of desire and physical vulnerability, at once publicly assertive and vulnerable.

I am not sure I know when mourning is successful, or when one has fully mourned another human being. I'm certain, though, that it does not mean that one has forgotten the person, or that something else comes along to take his or her place. I don't think it works that way. I think instead that one mourns when one accepts the fact that the loss one undergoes will be one that changes you, changes you possibly forever, and that mourning has to do with agreeing to undergo a transformation the full result of which you cannot know in advance. So there is losing, and there is the transformative effect of loss, and this latter cannot be charted or planned. I don't think, for instance, you can invoke a Protestant ethic when it comes to loss. You can't say, "Oh, I'll go through loss this way, and that will be the result, and I'll apply myself to the task, and I'll endeavor to achieve the resolution of grief that is before me." I think one is hit by waves, and that one starts out the day with an aim, a project, a plan, and one finds oneself foiled. One finds oneself fallen. One is exhausted but does not know why. Something is larger than one's own deliberate plan or project, larger than one's own knowing. Something takes hold, but is this something coming from the self, from the outside, or from some region where the difference between the two is indeterminable? What is it that claims us at such moments, such that we are not the masters of ourselves? To what are we tied? And by what are we seized?

It may seem that one is undergoing something temporary, but it could be that in this experience something about who we are is revealed, something that delineates the ties we have to others, that shows us that those ties constitute a sense of self, compose who we are, and that when we lose them, we lose our composure in some fundamental sense: we do not know who we are or what to do. Many people think that grief is privatizing, that it returns us to a solitary situation, but I think it exposes the constitutive sociality of the self, a basis for thinking a political community of a complex order.

It is not just that I might be said to "have" these relations, or that I might sit back and view them at a distance, enumerating them, explaining what this friendship means, what that lover meant or means to me. On the contrary, grief displays the way in which we are in the thrall of our relations with others that we cannot always recount or explain, that often interrupts the self-conscious account of ourselves we might try to provide in ways that challenge the very notion of ourselves as autonomous and in control. I might try to tell a story about what I am feeling, but it would have to be a story in which the very "I" who seeks to tell the story is stopped in the midst of the telling. The very "I" is called into question by its relation to the one to whom I address myself. This relation to the Other does not precisely ruin my story or reduce me to speechlessness, but it does, invariably, clutter my speech with signs of its undoing.

Let's face it. We're undone by each other. And if we're not, we're missing something. If this seems so clearly the case with grief, it is only because it was already the case with desire. One does not always stay intact. It may be that one wants to, or does, but it may also be that despite one's best efforts, one is undone, in the face of the other, by the touch, by the scent, by the feel, by the prospect of the touch, by the memory of the feel. And so when we speak about *my* sexuality or *my* gender, as we do (and as we must), we mean something complicated by it. Neither of these is precisely a possession, but both are to be understood as *modes of being dispossessed,* ways of being for another or, indeed, by virtue of another. It does not suffice to say that I am promoting a relational view of the self over an autonomous one, or trying to redescribe autonomy in terms of relationality. The term "relationality" sutures the rupture in the relation we seek to describe, a rupture that is constitutive of identity itself. This means that we will have to approach the problem of conceptualizing dispossession with circumspection. One way of doing this is through the notion of ecstasy.

We tend to narrate the history of the broader movement for sexual freedom in such a way that ecstasy figures in the 60s and 70s and persists midway through the 80s. But maybe ecstasy is more historically persistent than that, maybe it is with us all along. To be ec-static means, literally, to be outside oneself, and this can have several meanings: to be transported beyond oneself by a passion, but also to be *beside oneself* with rage or grief. I think that if I can still speak to a "we," and include myself within its terms, I am speaking to those of us who are living in certain ways *beside ourselves*, whether it is in sexual passion, or emotional grief, or political rage. In a sense, the predicament is to understand what kind of community is composed of those who are beside themselves.

We have an interesting political predicament, since most of the time when we hear about "rights," we understand them as pertaining to individuals, or when we argue for protection against discrimination, we argue as a group or a class. And in that language and in that context, we have to present ourselves as bounded beings, distinct, recognizable, delineated, subjects before the law, a community defined by sameness. Indeed, we had better be able to use that language to secure legal protections and entitlements. But perhaps we make a mistake if we take the definitions of who we are, legally, to be adequate descriptions of what we are about. Although this language might well establish our legitimacy within a legal framework ensconced in liberal versions of human ontology, it fails to do justice to passion and grief and rage, all of which tear us from ourselves, bind us to others, transport us, undo us, and implicate us in lives that are not our own, sometimes fatally, irreversibly.

It is not easy to understand how a political community is wrought from such ties. One speaks, and one speaks for another, to another, and yet there is no way to collapse the distinction between the other and myself. When we say "we" we do nothing more than designate this as very problematic. We do not solve it. And perhaps it is, and ought to be, insoluble. We ask that the state, for instance, keep its laws off our bodies, and we call for principles of bodily self-defense and bodily integrity to be accepted as political goods. Yet, it is through the body that gender and sexuality become exposed to others, implicated in social processes, inscribed by cultural norms, and apprehended in their social meanings. In a sense, to be a body is to be given over to others even as a body is, emphatically, "one's own," that over which we must claim rights of autonomy. This is as true for the claims made by lesbians, gays, and bisexuals in favor of sexual freedom as it is for transsexual and transgender claims to self-determination; as it is for intersex claims to be free of coerced medical, surgical, and psychiatric interventions; as it is for all claims to be free from racist attacks, physical and verbal; and as it is for feminism's claim to reproductive freedom. It is difficult, if not impossible, to make these claims without recourse to autonomy and, specifically, a sense of bodily autonomy. Bodily autonomy, however, is a lively paradox. I am not suggesting, though, that we cease to make these claims. We have to, we must. And I'm not saying that we have to make these claims reluctantly or strategically. They are part of the normative aspiration of any movement that seeks to maximize the protection and the freedoms of sexual and gender minorities, of women, defined with the broadest possible compass, of racial and ethnic minorities, especially as they cut across all the other categories. But is there another normative aspiration that we must also seek to articulate and to defend? Is there a way in which the place of the body in all of these struggles opens up a different conception of politics?

The body implies mortality, vulnerability, agency: the skin and the flesh expose us to the gaze of others but also to touch and to violence. The body can be the agency and instrument of all these as well, or the site where "doing" and "being done to" become equivocal. Although we struggle for rights over our own bodies, the very bodies for which we struggle are not quite ever only our own. The body has its invariably public dimension; constituted as a social phenomenon in the public sphere, my body is and is not mine. Given over from the start to the world of others, bearing their imprint, formed within the crucible of social life, the body is only later, and with some uncertainty, that to which I lay claim as my own. Indeed, if I seek to deny the fact that my body relates me — against my will and from the start — to others I do not choose to have in proximity to myself (the subway or the tube are excellent examples of this dimension of sociality), and if I build a notion of "autonomy" on the basis of the denial of this sphere or a primary and unwilled physical proximity with others, then do I precisely deny the social and political conditions of my embodiment in the name of autonomy? If I am struggling *for* autonomy, do I not need to be struggling for something else as well, a conception of myself as invariably in community, impressed upon by others, impressing them as well, and in ways that are not always clearly delineable, in forms that are not fully predictable?

Is there a way that we might struggle for autonomy in many spheres but also consider the demands that are imposed upon us by living in a world of beings who are, by definition, physically dependent on one another, physically vulnerable to one another? Is this not another way of imagining community in such a way that it becomes incumbent upon us to consider very carefully when and where we engage violence, for violence is, always, an exploitation of that primary tie, that primary way in which we are, as bodies, outside ourselves, for one another?

If we might then return to the problem of grief, to the moments in which one undergoes something outside of one's control and finds that one is beside oneself, not at one with oneself, we can say grief contains within it the possibility of apprehending the fundamental sociality of embodied life, the ways in which we are from the start, and by virtue of being a bodily being, already given over, beyond ourselves, implicated in lives that are not our own. Can this situation, one that is so dramatic for sexual minorities, one that establishes a very specific political perspective for anyone who works in the field of sexual and gender politics, supply a perspective with which to begin to apprehend the contemporary global situation?

Mourning, fear, anxiety, rage. In the United States after September 11, 2001, we have been everywhere surrounded with violence, of having perpetrated it, having suffered it, living in fear of it, planning more of it. Violence is surely a touch of the worst order, a way in which the human vulnerability to other humans is exposed in its most terrifying way, a way in which we are given over, without control, to the will of another, the way in which life itself can be expunged by the willful action of another. To the extent that we commit violence, we are acting upon another, putting others at risk, causing damage to others. In a way, we all live with this particular vulnerability, a vulnerability to the other that is part of bodily life, but this vulnerability becomes highly exacerbated under certain social and political conditions. Although the dominant mode in the United States has been to shore up sovereignty and security to minimize or, indeed, foreclose this vulnerability, it can serve another function and another ideal. The fact that our lives are dependent on others can become the basis of claims for nonmilitaristic political solutions, one which we cannot will away, one which we must attend to, even abide by, as we begin to think about what politics might be implied by staying with the thought of corporeal vulnerability itself.

Is there something to be gained from grieving, from tarrying with grief, remaining exposed to its apparent tolerability and not endeavoring to seek a resolution for grief through violence? Is there something to be gained in the political domain by maintaining grief as part of the framework by which we think our international ties? If we stay with the sense of loss, are we left feeling only passive and powerless, as some fear? Or are we, rather, returned to a sense of human vulnerability, to our collective responsibility for the physical lives of one another? The attempt to foreclose that vulnerability, to banish it, to make ourselves secure at the expense [of] every other human consideration, is surely also to eradicate one of the most important resources from which we must take our bearings and find our way.

To grieve, and to make grief itself into a resource for politics, is not to be resigned to a simple passivity or powerlessness. It is, rather, to allow oneself to extrapolate from this experience of vulnerability to the vulnerability that others suffer through military incursions, occupations, suddenly declared wars, and police brutality. That our very survival can be determined by those we do not know and over whom there is no final control means that life is precarious, and that politics must consider what forms of social and political organization seek best to sustain precarious lives across the globe.

There is a more general conception of the human at work here, one in which we are, from the start, given over to the other, one in which we are, from the start, even prior to individuation itself, and by virtue of our embodiment, given over to an other: this makes us vulnerable to violence, but also to another range of touch, a range that includes the eradication of our being at the one end, and the physical support for our lives, at the other.

We cannot endeavor to "rectify" this situation. And we cannot recover the source of this vulnerability, for it precedes the formation of "I." This condition of being laid bare from the start, dependent on those we do not know, is one with which we cannot precisely argue. We come into the world unknowing and dependent, and, to a certain degree, we remain that way. We can try, from the point of view of autonomy, to argue with this situation, but we are perhaps foolish, if not dangerous, when we do. Of course, we can say that for some this primary scene is extraordinary, loving, and receptive, a warm tissue of relations that support and nurture life in its infancy. For others, this is, however, a scene of abandonment or violence or starvation; they are bodies given over to nothing, or to brutality, or to no sustenance. No matter what the valence of that scene is, however, the fact remains that infancy constitutes a necessary dependency, one that we never fully leave behind. Bodies still must be apprehended as given over. Part of understanding the oppression of lives is precisely to understand that there is no way to argue away this condition of a primary vulnerability, of being given over to the touch of the other, even if, or precisely when, there is no other there, and no support for our lives. To counter oppression requires that one understand that lives are supported and maintained differentially, that there are radically different ways in which human physical vulnerability is distributed across the globe. Certain lives will be highly protected, and the abrogation of their claims to sanctity will be sufficient to mobilize the forces of war. And other lives will not find such fast and furious support and will not even qualify as "grievable."

What are the cultural contours of the notion of the human at work here? And how do the contours that we accept as the cultural frame for the human limit the extent to which we can avow loss as loss? This is surely a question that lesbian, gay, and bi-studies has asked in relation to violence against sexual minorities, and that transgendered people have asked as they have been singled out for harassment and sometimes murder, and that intersexed people have asked, whose formative years have so often been marked by an unwanted violence against their bodies in the name of a normative notion of human morphology. This is no doubt as well the basis of a profound affinity between movements centered on gender and sexuality with efforts to counter the normative human morphologies and capacities that condemn or efface those who are physically challenged. It must, as well, also be part of the affinity with antiracist struggles, given the racial differential that undergirds the culturally viable notions of the human — ones that we see acted out in dramatic and terrifying ways in the global arena at the present time.

So what is the relation between violence and what is "unreal," between violence and unreality that attends to those who become the victims of violence, and where does the notion of the ungrievable life come in? On the level of discourse, certain lives are not considered lives at all, they cannot be humanized; they fit no dominant frame for the human, and their dehumanization occurs first, at this level. This level then gives rise to a physical violence that in some sense delivers the message of dehumanization, which is already at work in the culture.

So it is not just that a discourse exists in which there is no frame and no story and no name for such a life, or that violence might be said to realize or apply this discourse. Violence against those who are already not quite lives, who are living in a state of suspension between life and death, leaves a mark that is no mark. If there is a discourse, it is a silent and melancholic writing in which there have been no lives, and no losses, there has been no common physical condition, no vulnerability that serves as the basis for an apprehension of our commonality, and there has been no sundering of that commonality. None of this takes place on the order of the event. None of this takes place. How many lives have been lost from AIDS in Africa in the last few years? Where are the media representations of this loss, the discursive elaborations of what these losses mean for communities there?

I began this chapter with a suggestion that perhaps the interrelated movements and modes of inquiry that collect here might need to consider autonomy as one dimension of their normative aspirations, one value to realize when we ask ourselves, in what direction ought we to proceed, and what kinds of values ought we to be realizing? I suggested as well that the way in which the body figures in gender and sexuality studies, and in the struggles for a less oppressive social world for the otherwise gendered and for sexual minorities of all kinds, is precisely to underscore the value of being beside oneself, of being a porous boundary, given over to others, finding oneself in a trajectory of desire in which one is taken out of oneself, and resituated irreversibly in a field of others in which one is not the presumptive center. The particular sociality that belongs to bodily life, to sexual life, and to becoming gendered (which is always, to a certain extent, becoming gendered *for others*) establishes a field of ethical enmeshment with others and a sense of disorientation for the first-person, that is, the perspective of the ego. As bodies, we are always for something more than, and other than, ourselves. To articulate this as an entitlement is not always easy, but perhaps not impossible. It suggests, for instance, that "association" is not a luxury, but one of the very conditions and prerogatives of freedom. Indeed, the kinds of associations we maintain importantly take many forms. It will not do to extol the marriage norm as the new ideal for this movement, as the Human Rights Campaign has erroneously done.[1] No doubt, marriage and same-sex domestic partnerships should certainly be available as options, but to install either as a model for sexual legitimacy is precisely to constrain the sociality of the body in acceptable ways. In light

> **AS BODIES, WE ARE ALWAYS FOR SOMETHING MORE THAN, AND OTHER THAN, OURSELVES.**

of seriously damaging judicial decisions against second parent adoptions in recent years, it is crucial to expand our notions of kinship beyond the heterosexual frame. It would be a mistake, however, to reduce kinship to family, or to assume that all sustaining community and friendship ties are extrapolations of kin relations.

I make the argument [elsewhere] . . . that kinship ties that bind persons to one another may well be no more or less than the intensification of community ties, may or may not be based on enduring or exclusive sexual relations, may well consist of ex-lovers, nonlovers, friends, and community members. The relations of kinship cross the boundaries between community and family and sometimes redefine the meaning of friendship as well. When these modes of intimate association produce sustaining webs of relationships, they constitute a "breakdown" of traditional kinship that displaces the presumption that biological and sexual relations structure kinship centrally. In addition, the incest taboo that governs kinship ties, producing a necessary exogamy, does not necessarily operate among friends in the same way or, for that matter, in networks of communities. Within these frames, sexuality is no longer exclusively regulated by the rules of kinship at the same time that the durable tie can be situated outside of the conjugal frame. Sexuality becomes open to a number of social articulations that do not always imply binding relations or conjugal ties. That not all of our relations last or are meant to, however, does not mean that we are immune to grief. On the contrary, sexuality outside the field of monogamy well may open us to a different sense of community, intensifying the question of where one finds enduring ties, and so become the condition for an attunement to losses that exceed a discretely private realm.

Nevertheless, those who live outside the conjugal frame or maintain modes of social organization for sexuality that are neither monogamous nor quasi-marital are more and more considered unreal, and their loves and losses less than "true" loves and "true" losses. The derealization of this domain of human intimacy and sociality works by denying reality and truth to the relations at issue.

The question of who and what is considered real and true is apparently a question of knowledge. But it is also, as Michel Foucault makes plain, a question of power. Having or bearing "truth" and "reality" is an enormously powerful prerogative within the social world, one way that power dissimulates as ontology. According to Foucault, one of the first tasks of a radical critique is to discern the relation "between mechanisms of coercion and elements of knowledge."[2] Here we are confronted with the limits of what is knowable, limits that exercise a certain force, but are not grounded in any necessity, limits that can only be read or interrogated by risking a certain security through departing from an established ontology: "[N]othing can exist as an element of knowledge if, on the one hand, it . . . does not conform to a set of rules and constraints characteristic, for example, of a given type of scientific discourse in a given period, and if, on the other hand, it does not possess the effects of coercion or simply the incentives peculiar to what is scientifically validated or simply rational or simply generally accepted, etc."[3] Knowledge and power are not finally separable but work together to establish a set of subtle and explicit criteria for thinking the world: "It is therefore not a matter of describing what knowledge is and what power is and how one would repress the other or how the other would abuse the one, but rather, a nexus of knowledge-power has to be described so that we can grasp what constitutes the acceptability of a system...."[4]

What this means is that one looks *both* for the conditions by which the object field is constituted, and for *the limits* of those conditions. The limits are to be found where the reproducibility of the conditions is not secure, the site where conditions are contingent, transformable. In Foucault's terms, "schematically speaking, we have perpetual mobility, essential fragility or rather the complex interplay between what replicates the same process and what transforms it."[5] To intervene in the name of transformation means precisely to disrupt what has become settled knowledge and knowable reality, and to use, as it were, one's unreality to make an otherwise impossible or illegible claim. I think that when the unreal lays claim to reality, or enters into its domain, something other than a simple assimilation into prevailing norms can and does take place. The norms themselves can become rattled, display their instability, and become open to resignification.

In recent years, the new gender politics has offered numerous challenges from transgendered and transsexual peoples to established feminist and lesbian/gay frameworks, and the intersex movement has rendered more complex the concerns and demands of sexual rights advocates. If some on the Left thought that these concerns were not properly or substantively political, they have been under pressure to rethink the political sphere in terms of its gendered and sexual presuppositions. The suggestion that butch, femme, and transgendered lives are not essential referents for a refashioning of political life, and for a more just and equitable society, fails to acknowledge the violence that the otherwise gendered suffer in the public world and fails as well to recognize that embodiment denotes a contested set of norms governing who will count as a viable subject within the sphere of politics. Indeed, if we consider that human bodies are not experienced without recourse to some ideality, some frame for experience itself, and that this is as true for the experience of one's own body as it is for experiencing another, and if we accept that that ideality and frame are socially articulated, we can see how it is that embodiment is not thinkable without a relation to a norm, or a set of norms. The struggle to rework the norms by which bodies are experienced is thus crucial not only to disability politics, but to the intersex and transgendered movements as they contest forcibly imposed ideals of what bodies ought to be like. The embodied relation to the norm exercises a transformative potential. To posit possibilities beyond the norm or, indeed, a different future for the norm itself, is part of the work of fantasy when we understand fantasy as taking the body as a point of departure for an articulation that is not always constrained by the body as it is. If we accept that altering these norms that decide normative human morphology gives differential "reality" to different kinds of humans as a result, then we are compelled to affirm that transgendered lives have a potential and actual impact on political life at its most fundamental level, that is, who counts as a human, and what norms govern the appearance of "real" humanness.

Moreover, fantasy is part of the articulation of the possible; it moves us beyond what is merely actual and present into a realm of possibility, the not yet actualized or the not actualizable. The struggle to survive is not really separable from the cultural life of fantasy, and the foreclosure of fantasy — through censorship, degradation, or other means — is one strategy for providing for the social death of persons. Fantasy is not the opposite of reality; it is what reality forecloses, and, as a result, it defines the limits of reality, constituting it as its constitutive outside. The critical promise of fantasy, when and where it exists, is to challenge the contingent limits of what will and will not be called reality. Fantasy is what allows us to imagine ourselves and others otherwise; it establishes the possible in excess of the real; it points elsewhere, and when it is embodied, it brings the elsewhere home.

How do drag, butch, femme, transgender, transsexual persons enter into the political field? They make us not only question what is real, and what "must" be, but they also show us how the norms that govern contemporary notions of reality can be questioned and how new modes of reality can become instituted. These practices of instituting new modes of reality take place in part through the scene of embodiment, where the body is not understood as a static and accomplished fact, but as an aging process, a mode of becoming that, in becoming otherwise, exceeds the norm, reworks the norm, and makes us see how realities to which we thought we were confined are not written in stone. Some people have asked me what is the use of increasing possibilities for gender. I tend to answer: Possibility is not a luxury; it is as crucial as bread. I think we should not underestimate what the thought of the possible does for those for whom the very issue of survival is most urgent. If the answer to the question, is life possible, is yes, that is surely something significant. It cannot, however, be taken for granted as the answer. That is a question whose answer is sometimes "no," or one that has no ready answer, or one that bespeaks an ongoing agony. For many who can and do answer the question in the affirmative, that answer is hard won, if won at all, an accomplishment that is fundamentally conditioned by reality being structured or restructured in such a way that the affirmation becomes possible.

One of the central tasks of lesbian and gay international rights is to assert in clear and public terms the reality of homosexuality, not as an inner truth, not as a sexual practice, but as one of the defining features of the social world in its very intelligibility. In other words, it is one thing to assert the reality of lesbian and gay lives as a reality, and to insist that these are lives worthy of protection in their specificity and commonality; but it is quite another to insist that the very public assertion of gayness calls into question what counts as reality and what counts as a human life. Indeed, the task of international lesbian and gay politics is no less than a remaking of reality, a reconstituting of the human, and a brokering of the question, what is and is not livable? So what is the injustice opposed by such work? I would put it this way: to be called unreal and to have that call, as it were, institutionalized as a form of differential treatment, is to become the other against whom (or against which) the human is made. It is the inhuman, the beyond the human, the less than human, the border that secures the human in its ostensible reality. To be called a copy, to be called unreal, is one way in which one can be oppressed, but consider that it is more fundamental than that. To be oppressed means that you already exist as a subject of some kind, you are there as the visible and oppressed other for the master subject, as a possible or potential subject, but to be unreal is something else again. To be oppressed you must first become intelligible. To find that you are fundamentally unintelligible (indeed, that the laws of culture and of language find you to be an impossibility) is to find that you have not yet achieved access to the human, to find yourself speaking only and always *as if you were* human, but with the sense that you are not, to find that your language is hollow, that no recognition is forthcoming because the norms by which recognition takes place are not in your favor.

We might think that the question of how one does one's gender is a merely cultural question, or an indulgence on the part of those who insist on exercising bourgeois freedom in excessive dimensions. To say, however, that gender is performative is not simply to insist on a right to produce a pleasurable and subversive spectacle but to allegorize the spectacular and consequential ways in which reality is both reproduced and contested. This has consequences for how gender presentations are criminalized and pathologized, how subjects who cross gender risk internment and imprisonment, why violence against transgendered subjects is not recognized as violence, and why this violence is sometimes inflicted by the very states that should be offering such subjects protection from violence.

What if new forms of gender are possible? How does this affect the ways that we live and the concrete needs of the human community? And how are we to distinguish between forms of gender possibility that are valuable and those that are not? I would say that it is not a question merely of producing a new future for genders that do not yet exist. The genders I have in mind have been in existence for a long time, but they have not been admitted into the terms that govern reality. So it is a question of developing within law, psychiatry, social, and literary theory a new legitimating lexicon for the gender complexity that we have been living for a long time. Because the norms governing reality have not admitted these forms to be real, we will, of necessity, call them "new."

What place does the thinking of the possible have within political theorizing? Is the problem that we have no norm to distinguish among kinds of possibility, or does that only appear to be a problem if we fail to comprehend "possibility" itself as a norm? Possibility is an aspiration, something we might hope will be equitably distributed, something that might be socially secured, something that cannot be taken for granted, especially if it is apprehended phenomenologically. The point is not to prescribe new gender norms, as if one were under an obligation to supply a measure, gauge, or norm for the adjudication of competing gender presentations. The normative aspiration at work here has to do with the ability to live and breathe and move and would no doubt belong somewhere in what is called a philosophy of freedom. The thought of a possible life is only an indulgence for those who already know themselves to be possible. For those who are still looking to become possible, possibility is a necessity.

It was Spinoza who claimed that every human being seeks to persist in his own being, and he made this principle of self-persistence, the *conatus,* into the basis of his ethics and, indeed, his politics. When Hegel made the claim that desire is always a desire for recognition, he was, in a way, extrapolating upon this Spinozistic point, telling us, effectively, that to persist in one's own being is only possible on the condition that we are engaged in receiving and offering recognition. If we are not recognizable, if there are no norms of recognition by which we are recognizable, then it is not possible to persist in one's own being, and we are not possible beings; we have been foreclosed from possibility. We think of norms of recognition perhaps as residing already in a cultural world into which we are born, but these norms change, and with the changes in these norms come changes in what does and does not count as recognizably human. To twist the Hegelian argument in a Foucaultian direction: norms of recognition function to produce and to deproduce the notion of the human. This is made true in a specific way when we consider how international norms work in the context of lesbian and gay human rights, especially as they insist that certain kinds of violences are impermissible, that certain lives are vulnerable and worthy of protection, that certain deaths are grievable and worthy of public recognition.

To say that the desire to persist in one's own being depends on norms of recognition is to say that the basis of one's autonomy, one's persistence as an "I" through time, depends fundamentally on a social norm that exceeds that "I," that positions that "I" ec-statically, outside of itself in a world of complex and historically changing norms. In effect, our lives, our very persistence, depend upon such norms or, at least, on the possibility that we will be able to negotiate within them, derive our agency from the field of their operation. In our very ability to persist, we are dependent on what is outside of us, on a broader sociality, and this dependency is the basis of our endurance and survivability. When we assert our "right," as we do and we must, we are not carving out a place for our autonomy — if by autonomy we mean a state of individuation, taken as self-persisting prior to and apart from any relations of dependency on the world of others. We do not negotiate with norms or with Others subsequent to our coming into the world. We come into the world on the condition that the social world is already there, laying the groundwork for us. This implies that I cannot persist without norms of recognition that support my persistence: the sense of possibility pertaining to me must first be imagined from some-where else before I can begin to imagine myself. My reflexivity is not only socially mediated, but socially constituted. I cannot be who I am without drawing upon the sociality of norms that precede and exceed me. In this sense, I am outside myself from the outset, and must be, in order to sur-vive, and in order to enter into the realm of the possible.

To assert sexual rights, then, takes on a specific meaning against this background. It means, for instance, that when we struggle for rights, we are not simply struggling for rights that attach to my person, but we are struggling *to be conceived as persons.* And there is a difference between the former and the latter. If we are struggling for rights that attach, or should attach, to my personhood, then we assume that per-sonhood as already constituted. But if we are struggling not only to be conceived as persons, but to create a social transformation of the very meaning of personhood, then the assertion of rights becomes a way of intervening into the social and political process by which the human is articulated. International human rights is always in the process of sub-jecting the human to redefinition and rene-gotiation. It mobilizes the human in the ser-vice of rights, but also rewrites the human and rearticulates the human when it comes up against the cultural limits of its work-ing conception of the human, as it does and must.

> **I CANNOT BE WHO I AM WITHOUT DRAWING UPON THE SOCIALITY OF NORMS THAT PRECEDE AND EXCEED ME.**

Lesbian and gay human rights takes sexuality, in some sense, to be its issue. Sexuality is not simply an attribute one has or a disposition or patterned set of inclinations. It is a mode of being disposed toward oth-ers, including in the mode of fantasy, and sometimes only in the mode of fantasy. If we are outside of ourselves as sexual beings, given over from the start, crafted in part through primary relations of dependency and attachment, then it would seem that our being beside ourselves, outside ourselves, is there as a function of sexuality itself, where sexu-ality is not this or that dimension of our existence, not the key or bedrock of our existence, but, rather, as coextensive with existence, as Merleau-Ponty once aptly suggested.[6]

I have tried here to argue that our very sense of personhood is linked to the desire for recognition, and that desire places us outside ourselves, in a realm of social norms that we do not fully choose, but that provides the horizon and the resource for any sense of choice that we have. *This means that the ec-static character of our existence is essential to the possi-bility of persisting as human.* In this sense, we can see how sexual rights brings together two related domains of ec-stasy, two connected ways of being outside of ourselves. As sexual, we are dependent on a world of oth-ers, vulnerable to need, violence, betrayal, compulsion, fantasy; we project desire, and we have it projected onto us. To be part of a sexual minority means, most emphatically, that we are also dependent on the protection of public and private spaces, on legal sanctions that protect us from violence, on safeguards of various institutional kinds against unwanted aggression imposed upon us, and the violent actions they sometimes instigate. In this sense, our very lives, and the persistence of our desire, depend on there being norms of recognition that produce and sustain our viability as human. Thus, when we speak about sexual rights, we are not merely talking about rights that pertain to our individual desires but to the norms on which our very individuality depends. That means that the discourse of rights avows our dependency, the mode of our being in the hands of others, a mode of being with and for others without which we cannot be.

I served for a few years on the board of the International Gay and Lesbian Human Rights Commission, a group that is located in San Francisco. It is part of a broad international coalition of groups and individuals who struggle to establish both equality and justice for sexual minorities, including transgender and intersexed individuals as well as persons with HIV or AIDS.[7] What astonished me time and again was how often the organization was asked to respond to immediate acts of violence against sexual minorities, especially when that violence was not redressed in any way by local police or government in various places in the globe. I had to reflect on what sort of anxiety is prompted by the public appearance of someone who is openly gay, or presumed to be gay, someone whose gender does not conform to norms, someone whose sexuality defies public prohibitions, someone whose body does not conform with certain morphological ideals. What motivates those who are driven to kill someone for being gay, to threaten to kill someone for being intersexed, or would be driven to kill because of the public appearance of someone who is transgendered?

The desire to kill someone, or killing someone, for not conforming to the gender norm by which a person is "supposed" to live suggests that life itself requires a set of sheltering norms, and that to be outside it, to live outside it, is to court death. The person who threatens violence proceeds from the anxious and rigid belief that a sense of world and a sense of self will be radically undermined if such a being, uncategorizable, is permitted to live within the social world. The negation, through violence, of that body is a vain and violent effort to restore order, to renew the social world on the basis of intelligible gender, and to refuse the challenge to rethink that world as something other than natural or necessary. This is not far removed from the threat of death, or the murder itself, of transsexuals in various countries, and of gay men who read as "feminine" or gay women who read as "masculine." These crimes are not always immediately recognized as criminal acts. Sometimes they are denounced by governments and international agencies; sometimes they are not included as legible or real crimes against humanity by those very institutions.

If we oppose this violence, then we oppose it in the name of what? What is the alternative to this violence, and for what transformation of the social world do I call? This violence emerges from a profound desire to keep the order of binary gender natural or necessary, to make of it a structure, either natural or cultural, or both, that no human can oppose, and still remain human. If a person opposes norms of binary gender not just by having a critical point of view about them, but by incorporating norms critically, and that stylized opposition is legible, then it seems that violence emerges precisely as the demand to undo that legibility, to question its possibility, to render it unreal and impossible in the face of its appearance to the contrary. This is, then, no simple difference in points of view. To counter that embodied opposition by violence is to say, effectively, that this body, this challenge to an accepted version of the world is and shall be unthinkable. The effort to enforce the boundaries of what will be regarded as real requires stalling what is contingent, frail, open to fundamental transformation in the gendered order of things.

An ethical query emerges in light of such an analysis: how might we encounter the difference that calls our grids of intelligibility into question without trying to foreclose the challenge that the difference delivers? What might it mean to learn to live in the anxiety of that challenge, to feel the surety of one's epistemological and ontological anchor go, but to be willing, in the name of the human, to allow the human to become something other than what it is traditionally assumed to be? This means that we must learn to live and to embrace the destruction and rearticulation of the human in the name of a more capacious and, finally, less violent world, not knowing in advance what precise form our humanness does and will take. It means we must be open to its permutations, in the name of nonviolence. As Adriana Cavarero points out, paraphrasing Arendt, the question we pose to the Other is simple and unanswerable: "who are you?"[8] The violent response is the one that does not ask, and does not seek to know. It wants to shore up what it knows, to expunge what threatens it with not-knowing, what forces it to reconsider the presuppositions of its world, their contingency, their malleability. The nonviolent response lives with its unknowingness about the Other in the face of the Other, since sustaining the bond that the question opens is finally more valuable than knowing in advance what holds us in common, as if we already have all the resources we need to know what defines the human, what its future life might be.

That we cannot predict or control what permutations of the human might arise does not mean that we must value all possible permutations of the human; it does not mean that we cannot struggle for the realization of certain values, democratic and nonviolent, international and antiracist. The point is only that to struggle for those values is precisely to avow that one's own position is not sufficient to elaborate the spectrum of the human, that one must enter into a collective work in which one's own status as a subject must, for democratic reasons, become disoriented, exposed to what it does not know.

The point is not to apply social norms to lived social instances, to order and define them (as Foucault has criticized), nor is it to find justificatory mechanisms for the grounding of social norms that are extrasocial (even as they operate under the name of the social). There are times when both of these activities do and must take place: we level judgments against criminals for illegal acts, and so subject them to a normalizing procedure; we consider our grounds for action in collective contexts and try to find modes of deliberation and reflection about which we can agree. But neither of these is all we do with norms. Through recourse to norms, the sphere of the humanly intelligible is circumscribed, and this circumscription is consequential for any ethics and any conception of social transformation. We might try to claim that we must *first* know the fundamentals of the human in order to preserve and promote human life as we know it. But what if the very categories of the human have excluded those who should be described and sheltered within its terms? What if those who ought to belong to the human do not operate within the modes of reasoning and justifying validity claims that have been proffered by western forms of rationalism? Have we ever yet known the human? And what might it take to approach that knowing? Should we be wary of knowing it too soon or of any final or definitive knowing? If we take the field of the human for granted, then we fail to think critically and ethically about the consequential ways that the human is being produced, reproduced, and deproduced. This latter inquiry does not exhaust the field of ethics, but I cannot imagine a responsible ethics or theory of social transformation operating without it.

The necessity of keeping our notion of the human open to a future articulation is essential to the project of international human rights discourse and politics. We see this time and again when the very notion of the human is presupposed; the human is defined in advance, in terms that are distinctively western, very often American, and, therefore, partial and parochial. When we start with the human as a foundation, then the human at issue in human rights is already known, already defined. And yet, the human is supposed to be the ground for a set of rights and obligations that are global in reach. How we move from the local to the international (conceived globally in such a way that it does not recirculate the presumption that all humans belong to established nation-states) is a major question for international politics, but it takes a specific form for international lesbian, gay, bi-, trans-, and intersex struggles as well as for feminism. An anti-imperialist or, minimally, nonimperialist conception of international human rights must call into question what is meant by the human and learn from the various ways and means by which it is defined across cultural venues. This means that local conceptions of what is human or, indeed, of what the basic conditions and needs of human life are, must be subjected to reinterpretation, since there are historical and cultural circumstances in which the human is defined differently. Its basic needs and, hence, basic entitlements are made known through various media, through various kinds of practices, spoken and performed.

A reductive relativism would say that we cannot speak of the human or of international human rights, since there are only and always local and provisional understandings of these terms, and that the generalizations themselves do violence to the specificity of the meanings in question. This is not my view. I'm not ready to rest there. Indeed, I think we are compelled to speak of the human, and of the international, and to find out in particular how human rights do and do not work, for example, in favor of women, of what women are, and what they are not. But to speak in this way, and to call for social transformations in the name of women, we must also be part of a critical democratic project. Moreover, the category of women has been used differentially and with exclusionary aims, and not all women have been included within its terms; women have not been fully incorporated into the human. Both categories are still in process, underway, unfulfilled, thus we do not yet know and cannot ever definitively know in what the human finally consists. This means that we must follow a double path in politics: we must use this language to assert an entitlement to conditions of life in ways that affirm the constitutive role of sexuality and gender in political life, and we must also subject our very categories to critical scrutiny. We must find out the limits of their inclusivity and translatability, the presuppositions they include, the ways in which they must be expanded, destroyed, or reworked both to encompass and open up what it is to be human and gendered. When the United Nations conference at Beijing met a few years ago, there was a discourse on "women's human rights" (or when we hear of the International Gay and Lesbian Human Rights Commission), which strikes many people as a paradox. Women's human rights? Lesbian and gay human rights? But think about what this coupling actually does. It performs the human as contingent, a category that has in the past, and continues in the present, to define a variable and restricted population, which may or may not include lesbians and gays, may or may not include women, which has several racial and ethnic differentials at work in its operation. It says that such groups have their own set of human rights, that what human may mean when we think about the humanness of women is perhaps different from what human has meant when it has functioned as presumptively male. It also says that these terms are defined, variably, in relation to one another. And we could certainly make a similar argument about race. Which populations have qualified as the human and which have not? What is the history of this category? Where are we in its history at this time?

I would suggest that in this last process, we can only rearticulate or resignify the basic categories of ontology, of being human, of being gendered, of being recognizably sexual, to the extent that we submit ourselves to a process of cultural translation. The point is not to assimilate foreign or unfamiliar notions of gender or humanness into our own as if it is simply a matter of incorporating alienness into an established lexicon. Cultural translation is also a process of yielding our most fundamental categories, that is, seeing how and why they break up, require resignification when they encounter the limits of an available episteme: what is unknown or not yet known. It is crucial to recognize that the notion of the human will only be built over time in and by the process of cultural translation, where it is not a translation between two languages that stay enclosed, distinct, unified. But rather, *translation will compel each language to change in order to apprehend the other,* and this apprehension, at the limit of what is familiar, parochial, and already known, will be the occasion for both an ethical and social transformation. It will constitute a loss, a disorientation, but one in which the human stands a chance of coming into being anew.

When we ask what makes a life livable, we are asking about certain normative conditions that must be fulfilled for life to become life. And so there are at least two senses of life, the one that refers to the minimum biological form of living, and another that intervenes at the start, which establishes minimum conditions for a livable life with regard to human life.[9] And this does not imply that we can disregard the merely living in favor of the livable life, but that we must ask, as we asked about gender violence, what humans require in order to maintain and reproduce the conditions of their own livability. And what are our politics such that we are, in whatever way is possible, both conceptualizing the possibility of the livable life, and arranging for its institutional support? There will always be disagreement about what this means, and those who claim that a single political direction is necessitated by virtue of this commitment will be mistaken. But this is only because to live is to live a life politically, in relation to power, in relation to others, in the act of assuming responsibility for a collective future. To assume responsibility for a future, however, is not to know its direction fully in advance, since the future, especially the future with and for others, requires a certain openness and unknowingness; it implies becoming part of a process the outcome of which no one subject can surely predict. It also implies that a certain agonism and contestation over the course of direction will and must be in play. Contestation must be in play for politics to become democratic. Democracy does not speak in unison; its tunes are dissonant, and necessarily so. It is not a predictable process; it must be undergone, like a passion must be undergone. It may also be that life itself becomes foreclosed when the right way is decided in advance, when we impose what is right for everyone and without finding a way to enter into community, and to discover there the "right" in the midst of cultural translation. It may be that what is right and what is good consist in staying open to the tensions that beset the most fundamental categories we require, in knowing unknowingness at the core of what we know, and what we need, and in recognizing the sign of life in what we undergo without certainty about what will come.

NOTES

[1] The Human Rights Campaign is the main lobbying organization for lesbian and gay rights in the United States. Situated in Washington, D.C., it has maintained that gay marriage is the number one priority of lesbian and gay politics in the U.S. See www.hrc.org. [All notes are Butler's.]

[2] Michel Foucault, "What Is Critique?" in *The Politics of Truth,* 50. This essay is reprinted with an essay by me entitled "Critique as Virtue" in David Ingram, *The Political.*

[3] "What Is Critique?" 52.

[4] Ibid., 52–53.

[5] Ibid., 58.

[6] Maurice Merleau-Ponty, *The Phenomenology of Perception.*

[7] See www.iglhrc.org for more information on the mission and accomplishments of this organization.

[8] See Adriana Cavarero, *Relating Narratives,* 20–29 and 87–92.

[9] See Giorgio Agamben, *Homo Sacer: Sovereign Power and Bare Life,* 1–12.

BIBLIOGRAPHY

Agamben, Giorgio. *Homo Sacer: Sovereign Power and Bare Life.* Translated by Daniel Heller-Roazen. Stanford: Stanford University Press, 1998.

Cavarero, Adriana. *Relating Narratives: Storytelling and Selfhood.* Translated by Paul A. Kottman. London: Routledge, 2000.

Foucault, Michel. "What Is Critique?" *The Politics of Truth,* edited by Sylvere Lotringer and Lysa Hochroth. New York: Semiotext(e), 1997.

Ingram, David. *The Political.* San Francisco: Wiley-Blackwell, 2002.

Merleau-Ponty, Maurice. "The Body in Its Sexual Being." *The Phenomenology of Perception.* Translated by Colin Smith. New York: Routledge, 1967.

• • • ● ● ● • •

QUESTIONS FOR A SECOND READING

1. Butler's "Beside Oneself: On the Limits of Sexual Autonomy" is a philosophical essay, and one of the difficulties it presents to a reader is its emphasis on conceptual language. The sentences most often refer to concepts or ideas rather than to people, places, or events in the concrete, tangible, or observable world. It refers to the *human* or to the *body*, but without telling the stories of particular humans or particular bodies. And this can be frustrating. Without something concrete, without some situation or context in which the conceptual can take shape, these conceptual terms can lose their force or meaning. (If there is a story here, it is the story of a struggle to understand and to articulate a response to the essay's opening question: What makes for a livable world?)

   As you reread Butler, pay attention to the conceptual terms that recur. Words like *ethics, power, life, grief, agency,* and *possibility* punctuate this essay, and it is through these key terms that Butler attempts to describe and theorize the world we live in. Pick one of these terms (or one of your own choosing) and pay particular attention to the ways it is used. How is it defined in its initial context? Beyond its dictionary definition, what does this particular term come to mean for Butler? for you as a reader? And how is its meaning elaborated or consolidated or complicated by its uses later in the text?

2. At one point Butler says, "I might try to tell a story about what I am feeling, but it would have to be a story in which the very 'I' who seeks to tell the story is stopped in the midst of the telling. The very 'I' is called into question by its relation to the one to whom I address myself" (p. 239).

   As you reread, pay attention to personal pronouns, such as "I," "we," "one," "you," "our," "my," and "your." In an essay about how we are "constituted," the struggle to claim identity in relation to others is played out in the arena of the sentence. Choose a paragraph where the play of personal pronouns is particularly odd or rich, and be prepared to describe what Butler is doing. And be prepared to think out loud (or to think on the page) about the relationship between what the writer is doing (the deed of writing) and what the paragraph says.

3. Butler writes in the field of Queer Theory. Queer theorists are concerned with queer lives, queer writing, and the study of gender and sexuality. In "Beside Oneself: On the Limits of Sexual Autonomy," Butler raises questions about the visibility, intelligibility, and recognition of gays and lesbians and also about the lives of those who may not conform to any fixed or binary gender norms. She writes:

> To find that you are fundamentally unintelligible (indeed, that the laws of culture and of language find you to be an impossibility) is to find that you have not yet achieved access to the human, to find yourself speaking only and always *as if you were* human, but with the sense that you are not, to find that your language is hollow, that no recognition is forthcoming because the norms by which recognition takes place are not in your favor. (p. 248)

This is a long sentence, and a complicated one. Butler knows this; she knows that it will be difficult for a reader, so she provides what help she can with the parenthetical phrase and the italics. It is useful, as Butler's reader, to practice reading and rereading her sentences, to unfold them slowly, word by word. What does it mean to be "unintelligible"? Why might being unintelligible also mean not having "access to the human" or having a "hollow" language? What examples can you think of that might help someone better understand Butler's claim about gender and sexuality? And, finally, what seems to be at stake in making this claim?

As an exercise in reading and in understanding, write a paraphrase, a translation of this sentence (or a Butler sentence of your own choosing). And in the sentence or sentences of your paraphrase, imitate Butler's rhythm and style.

4. The opening lines of Butler's essay might be understood as an invitation to participate with her in one of the traditions of philosophy. She writes:

> What makes for a livable world is no idle question. It is not merely a question for philosophers. It is posed in various idioms all the time by people in various walks of life. If that makes them all philosophers, then that is a conclusion I am happy to embrace. (p. 238)

Stylistically, Butler makes use of questions as a way of enacting philosophical inquiry. As you reread, pay attention to Butler's questions and, through these, to the method and the rhythm of philosophical inquiry. How would you describe the use, placement, and pacing of her questions? How does one question seem to lead to another? Where do they come from? How do they work together to make an argument?

• • ● • •

ASSIGNMENTS FOR WRITING

1.   The opening lines of Butler's essay might be understood as an invitation to participate with her in one of the traditions of philosophy. She writes:

> What makes for a livable world is no idle question. It is not merely a question for philosophers. It is posed in various idioms all the time by people in various walks of life. If that makes them all philosophers, then that is a conclusion I am happy to embrace. It becomes a question for ethics, I think, not only when we ask the personal question, what makes my own life bearable, but when we ask, from a position of power, and from the point of view of distributive justice, what makes, or ought to make, the lives of others bearable? Somewhere in the answer we find ourselves not only committed to a certain view of what life is, and what it should be, but also of what constitutes the human, the distinctively human life, and what does not. (p. 238)

Write an essay that takes up this invitation — and that takes it up in specific reference to what Butler has offered in "Beside Oneself: On the Limits of Sexual Autonomy." You will need, then, to take some time to represent her essay — both what it says and what it does. The "Questions for a Second Reading" should be helpful in preparing for this. Imagine an audience of smart people, people who may even know something about Butler but who have not read this essay. You have read it, and you want to give them a sense of how and why you find it interesting and important. But you'll also need to take time to address her questions in your own terms: What makes for a livable world? What constitutes the human? Don't slight this part of your essay. Give yourself as many pages as you gave Butler. You should, however, make it clear that you are writing in response to what you have read. You'll want to indicate, both directly and indirectly, how your thoughts are shaped by, indebted to, or in response to hers.

2.   Consider the following passage from Butler's "Beside Oneself: On the Limits of Sexual Autonomy":

> To be ec-static means, literally, to be outside oneself, and this can have several meanings: to be transported beyond oneself by a passion, but also to be *beside oneself* with rage or grief. I think that if I can still speak to a "we," and include myself within its terms, I am speaking to those of us who are living in certain ways *beside ourselves*, whether it is in sexual passion, or emotional grief, or political rage. In a sense, the predicament is to understand what kind of community is composed of those who are beside themselves. (p. 240)

To be *beside oneself* is an idiomatic phrase — which suggests that the meaning of the phrase cannot be determined literally but rather has some figurative connotation. In this sense, for someone not familiar with the idiom, the phrase might even be misleading or misunderstood. Butler takes this idiomatic phrase to its theoretical and social conclusions, thinking carefully about what exactly the figurative expression means to say, what it wants us to say, how it has been used, and how it might be made to serve as a fresh tool for thinking. This is a bold project, and one that takes both a critical eye and creative thought.

We might think of all idiomatic expressions as carrying important social, political, and emotional meanings that, while they might not always be visible on the surface or in everyday conversation, propose a way of thinking: *Blood is thicker than water. I was out of my mind. He is out of touch. She has gone out on a limb. It is all water under the bridge.* For this assignment, write an essay that takes up a particular idiomatic phrase as a tool for thinking through an issue that is important to you. Choose carefully — both the issue and the idiom. There should be an urgency in your writing, as there is in Butler's. And, to locate your essay as a reading of Butler, the urgency should be similarly thoughtful and modulated. You are offering your essay as a response to hers, as a similar exercise in thinking.

· • ● ● ● · ·

MAKING CONNECTIONS

1. At a key point in her essay, Butler refers to the work of Michel Foucault:

> The question of who and what is considered real and true is apparently a question of knowledge. But it is also, as Michel Foucault makes plain, a question of power. Having or bearing "truth" and "reality" is an enormously powerful prerogative within the social world, one way that power dissimulates as ontology. According to Foucault, one of the first tasks of a radical critique is to discern the relation "between mechanisms of coercion and elements of knowledge." (p. 245)

And she goes on for some length to work with passages from Foucault, although not from his book *Discipline and Punish*. One of its chapters, "Panopticism," is a selection in *Ways of Reading* (p. 328). Take some time to reread Butler's essay, paying particular attention to her use of Foucault. Where and why is Foucault helpful to her? In what ways is she providing a new argument or a counterargument? And take time to reread "Panopticism." What passages might be useful in extending or challenging Butler's argument in "Beside Oneself"? Using these two sources, write an essay in which you talk about Butler and Foucault and their engagement with what might be called "radical critique," an effort (in the terms offered above) to "discern the relation 'between mechanisms of coercion and elements of knowledge.'"

Note: The assignment limits you to these two sources, the two selections in the textbook. Butler and Foucault have written much, and their work circulates widely. You are most likely not in a position to speak about every-thing they have written or about all that has been written about them. We wanted to define a starting point that was manageable. Still, if you want to do more research, you might begin by reading the Foucault essay that Butler cites, "What Is Critique?"; you might go to the library to look through books by Butler and Foucault, choosing one or two that seem to offer themselves as next steps; or you could go to essays written by scholars who, like you, are trying to think about the two together.

2. In his essay "States" (p. 559), Edward Said theorizes about the notion of exile in relation to Palestinian identity, offering a study of exile and dislocation through his analysis of photographs taken by Jean Mohr. Consider the fol-lowing passage:

> We turn ourselves into objects not for sale, but for scrutiny. People ask us, as if looking into an exhibit case, "What is it you Palestinians want?" — as if we can put our demands into a single neat phrase. All of us speak of *awdah*, "return," but do we mean that literally, or do we mean "we must restore ourselves to ourselves"? (p. 578)

When Said talks about being looked at as though in an exhibit case, we might understand him as being concerned with the problem of dehuman-ization. After all, to be in an exhibit case is to be captured, trapped, or even dead. We might understand Butler as also wrestling with the problem of dehumanization; she writes: "I would like to start, and to end, with the ques-tion of the human, of who counts as the human, and the related question of whose lives count as lives, and with a question that has preoccupied many of us for years: what makes for a grievable life?" (p. 238).

Write an essay in which you consider the ways Said and Butler might be said to be speaking with each other. How might the condition of exile be like the condition of being *beside oneself*? What kind of connections — whether you see them as productive or problematic, or both at once — can be made between the ways Said talks about nation, identity, and home, and the ways Butler talks about gender and sexuality? What passages from each seem to have the other in mind? How does each struggle with reference, with pro-nouns like "we" and "our"?

3. Richard E. Miller, in "The Dark Night of the Soul" (p. 435), asks a simple and disturbing question. Institutions of higher education teach, and have taught, the "literate arts," reading and writing, always with the assumption that they improve our lives and make us better as human beings. But do they? Miller asks, "Is there any way to justify or explain a life spent working with — and teaching others to work with — texts?" (p. 439).

Miller's essay is divided into sections; most sections consider a particular text: Krakauer's *Into the Wild*, Descartes's *Meditations*, Mary Karr's *The Liar's*

Club. Reread Miller in order to get a sense of his argument, style, and method, and then write a section that could be added to "The Dark Night of the Soul" with Butler's "Beside Oneself" as its subject. You could talk about your reading of the text — and what it has to offer. You could talk about its use, as represented in this textbook, in your class, or in the writing of your colleagues. You might also talk about where you might insert your entry into the essay "The Dark Night of the Soul."

Joy Castro

JOY
Castro

Joy Castro was born in Miami, Florida, in 1967. She writes nonfiction as well as poetry and short fiction. She is currently a full professor at the University of Nebraska–Lincoln, where she teaches creative writing and literature in the department of English and serves as the director of the Institute for Ethnic Studies. Castro has authored two memoirs, *The Truth Book: Escaping a Childhood of Abuse among Jehovah's Witnesses* (2005) and *Island of Bones* (2012), a collection of essays — two of which we reprint here. Castro has also written two novels, *Hell or High Water* (2012) and *Nearer Home* (2013), and, most recently, a short story collection, *How Winter Began* (2015). She has been a visiting writer at numerous institutions and has given talks, readings, lectures, and workshops across the country. Her writing has won the International Latino Book Award and the Nebraska Book Award and has been selected as a finalist for the PEN Center USA Literary Award.

Author Sandra Cisneros writes that "Joy Castro's writing is like watching an Acapulco cliff diver. It takes my breath away." Aaron Westerman declares that "there's nothing even remotely safe about Joy Castro's writing. You may be emotionally harmed by these stories. You will be changed by them. That's their purpose. That's her gift."

Castro often chooses to reflect on issues that affect her personally and affect all of us culturally and politically, yet she maintains intellectual curiosity and quiet attentiveness in the face of social injustice and outright antagonism. Castro is best

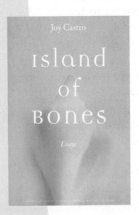

Joy Castro

island
of
Bones

Essays

known for her memoir *The Truth Book*. This memoir details her childhood experiences with her abusive stepfather and the church of Jehovah's Witnesses. In an interview for the *Los Angeles Review of Books*, Castro says she has "always been plagued by a tendency toward extreme alertness and openness to sensation, to intensity — to exploring without judgment." Interviewer Alex Espinoza remarks that "confronting hard truths is something author Joy Castro does especially well."

The pieces that follow deal with Castro's experiences as a first-generation college student. Even as she addresses the inadequacies and prejudices of "the academy," Castro's passion for education and learning is fully palpable throughout. Her work is imbued with social imperative.

Hungry

I came to college hungry.

"The kids look like they're in a concentration camp," a mutual friend told our father, who lived in another part of the state and had failed to get custody. During the late years of my childhood, literal starvation had been both a punishment and a way of life, enforced by our abusive Jehovah's Witness stepfather and mother. Gaunt, malnourished, beaten, suffering from the lack of medical and dental care, my brother and I rattled around our classrooms, the school bus, the Kingdom Hall, and no one intervened. At fourteen, I ran away from that trailer, and with the police, the courts, and my father's help, we got my little brother out. For two more years, I lived with my father and his wife, devouring tuna, wheat bread, peanut butter, putting on weight, putting on the clothes they bought for me in bulk at the outlet store, since I'd run away with nothing.

With time, I began to pass for normal. I was the only Latina I knew at my West Virginia high school, but with my pale skin and dark hair and eyes, I looked like just another Italian American, a descendant of those waves of immigrants who'd come to work the mountains' coal mines. Some of my high-school friends went into the mines themselves. Some joined the military. By graduation, many of the girls were engaged.

I came to college hungry for knowledge, for experience.

Jehovah's Witnesses don't believe in evolution, don't participate in politics, don't celebrate any of the myriad Judeo-Christian traditional holidays that brighten most people's lives in the United States: birthdays, Christmas, Chanukah, Easter, Thanksgiving. Intellectually, I was nearly a blank slate, and eager to fill in the gaps, but Jehovah's Witnesses don't believe that college is necessary, and my mother had always forbidden me to dream of it. For me, she envisioned only a good, virginal marriage in the Kingdom Hall and a life of stay-at-home motherhood, of scripture and subservience, of knowing my place and keeping it. In return, I'd be rewarded — eventually — with eternal life on a perfect paradise earth, unburdened by racial injustice, poverty, environmental degradation, or war.

It was the same promise that had lured my Cuban American grandmother away from Catholicism when a Jehovah's Witness climbed the steps of her front porch long ago. A Key West housewife with a seventh-grade education, raising five children and caring for more, my *abuela* chose an idealized vision of this life, this earth — and for her children: peace, justice, and plenty. She died clinging to that dream.

I have not kept my place. Like my mother and grandmother, I chose the earth — but the real earth, complicated and torn, not a post-Armageddon fantasy purveyed by a global religious organization with its own political and financial ends. I chose education, although, growing up, I knew no one who had graduated from college, aside from my schoolteachers and, briefly, my father's lawyer. My parents had only their high school diplomas. None of my relatives and none of my parents' friends had been to college. It was a mysterious, forbidden world, which is perhaps why I wanted it so badly. I chose worldly knowledge and worldly pleasures — and, since my father believed you didn't need a college education, much less graduate school, I did it at my own expense, with generous scholarships, tedious jobs, and enormous loans.

This labor and debt often set me apart from my friends at the groomed green campus of the elite university in Texas that I attended, a school that liked to be called the Harvard of the South and was renowned for golf and tennis — rich people's sports, games I couldn't play. There were no Latina sororities at my university then, and the sororities that did exist seemed stocked with a breed of weird, beautiful aliens. I couldn't relate. I hung out mostly with other scholarship kids, but even they tended to come from comfortable middle-class homes.

When I became pregnant at twenty, the baby's father and I moved into a two-hundred-dollar-a-month apartment in a predominantly Mexican American barrio. My college friends stopped coming around. Most of them who entered my new neighborhood did so only to buy drugs.

But while the area had its problems with crime — the drugs, the wooden houses lit ablaze, the occasional gunshot — there were things about it that I liked. The landlord had my brother's name, and I liked the alleys where women in dusty backyards trimmed their husbands' hair. I liked our sweet neighbors Meiyo and Yoli, finding myself more at ease with them than with my college peers who drove Volvos and Mercedes and went to Vail for spring break. I liked lugging the baby on one hip and the laundry on the other down the rickety wooden stairs and across the street to the open-air laundromat — just a couple of washers and dryers in a guy's carport — and chatting in my battered Spanglish with the other mamas. The crime did scare me, true — but I felt sort of at home.

Yet I felt sort of at home, too, in the seminar rooms at the university, arguing about the politics of texts, or doing research in the library. My mind felt like it was finally stretching and working in the way it was born to work. Though my professors did not, in the 1980s, offer courses on Latina/o literature or women's literature or working-class literature, I could still use the skills I learned to analyze the literature

MY MIND FELT LIKE IT WAS FINALLY STRETCHING AND WORKING IN THE WAY IT WAS BORN TO WORK.

of my own choosing. I rode the bus back and forth between the manicured campus and my shabby street, confused but happy.

Two homes. Sort of. As Latinas in higher education, we don't have to make an either-or choice about what we want or who we will become. We can choose to be both-and. Our challenge is finding and balancing the right ingredients: the ones that nourish us, the ones that taste right.

Today I am a professor with a joint appointment in English and ethnic studies. I teach Latina/o literature, Latina/o studies, women's literature, and creative writing, and I move with comfort and pleasure between my two departments. The student body at the university in Nebraska where I teach is over 90 percent non-Hispanic white, but I'm okay with that. I'm used to it, and I can be useful here, sharing texts, ideas, and perspectives with students who wouldn't otherwise encounter them — and nurturing and mentoring with special pride those Latino and Latina students who do make it through the door. I can help make college a place where they can envision themselves, a place where they, too, can feel at home. I can help recruit them and tell them the truth about the hard parts as well as the rewards.

I went to college at sixteen, hungry for so many things. Now in my forties, I have tasted so much. So much has nourished me. And I am still hungry, still learning.

On Becoming Educated

In graduate school in the 1990s, I am introduced to a feminist professor of law. We're in a bagel shop. It's sunny. Wiry, with cropped sandy hair and glasses, she looks exactly like my nascent concept of a feminist.

She's working on an article about a little-known provision in the Violence Against Women Act, which President Clinton has just signed into law. The new legislation makes employers responsible for providing workplace protection for women whose partners have threatened them with violence. In the past, violent men had ignored restraining orders to assault and even kill women at their workplaces. This new legislation requires employers, if notified that a targeted woman is in their employ, to provide appropriate security rather than leaving it to the individual woman to defend herself.

I know about men who hurt women.

This is marvelous, I tell the professor. Her article will help protect thousands of women — hundreds of thousands, maybe. I think of my mother, my friend Cindy, my neighbor Diana. Battering happens in every stratum of society, but under the poverty level, domestic violence increases by a factor of five. In the trailer park and barrio and rural towns where I've lived, I've seen my share.

But the professor grimaces and shakes her head. Her article, she explains, is for a law journal, an academic journal. Only other scholars will read it.

But since this new legislative provision isn't widely known, I suggest she could write an article for a mass-market women's magazine, one that will reach millions of woman. Not *Ms.*, which is hard to find, but the kind of magazine available at drugstores and supermarkets, the kind that sits in stacks at inexpensive beauty salons, *Cosmopolitan* or *Redbook*; the kind that reaches ordinary women, women who might be getting beaten. She could save actual women's lives.

Her face wrinkles. That's not the kind of article she writes, she explains with exaggerated patience. Someone else will do that, eventually. A writer who does commercial, popular articles for a general audience.

Her own work, she says, will trickle down.

I take a graduate course in feminist theory. Our professor, educated at one of the world's most prestigious universities, is intimidatingly brilliant in the seminar she runs like a Socratic inquisition one evening a week. I admire her; I like her; I want to be her — but as the semester winds on, my eagerness dissipates because I don't understand Toril Moi or Luce Irigaray or any of the feminists (after Virginia Woolf) whose work we're reading.

I'm a first-generation college student, here by fluke on fellowship, and the theorists' English seems foreign to me, filled with jargon and abstractions at which I can only guess. They say nothing about wife-beating or rape or unequal wages or child molesting, which is the charge that finally got my stepfather sent to prison. They say nothing about being a single mother on ten thousand dollars a year, which is my own situation. The feminist writers respond to male theorists — Lacan, Derrida — whose work I haven't read. I can't parse their sentences or recognize their allusions, and I don't know what they mean or how they're helpful to the strippers and dropouts and waitresses I know, the women I care about the most, to my aunt Lettie who worked the register at Winn-Dixie and my aunt Linda who cleaned houses.

It's true that the complexity and jargon are alluring, like another country, safe and leisured, with a strange, beautiful language that means only abstract things, where a dozen bright young women and their interlocutor can spend three hours conversing around a big table in a comfortable, air-conditioned room that looks like a corporate boardroom in a movie. But I climb the stairs each week in grim frustration.

bell hooks's piece "Out of the Academy and Into the Streets" appears in *Ms.*, and I'm relieved that someone has expressed the inchoate things rumbling inside me. I make photocopies and take it to my professor, asking if we could please read and discuss it in class. She takes the copies and says she'll see.

One evening, our discussion has strayed to Stephen Greenblatt, who, I'll learn later, is the paradigm-shifting Renaissance scholar who initiated New Historicism, a scholarly approach to literary texts. At the time, I know none of this; he's just another male name. I have no context, but the professor and some of the older students seem to have read his work, perhaps in other classes. The professor is intense, lively. She presses her fist to the seminar table. "How do we, as feminist theorists, *respond* to Stephen Greenblatt?"

"What if we don't respond?" I say in frustration. "What if we just keep working on issues that are focused on actual women, issues we actually care about?"

Her eyes are wide. "You can't just *ignore* Stephen Greenblatt," she says. The oldest graduate student, the smart one I admire, shakes her head and smiles faintly.

I disengage. At the end of the term, I write my paper on Woolf's *A Room of One's Own*, the only book that was clear to me.

We never do discuss the piece by bell hooks.

In a different class, a graduate seminar on multicultural literature, our professor assigns Gloria Anzaldúa's *Borderlands/La Frontera: The New Mestiza*. I enter the seminar room that day with excitement. For the first time in my graduate career, I've encountered a text that speaks passionately to me, a text radical and thrilling, an author whose feminist, ethnic, sexual, and working-class concerns correspond to my own, a book that acknowledges real-world prejudice, poverty, and sexual violation, that mixes poetry and history, memoir and argument. I have fallen in love. In cursive, I've gushed onto the title page of the black paperback: *The most incredible book I've ever read. It speaks straight to me.*

At last. I can't wait to talk about it.

But the professor, whom I've always admired, opens class by apologizing for having assigned the book at all. He'd included it, he explains, only because he'd heard it was important. But if he'd read it first, he would never have put it on the syllabus: it was too disjointed, too polemical. Students quickly chime in with their discomfort over the book's "angry" content.

I'm confused. My professor and classmates hadn't stumbled over W. E. B. Du Bois, Zora Neale Hurston, or Maxine Hong Kingston, but Gloria Anzaldúa is somehow too different, too much.

It's the anger in the text, I learn, that bothers them. "She's so *angry*," they keep saying. For the whole session, I find myself arguing in defense of the book's worth, trying to articulate the difference between being angry by temperament and expressing justified anger in response to violation.

The experience is both alienating and illuminating. *Did you think we weren't angry?*

Maybe if you're a distinguished professor of law, the notion of your name next to a piece in *Cosmo* makes you cringe. Maybe if your educational pedigree is immaculate, the remedial intellectual needs of people who grew up with food stamps aren't your problem. Maybe if you're a well-meaning professor teaching ethnic literature, Anzaldúa's anger is the only thing visible. Maybe you can't feel the burn of every injustice she inherited and lived, much less appreciate the elegance of her complex aesthetic.

> AT THE TIME, I DIDN'T REALIZE THAT THESE SMALL INCIDENTS WERE NEGOTIATIONS OF POWER, CONTESTS OVER WHOSE PERSPECTIVES MATTERED AND WHOSE VOICES WOULD BE PERMITTED AND WELCOMED AT THE TABLE.

At the time, I didn't realize that these small incidents were negotiations of power, contests over whose perspective mattered and whose voices would be permitted and welcomed at the table. At the institution where I did my graduate work in the 1990s, Third World feminism, women-of-color feminism, and transnational feminism hadn't yet trickled down.

After earning a doctorate, I was hired by a small men's college in rural Indiana. At Wabash, which prided itself on its maintenance of tradition, men comprised not only the entire student body but also most of the faculty and almost the whole administrative structure.

Students asked, while I was sitting at my desk in my office, whose secretary I was. Alumni at luncheons asked what a "purty young thing" like me was doing there. All-campus emails by drunk freshmen asked for the best place on campus to beat their meat.

I taught there for ten years, the only tenure-line woman in my department for the first nine. I earned tenure; I chaired my department. We hired more women.

I also got to teach women's literature, including Latina literature, and feminist theory to classrooms of thirty-five men at a time. Farm-boys and lawyers' sons took my classes. Some came with the expressed intention of debunking feminism. Some wanted to know, when we read the novels of Jean Rhys, why we had to read a book by a slut. Some questioned women's right to vote. Yes. When I taught Gloria Anzaldúa's *Borderlands/La Frontera*, I was under no illusion that its insights would be met with joy.

I value those voices, those questions, that red-state hostility, because they taught me how to make feminism's insights relevant to people outside a closed, snug room of agreement. I learned how to make feminist theory, critical race theory, and observations about class privilege relevant, exciting, and even needful to people who had no material reason to care. I learned diplomacy. I learned not to back down.

As academics, we can forget the urgency and hunger people have for the knowledge we hold. We can forget that even those who claim to be hostile may need what we offer to help them make sense of a complicated world.

Academics don't share a monolithic experience. Many of us are adjuncts or lecturers, forced to piece together work with few benefits and little security, while the fortunate percentage of us with tenure-track positions have to hustle to build our vitas and merit files as our institutions require. Either way, the thick busyness of our lives can induce a sweet, privileged forgetfulness, a smug sense of how worthwhile our work of "knowledge production" is. Over the years, I've known many dedicated and creative teachers, eager to reach and engage every student, yet I've also known academics who view students as an obstacle to their real work of research or see teaching as a process of simply culling the best from the herd.

But I speak now as one of that herd. The herd is made up of smart, desperate, and intellectually eager individuals — if they are met halfway, if they are spoken to with respect and in language they can understand. They have not been to Harvard, and if we make them feel stupid, inadequate, and ashamed for not knowing its vocabularies and sharing its assumptions, they will retreat. (My brother, living in a trailer with friends and putting himself through college, dropped out after a year.) If our concerns seem too abstract, effete, and irrelevant, they will turn away in disgust.

Yet we need them. Their voices are vital. The academy — as we fondly, misguidedly call it, as if it were some great, unified thing — is lumbering along amid eviscerating budget cuts, pressures to corporatize, to streamline, to justify its existence to hostile anti-intellectual factions and a skeptical public, to become purely instrumental, a machine that grants job credentials to twenty-two-year-olds so they can get on with their lives. In the face of such intense and varied pressures, the academy must find ways to preserve itself as a place for thought to flourish — yet *everyone* needs to be invited to think. The discussion has to matter to everyone, and everyone's voice must be heard.

> **IN THE FACE OF SUCH INTENSE AND VARIED PRESSURES, THE ACADEMY MUST FIND WAYS TO PRESERVE ITSELF AS A PLACE FOR THOUGHT TO FLOURISH — YET *EVERYONE* NEEDS TO BE INVITED TO THINK.**

Last spring, my son graduated from Oberlin College, and in only a few more months, I'll have paid off my own enormous student loans. That is, I believe deeply in the intellectual benefits of higher education and have willingly indentured myself to attain them. On the other hand, I loathe the academy's blind spots.

A few years ago, Stephen Greenblatt — *the* Stephen Greenblatt — said in an interview, "I've been at this for 40 years. And, as an academic, I've been content with relatively small audiences, with the thought that the audience I long for will find its way eventually to what I have written, provided that what I have written is good enough."

On the one hand, there's a lovely quiet confidence in the long view Greenblatt takes, a modest surety of purpose, but it's also a position freighted with an absence of urgency. That unacknowledged absence is a luxury, a privilege, that too many academics ignore, not at their own peril, but at the peril of others, others like the women who would have been very grateful to learn about that provision in the Violence Against Women Act about employers' responsibilities to protect them. "The audience I long for will find its way eventually to what I have written," Greenblatt writes. *Eventually.* There's no rush. And the burden of finding knowledge, you'll note, is on the audience. Seeking the audience out is not configured as the thinker's job. *Eventually, if I am superb enough, the chosen few will manage to discover my work.*

Sitting on my sofa on a Saturday morning, writing, it still surprises and honors me that an editor has asked me to write an essay for a prestigious college's online journal. I was raised to be seen and not heard. Now someone wants my voice?

That's the key, I think: to remain surprised, to remain honored. Our public voices are an extraordinary privilege. We can make the choice to carry with us and be shaped by the voices we've heard — the strippers and dropouts and battered mothers — and we can act so that what we do will matter to them. We can continue to choose — no matter what islands of remove our positions may afford us — to keep inviting those voices: to teach free classes to the poor, for example, and to listen to what the poor tell us when they read our cherished texts. We can teach texts written by poor women in our classrooms. We can remember that torture and abuse traumatize humans into silence, and that humiliation and subordination train people into reticence, but that their voices, those valuable voices, can be fished to the surface again, if we are patient, if we are kind. If we care.

In graduate school, professors said you had to choose one thing or the other: you could be a creative writer or a scholar, not both. The creative writing professors said you had to choose a genre: poetry or fiction, not both. You could be a feminist professor in a classroom or a feminist activist on the streets, not both.

It was all too reminiscent of the old divisions long demanded of us: you must think or feel, not both. You must be a mind or a body, not both. You can be pretty or smart, not both. You can have a family or a career. Why did intellectuals in the 1990s continue to invest in such reductive binaries? Why the urge to bifurcate, to build retaining walls between the multiple truths of our experience?

They were wrong. It isn't necessary. Today we publish scholarship and creative work. We write for general audiences and trained specialists in our field. We publish in glossy magazines, and the local newspaper, and academic journals; we publish scholarly articles, and poetry, and fiction, and memoir.

For me, all of feminism's waves and permutations — as well as the voices that contest it — are essential. All of our varied feminisms seek a more just world, and there's no need to limit our efforts to particular spheres, no need to cut ties with parts of ourselves. While I serve on the advisory board of a university press with other professors, vetting scholarly projects for publication, I also serve as a mentor to a Latina-Lakota teenager whose mother, a meth addict, lost custody.

She lives with her father, stepmother, and two brothers in their small mobile home in a trailer park. When I drive to see her, it feels like I am driving into my own past.

· · · ● · · ·

QUESTIONS FOR A SECOND READING

1. In both of these short essays, Castro troubles many binary understandings of the world, particularly the understanding of the university (or the "academy") and the world(s) "outside" the academy. Reread Castro's essays and underline passages that would appear to you to fit a definition you have of "academic." What are the markers of "academic" prose as you understand it? Additionally, which passages seem to resist rather than adhere to conventions of academic writing? What writerly moves does Castro make that either conform to or resist what you have come to think of as writing that belongs in "the academy"?

2. Castro mentions quite a few writers in her work: Toril Moi, Luce Irigaray, bell hooks, Stephen Greenblatt, Jean Rhys, Zora Neale Hurston, and others. As you look back at Castro's references to these authors, what can you tell about them from the context of Castro's essays? Once you have found a few examples, go online and find out about a few of these authors. It is likely you will even be able to find examples of their writing. How does reading these authors' work or reading about them help you further understand the specific moments of Castro's essays or her essays as a whole?

3. Alex Espinoza has said that "confronting hard truths is something author Joy Castro does especially well." As you read Castro's essays again, what do you identify as the "hard truths" in this work? What signals to you that the truth you are noticing is "hard" either for Castro or for all of us? And how would you describe the way that Castro "confronts" these hard truths?

4. What is remarkable about Castro's work here is how many subjects she attends to quite carefully in such a short amount of space. Gather a few fellow readers together and make a list of as many things as you can think of that these essays seem to be about. What subjects does Castro bring up? How does she manage to address so many subjects in so few pages?

· · · ● · · ·

ASSIGNMENTS FOR WRITING

1. One way to read Castro's pieces is to see them as narrative, as two short essays that tell the stories of Castro's journey as a student and educator. But another way to understand Castro's writing is to imagine these essays as making an argument (or several arguments) about many different things: education, race, class, higher education, social justice, gender, and any other subjects you might have thought of while you considered the fourth "Question for a Second Reading."

    Write an essay in which you make an argument about what the most urgent argument of Castro's essays seems to be. Of course, she makes more than one argument. But for the essay you will write, try to prioritize. What is her central argument? Or which of her arguments are most central to you? Why? How can you tell? What passages would you point to in order to support your own argument about what is most important in Castro's work? What is Castro's work *really* about in this selection?

2. Castro has a very lively online presence—a website, an active Twitter account, many online publications, interviews, and book reviews. Spend some time reading from these many sources—read at least one book review of *Island of Bones* (the book you read excerpts from here), one interview with Castro, and whatever other kinds of materials about Castro or her work you can find.

    Write an essay in which you consider the following: What does your research help you see? How does reading what Castro has said about her own work, or what others have said about it, transform or affirm your initial reading of these essays? You might then make a move to talk more conceptually about reading—about *how* we read, and how it changes our reading to learn more about a writer or his or her other work. What kind of enterprise is reading? How does the movement between these printed essays and your online reading enrich your reading of Castro? Imagine that after your online research, you were able to create hyperlinks or footnotes in Castro's essays: what kinds of interventions would you make to help other readers read more closely and more richly?

3. Castro's essays, in two places, refer to the concept of "trickling down." You might be most familiar with this term from the study of economics, if you have ever taken such a course. If you have not taken such a course, some online reading will help you get a sense of what this means. Once you feel like you have a handle on the history and meaning of "trickle-down economics," look carefully at the places in the essay where Castro refers to "trickling down." Write an essay in which you consider why Castro might pay attention to this term. How does it come up in the essay the first time? How does it come up the second time? How might this notion of "trickling down" be a part of Castro's larger critiques and arguments? Why do you think Castro might want us to pay attention to such a concept?

• • ● • • ⁃

MAKING CONNECTIONS

1. W. E. B. Du Bois, in the selections from *The Souls of Black Folk* (p. 294), writes to reform American education. There are many other writers in *Ways of Reading* who write as agents of change, although with different starting points, different concerns, and different agendas: Joy Castro is just one example.

    Write an essay in which you put Castro's work into conversation with the three chapters from Du Bois's *The Souls of Black Folk*. Where and how do they speak to the same issues? Where and how do they differ in their arguments and in their approach? How are they different as pieces of writing—different in style and in intent? You will need to represent carefully the positions of each. You will need to think about differences as well as similarities. And you should think about how and why the differences might be attributed to history, to race, or to gender.

2. We might read both Joy Castro's work and Susan Griffin's "Our Secret" (p. 381) as containing elements of autobiography. Each writer relies on stories from her own life to demonstrate the relationship between one individual life and the larger cultural and political implications. Griffin writes, "To a certain kind of mind, what is hidden away ceases to exist" (p. 404). As readers, we are struck by the ways this statement (and so many of Griffin's statements) pertains both to her own life story and to the larger historical narrative of the Holocaust.

   Reread both Castro and Griffin, looking for sentences and phrases that seem to work on two levels (the personal and the political/cultural). Which sentences or phrases suggest to you that they are both about the writer's life *and* about all of our lives, about the world? How can you tell?

   Write an essay in which you illuminate, through the work of these two writers, the relationship between one life and what happens in the world at large. How do these writers help us understand ourselves as individuals and also as parts of larger systems, cultures, or worlds?

3. Joy Castro writes about her experience with discussing Gloria Anzaldúa's book *Borderlands/La Frontera* (from which the essay "How to Tame a Wild Tongue" is excerpted; see p. 26) as both a student and a teacher. Castro writes, "I find myself arguing in defense of the book's worth, trying to articulate the difference between being angry by temperament and expressing justified anger in response to violation" (p. 268). Both Anzaldúa and Castro are writers and both are scholars, academics who have developed theories and philosophies about education, class, culture, race, language, and identity.

   Write an essay in which you talk about the relationship between Castro's essays and Anzaldúa's essay. To give yourself a starting point, you might begin with what Castro directly says about Anzaldúa. But your job is to imagine these two texts as having a conversation. What are their common threads? How can Anzaldúa's essay illuminate Castro's essays, which were written twenty-five years later? How would you describe each writer's relationship to anger? What are Castro and Anzaldúa angry about? How can you tell? And, finally, what is your response? Given Castro's critique of readers who are bothered by "the anger in the text," what would you say to those readers? How do you understand the relationship between writing, identity, social justice, and emotion?

TA-NEHISI
Coates

Ta-Nehisi Coates (b. 1975), a national correspondent for *The Atlantic*, is the author of the memoir *The Beautiful Struggle: A Father, Two Sons, and an Unlikely Road to Manhood* (2008) and the *New York Times* bestseller *Between the World and Me* (2015). He has served as Journalist in Residence at the Graduate School of Journalism at City University of New York and has received numerous writing awards, including the 2016 PEN/Diamonstein-Spielvogel Award for the Art of the Essay and the 2015 National Book Award for Nonfiction for *Between the World and Me*. In 2015, he received a MacArthur "Genius" Fellowship.

Coates also authors a run of the Marvel Comic *Black Panther*, about the first major black superhero. The Black Panther rules Wakanda, a fictional technologically advanced nation, but Coates says he pulls the series's story lines from "the very real history of society." When the first issue was released on April 6, 2016, Marvel editor-in-chief Axel Alonso called it "the buzz book of the industry."

Both of Coates's books ground readers in his experiences growing up in the Mondawmin neighborhood of Baltimore, Maryland. *Between the World and Me* takes the form of a series of essays written to Coates's son. Toni Morrison has called it "required reading" and "as profound as it is revelatory" in "its examination of the hazards and hopes of black male life." *Publishers Weekly* named it "a classic of our time," and the *New York Observer* called Coates "the single best writer on the subject of race in the United States."

Our excerpt from *Between the World and Me* presents readers with Coates's thinking about what it might mean for him, a black man, to literally and figuratively lose his body, and what it means to live in an American reality where people "believe" themselves to be white, where "race is the child of racism," and where fear inflects the stories he tells his son about his past and those on the front pages of newspapers about brutal murders and beatings of African Americans by police.

Speaking in a 2013 taped interview for *The Atlantic* about writing, Coates shares his struggles and the difficulty of writing openly. He says,

> Breakthroughs come from stress . . . from putting an inordinate amount of pressure on yourself and seeing what you can take and hoping that you grow some new muscles. It's not really that mystical. . . . It's like repeated practice over and over again. . . . I strongly believe that writing is an act of courage. . . . Perseverance is so key to writing.

Between the World and Me

Son,

Last Sunday the host of a popular news show asked me what it meant to lose my body. The host was broadcasting from Washington, D.C., and I was seated in a remote studio on the far west side of Manhattan. A satellite closed the miles between us, but no machinery could close the gap between her world and the world for which I had been summoned to speak. When the host asked me about my body, her face faded from the screen, and was replaced by a scroll of words, written by me earlier that week.

The host read these words for the audience, and when she finished she turned to the subject of my body, although she did not mention it specifically. But by now I am accustomed to intelligent people asking about the condition of my body without realizing the nature of their request. Specifically, the host wished to know why I felt that white America's progress, or rather the progress of those Americans who believe that they are white, was built on looting and violence. Hearing this, I felt an old and indistinct sadness well up in me. The answer to this question is the record of the believers themselves. The answer is American history.

There is nothing extreme in this statement. Americans deify democracy in a way that allows for a dim awareness that they have, from time to time, stood in defiance of their God. But democracy is a forgiving God and America's heresies — torture, theft, enslavement — are so common among individuals and nations that none can declare themselves immune. In fact, Americans, in a real sense, have never betrayed their God. When Abraham Lincoln declared, in 1863, that the battle of Gettysburg must ensure "that government of the people, by the people, for the people, shall not perish from the earth," he was not merely being aspirational; at the onset of the Civil War, the United States of America had one of the highest rates of suffrage in the world. The question is not whether Lincoln truly meant "government of the people" but what our country has, throughout its history, taken the political term "people" to actually mean. In 1863 it did not mean your mother or your grandmother, and it did not mean you and me. Thus America's problem is not its betrayal of "government of the people," but the means by which "the people" acquired their names.

This leads us to another equally important ideal, one that Americans implicitly accept but to which they make no conscious claim. Americans believe in the reality of "race" as a defined, indubitable feature of the natural world. Racism — the need to ascribe bone-deep features to people and then humiliate, reduce, and destroy them — inevitably follows from this inalterable condition. In this way, racism is rendered as the innocent daughter of Mother Nature, and one is left to deplore the Middle Passage or the Trail of Tears the way one deplores an earthquake, a tornado, or any other phenomenon that can be cast as beyond the handiwork of men.

But race is the child of racism, not the father. And the process of naming "the people" has never been a matter of genealogy and physiognomy so much as one of hierarchy. Difference in hue and hair is old. But the belief in the preeminence of hue and hair, the notion that these factors can correctly organize a society and that they signify deeper attributes, which are indelible — this is the new idea at the heart of these new people who have been brought up hopelessly, tragically, deceitfully, to believe that they are white.

AMERICANS BELIEVE IN THE REALITY OF "RACE" AS A DEFINED, INDUBITABLE FEATURE OF THE NATURAL WORLD.

These new people are, like us, a modern invention. But unlike us, their new name has no real meaning divorced from the machinery of criminal power. The new people were something else before they were white — Catholic, Corsican, Welsh, Mennonite, Jewish — and if all our national hopes have any fulfillment, then they will have to be something else again. Perhaps they will truly become American and create a nobler basis for their myths. I can not call it. As for now, it must be said that the process of washing the disparate tribes white, the elevation of the belief in being white, was not achieved through wine tastings and ice cream socials, but rather through the pillaging of life, liberty, labor, and land; through the flaying of backs; the chaining of limbs; the strangling of dissidents; the destruction of families; the rape of mothers; the sale of children; and various other acts meant, first and foremost, to deny you and me the right to secure and govern our own bodies.

The new people are not original in this. Perhaps there has been, at some point in history, some great power whose elevation was exempt from the violent exploitation of other human bodies. If there has been, I have yet to discover it. But this banality of violence can never excuse America, because America makes no claim to the banal. America believes itself exceptional, the greatest and noblest nation ever to exist, a lone champion standing between the white city of democracy and the terrorists, despots, barbarians, and other enemies of civilization. One cannot, at once, claim to be superhuman and then plead mortal error. I propose to take our countrymen's claims of American exceptionalism seriously, which is to say I propose subjecting our country to an exceptional moral standard. This is difficult because there exists, all around us, an apparatus urging us to accept American innocence at face value and not to inquire too much. And it is so easy to look away, to live with the fruits of our history and to ignore the great evil done in all of our names. But you and I have never truly had that luxury. I think you know.

I write you in your fifteenth year. I am writing you because this was the year you saw Eric Garner choked to death for selling cigarettes; because you know now that Renisha McBride was shot for seeking help, that John Crawford was shot down for browsing in a department store. And you have seen men in uniform drive by and murder Tamir Rice, a twelve-year-old child whom they were oath-bound to protect. And you have seen men in the same uniforms pummel Marlene Pinnock, someone's grandmother, on the side of a road. And you know now, if you did not before, that the police departments of your country have been endowed with the authority to destroy your body. It does not matter if the destruction is the result of an unfortunate overreaction. It does not matter if it originates in a misunderstanding. It does not matter if the destruction springs from a foolish policy. Sell cigarettes without the proper authority and your body can be destroyed. Resent the people trying to entrap your body and it can be destroyed. Turn into a dark stairwell and your body can be destroyed. The destroyers will rarely be held accountable. Mostly they will receive pensions. And destruction is merely the superlative form of a dominion whose prerogatives include friskings, detainings, beatings, and humiliations. All of this is common to black people. And all of this is old for black people. No one is held responsible.

There is nothing uniquely evil in these destroyers or even in this moment. The destroyers are merely men enforcing the whims of our country, correctly interpreting its heritage and legacy. It is hard to face this. But all our phrasing — race relations, racial chasm, racial justice, racial profiling, white privilege, even white supremacy — serves to obscure that racism is a visceral experience, that it dislodges brains, blocks airways, rips muscle, extracts organs, cracks bones, breaks teeth. You must never look away from this. You must always remember that the sociology, the history, the economics, the graphs, the charts, the regressions all land, with great violence, upon the body.

That Sunday, with that host, on that news show, I tried to explain this as best I could within the time allotted. But at the end of the segment, the host flashed a widely shared picture of an eleven-year-old black boy tearfully hugging a white police officer. Then she asked me about "hope." And I knew then that I had failed. And I remembered that I had expected to fail. And I wondered again at the indistinct sadness welling up in me. Why exactly was I sad? I came out of the studio and walked for a while. It was a calm December day. Families, believing themselves white, were out on the streets. Infants, raised to be white, were bundled in strollers. And I was sad for these people, much as I was sad for the host and sad for all the people out there watching and reveling in a specious hope. I realized then why I was sad. When the journalist asked me about my body, it was like she was asking me to awaken her from the most gorgeous dream. I have seen that dream all my life. It is perfect houses with nice lawns. It is Memorial Day cookouts, block associations, and driveways. The Dream is treehouses and the Cub Scouts. The Dream smells like peppermint but tastes like strawberry shortcake. And for so long I have wanted to escape into the Dream, to fold my country over my head like a blanket. But this has never been an option because the Dream rests on our backs, the bedding made from our bodies. And knowing this, knowing that the Dream persists by warring with the known world, I was sad for the host, I was sad for all those families, I was sad for my country, but above all, in that moment, I was sad for you.

That was the week you learned that the killers of Michael Brown would go free. The men who had left his body in the street like some awesome declaration of their inviolable power would never be punished. It was not my expectation that anyone would ever be punished. But you were young and still believed. You stayed up till 11 P.M. that night, waiting for the announcement of an indictment, and when instead it was announced that there was none you said, "I've got to go," and you went into your room, and I heard you crying. I came in five minutes after, and I didn't hug you, and I didn't comfort you, because I thought it would be wrong to comfort you. I did not tell you that it would be okay, because I have never believed it would be okay. What I told you is what your grandparents tried to tell me: that this is your country, that this is your world, that this is your body, and you must find some way to live within the all of it. I tell you now that the question of how one should live within a black body, within a country lost in the Dream, is the question of my life, and the pursuit of this question, I have found, ultimately answers itself.

This must seem strange to you. We live in a "goal-oriented" era. Our media vocabulary is full of hot takes, big ideas, and grand theories of everything. But some time ago I rejected magic in all its forms. This rejection was a gift from your grandparents, who never tried to console me with ideas of an afterlife and were skeptical of preordained American glory. In accepting both the chaos of history and the fact of my total end, I was freed to truly consider how I wished to live — specifically, how do I live free in this black body? It is a profound question because America understands itself as God's handiwork, but the black body is the clearest evidence that America is the work of men. I have asked the question through my reading and writings, through the music of my youth, through arguments with your grandfather, with your mother, your aunt Janai, your uncle Ben. I have searched for answers in nationalist myth, in classrooms, out on the streets,

and on other continents. The question is unanswerable, which is not to say futile. The greatest reward of this constant interrogation, of confrontation with the brutality of my country, is that it has freed me from ghosts and girded me against the sheer terror of disembodiment.

And I am afraid. I feel the fear most acutely whenever you leave me. But I was afraid long before you, and in this I was unoriginal. When I was your age the only people I knew were black, and all of them were powerfully, adamantly, dangerously afraid. I had seen this fear all my young life, though I had not always recognized it as such.

It was always right in front of me. The fear was there in the extravagant boys of my neighborhood, in their large rings and medallions, their big puffy coats and full-length fur-collared leathers, which was their armor against their world. They would stand on the corner of Gwynn Oak and Liberty, or Cold Spring and Park Heights, or outside Mondawmin Mall, with their hands dipped in Russell sweats. I think back on those boys now and all I see is fear, and all I see is them girding themselves against the ghosts of the bad old days when the Mississippi mob gathered 'round their grandfathers so that the branches of the black body might be torched, then cut away. The fear lived on in their practiced bop, their slouching denim, their big T-shirts, the calculated angle of their baseball caps, a catalog of behaviors and garments enlisted to inspire the belief that these boys were in firm possession of everything they desired.

> WHEN I WAS YOUR AGE THE ONLY PEOPLE I KNEW WERE BLACK, AND ALL OF THEM WERE POWERFULLY, ADAMANTLY, DANGEROUSLY AFRAID.

I saw it in their customs of war. I was no older than five, sitting out on the front steps of my home on Woodbrook Avenue, watching two shirtless boys circle each other close and buck shoulders. From then on, I knew that there was a ritual to a street fight, bylaws and codes that, in their very need, attested to all the vulnerability of the black teenage bodies.

I heard the fear in the first music I ever knew, the music that pumped from boom boxes full of grand boast and bluster. The boys who stood out on Garrison and Liberty up on Park Heights loved this music because it told them, against all evidence and odds, that they were masters of their own lives, their own streets, and their own bodies. I saw it in the girls, in their loud laughter, in their gilded bamboo earrings that announced their names thrice over. And I saw it in their brutal language and hard gaze, how they would cut you with their eyes and destroy you with their words for the sin of playing too much. "Keep my name out your mouth," they would say. I would watch them after school, how they squared off like boxers, vaselined up, earrings off, Reeboks on, and leaped at each other.

I felt the fear in the visits to my Nana's home in Philadelphia. You never knew her. I barely knew her, but what I remember is her hard manner, her rough voice. And I knew that my father's father was dead and that my uncle Oscar was dead and that my uncle David was dead and that each of these instances was unnatural. And I saw it in my own father, who loves you, who counsels you, who slipped me money to care for you. My father was so very afraid. I felt it in the sting of his black leather belt, which he applied with more anxiety than anger, my father who beat me as if someone might steal me away, because that is exactly what was happening all around us. Everyone had lost a child, somehow, to the streets, to jail, to drugs, to guns. It was said that these lost girls were sweet as honey and would not hurt a fly. It was said that these lost boys had just received a GED and had begun to turn their lives around. And now they were gone, and their legacy was a great fear.

Have they told you this story? When your grandmother was sixteen years old a young man knocked on her door. The young man was your Nana Jo's boyfriend. No one else was home. Ma allowed this young man to sit and wait until your Nana Jo returned. But your great-grandmother got there first. She asked the young man to leave. Then she beat your grandmother terrifically, one last time, so that she might remember how easily she could lose her body. Ma never forgot. I remember her clutching my small hand tightly as we crossed the street. She would tell me that if I ever let go and were killed by an onrushing car, she would beat me back to life. When I was six, Ma and Dad took me to a local park. I slipped from their gaze and found a playground. Your grandparents spent anxious minutes looking for me. When they found me, Dad did what every parent I knew would have done — he reached for his belt. I remember watching him in a kind of daze, awed at the distance between punishment and offense. Later, I would hear it in Dad's voice — "Either I can beat him, or the police." Maybe that saved me. Maybe it didn't. All I know is, the violence rose from the fear like smoke from a fire, and I cannot say whether that violence, even administered in fear and love, sounded the alarm or choked us at the exit. What I know is that fathers who slammed their teenage boys for sass would then release them to streets where their boys employed, and were subject to, the same justice. And I knew mothers who belted their girls, but the belt could not save these girls from drug dealers twice their age. We, the children, employed our darkest humor to cope. We stood in the alley where we shot basketballs through hollowed crates and cracked jokes on the boy whose mother wore him out with a beating in front of his entire fifth-grade class. We sat on the number five bus, headed downtown, laughing at some girl whose mother was known to reach for anything — cable wires, extension cords, pots, pans. We were laughing, but I know that we were afraid of those who loved us most. Our parents resorted to the lash the way flagellants in the plague years resorted to the scourge.

To be black in the Baltimore of my youth was to be naked before the elements of the world, before all the guns, fists, knives, crack, rape, and disease. The nakedness is not an error, nor pathology. The nakedness is the correct and intended result of policy, the predictable upshot of people forced for centuries to live under fear. The law did not protect us. And now, in your time, the law has become an excuse for stopping and frisking you, which is to say, for furthering the assault on your body. But a society that protects some people through a safety net of schools, government-backed home loans, and ancestral wealth but can only protect you with the club of criminal justice has either failed at enforcing its good intentions or has succeeded at something much darker. However you call it, the result was our infirmity before the criminal forces of the world. It does not matter if the agent of those forces is white or black — what matters is our condition, what matters is the system that makes your body breakable.

The revelation of these forces, a series of great changes, has unfolded over the course of my life. The changes are still unfolding and will likely continue until I die. I was eleven years old, standing out in the parking lot in front of the 7-Eleven, watching a crew of older boys standing near the street. They yelled and gestured at . . . who? . . . another boy, young, like me, who stood there, almost smiling, gamely throwing up his hands. He had already learned the lesson he would teach me that day: that his body was in constant jeopardy. Who knows what brought him to that knowledge? The projects, a drunken stepfather, an older brother concussed by police, a cousin pinned in the city jail. That he was outnumbered did not matter because the whole world had outnumbered him long ago, and what do numbers matter? This was a war for the possession of his body and that would be the war of his whole life.

I stood there for some seconds, marveling at the older boys' beautiful sense of fashion. They all wore ski jackets, the kind which, in my day, mothers put on layaway in September, then piled up overtime hours so as to have the thing wrapped and ready for Christmas. I focused in on a light-skinned boy with a long head and small eyes. He was scowling at another boy, who was standing close to me. It was just before three in the afternoon. I was in sixth grade. School had just let out, and it was not yet the fighting weather of early spring. What was the exact problem here? Who could know?

The boy with the small eyes reached into his ski jacket and pulled out a gun. I recall it in the slowest motion, as though in a dream. There the boy stood, with the gun brandished, which he slowly untucked, tucked, then untucked once more, and in his small eyes I saw a surging rage that could, in an instant, erase my body. That was 1986. That year I felt myself to be drowning in the news reports of murder. I was aware that these murders very often did not land upon the intended targets but fell upon great-aunts, PTA mothers, overtime uncles, and joyful children — fell upon them random and relentless, like great sheets of rain. I knew this in theory but could not understand it as fact until the boy with the small eyes stood across from me holding my entire body in his small hands. The boy did not shoot. His friends pulled him back. He did not need to shoot. He had affirmed my place in the order of things. He had let it be known how easily I could be selected. I took the subway home that day, processing the episode all alone. I did not tell my parents. I did not tell my teachers, and if I told my friends I would have done so with all the excitement needed to obscure the fear that came over me in that moment.

I remember being amazed that death could so easily rise up from the nothing of a boyish afternoon, billow up like fog. I knew that West Baltimore, where I lived; that the north side of Philadelphia, where my cousins lived; that the South Side of Chicago, where friends of my father lived, comprised a world apart. Somewhere out there beyond the firmament, past the asteroid belt, there were other worlds where children did not regularly fear for their bodies. I knew this because there was a large television resting in my living room. In the evenings I would sit before this television bearing witness to the dispatches from this other world. There were little white boys with complete collections of football cards, and their only want was a popular girlfriend and their only worry was poison oak. That other world was suburban and endless, organized around pot roasts, blueberry pies, fireworks, ice cream sundaes, immaculate bathrooms, and small toy trucks that were loosed in wooded backyards with streams and glens. Comparing these dispatches with the facts of my native world, I came to understand that my country was a galaxy, and this galaxy stretched from the pandemonium of West Baltimore to the happy hunting grounds of *Mr. Belvedere*. I obsessed over the distance between that other sector of space and my own. I knew that my portion of the American galaxy, where bodies were enslaved by a tenacious gravity, was black and that the other, liberated portion was not. I knew that some inscrutable energy preserved the breach. I felt, but did not yet understand, the relation between that other world and me. And I felt in this a cosmic injustice, a profound cruelty, which infused an abiding, irrepressible desire to unshackle my body and achieve the velocity of escape.

Do you ever feel that same need? Your life is so very different from my own. The grandness of the world, the real world, the whole world, is a known thing for you. And you have no need of dispatches because you have seen so much of the American galaxy and its inhabitants — their homes, their hobbies — up close. I don't know what it means to grow up with a black president, social networks, omnipresent media, and black women everywhere in their natural hair. What I know is that when they loosed the killer of Michael Brown, you said, "I've got to go." And that cut me because, for all our differing worlds, at your age my feeling was exactly the same. And I recall that even then I had not yet begun to imagine the perils that tangle us. You still believe the injustice was Michael Brown. You have not yet grappled with your own myths and narratives and discovered the plunder everywhere around us.

Before I could discover, before I could escape, I had to survive, and this could only mean a clash with the streets, by which I mean not just physical blocks, nor simply the people packed into them, but the array of lethal puzzles and strange perils that seem to rise up from the asphalt itself. The streets transform every ordinary day into a series of trick questions, and every incorrect answer risks a beatdown, a shooting, or a pregnancy. No one survives unscathed. And yet the heat that springs from the constant danger, from a lifestyle of near-death experience, is thrilling. This is what the rappers mean when they pronounce themselves addicted to "the streets" or in love with "the game." I imagine they feel something akin to parachutists, rock climbers, BASE jumpers, and others who choose to live on the edge. Of course we chose nothing. And I have never believed the brothers who claim to "run," much less "own," the city. We did not design the streets. We do not fund them. We do not preserve them. But I was there, nevertheless, charged like all the others with the protection of my body.

The crews, the young men who'd transmuted their fear into rage, were the greatest danger. The crews walked the blocks of their neighborhood, loud and rude, because it was only through their loud rudeness that they might feel any sense of security and power. They would break your jaw, stomp your face, and shoot you down to feel that power, to revel in the might of their own bodies. And their wild reveling, their astonishing acts made their names ring out. Reps were made, atrocities recounted. And so in my Baltimore it was known that when Cherry Hill rolled through you rolled the other way, that North and Pulaski was not an intersection but a hurricane, leaving only splinters and shards in its wake. In that fashion, the security of these neighborhoods flowed downward and became the security of the bodies living there. You steered clear of Jo-Jo, for instance, because he was cousin to Keon, the don of Murphy Homes. In other cities, indeed in other Baltimores, the neighborhoods had other handles and the boys went by other names, but their mission did not change: prove the inviolability of their block, of their bodies, through their power to crack knees, ribs, and arms. This practice was so common that today you can approach any black person raised in the cities of that era and they can tell you which crew ran which hood in their city, and they can tell you the names of all the captains and all their cousins and offer an anthology of all their exploits.

To survive the neighborhoods and shield my body, I learned another language consisting of a basic complement of head nods and handshakes. I memorized a list of prohibited blocks. I learned the smell and feel of fighting weather. And I learned that "Shorty, can I see your bike?" was never a sincere question, and "Yo, you was messing with my cousin" was neither an earnest accusation nor a misunderstanding of the facts. These were the summonses that you answered with your left foot forward, your right foot back, your hands guarding your face, one slightly lower than the other, cocked like a hammer. Or they were answered by breaking out, ducking through alleys, cutting through backyards, then bounding through the door past your kid

> I RECALL LEARNING THESE LAWS CLEARER THAN I RECALL LEARNING MY COLORS AND SHAPES, BECAUSE THESE LAWS WERE ESSENTIAL TO THE SECURITY OF MY BODY.

brother into your bedroom, pulling the tool out of your lambskin or from under your mattress or out of your Adidas shoebox, then calling up your own cousins (who really aren't) and returning to that same block, on that same day, and to that same crew, hollering out, "Yeah, nigger, what's up now?" I recall learning these laws clearer than I recall learning my colors and shapes, because these laws were essential to the security of my body.

I think of this as a great difference between us. You have some acquaintance with the old rules, but they are not as essential to you as they were to me. I am sure that you have had to deal with the occasional roughneck on the subway or in the park, but when I was about your age, each day, fully one-third of my brain was concerned with who I was walking to school with, our precise number, the manner of our walk, the number of times I smiled, who or what I smiled at, who offered a pound and who did not—all of which is to say that I practiced the culture of the streets, a culture concerned chiefly with securing the body. I do not long for those days. I have no desire to make you "tough" or "street," perhaps because any "toughness" I garnered came reluctantly. I think I was always, somehow, aware of the price. I think I somehow knew that that third of my brain should have been concerned with more beautiful things. I think I felt that something out there, some force, nameless and vast, had robbed me of . . . what? Time? Experience? I think you know something of what that third could have done, and I think that is why you may feel the need for escape even more than I did. You have seen all the wonderful life up above the tree-line, yet you understand that there is no real distance between you and Trayvon Martin, and thus Trayvon Martin must terrify you in a way that he could never terrify me. You have seen so much more of all that is lost when they destroy your body.

• • • ● • •

QUESTIONS FOR A SECOND READING

1. The book *Between the World and Me* makes direct reference to a poem of the same title by Richard Wright, and many reviewers of *Between the World and Me* have thought about James Baldwin's *The Fire Next Time*, a book that also features an older African American addressing a young man, in this case a nephew. Wright's poem is readily available online, and your college or university library likely has a copy of Baldwin's book. Select one of the two—the Wright poem or the Baldwin book—and, perhaps in a group, prepare an informal presentation on how you see Coates responding to, or in conversation with, this prior text.

2. At one point in this selection, recalling his past, Coates says, "I came out of the studio and walked for a while. It was a calm December day. Families, believing themselves white, were out on the streets. Infants, raised to be white, were bundled in strollers" (p. 279). What does Coates mean by "believing themselves white"? As you reread, let this phrase stand as an invitation to you as a reader. How does this construction function as a central aspect of Coates's arguments about race and identity?

3. Coates argues that "Americans believe in the reality of 'race' as a defined, indubitable feature of the natural world. . . . In this way, racism is rendered as the innocent daughter of Mother Nature, and one is left to deplore [it] the

way one deplores . . . any other phenomenon that can be cast as beyond the handiwork of men" (pp. 277–78). In the paragraph that follows, he writes that "race is the child of racism, not the father." If the reality of race is not this "defined, indubitable feature of the natural world" that Americans believe it is, then what is it? And how, then, is race "the child of racism"? How, in other words, is Coates asking you as a reader to understand Americans' rendering of race and racism?

4. As he recalls his own childhood, Coates says,

> I remember being amazed that death could so easily rise up from the nothing of a boyish afternoon, billow up like fog. I knew that West Baltimore, where I lived; that the north side of Philadelphia, where my cousins lived; that the South Side of Chicago, where friends of my father lived, comprised a world apart. Somewhere out there beyond the firmament, past the asteroid belt, there were other worlds where children did not regularly fear for their bodies. I knew this because there was a large television resting in my living room. In the evenings I would sit before this television bearing witness to the dispatches from this other world. There were little white boys with complete collections of football cards, and their only want was a popular girlfriend and their only worry was poison oak. That other world was suburban and endless, organized around pot roasts, blueberry pies, fireworks, ice cream sundaes, immaculate bathrooms, and small toy trucks that were loosed in wooded backyards with streams and glens. (pp. 283–84).

There is every reason to believe that the speaker in this passage knows that white boys, too, grow up in various circumstances, including neighborhoods like West Baltimore or the South Side of Chicago, though these stories are also not likely to appear on television. As you reread, think about the strategy of a passage like this one—both for the immediate audience, Coates's son, and the larger audience, you and people like you. What is Coates doing here? What might this text be asking of a reader in response?

5. As you reread Coates's selection, mark those moments where he refers to bodies, the "condition of [his] body," the bodies of African Americans, his son's body, living in a black body, and the nakedness of black bodies. Make a two-column chart. In the left column, write out the references to bodies that strike you as significant. In the right column, jot down what you understand each reference to be saying. After you've done this, step back from your chart and notes. What is Coates saying about the bodies of African Americans—literally and figuratively? Why do you think he says he is "accustomed to intelligent people asking about the condition of [his] body without realizing the nature of their request" (p. 277)? What, to Coates, is the nature of this request?

· · · ● · · ·

ASSIGNMENTS FOR WRITING

1. Coates's "Between the World and Me" is written as a direct address between an African American father and his son — and not just a generic African American father and son but, we learn as we read, a very specific pair defined by family, circumstance, place, and time.

    Whatever your race or gender, where, as a reader, do you locate yourself in this exchange? Where do you find yourself most engaged? Where do you feel that you, too, are being addressed or invited to respond? As you reread, mark places where you feel, as a reader, an opening in this selection. What does it mean, or what does it take, to be a reader in the face of a text like this one?

    Write an essay, perhaps in the shape of a review for a magazine or newspaper, in which you consider this book's considerable success and the demands it places on its readers.

2. Coates writes to his son,

    > I propose to take our countrymen's claims of American exceptionalism seriously, which is to say I propose subjecting our country to an exceptional moral standard. This is difficult because there exists, all around us, an apparatus urging us to accept American innocence at face value and not to inquire too much. And it is so easy to look away, to live with the fruits of our history and to ignore the great evil done in all of our names. But you and I have never truly had that luxury. (p. 278)

    What, in your experience, is this apparatus that urges us "to accept American innocence at face value and not to inquire too much" about "the great evil done in all of our names"? Coates offers us examples. He points to the actions of police that cover up brutal killings of black people. He points to "the Dream," as he calls it, that "persists by warring with the known world" (pp. 279–80). And he points to policies and practices directed at "people forced for centuries to live under fear" (p. 282).

    Work with a partner to point to and name the apparatuses — the policies and practices and beliefs and histories — that urge you not to inquire too much about race and racism. Once you've identified and talked through your examples, each of you should write an essay in which you explain these apparatuses and the ways that they urge *you* not to inquire too much. Imagine that you are writing for readers who have read Coates's selection but haven't thought through the question and examples you are working with.

3. Write an essay in which you explain Coates's key arguments, his passionate pleas to his son, about race, racism, and the idea that people "have been brought up hopelessly, tragically, deceitfully, to believe that they are white" (p. 278). Imagine that you are writing to an audience of readers who have not

read Coates's selection and who have not thought about it or worked with it in the ways that you have.

You might also consider these questions: How can you tell, as a reader, that an argument in Coates's work is a "key" argument? What moves does Coates make, as a writer, to signal to you that particular passages or points are central to his work?

4. Coates's expertise as a writer invites us into scenes and landscapes to see what he sees, to recognize fear, to see grandfathers and "extravagant boys" and his neighborhoods, to catch the glint of "gilded bamboo earrings" and a father's worry in a few spoken sentences.

For this assignment, reread paragraphs 13–23 on pages 281–84 (beginning with "And I am afraid. I feel the fear most acutely whenever you leave me" and ending with "And I felt in this a cosmic injustice, a profound cruelty, which infused an abiding, irrepressible desire to unshackle my body and achieve the velocity of escape"). Coates, in these pages, is working with fear through moments and landscapes that he re-creates in paragraphs, often beginning with invocations such as "I heard the fear in the first music I ever knew," "It was always right in front of me," "I felt the fear in the visits to my Nana's home," and "Have they told you this story?" He writes spare, compelling sentences. They make use of such devices as repetition, questions, quoted language, and, of course, descriptions of events and people.

Reread these paragraphs a couple of times to identify a moment or a landscape or an event that you'd like to work with in the spirit of Coates. Imagine that you are taking his decisions, movements, and qualities as a writer as your writing teacher. Allow Coates's writerly approach to become your model. Once you've identified the section you'd like to work with, write it out on a sheet of paper. Write by hand. Don't type. Writing it out will slow you down so that you can notice the language and sentence structures, the way the section begins and evolves. Once you've written it out and studied its craft, write a section of your own that imitates Coates. Work toward writing sentences like his, with the same structure and punctuation, the same rhythms, and work toward writing your section with the same number of sentences and the same overall evolving structure. His stories of fear resonate emotionally; they give us fear in words. When you choose what you'll write about, you may or may not be able to create that kind of emotional resonance; don't be concerned about it. You're working here as a writer apprentice to Coates.

— • • • ● • • • —

MAKING CONNECTIONS

1. As Kwame Anthony Appiah prepares for the final section of his essay "Racial Identities" (p. 42), he offers a surprising list to counter what he refers to as the "imperialism of identity":

> In policing this imperialism of identity — an imperialism as visible in racial identities as anywhere else — it is crucial to remember always

that we are not simply black or white or yellow or brown, gay or straight or bisexual, Jewish, Christian, Moslem, Buddhist, or Confucian but that we are also brothers and sisters; parents and children; liberals, conservatives, and leftists; teachers and lawyers and auto-makers and gardeners; fans of the Padres and the Bruins; amateurs of grunge rock and lovers of Wagner; movie buffs; MTV-holics; mystery-readers; surfers and singers; poets and pet-lovers; students and teachers; friends and lovers. Racial identity can be the basis of resistance to racism; but even as we struggle against racism — and though we have made great progress, we have further still to go — let us not let our racial identities subject us to new tyrannies. (p. 62)

Ta-Nehisi Coates also raises questions about racial identity, although in a different register and defined in terms of a different dramatic encounter. If Appiah were to select a passage from "Between the World and Me" to bring into his essay, what might it be? If the speaker in "Between the World and Me" were to speak to his son about Appiah's essay, perhaps reciting a passage, what might it be?

Write an essay in which you consider Appiah's argument from the point of view of Coates, the father, speaking to his son in "Between the World and Me."

2. Like Edward Said in "States" (p. 559), Ta-Nehisi Coates includes photographs in "Between the World and Me." (One image is included in our selection. You might look through a copy of the book *Between the World and Me* at your library to see the others.) Both Said and Coates are trying to represent a world — present, past, and future — and both rely on visual images. Write an essay in which you consider the different uses of the photograph in these two selections. How do they function for you, as a reader? What do you imagine the authors had in mind when they selected these images and brought them into the text?

3. Both John Edgar Wideman in "Our Time" (p. 622) and Ta-Nehisi Coates in "Between the World and Me" can be seen as writing to understand the places in which they grew up and the ideas about the world and family that circulated in those places at those times. Wideman takes on this work by writing *about* his brother (sometimes in the voice of his brother), while Coates takes on this work by writing *to* his son. Write an essay in which you consider the following questions: What ideas, arguments, or approaches do Wideman and Coates have in common, despite more than thirty years between the publications of their books? What do their commonalities suggest to you? How does Wideman's writing about his brother make his work different from Coates's work, in which Coates is talking to his son? How might Coates's perspective address Wideman's concerns about getting to the truth of his brother's story?

W. E. B.
Du Bois

William Edward Burghardt Du Bois (1868–1963) was the most significant African American intellectual of the first half of the twentieth century. He stands among the most widely read and admired and the most prolific and influential writers of our nation. He was a historian and sociologist, a journalist and political activist, a novelist and playwright. He was the founder and editor of *The Crisis*, the journal of the National Association for the Advancement of Colored People (NAACP), and the author of over two dozen books. He wrote on virtually every aspect of American political, social, and economic life.

In a tribute on the anniversary of Du Bois's one hundredth birthday, Martin Luther King Jr. said:

> Dr. Du Bois was a man possessed of priceless dedication to his people. The vast accumulation of achievement and public recognition were not for him pathways to personal affluence and a diffusion of identity. Whatever else he was, with his multitude of careers and professional titles, he was first and always a Black man. He used his richness of talent as a trust for his people. He saw that Negroes were robbed of so many things decisive to their existence that the theft of their history seemed only a small part of their losses. But Dr. Du Bois knew that to lose one's history is to lose one's self-understanding and with it the roots for pride. This drove him to become a historian of Negro life, and the combination of his unique zeal and intellect rescued for all of us a heritage whose loss would have profoundly impoverished us.

W. E. B. Du Bois was born in Massachusetts. His mother was a domestic servant; his relatives on his mother's side owned and worked a small farm. As a child he attended predominantly white schools and churches. It was there, he wrote, that he first felt the peculiar experience of being "a problem" by being black. Reflecting on a moment of discrimination at school, he wrote, "It dawned upon me with a certain suddenness that I was different from others; or like, mayhap, in heart and life and longing, but shut out from their world by a vast veil." The immediate effect on the young Du Bois was a deep determination to succeed "by reading law, by healing the sick, by telling the wonderful tales that swam in [his] head, — some way." He grew up, however, with the peculiar sensation of "double-consciousness, this sense of always looking at one's self through the eyes of others, of measuring one's soul by the tape of a world that looks on in amused contempt and pity. One ever feels his two-ness, — an American, a Negro; two souls, two thoughts, two unreconciled strivings; two warring ideals in one dark body, whose dogged strength alone keeps it from being torn asunder."

In 1885 he left the North to attend Fisk University in Nashville, Tennessee. It was there that he first became immersed in the life and culture of black Americans. For two summers, he taught school in a small black community near Alexandria, Tennessee, and began a lifelong interest in African American folk songs and spirituals. From Fisk, Du Bois went to Harvard University, then to the University of Berlin. He received his PhD in history from Harvard in 1895, becoming the first black American to receive a Harvard PhD. In 1896, Du Bois published his dissertation, *The Suppression of the African Slave-Trade to the United States.*

Du Bois's first teaching position was at Wilberforce University in Ohio, and his next book was a sociological study of the African American community in Philadelphia, *The Philadelphia Negro* (1899). By this time Du Bois had begun to write as a journalist and essayist in magazines such as the *Atlantic Monthly*, *The Dial*, *The New World*, the *Annals of the American Academy of Political and Social Science*, and *World's Work*, speaking for the experience of black Americans and speaking against racial violence and segregation. All this was in preparation for his masterwork, *The Souls of Black Folk* (1903). *The Souls of Black Folk* is a mixture of reverie and history, prophecy and autobiography. It is an eloquent and unconventional work of writing designed to introduce both black and white readers to the distinctive history and heritage of black America, its culture, religion, values, and forms of expression.

Perhaps the best way to introduce the project of the book and the selections that follow, Chapters 4, 5, and 6 of *The Souls of Black Folk*, is to reproduce a section of Du Bois's introduction, called "The Forethought." In it he describes the outline and intent of his book and introduces the metaphor of the "Veil," a figure of speech that comes to represent the forces of mind, politics, and economy that divide black from white Americans. He ends with a reference to the "Sorrow Songs," his term for the spirituals created and sung by African American slaves:

Herein lie buried many things which if read with patience may show the strange meaning of being black here in the dawning of the Twentieth Century. This meaning is not without interest to you, Gentle Reader; for the problem of the Twentieth Century is the problem of the color-line.

I pray you, then, receive my little book in all charity, studying my words with me, forgiving mistake and foible for sake of the faith and passion that is in me, and seeking the grain of truth hidden there.

I have sought to sketch, in vague, uncertain outline, the spiritual world in which ten thousand Americans live and strive. First, in two chapters I have tried to show what Emancipation meant to them, and what was its aftermath. In a third chapter I have pointed out the slow rise of personal leadership, and criticised candidly the leader who bears the chief burden of his race today [Booker T. Washington]. Then, in two other chapters I have sketched in swift outline the two worlds within and without the Veil, and thus have come to the central problem of training men for life. Venturing now into deeper detail, I have in two chapters studied the struggles of the massed millions of the black peasantry, and in another have sought to make clear the present relations of the sons of master and man.

Leaving, then, the world of the white man, I have stepped within the Veil, raising it that you may view faintly its deeper recesses, — the meaning of its religion, the passion of its human sorrow, and the struggle of its greater souls. . . .

Before each chapter, as now printed, stands a bar from the Sorrow Songs, — some echo of haunting melody from the only American music which welled up from black souls in the dark past. And, finally, need I add that I who speak here am bone of the bone and flesh of the flesh of them that live within the Veil?

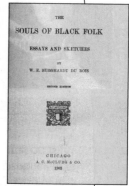

Of the Meaning of Progress

Willst Du Deine Macht verkünden,
Wähle sie die frei von Sünden,
Steh'n in Deinem ew' gen Haus!
Deine Geister sende aus!
Die Unsterblichen, die Reinen,
Die nicht fühlen, die nicht weinen!
Nicht die zarte Jungfrau wähle,
Nicht der Hirtin weiche Seele!

—SCHILLER

Once upon a time I taught school in the hills of Tennessee, where the broad dark vale of the Mississippi begins to roll and crumple to greet the Alleghanies. I was a Fisk student then, and all Fisk men thought that Tennessee — beyond the Veil — was theirs alone, and in vacation time they sallied forth in lusty bands to meet the county school-commissioners. Young and happy, I too went, and I shall not soon forget that summer, seventeen years ago.

First, there was a Teachers' Institute at the county-seat; and there distinguished guests of the superintendent taught the teachers fractions and spelling and other mysteries, — white teachers in the morning, Negroes at night. A picnic now and then, and a supper, and the rough world was softened by laughter and song. I remember how — But I wander.

There came a day when all the teachers left the Institute and began the hunt for schools. I learn from hearsay (for my mother was mortally afraid of fire-arms) that the hunting of ducks and bears and men is wonderfully interesting, but I am sure that the man who has never hunted a country school has something to learn of the pleasures of the chase. I see now the white, hot roads lazily rise and fall and wind before me under the burning July sun; I feel the deep weariness of heart and limb as ten, eight, six miles stretch relentlessly ahead; I feel my heart sink heavily as I hear again and again, "Got a teacher? Yes." So I walked on and on — horses were too expensive until I had wandered beyond railways, beyond stage lines, to a land of "varmints" and rattlesnakes, where the coming of a stranger was an event, and men lived and died in the shadow of one blue hill.

Sprinkled over hill and dale lay cabins and farmhouses, shut out from the world by the forests and the rolling hills toward the east. There I found at last a little school. Josie told me of it; she was a thin, homely girl of twenty, with a dark-brown face and thick, hard hair. I had crossed the stream at Watertown, and rested under the great willows; then I had gone to the little cabin in the lot where Josie was resting on her way to town. The gaunt farmer made me welcome, and Josie, hearing my errand, told me anxiously that they wanted a school over the hill; that but once since the war had a teacher been there; that she herself longed to learn, — and thus she ran on, talking fast and loud, with much earnestness and energy.

Next morning I crossed the tall round hill, lingered to look at the blue and yellow mountains stretching toward the Carolinas, then plunged into the wood, and came out at Josie's home. It was a dull frame cottage with four rooms, perched just below the brow of the hill, amid peach-trees. The father was a quiet, simple soul, calmly ignorant, with no touch of vulgarity. The mother was different, — strong, bustling, and energetic, with a quick, restless tongue, and an ambition to live "like folks." There was a crowd of children. Two boys had gone away. There remained two growing girls; a shy midget of eight; John, tall, awkward, and eighteen; Jim, younger, quicker, and better looking; and two babies of indefinite age. Then there was Josie herself. She seemed to be the centre of the family: always busy at service, or at home, or berry-picking; a little nervous and inclined to scold, like her mother, yet faithful, too, like her father. She had about her a certain fineness, the shadow of an unconscious moral heroism that would willingly give all of life to make life broader, deeper, and fuller for her and hers. I saw much of this family afterwards, and grew to love them for their honest efforts to be decent and comfortable, and for their knowledge of their own ignorance. There was with them no affectation. The mother would scold the father for being so "easy"; Josie would roundly berate the boys for carelessness; and all knew that it was a hard thing to dig a living out of a rocky sidehill.

I secured the school. I remember the day I rode horseback out to the commissioner's house with a pleasant young white fellow who wanted the white school. The road ran down the bed of a stream; the sun laughed and the water jingled, and we rode on. "Come in," said the commissioner, — "come in. Have a seat. Yes, that certificate will do. Stay to dinner. What do you want a month?" "Oh," thought I, "this is lucky"; but even then fell the awful shadow of the Veil, for they ate first, then I — alone.

> "OH," THOUGHT I, "THIS IS LUCKY"; BUT EVEN THEN FELL THE AWFUL SHADOW OF THE VEIL.

The schoolhouse was a log hut, where Colonel Wheeler used to shelter his corn. It sat in a lot behind a rail fence and thorn bushes, near the sweetest of springs. There was an entrance where a door once was, and within, a massive rickety fireplace; great chinks between the logs served as windows. Furniture was scarce. A pale blackboard crouched in the corner. My desk was made of three boards, reinforced at critical points, and my chair, borrowed from the landlady, had to be returned every night. Seats for the children — these puzzled me much. I was haunted by a New England vision of neat little desks and chairs, but, alas! the reality was rough plank benches without backs, and at times without legs. They had the one virtue of making naps dangerous, — possibly fatal, for the floor was not to be trusted.

It was a hot morning late in July when the school opened. I trembled when I heard the patter of little feet down the dusty road, and saw the growing row of dark solemn faces and bright eager eyes facing me. First came Josie and her brothers and sisters. The longing to know, to be a student in the great school at Nashville, hovered like a star above this child-woman amid her work and worry, and she studied doggedly. There were the Dowells from their farm over toward Alexandria, — Fanny, with her smooth black face and wondering eyes; Martha, brown and dull; the pretty girl-wife of a brother, and the younger brood.

There were the Burkes, — two brown and yellow lads, and a tiny haughty-eyed girl. Fat Reuben's little chubby girl came, with golden face and old-gold hair, faithful and solemn. 'Thenie was on hand early, — a jolly, ugly, good-hearted girl, who slyly dipped snuff and looked after her little bow-legged brother. When her mother could spare her, 'Tildy came, — a midnight beauty, with starry eyes and tapering limbs; and her brother, correspondingly homely. And then the big boys, — the hulking Lawrences; the lazy Neills, unfathered sons of mother and daughter; Hickman, with a stoop in his shoulders; and the rest.

There they sat, nearly thirty of them, on the rough benches, their faces shading from a pale cream to a deep brown, the little feet bare and swinging, the eyes full of expectation, with here and there a twinkle of mischief, and the hands grasping Webster's blue-back spelling-book. I loved my school, and the fine faith the children had in the wisdom of their teacher was truly marvellous. We read and spelled together, wrote a little, picked flowers, sang, and listened to stories of the world beyond the hill. At times the school would dwindle away, and I would start out. I would visit Mun Eddings, who lived in two very dirty rooms, and ask why little Lugene, whose flaming face seemed ever ablaze with the dark-red hair uncombed, was absent all last week, or why I missed so often the inimitable rags of Mack and Ed. Then the father, who worked Colonel Wheeler's farm on shares, would tell me how the crops needed the boys; and the thin, slovenly mother, whose face was pretty when washed, assured me that Lugene must mind the baby. "But we'll start them again next week." When the Lawrences stopped, I knew that the doubts of the old folks about book-learning had conquered again, and so, toiling up the hill, and getting as far into the cabin as possible, I put Cicero "pro Archia Poeta" into the simplest English with local applications, and usually convinced them — for a week or so.

On Friday nights I often went home with some of the children, — sometimes to Doc Burke's farm. He was a great, loud, thin Black, ever working, and trying to buy the seventy-five acres of hill and dale where he lived; but people said that he would surely fail, and the "white folks would get it all." His wife was a magnificent Amazon, with saffron face and shining hair, uncorseted and barefooted, and the children were strong and beautiful. They lived in a one-and-a-half-room cabin in the hollow of the farm, near the spring. The front room was full of great fat white beds, scrupulously neat; and there were bad chromos on the walls, and a tired centre-table. In the tiny back kitchen I was often invited to "take out and help" myself to fried chicken and wheat biscuit, "meat" and corn pone, string-beans and berries. At first I used to be a little alarmed at the approach of bedtime in the one lone bedroom, but embarrassment was very deftly avoided. First, all the children nodded and slept, and were stowed away in one great pile of goose feathers; next, the mother and the father discreetly slipped away to the kitchen while I went to bed; then, blowing out the dim light, they retired in the dark. In the morning all were up and away before I thought of awaking. Across the road, where fat Reuben lived, they all went outdoors while the teacher retired, because they did not boast the luxury of a kitchen.

I liked to stay with the Dowells, for they had four rooms and plenty of good country fare. Uncle Bird had a small, rough farm, all woods and hills, miles from the big road; but he was full of tales, — he preached now and then, — and with his children, berries, horses, and wheat he was happy and prosperous. Often, to keep the peace, I must go where life was less lovely; for instance, 'Tildy's mother was incorrigibly dirty, Reuben's larder was limited seriously, and herds of untamed insects wandered over the Eddingses' beds. Best of all I loved to go to Josie's, and sit on the porch, eating peaches, while the mother bustled and talked: how Josie had bought the sewing-machine; how Josie worked at service in winter, but that four dollars a month was "mighty little" wages; how Josie longed to go away to school, but that it "looked like" they never could get far enough ahead to let her; how the crops failed and the well was yet unfinished; and, finally, how "mean" some of the white folks were.

For two summers I lived in this little world; it was dull and humdrum. The girls looked at the hill in wistful longing, and the boys fretted and haunted Alexandria. Alexandria was "town," — a straggling, lazy village of houses, churches, and shops, and an aristocracy of Toms, Dicks, and Cap-tains. Cuddled on the hill to the north was the village of the colored folks, who lived in three- or four-room unpainted cottages, some neat and home-like, and some dirty. The dwellings were scattered rather aimlessly, but they centred about the twin temples of the hamlet, the Methodist, and the Hard-Shell Baptist churches. These, in turn, leaned gingerly on a sad-colored schoolhouse. Hither my little world wended its crooked way on Sunday to meet other worlds, and gossip, and wonder, and make the weekly sacrifice with frenzied priest at the altar of the "old-time religion." Then the soft melody and mighty cadences of Negro song fluttered and thundered.

I have called my tiny community a world, and so its isolation made it; and yet there was among us but a half-awakened common consciousness, sprung from common joy and grief, at burial, birth, or wedding; from a common hardship in poverty, poor land, and low wages; and, above all, from the sight of the Veil that hung between us and Opportunity. All this caused us to think some thoughts together; but these, when ripe for speech, were spoken in various languages. Those whose eyes twenty-five and more years before had seen "the glory of the coming of the Lord," saw in every present hindrance or help a dark fatalism bound to bring all things right in His own good time. The mass of those to whom slavery was a dim recollection of childhood found the world a puzzling thing: it asked little of them, and they answered with little, and yet it ridiculed their offering. Such a paradox they could not understand, and therefore sank into listless indifference, or shiftlessness, or reckless bravado. There were, however, some — such as Josie, Jim, and Ben — to whom War, Hell, and Slavery were but childhood tales, whose young appetites had been whetted to an edge by school and story and half-awakened thought. Ill could they be content, born without and beyond the World. And their weak wings beat against their barriers, — barriers of caste, of youth, of life; at last, in dangerous moments, against everything that opposed even a whim.

> **AND YET THERE WAS AMONG US BUT A HALF-AWAKENED COMMON CONSCIOUSNESS.**

The ten years that follow youth, the years when first the realization comes that life is leading somewhere, — these were the years that passed after I left my little school. When they were past, I came by chance once more to the walls of Fisk University, to the halls of the chapel of melody. As I lingered there in the joy and pain of meeting old school-friends, there swept over me a sudden longing to pass again beyond the blue hill, and to see the homes and the school of other days, and to learn how life had gone with my school-children; and I went.

Josie was dead, and the gray-haired mother said simply, "We've had a heap of trouble since you've been away." I had feared for Jim. With a cultured parentage and a social caste to uphold him, he might have made a venturesome merchant or a West Point cadet. But here he was, angry with life and reckless; and when Farmer Durham charged him with stealing wheat, the old man had to ride fast to escape the stones which the furious fool hurled after him. They told Jim to run away; but he would not run, and the constable came that afternoon. It grieved Josie, and great awkward John walked nine miles every day to see his little brother through the bars of Lebanon jail. At last the two came back together in the dark night. The mother cooked supper, and Josie emptied her purse, and the boys stole away. Josie grew thin and silent, yet worked the more. The hill became steep for the quiet old father, and with the boys away there was little to do in the valley. Josie helped them to sell the old farm, and they moved nearer town. Brother Dennis, the carpenter, built a new house with six rooms;

Josie toiled a year in Nashville, and brought back ninety dollars to furnish the house and change it to a home.

When the spring came, and the birds twittered, and the stream ran proud and full, little sister Lizzie, bold and thoughtless, flushed with the passion of youth, bestowed herself on the tempter, and brought home a nameless child. Josie shivered and worked on, with the vision of school-days all fled, with a face wan and tired, — worked until, on a summer's day, some one married another; then Josie crept to her mother like a hurt child, and slept — and sleeps.

I paused to scent the breeze as I entered the valley. The Lawrences have gone, — father and son forever, — and the other son lazily digs in the earth to live. A new young widow rents out their cabin to fat Reuben. Reuben is a Baptist preacher now, but I fear as lazy as ever, though his cabin has three rooms; and little Ella has grown into a bouncing woman, and is ploughing corn on the hot hillside. There are babies a-plenty, and one half-witted girl. Across the valley is a house I did not know before, and there I found, rocking one baby and expecting another, one of my schoolgirls, a daughter of Uncle Bird Dowell. She looked somewhat worried with her new duties, but soon bristled into pride over her neat cabin and the tale of her thrifty husband, the horse and cow, and the farm they were planning to buy.

My log schoolhouse was gone. In its place stood Progress; and Progress, I understand, is necessarily ugly. The crazy foundation stones still marked the former site of my poor little cabin, and not far away, on six weary boulders, perched a jaunty board house, perhaps twenty by thirty feet, with three windows and a door that locked. Some of the window-glass was broken, and part of an old iron stove lay mournfully under the house. I peeped through the window half reverently, and found things that were more familiar. The blackboard had grown by about two feet, and the seats were still without backs. The county owns the lot now, I hear, and every year there is a session of school. As I sat by the spring and looked on the Old and the New I felt glad, very glad, and yet —

After two long drinks I started on. There was the great double log-house on the corner. I remembered the broken, blighted family that used to live there. The strong, hard face of the mother, with its wilderness of hair, rose before me. She had driven her husband away, and while I taught school a strange man lived there, big and jovial, and people talked. I felt sure that Ben and 'Tildy would come to naught from such a home. But this is an odd world; for Ben is a busy farmer in Smith County, "doing well, too," they say, and he had cared for little 'Tildy until last spring, when a lover married her. A hard life the lad had led, toiling for meat, and laughed at because he was homely and crooked. There was Sam Carlon, an impudent old skinflint, who had definite notions about "niggers," and hired Ben a summer and would not pay him. Then the hungry boy gathered his sacks together, and in broad daylight went into Carlon's corn; and when the hard-fisted farmer set upon him, the angry boy flew at him like a beast. Doc Burke saved a murder and a lynching that day.

The story reminded me again of the Burkes, and an impatience seized me to know who won in the battle, Doc or the seventy-five acres. For it is a hard thing to make a farm out of nothing, even in fifteen years. So I hurried on, thinking of the Burkes. They used to have a certain magnificent barbarism about them that I liked. They were never vulgar, never immoral, but rather rough and primitive, with an unconventionality that spent itself in loud guffaws, slaps on the back, and naps in the corner. I hurried by the cottage of the misborn Neill boys. It was empty, and they were grown into fat, lazy farm-hands. I saw the home of the Hickmans, but Albert, with his stooping shoulders, had passed from the world. Then I came to the Burkes' gate and peered through; the inclosure looked rough and untrimmed, and yet there were the same fences around the old farm save to the left, where lay twenty-five other acres. And lo! the cabin in the hollow had climbed the hill and swollen to a half-finished six-room cottage.

The Burkes held a hundred acres, but they were still in debt. Indeed, the gaunt father who toiled night and day would scarcely be happy out of debt, being so used to it. Some day he must stop, for his massive frame is showing decline. The mother wore shoes, but the lion-like physique of other days was broken. The children had grown up. Rob, the image of his father, was loud and rough with laughter. Birdie, my school baby of six, had grown to a picture of maiden beau, tall and tawny. "Edgar is gone," said the mother, with head half bowed, — "gone to work in Nashville; he and his father couldn't agree."

Little Doc, the boy born since the time of my school, took me horseback down the creek next morning toward Farmer Dowell's. The road and the stream were battling for mastery, and the stream had the better of it. We splashed and waded, and the merry boy, perched behind me, chattered and laughed. He showed me where Simon Thompson had bought a bit of ground and a home; but his daughter Lana, a plump, brown, slow girl, was not there. She had married a man and a farm twenty miles away. We wound on down the stream till we came to a gate that I did not recognize, but the boy insisted that it was "Uncle Bird's." The farm was fat with the growing crop. In that little valley was a strange stillness as I rode up; for death and marriage had stolen youth and left age and childhood there. We sat and talked that night after the chores were done. Uncle Bird was grayer, and his eyes did not see so well, but he was still jovial. We talked of the acres bought, — one hundred and twenty-five, — of the new guest-chamber added, of Martha's marrying. Then we talked of death: Fanny and Fred were gone; a shadow hung over the other daughter, and when it lifted she was to go to Nashville to school. At last we spoke of the neighbors, and as night fell, Uncle Bird told me how, on a night like that, 'Thenie came wandering back to her home over yonder, to escape the blows of her husband. And next morning she died in the home that her little bow-legged brother, working and saving, had bought for their widowed mother.

My journey was done, and behind me lay hill and dale, and Life and Death. How shall man measure Progress there where the dark-faced Josie lies? How many heartfuls of sorrow shall balance a bushel of wheat? How hard a thing is life to the lowly, and yet how human and real! And all this life and love and strife and failure, — is it the twilight of nightfall or the flush of some faint-dawning day?

Thus sadly musing, I rode to Nashville in the Jim Crow car.

Of the Wings of Atalanta

O black boy of Atlanta!
    But half was spoken;
The slave's chains and the master's
    Alike are broken;
The one curse of the races
    Held both in tether;
They are rising — all are rising —
    The black and white together.

                 —WHITTIER

South of the North, yet north of the South, lies the City of a Hundred Hills, peering out from the shadows of the past into the promise of the future. I have seen her in the morning, when the first flush of day had half-roused her; she lay gray and still on the crimson soil of Georgia; then the blue smoke began to curl from her chimneys, the tinkle of bell and scream of whistle broke the silence, the rattle and roar of busy life slowly gathered and swelled, until the seething whirl of the city seemed a strange thing in a sleepy land.

Once, they say, even Atlanta slept dull and drowsy at the foot-hills of the Alleghanies, until the iron baptism of war awakened her with its sullen waters, aroused and maddened her, and left her listening to the sea. And the sea cried to the hills and the hills answered the sea, till the city rose like a widow and cast away her weeds, and toiled for her daily bread; toiled steadily, toiled cunningly, — perhaps with some bitterness, with a touch of *réclame*, — and yet with real earnestness, and real sweat.

It is a hard thing to live haunted by the ghost of an untrue dream; to see the wide vision of empire fade into real ashes and dirt; to feel the pang of the conquered, and yet know that with all the Bad that fell on one black day, something was vanquished that deserved to live, something killed that in justice had not dared to die; to know that with the Right that triumphed, triumphed something of Wrong, something sordid and mean, something less than the broadest and best. All this is bitter hard; and many a man and city and people have found in it excuse for sulking, and brooding, and listless waiting.

IT IS A HARD THING TO LIVE HAUNTED BY THE GHOST OF AN UNTRUE DREAM.

Such are not men of the sturdier make; they of Atlanta turned reso-lutely toward the future; and that future held aloft vistas of purple and gold: — Atlanta, Queen of the cotton kingdom; Atlanta, Gateway to the Land of the Sun; Atlanta, the new Lachesis, spinner of web and woof for the world. So the city crowned her hundred hills with factories, and stored her shops with cunning handiwork, and stretched long iron ways to greet the busy Mercury in his coming. And the Nation talked of her striving.

Perhaps Atlanta was not christened for the winged maiden of dull Bœotia; you know the tale, — how swarthy Atalanta, tall and wild, would marry only him who out-raced her; and how the wily Hippomenes laid three apples of gold in the way. She fled like a shadow, paused, startled over the first apple, but even as he stretched his hand, fled again; hovered over the second, then, slipping from his hot grasp, flew over river, vale, and hill; but as she lingered over the third, his arms fell round her, and looking on each other, the blazing passion of their love profaned the sanctuary of Love, and they were cursed. If Atlanta be not named for Atalanta, she ought to have been.

Atalanta is not the first or the last maiden whom greed of gold has led to defile the temple of Love; and not maids alone, but men in the race of life, sink from the high and generous ideals of youth to the gambler's code of the Bourse; and in all our Nation's striving is not the Gospel of Work befouled by the Gospel of Pay? So common is this that one-half think it normal; so unquestioned, that we almost fear to question if the end of racing is not gold, if the aim of man is not rightly to be rich. And if this is the fault of America, how dire a danger lies before a new land and a new city, lest Atlanta, stooping for mere gold, shall find that gold accursed!

It was no maiden's idle whim that started this hard racing; a fearful wilderness lay about the feet of that city after the War, — feudalism, pov-erty, the rise of the Third Estate, serfdom, the re-birth of Law and Order, and above and between all, the Veil of Race. How heavy a journey for weary feet! what wings must Atalanta have to flit over all this hollow and hill, through sour wood and sullen water, and by the red waste of sun-baked clay! How fleet must Atalanta be if she will not be tempted by gold to profane the Sanctuary!

The Sanctuary of our fathers has, to be sure, few Gods, — some sneer, "all too few." There is the thrifty Mercury of New England, Pluto of the North, and Ceres of the West; and there, too, is the half-forgotten Apollo of the South, under whose ægis the maiden ran, — and as she ran she forgot him, even as there in Bœotia Venus was forgot. She forgot the old ideal of the Southern gentleman, — that new-world heir of the grace and courtliness of patrician, knight, and noble; forgot his honor with his foi-bles, his kindliness with his carelessness, and stooped to apples of gold, — to men busier and sharper, thriftier and more unscrupulous. Golden apples are beautiful — I remember the lawless days of boyhood, when orchards in crimson and gold tempted me over fence and field — and, too, the merchant who has dethroned the planter is no despicable *parvenu*. Work and wealth are the mighty levers to lift this old new land; thrift and toil and saving are the highways to new hopes and new possibilities; and yet the warning is needed lest the wily Hippomenes tempt Atalanta to thinking that golden apples are the goal of racing, and not mere incidents by the way.

Atlanta must not lead the South to dream of material prosperity as the touchstone of all success; already the fatal might of this idea is beginning to spread; it is replacing the finer type of Southerner with vulgar money-getters; it is burying the sweeter beauties of Southern life beneath pretence and ostentation. For every social ill the panacea of Wealth has been urged, — wealth to overthrow the remains of the slave feudalism; wealth to raise the "cracker" Third Estate; wealth to employ the black serfs, and the prospect of wealth to keep them working; wealth as the end and aim of politics, and as the legal tender for law and order; and, finally, instead of Truth, Beauty, and Goodness, wealth as the ideal of the Public School.

> **ATLANTA MUST NOT LEAD THE SOUTH TO DREAM OF MATERIAL PROSPERITY AS THE TOUCHSTONE OF ALL SUCCESS.**

Not only is this true in the world which Atlanta typifies, but it is threatening to be true of a world beneath and beyond that world, — the Black World beyond the Veil. To-day it makes little difference to Atlanta, to the South, what the Negro thinks or dreams or wills. In the soul-life of the land he is to-day, and naturally will long remain, unthought of, half forgotten; and yet when he does come to think and will and do for himself, — and let no man dream that day will never come, — then the part he plays will not be one of sudden learning, but words and thoughts he has been taught to lisp in his race-childhood. To-day the ferment of his striving toward self-realization is to the strife of the white world like a wheel within a wheel: beyond the Veil are smaller but like problems of ideals, of leaders and the led, of serfdom, of poverty, of order and subordination, and, through all, the Veil of Race. Few know of these problems, few who know notice them; and yet there they are, awaiting student, artist, and seer, — a field for somebody sometime to discover. Hither has the temptation of Hippomenes penetrated; already in this smaller world, which now indirectly and anon directly must influence the larger for good or ill, the habit is forming of interpreting the world in dollars. The old leaders of Negro opinion, in the little groups where there is a Negro social consciousness, are being replaced by new; neither the black preacher nor the black teacher leads as he did two decades ago. Into their places are pushing the farmers and gardeners, the well-paid porters and artisans, the businessmen, — all those with property and money. And with all this change, so curiously parallel to that of the Other-world, goes too the same inevitable change in ideals. The South laments to-day the slow, steady disappearance of a certain type of Negro, — the faithful, courteous slave of other days, with his incorruptible honesty and dignified humility. He is passing away just as surely as the old type of Southern gentleman is passing, and from not dissimilar causes, — the sudden transformation of a fair far-off ideal of Freedom into the hard reality of bread-winning and the consequent deification of Bread.

In the Black World, the Preacher and Teacher embodied once the ideals of this people, — the strife for another and a juster world, the vague dream of righteousness, the mystery of knowing; but to-day the danger is that these ideals, with their simple beauty and weird inspiration, will suddenly sink to a question of cash and a lust for gold. Here stands this black young Atalanta, girding herself for the race that must be run; and if her eyes be still toward the hills and sky as in the days of old, then we may look for noble running; but what if some ruthless or wily or even thoughtless Hippomenes lay golden apples before her? What if the Negro people be wooed from a strife for righteousness, from a love of knowing, to regard dollars as the be-all and end-all of life? What if to the Mammonism of America be added the rising Mammonism of the re-born South, and the Mammonism of this South be reinforced by the budding Mammonism of its half-awakened black millions? Whither, then, is the new-world quest of Goodness and Beauty and Truth gone glimmering? Must this, and that fair flower of Freedom which, despite the jeers of latter-day striplings, sprung from our fathers' blood, must that too degenerate into a dusty quest of gold, — into lawless lust with Hippomenes?

The hundred hills of Atlanta are not all crowned with factories. On one, toward the west, the setting sun throws three buildings in bold relief against the sky. The beauty of the group lies in its simple unity: — a broad lawn of green rising from the red street with mingled roses and peaches; north and south, two plain and stately halls; and in the midst, half hidden in ivy, a larger building, boldly graceful, sparingly decorated, and with one low spire. It is a restful group, — one never looks for more; it is all here, all intelligible. There I live, and there I hear from day to day the low hum of restful life. In winter's twilight, when the red sun glows, I can see the dark figures pass between the halls to the music of the night-bell. In the morning, when the sun is golden, the clang of the day-bell brings the hurry and laughter of three hundred young hearts from hall and street, and from the busy city below, — children all dark and heavy-haired, — to join their clear young voices in the music of the morning sacrifice. In a half-dozen classrooms they gather then, — here to follow the love-song of Dido, here to listen to the tale of Troy divine; there to wander among the stars, there to wander among men and nations, — and elsewhere other well-worn ways of knowing this

NOTHING NEW, NO TIME-SAVING DEVICES, — SIMPLY OLD TIME-GLORIFIED METHODS OF DELVING FOR TRUTH.

queer world. Nothing new, no time-saving devices, — simply old time-glorified methods of delving for Truth, and searching out the hidden beauties of life, and learning the good of living. The riddle of existence is the college curriculum that was laid before the Pharaohs, that was taught in the groves by Plato, that formed the *trivium* and *quadrivium*, and is to-day laid before the freedmen's sons by Atlanta University. And this course of study will not change; its methods will grow more deft and effectual, its content richer by toil of scholar and sight of seer; but the true college will ever have one goal, — not to earn meat, but to know the end and aim of that life which meat nourishes.

The vision of life that rises before these dark eyes has in it nothing mean or selfish. Not at Oxford or at Leipsic, not at Yale or Columbia, is there an air of higher resolve or more unfettered striving; the determination to realize for men, both black and white, the broadest possibilities of life, to seek the better and the best, to spread with their own hands the Gospel of Sacrifice, — all this is the burden of their talk and dream. Here, amid a wide desert of caste and proscription, amid the heart-hurting slights and jars and vagaries of a deep race-dislike, lies this green oasis, where hot anger cools, and the bitterness of disappointment is sweetened by the springs and breezes of Parnassus; and here men may lie and listen, and learn of a future fuller than the past, and hear the voice of Time:

"Entbehren sollst du, sollst entbehren."

They made their mistakes, those who planted Fisk and Howard and Atlanta before the smoke of battle had lifted; they made their mistakes, but those mistakes were not the things at which we lately laughed somewhat uproariously. They were right when they sought to found a new educational system upon the University: where, forsooth, shall we ground knowledge save on the broadest and deepest knowledge? The roots of the tree, rather than the leaves, are the sources of its life; and from the dawn of history, from Academus to Cambridge, the culture of the University has been the broad foundation-stone on which is built the kindergarten's A B C.

But these builders did make a mistake in minimizing the gravity of the problem before them; in thinking it a matter of years and decades; in therefore building quickly and laying their foundation carelessly, and lowering the standard of knowing, until they had scattered haphazard through the South some dozen poorly equipped high schools and miscalled them universities. They forgot, too, just as their successors are forgetting, the rule of inequality: — that of the million black youth, some were fitted to know and some to dig; that some had the talent and capacity of university men, and some the talent and capacity of blacksmiths; and that true training meant neither that all should be college men nor all artisans, but that the one should be made a missionary of culture to an untaught people, and the other a free workman among serfs. And to seek to make the blacksmith a scholar is almost as silly as the more modern scheme of making the scholar a blacksmith; almost, but not quite.

The function of the university is not simply to teach breadwinning, or to furnish teachers for the public schools, or to be a centre of polite society; it is, above all, to be the organ of that fine adjustment between real life and the growing knowledge of life, an adjustment which forms the secret of civilization. Such an institution the South of to-day sorely needs. She has religion, earnest, bigoted: — religion that on both sides the Veil often omits the sixth, seventh, and eighth command-ments, but substitutes a dozen supplementary ones. She has, as Atlanta shows, growing thrift and love of toil; but she lacks that broad knowl-edge of what the world knows and knew of human living and doing, which she may apply to the thousand problems of real life to-day con-fronting her. The need of the South is knowledge and culture, — not in dainty limited quantity, as before the war, but in broad busy abundance in the world of work; and until she has this, not all the Apples of Hesperides, be they golden and bejewelled, can save her from the curse of the Bœotian lovers.

> THE FUNCTION OF THE UNIVERSITY IS NOT SIMPLY TO TEACH BREADWINNING.

The Wings of Atalanta are the coming universities of the South. They alone can bear the maiden past the temptation of golden fruit. They will not guide her flying feet away from the cotton and gold; for — ah, thought-ful Hippomenes! — do not the apples lie in the very Way of Life? But they will guide her over and beyond them, and leave her kneeling in the Sanctuary of Truth and Freedom and broad Humanity, virgin and unde-filed. Sadly did the Old South err in human education, despising the edu-cation of the masses, and niggardly in the support of colleges. Her ancient university foundations dwindled and withered under the foul breath of slavery; and even since the war they have fought a failing fight for life in the tainted air of social unrest and commercial selfishness, stunted by the death of criticism, and starving for lack of broadly cultured men. And if this is the white South's need and danger, how much heavier the danger and need of the freedmen's sons! how pressing here the need of broad ideals and true culture, the conservation of soul from sordid aims and petty passions! Let us build the Southern university — William and Mary, Trinity, Georgia, Texas, Tulane, Vanderbilt, and the others — fit to live; let us build, too, the Negro universities: — Fisk, whose foundation was ever broad; Howard, at the heart of the Nation; Atlanta at Atlanta, whose ideal of scholarship has been held above the temptation of numbers. Why not here, and perhaps elsewhere, plant deeply and for all time centres of learning and living, colleges that yearly would send into the life of the South a few white men and a few black men of broad culture, catholic tolerance, and trained ability, joining their hands to other hands, and giv-ing to this squabble of the Races a decent and dignified peace?

Patience, Humility, Manners, and Taste, common schools and kinder-gartens, industrial and technical schools, literature and tolerance, — all these spring from knowledge and culture, the children of the university. So must men and nations build, not otherwise, not upside down.

Teach workers to work, — a wise saying; wise when applied to German boys and American girls; wiser when said of Negro boys, for they have less knowledge of working and none to teach them. Teach thinkers to think, — a needed knowledge in a day of loose and careless logic; and they whose lot is gravest must have the carefulest training to think aright. If these things are so, how foolish to ask what is the best education for one or seven or sixty million souls! shall we teach them trades, or train them in liberal arts? Neither and both: teach the workers to work and the thinkers to think; make carpenters of carpenters, and philosophers of philosophers, and fops of fools. Nor can we pause here. We are training not isolated men but a living group of men, — nay, a group within a group. And the final product of our training must be neither a psychologist nor a brickmason, but a man. And to make men, we must have ideals, broad, pure, and inspiring ends of living, — not sordid money-getting, not apples of gold. The worker must work for the glory of his handiwork, not simply for pay; the thinker must think for truth, not for fame. And all this is gained only by human strife and longing; by ceaseless training and education; by founding Right on righteousness and Truth on the unhampered search for Truth; by founding the common school on the university, and the industrial school on the common school; and weaving thus a system, not a distortion, and bringing a birth, not an abortion.

When night falls on the City of a Hundred Hills, a wind gathers itself from the seas and comes murmuring westward. And at its bidding, the smoke of the drowsy factories sweeps down upon the mighty city and covers it like a pall, while yonder at the University the stars twinkle above Stone Hall. And they say that yon gray mist is the tunic of Atalanta pausing over her golden apples. Fly, my maiden, fly, for yonder comes Hippomenes!

Of the Training of Black Men

Why, if the Soul can fling the Dust aside,
And naked on the Air of Heaven ride,
   Were 't not a Shame — were 't not a Shame for him
In this clay carcase crippled to abide?

                     —OMAR KHAYYÁM (FITZGERALD)

From the shimmering swirl of waters where many, many thoughts ago the slave-ship first saw the square tower of Jamestown, have flowed down to our day three streams of thinking: one swollen from the larger world here and overseas, saying, the multiplying of human wants in culture-lands calls for the world-wide coöperation of men in satisfying them. Hence arises a new human unity, pulling the ends of earth nearer, and all men, black, yellow, and white. The larger humanity strives to feel in this contact of living Nations and sleeping hordes a thrill of new life in the world, crying, "If the contact of Life and Sleep be Death, shame on such Life." To be sure, behind this thought lurks the afterthought of force and dominion, — the making of brown men to delve when the temptation of beads and red calico cloys.

The second thought streaming from the death-ship and the curving river is the thought of the older South, — the sincere and passionate belief that somewhere between men and cattle, God created a *tertium quid*, and called it a Negro, — a clownish, simple creature, at times even lovable within its limitations, but straitly foreordained to walk within the Veil. To be sure, behind the thought lurks the afterthought, — some of them with favoring chance might become men, but in sheer self-defence we dare not let them, and we build about them walls so high, and hang between them and the light a veil so thick, that they shall not even think of breaking through.

And last of all there trickles down that third and darker thought, — the thought of the things themselves, the confused, half-conscious mutter of men who are black and whitened, crying "Liberty, Freedom, Opportunity — vouchsafe to us, O boastful World, the chance of living men!" To be sure, behind the thought lurks the afterthought, — suppose, after all, the World is right and we are less than men? Suppose this mad impulse within is all wrong, some mock mirage from the untrue?

So here we stand among thoughts of human unity, even through conquest and slavery; the inferiority of black men, even if forced by fraud; a shriek in the night for the freedom of men who themselves are not yet sure of their right to demand it. This is the tangle of thought and after-thought wherein we are called to solve the problem of training men for life.

Behind all its curiousness, so attractive alike to sage and *dilettante*, lie its dim dangers, throwing across us shadows at once grotesque and awful. Plain it is to us that what the world seeks through desert and wild we have within our threshold, — a stalwart laboring force, suited to the semi-tropics; if, deaf to the voice of the Zeitgeist, we refuse to use and develop these men, we risk poverty and loss. If, on the other hand, seized by the brutal afterthought, we debauch the race thus caught in our talons, selfishly suck-ing their blood and brains in the future as in the past, what shall save us from national deca-dence? Only that saner selfishness, which Education teaches men, can find the rights of all in the whirl of work.

> **THIS IS THE TANGLE OF THOUGHT AND AFTERTHOUGHT WHEREIN WE ARE CALLED TO SOLVE THE PROBLEM OF TRAINING MEN FOR LIFE.**

Again, we may decry the color-prejudice of the South, yet it remains a heavy fact. Such curious kinks of the human mind exist and must be reckoned with soberly. They cannot be laughed away, nor always success-fully stormed at, nor easily abolished by act of legislature. And yet they must not be encouraged by being let alone. They must be recognized as facts, but unpleasant facts; things that stand in the way of civilization and religion and common decency. They can be met in but one way, — by the breadth and broadening of human reason, by catholicity of taste and cul-ture. And so, too, the native ambition and aspiration of men, even though they be black, backward, and ungraceful, must not lightly be dealt with. To stimulate wildly weak and untrained minds is to play with mighty fires; to flout their striving idly is to welcome a harvest of brutish crime and shameless lethargy in our very laps. The guiding of thought and the deft coordination of deed is at once the path of honor and humanity.

And so, in this great question of reconciling three vast and partially contradictory streams of thought, the one panacea of Education leaps to the lips of all: — such human training as will best use the labor of all men without enslaving or brutalizing; such training as will give us poise to encourage the prejudices that bulwark society, and to stamp out those that in sheer barbarity deafen us to the wail of prisoned souls within the Veil, and the mounting fury of shackled men.

But when we have vaguely said that Education will set this tangle straight, what have we uttered but a truism? Training for life teaches liv-ing; but what training for the profitable living together of black men and white? A hundred and fifty years ago our task would have seemed easier.

Then Dr. Johnson blandly assured us that education was needful solely for the embellishments of life, and was useless for ordinary vermin. To-day we have climbed to heights where we would open at least the outer courts of knowledge to all, display its treasures to many, and select the few to whom its mystery of Truth is revealed, not wholly by birth or the accidents of the stock market, but at least in part according to deftness and aim, talent and character. This programme, however, we are sorely puzzled in carrying out through that part of the land where the blight of slavery fell hardest, and where we are dealing with two backward peoples. To make here in human education that ever necessary combination of the permanent and the contingent — of the ideal and the practical in workable equilibrium — has been there, as it ever must be in every age and place, a matter of infinite experiment and frequent mistakes.

In rough approximation we may point out four varying decades of work in Southern education since the Civil War. From the close of the war until 1876, was the period of uncertain groping and temporary relief. There were army schools, mission schools, and schools of the Freedman's Bureau in chaotic disarrangement seeking system and coöperation. Then followed ten years of constructive definite effort toward the building of complete school systems in the South. Normal schools and colleges were founded for the freedmen, and teachers trained there to man the public schools. There was the inevitable tendency of war to underestimate the prejudices of the master and the ignorance of the slave, and all seemed clear sailing out of the wreckage of the storm. Meantime, starting in this decade yet especially developing from 1885 to 1895, began the industrial revolution of the South. The land saw glimpses of a new destiny and the stirring of new ideals. The educational system striving to complete itself saw new obstacles and a field of work ever broader and deeper. The Negro colleges, hurriedly founded, were inadequately equipped, illogically distributed, and of varying efficiency and grade; the normal and high schools were doing little more than common-school work, and the common schools were training but a third of the children who ought to be in them, and training these too often poorly. At the same time the white South, by reason of its sudden conversion from the slavery ideal, by so much the more became set and strengthened in its racial prejudice, and crystallized it into harsh law and harsher custom; while the marvellous pushing forward of the poor white daily threatened to take even bread and butter from the mouths of the heavily handicapped sons of the freedmen. In the midst, then, of the larger problem of Negro education sprang up the more practical question of work, the inevitable economic quandary that faces a people in the transition from slavery to freedom, and especially those who make that change amid hate and prejudice, lawlessness and ruthless competition.

The industrial school springing to notice in this decade, but coming to full recognition in the decade beginning with 1895, was the proffered answer to this combined educational and economic crisis, and an answer of singular wisdom and timeliness. From the very first in nearly all the schools some attention had been given to training in handiwork, but now was this training first raised to a dignity that brought it in direct touch with the South's magnificent industrial development, and given an emphasis which reminded black folk that before the Temple of Knowledge swing the Gates of Toil.

Yet after all they are but gates, and when turning our eyes from the temporary and the contingent in the Negro problem to the broader question of the permanent uplifting and civilization of black men in America, we have a right to inquire, as this enthusiasm for material advancement mounts to its height, if after all the industrial school is the final and sufficient answer in the training of the Negro race; and to ask gently, but in all sincerity, the ever-recurring query of the ages, Is not life more than meat, and the body more than raiment? And men ask this to-day all the more eagerly because of sinister signs in recent educational movements. The tendency is here, born of slavery and quickened to renewed life by the crazy imperialism of the day, to regard human beings as among the material resources of a land to be trained with an eye single to future dividends. Race-prejudices, which keep brown and black men in their "places," we are coming to regard as useful allies with such a theory, no matter how much they may dull the ambition and sicken the hearts of struggling human beings. And above all, we daily hear that an education that encourages aspiration, that sets the loftiest of ideals and seeks as an end culture and character rather than breadwinning, is the privilege of white men and the danger and delusion of black.

WE DAILY HEAR THAT AN EDUCATION THAT ENCOURAGES ASPIRATION . . . IS THE PRIVILEGE OF WHITE MEN AND THE DANGER AND DELUSION OF BLACK.

Especially has criticism been directed against the former educational efforts to aid the Negro. In the four periods I have mentioned, we find first, boundless, planless enthusiasm and sacrifice; then the preparation of teachers for a vast public-school system; then the launching and expansion of that school system amid increasing difficulties; and finally the training of workmen for the new and growing industries. This development has been sharply ridiculed as a logical anomaly and flat reversal of nature. Soothly we have been told that first industrial and manual training should have taught the Negro to work, then simple schools should have taught him to read and write, and finally, after years, high and normal schools could have completed the system, as intelligence and wealth demanded.

That a system logically so complete was historically impossible, it needs but a little thought to prove. Progress in human affairs is more often a pull than a push, surging forward of the exceptional man, and the lifting of his duller brethren slowly and painfully to his vantage-ground. Thus it was no accident that gave birth to universities centuries before the common schools, that made fair Harvard the first flower of our wilderness. So in the South: the mass of the freedmen at the end of the war lacked the intelligence so necessary to modern workingmen. They must first have the common school to teach them to read, write, and cipher; and they must have higher schools to teach teachers for the common schools. The white teachers who flocked South went to establish such a common-school system. Few held the idea of founding colleges; most of them at first would have laughed at the idea. But they faced, as all men since them have faced, that central paradox of the South, — the social separation of the races. At that time it was the sudden volcanic rupture of nearly all relations between black and white, in work and government and family life. Since then a new adjustment of relations in economic and political affairs has grown up, — an adjustment subtle and difficult to grasp, yet singularly ingenious, which leaves still that frightful chasm at the color-line across which men pass at their peril. Thus, then and now, there stand in the South two separate worlds; and separate not simply in the higher realms of social intercourse, but also in church and school, on railway and street-car, in hotels and theatres, in streets and city sections, in books and newspapers, in asylums and jails, in hospitals and graveyards. There is still enough of contact for large economic and group coöperation, but the separation is so thorough and deep that it absolutely precludes for the present between the races anything like that sympathetic and effective group-training and leadership of the one by the other, such as the American Negro and all backward peoples must have for effectual progress.

This the missionaries of '68 soon saw; and if effective industrial and trade schools were impracticable before the establishment of a common-school system, just as certainly no adequate common schools could be founded until there were teachers to teach them. Southern whites would not teach them; Northern whites in sufficient numbers could not be had. If the Negro was to learn, he must teach himself, and the most effective help that could be given him was the establishment of schools to train Negro teachers. This conclusion was slowly but surely reached by every student of the situation until simultaneously, in widely separated regions, without consultation or systematic plan, there arose a series of institutions designed to furnish teachers for the untaught. Above the sneers of critics at the obvious defects of this procedure must ever stand its one crushing rejoinder: in a single generation they put thirty thousand black teachers in the South; they wiped out the illiteracy of the majority of the black people of the land, and they made Tuskegee possible.

Such higher training-schools tended naturally to deepen broader development: at first they were common and grammar schools, then some became high schools. And finally, by 1900, some thirty-four had one year or more of studies of college grade. This development was reached with different degrees of speed in different institutions: Hampton is still a high school, while Fisk University started her college in 1871, and Spelman Seminary about 1896. In all cases the aim was identical, — to maintain the standards of the lower training by giving teachers and leaders the best practicable training; and above all, to furnish the black world with adequate standards of human culture and lofty ideals of life. It was not enough that the teachers of teachers should be trained in technical normal methods; they must also, so far as possible, be broad-minded, cultured men and women, to scatter civilization among a people whose ignorance was not simply of letters, but of life itself.

It can thus be seen that the work of education in the South began with higher institutions of training, which threw off as their foliage common schools, and later industrial schools, and at the same time strove to shoot their roots ever deeper toward college and university training. That this was an inevitable and necessary development, sooner or later, goes without saying; but there has been, and still is, a question in many minds if the natural growth was not forced, and if the higher training was not either overdone or done with cheap and unsound methods. Among white Southerners this feeling is widespread and positive. A prominent Southern journal voiced this in a recent editorial.

> The experiment that has been made to give the colored students classical training has not been satisfactory. Even though many were able to pursue the course, most of them did so in a parrot-like way, learning what was taught, but not seeming to appropriate the truth and import of their instruction, and graduating without sensible aim or valuable occupation for their future. The whole scheme has proved a waste of time, efforts, and the money of the state.

While most fair-minded men would recognize this as extreme and overdrawn, still without doubt many are asking, Are there a sufficient number of Negroes ready for college training to warrant the undertaking? Are not too many students prematurely forced into this work? Does it not have the effect of dissatisfying the young Negro with his environment? And do these graduates succeed in real life? Such natural questions cannot be evaded, nor on the other hand must a Nation naturally skeptical as to Negro ability assume an unfavorable answer without careful inquiry and patient openness to conviction. We must not forget that most Americans answer all queries regarding the Negro *a priori*, and that the least that human courtesy can do is to listen to evidence.

The advocates of the higher education of the Negro would be the last to deny the incompleteness and glaring defects of the present system: too many institutions have attempted to do college work, the work in some cases has not been thoroughly done, and quantity rather than quality has sometimes been sought. But all this can be said of higher education throughout the land; it is the almost inevitable incident of educational growth, and leaves the deeper question of the legitimate demand for the higher training of Negroes untouched. And this latter question can be settled in but one way, — by a first-hand study of the facts. If we leave out of view all institutions which have not actually graduated students from a course higher than that of a New England high school, even though they be called colleges; if then we take the thirty-four remaining institutions, we may clear up many misapprehensions by asking searchingly, What kind of institutions are they? what do they teach? and what sort of men do they graduate?

And first we may say that this type of college, including Atlanta, Fisk, and Howard, Wilberforce and Lincoln, Biddle, Shaw, and the rest, is peculiar, almost unique. Through the shining trees that whisper before me as I write, I catch glimpses of a boulder of New England granite, covering a grave, which graduates of Atlanta University have placed there, with this inscription:

> IN GRATEFUL MEMORY OF THEIR
> FORMER TEACHER AND FRIEND
> AND OF THE UNSELFISH LIFE HE
> LIVED, AND THE NOBLE WORK HE
> WROUGHT; THAT THEY, THEIR
> CHILDREN, AND THEIR CHIL-
> DREN'S CHILDREN MIGHT BE
> BLESSED.

This was the gift of New England to the freed Negro: not alms, but a friend; not cash, but character. It was not and is not money these seething millions want, but love and sympathy, the pulse of hearts beating with red blood; — a gift which to-day only their own kindred and race can bring to the masses, but which once saintly souls brought to their favored children in the crusade of the sixties, that finest thing in American history, and one of the few things untainted by sordid greed and cheap vainglory. The teachers in these institutions came not to keep the Negroes in their place, but to raise them out of the defilement of the places where slavery had wallowed them. The colleges they founded were social settlements; homes where the best of the sons of the freedmen came in close and sympathetic touch with the best traditions of New England. They lived and ate together, studied and worked, hoped and harkened in the dawning light. In actual formal content their curriculum was doubtless old-fashioned, but in educational power it was supreme, for it was the contact of living souls.

From such schools about two thousand Negroes have gone forth with the bachelor's degree. The number in itself is enough to put at rest the argument that too large a proportion of Negroes are receiving higher training. If the ratio to population of all Negro students throughout the land, in both college and secondary training, be counted, Commissioner Harris assures us "it must be increased to five times its present average" to equal the average of the land.

Fifty years ago the ability of Negro students in any appreciable numbers to master a modern college course would have been difficult to prove. To-day it is proved by the fact that four hundred Negroes, many of whom have been reported as brilliant students, have received the bachelor's degree from Harvard, Yale, Oberlin, and seventy other leading colleges. Here we have, then, nearly twenty-five hundred Negro graduates, of whom the crucial query must be made, How far did their training fit them for life? It is of course extremely difficult to collect satisfactory data on such a point, — difficult to reach the men, to get trustworthy testimony, and to gauge that testimony by any generally acceptable criterion of success. In 1900, the Conference at Atlanta University undertook to study these graduates, and published the results. First they sought to know what these graduates were doing, and succeeded in getting answers from nearly two-thirds of the living. The direct testimony was in almost all cases corroborated by the reports of the colleges where they graduated, so that in the main the reports were worthy of credence. Fifty-three per cent of these graduates were teachers, — presidents of institutions, heads of normal schools, principals of city school-systems, and the like. Seventeen per cent were clergymen; another seventeen per cent were in the professions, chiefly as physicians. Over six per cent were merchants, farmers, and artisans, and four per cent were in the government civil-service. Granting even that a considerable proportion of the third unheard from are unsuccessful, this is a record of usefulness. Personally I know many hundreds of these graduates, and have corresponded with more than a thousand; through others I have followed carefully the life-work of scores; I have taught some of them and some of the pupils whom they have taught, lived in homes which they have builded, and looked at life through their eyes. Comparing them as a class with my fellow students in New England and in Europe, I cannot hesitate in saying that nowhere have I met men and women with a broader spirit of helpfulness, with deeper devotion to their life-work, or with more consecrated determination to succeed in the face of bitter difficulties than among Negro college-bred men. They have, to be sure, their proportion of ne'er-do-weels, their pedants and lettered fools, but they have a surprisingly small proportion of them; they have not that culture of manner which we instinctively associate with university men, forgetting that in reality it is the heritage from cultured homes, and that no people a generation removed from slavery can escape a certain unpleasant rawness and *gaucherie*, despite the best of training.

With all their larger vision and deeper sensibility, these men have usually been conservative, careful leaders. They have seldom been agitators, have withstood the temptation to head the mob, and have worked steadily and faithfully in a thousand communities in the South. As teachers, they have given the South a commendable system of city schools and large numbers of private normal-schools and academies. Colored college-bred men have worked side by side with white college graduates at Hampton; almost from the beginning the backbone of Tuskegee's teaching force has been formed of graduates from Fisk and Atlanta. And to-day the institute is filled with college graduates, from the energetic wife of the principal down to the teacher of agriculture, including nearly half of the executive council and a majority of the heads of departments. In the professions, college men are slowly but surely leavening the Negro church, are healing and preventing the devastations of disease, and beginning to furnish legal protection for the liberty and property of the toiling masses. All this is needful work. Who would do it if Negroes did not? How could Negroes do it if they were not trained carefully for it? If white people need colleges to furnish teachers, ministers, lawyers, and doctors, do black people need nothing of the sort?

If it is true that there are an appreciable number of Negro youth in the land capable by character and talent to receive that higher training, the end of which is culture, and if the two and a half thousand who have had something of this training in the past have in the main proved themselves useful to their race and generation, the question then comes, What place in the future development of the South ought the Negro college and college-bred man to occupy? That the present social separation and acute race-sensitiveness must eventually yield to the influences of culture, as the South grows civilized, is clear. But such transformation calls for singular wisdom and patience. If, while the healing of this vast sore is progressing, the races are to live for many years side by side, united in economic effort, obeying a common government, sensitive to mutual thought and feeling, yet subtly and silently separate in many matters of deeper human intimacy, — if this unusual and dangerous development is to progress amid peace and order, mutual respect and growing intelligence, it will call for social surgery at once the delicatest and nicest in modern history. It will demand broad-minded, upright men, both white and black, and in its final accomplishment American civilization will triumph. So far as white men are concerned, this fact is to-day being recognized in the South, and a happy renaissance of university education seems imminent. But the very voices that cry hail to this good work are, strange to relate, largely silent or antagonistic to the higher education of the Negro.

> SUCH TRANSFORMATION CALLS FOR SINGULAR WISDOM AND PATIENCE.

Strange to relate! for this is certain, no secure civilization can be built in the South with the Negro as an ignorant, turbulent proletariat. Suppose we seek to remedy this by making them laborers and nothing more: they are not fools, they have tasted of the Tree of Life, and they will not cease to think, will not cease attempting to read the riddle of the world. By taking away their best equipped teachers and leaders, by slamming the door of opportunity in the faces of their bolder and brighter minds, will you make them satisfied with their lot? or will you not rather transfer their leading from the hands of men taught to think to the hands of untrained demagogues? We ought not to forget that despite the pressure of poverty, and despite the active discouragement and even ridicule of friends, the demand for higher training steadily increases among Negro youth: there were, in the years from 1875 to 1880, 22 Negro graduates from Northern colleges; from 1885 to 1890 there were 43, and from 1895 to 1900, nearly 100 graduates. From Southern Negro colleges there were, in the same three periods, 143, 413, and over 500 graduates. Here, then, is the plain thirst for training; by refusing to give this Talented Tenth the key to knowledge, can any sane man imagine that they will lightly lay aside their yearning and contentedly become hewers of wood and drawers of water?

No. The dangerously clear logic of the Negro's position will more and more loudly assert itself in that day when increasing wealth and more intricate social organization preclude the South from being, as it so largely is, simply an armed camp for intimidating black folk. Such waste of energy cannot be spared if the South is to catch up with civilization. And as the black third of the land grows in thrift and skill, unless skilfully guided in its larger philosophy, it must more and more brood over the red past and the creeping, crooked present, until it grasps a gospel of revolt and revenge and throws its new-found energies athwart the current of advance. Even to-day the masses of the Negroes see all too clearly the anomalies of their position and the moral crookedness of yours. You may marshal strong indictments against them, but their counter-cries, lacking though they be in formal logic, have burning truths within them which you may not wholly ignore, O Southern Gentlemen! If you deplore their presence here, they ask, Who brought us? When you cry, Deliver us from the vision of intermarriage, they answer that legal marriage is infinitely better than systematic concubinage and prostitution. And if in just fury you accuse their vagabonds of violating women, they also in fury quite as just may reply: The wrong which your gentlemen have done against helpless black women in defiance of your own laws is written on the foreheads of two millions of mulattoes, and written in ineffaceable blood. And finally, when you fasten crime upon this race as its peculiar trait, they answer that slavery was the arch-crime, and lynching and lawlessness its twin abortion; that color and race are not crimes, and yet they it is which in this land receives most unceasing condemnation, North, East, South, and West.

I will not say such arguments are wholly justified, — I will not insist that there is no other side to the shield; but I do say that of the nine millions of Negroes in this nation, there is scarcely one out of the cradle to whom these arguments do not daily present themselves in the guise of terrible truth. I insist that the question of the future is how best to keep these millions from brooding over the wrongs of the past and the difficulties of the present, so that all energies may be bent toward a cheerful striving and co-operation with their white neighbors toward a larger, juster, and fuller future. That one wise method of doing this lies in the closer knitting of the Negro to the great industrial possibilities of the South is a great truth. And this the common schools and the manual training and trade schools are working to accomplish. But these alone are not enough. The foundations of knowledge in this race, as in others, must be sunk deep in the college and university if we would build a solid, permanent structure. Internal problems of social advance must inevitably come, — problems of work and wages, of families and homes, of morals and the true valuing of the things of life; and all these and other inevitable problems of civilization the Negro must meet and solve largely for himself, by reason of his isolation; and can there be any possible solution other than by study and thought and an appeal to the rich experience of the past? Is there not, with such a group and in such a crisis, infinitely more danger to be apprehended from half-trained minds and shallow thinking than from over-education and over-refinement? Surely we have wit enough to found a Negro college so manned and equipped as to steer successfully between the *dilettante* and the fool. We shall hardly induce black men to believe that if their stomachs be full, it matters little about their brains. They already dimly perceive that the paths of peace winding between honest toil and dignified manhood call for the guidance of skilled thinkers, the loving, reverent comradeship between the black lowly and the black men emancipated by training and culture.

The function of the Negro college, then, is clear: it must maintain the standards of popular education, it must seek the social regeneration of the Negro, and it must help in the solution of problems of race contact and co-operation. And finally, beyond all this, it must develop men. Above our modern socialism, and out of the worship of the mass, must persist and evolve that higher individualism which the centres of culture protect; there must come a loftier respect for the sovereign human soul that seeks to know itself and the world about it; that seeks a freedom for expansion and self-development; that will love and hate and labor in its own way, untrammeled alike by old and new. Such souls aforetime have inspired and guided worlds, and if we be not wholly bewitched by our Rhine-gold, they shall again. Herein the longing of black men must have respect: the rich and bitter depth of their experience, the unknown treasures of their inner life, the strange rendings of nature they have seen, may give the world new points of view and make their loving, living, and doing precious to all human hearts. And to themselves in these the days that try their souls, the chance to soar in the dim blue air above the smoke is to their finer spirits boon and guerdon for what they lose on earth by being black.

I sit with Shakespeare and he winces not. Across the color line I move arm in arm with Balzac and Dumas, where smiling men and welcoming women glide in gilded halls. From out the caves of evening that swing between the strong-limbed earth and the tracery of the stars, I summon Aristotle and Aurelius and what soul I will, and they come all graciously with no scorn nor condescension. So, wed with Truth, I dwell above the Veil. Is this the life you grudge us, O knightly America? Is this the life you long to change into the dull red hideousness of Georgia? Are you so afraid lest peering from this high Pisgah, between Philistine and Amalekite, we sight the Promised Land?

its function is to sort out every possible confusion: that of the disease, which is transmitted when bodies are mixed together; that of the evil, which is increased when fear and death overcome prohibitions. It lays down for each individual his place, his body, his disease, and his death, his well-being, by means of an omnipresent and omniscient power that subdivides itself in a regular, uninterrupted way even to the ultimate determination of the individual, of what characterizes him, of what belongs to him, of what happens to him. Against the plague, which is a mixture, discipline brings into play its power, which is one of analysis. A whole literary fiction of the festival grew up around the plague: suspended laws, lifted prohibitions, the frenzy of passing time, bodies mingling together without respect, individuals unmasked, abandoning their statutory identity and the figure under which they had been recognized, allowing a quite different truth to appear. But there was also a political dream of the plague, which was exactly its reverse: not the collective festival, but strict divisions; not laws transgressed, but the penetration of regulation into even the smallest details of everyday life through the mediation of the complete hierarchy that assured the capillary functioning of power; not masks that were put on and taken off, but the assignment to each individual of his "true" name, his "true" place, his "true" body, his "true" disease. The plague as a form, at once real and imaginary, of disorder had as its medical and political correlative discipline. Behind the disciplinary mechanisms can be read the haunting memory of "contagions," of the plague, of rebellions, crimes, vagabondage, desertions, people who appear and disappear, live and die in disorder.

If it is true that the leper gave rise to rituals of exclusion, which to a certain extent provided the model for and general form of the great Confinement, then the plague gave rise to disciplinary projects. Rather than the massive, binary division between one set of people and another, it called for multiple separations, individualizing distributions, an organization in depth of surveillance and control, an intensification and a ramification of power. The leper was caught up in a practice of rejection, of exile-enclosure; he was left to his doom in a mass among which it was useless to differentiate; those sick of the plague were caught up in a meticulous tactical partitioning in which individual differentiations were the constricting effects of a power that multiplied, articulated, and subdivided itself; the great confinement on the one hand; the correct training on the other. The leper and his separation; the plague and its segmentations. The first is marked; the second analyzed and distributed. The exile of the leper and the arrest of the plague do not bring with them the same political dream. The first is that of a pure community, the second that of a disciplined society. Two ways of exercising power over men, of controlling their relations, of separating out their dangerous mixtures. The plague-stricken town, traversed throughout with hierarchy, surveillance, observation, writing; the town immobilized by the functioning of an extensive power that bears in a distinct way over all individual bodies — this is the utopia of the perfectly governed city. The plague (envisaged as a possibility at least) is the trial in the course of which one may define ideally the exercise of disciplinary power. In order to make rights and laws function according to pure theory, the jurists place themselves in imagination in the state of nature; in order to see perfect disciplines functioning, rulers dreamed of the state of plague. Underlying disciplinary projects the image of the plague stands for all forms of confusion and disorder; just as the image of the leper, cut off from all human contact, underlies projects of exclusion.

They are different projects, then, but not incompatible ones. We see them coming slowly together, and it is the peculiarity of the nineteenth century that it applied to the space of exclusion of which the leper was the symbolic inhabitant (beggars, vagabonds, madmen, and the disorderly formed the real population) the technique of power proper to disciplinary partitioning. Treat "lepers" as "plague victims," project the subtle segmentations of discipline onto the confused space of internment, combine it with the methods of analytical distribution proper to power, individualize the excluded, but use procedures of individualization to mark exclusion — this is what was operated regularly by disciplinary power from the beginning of the nineteenth century in the psychiatric asylum, the penitentiary, the reformatory, the approved school, and to some extent, the hospital. Generally speaking, all the authorities exercising individual control function according to a double mode; that of binary division and branding (mad/sane; dangerous/harmless; normal/ abnormal); and that of coercive assignment, of differential distribution (who he is; where he must be; how he is to be characterized; how he is to be recognized; how a constant surveillance is to be exercised over him in an individual way, etc.). On the one hand, the lepers are treated as plague victims; the tactics of individualizing disciplines are imposed on the excluded; and, on the other hand, the universality of disciplinary controls makes it possible to brand the "leper" and to bring into play against him the dualistic mechanisms of exclusion. The constant division between the normal and the abnormal, to which every individual is subjected, brings us back to our own time, by applying the binary branding and exile of the leper to quite different objects; the existence of a whole set of techniques and institutions for measuring, supervising, and correcting the abnormal brings into play the disciplinary mechanisms to which the fear of the plague gave rise. All the mechanisms of power which, even today, are disposed around the abnormal individual, to brand him and to alter him, are composed of those two forms from which they distantly derive.

Bentham's *Panopticon* is the architectural figure of this composition. We know the principle on which it was based: at the periphery, an annular building; at the center, a tower; this tower is pierced with wide windows that open onto the inner side of the ring; the peripheric building is divided into cells, each of which extends the whole width of the building; they have two windows, one on the inside, corresponding to the windows of the tower; the other, on the outside, allows the light to cross the cell from one end to the other. All that is needed, then, is to place a supervisor in a central tower and to shut up in each cell a madman, a patient, a condemned

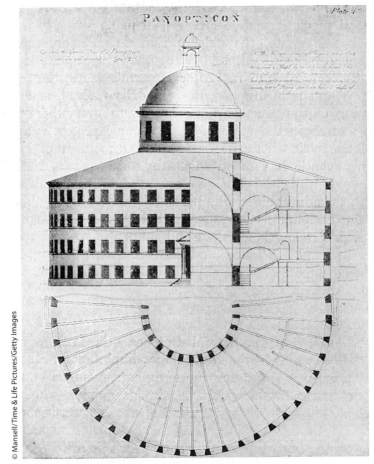

Plan of the Panopticon by J. Bentham (*The Works of Jeremy Bentham*, ed. Bowring, vol. IV, 1843, 172–73).

man, a worker, or a schoolboy. By the effect of backlighting, one can observe from the tower, standing out precisely against the light, the small captive shadows in the cells of the periphery. They are like so many cages, so many small theaters, in which each actor is alone, perfectly individualized and constantly visible. The panoptic mechanism arranges spatial unities that make it possible to see constantly and to recognize immediately. In short, it reverses the principle of the dungeon; or rather of its three functions — to enclose, to deprive of light, and to hide — it preserves only the first and eliminates the other two. Full lighting and the eye of a supervisor capture better than darkness, which is ultimately protected. Visibility is a trap.

To begin with, this made it possible — as a negative effect — to avoid those compact, swarming, howling masses that were to be found in places of confinement, those painted by Goya or described by Howard. Each individual, in his place, is securely confined to a cell from which he is seen from the front by the supervisor; but the side walls prevent him from coming into contact with his companions. He is seen, but he does not see; he is the object of information, never a subject in communication. The arrangement of his room, opposite the central tower, imposes on him an axial visibility; but the divisions of the ring, those separated cells, imply a lateral invisibility. And this invisibility is a guarantee of order. If the inmates are convicts, there is no danger of a plot, an attempt at collective escape, the planning of new crimes for the future, bad reciprocal influences; if they are patients, there is no danger of contagion; if they are madmen, there is no risk of their committing violence upon one another;

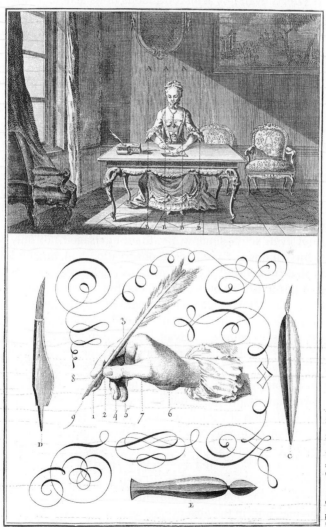

Handwriting model. *Collections historiques de l'I.N.R.D.P.*

if they are schoolchildren, there is no copying, no noise, no chatter, no waste of time; if they are workers, there are no disorders, no theft, no coalitions, none of those distractions that slow down the rate of work, make it less perfect, or cause accidents. The crowd, a compact mass, a locus of multiple exchanges, individualities merging together, a collective effect, is abolished and replaced by a collection of separated individualities. From the point of view of the guardian, it is replaced by a multiplicity that can be numbered and supervised; from the point of view of the inmates, by a sequestered and observed solitude (Bentham 60–64).

Hence the major effect of the Panopticon: to induce in the inmate a state of conscious and permanent visibility that assures the automatic functioning of power. So to arrange things that the surveillance is permanent in its effects even if it is discontinuous in its action; that the perfection of power should tend to render its actual exercise unnecessary; that this architectural apparatus should be a machine for creating and sustaining a power relation independent of the person who exercises it; in short, that the inmates should be caught up in a power situation of which they are themselves the bearers. To achieve this, it is at once too much and too little that the prisoner should be constantly observed by an inspector: too little, for what matters is that he knows himself to be observed; too much, because he has no need in fact of being so. In view of this, Bentham laid down the principle that power should be visible and unverifiable. Visible: the inmate will constantly have before his eyes the tall outline of the central tower from which he is spied upon. Unverifiable: the inmate must never know whether he is being looked at at any one moment; but he must be sure that he may always be so. In order to make the presence or absence of the inspector unverifiable, so that the prisoners, in their cells, cannot even see a shadow, Bentham envisaged not only venetian blinds on the windows of the central observation hall, but, on the inside, partitions that intersected the hall at right angles and, in order to pass from one quarter to the other, not doors but zigzag openings; for the slightest noise, a gleam of light, a brightness in a half-opened door would betray the presence of the guardian.[2] The Panopticon is a machine for dissociating the see/being seen dyad: in the peripheric ring, one is totally seen, without ever seeing; in the central tower, one sees everything without ever being seen.[3]

It is an important mechanism, for it automatizes and disindividualizes power. Power has its principle not so much in a person as in a certain concerted distribution of bodies, surfaces, lights, gazes; in an arrangement whose internal mechanisms produce the relation in which individuals are caught up. The ceremonies, the rituals, the marks by which the sovereign's surplus power was manifested are useless. There is a machinery that assures dissymmetry, disequilibrium, difference. Consequently, it does not matter who exercises power. Any individual, taken almost at random, can operate the machine: in the absence of the director, his family, his friends, his visitors, even his servants (Bentham 45). Similarly, it does not matter what motive animates him: the curiosity of the indiscreet, the malice of a

Interior of the penitentiary at Stateville, United States, twentieth century.

child, the thirst for knowledge of a philosopher who wishes to visit this museum of human nature, or the perversity of those who take pleasure in spying and punishing. The more numerous those anonymous and temporary observers are, the greater the risk for the inmate of being surprised and the greater his anxious awareness of being observed. The Panopticon is a marvelous machine which, whatever use one may wish to put it to, produces homogeneous effects of power.

A real subjection is born mechanically from a fictitious relation. So it is not necessary to use force to constrain the convict to good behavior, the madman to calm, the worker to work, the schoolboy to application, the patient to the observation of the regulations. Bentham was surprised that panoptic institutions could be so light: there were no more bars, no more

Lecture on the evils of alcoholism in the auditorium of Fresnes prison.

chains, no more heavy locks; all that was needed was that the separations should be clear and the openings well arranged. The heaviness of the old "houses of security," with their fortresslike architecture, could be replaced by the simple, economic geometry of a "house of certainty." The efficiency of power, its constraining force have, in a sense, passed over to the other side — to the side of its surface of application. He who is subjected to a field of visibility, and who knows it, assumes responsibility for the constraints of power; he makes them play spontaneously upon himself; he inscribes in himself the power relation in which he simultaneously plays both roles; he becomes the principle of his own subjection. By this very fact, the external power may throw off its physical

> **HE WHO IS SUBJECTED TO A FIELD OF VISIBILITY, AND WHO KNOWS IT, ASSUMES RESPONSIBILITY FOR THE CONSTRAINTS OF POWER.**

weight; it tends to the noncorporal; and, the more it approaches this limit, the more constant, profound, and permanent are its effects: it is a perpetual victory that avoids any physical confrontation and which is always decided in advance.

Bentham does not say whether he was inspired, in his project, by Le Vaux's menagerie at Versailles: the first menagerie in which the different elements are not, as they traditionally were, distributed in a park (Loisel 104–7). At the center was an octagonal pavilion which, on the first floor, consisted of only a single room, the king's *salon*; on every side large windows looked out onto seven cages (the eighth side was reserved for the entrance), containing different species of animals. By Bentham's time, this menagerie had disappeared. But one finds in the program of the Panopticon a similar concern with individualizing observation, with characterization and classification, with the analytical arrangement of space. The Panopticon is a royal menagerie; the animal is replaced by man, individual distribution by specific grouping, and the king by the machinery of a furtive power. With this exception, the Panopticon also does the work of a naturalist. It makes it possible to draw up differences: among patients, to observe the symptoms of each individual, without the proximity of beds, the circulation of miasmas, the effects of contagion confusing the clinical tables; among schoolchildren, it makes it possible to observe performances (without there being any imitation or copying), to map aptitudes, to assess characters, to draw up rigorous classifications, and in relation to normal development, to distinguish "laziness and stubbornness" from "incurable imbecility"; among workers, it makes it possible to note the aptitudes of each worker, compare the time he takes to perform a task, and if they are paid by the day, to calculate their wages (Bentham 60–64).

So much for the question of observation. But the Panopticon was also a laboratory; it could be used as a machine to carry out experiments, to alter behavior, to train or correct individuals. To experiment with medicines and monitor their effects. To try out different punishments on prisoners, according to their crimes and character, and to seek the most effective ones. To teach different techniques simultaneously to the workers, to decide which is the best. To try out pedagogical experiments — and in particular to take up once again the well-debated problem of secluded education, by using orphans. One would see what would happen when, in their sixteenth or eighteenth year, they were presented with other boys or girls; one could verify whether, as Helvetius thought, anyone could learn anything; one would follow "the genealogy of every observable idea"; one could bring up different children according to different systems of thought, making certain children believe that two and two do not make four or that the moon is a cheese, then put them together when they are twenty or twenty-five years old; one would then have discussions that would be worth a great deal more than the sermons or lectures on which so much money is spent; one would have at least an opportunity of making discoveries in the domain of metaphysics. The Panopticon is a privileged place for experiments on men, and for analyzing with complete certainty the transformations that may be obtained from them. The Panopticon may even provide an apparatus for supervising its own mechanisms. In this central tower, the director may spy on all the employees that he has under his orders: nurses, doctors, foremen, teachers, warders; he will be able to judge them continuously, alter their behavior, impose upon them the methods he thinks best; and it will even be possible to observe the director himself. An inspector arriving unexpectedly at the center of the Panopticon will be able to judge at a glance, without anything being concealed from him, how the entire establishment is functioning. And, in any case, enclosed as he is in the middle of this architectural mechanism, is not the director's own fate entirely bound up with it? The incompetent physician who has allowed contagion to spread, the incompetent prison governor or workshop manager will be the first victims of an epidemic or a revolt. "'By every tie I could devise,' said the master of the Panopticon, 'my own fate had been bound up by me with theirs'" (Bentham 177). The Panopticon functions as a kind of laboratory of power. Thanks to its mechanisms of observation, it gains in efficiency and in the ability to penetrate into men's behavior; knowledge follows the advances of power, discovering new objects of knowledge over all the surfaces on which power is exercised.

The plague-stricken town, the panoptic establishment — the differences are important. They mark, at a distance of a century and a half, the transformations of the disciplinary program. In the first case, there is an exceptional situation: against an extraordinary evil, power is mobilized; it makes itself everywhere present and visible; it invents new mechanisms; it separates, it immobilizes, it partitions; it constructs for a time what is both a counter-city and the perfect society; it imposes an ideal functioning, but one that is reduced, in the final analysis, like the evil that it combats, to a simple dualism of life and death: that which moves brings death, and one kills that which moves. The Panopticon, on the other hand, must be understood as a generalizable model of functioning; a way of defining power relations in terms of the everyday life of men. No doubt Bentham presents it as a particular institution, closed in upon itself. Utopias, perfectly closed in upon themselves, are common enough. As opposed to the ruined prisons, littered with mechanisms of torture, to be seen in Piranese's engravings, the Panopticon presents a cruel, ingenious cage. The fact that it should have given rise, even in our own time, to so many variations, projected or realized, is evidence of the imaginary intensity that it has possessed for almost two hundred years. But the Panopticon must not be understood as a dream building: it is the diagram of a mechanism of power reduced to its ideal form; its functioning, abstracted from any obstacle, resistance, or friction, must be represented as a pure architectural and optical system: it is in fact a figure of political technology that may and must be detached from any specific use.

It is polyvalent in its applications; it serves to reform prisoners, but also to treat patients, to instruct schoolchildren, to confine the insane, to supervise workers, to put beggars and idlers to work. It is a type of location of bodies in space, of distribution of individuals in relation to one another, of hierarchical organization, of disposition of centers and channels of power, of definition of the instruments and modes of intervention of power, which can be implemented in hospitals, workshops, schools, prisons. Whenever one is dealing with a multiplicity of individuals on whom a task or a particular form of behavior must be imposed, the panoptic schema may be used. It is — necessary modifications apart — applicable "to all establishments whatsoever, in which, within a space not too large to be covered or commanded by buildings, a number of persons are meant to be kept under inspection" (Bentham 40; although Bentham takes the penitentiary house as his prime example, it is because it has many different functions to fulfill — safe custody, confinement, solitude, forced labor, and instruction).

In each of its applications, it makes it possible to perfect the exercise of power. It does this in several ways: because it can reduce the number of those who exercise it, while increasing the number of those on whom it is exercised. Because it is possible to intervene at any moment and because the constant pressure acts even before the offenses, mistakes, or crimes have been committed. Because, in these conditions, its strength is that it never intervenes, it is exercised spontaneously and without noise, it constitutes a mechanism whose effects follow from one another. Because, without any physical instrument other than architecture and geometry, it acts directly on individuals; it gives "power of mind over mind." The panoptic schema makes any apparatus of power more intense: it assures its economy (in material, in personnel, in time); it assures its efficacity by its preventative character, its continuous functioning, and its automatic mechanisms. It is a way of obtaining from power "in hitherto unexampled quantity," "a great and new instrument of government . . . ; its great excellence consists in the great strength it is capable of giving to *any* institution it may be thought proper to apply it to" (Bentham 66).

It's a case of "it's easy once you've thought of it" in the political sphere. It can in fact be integrated into any function (education, medical treatment, production, punishment); it can increase the effect of this function, by being linked closely with it; it can constitute a mixed mechanism in which relations of power (and of knowledge) may be precisely adjusted, in the smallest detail, to the processes that are to be supervised; it can establish a direct proportion between "surplus power" and "surplus production." In short, it arranges things in such a way that the exercise of power is not added on from the outside, like a rigid, heavy constraint, to the functions it invests, but is so subtly present in them as to increase their efficiency by itself increasing its own points of contact. The panoptic mechanism is not simply a hinge, a point of exchange between a mechanism of power and a function; it is a way of making power relations function in a function, and of making a function function through these power relations. Bentham's preface to *Panopticon* opens with a list of the benefits to be obtained from his "inspection-house": *"Morals reformed — health preserved — industry invigorated — instruction diffused — public burthens lightened —* Economy seated, as it were, upon a rock — the Gordian knot of the Poor-Laws not cut, but untied — all by a simple idea in architecture!" (Bentham 39).

Furthermore, the arrangement of this machine is such that its enclosed nature does not preclude a permanent presence from the outside: we have seen that anyone may come and exercise in the central tower the functions of surveillance, and that, this being the case, he can gain a clear idea of the way in which the surveillance is practiced. In fact, any panoptic institution, even if it is as rigorously closed as a penitentiary, may without difficulty be subjected to such irregular and constant inspections: and not only by the appointed inspectors, but also by the public; any member of society will have the right to come and see with his own eyes how the schools, hospitals, factories, prisons function. There is no risk, therefore, that the increase of power created by the panoptic machine may degenerate into tyranny; the disciplinary mechanism will be democratically controlled, since it will be constantly accessible "to the great tribunal committee of the world."[4] This Panopticon, subtly arranged so that an observer may observe, at a glance, so many different individuals, also enables everyone to come and observe any of the observers. The seeing machine was once a sort of dark room into which individuals spied; it has become a transparent building in which the exercise of power may be supervised by society as a whole.

The panoptic schema, without disappearing as such or losing any of its properties, was destined to spread throughout the social body; its vocation was to become a generalized function. The plague-stricken town provided an exceptional disciplinary model: perfect, but absolutely violent; to the disease that brought death, power opposed its perpetual threat of death; life inside it was reduced to its simplest expression; it was, against the power of death, the meticulous exercise of the right of the sword. The Panopticon, on the other hand, has a role of amplification; although it arranges power, although it is intended to make it more economic and more effective, it does so not for power itself, nor for the immediate salvation of a threatened society: its aim is to strengthen the social forces — to increase production, to develop the economy, spread education, raise the level of public morality; to increase and multiply.

How is power to be strengthened in such a way that, far from impeding progress, far from weighing upon it with its rules and regulations, it actually facilitates such progress? What intensificator of power will be able at the same time to be a multiplicator of production? How will power, by increasing its forces, be able to increase those of society instead of confiscating them or impeding them? The Panopticon's solution to this problem is that the productive increase of power can be assured only if, on the one hand, it can be exercised continuously in the very foundations of society, in the subtlest possible way, and if, on the other hand, it functions outside these sudden, violent, discontinuous forms that are bound up with the exercise of sovereignty. The body of the king, with its strange material and physical presence, with the force that he himself deploys or transmits to some few others, is at the opposite extreme of this new physics of power represented by panopticism; the domain of panopticism is, on the contrary, that whole lower region, that region of irregular bodies, with their details, their multiple movements, their heterogeneous forces, their spatial relations; what are required are mechanisms that analyze distributions, gaps, series, combinations, and which use instruments that render visible, record, differentiate, and compare: a physics of a relational and multiple power, which has its maximum intensity not in the person of the king, but in the bodies that can be individualized by these relations. At the theoretical level, Bentham defines another way of analyzing the social body and the power relations that traverse it; in terms of practice, he defines a procedure of subordination of bodies and forces that must increase the utility of power while practicing the economy of the prince. Panopticism is the general principle of a new "political anatomy" whose object and end are not the relations of sovereignty but the relations of discipline.

The celebrated, transparent, circular cage, with its high tower, powerful and knowing, may have been for Bentham a project of a perfect disciplinary institution; but he also set out to show how one may "unlock" the disciplines and get them to function in a diffused, multiple, polyvalent way throughout the whole social body. These disciplines, which the classical age had elaborated in specific, relatively enclosed places — barracks, schools, workshops — and whose total implementation had been imagined only at the limited and temporary scale of a plague-stricken town, Bentham dreamed of transforming into a network of mechanisms that would be everywhere and always alert, running through society without interruption in space or in time. The panoptic arrangement provides the formula for this generalization. It programs, at the level of an elementary and easily transferable mechanism, the basic functioning of a society penetrated through and through with disciplinary mechanisms.

There are two images, then, of discipline. At one extreme, the discipline-blockade, the enclosed institution, established on the edges of society, turned inwards towards negative functions: arresting evil, breaking communications, suspending time. At the other extreme, with panopticism, is the discipline-mechanism: a functional mechanism that must improve the exercise of power by making it lighter, more rapid, more effective, a design of subtle coercion for a society to come. The movement from one project to the other, from a schema of exceptional discipline to one of a generalized surveillance, rests on a historical transformation: the gradual extension of the mechanisms of discipline throughout the seventeenth and eighteenth centuries, their spread throughout the whole social body, the formation of what might be called in general the disciplinary society.

A whole disciplinary generalization — the Benthamite physics of power represents an acknowledgment of this — had operated throughout the classical age. The spread of disciplinary institutions, whose network was beginning to cover an ever larger surface and occupying above all a less and less marginal position, testifies to this: what was an islet, a privileged place, a circumstantial measure, or a singular model, became a general formula; the regulations characteristic of the Protestant and pious armies of William of Orange or of Gustavus Adolphus were transformed into regulations for all the armies of Europe; the model colleges of the Jesuits, or the schools of Batencour or Demia, following the example set by Sturm, provided the outlines for the general forms of educational discipline; the ordering of the naval and military hospitals provided the model for the entire reorganization of hospitals in the eighteenth century.

But this extension of the disciplinary institutions was no doubt only the most visible aspect of various, more profound processes.

1. *The functional inversion of the disciplines.* At first, they were expected to neutralize dangers, to fix useless or disturbed populations, to avoid the inconveniences of over-large assemblies; now they were being asked to play a positive role, for they were becoming able to do so, to increase the possible utility of individuals. Military discipline is no longer a mere means of preventing looting, desertion, or failure to obey orders among the troops; it has become a basic technique to enable the army to exist, not as an assembled crowd, but as a unity that derives from this very unity an increase in its forces; discipline increases the skill of each individual, coordinates these skills, accelerates movements, increases fire power, broadens the fronts of attack without reducing their vigor, increases the capacity for resistance, etc. The discipline of the workshop, while remaining a way of enforcing respect for the regulations and authorities, of preventing thefts or losses, tends to increase aptitudes, speeds, output, and therefore profits; it still exerts a moral influence over behavior, but more and more it treats actions in terms of their results, introduces bodies into a machinery, forces into an economy. When, in the seventeenth century, the provincial schools or the Christian elementary schools were founded, the justifications given for them were above all negative: those poor who were unable to bring up their children left them "in ignorance of their obligations: given the difficulties they have in earning a living, and themselves having been badly brought up, they are unable to communicate a sound upbringing that they themselves never had"; this involves three major inconveniences: ignorance of God, idleness (with its consequent drunkenness, impurity, larceny, brigandage), and the formation of those gangs of beggars, always ready to stir up public disorder and "virtually to exhaust the funds of the Hôtel-Dieu" (Demia 60–61). Now, at the beginning of the Revolution, the end laid down for primary education was to be, among other things, to "fortify," to "develop the body," to prepare the child "for a future in some mechanical work," to give him "an observant eye, a sure hand and prompt habits" (Talleyrand's Report to the Constituent Assembly, 10 September 1791, quoted by Léon 106). The disciplines function increasingly as techniques for making useful individuals. Hence their emergence from a marginal position on the confines of society, and detachment from the forms of exclusion or expiation, confinement, or retreat. Hence the slow loosening of their kinship with religious regularities and enclosures. Hence also their

rooting in the most important, most central, and most productive sectors of society. They become attached to some of the great essential functions: factory production, the transmission of knowledge, the diffusion of aptitudes and skills, the war-machine. Hence, too, the double tendency one sees developing throughout the eighteenth century to increase the number of disciplinary institutions and to discipline the existing apparatuses.

2. *The swarming of disciplinary mechanisms*. While, on the one hand, the disciplinary establishments increase, their mechanisms have a certain tendency to become "deinstitutionalized," to emerge from the closed fortresses in which they once functioned and to circulate in a "free" state; the massive, compact disciplines are broken down into flexible methods of control, which may be transferred and adapted. Sometimes the closed apparatuses add to their internal and specific function a role of external surveillance, developing around themselves a whole margin of lateral controls. Thus the Christian School must not simply train docile children; it must also make it possible to supervise the parents, to gain information as to their way of life, their resources, their piety, their morals. The school tends to constitute minute social observatories that penetrate even to the adults and exercise regular supervision over them: the bad behavior of the child, or his absence, is a legitimate pretext, according to Demia, for one to go and question the neighbors, especially if there is any reason to believe that the family will not tell the truth; one can then go and question the parents themselves, to find out whether they know their catechism and the prayers, whether they are determined to root out the vices of their children, how many beds there are in the house and what the sleeping arrangements are; the visit may end with the giving of alms, the present of a religious picture, or the provision of additional beds (Demia 39–40). Similarly, the hospital is increasingly conceived of as a base for the medical observation of the population outside; after the burning down of the Hôtel-Dieu in 1772, there were several demands that the large buildings, so heavy and so disordered, should be replaced by a series of smaller hospitals; their function would be to take in the sick of the quarter, but also to gather information, to be alert to any endemic or epidemic phenomena, to open dispensaries, to give advice to the inhabitants, and to keep the authorities informed of the sanitary state of the region.[5]

> ONE ALSO SEES THE SPREAD OF DISCIPLINARY PROCEDURES, NOT IN THE FORM OF ENCLOSED INSTITUTIONS, BUT AS CENTERS OF OBSERVATION DISSEMINATED THROUGHOUT SOCIETY.

One also sees the spread of disciplinary procedures, not in the form of enclosed institutions, but as centers of observation disseminated throughout society. Religious groups and charity organizations had long played this role of "disciplining" the population. From the Counter-Reformation to the philanthropy of the July monarchy, initiatives of this type continued to increase; their aims were religious (conversion and moralization), economic (aid and encouragement to work), or political (the struggle against discontent or agitation). One has only to cite by way of example the regulations for the charity associations in the Paris parishes. The territory to be covered was divided into quarters and cantons and the members of the associations divided themselves up along the same lines. These members had to visit their respective areas regularly. "They will strive to eradicate places of ill-repute, tobacco shops, life-classes, gaming houses, public scandals, blasphemy, impiety, and any other disorders that may come to their knowledge." They will also have to make individual visits to the poor; and the information to be obtained is laid down in regulations: the stability of the lodging, knowledge of prayers, attendance at the sacraments, knowledge of a trade, morality (and "whether they have not fallen into poverty through their own fault"); lastly, "one must learn by skillful questioning in what way they behave at home. Whether there is peace between them and their neighbors, whether they are careful to bring up their children in the fear of God . . . , whether they do not have their older children of different sexes sleeping together and with them, whether they do not allow licentiousness and cajolery in their families, especially in their older daughters. If one has any doubts as to whether they are married, one must ask to see their marriage certificate."[6]

3. *The state-control of the mechanisms of the discipline*. In England, it was private religious groups that carried out, for a long time, the functions of social discipline (cf. Radzinovitz 203–14); in France, although a part of this role remained in the hands of parish guilds or charity associations, another — and no doubt the most important part — was very soon taken over by the police apparatus.

The organization of a centralized police had long been regarded, even by contemporaries, as the most direct expression of royal absolutism; the sovereign had wished to have "his own magistrate to whom he might directly entrust his orders, his commissions, intentions, and who was entrusted with the execution of orders and orders under the King's private seal" (a note by Duval, first secretary at the police magistrature, quoted in Funck-Brentano, I). In effect, in taking over a number of preexisting functions — the search for criminals, urban surveillance, economic and political supervision — the police magistratures and the magistrature-general that presided over them in Paris transposed them into a single, strict, administrative machine: "All the radiations of force and information that spread from the circumference culminate in the magistrate-general. . . . It is he who operates all the wheels that together produce order and harmony. The effects of his administration cannot be better compared than to the movement of the celestial bodies" (Des Essarts 344, 528).

But, although the police as an institution were certainly organized in the form of a state apparatus, and although this was certainly linked directly to the center of political sovereignty, the type of power that it exercises, the mechanisms it operates, and the elements to which it applies them are specific. It is an apparatus that must be coextensive with the entire social body and not only by the extreme limits that it embraces, but by the minuteness of the details it is concerned with. Police power must bear "over everything": it is not, however, the totality of the state nor of the kingdom as visible and invisible body of the monarch; it is the dust of events, actions, behavior, opinions — "everything that happens";[7] the police are concerned with "those things of every moment," those "unimportant things," of which Catherine II spoke in her Great Instruction (Supplement to the *Instruction for the Drawing Up of a New Code*, 1769, article 535). With the police, one is in the indefinite world of a supervision that seeks ideally to reach the most elementary particle, the most passing phenomenon of the social body: "The ministry of the magistrates and police officers is of the greatest importance; the objects that it embraces are in a sense definite, one may perceive them only by a sufficiently detailed examination" (Delamare, unnumbered preface): the infinitely small of political power.

And, in order to be exercised, this power had to be given the instrument of permanent, exhaustive, omnipresent surveillance, capable of making all visible, as long as it could itself remain invisible. It had to be like a faceless gaze that transformed the whole social body into a field of perception: thousands of eyes posted everywhere, mobile attentions ever on the alert, a long, hierarchized network which, according to Le Maire, comprised for Paris the forty-eight *commissaires*, the twenty *inspecteurs*, then the "observers," who were paid regularly, the *"basses mouches,"* or secret agents, who were paid by the day, then the informers, paid according to the job done, and finally the prostitutes. And this unceasing observation had to be accumulated in a series of reports and registers; throughout the eighteenth century, an immense police text increasingly covered society by means of a complex documentary organization (on the police registers in the eighteenth century, cf. Chassaigne). And, unlike the methods of judicial or administrative writing, what was registered in this way were forms of behavior, attitudes, possibilities, suspicions — a permanent account of individuals' behavior.

Now, it should be noted that, although this police supervision was entirely "in the hands of the king," it did not function in a single direction. It was in fact a double-entry system: it had to correspond, by manipulating the machinery of justice, to the immediate wishes of the king, but it was also capable of responding to solicitations from below; the celebrated *lettres de cachet*, or orders under the king's private seal, which were long the symbol of arbitrary royal rule and which brought detention into disrepute on political grounds, were in fact demanded by families, masters, local notables, neighbors, parish priests; and their function was to punish by confinement a whole infrapenality, that of disorder, agitation, disobedience, bad conduct; those things that Ledoux wanted to exclude from his architecturally perfect city and which he called "offenses of nonsurveillance." In short, the eighteenth-century police added a disciplinary function to its role as the auxiliary of justice in the pursuit of criminals and as an instrument for the political supervision of plots, opposition movements, or revolts. It was a complex function since it linked the absolute power of the monarch to the lowest levels of power disseminated in society; since, between these different, enclosed institutions of discipline (workshops, armies, schools), it extended an intermediary network, acting where they could not intervene, disciplining the nondisciplinary spaces; but it filled in the gaps, linked them together, guaranteed with its armed force an interstitial discipline and a metadiscipline. "By means of a wise police, the sovereign accustoms the people to order and obedience" (Vattel 162).

The organization of the police apparatus in the eighteenth century sanctioned a generalization of the disciplines that became coextensive with the state itself. Although it was linked in the most explicit way with everything in the royal power that exceeded the exercise of regular justice, it is understandable why the police offered such slight resistance to the rearrangement of the judicial power; and why it has not ceased to impose its prerogatives upon it, with ever-increasing weight, right up to the present day; this is no doubt because it is the secular arm of the judiciary; but it is also because, to a far greater degree than the judicial institution, it is identified, by reason of its extent and mechanisms, with a society of the disciplinary type. Yet it would be wrong to believe that the disciplinary functions were confiscated and absorbed once and for all by a state apparatus.

"Discipline" may be identified neither with an institution nor with an apparatus; it is a type of power, a modality for its exercise, comprising a whole set of instruments, techniques, procedures, levels of application, targets; it is a "physics" or an "anatomy" of power, a technology. And it may be taken over either by "specialized" institutions (the penitentiaries or "houses of correction" of the nineteenth century), or by institutions that use it as an essential instrument for a particular end (schools, hospitals), or by preexisting authorities that find in it a means of reinforcing or reorganizing their internal mechanisms of power (one day we should show how intrafamilial relations, essentially in the parents-children cell, have become "disciplined," absorbing since the classical age external schemata, first educational and military, then medical, psychiatric, psychological, which have made the family the privileged locus of emergence for the disciplinary question of the normal and the abnormal), or by apparatuses that have made discipline their principle of internal functioning (the disciplinarization of the administrative apparatus from the Napoleonic period), or finally by state apparatuses whose major, if not exclusive, function is to assure that discipline reigns over society as a whole (the police).

On the whole, therefore, one can speak of the formation of a disciplinary society in this movement that stretches from the enclosed disciplines, a sort of social "quarantine," to an indefinitely generalizable mechanism of "panopticism." Not because the disciplinary modality of power has replaced all the others; but because it has infiltrated the others, sometimes undermining them, but serving as an intermediary between them, linking them together, extending them, and above all making it possible to bring the effects of power to the most minute and distant elements. It assures an infinitesimal distribution of the power relations.

A few years after Bentham, Julius gave this society its birth certificate (Julius 384–86). Speaking of the panoptic principle, he said that there was much more there than architectural ingenuity: it was an event in the "history of the human mind." In appearance, it is merely the solution of a technical problem; but, through it, a whole type of society emerges. Antiquity had been a civilization of spectacle. "To render accessible to a multitude of men the inspection of a small number of objects": this was the problem to which the architecture of temples, theaters, and circuses responded. With spectacle, there was a predominance of public life, the intensity of festivals, sensual proximity. In these rituals in which blood flowed, society found new vigor and formed for a moment a single great body. The modern age poses the opposite problem: "To procure for a small number, or even for a single individual, the instantaneous view of a great multitude." In a society in which the principal elements are no longer the community and public life, but, on the one hand, private individuals and, on the other, the state, relations can be regulated only in a form that is the exact reverse of the spectacle: "It was to the modern age, to the ever-growing influence of the state, to its ever more profound intervention in all the details and all the relations of social life, that was reserved the task of increasing and perfecting its guarantees, by using and directing towards that great aim the building and distribution of buildings intended to observe a great multitude of men at the same time."

Julius saw as a fulfilled historical process that which Bentham had described as a technical program. Our society is one not of spectacle, but of surveillance; under the surface of images, one invests bodies in depth; behind the great abstraction of exchange, there continues the meticulous, concrete training of useful forces; the circuits of communication are the supports of an accumulation and a centralization of knowledge; the play of signs defines the anchorages of power; it is not that the beautiful totality of the individual is amputated, repressed, altered by our social order, it is rather that the individual is carefully fabricated in it, according to a whole technique of forces and bodies. We are much less Greeks than we believe. We are neither in the amphitheater, nor on the stage, but in the panoptic machine, invested by its effects of power, which we bring to ourselves since we are part of its mechanism. The importance, in historical mythology, of the Napoleonic character probably derives from the fact that it is at the point of junction of the monarchical, ritual exercise of sovereignty and the hierarchical, permanent exercise of indefinite discipline. He is the individual who looms over everything with a single gaze which no detail, however minute, can escape: "You may consider that no part of the Empire is without surveillance, no crime, no offense, no contravention that remains unpunished, and that the eye of the genius who can enlighten all embraces the whole of this vast machine, without, however, the slightest detail escaping his attention" (Treilhard 14). At the moment of its full blossoming, the disciplinary society still assumes with the Emperor the old aspect of the power of spectacle. As a monarch who is at one and the same time a usurper of the ancient throne and the organizer of the new state, he combined into a single symbolic, ultimate figure the whole of the long process by which the pomp of sovereignty, the necessarily spectacular manifestations of power, were extinguished one by one in the daily exercise of surveillance, in a panopticism in which the vigilance of intersecting gazes was soon to render useless both the eagle and the sun.

The formation of the disciplinary society is connected with a number of broad historical processes — economic, juridico-political, and lastly, scientific — of which it forms part.

1. Generally speaking, it might be said that the disciplines are techniques for assuring the ordering of human multiplicities. It is true that there is nothing exceptional or even characteristic in this: every system of power is presented with the same problem. But the peculiarity of the disciplines is that they try to define in relation to the multiplicities a tactics of power that fulfills three criteria: firstly, to obtain the exercise of power at the lowest possible cost (economically, by the low expenditure it involves; politically, by its discretion, its low exteriorization, its relative invisibility, the little resistance it arouses); secondly, to bring the effects of this social power to their maximum intensity and to extend them as far as possible, without either failure or interval; thirdly, to link this "economic" growth of power with the output of the apparatuses (educational, military, industrial, or medical) within which it is exercised; in short, to increase both the docility and the utility of all the elements of the system. This triple objective of the disciplines corresponds to a well-known historical conjuncture. One aspect of this conjuncture was the large demographic thrust of the eighteenth century; an increase in the floating population (one of the primary objects of discipline is to fix; it is an antinomadic technique); a change of quantitative scale in the groups to be supervised or manipulated (from the beginning of the seventeenth century to the eve of the French Revolution, the school population had been increasing rapidly, as had no doubt the hospital population; by the end of the eighteenth century, the peacetime army exceeded 200,000 men). The other aspect of the conjuncture was the growth in the apparatus of production, which was becoming more and more extended and complex; it was also becoming more costly and its profitability had to be increased. The development of the disciplinary methods corresponded to these two processes, or rather, no doubt, to the new need to adjust their correlation. Neither the residual forms of feudal power nor the structures of the administrative monarchy, nor the local mechanisms of supervision, nor the unstable, tangled mass they all formed together could carry out this role: they were hindered from doing so by the irregular and inadequate extension of their network, by their often conflicting functioning, but above all by the "costly" nature of the power that was exercised in them. It was costly in several senses: because directly it cost a great deal to the Treasury; because the system of corrupt offices and farmed-out taxes weighed indirectly, but very heavily, on the population; because the resistance it encountered forced it into a cycle of perpetual reinforcement; because it proceeded essentially by levying (levying on money or products by royal, seigniorial, ecclesiastical taxation; levying on men or time by *corvées* of press-ganging, by locking up or banishing vagabonds). The development of the disciplines marks

the appearance of elementary techniques belonging to a quite different economy: mechanisms of power which, instead of proceeding by deduction, are integrated into the productive efficiency of the apparatuses from within, into the growth of this efficiency and into the use of what it produces. For the old principle of "levying-violence," which governed the economy of power, the disciplines substitute the principle of "mildness-production-profit." These are the techniques that make it possible to adjust the multiplicity of men and the multiplication of the apparatuses of production (and this means not only "production" in the strict sense, but also the production of knowledge and skills in the school, the production of health in the hospitals, the production of destructive force in the army).

In this task of adjustment, discipline had to solve a number of problems for which the old economy of power was not sufficiently equipped. It could reduce the inefficiency of mass phenomena: reduce what, in a multiplicity, makes it much less manageable than a unity; reduce what is opposed to the use of each of its elements and of their sum; reduce everything that may counter the advantages of number. That is why discipline fixes; it arrests or regulates movements; it clears up confusion; it dissipates compact groupings of individuals wandering about the country in unpredictable ways; it establishes calculated distributions. It must also master all the forces that are formed from the very constitution of an organized multiplicity; it must neutralize the effects of counterpower that spring from them and which form a resistance to the power that wishes to dominate it: agitations, revolts, spontaneous organizations, coalitions — anything that may establish horizontal conjunctions. Hence the fact that the disciplines use procedures of partitioning and verticality, that they introduce, between the different elements at the same level, as solid separations as possible, that they define compact hierarchical networks, in short, that they oppose to the intrinsic, adverse force of multiplicity the technique of the continuous, individualizing pyramid. They must also increase the particular utility of each element of the multiplicity, but by means that are the most rapid and the least costly, that is to say, by using the multiplicity itself as an instrument of this growth. Hence, in order to extract from bodies the maximum time and force, the use of those overall methods known as timetables, collective training, exercises, total and detailed surveillance. Furthermore, the disciplines must increase the effect of utility proper to the multiplicities, so that each is made more useful than the simple sum of its elements: it is in order to increase the utilizable effects of the multiple that the disciplines define tactics of distribution, reciprocal adjustment of bodies, gestures, and rhythms, differentiation of capacities, reciprocal coordination in relation to apparatuses or tasks. Lastly, the disciplines have to bring into play the power relations, not above but inside the very texture of the multiplicity, as discreetly as possible, as well articulated on the other functions of these multiplicities and also in the least expensive way possible: to this correspond anonymous instruments of power, coextensive with the multiplicity that they regiment, such as hierarchical surveillance, continuous registration, perpetual assessment, and classification.

In short, to substitute for a power that is manifested through the brilliance of those who exercise it, a power that insidiously objectifies those on whom it is applied; to form a body of knowledge about these individuals, rather than to deploy the ostentatious signs of sovereignty. In a word, the disciplines are the ensemble of minute technical inventions that made it possible to increase the useful size of multiplicities by decreasing the inconveniences of the power which, in order to make them useful, must control them. A multiplicity, whether in a workshop or a nation, an army or a school, reaches the threshold of a discipline when the relation of the one to the other becomes favorable.

If the economic take-off of the West began with the techniques that made possible the accumulation of capital, it might perhaps be said that the methods for administering the accumulation of men made possible a political take-off in relation to the traditional, ritual, costly, violent forms of power, which soon fell into disuse and were superseded by a subtle, calculated technology of subjection. In fact, the two processes — the accumulation of men and the accumulation of capital — cannot be separated; it would not have been possible to solve the problem of the accumulation of men without the growth of an apparatus of production capable of both sustaining them and using them; conversely, the techniques that made the cumulative multiplicity of men useful accelerated the accumulation of capital. At a less general level, the technological mutations of the apparatus of production, the division of labor and the elaboration of the disciplinary techniques sustained an ensemble of very close relations (cf. Marx, *Capital*, vol. I, chapter XIII and the very interesting analysis in Guerry and Deleule). Each makes the other possible and necessary; each provides a model for the other. The disciplinary pyramid constituted the small cell of power within which the separation, coordination, and supervision of tasks was imposed and made efficient; and analytical partitioning of time, gestures, and bodily forces constituted an operational schema that could easily be transferred from the groups to be subjected to the mechanisms of production; the massive projection of military methods onto industrial organization was an example of this modeling of the division of labor following the model laid down by the schemata of power. But, on the other hand, the technical analysis of the process of production, its "mechanical" breaking-down, were projected onto the labor force whose task it was to implement it: the constitution of those disciplinary machines in which the individual forces that they bring together are composed into a whole and therefore increased is the effect of this projection. Let us say that discipline is the unitary technique by which the body is reduced as a "political" force at the least cost and maximized as a useful force. The growth of a capitalist economy gave rise to the specific modality of disciplinary power, whose general formulas, techniques of submitting forces and bodies, in short, "political anatomy," could be operated in the most diverse political regimes, apparatuses, or institutions.

2. The panoptic modality of power — at the elementary, technical, merely physical level at which it is situated — is not under the immediate

dependence or a direct extension of the great juridico-political structures of a society; it is nonetheless not absolutely independent. Historically, the process by which the bourgeoisie became in the course of the eighteenth century the politically dominant class was masked by the establishment of an explicit, coded, and formally egalitarian juridical framework, made possible by the organization of a parliamentary, representative regime. But the development and generalization of disciplinary mechanisms constituted the other, dark side of these processes. The general juridical form that guaranteed a system of rights that were egalitarian in principle was supported by these tiny, everyday, physical mechanisms, by all those systems of micropower that are essentially nonegalitarian and asymmetrical that we call the disciplines. And although, in a formal way, the representative regime makes it possible, directly or indirectly, with or without relays, for the will of all to form the fundamental authority of sovereignty, the disciplines provide, at the base, a guarantee of the submission of forces and bodies. The real, corporal disciplines constituted the foundation of the formal, juridical liberties. The contract may have been regarded as the ideal foundation of law and political power; panopticism constituted the technique, universally widespread, of coercion. It continued to work in depth on the juridical structures of society, in order to make the effective mechanisms of power function in opposition to the formal framework that it had acquired. The "Enlightenment," which discovered the liberties, also invented the disciplines.

In appearance, the disciplines constitute nothing more than an infra-law. They seem to extend the general forms defined by law to the infinitesimal level of individual lives; or they appear as methods of training that enable individuals to become integrated into these general demands. They seem to constitute the same type of law on a different scale, thereby making it more meticulous and more indulgent. The disciplines should be regarded as a sort of counterlaw. They have the precise role of introducing insuperable asymmetries and excluding reciprocities. First, because discipline creates between individuals a "private" link, which is a relation of constraints entirely different from contractual obligation; the acceptance of a discipline may be underwritten by contract; the way in which it is imposed, the mechanisms it brings into play, the nonreversible subordination of one group of people by another, the "surplus" power that is always fixed on the same side, the inequality of position of the different "partners" in relation to the common regulation, all these distinguish the disciplinary link from the contractual link, and make it possible to distort the contractual link systematically from the moment it has as its content a mechanism of discipline. We know, for example, how many real procedures undermine the legal fiction of the work contract: workshop discipline is not the least important. Moreover, whereas the juridical systems

> THE DEVELOPMENT AND GENERALIZATION OF DISCIPLINARY MECHANISMS CONSTITUTED THE OTHER, DARK SIDE OF THESE PROCESSES.

define juridical subjects according to universal norms, the disciplines characterize, classify, specialize; they distribute along a scale, around a norm, hierarchize individuals in relation to one another and, if necessary, disqualify and invalidate. In any case, in the space and during the time in which they exercise their control and bring into play the asymmetries of their power, they effect a suspension of the law that is never total, but is never annulled either. Regular and institutional as it may be, the discipline, in its mechanism, is a "counterlaw." And, although the universal juridicism of modern society seems to fix limits on the exercise of power, its universally widespread panopticism enables it to operate, on the underside of the law, a machinery that is both immense and minute, which supports, reinforces, multiplies the asymmetry of power and undermines the limits that are traced around the law. The minute disciplines, the panopticisms of every day may well be below the level of emergence of the great apparatuses and the great political struggles. But, in the genealogy of modern society, they have been, with the class domination that traverses it, the political counterpart of the juridical norms according to which power was redistributed. Hence, no doubt, the importance that has been given for so long to the small techniques of discipline, to those apparently insignificant tricks that it has invented, and even to those "sciences" that give it a respectable face; hence the fear of abandoning them if one cannot find any substitute; hence the affirmation that they are at the very foundation of society, and an element in its equilibrium, whereas they are a series of mechanisms for unbalancing power relations definitively and everywhere; hence the persistence in regarding them as the humble, but concrete form of every morality, whereas they are a set of physico-political techniques.

To return to the problem of legal punishments, the prison with all the corrective technology at its disposal is to be resituated at the point where the codified power to punish turns into a disciplinary power to observe; at the point where the universal punishments of the law are applied selectively to certain individuals and always the same ones; at the point where the redefinition of the juridical subject by the penalty becomes a useful training of the criminal; at the point where the law is inverted and passes outside itself, and where the counterlaw becomes the effective and institutionalized content of the juridical forms. What generalizes the power to punish, then, is not the universal consciousness of the law in each juridical subject; it is the regular extension, the infinitely minute web of panoptic techniques.

3. Taken one by one, most of these techniques have a long history behind them. But what was new, in the eighteenth century, was that, by being combined and generalized, they attained a level at which the formation of knowledge and the increase of power regularly reinforce one another in a circular process. At this point, the disciplines crossed the "technological" threshold. First the hospital, then the school, then, later, the workshop were not simply "reordered" by the disciplines; they became, thanks to them, apparatuses such that any mechanism of

objectification could be used in them as an instrument of subjection, and any growth of power could give rise in them to possible branches of knowledge; it was this link, proper to the technological systems, that made possible within the disciplinary element the formation of clinical medicine, psychiatry, child psychology, educational psychology, the rationalization of labor. It is a double process, then: an epistemological "thaw" through a refinement of power relations; a multiplication of the effects of power through the formation and accumulation of new forms of knowledge.

The extension of the disciplinary methods is inscribed in a broad historical process: the development at about the same time of many other technologies — agronomical, industrial, economic. But it must be recognized that, compared with the mining industries, the emerging chemical industries or methods of national accountancy, compared with the blast furnaces or the steam engine, panopticism has received little attention. It is regarded as not much more than a bizarre little utopia, a perverse dream — rather as though Bentham had been the Fourier of a police society, and the Phalanstery had taken on the form of the Panopticon. And yet this represented the abstract formula of a very real technology, that of individuals. There were many reasons why it received little praise; the most obvious is that the discourses to which it gave rise rarely acquired, except in the academic classifications, the status of sciences; but the real reason is no doubt that the power that it operates and which it augments is a direct, physical power that men exercise upon one another. An inglorious culmination had an origin that could be only grudgingly acknowledged. But it would be unjust to compare the disciplinary techniques with such inventions as the steam engine or Amici's microscope. They are much less; and yet, in a way, they are much more. If a historical equivalent or at least a point of comparison had to be found for them, it would be rather in the "inquisitorial" technique.

The eighteenth century invented the techniques of discipline and the examination, rather as the Middle Ages invented the judicial investigation. But it did so by quite different means. The investigation procedure, an old fiscal and administrative technique, had developed above all with the reorganization of the Church and the increase of the princely states in the twelfth and thirteenth centuries. At this time it permeated to a very large degree the jurisprudence first of the ecclesiastical courts, then of the lay courts. The investigation as an authoritarian search for a truth observed or attested was thus opposed to the old procedures of the oath, the ordeal, the judicial duel, the judgment of God, or even of the transaction between private individuals. The investigation was the sovereign power arrogating to itself the right to establish the truth by a number of regulated techniques. Now, although the investigation has since then been an integral part of Western justice (even up to our own day), one must not forget either its political origin, its link with the birth of the states and of monarchical sovereignty, or its later extension and its role in the formation of knowledge. In fact, the investigation has been the no doubt crude, but fundamental, element in the constitution of the empirical sciences; it has been the juridico-political matrix of this experimental knowledge, which, as we know, was very rapidly released at the end of the Middle Ages. It is perhaps true to say that, in Greece, mathematics were born from techniques of measurement; the sciences of nature, in any case, were born, to some extent, at the end of the Middle Ages, from the practices of investigation. The great empirical knowledge that covered the things of the world and transcribed them into the ordering of an indefinite discourse that observes, describes, and establishes the "facts" (at a time when the Western world was beginning the economic and political conquest of this same world) had its operating model no doubt in the Inquisition — that immense invention that our recent mildness has placed in the dark recesses of our memory. But what this politico-juridical, administrative, and criminal, religious and lay, investigation was to the sciences of nature, disciplinary analysis has been to the sciences of man. These sciences, which have so delighted our "humanity" for over a century, have their technical matrix in the petty, malicious minutiae of the disciplines and their investigations. These investigations are perhaps to psychology, psychiatry, pedagogy, criminology, and so many other strange sciences, what the terrible power of investigation was to the calm knowledge of the animals, the plants, or the earth. Another power, another knowledge. On the threshold of the classical age, Bacon, lawyer and statesman, tried to develop a methodology of investigation for the empirical sciences. What Great Observer will produce the methodology of examination for the human sciences? Unless, of course, such a thing is not possible. For, although it is true that, in becoming a technique for the empirical sciences, the investigation has detached itself from the inquisitorial procedure, in which it was historically rooted, the examination has remained extremely close to the disciplinary power that shaped it. It has always been and still is an intrinsic element of the disciplines. Of course it seems to have undergone a speculative purification by integrating itself with such sciences as psychology and psychiatry. And, in effect, its appearance in the form of tests, interviews, interrogations, and consultations is apparently in order to rectify the mechanisms of discipline: educational psychology is supposed to correct the rigors of the school, just as the medical or psychiatric interview is supposed to rectify the effects of the discipline of work. But we must not be misled; these techniques merely refer individuals from one disciplinary authority to another, and they reproduce, in a concentrated or formalized form, the schema of power-knowledge proper to each discipline (on this subject, cf. Tort). The great investigation that gave rise to the sciences of nature has become detached from its politico-juridical model; the examination, on the other hand, is still caught up in disciplinary technology.

In the Middle Ages, the procedure of investigation gradually superseded the old accusatory justice, by a process initiated from above; the disciplinary technique, on the other hand, insidiously and as if from below, has invaded a penal justice that is still, in principle, inquisitorial. All the great movements of extension that characterize modern penality — the problematization of the criminal behind his crime, the concern with a punishment that is a correction, a therapy, a normalization, the division of the act of judgment between various authorities that are supposed to measure, assess, diagnose, cure, transform individuals — all this betrays the penetration of the disciplinary examination into the judicial inquisition.

What is now imposed on penal justice as its point of application, its "useful" object, will no longer be the body of the guilty man set up against the body of the king; nor will it be the juridical subject of an ideal contract; it will be the disciplinary individual. The extreme point of penal justice under the Ancien Régime was the infinite segmentation of the body of the regicide: a manifestation of the strongest power over the body of the greatest criminal, whose total destruction made the crime explode into its truth. The ideal point of penality today would be an indefinite discipline: an interrogation without end, an investigation that would be extended without limit to a meticulous and ever more analytical observation, a judgment that would at the same time be the constitution of a file that was never closed, the calculated leniency of a penalty that would be interlaced with the ruthless curiosity of an examination, a procedure that would be at the same time the permanent measure of a gap in relation to an inaccessible norm and the asymptotic movement that strives to meet in infinity. The public execution was the logical culmination of a procedure governed by the Inquisition. The practice of placing individuals under "observation" is a natural extension of a justice imbued with disciplinary methods and examination procedures. Is it surprising that the cellular prison, with its regular chronologies, forced labor, its authorities of surveillance and registration, its experts in normality, who continue and multiply the functions of the judge, should have become the modern instrument of penalty? Is it surprising that prisons resemble factories, schools, barracks, hospitals, which all resemble prisons?

NOTES

[1] Archives militaires de Vincennes, A 1,516 91 sc. Pièce. This regulation is broadly similar to a whole series of others that date from the same period and earlier. [All notes are Foucault's.]

[2] In the *Postscript to the Panopticon*, 1791, Bentham adds dark inspection galleries painted in black around the inspector's lodge, each making it possible to observe two stories of cells.

[3] In his first version of the *Panopticon*, Bentham had also imagined an acoustic surveillance, operated by means of pipes leading from the cells to the central tower. In the *Postscript* he abandoned the idea, perhaps because he could not introduce into it the principle of dissymmetry and prevent the prisoners from hearing the inspector as well as the inspector hearing them. Julius tried to develop a system of dissymmetrical listening (Julius 18).

[4] Imagining this continuous flow of visitors entering the central tower by an underground passage and then observing the circular landscape of the Panopticon, was Bentham aware of the Panoramas that Barker was constructing at exactly the same period (the first seems to have dated from 1787) and in which the visitors, occupying the central place, saw unfolding around them a landscape, a city, or a battle? The visitors occupied exactly the place of the sovereign gaze.

[5] In the second half of the eighteenth century, it was often suggested that the army should be used for the surveillance and general partitioning of the population. The army, as yet to undergo discipline in the seventeenth century, was regarded as a force capable of instilling it. Cf., for example, Servan, *Le Soldat citoyen*, 1780.

[6] Arsenal, MS. 2565. Under this number, one also finds regulations for charity associations of the seventeenth and eighteenth centuries.

[7] Le Maire in a memorandum written at the request of Sartine, in answer to sixteen questions posed by Joseph II on the Parisian police. This memorandum was published by Gazier in 1879.

BIBLIOGRAPHY

Archives militaires de Vincennes, A 1,516 91 sc.
Bentham, J., *Works*, ed. Bowring, IV, 1843.
Chassaigne, M., *La Lieutenance générale de police*, 1906.
Delamare, N., *Traité de police*, 1705.
Demia, C., *Règlement pour les écoles de la ville de Lyon*, 1716.
Des Essarts, T. N., *Dictionnaire universel de police*, 1787.
Funck-Brentano, F., *Catalogue des manuscrits de la bibliothèque de l'Arsenal*, IX.
Guerry, F., and Deleule, D., *Le Corps productif*, 1973.
Julius, N. H., *Leçons sur les prisons*, I, 1831 (Fr. trans.).
Léon, A., *La Révolution française et l'éducation technique*, 1968.
Loisel, G., *Histoire des ménageries*, II, 1912.
Marx, Karl, *Capital*, vol. I, ed. 1970.
Radzinovitz, L., *The English Criminal Law*, II, 1956.
Servan, J., *Le Soldat citoyen*, 1780.
Tort, Michel, *Q.I.*, 1974.
Treilhard, J. B., *Motifs du code d'instruction criminelle*, 1808.
Vattel, E. de, *Le Droit des gens*, 1768.

• • • ● • • •

QUESTIONS FOR A SECOND READING

1. Foucault's text begins with an account of a system enacted in the seventeenth century to control the spread of plague. After describing this system of surveillance, he compares it to the "rituals of exclusion" used to control lepers. He says, "The exile of the leper and the arrest of the plague do not bring with them the same political dream" (p. 330). At many points he sets up similar pairings, all in an attempt to understand the relations of power and knowledge in modern public life.

   As you reread, mark the various points at which Foucault works out the differences between a prior and the current "political dream" of order. What techniques or instruments belong to each? What moments in history are defined by each? How and where are they visible in public life?

2. Toward the end of the chapter, Foucault says, "The extension of the disciplinary methods is inscribed in a broad historical process" (p. 353). Foucault writes a difficult kind of history (at one point he calls it a genealogy), since it does not make use of the usual form of historical narrative — with characters, plots, scenes, and action. As you reread, take notes that will allow you to trace time, place, and sequence (and, if you can, agents and agency) in Foucault's account of the formation of the disciplinary society based on technologies of surveillance. Why do you think he avoids a narrative mode of presentation?

3. As you reread Foucault's text, bring forward the stages in his presentation (or the development of his argument). Mark those moments that you consider

key or central to the working out of his argument concerning the panopticon. What sentences of his would you use to represent key moments in the text? The text at times turns to numbered sections. How, for example, do they function? Describe the beginning, middle, and end of the essay. Describe the skeleton or understructure of the chapter. What are its various stages or steps? How do they relate to one another?

· · ● · ·

ASSIGNMENTS FOR WRITING

1. About three-quarters of the way into this chapter, Foucault says,

> Our society is one not of spectacle, but of surveillance; under the surface of images, one invests bodies in depth; behind the great abstraction of exchange, there continues the meticulous, concrete training of useful forces; the circuits of communication are the supports of an accumulation and a centralization of knowledge; the play of signs defines the anchorages of power; it is not that the beautiful totality of the individual is amputated, repressed, altered by our social order, it is rather that the individual is carefully fabricated in it, according to a whole technique of forces and bodies. (p. 347)

This prose is eloquent and insists on its importance to our moment and our society; it is also very hard to read or to paraphrase. Who is doing what to whom? How do we think about the individual's being carefully fabricated in the social order?

Take this chapter as a problem to solve. What is it about? What are its key arguments? its examples and conclusions? Write an essay that summarizes "Panopticism." Imagine that you are writing for readers who have read the chapter (although they won't have the pages in front of them). You will need to take time to present and discuss examples from the text. Your job is to help your readers figure out what it says. You get the chance to take the lead and be the teacher. You should feel free to acknowledge that you don't understand certain sections even as you write about them.

So, how do you write about something you don't completely understand? Here's a suggestion: when you have completed your summary, read it over and treat it as a draft. Ask questions like these: What have I left out? What was I tempted to ignore or finesse? Go back to those sections of the chapter that you ignored and bring them into your essay. Revise by adding discussions of some of the very sections you don't understand. You can write about what you think Foucault *might* be saying — you can, that is, be cautious and tentative; you can admit that the text is what it is, hard to read. You don't have to master this text. You do, however, need to see what you can make of it.

2. About a third of the way through his text, Foucault asserts, "The Panopticon is a marvelous machine which, whatever use one may wish to put it to,

produces homogeneous effects of power" (p. 335). Write an essay in which you explain the machinery of the panopticon as a mechanism of power. Paraphrase Foucault and, where it seems appropriate, use his words. Present Foucault's account as you understand it. As part of your essay, and in order to explain what he is getting at, include two examples — one of his, perhaps, and then one of your own.

3. Perhaps the most surprising thing about Foucault's argument in "Panopticism" is the way it equates prisons with schools, hospitals, and workplaces, sites we are accustomed to imagining as very different from a prison. Foucault argues against our commonly accepted understanding of such things.

At the end of the chapter Foucault asks two questions. These are rhetorical questions, strategically placed at the end. Presumably we are prepared to feel their force and to think of possible answers.

> Is it surprising that the cellular prison, with its regular chronologies, forced labor, its authorities of surveillance and registration, its experts in normality, who continue and multiply the functions of the judge, should have become the modern instrument of penalty? Is it surprising that prisons resemble factories, schools, barracks, hospitals, which all resemble prisons? (p. 355)

For this assignment, take the invitation of Foucault's conclusion. No, you want to respond, it is not surprising that "experts in normality, who continue and multiply the functions of the judge, should have become the modern instrument of penalty." No, it is not surprising that "prisons resemble factories, schools, barracks, hospitals, which all resemble prisons." Why isn't it surprising? Or, why isn't it surprising if you are thinking along with Foucault?

Write an essay in which you explore one of these possible resemblances. You may, if you choose, cite Foucault. You can certainly pick up some of his key terms or examples and put them into play. You should imagine, however, that it is your turn. With your work on Foucault behind you, you are writing to a general audience about "experts in normality" and the key sites of surveillance and control.

· · • · · ·

MAKING CONNECTIONS

1. Both John Berger in "Ways of Seeing" (p. 142) and Michel Foucault in "Panopticism" discuss what Foucault calls "power relations." Berger claims that "the entire art of the past has now become a political issue," and he makes a case for the evolution of a "new language of images" that could "confer a new kind of power" if people were to understand history in art. Foucault argues that the Panopticon signals an "inspired" change in power relations. "It is," he says,

> an important mechanism, for it automatizes and disindividualizes power. Power has its principle not so much in a person as in a certain concerted distribution of bodies, surfaces, lights, gazes; in an

arrangement whose internal mechanisms produce the relation in which individuals are caught up. (p. 334)

Both Berger and Foucault create arguments about power, its methods and goals. As you read through their essays, mark passages you might use to explain how each author thinks about power — where it comes from, who has it, how it works, where you look for it, how you know when you see it, what it does, where it goes. You should reread the essays as a pair, as part of a single project in which you are looking to explain theories of power.

Write an essay in which you present and explain "Ways of Seeing" and "Panopticism" as examples of Berger's and Foucault's theories of power. Both Berger and Foucault are arguing against usual understandings of power and knowledge and history. In this sense, their projects are similar. You should be sure, however, to look for differences as well as similarities.

2.   At a key point in her essay "Beside Oneself: On the Limits of Sexual Autonomy" (p. 238), Judith Butler refers to the work of Michel Foucault:

> The question of who and what is considered real and true is apparently a question of knowledge. But it is also, as Michel Foucault makes plain, a question of power. Having or bearing "truth" and "reality" is an enormously powerful prerogative within the social world, one way that power dissimulates as ontology. According to Foucault, one of the first tasks of a radical critique is to discern the relation "between mechanisms of coercion and elements of knowledge." (p. 245)

And she goes on for some length to work with passages from Foucault, although not from his book *Discipline and Punish*.

Take some time to reread Butler's essay, paying particular attention to her use of Foucault. Where and why is Foucault helpful to her? In what ways is she providing a new argument or a counterargument? And take time to reread "Panopticism." What passages might be useful in extending or challenging Butler's argument in "Beside Oneself"? Using these two sources, write an essay in which you talk about Butler and Foucault and their engagement with what might be called "radical critique," an effort (in the terms offered above) to "discern the relation 'between mechanisms of coercion and elements of knowledge.'"

Note: The assignment limits you to these two sources, the two selections in the textbook. Butler and Foucault have written much, and their work circulates widely. You are most likely not in a position to speak about everything they have written or about all that has been written about them. We wanted to define a starting point that was manageable. Still, if you want to do more research, you might begin by reading the Foucault essay that Butler cites, "What Is Critique?"; you might go to the library to look through books by Butler and Foucault, choosing one or two that seem to offer themselves as next steps; or you could go to essays written by scholars who, as you are, are trying to think about the two together.

3. One way to think about Foucault's text is to see Foucault as developing a theory of discipline, raising questions about the way discipline works — as a metaphor, as institutional regulation, and perhaps also as societal norms. Foucault tells us: "One also sees the spread of disciplinary procedures, not in the form of enclosed institutions, but as centers of observation disseminated throughout society" (p. 343). One might say that Susan Griffin's "Our Secret" (p. 381) is also about this idea of discipline.

Reread "Our Secret," marking in the margins any passages that seem connected to Foucault's theory of discipline. Choose three particular passages from Griffin that strike you as good examples through which to explore Foucault's theory. Write an essay that further theorizes discipline by involving Griffin's passages in the conversation. What does Griffin have to offer to this theory? How are Griffin and Foucault doing the same kind of work? Where, if anywhere, might they diverge?

ATUL
Gawande

Atul Gawande (b. 1965), a surgeon at Brigham and Women's Hospital in Boston and the Samuel O. Thier Professor of Surgery at Harvard Medical School as well as a writer for *The New Yorker*, is the author of *Complications: A Surgeon's Notes on an Imperfect Science* (2002), *Better: A Surgeon's Notes on Performance* (2007), the *New York Times* bestseller *The Checklist Manifesto: How to Get Things Right* (2009), and *Being Mortal: Medicine and What Matters in the End* (2014).

Gawande was named one of the world's hundred most influential thinkers by *Time* magazine. He has won a MacArthur "Genius" Fellowship and two National Magazine Awards, has been a finalist for the National Book Award, and has received the Lewis Thomas Award for science writing. He cofounded and chairs Lifebox, an international nonprofit dedicated to making surgeries safer.

A number of Gawande's books and essays take up the question of how we can best teach and learn. His book *The Checklist Manifesto* offers readers the simple checklist as a teaching and learning tool that saves lives in surgery and can help people prioritize and organize their lives. "Slow Ideas," an essay published in *The New Yorker* in 2013, poses questions about teaching and learning in relation to life-and-death innovations that are both fast and slow to take hold. In "Slow Ideas," as Gawande writes about the challenges in changing medical practices, we see him, in what is signature Gawande writing, using his examples to think on the page about the conditions of teaching and learning.

Slow Ideas

Why do some innovations spread so swiftly and others so slowly? Consider the very different trajectories of surgical anesthesia and antiseptics, both of which were discovered in the nineteenth century. The first public demonstration of anesthesia was in 1846. The Boston surgeon Henry Jacob Bigelow was approached by a local dentist named William Morton, who insisted that he had found a gas that could render patients insensible to the pain of surgery. That was a dramatic claim. In those days, even a minor tooth extraction was excruciating. Without effective pain control, surgeons learned to work with slashing speed. Attendants pinned patients down as they screamed and thrashed, until they fainted from the agony. Nothing ever tried had made much difference. Nonetheless, Bigelow agreed to let Morton demonstrate his claim.

On October 16, 1846, at Massachusetts General Hospital, Morton administered his gas through an inhaler in the mouth of a young man undergoing the excision of a tumor in his jaw. The patient only muttered to himself in a semi-conscious state during the procedure. The following day, the gas left a woman, undergoing surgery to cut a large tumor from her upper arm, completely silent and motionless. When she woke, she said she had experienced nothing at all.

Four weeks later, on November 18th, Bigelow published his report on the discovery of "insensibility produced by inhalation" in the *Boston Medical and Surgical Journal*. Morton would not divulge the composition of the gas, which he called Letheon, because he had applied for a patent. But Bigelow reported that he smelled ether in it (ether was used as an ingredient in certain medical preparations), and that seems to have been enough. The idea spread like a contagion, travelling through letters, meetings, and periodicals. By mid-December, surgeons were administering ether to patients in Paris and London. By February, anesthesia had been used in almost all the capitals of Europe, and by June in most regions of the world.

There were forces of resistance, to be sure. Some people criticized anesthesia as a "needless luxury"; clergymen deplored its use to reduce pain during childbirth as a frustration of the Almighty's designs. James Miller, a nineteenth-century Scottish surgeon who chronicled the advent of anesthesia, observed the opposition of elderly surgeons: "They closed their ears, shut their eyes, and folded their hands. . . . They had quite made up their minds that pain was a necessary evil, and must be endured." Yet soon even the obstructors, "with a run, mounted behind — hurrahing and shouting with the best." Within seven years, virtually every hospital in America and Britain had adopted the new discovery.

Sepsis — infection — was the other great scourge of surgery. It was the single biggest killer of surgical patients, claiming as many as half of those who underwent major operations, such as a repair of an open fracture or the amputation of a limb. Infection was so prevalent that suppuration — the discharge of pus from a surgical wound — was thought to be a necessary part of healing.

In the eighteen-sixties, the Edinburgh surgeon Joseph Lister read a paper by Louis Pasteur laying out his evidence that spoiling and fermentation were the consequence of microorganisms. Lister became convinced that the same process accounted for wound sepsis. Pasteur had observed that, besides filtration and the application of heat, exposure to certain chemicals could eliminate germs. Lister had read about the city of Carlisle's success in using a small amount of carbolic acid to eliminate the odor of sewage, and reasoned that it was destroying germs. Maybe it could do the same in surgery.

During the next few years, he perfected ways to use carbolic acid for cleansing hands and wounds and destroying any germs that might enter the operating field. The result was strikingly lower rates of sepsis and death. You would have thought that, when he published his observations in a groundbreaking series of reports in *The Lancet*, in 1867, his antiseptic method would have spread as rapidly as anesthesia.

Far from it. The surgeon J. M. T. Finney recalled that, when he was a trainee at Massachusetts General Hospital two decades later, hand washing was still perfunctory. Surgeons soaked their instruments in carbolic acid, but they continued to operate in black frock coats stiffened with the blood and viscera of previous operations — the badge of a busy practice. Instead of using fresh gauze as sponges, they reused sea sponges without sterilizing them. It was a generation before Lister's recommendations became routine and the next steps were taken toward the modern standard of asepsis — that is, entirely excluding germs from the surgical field, using heat-sterilized instruments and surgical teams clad in sterile gowns and gloves.

In our era of electronic communications, we've come to expect that important innovations will spread quickly. Plenty do: think of in-vitro fertilization, genomics, and communications technologies themselves. But there's an equally long list of vital innovations that have failed to catch on. The puzzle is why.

Did the spread of anesthesia and antisepsis differ for economic reasons? Actually, the incentives for both ran in the right direction. If painless surgery attracted paying patients, so would a noticeably lower death rate. Besides, live patients were more likely to make good on their surgery bill. Maybe ideas that violate prior beliefs are harder to embrace. To nineteenth-century surgeons, germ theory seemed as illogical as, say, Darwin's theory that human beings evolved from primates. Then again, so did the idea that you could inhale a gas and enter a pain-free state of suspended animation. Proponents of anesthesia overcame belief by encouraging surgeons to try ether on a patient and witness the results for themselves — to take a test drive. When Lister tried this strategy, however, he made little progress.

The technical complexity might have been part of the difficulty. Giving Lister's methods "a try" required painstaking attention to detail. Surgeons had to be scrupulous about soaking their hands, their instruments, and even their catgut sutures in antiseptic solution. Lister also set up a device that continuously sprayed a mist of antiseptic over the surgical field.

But anesthesia was no easier. Obtaining ether and constructing the inhaler could be difficult. You had to make sure that the device delivered an adequate dosage, and the mechanism required constant tinkering. Yet most surgeons stuck with it — or else they switched to chloroform, which was found to be an even more powerful anesthetic, but posed its own problems. (An imprecise dosage killed people.) Faced with the complexities, they didn't give up; instead, they formed an entire new medical specialty — anesthesiology.

So what were the key differences? First, one combatted a visible and immediate problem (pain); the other combatted an invisible problem (germs) whose effects wouldn't be manifest until well after the operation. Second, although both made life better for patients, only one made life better for doctors. Anesthesia changed surgery from a brutal, time-pressured assault on a shrieking patient to a quiet, considered procedure. Listerism, by contrast, required the operator to work in a shower of carbolic acid. Even low dilutions burned the surgeons' hands. You can imagine why Lister's crusade might have been a tough sell.

This has been the pattern of many important but stalled ideas. They attack problems that are big but, to most people, invisible; and making them work can be tedious, if not outright painful. The global destruction wrought by a warming climate, the health damage from our over-sugared modern diet, the economic and social disaster of our trillion dollars in unpaid student debt — these things worsen imperceptibly every day. Meanwhile, the carbolic-acid remedies to them, all requiring individual sacrifice of one kind or another, struggle to get anywhere.

> **THIS HAS BEEN THE PATTERN OF MANY IMPORTANT BUT STALLED IDEAS. THEY ATTACK PROBLEMS THAT ARE BIG BUT, TO MOST PEOPLE, INVISIBLE; AND MAKING THEM WORK CAN BE TEDIOUS, IF NOT OUTRIGHT PAINFUL.**

The global problem of death in childbirth is a pressing example. Every year, three hundred thousand mothers and more than six million children die around the time of birth, largely in poorer countries. Most of these deaths are due to events that occur during or shortly after delivery. A mother may hemorrhage. She or her baby may suffer an infection. Many babies can't take their first breath without assistance, and newborns, especially those born small, have trouble regulating their body temperature after birth. Simple, lifesaving solutions have been known for decades. They just haven't spread.

Many solutions aren't ones you can try at home, and that's part of the problem. Increasingly, however, women around the world are giving birth in hospitals. In India, a government program offers mothers up to fourteen hundred rupees — more than what most Indians live on for a month — when they deliver in a hospital, and now, in many areas, the majority of births are in facilities. Death rates in India have fallen, but they're still ten times greater than in high-income countries like our own.

Not long ago, I visited a few community hospitals in north India, where just one-third of mothers received the medication recommended to prevent hemorrhage; less than ten per cent of the newborns were given adequate warming; and only four per cent of birth attendants washed their hands for vaginal examination and delivery. In an average childbirth, clinicians followed only about ten of twenty-nine basic recommended practices.

Here we are in the first part of the twenty-first century, and we're still trying to figure out how to get ideas from the first part of the twentieth century to take root. In the hopes of spreading safer childbirth practices, several colleagues and I have teamed up with the Indian government, the World Health Organization, the Gates Foundation, and Population Services International to create something called the BetterBirth Project. We're working in Uttar Pradesh, which is among India's poorest states. One afternoon in January, our team travelled a couple of hours from the state's capital, Lucknow, with its bleating cars and ramshackle shops, to a rural hospital surrounded by lush farmland and thatched-hut villages. Although the sun was high and the sky was clear, the temperature was near freezing. The hospital was a one-story concrete building painted goldenrod yellow. (Our research agreement required that I keep it unnamed.) The entrance is on a dirt road lined with rows of motorbikes, the primary means of long-distance transportation. If an ambulance or an auto-rickshaw can't be found, women in labor sit sidesaddle on the back of a bike.

> **HERE WE ARE IN THE FIRST PART OF THE TWENTY-FIRST CENTURY, AND WE'RE STILL TRYING TO FIGURE OUT HOW TO GET IDEAS FROM THE FIRST PART OF THE TWENTIETH CENTURY TO TAKE ROOT.**

The hospital delivers three thousand newborns a year, a typical volume in India but one that would put it in the top fifth of American hospitals. Yet it had little of the amenities that you'd associate with a modern hospital. I met the physician in charge, a smart and capable internist in his early thirties who had trained in the capital. He was clean-shaven and buzz-cut, with an Argyle sweater, track shoes, and a habitual half smile. He told me, apologetically, that the hospital staff had no ability to do blood tests, to give blood transfusions, or to perform emergency obstetrics procedures such as Cesarean sections. There was no electricity during the day. There was certainly no heating, even though the temperature was barely forty degrees that day, and no air-conditioning, even though summer temperatures routinely reach a hundred degrees. There were two blood-pressure cuffs for the entire facility. The nurse's office in my neighborhood elementary school was better equipped.

The hospital was severely understaffed, too. The doctor said that half of the staff positions were vacant. To help with child deliveries for a local population of a quarter of a million people, the hospital had two nurses and one obstetrician, who happened to be his wife. The nurses, who had six months of childbirth training, did most of the deliveries, swapping shifts year-round. The obstetrician covered the outpatient clinic, and helped with complicated births whenever she was required, day or night. During holidays or sickness, the two nurses covered for each other, but, if no one was available, laboring women were either sent to another hospital, miles away, or an untrained assistant might be forced to step in.

It may be surprising that mothers are better off delivering in such places than at home in a village, but studies show a consistently higher survival rate when they do. The staff members I met in India had impressive experience. Even the youngest nurses had done more than a thousand child deliveries. They've seen and learned to deal with countless problems — a torn placenta, an umbilical cord wrapped around a baby's neck, a stuck shoulder. Seeing the daily heroism required to keep such places going, you feel foolish and ill-mannered asking how they could do things better.

But then we hung out in the wards for a while. In the delivery room, a boy had just been born. He and his mother were lying on a cot, bundled under woollen blankets, resting. The room was coffin-cold; I was having trouble feeling my toes. I tried to imagine what that baby must have felt like. Newborns have a high body-surface area and lose heat rapidly. Even in warm weather, hypothermia is common, and it makes newborns weak and less responsive, less able to breast-feed adequately and more prone to infection. I noticed that the boy was swaddled separately from his mother. Voluminous evidence shows that it is far better to place the child on the mother's chest or belly, skin to skin, so that the mother's body can regulate the baby's until it is ready to take over. Among small or premature babies, kangaroo care (as it is known) cuts mortality rates by a third.

So why hadn't the nurse swaddled the two together? She was a skilled and self-assured woman in her mid-thirties with twinkly eyes, a brown knit hat, and a wool sweater over her shalwar kameez. Resources clearly weren't the issue — kangaroo care costs nothing. Had she heard of it? Oh, yes, she said. She'd taken a skilled-birth-attendant class that taught it. Had she forgotten about it? No. She had actually offered to put the baby skin to skin with the mother, and showed me where she'd noted this in the record.

"The mother didn't want it," she explained. "She said she was too cold."

The nurse seemed to think it was strange that I was making such an issue of this. The baby was fine, wasn't he? And he was. He was sleeping sweetly, a tightly wrapped peanut with a scrunched brown face and his mouth in a lowercase "o."

But had his temperature been taken? It had not. The nurse said that she had been planning to do so. Our visit had disrupted her routine. Suppose she had, though, and his temperature was low. Would she have done anything differently? Would she have made the mom unswaddle the child and put him to her chest?

Everything about the life the nurse leads — the hours she puts in, the circumstances she endures, the satisfaction she takes in her abilities — shows that she cares. But hypothermia, like the germs that Lister wanted surgeons to battle, is invisible to her. We picture a blue child, suffering right before our eyes. That is not what hypothermia looks like. It is a child who is just a few degrees too cold, too sluggish, too slow to feed. It will be some time before the baby begins to lose weight, stops making urine, develops pneumonia or a bloodstream infection. Long before that happens — usually the morning after the delivery, perhaps the same night — the mother will have hobbled to an auto-rickshaw, propped herself beside her husband, held her new baby tight, and ridden the rutted roads home.

From the nurse's point of view, she'd helped bring another life into the world. If four per cent of the newborns later died at home, what could that possibly have to do with how she wrapped the mother and child? Or whether she washed her hands before putting on gloves? Or whether the blade with which she cut the umbilical cord was sterilized?

We're infatuated with the prospect of technological solutions to these problems — baby warmers, say. You can still find high-tech incubators in rural hospitals that sit mothballed because a replacement part wasn't available, or because there was no electricity for them. In recent years, though, engineers have produced designs specifically for the developing world. Dr. Steven Ringer, a neonatologist and BetterBirth leader, was an adviser for a team that made a cheap, ingenious, award-winning incubator from old car parts that are commonly available and easily replaced in low-income environments. Yet it hasn't taken off, either. "It's in more museums than delivery rooms," he laments.

As with most difficulties in global health care, lack of adequate technology is not the biggest problem. We already have a great warming technology: a mother's skin. But even in high-income countries we do not consistently use it. In the United States, according to Ringer, more than half of newborns needing intensive care arrive hypothermic. Preventing hypothermia is a perfect example of an unsexy task: it demands painstaking effort without immediate reward. Getting hospitals and birth attendants to carry out even a few of the tasks required for safer childbirth would save hundreds of thousands of lives. But how do we do that?

> GETTING HOSPITALS AND BIRTH ATTENDANTS TO CARRY OUT EVEN A FEW OF THE TASKS REQUIRED FOR SAFER CHILDBIRTH WOULD SAVE HUNDREDS OF THOUSANDS OF LIVES. BUT HOW DO WE DO THAT?

The most common approach to changing behavior is to say to people, "Please do X." Please warm the newborn. Please wash your hands. Please follow through on the twenty-seven other childbirth practices that you're not doing. This is what we say in the classroom, in instructional videos, and in public-service campaigns, and it works, but only up to a point.

Then, there's the law-and-order approach: "You must do X." We establish standards and regulations, and threaten to punish failures with fines, suspensions, the revocation of licenses. Punishment can work. Behavioral economists have even quantified how averse people are to penalties. In experimental games, they will often quit playing rather than risk facing negative consequences. And that is the problem with threatening to discipline birth attendants who are taking difficult-to-fill jobs under intensely trying conditions. They'll quit.

The kinder version of "You must do X" is to offer incentives rather than penalties. Maybe we could pay birth attendants a bonus for every healthy child who makes it past a week of life. But then you think about how hard it would be to make a scheme like that work, especially in poor settings. You'd need a sophisticated tracking procedure, to make sure that people aren't gaming the system, and complex statistical calculations, to take prior risks into account. There's also the impossible question of how you split the reward among all the people involved. How much should the community health worker who provided the prenatal care get? The birth attendant who handled the first twelve hours of labor? The one who came on duty and handled the delivery? The doctor who was called in when things got complicated? The pharmacist who stocked the antibiotic that the child required?

Besides, neither penalties nor incentives achieve what we're really after: a system and a culture where X is what people do, day in and day out, even when no one is watching. "You must" rewards mere compliance. Getting to "X is what we do" means establishing X as the norm. And that's what we want: for skin-to-skin warming, hand washing, and all the other lifesaving practices of childbirth to be, quite simply, the norm.

To create new norms, you have to understand people's existing norms and barriers to change. You have to understand what's getting in their way. So what about just working with health-care workers, one by one, to do just that? With the BetterBirth Project, we wondered, in particular, what would happen if we hired a cadre of childbirth-improvement workers to visit birth attendants and hospital leaders, show them why and how to follow a checklist of essential practices, understand their difficulties and objections, and help them practice doing things differently. In essence, we'd give them mentors.

The experiment is just getting under way. The project has recruited only the first few of a hundred or so workers whom we are sending out to hospitals across six regions of Uttar Pradesh in a trial that will involve almost two hundred thousand births over two years. There's no certainty that our approach will succeed. But it seemed worth trying.

Reactions that I've heard both abroad and at home have been interestingly divided. The most common objection is that, even if it works, this kind of one-on-one, on-site mentoring "isn't scalable." But that's one thing it surely is. If the intervention saves as many mothers and newborns as we're hoping — about a thousand lives in the course of a year at the target hospitals — then all that need be done is to hire and develop similar cadres of childbirth-improvement workers for other places around the country and potentially the world. To many people, that doesn't sound like much of a solution. It would require broad mobilization, substantial expense, and perhaps even the development of a new profession. But, to combat the many antisepsis-like problems in the world, that's exactly what has worked. Think about the creation of anesthesiology: it meant doubling the number of doctors in every operation, and we went ahead and did so. To reduce illiteracy, countries, starting with our own, built schools, trained professional teachers, and made education free and compulsory for all children. To improve farming, governments have sent hundreds of thousands of agriculture extension agents to visit farmers across America and every corner of the world and teach them up-to-date methods for increasing their crop yields. Such programs have been extraordinarily effective. They have cut the global illiteracy rate from one in three adults in 1970 to one in six today, and helped give us a Green Revolution that saved more than a billion people from starvation.

In the era of the iPhone, Facebook, and Twitter, we've become enamored of ideas that spread as effortlessly as ether. We want frictionless, "turnkey" solutions to the major difficulties of the world — hunger, disease, poverty. We prefer instructional videos to teachers, drones to troops, incentives to institutions. People and institutions can feel messy and anachronistic. They introduce, as the engineers put it, uncontrolled variability.

But technology and incentive programs are not enough. "Diffusion is essentially a social process through which people talking to people spread an innovation," wrote Everett Rogers, the great scholar of how new ideas are communicated and spread. Mass media can introduce a new idea to people. But, Rogers showed, people follow the lead of other people they know and trust when they decide whether to take it up. Every change requires effort, and the decision to make that effort is a social process.

> IN THE ERA OF THE IPHONE, FACEBOOK, AND TWITTER, WE'VE BECOME ENAMORED OF IDEAS THAT SPREAD AS EFFORTLESSLY AS ETHER. WE WANT FRICTIONLESS, "TURNKEY" SOLUTIONS TO THE MAJOR DIFFICULTIES OF THE WORLD — HUNGER, DISEASE, POVERTY.

This is something that salespeople understand well. I once asked a pharmaceutical rep how he persuaded doctors — who are notoriously stubborn — to adopt a new medicine. Evidence is not remotely enough, he said, however strong a case you may have. You must also apply "the rule of seven touches." Personally "touch" the doctors seven times, and they will come to know you; if they know you, they might trust you; and, if they trust you, they will change. That's why he stocked doctors' closets with free drug samples in person. Then he could poke his head around the corner and ask, "So how did your daughter Debbie's soccer game go?" Eventually, this can become "Have you seen this study on our new drug? How about giving it a try?" As the rep had recognized, human interaction is the key force in overcoming resistance and speeding change.

In 1968, *The Lancet* published the results of a modest trial of what is now regarded as among the most important medical advances of the twentieth century. It wasn't a new drug or vaccine or operation. It was basically a solution of sugar, salt, and water that you could make in your kitchen. The researchers gave the solution to victims of a cholera outbreak in Dhaka, the capital of what is now Bangladesh, and the results were striking.

Cholera is a violent and deadly diarrheal illness, caused by the bacterium *Vibrio cholera*, which the victim usually ingests from contaminated water. The bacteria secrete a toxin that triggers a rapid outpouring of fluid into the intestine. The body, which is sixty per cent water, becomes like a sponge being wrung out. The fluid pouring out is a cloudy white, likened to the runoff of washed rice. It produces projectile vomiting and explosive diarrhea. Children can lose a third of their body's water in less than twenty-four hours, a fatal volume. Drinking water to replace the fluid loss is ineffective, because the intestine won't absorb it. As a result, mortality commonly reached seventy per cent or higher. During the nineteenth century, cholera pandemics killed millions across Asia, Europe, Africa, and North America. The disease was dubbed the Blue Death because of the cyanotic blue-gray color of the skin from extreme dehydration.

In 1906, a partially effective treatment was found: intravenous fluid solutions reduced mortality to thirty per cent. Prevention was the most effective approach. Modern sewage and water treatment eliminated the disease in affluent countries. Globally, though, millions of children continued to die from diarrheal illness each year. Even if victims made it to a medical facility, the needles, plastic tubing, and litres of intravenous fluid required for treatment were expensive, in short supply, and dependent on medical workers who were themselves in short supply, especially in outbreaks that often produced thousands of victims.

Then, in the nineteen-sixties, scientists discovered that sugar helps the gut absorb fluid. Two American researchers, David Nalin and Richard Cash, were in Dhaka during a cholera outbreak. They decided to test the scientific findings, giving victims an oral rehydration solution containing sugar as well as salt. Many people doubted that victims could drink enough of it to restore their fluid losses, typically ten to twenty litres a day. So the researchers confined the Dhaka trial to twenty-nine patients. The subjects proved to have no trouble drinking enough to reduce or even eliminate the need for intravenous fluids, and none of them died.

Three years later, in 1971, an Indian physician named Dilip Mahalanabis was directing medical assistance at a West Bengal camp of three hundred and fifty thousand refugees from Bangladesh's war of independence when cholera struck. Intravenous-fluid supplies ran out. Mahalanabis instructed his team to try the Dhaka solution. Just 3.6 per cent died, an unprecedented reduction from the usual thirty per cent. The solution was actually better than intravenous fluids. If cholera victims were alert, able to drink, and supplied with enough of it, they could almost always save their own lives.

One might have expected people to clamor for the recipe after these results were publicized. Oral rehydration solution seems like ether: a miraculous fix for a vivid, immediate, and terrifying problem. But it wasn't like ether at all.

To understand why, you have to imagine having a child throwing up and pouring out diarrhea like you've never seen before. Making her drink seems only to provoke more vomiting. Chasing the emesis and the diarrhea seems both torturous and futile. Many people's natural inclination is to not feed the child anything.

Furthermore, why believe that this particular mixture of sugar and salt would be any different from water or anything else you might have tried? And it *is* particular. Throw the salt concentration off by a couple of teaspoons and the electrolyte imbalance could be dangerous. The child must also keep drinking the stuff even after she feels better, for as long as the diarrhea lasts, which is up to five days. Nurses routinely got these steps wrong. Why would villagers do any better?

A decade after the landmark findings, the idea remained stalled. Nothing much had changed. Diarrheal disease remained the world's biggest killer of children under the age of five.

In 1980, however, a Bangladeshi nonprofit organization called BRAC decided to try to get oral rehydration therapy adopted nationwide. The campaign required reaching a mostly illiterate population. The most recent public-health campaign — to teach family planning — had been deeply unpopular. The messages the campaign needed to spread were complicated.

Nonetheless, the campaign proved remarkably successful. A gem of a book published in Bangladesh, "A Simple Solution," tells the story. The organization didn't launch a mass-media campaign — only twenty per cent of the population had a radio, after all. It attacked the problem in a way that is routinely dismissed as impractical and inefficient: by going door to door, person by person, and just talking.

It started with a pilot project that set out to reach some sixty thousand women in six hundred villages. The logistics were daunting. Who, for instance, would do the teaching? How were those workers going to travel? How was their security to be assured? The BRAC leaders planned the best they could and then made adjustments on the fly.

They recruited teams of fourteen young women, a cook, and a male supervisor, figuring that the supervisor would protect them from others as they travelled, and the women's numbers would protect them from the supervisor. They travelled on foot, pitched camp near each village, fanned out door to door, and stayed until they had talked to women in every hut. They worked long days, six days a week. Each night after dinner, they held a meeting to discuss what went well and what didn't and to share ideas on how to do better. Leaders periodically debriefed them, as well.

The workers were only semi-literate, but they helped distill their sales script into seven easy-to-remember messages: for instance, severe diarrhea leads to death from dehydration; the signs of dehydration include dry tongue, sunken eyes, thirst, severe weakness, and reduced urination; the way to treat dehydration is to replace salt and water lost from the body, starting with the very first loose stool; a rehydration solution provides the most effective way to do this. BRAC's scientists had to figure out how the workers could teach the recipe for the solution. Villagers had no precise measuring implements — spoons were locally made in nonstandard sizes. The leaders considered issuing special measuring spoons with the recipe on the handle. But these would be costly; most people couldn't read the recipe; and how were the spoons to be replaced when lost? Eventually, the team hit upon using finger measures: a fistful of raw sugar plus a three-finger pinch of salt mixed in half a "seer" of water — a pint measure commonly used by villagers when buying milk and oil. Tests showed that mothers could make this with sufficient accuracy.

Initially, the workers taught up to twenty mothers per day. But monitors visiting the villages a few weeks later found that the quality of teaching suffered on this larger scale, so the workers were restricted to ten households a day. Then a new salary system was devised to pay each worker according to how many of the messages the mothers retained when the monitor followed up. The quality of teaching improved substantially. The field workers soon realized that having the mothers make the solution themselves was more effective than just showing them. The workers began looking for diarrhea cases when they arrived in a village, and treating them to show how effective and safe the remedy was. The scientists also investigated various questions that came up, such as whether clean water was required. (They found that, although boiled water was preferable, contaminated water was better than nothing.)

Early signs were promising. Mothers seemed to retain the key messages. Analysis of their sugar solutions showed that three-quarters made them properly, and just four in a thousand had potentially unsafe salt levels. So BRAC and the Bangladeshi government took the program nationwide. They hired, trained, and deployed thousands of workers region by region. The effort was, inevitably, imperfect. But, by going door to door through more than seventy-five thousand villages, they showed twelve million families how to save their children.

The program was stunningly successful. Use of oral rehydration therapy skyrocketed. The knowledge became self-propagating. The program had changed the norms.

Coaxing villagers to make the solution with their own hands and explain the messages in their own words, while a trainer observed and guided them, achieved far more than any public-service ad or instructional video could have done. Over time, the changes could be sustained with television and radio, and the growth of demand led to the development of a robust market for manufactured oral rehydration salt packets. Three decades later, national surveys have found that almost ninety per cent of children with severe diarrhea were given the solution. Child deaths from diarrhea plummeted more than eighty per cent between 1980 and 2005.

COAXING VILLAGERS TO MAKE THE SOLUTION WITH THEIR OWN HANDS AND EXPLAIN THE MESSAGES IN THEIR OWN WORDS, WHILE A TRAINER OBSERVED AND GUIDED THEM, ACHIEVED FAR MORE THAN ANY PUBLIC-SERVICE AD OR INSTRUCTIONAL VIDEO COULD HAVE DONE.

As other countries adopted Bangladesh's approach, global diarrheal deaths dropped from five million a year to two million, despite a fifty-per-cent increase in the world's population during the past three decades. Nonetheless, only a third of children in the developing world receive oral rehydration therapy. Many countries tried to implement at arm's length, going "low touch," without sandals on the ground. As a recent study by the Gates Foundation and the University of Washington has documented, those countries have failed almost entirely. People talking to people is still how the world's standards change.

Surgeons finally did upgrade their antiseptic standards at the end of the nineteenth century. But, as is often the case with new ideas, the effort required deeper changes than anyone had anticipated. In their blood-slick, viscera-encrusted black coats, surgeons had seen themselves as warriors doing hemorrhagic battle with little more than their bare hands. A few pioneering Germans, however, seized on the idea of the surgeon as scientist. They traded in their black coats for pristine laboratory whites, refashioned their operating rooms to achieve the exacting sterility of a bacteriological lab, and embraced anatomic precision over speed.

The key message to teach surgeons, it turned out, was not how to stop germs but how to think like a laboratory scientist. Young physicians from America and elsewhere who went to Germany to study with its surgical luminaries became fervent converts to their thinking and their standards. They returned as apostles not only for the use of antiseptic practice (to kill germs) but also for the much more exacting demands of aseptic practice (to prevent germs), such as wearing sterile gloves, gowns, hats, and masks. Proselytizing through their own students and colleagues, they finally spread the ideas worldwide.

In childbirth, we have only begun to accept that the critical practices aren't going to spread themselves. Simple "awareness" isn't going to solve anything. We need our sales force and our seven easy-to-remember messages. And in many places around the world the concerted, person-by-person effort of changing norms is under way.

I recently asked BetterBirth workers in India whether they'd yet seen a birth attendant change what she does. Yes, they said, but they've found that it takes a while. They begin by providing a day of classroom training for birth attendants and hospital leaders in the checklist of practices to be followed. Then they visit them on site to observe as they try to apply the lessons.

Sister Seema Yadav, a twenty-four-year-old, round-faced nurse three years out of school, was one of the trainers. (Nurses are called "sisters" in India, a carryover from the British usage.) Her first assignment was to follow a thirty-year-old nurse with vastly more experience than she had. Watching the nurse take a woman through labor and delivery, she saw how little of the training had been absorbed. The room had not been disinfected; blood from a previous birth remained in a bucket. When the woman came in — moaning, contractions speeding up — the nurse didn't check her vital signs. She didn't wash her hands. She prepared no emergency supplies. After delivery, she checked the newborn's temperature with her hand, not a thermometer. Instead of warming the baby against the mother's skin, she handed the newborn to the relatives.

When Sister Seema pointed out the discrepancy between the teaching and the practice, the nurse was put out. She gave many reasons that steps were missed — there was no time, they were swamped with deliveries, there was seldom a thermometer at hand, the cleaners never did their job. Sister Seema — a cheerful, bubbly, fast talker — took her to the cleaner on duty and together they explained why cleaning the rooms between deliveries was so important. They went to the medical officer in charge and asked for a thermometer to be supplied. At her second and third visits, disinfection seemed more consistent. A thermometer had been found in a storage closet. But the nurse still hadn't changed much of her own routine.

By the fourth or fifth visit, their conversations had shifted. They shared cups of chai and began talking about why you must wash hands even if you wear gloves (because of holes in the gloves and the tendency to touch equipment without them on), and why checking blood pressure matters (because hypertension is a sign of eclampsia, which, when untreated, is a common cause of death among pregnant women). They learned a bit about each other, too. Both turned out to have one child — Sister Seema a four-year-old boy, the nurse an eight-year-old girl. The nurse lived in the capital, a two-hour bus ride away. She was divorced, living with her mother, and struggled with the commute. She'd been frustrated not to find a hospital posting in the city. She worked for days at a stretch, sleeping on a cot when she got a break. Sister Seema commiserated, and shared her own hopes for her family and her future. With time, it became clearer to the nurse that Sister Seema was there only to help and to learn from the experience herself. They even exchanged mobile-phone numbers and spoke between visits. When Sister Seema didn't have the answer to a question, she made sure she got one.

Soon, she said, the nurse began to change. After several visits, she was taking temperatures and blood pressures properly, washing her hands, giving the necessary medications — almost everything. Sister Seema saw it with her own eyes.

She'd had to move on to another pilot site after that, however. And although the project is tracking the outcomes of mothers and newborns, it will be a while before we have enough numbers to know if a difference has been made. So I got the nurse's phone number and, with a translator to help with the Hindi, I gave her a call.

It had been four months since Sister Seema's visit ended. I asked her whether she'd made any changes. Lots, she said.

"What was the most difficult one?" I asked.

"Washing hands," she said. "I have to do it so many times!"

"What was the easiest?"

"Taking the vital signs properly." Before, she said, "we did it haphazardly." Afterward, "everything became much more systematic."

She said that she had eventually begun to see the effects. Bleeding after delivery was reduced. She recognized problems earlier. She rescued a baby who wasn't breathing. She diagnosed eclampsia in a mother and treated it. You could hear her pride as she told her stories.

Many of the changes took practice for her, she said. She had to learn, for instance, how to have all the critical supplies — blood-pressure cuff, thermometer, soap, clean gloves, baby respiratory mask, medications — lined up and ready for when she needed them; how to fit the use of them into her routine; how to convince mothers and their relatives that the best thing for a child was to be bundled against the mother's skin. But, step by step, Sister Seema had helped her to do it. "She showed me how to get things done practically," the nurse said.

"Why did you listen to her?" I asked. "She had only a fraction of your experience."

In the beginning, she didn't, the nurse admitted. "The first day she came, I felt the workload on my head was increasing." From the second time, however, the nurse began feeling better about the visits. She even began looking forward to them.

"Why?" I asked.

All the nurse could think to say was "She was nice."

"She was nice?"

"She smiled a lot."

"That was it?"

"It wasn't like talking to someone who was trying to find mistakes," she said. "It was like talking to a friend."

That, I think, was the answer. Since then, the nurse had developed her own way of explaining why newborns needed to be warmed skin to skin. She said that she now tells families, "Inside the uterus, the baby is very warm. So when the baby comes out it should be kept very warm. The mother's skin does this."

I hadn't been sure if she was just telling me what I wanted to hear. But when I heard her explain how she'd put her own words to what she'd learned, I knew that the ideas had spread. "Do the families listen?" I asked.

"Sometimes they don't," she said. "Usually, they do."

· · ● · · ·

QUESTIONS FOR A SECOND READING

1. Gawande's essay proceeds as a series of case examples. He begins with a case in which he compares the spread of anesthesia and antisepsis. Why do you think he begins with these? What does his introduction of these two case examples allow him to do before he goes on to the longer cases involving childbirth and cholera?

2. After you've read the essay, go back to it for a second reading with Gawande's question from his first paragraph in mind: "Why do some innovations spread so swiftly and others so slowly?" Take notes or annotate the essay as you reread. Now that you've had an opportunity to reread "Slow Ideas," what would you say to someone who hasn't read it about how to speed ideas that don't spread quickly? What solutions does Gawande offer after his explanations of the four examples — anesthesia, antisepsis, childbirth, and

cholera — that he presents? What order of priority might he give his solutions? How would you explain such an order based on what you've learned from his cases?

3. Gawande is a surgeon, a writer, and a teacher at a teaching hospital. We can think of this essay as Gawande the research physician writing to teach us. We might claim that he expects us to learn about innovations and why some stick and others don't, but we might also claim that he expects us to come away from his essay with lessons about best practices for teaching and learning. In order for innovations to stick, people have to be taught and they have to learn. This much is true of all the case examples he presents.

Working from both his childbirth and cholera examples, what would you say he's arguing for as best teaching practices for change? What would you argue, then, are his claims about the best conditions for learning? Be sure to work closely from both of these case examples, referring to them when it's useful to your own arguments.

4. Step back from Gawande's essay after you've reread it. Think of it as purposeful in its arguments, examples, and structure. For this assignment, focus on the structure of his essay and the ways that it could be said to contribute to his arguments. To do this, circle or mark what you see as the major chunks or movements. There are breaks in the text, so you might begin with those, but you shouldn't limit yourself to them. Give the major chunks or movements names or labels so that you can refer to them easily. What are they? How would you describe the structure or organization of Gawande's essay? How would you say that the structure contributes to his arguments about innovations that stick and those that don't?

— • • ● • • —

ASSIGNMENTS FOR WRITING

1. As we said earlier, Gawande's essay can be thought of as a teaching tool. Gawande has things for us to learn about innovation and change in medical practices. He also has things for us to learn about the teaching and learning that made innovation and successful change possible in life-and-death situations. This assignment invites you to write about Gawande's arguments for best practices in teaching for innovation and change and to situate those practices in the conditions for learning that you might call necessary or at least helpful to the success of the teaching.

When you reread "Slow Ideas," mark the moments when Gawande seems to be drawing lessons about best teaching practices from his case examples. It might be that the teaching practices are specific to the cases, or it might be that he's making larger claims about what's effective for teaching others. You'll have to decide how to situate his claims for best teaching practices, but you should at the least situate them in the conditions that seem to be necessary for learning to occur. What is it, in other words, about learners and their situations that has to be present for the best teaching practices to take hold?

Write an essay in which you make a case for what you think Gawande is saying about the best teaching practices for supporting others to innovate and change. Work closely from Gawande's case examples and situate your thinking in the conditions for learning that seem to be necessary for the best practices to work, to take hold.

2. This assignment is an invitation to take up Gawande's project by doing research of your own on innovations that have spread quickly and others that have not. You'll need to identify two or three innovations that interest you and that have spread fairly quickly. You'll also need to identify two or three innovations that haven't spread quickly. It can certainly be the case that the ones that didn't spread quickly took hold after a while. You'll have to decide on the cases that you present to test Gawande's ideas about why some innovations spread quickly and others don't.

Once you've identified cases of innovations that spread quickly and cases of those that didn't, you'll need to dig into them through research. You'll want to imagine that your readers don't know what you do about the case examples, so you'll be writing partly as a researcher presenting the history of the innovations and partly as an essayist presenting complex innovations in a handful of paragraphs that describe and summarize them for readers. Before you present your case examples in writing, you'll want to study the ways Gawande presents his examples so you can follow his lead in terms of writing strategies.

Write an essay in which you present at least one example each of fast- and slow-spreading innovations. What are the reasons that your quickly spreading example(s) spread so swiftly? What are the reasons that your slow-spreading innovation(s) didn't take hold? What kinds of teaching and learning were involved in the spreading of the innovations? Do the teaching and learning involved fit Gawande's thinking about best practices for teaching others to innovate and change?

3. Imagine that you're writing this essay for others who haven't read "Slow Ideas." Take up Gawande's question, "Why do some innovations spread so swiftly and others so slowly?" and write an essay in which you answer this question. Work closely from all of Gawande's case examples. You'll want to give your readers substantial descriptions of each of his case examples in your own words, and you'll also want to comment on each, as he does, to point out the teaching and the procedures that enabled others to adopt the innovations and to change. Finally, you'll want to be sure to account for what gets in the way of innovations' spreading by weaving those obstacles into your retellings of his cases as he does.

4. What gets in the way of innovations' spreading quickly? Gawande introduces us to some of his ideas about this early on in his essay when he's writing about the spread of anesthesia and antisepsis, but he also leaves work for us to do as readers on this question when he writes about childbirth and cholera. Write an essay in which you work from Gawande's case examples on childbirth and cholera to test his ideas in the beginning pages of his essay on

the things that get in the way of innovations and change. What do you see in these two cases that he thinks of as patterns of "important but stalled ideas"? What else do you learn from these cases that doesn't seem to fit these patterns? or that seems unique to the specific case examples?

— • • ● • • —

MAKING CONNECTIONS

1. Like Atul Gawande, Michael Pollan in "Nutritionism Defined" (p. 490) and Michael Specter in "The Gene Hackers" (p. 602) write about science and public policy. Pollan and Specter are journalists; Gawande is a physician; all three are writers.

    Write an essay that looks at one of these two selections, either "Nutritionism Defined" or "The Gene Hackers," from the perspective of "Slow Ideas." Where and how might they be said to speak to each other? How do they each understand the key issues in science as they relate to public policy? How do they represent the role of the essay as a form of engagement with science and with public policy? If you had to choose one of the two as exemplary — as an example of what we need more of if, as a nation, we are going to be able to make informed decisions about scientific research — which would you choose? and why?

    One possible shape for your essay is to present your take, your point of view, on each reading, with summary and block quotation, and then to turn, in a third section, to the larger questions about journalism, science, and public policy.

2. In "Arts of the Contact Zone" (p. 512), Mary Louise Pratt defines contact zones as "social spaces where cultures meet, clash, and grapple with each other, often in contexts of highly asymmetrical relations of power." Atul Gawande, in "Slow Ideas," chronicles the ways that lifesaving innovations and changes for childbirth in India and the treatment of cholera in Bangladesh take hold. At one point in his essay, he writes that the physicians involved in these projects want to change systems in cultures so that particular practices and treatments become daily routines or the norm. "To create new norms," he writes, "you have to understand people's existing norms and barriers to change" (p. 368).

    Pratt might argue that those involved in the childbirth and cholera projects interacted in a context of "highly asymmetrical relations of power," where the health-care providers in India and Bangladesh hold the dominant position, trying to get medical treatments to take hold in systems in cultures where neither incentives nor penalties work.

    Write an essay in which you consider how Pratt's concept of the contact zone might be useful in helping us understand the ways that change came about in childbirth practices in India and the treatment of cholera in Bangladesh. What might be the "autoethnographic texts" produced during the evolutions of these changes, and how might you say that the caregivers, including Gawande, learned to read them? And, finally, what conclusions might you draw about Gawande's understanding of systemic or cultural change as the development of social and intellectual understanding in a contact zone?

SUSAN
Griffin

Susan Griffin (b. 1943) is a well-known and respected feminist writer, poet, essayist, lecturer, teacher, playwright, and filmmaker. She has published more than twenty books, including an Emmy Award–winning play, *Voices*, with a preface by Adrienne Rich (1975); three books of poetry, *Like the Iris of an Eye* (1976), *Unremembered Country* (1987), and *Bending Home: Selected and New Poems* (1998); and four books of nonfiction that have become key feminist texts, *Women and Nature: The Roaring inside Her* (1978), *Rape: The Power of Consciousness* (1979), *Pornography and Silence: Culture's Revenge against Nature* (1981), and *A Chorus of Stones: The Private Life of War* (1992). Her most recent books are *What Her Body Thought: A Journey into the Shadows* (1999), on her battle with illness; *The Book of the Courtesans: A Catalog of Their Virtues* (2001), which includes biographies of courtesans throughout history; *Wrestling with the Angel of Democracy: On Being an American Citizen* (2008), an examination of democratic ideals; and, with Karin Lofthus Carrington, *Transforming Terror: Remembering the Soul of the World* (2011), a meditation on the ways in which human interdependence and compassion can overcome violence.

We've included here an abridged version of "Our Secret," which is taken from a chapter from Susan Griffin's moving and powerful book *A Chorus of Stones*, winner of the Bay Area Book Reviewers Association Award and a finalist for the Pulitzer Prize in nonfiction. The book explores the connections between present and past, public life and private life, an individual life and the lives of others. Griffin writes, for example, "I do not see my life as separate from history. In my mind my family secrets mingle with the secrets of statesmen and bombers." In one section of the book she writes of her mother's alcoholism and her father's response to it. In another she writes of her paternal grandmother, who was banished from the family for reasons never spoken. Next to these she thinks about Heinrich Himmler, head of the Nazi secret police, or Hugh Trenchard of the British Royal Air Force, who introduced the saturation bombing of cities and civilians to modern warfare, or Wernher von Braun and the development of rockets and rocketry. "As I held these [figures and scenes] in my mind," she writes, "a certain energy was generated between them. There were two subjects but one theme: denying and bearing witness."

A Chorus of Stones combines the skills of a careful researcher working with the documentary records of war, the imaginative powers of a novelist entering the lives and experiences of those long dead, and a poet's attention to language. It is a remarkable piece of writing, producing in its form and style the very experience of surprise and connectedness that Griffin presents as the product of her research. "It's not a historian's history," she once told an interviewer. "What's in it is true, but I think of it as a book that verges on myth and legend, because those are the ways we find the deepest meanings and significance of events."

Griffin's history is not a historian's history; her sociology is not a sociologist's; her psychology is not written in conventional forms or registers. She is actively engaged in the key research projects of our time, providing new knowledge and new ways of thinking and seeing, but she works outside the usual forms and boundaries of the academic disciplines. There are other ways of thinking about this, she seems to say. There are other ways to do this work. Her book on rape, for example, ends with a collage of women's voices, excerpts from public documents, and bits and pieces from the academy.

"Our Secret" has its own peculiar structure and features — the sections in italics, for example. As a piece of writing, it proceeds with a design that is not concerned to move quickly or efficiently from introduction to conclusion. It is, rather, a kind of collage or collection of stories, sketches, anecdotes, fragments. While the sections in the essay are presented as fragments, the essay is not, however, deeply confusing or disorienting. The pleasure of the text, in fact, is moving from here to there, feeling a thread of connection at one point, being surprised by a new direction at another. The writing is careful, thoughtful, controlled, even if this is not the kind of essay that announces its thesis and then collects examples for support. It takes a different attitude toward examples — and toward the kind of thinking one might bring to bear in gathering them and thinking them through. As Griffin says, "The telling and hearing of a story is not a simple act." It is not simple and, as her writing teaches us, it is not straightforward. As you read this essay, think of it as a lesson in reading, writing, and thinking. Think of it as a lesson in working differently. And you might ask why it is that this kind of writing is seldom taught in school.

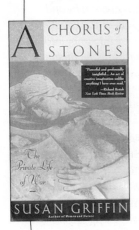

A CHORUS of STONES

"Powerful and profoundly insightful.... An act of creative imagination unlike anything I have ever read."
—Richard Rorlek
New York Times Book Review

The Private Life of War

SUSAN GRIFFIN
Author of Woman and Nature

Our Secret

The nucleus of the cell derives its name from the Latin nux, *meaning nut. Like the stone in a cherry, it is found in the center of the cell, and like this stone, keeps its precious kernel in a shell.*

She is across the room from me. I am in a chair facing her. We sit together in the late darkness of a summer night. As she speaks the space between us grows larger. She has entered her past. She is speaking of her childhood. Her father. The war. Did I know her father fought in the Battle of the Bulge? What was it for him, this great and terrible battle? She cannot say. He never spoke of it at home. They knew so little, her mother, her brothers, herself. Outside, the sea has disappeared. One finds the water now only by the city lights that cease to shine at its edges. California. She moved here with her family when her father became the commander of a military base. There were nuclear missiles standing just blocks from where she lived. But her father never spoke about them. Only after many years away from home did she learn what these weapons were.

The first guided missile is developed in Germany, during World War II. It is known as the Vergeltungswaffe, *or the Vengeance weapon. Later, it will be called the V-1 rocket.*

She is speaking of another life, another way of living. I give her the name Laura here. She speaks of the time after the war, when the cold war was just beginning. The way we are talking now, Laura tells me, was not possible in her family. I nod in recognition. Certain questions were never answered. She learned what not to ask. She begins to tell me a story. Once when she was six years old she went out with her father on a long trip. It was not even a year since the war ended. They were living in Germany.

 They drove for miles and miles. Finally they turned into a small road at the edge of a village and drove through a wide gate in a high wall. The survivors were all gone. But there were other signs of this event beyond and yet still within her comprehension. Shoes in great piles. Bones. Women's hair, clothes, stains, a terrible odor. She began to cry a child's frightened tears and then to scream. She had no words for what she saw. Her father admonished her to be still. Only years later, and in a classroom, did she find out the name of this place and what had happened here.

The shell surrounding the nucleus is not hard and rigid; it is a porous membrane. These pores allow only some substances to pass through them, mediating the movement of materials in and out of the nucleus.

Often I have looked back into my past with a new insight only to find that some old, hardly recollected feeling fits into a larger pattern of meaning. Time can be measured in many ways. We see time as moving forward and hope that by our efforts this motion is toward improvement. When the atomic bomb exploded, many who survived the blast say time stopped with the flash of light and was held suspended until the ash began to descend. Now, in my mind, I can feel myself moving backward in time. I am as if on a train. And the train pushes into history. This history seems to exist somewhere, waiting, a foreign country behind a border and, perhaps, also inside me. From the windows of my train, I can see what those outside do not see. They do not see each other, or the whole landscape through which the track is laid. This is a straight track, but still there are bends to fit the shape of the earth. There are even circles. And returns.

The missile is guided by a programmed mechanism. There is no electronic device that can be jammed. Once it is fired it cannot stop.

It is 1945 and a film is released in Germany. This film has been made for other nations to see. On the screen a train pulls into a station. The train is full of children. A man in a uniform greets the children warmly as they step off the train. Then the camera cuts to boys and girls who are swimming. The boys and girls race to see who can reach the other side of the pool first. Then a woman goes to a post office. A man goes to a bank. Men and women sit drinking coffee at a cafe. The film is called *The Führer Presents the Jews with a City*. It has been made at Terezin concentration camp.

Through the pores of the nuclear membrane a steady stream of ribonucleic acid, RNA, the basic material from which the cell is made, flows out.

It is wartime and a woman is writing a letter. *Everyone is on the brink of starvation*, she says. In the right-hand corner of the page she has written *Nordhausen, Germany 1944*. She is writing to Hans. *Do you remember*, she asks, the day this war was declared? The beauty of the place. The beauty of the sea. *And I bathed in it that day, for the last time.*

In the same year, someone else is also writing a letter. In the right-hand corner he has put his name followed by a title. *Heinrich Himmler. Reichsführer, SS. Make no mention of the special treatment of the Jews*, he says, use only the words Transportation of the Jews toward the Russian East.

A few months later this man will deliver a speech to a secret meeting of leaders in the district of Posen. *Now you know all about it, and you will keep quiet*, he will tell them. Now we share a secret and *we should take our secret to our graves.*

The missile flies from three to four thousand feet above the earth and this makes it difficult to attack from the ground.

The woman who writes of starvation is a painter in her seventy-seventh year. She has lost one grandchild to this war. And a son to the war before. Both boys were named Peter. Among the drawings she makes which have already become famous: a terrified mother grasps a child, *Death Seizes Children*; an old man curls over the bent body of an old woman, *Parents*; a thin face emerges white from charcoal, *Beggars*.

A small but critical part of the RNA flowing out of the pores holds most of the knowledge issued by the nucleus. These threads of RNA act as messengers.

Encountering such images, one is grateful to be spared. But is one ever really free of the fate of others? I was born in 1943, in the midst of this war. And I sense now that my life is still bound up with the lives of those who lived and died in this time. Even with Heinrich Himmler. All the details of his existence, his birth, childhood, adult years, death, still resonate here on earth.

The V-1 rocket is a winged plane powered by a duct motor with a pulsating flow of fuel.

It is April 1943, Heinrich Himmler, Reichsführer SS, has gained control of the production of rockets for the Third Reich. The SS Totenkampf stand guard with machine guns trained at the entrance to a long tunnel, two miles deep, fourteen yards wide and ten yards high, sequestered in the Harz Mountains near Nordhausen. Once an old mining shaft, this tunnel serves now as a secret factory for the manufacture of V-1 and V-2 missiles. The guards aim their machine guns at the factory workers who are inmates of concentration camp Dora.

> I SENSE NOW THAT MY LIFE IS STILL BOUND UP WITH THE LIVES OF THOSE WHO LIVED AND DIED IN THIS TIME. EVEN WITH HEINRICH HIMMLER.

Most of the RNA flowing out of the cell is destined for the construction of a substance needed to compensate for the continual wearing away of the cell.

It is 1925. Heinrich Himmler, who is now twenty-five years old, has been hired as a secretary by the chief of the Nazi Party in Landshut. He sits behind a small desk in a room overcrowded with party records, correspondence, and newspaper files. On the wall facing him he can see a portrait of Adolf Hitler. He hopes one day to meet the Führer. In anticipation of that day, while he believes no one watches, he practices speaking to this portrait.

It is 1922. Heinrich visits friends who have a three-year-old child. Before going to bed this child is allowed to run about naked. And this disturbs Heinrich. He writes in his diary, *One should teach a child a sense of shame.*

It is the summer of 1910. Heinrich begins his first diary. He is ten years old. He has just completed elementary school. His father tells him his childhood is over now. In the fall he will enter Wilhelms Gymnasium. There the grades he earns will determine his prospects for the future. From now on he must learn to take himself seriously.

· · ● ● · · ·

Eight out of ten of the guided missiles will land within eight miles of their targets.

His father Gebhard is a schoolmaster. He knows the requirements. He provides the boy with pen and ink. Gebhard was once a tutor for Prince Heinrich of Wittelsbach. He has named his son Heinrich after this prince. He is grateful that the prince consented to be Heinrich's godparent. Heinrich is to write in his diary every day. Gebhard writes the first entry in his son's diary, to show the boy how it is to be done.

July 13, Departed at 11:50 and arrive safely on the bus in L. We have a very pretty house. In the afternoon we drink coffee at the coffee house.

I open the cover of the journal I began to keep just as I started my work on this book. I want to see what is on the first page. *It is here I begin a new life*, I wrote. Suffering many losses at once, I was alone and lonely. Yet suddenly I felt a new responsibility for myself. *The very act of keeping a journal*, I sensed, would help me into this life that would now be my own.

Inside the nucleus is the nucleolus where the synthesis of RNA takes place. Each nucleolus is filled with a small jungle of fern-like structures all of whose fronds and stalks move and rotate in perfect synchrony.

It is 1910. The twenty-second of July. Gebhard adds the words *first swim* to his son's brief entry, *thirteenth wedding anniversary of my dear parents.* 1911. Over several entries Heinrich lists each of thirty-seven times he takes a swim, in chronological order. *11:37 A.M. Departed for Lindau.* He does not write of his feelings. *August 8, Walk in the park.* Or dreams. *August 10, Bad weather.*

In the last few years I have been searching, though for what precisely I cannot say. Something still hidden which lies in the direction of Heinrich Himmler's life. I have been to Berlin and Munich on this search, and I have walked over the gravel at Dachau. Now as I sit here I read once again the fragments from Heinrich's boyhood diary that exist in English. I have begun to think of these words as ciphers. Repeat them to myself, hoping to find a door into the mind of this man, even as his character first forms so that I might learn how it is he becomes himself.

The task is not easy. The earliest entries in this diary betray so little. Like the words of a schoolboy commanded to write what the teacher

requires of him, they are wooden and stiff. The stamp of his father's character is so heavy on this language that I catch not even a breath of a self
here. It is easy to see how this would be true. One simply has to imagine
Gebhard standing behind Heinrich and tapping his foot.

His father must have loomed large to him. Did Gebhard lay his hand
on Heinrich's shoulder? The weight of that hand would not be comforting.
It would be a warning. A reminder. Heinrich must straighten up now and
be still. Yet perhaps he turns his head. Maybe there is a sound outside. A
bird. Or his brother Gebhard's voice. But from the dark form behind him
he hears a name pronounced. This is his name, *Heinrich*. The sound rolls
sharply off his father's tongue. He turns his head back. He does not know
what to write. He wants to turn to this form and beseech him, but this man
who is his father is more silent than stone. And now when Heinrich can
feel impatience all around him, he wants to ask, *What should I write?* The
edge of his father's voice has gotten sharper. *Why can't you remember?* Just
write what happened yesterday. And make sure you get the date right.
Don't you remember? We took a walk in the park together and we ran into
the duchess. Be certain you spell her name correctly. And look here, you
must get the title right. That is extremely important. Cross it out. Do it
again. *The title.*

The boy is relieved. His mind has not been working. His thoughts
were like paralyzed limbs, immobile. Now he is in motion again. He writes
the sentences as they are dictated to him. *The park.* He crosses out the
name. He writes it again. Spelling it right. *The duchess.* And his father
makes one more correction. The boy has not put down the correct time for
their walk in the park.

And who is the man standing behind? In a photograph I have before
me of the aging Professor and Frau Himmler, as they pose before a wall
carefully composed with paintings and family portraits, Frau Himmler
adorned with a demure lace collar, both she and the professor smiling
kindly from behind steel-rimmed glasses, the professor somewhat rounded
with age, in a dark three-piece suit and polka-dot tie, looks so ordinary.

*The missile carries a warhead weighing 1,870 pounds. It has three different
fuses to insure detonation.*

Ordinary. What an astonishing array of images hide behind this word. The
ordinary is of course never ordinary. I think of it now as a kind of mask,
not an animated mask that expresses the essence of an inner truth, but a
mask that falls like dead weight over the human face, making flesh
a stationary object. One has difficulty penetrating the heavy mask that
Gebhard and his family wore, difficulty piercing through to the creatures
behind.

It must not have been an easy task to create this mask. One detects
the dimensions of the struggle in the advice of German child-rearing experts from this and the last century. *Crush the will*, they write. *Establish
dominance. Permit no disobedience. Suppress everything in the child.*

I have seen illustrations from the books of one of these experts, perhaps the most famous of these pedagogues, Dr. Daniel Gottlieb Moritz Schreber. At first glance these pictures recall images of torture. But they are instead pictures of children whose posture or behavior is being corrected. A brace up the spine, a belt tied to a waist and the hair at the back of the neck so the child will be discouraged from slumping, a metal plate at the edge of a desk keeping the child from curling over her work, a child tied to a bed to prevent poor sleeping posture or masturbation. And there are other methods recommended in the text. An enema to be given before bedtime. The child immersed in ice-cold water up to the hips, before sleep.

The nightmare images of the German child-rearing practices that one discovers in this book call to mind the catastrophic events of recent German history. I first encountered this pedagogy in the writing of Alice Miller. At one time a psychoanalyst, she was haunted by the question, *What could make a person conceive the plan of gassing millions of human beings to death?* In her work, she traces the origins of this violence to childhood.

Of course there cannot be one answer to such a monumental riddle, nor does any event in history have a single cause. Rather a field exists, like a field of gravity that is created by the movements of many bodies. Each life is influenced and it in turn becomes an influence. Whatever is a cause is also an effect. Childhood experience is just one element in the determining field.

As a man who made history, Heinrich Himmler shaped many childhoods, including, in the most subtle of ways, my own. And an earlier history, a history of governments, of wars, of social customs, an idea of gender, the history of a religion leading to the idea of original sin, shaped Heinrich Himmler's childhood as certainly as any philosophy of child raising. One can take for instance any formative condition of his private life, the fact that he was a frail child, for example, favored by his mother, who could not meet masculine standards, and show that this circumstance derived its real meaning from a larger social system that gave inordinate significance to masculinity.

Yet to enter history through childhood experience shifts one's perspective not away from history but instead to an earlier time just before history has finally shaped us. Is there a child who existed before the conventional history that we tell of ourselves, one who, though invisible to us, still shapes events, even through this absence? How does our sense of history change when we consider childhood, and perhaps more important, why is it that until now we have chosen to ignore this point of origination, the birthplace and womb of ourselves, in our consideration of public events?

In the silence that reverberates around this question, an image is born in my mind. I can see a child's body, small, curled into itself, knees bent toward the chest, head bending softly into pillows and blankets, in a posture thought unhealthy by Dr. Schreber, hand raised to the face, delicate mouth making a circle around the thumb. There is comfort as well as sadness in this image. It is a kind of a self-portrait, drawn both from memory and from a feeling that is still inside me. As I dwell for a moment with this image I can imagine Heinrich in this posture, silent, curled, fetal, giving comfort to himself.

But now, alongside this earlier image, another is born. It is as if these two images were twins, always traveling in the world of thought together. One does not come to mind without the other. In this second portrait, which is also made of feeling and memory, a child's hands are tied into mittens. And by a string extending from one of the mittens, her hand is tied to the bars of her crib. She is not supposed to be putting her finger in her mouth. And she is crying out in rage while she yanks her hand violently trying to free herself of her bonds.

To most of existence there is an inner and an outer world. Skin, bark, surface of the ocean open to reveal other realities. What is inside shapes and sustains what appears. So it is too with human consciousness. And yet the mind rarely has a simple connection to the inner life. At a certain age we begin to define ourselves, to choose an image of who we are. I am this and not that, we say, attempting thus to erase whatever is within us that does not fit our idea of who we should be. In time we forget our earliest selves and replace that memory with the image we have constructed at the bidding of others.

One can see this process occur in the language of Heinrich's diaries. If in the earliest entries, except for the wooden style of a boy who obeys authority, Heinrich's character is hardly apparent, over time this stilted style becomes his own. As one reads on, one no longer thinks of a boy who is forced to the task, but of a prudish and rigid young man.

In Heinrich's boyhood diaries no one has been able to find any record of rage or of events that inspire such rage. Yet one cannot assume from this evidence that such did not exist. His father would have permitted neither anger nor even the memory of it to enter these pages. That there must be no visible trace of resentment toward the parent was the pedagogy of the age. Dr. Schreber believed that children should learn to be grateful. The pain and humiliation children endure are meant to benefit them. The parent is only trying to save the child's soul.

Now, for different reasons, I too find myself on the track of a child's soul. The dimensions of Heinrich Himmler's life have put me on this track. I am trying to grasp the inner state of his being. For a time the soul ceased to exist in the modern mind. One thought of a human being as a kind of machine, or as a cog in the greater mechanism of society, operating within another machine, the earth, which itself operates within the greater mechanical design of the universe.

When I was in Berlin, I spoke to a rabbi who had, it seemed to me, lost his faith. When I asked him if he still believed in God, he simply shook his head and widened his eyes as if to say, *How is this possible?* He had been telling me about his congregation: older people, many of Polish origin, survivors of the holocaust who were not able to leave Germany after the war because they were too ill to travel. He was poised in this painful place by choice. He had come to lead this congregation only temporarily but, once feeling the condition of his people, decided to stay. Still, despite his answer, and as much as the holocaust made a terrible argument for the death of the spirit, talking in that small study with this man, I could feel from him the light of something surviving.

The religious tradition that shaped Heinrich's childhood argues that the soul is not part of flesh but is instead a prisoner of the body. But suppose the soul is meant to live in and through the body and to know itself in the heart of earthly existence?

Then the soul is an integral part of the child's whole being, and its growth is thus part of the child's growth. It is, for example, like a seed planted underground in the soil, naturally moving toward the light. And it comes into its fullest manifestation thus only when seen, especially when self meeting self returns a gaze.

What then occurs if the soul in its small beginnings is forced to take on a secret life? A boy learns, for instance, to hide his thoughts from his father simply by failing to record them in his journals. He harbors his secrets in fear and guilt, confessing them to no one until in time the voice of his father chastising him becomes his own. A small war is waged in his mind. Daily implosions take place under his skin, by which in increments something in him seems to disappear. Gradually his father's voice subsumes the vitality of all his desires and even his rage, so that now what he wants most passionately is his own obedience, and his rage is aimed at his own failures. As over time his secrets fade from memory, he ceases to tell them, even to himself, so that finally a day arrives when he believes the image he has made of himself in his diaries is true.

The child, Dr. Schreber advised, *should be permeated by the impossibility of locking something in his heart.* The doctor who gave this advice had a son who was hospitalized for disabling schizophrenia. Another of his children committed suicide. But this was not taken as a warning against his approach. His methods of educating children were so much a part of the canon of everyday life in Germany that they were introduced into the state school system.

That this philosophy was taught in school gives me an interior view of the catastrophe to follow. It adds a certain dimension to my image of these events to know that a nation of citizens learned that no part of themselves could be safe from the scrutiny of authority, nothing locked in the heart, and at the same time to discover that the head of the secret police of this nation was the son of a schoolmaster. It was this man, after all, Heinrich Himmler, Reichsführer SS, who was later to say, speaking of the mass arrests of Jews, *Protective custody is an act of care.*

The polite manner of young Heinrich's diaries reminds me of life in my grandmother's home. Not the grandmother I lost and later found, but the one who, for many years, raised me. She was my mother's mother. The family would assemble in the living room together, sitting with a certain reserve, afraid to soil the surfaces. What was it that by accident might have been made visible?

All our family photographs were posed. We stood together in groups of three or four and squinted into the sun. My grandmother directed us to smile. I have carried one of these photographs with me for years without acknowledging to myself that in it my mother has the look she always had when she drank too much. In another photograph, taken near the time of my parents' divorce, I can see that my father is almost crying, though I could not see this earlier. I must have felt obliged to see only what my grandmother wanted us to see. Tranquil, domestic scenes.

In the matrix of the mitochondria all the processes of transformation join together in a central vortex.

We were not comfortable with ourselves as a family. There was a great shared suffering and yet we never wept together, except for my mother, who would alternately weep and then rage when she was drunk. Together, under my grandmother's tutelage, we kept up appearances. Her effort was ceaseless.

When at the age of six I went to live with her, my grandmother worked to reshape me. I learned what she thought was correct grammar. The manners she had studied in books of etiquette were passed on to me, not by casual example but through anxious memorization and drill. Napkin to be lifted by the corner and swept onto the lap. Hand to be clasped firmly but not too firmly.

We were not to the manner born. On one side my great-grandfather was a farmer, and on the other a butcher newly emigrated from Ireland, who still spoke with a brogue. Both great-grandfathers drank too much, the one in public houses, the other more quietly at home. The great-grandfather who farmed was my grandmother's father. He was not wealthy but he aspired to gentility. My grandmother inherited both his aspiration and his failure.

We considered ourselves finer than the neighbors to our left with their chaotic household. But when certain visitors came, we were as if driven by an inward, secret panic that who we really were might be discovered. Inadvertently, by some careless gesture, we might reveal to these visitors who were our betters that we did not belong with them, that we were not real. Though of course we never spoke of this, to anyone, not even ourselves.

Gebhard Himmler's family was newly risen from poverty. Just as in my family, the Himmlers' gentility was a thinly laid surface, maintained no doubt only with great effort. Gebhard's father had come from a family of peasants and small artisans. Such a living etched from the soil, and by one's hands, is tenuous and hard. As is frequently the case with young men born to poverty, Johann became a soldier. And, like many young soldiers, he got himself into trouble more than once for brawling and general mischief. On one occasion he was reproved for what was called *immoral behavior with a low woman.* But nothing of this history survived in his son's version of him. By the time Gebhard was born, Johann was fifty-six years old and had reformed his ways. Having joined the royal police force of Bavaria, over the years he rose to the rank of sergeant. He was a respectable man, with a respectable position.

Perhaps Gebhard never learned of his father's less than respectable past. He was only three years old when Johann died. If he had the slightest notion, he did not breathe a word to his own children. Johann became the icon of the Himmler family, the heroic soldier who single-handedly brought his family from the obscurity of poverty into the warm light of the favored. Yet obscure histories have a way of casting a shadow over the present. Those who are born to propriety have a sense of entitlement, and this affords them some ease as they execute the correct mannerisms of their class. More recent members of the elect are less certain of themselves; around the edges of newly minted refinement one discerns a certain fearfulness, expressed perhaps as uncertainty, or as its opposite, rigidity.

One can sense that rigidity in Gebhard's face as a younger man. In a photograph of the Himmler family, Gebhard, who towers in the background, seems severe. He has the face of one who looks for mistakes. He is vigilant.

HE HAS THE FACE OF ONE WHO LOOKS FOR MISTAKES. HE IS VIGILANT.

Heinrich's mother looks very small next to him, almost as if she is cowering. She has that look I have seen many times on my father's face, which one can only describe as ameliorating. Heinrich is very small. He stands closest to the camera, shimmering in a white dress. His face is pretty, even delicate.

I am looking now at the etching called *Poverty*, made in 1897. Near the center, calling my attention, a woman holds her head in her hands. She stares through her hands into the face of a sleeping infant. Though the infant and the sheet and pillow around are filled with light, one recognizes that the child is dying. In a darker corner, two worried figures huddle, a father and another child. Room, mother, father, child exist in lines, a multitude of lines, and each line is filled with a rare intelligence.

Just as the physicist's scrutiny changes the object of perception, so does art transmute experience. One cannot look upon what Käthe Kollwitz has drawn without feeling. The lines around the child are bleak with unreason. Never have I seen so clearly that what we call poverty is simply a raw exposure to the terror and fragility of life. But there is more in this image. There is meaning in the frame. One can feel the artist's eyes. Her gaze is in one place soft, in another intense. Like the light around the infant, her attention interrupts the shadow that falls across the room.

The artist's choice of subject and the way she saw it were both radical departures, not only from certain acceptable assumptions in the world of art, but also from established social ideas because the poor were thought of as less than human. The death of a child to a poor parent was supposed to be a less painful event. In her depiction, the artist told a different story.

Heinrich is entering a new school now, and so his father makes a list of all his future classmates. Beside the name of each child he writes the child's father's name, what this father does for a living, and his social position. Heinrich must be careful, Gebhard tells him, to choose whom he befriends. In his diaries the boy seldom mentions his friends by name. Instead he writes that he played, for instance, with the landlord's child.

There is so much for Heinrich to learn. Gebhard must teach him the right way to bow. The proper forms of greeting. The history of his family; the history of his nation. Its heroes. His grandfather's illustrious military past. There is an order in the world and Heinrich has a place in this order which he must be trained to fill. His life is strictly scheduled. At this hour a walk in the woods so that he can appreciate nature. After that a game of chess to develop his mind. And after that piano, so that he will be cultured.

If a part of himself has vanished, that part of the self that feels and wants, and from which hence a coherent life might be shaped, Heinrich is not at sea yet. He has no time to drift or feel lost. Each moment has been spoken for, every move prescribed. He has only to carry out his father's plans for him.

But everything in his life is not as it should be. He is not popular among his classmates. Should it surprise us to learn that he has a penchant for listening to the secrets of his companions, and that afterward he repeats these secrets to his father, the schoolmaster? There is perhaps a secret he would like to learn and one he would like to tell, but this has long since been forgotten. Whatever he learns now he must tell his father. He must not keep anything from him. He must keep his father's good will at all costs. For, without his father, he does not exist.

And there is another reason Heinrich is not accepted by his classmates. He is frail. As an infant, stricken by influenza, he came close to perishing and his body still retains the mark of that illness. He is not strong. He is not good at the games the other boys play. At school he tries over and over to raise himself on the crossbars, unsuccessfully. He covets the popularity of his stronger, more masculine brother, Gebhard. But he cannot keep up with his brother. One day, when they go out for a simple bicycle ride together, Heinrich falls into the mud and returns with his clothes torn.

It is 1914. A war begins. There are parades. Young men marching in uniform. Tearful ceremonies at the railway station. Songs. Decorations. Heinrich is enthusiastic. The war has given him a sense of purpose in life. Like other boys, he plays at soldiering. He follows the war closely, writing in his diary of the progress of armies, *This time with 40 Army Corps and Russia and France against Germany*. The entries he makes do not seem so listless now; they have a new vigor. As the war continues, a new ambition gradually takes the shape of determination. Is this the way he will finally prove himself? Heinrich wants to be a soldier. And above all he wants a uniform.

It is 1915. In her journal Käthe Kollwitz records a disturbing sight. The night before at the opera she found herself sitting next to a young soldier. He was blinded. He sat *without stirring, his hands on his knees, his head erect.* She could not stop looking at him, and the memory of him, she writes now, *cuts her to the quick.*

It is 1916. As Heinrich comes of age he implores his father to help him find a regiment. He has many heated opinions about the war. But his thoughts are like the thoughts and feelings of many adolescents; what he expresses has no steady line of reason. His opinions are filled with contradictions, and he lacks that awareness of self which can turn ambivalence into an inner dialogue. Yet, beneath this amorphous bravado, there is a pattern. As if he were trying on different attitudes, Heinrich swings from harshness to compassion. In one place he writes, *The Russian prisoners multiply like vermin.* (Should I write here that this is a word he will one day use for Jews?) But later he is sympathetic to the same prisoners because they are so far away from home. Writing once of *the silly old women and petty bourgeois ... who so dislike war,* in another entry, he remembers the young men he has seen depart on trains and he asks, *How many are alive today?*

Is the direction of any life inevitable? Or are there crossroads, points at which the direction might be changed? I am looking again at the Himmler family. Heinrich's infant face resembles the face of his mother. His face is soft. And his mother? In the photograph she is a fading presence. She occupied the same position as did most women in German families, secondary and obedient to the undisputed power of her husband. She has a slight smile which for some reason reminds me of the smile of a child I saw in a photograph from an album made by the SS. This child's image was captured as she stood on the platform at Auschwitz. In the photograph she emanates a certain frailty. Her smile is a very feminine smile. Asking, or perhaps pleading, *Don't hurt me.*

Is it possible that Heinrich, looking into that child's face, might have seen himself there? What is it in a life that makes one able to see oneself in others? Such affinities do not stop with obvious resemblance. There is a sense in which we all enter the lives of others.

It is 1917, and a boy who will be named Heinz is born to Catholic parents living in Vienna. Heinz's father bears a certain resemblance to Heinrich's father. He is a civil servant and, also like Gebhard, he is pedantic and correct in all he does. Heinrich will never meet this boy. And yet their paths will cross.

Early in the same year as Heinz's birth, Heinrich's father has finally succeeded in getting him into a regiment. As the war continues for one more year, Heinrich comes close to achieving his dream. He will be a soldier. He is sent to officer's training. Yet he is not entirely happy. *The food is bad*, he writes to his mother, *and there is not enough of it. It is cold. There are bedbugs. The room is barren.* Can she send him food? A blanket? Why doesn't she write him more often? Has she forgotten him? They are calling up troops. Suppose he should be called to the front and die?

But something turns in him. Does he sit on the edge of a neat, narrow military bunk bed as he writes in his diary that he does not want to be like a boy who whines to his mother? Now, he writes a different letter: *I am once more a soldier body and soul.* He loves his uniform; the oath he has learned to write; the first inspection he passes. He signs his letters now, *Miles Heinrich.* Soldier Heinrich.

I am looking at another photograph. It is of two boys. They are both in military uniform. Gebhard, Heinrich's older brother, is thicker and taller. Next to him Heinrich is still diminutive. But his face has become harder, and his smile, though faint like his mother's smile, has gained a new quality, harsh and stiff like the little collar he wears.

Most men can remember a time in their lives when they were not so different from girls, and they also remember when that time ended. In ancient Greece a young boy lived with his mother, practicing a feminine life in her household, until the day he was taken from her into the camp of men. From this day forward the life that had been soft and graceful became rigorous and hard, as the older boy was prepared for the life of a soldier.

My grandfather on my mother's side was a contemporary of Heinrich Himmler. He was the youngest boy in the family and an especially pretty child. Like Heinrich and all small boys in this period, he was dressed in a lace gown. His hair was long and curled about his face. Like Heinrich, he was his mother's favorite. She wanted to keep him in his finery. He was so beautiful in it, and he was her last child. My great-grandmother Sarah had a dreamy, artistic nature, and in his early years my grandfather took after her. But all of this made him seem girlish. And his father and older brothers teased him mercilessly. Life improved for him only when he graduated to long pants. With them he lost his dreamy nature too.

The soul is often imagined to be feminine. All those qualities thought of as soulful, a dreaminess or artistic sensibility, are supposed to come more naturally to women. Ephemeral, half seen, half present, nearly ghostly, with only the vaguest relation to the practical world of physical law, the soul appears to us as lost. The hero, with his more masculine virtues, must go in search of her. But there is another, older story of the soul. In this story she is firmly planted on the earth. She is incarnate and visible everywhere. Neither is she faint of heart, nor fading in her resolve. It is she, in fact, who goes bravely in search of desire.

1918. Suddenly the war is over. Germany has lost. Heinrich has failed to win his commission. He has not fought in a single battle. Prince Heinrich, his namesake, has died. The prince will be decorated for heroism, after his death. Heinrich returns home, not an officer or even a soldier any longer. He returns to school, completing his studies at the gymnasium and then the university. But he is adrift. Purposeless. And like the world he belongs to, dissatisfied. Neither man nor boy, he does not know what he wants.

Until now he could rely on a strict regimen provided by his father. Nothing was left uncertain or undefined for long in his father's house. The thoroughness of Gebhard's hold over his family comes alive for me through this procedure: every package, letter, or money order to pass through the door was by Gebhard's command to be duly recorded. And I begin to grasp a sense of Gebhard's priorities when I read that Heinrich, on one of his leaves home during the war, assisted his mother in this task. The shadow of his father's habits will stretch out over history. They will fall over an office in Berlin through which the SS, and the entire network of concentration camps, are administered. Every single piece of paper issued with regard to this office will pass over Heinrich's desk, and to each page he will add his own initials. Schedules for trains. Orders for building supplies. Adjustments in salaries. No detail will escape his surmise or fail to be recorded.

But at this moment in his life Heinrich is facing a void. I remember a similar void, when a long and intimate relationship ended. What I felt then was fear. And at times panic. In a journal I kept after this separation, I wrote, *Direct knowledge of the illusory nature of panic. The feeling that I had let everything go out of control.* I could turn in only one direction: inward. Each day I abated my fears for a time by observing myself. But what exists in that direction for Heinrich? He has not been allowed to inhabit that terrain. His inner life has been sealed off both from his father and himself.

I am not certain what I am working for, he writes, and then, not able to let this uncertainty remain, he adds, *I work because it is my duty.* He spends long hours in his room, seldom leaving the house at all. He is at sea. Still somewhat the adolescent, unformed, not knowing what face he should put on when going out into the world, in his journal he confesses that he still lacks that *naturally superior kind of manner that he would dearly like to possess.*

Is it any wonder then that he is so eager to rejoin the army? The army gave purpose and order to his life. He wants his uniform again. In his uniform he knows who he is. But his frailty haunts him. Over and over he shows up at recruiting stations throughout Bavaria only to be turned away each time, with the single word, *Untauglich.* Unfit. At night the echo of this word keeps him awake.

When he tries to recover his pride, he suffers another failure of a similar kind. A student of agriculture at the university, now he dreams of becoming a farmer. He believes he can take strength and vitality from the soil. After all his own applications are rejected, his father finds him a position in the countryside. He rides toward his new life on his motorcycle and is pelted by torrents of rain. Though he is cold and hungry, he is also exuberant. He has defeated his own weakness. But after only a few weeks his body fails him again. He returns home ill with typhus and must face the void once more.

What Germany needs now is a man of iron. How easy it is to hear the irony of these words Heinrich records in his journal. But at this moment in history, he is hearing another kind of echo. There are so many others who agree with him. The treaty of Versailles is taken as a humiliation. An unforgivable weakness, it is argued, has been allowed to invade the nation.

1920. 1922. 1923. Heinrich is twenty, twenty-two, twenty-three. He is growing up with the century. And he starts to adopt certain opinions popular at this time. As I imagine myself in his frame of mind, facing a void, cast into unknown waters, these opinions appear like rescue ships on the horizon, a promise of *terra firma*, the known.

It is for instance fashionable to argue that the emergence of female equality has drained the nation of its strength. At social gatherings Heinrich likes to discuss the differences between men and women. That twilight area between the certainties of gender, homosexuality, horrifies him. A man should be a man and a woman a woman. Sexually explicit illustrations in a book by Oscar Wilde horrify him. Uncomfortable with the opposite sex, so much so that one of his female friends believes he hates women, he has strong feelings about how men and women ought to relate. *A real man,* he sets down in his diary, *should love a woman as a child who must be admonished perhaps even punished, when she is foolish, though she must also be protected and looked after because she is so weak.*

As I try to enter Heinrich's experience, the feeling I sense behind these words is of immense comfort. I know who I am. My role in life, what I am to feel, what I am to be, has been made clear. I am a man. I am the strong protector. And what's more, I am needed. There is one who is weak. One who is weaker than I am. And I am the one who must protect her.

And yet behind the apparent calm of my present mood, there is an uneasiness. Who is this one that I protect? Does she tell me the truth about herself? I am beginning to suspect that she hides herself from me. There is something secretive in her nature. She is an unknown, even dangerous, territory.

The year is 1924. And Heinrich is still fascinated with secrets. He discovers that his brother's fiancée has committed one or maybe even two indiscretions. At his urging, Gebhard breaks off the engagement. But

Heinrich is still not satisfied. He writes a friend who lives near his brother's former fiancée, *Do you know of any other shameful stories?* After this, he hires a private detective to look into her past.

Is it any coincidence that in the same year he writes in his diary that he has met a *great man, genuine and pure*? This man, he notes, may be the new leader Germany is seeking. He finds he shares a certain drift of thought with this man. He is discovering who he is now, partly by affinity and partly by negation. In his picture of himself, a profile begins to emerge cast in light and shadow. He knows now who he is and who he is not. He is not Jewish.

And increasingly he becomes obsessed with who he is not. In this pursuit, his curiosity is fed by best-selling books, posters, films, journals; he is part of a larger social movement, and this no doubt gives him comfort, and one cannot, in studying the landscape of his mind as set against the landscape of the social body, discover where he ends and the milieu of this time begins. He is perhaps like a particle in a wave, a wave which has only the most elusive relationship with the physical world, existing as an afterimage in the mind.

I can imagine him sitting at a small desk in his bedroom, still in his father's home. Is it the same desk where he was required to record some desultory sentences in his diary every day? He is bent over a book. It is evening. The light is on, shining on the pages of the book. Which book among the books he has listed in his journal does he read now? Is it *Das Liebesnest* (*The Lovenest*), telling the story of a liaison between a Jewish man and a gentile woman? *Rasse*? Explaining the concept of racial superiority? Or is it *Juden Schuldbuch* (*The Book of Jewish Guilt*). Or *Die Sünde wider das Blut* (*The Sin Against the Blood*).

One can follow somewhat his train of thought here and there where he makes comments on what he reads in his journal. When he reads *Tscheka*, for instance, a history of the secret police in Russia, he says he is disappointed. *Everyone knows*, he writes, that the Jews control the secret police in Russia. But nowhere in the pages of this book does he find a mention of this "fact."

His mind has begun to take a definite shape, even a predictable pattern. Everywhere he casts his eyes he will discover a certain word. Wherever his thoughts wander he brings them back to this word. *Jew. Jude. Jew.* With this word he is on firm ground again. In the sound of the word, a box is closed, a box with all the necessary documents, with all the papers in order.

My grandfather was an anti-Semite. He had a long list of enemies that he liked to recite. Blacks were among them. And Catholics. And the English. He was Protestant and Irish. Because of his drinking he retired early (though we never discussed the cause). In my childhood I often found him sitting alone in the living room that was darkened by closed venetian blinds which kept all our colors from fading. Lonely myself, I would try to speak with him. His repertoire was small. When I was younger he would tell me stories of his childhood, and I loved those stories. He talked about the dog named Blackie that was his then. A ceramic statue of a small black dog resembling him stood near the fireplace. He loved this dog in a way that was almost painful to hear. But he could never enter that intricate world of expressed emotion in which the shadings of one's life as it is felt and experienced become articulated. This way of speaking was left to the women of our family. As I grew older and he could no longer tell me the story of his dog, he would talk to me about politics. It was then that, with a passion he revealed nowhere else, he would recite to me his long list filled with everyone he hated.

I did not like to listen to my grandfather speak this way. His face would get red, and his voice took on a grating tone that seemed to abrade not only the ears but some other slower, calmer velocity within the body of the room. His eyes, no longer looking at me, blazed with a kind of blindness. There was no reaching him at these moments. He was beyond any kind of touch or remembering. Even so, reciting the long list of those he hated, he came temporarily alive. Then,

> **THERE WAS NO REACHING HIM AT THESE MOMENTS. HE WAS BEYOND ANY KIND OF TOUCH OR REMEMBERING.**

once out of this frame of mind, he lapsed into a kind of fog which we called, in the family, his retirement.

There was another part of my grandfather's mind that also disturbed me. But this passion was veiled. I stood at the borders of it occasionally catching glimpses. He had a stack of magazines by the chair he always occupied. They were devoted to the subject of crime, and the crimes were always grisly, involving photographs of women or girls uncovered in ditches, hacked to pieces or otherwise mutilated. I was never supposed to look in these magazines, but I did. What I saw there could not be reconciled with the other experience I had of my grandfather, fond of me, gentle, almost anachronistically protective.

Heinrich Himmler was also fascinated with crime. Along with books about Jews, he read avidly on the subjects of police work, espionage, torture. Despite his high ideals regarding chastity, he was drawn to torrid, even pornographic fiction, including *Ein Sadist im Priesterrock* (*A Sadist in Priestly Attire*) which he read quickly, noting in his journal that it was a book *about the corruption of women and girls . . . in Paris.*

Entering the odd and often inconsistent maze of his opinions, I feel a certain queasiness. I cannot find a balance point. I search in vain for some center, that place which is in us all, and is perhaps even beyond nationality, or even gender, the felt core of existence, which seems to be at the same time the most real. In Heinrich's morass of thought there are no connecting threads, no integrated whole. I find only the opinions themselves, standing in an odd relation to gravity, as if hastily formed, a rickety, perilous structure.

I am looking at a photograph. It was taken in 1925. Or perhaps 1926. A group of men pose before a doorway in Landshut. Over this doorway is a wreathed swastika. Nearly all the men are in uniform. Some wear shiny black boots. Heinrich is among them. He is the slightest, very thin. Heinrich Himmler. He is near the front. At the far left there is the blurred figure of a man who has been caught in motion as he rushes to join the other men. Of course I know his feeling. The desire to partake, and even to be part of memory.

Photographs are strange creations. They are depictions of a moment that is always passing; after the shutter closes, the subject moves out of the frame and begins to change outwardly or inwardly. One ages. One shifts to a different state of consciousness. Subtle changes can take place in an instant, perhaps one does not even feel them — but they are perceptible to the camera.

The idea we have of reality as a fixed quantity is an illusion. Everything moves. And the process of knowing oneself is in constant motion too, because the self is always changing. Nowhere is this so evident as in the process of art which takes one at once into the self and into *terra incognita*, the land of the unknown. *I am groping in the dark*, the artist Käthe Kollwitz writes in her journal. Here, I imagine she is not so much uttering a cry of despair as making a simple statement. A sense of emptiness always precedes creation.

Now, as I imagine Himmler, dressed in his neat uniform, seated behind his desk at party headquarters, I can feel the void he feared begin to recede. In every way his life has taken on definition. He has a purpose and a schedule. Even the place left by the cessation of his father's lessons has now been filled. He is surrounded by men whose ideas he begins to adopt. From Alfred Rosenberg he learns about the history of Aryan blood, a line Rosenberg traces back to thousands of years before Christ. From Walther Darré he learns that the countryside is a source of Nordic strength. (And that Jews gravitate toward cities.)

Yet I do not find the calmness of a man who has found himself in the descriptions I have encountered of Heinrich Himmler. Rather, he is filled with an anxious ambivalence. If there was once someone in him who felt strongly one way or the other, this one has long ago vanished. In a room filled with other leaders, he seems to fade into the woodwork, his manner obsequious, his effect inconsequential. He cannot make a decision alone. He is known to seek the advice of other men for even the smallest decisions. In the years to come it will be whispered that he is being led by his own assistant, Reinhard Heydrich. He has made only one decision on his own with a consistent resolve. Following Hitler with unwavering loyalty, he is known as *der treue Heinrich*, true Heinrich. He describes himself as an instrument of the Führer's will.

But still he has something of his own. Something hidden. And this will make him powerful. He is a gatherer of secrets. As he supervises the sale of advertising space for the Nazi newspaper, *Völkischer Beobachter*, he instructs the members of his staff to gather information, not only on the party enemies, the socialists and the communists, but on Nazi Party members themselves. In his small office he sits surrounded by voluminous files that are filled with secrets. From this he will build his secret police. By 1925, with an order from Adolf Hitler, the Schutzstaffel, or SS, has become an official institution.

His life is moving now. Yet in this motion one has the feeling not of a flow, as in the flow of water in a cell, nor as the flow of rivers toward an ocean, but of an engine, a locomotive moving at high speed, or even a missile, traveling above the ground. History has an uncanny way of creating its own metaphors. In 1930, months after Himmler is elected to the Reichstag, Wernher von Braun begins his experiments with liquid fuel missiles that will one day soon lead to the development of the V-2 rocket.

The successful journey of a missile depends upon the study of ballistics. Gravitational fields vary at different heights. The relationship of a projectile to the earth's surface will determine its trajectory. The missile may give the illusion of liberation from the earth, or even abandon. Young men dreaming of space often invest the missile with these qualities. Yet, paradoxically, one is more free of the consideration of gravity while traveling the surface of the earth on foot. There is no necessity for mathematical calculation for each step, nor does one need to apply Newton's laws to take a walk. But the missile has in a sense been forced away from its own presence; the wisdom that is part of its own weight has been transgressed. It finds itself thus careening in a space devoid of memory, always on the verge of falling, but not falling and hence like one who is constantly afraid of illusion, gripped by an anxiety that cannot be resolved even by a fate that threatens catastrophe.

The catastrophes which came to pass after Heinrich Himmler's astonishing ascent to power did not occur in his own life, but came to rest in the lives of others, distant from him, and out of the context of his daily world. It is 1931. Heinz, the boy born in Vienna to Catholic parents, has just turned sixteen, and he is beginning to learn something about himself. All around him his school friends are falling in love with girls. But when he searches inside himself, he finds no such feelings. He is pulled in a different direction. He finds that he is still drawn to another boy. He does not yet know, or even guess, that these feelings will one day place him in the territory of a target.

It is 1933. Heinrich Himmler, Reichsführer SS, has become President of the Bavarian police. In this capacity he begins a campaign against *subversive elements*. Opposition journalists, Jewish business owners, Social Democrats, Communists — names culled from a list compiled on index cards by Himmler's deputy, Reinhard Heydrich — are rounded up and arrested. When the prisons become too crowded, Himmler builds temporary camps. Then, on March 22, the Reichsführer opens the first official and permanent concentration camp at Dachau.

It is 1934. Himmler's power and prestige in the Reich are growing. Yet someone stands in his way. Within the hierarchy of the state police forces,

Ernst Röhm, Commandant of the SA, stands over him. But Himmler has made an alliance with Hermann Göring, who as President Minister of Prussia controls the Prussian police, known as the Gestapo. Through a telephone-tapping technique Göring has uncovered evidence of a seditious plot planned by Röhm against the Führer, and he brings this evidence to Himmler. The Führer, having his own reasons to proceed against Röhm, a notorious homosexual and a socialist, empowers the SS and the Gestapo to form an execution committee. This committee will assassinate Röhm, along with the other leaders of the SA. And in the same year, Göring transfers control of the Gestapo to the SS.

But something else less easy to conquer stands in the way of his dreams for himself. It is his own body. I can see him now as he struggles. He is on a playing field in Berlin. And he has broken out in a sweat. He has been trying once again to earn the Reich's sports badge, an honor whose requirements he himself established but cannot seem to fulfill. For three years he has exercised and practiced. On one day he will lift the required weights or run the required laps, but at every trial he fails to throw the discus far enough. His attempt is always a few centimeters short.

And once he is Reichsführer, he will set certain other standards for superiority that, no matter how heroic his efforts, he will never be able to meet. A sign of the *Übermensch*, he says, is blondness, but he himself is dark. He says he is careful to weed out any applicant for the SS who shows traces of a mongolian ancestry, but he himself has the narrow eyes he takes as a sign of such a descent. *I have refused to accept any man whose size was below six feet because I know only men of a certain size have the necessary quality of blood*, he declares, standing just five foot seven behind the podium.

It is the same year, and Heinz, who is certain now that he is a homosexual, has decided to end the silence which he feels to be a burden to him. From the earliest years of his childhood he has trusted his mother with all of his secrets. Now he will tell her another secret, the secret of whom he loves. *My dear child*, she tells him, *it is your life and you must live it.*

It is 1936. Though he does not know it, Himmler is moving into the sphere of Heinz's life now. He has organized a special section of the Gestapo to deal with homosexuality and abortion. On October 11, he declares in a public speech, *Germany's forebears knew what to do with homosexuals. They drowned them in bogs.* This was not punishment, he argues, but *the extermination of unnatural existence.*

As I read these words from Himmler's speech, they call to mind an image from a more recent past, an event I nearly witnessed. On my return from Berlin and after my search for my grandmother, I spent a few days in Maine, close to the city of Bangor. This is a quiet town, not much used to violence. But just days before I arrived a young man had been murdered there. He was a homosexual. He wore an earring in one ear. While he walked home one evening with another man, three boys stopped him on the street. They threw him to the ground and began to kick him. He had trouble catching his breath. He was asthmatic. They picked him up and carried him to a railing of a nearby bridge. He told them he could not swim. Yet still, they threw him over the railing of the bridge into the stream, and he drowned. I saw a picture of him printed in the newspaper. That kind of beauty only very graceful children possess shined through his adult features. It was said that he had come to New England to live with his lover. But the love had failed, and before he died he was piecing his life back together.

When Himmler heard that one of his heroes, Frederick the Great, was a homosexual, he refused to believe his ears. I remember the year when my sister announced to my family that she was a lesbian. I can still recall the chill of fear that went up my spine at the sound of the word "queer." We came of age in the fifties; this was a decade of conformity, awash with mood both public and private, bearing on the life of the body and the body politic. Day after day my grandfather would sit in front of the television set watching as Joseph McCarthy interrogated witnesses about their loyalty to the flag. At the same time, a strict definition of what a woman or a man is had returned to capture the shared imagination. In school I was taught sewing and cooking, and I learned to carry my books in front of my chest to strengthen the muscles which held up my breasts.

I was not happy to hear that my sister was a homosexual. Moved from one member of my family to another, I did not feel secure in the love of others. As the child of divorce I was already different. *Where are your mother and father? Why don't you live with them?* I dreaded these questions. Now my sister, whom I adored and in many ways had patterned myself after, had become an outcast, moved even further out of the circle than I.

It is March 1938. Germany has invaded Austria. Himmler has put on a field-gray uniform for the occasion. Two hand grenades dangle from his Sam Browne belt. Accompanied by a special command unit of twenty-eight men armed with tommy guns and light machine guns, he proceeds to Vienna. Here he will set up Gestapo headquarters in the Hotel Metropole before he returns to Berlin.

It is a Friday, in March of 1939. Heinz, who is twenty-two years old now, and a university student, has received a summons. He is to appear for questioning at the Hotel Metropole. Telling his mother it can't be anything serious, he leaves. He enters a room and stands before a desk. The man behind the desk does not raise his head to nod. He continues to write. When he puts his pen down and looks up at the young man, he tells him, *You are a queer, homosexual, admit it.* Heinz tries to deny this. But the man behind the desk pulls out a photograph. He sees two faces here he knows. His own face and the face of his lover. He begins to weep.

I have come to believe that every life bears in some way on every other. The motion of cause and effect is like the motion of a wave in water, continuous, within and not without the matrix of being, so that all consequences, whether we know them or not, are intimately embedded in our experience. But the missile, as it hurls toward its target, has lost its context. It has been driven farther than the eye can see. How can one speak of direction any longer? Nothing in the space the missile passes through can seem familiar. In the process of flight, alienated by terror, this motion has become estranged from life, has fallen out of the natural rhythm of events.

I am imagining Himmler as he sits behind his desk in January of 1940. The procedures of introduction into the concentration camps have all been outlined or authorized by Himmler himself. He supervises every detail of these operations. Following his father's penchant for order, he makes many very explicit rules, and requires that reports be filed continually. Train schedules, orders for food supplies, descriptions of punishments all pass over his desk. He sits behind a massive door of carved wood, in his office, paneled in light, unvarnished oak, behind a desk that is normally empty, and clean, except for the bust of Hitler he displays at one end, and a little drummer boy at the other, between which he reads, considers and initials countless pieces of paper.

One should teach a child a sense of shame. These words of Himmler's journals come back to me as I imagine Heinz now standing naked in the snow. The weather is below zero. After a while he is taken to a cold shower, and then issued an ill-fitting uniform. Now he is ordered to stand with the other prisoners once more out in the cold while the commandant reads the rules. All the prisoners in these barracks are homosexuals. There are pink triangles sewn to their uniforms. They must sleep with the light on, they are told, and with their hands outside their blankets. This is a rule made especially for homosexual men. Any man caught with his hands under his blankets will be taken outside into the icy night where several bowls of water will be poured over him, and where he will be made to stand for an hour.

Except for the fact that this punishment usually led to death from cold and exposure, this practice reminds me of Dr. Schreber's procedure for curing children of masturbation. Just a few nights ago I woke up with this thought: *Was Dr. Schreber afraid of children?* Or the child he once was? Fear is often just beneath the tyrant's fury, a fear that must grow with the trajectory of his flight from himself. At Dachau I went inside a barrack. It was a standard design, similar in many camps. The plan of the camps too was standard, and resembled, so I was told by a German friend, the camp sites designed for the Hitler Youth. This seemed to me significant, not as a clue in an analysis, but more like a gesture that colors and changes a speaker's words.

· · · ● · · ·

It is 1941. And Heinrich Himmler pays a visit to the Russian front. He has been put in charge of organizing the *Einsatzgruppen*, moving groups of men who carry out the killing of civilians and partisans. He watches as a deep pit is dug by the captured men and women. Then, suddenly, a young man catches his eye. He is struck by some quality the man possesses. He takes a liking to him. He has the commandant of the *Einsatzgruppen* bring the young man to him. *Who was your father?* he asks. *Your mother? Your grandparents? Do you have at least one grandparent who was not Jewish?* He is trying to save the young man. But he answers no to all the questions. So Himmler, strictly following the letter of the law, watches as the young man is put to death.

The captured men, women, and children are ordered to remove their clothing then. Naked, they stand before the pit they have dug. Some scream. Some attempt escape. The young men in uniform place their rifles against their shoulders and fire into the naked bodies. They do not fall silently. There are cries. There are open wounds. There are faces blown apart. Stomachs opened up. The dying groan. Weep. Flutter. Open their mouths.

There is no photograph of the particular moment when Heinrich Himmler stares into the face of death. What does he look like? Is he pale? He is stricken, the accounts tell us, and more than he thought he would be. He has imagined something quieter, more efficient, like the even rows of numbers, the alphabetical lists of names he likes to put in his files. Something he might be able to understand and contain. But one cannot contain death so easily.

· · · ● · · ·

Death with Girl in Her Lap. One of many studies the artist did of death. A girl is drawn, her body dead or almost dead, in that suspended state where the breath is almost gone. There is no movement. No will. The lines the artist has drawn are simple. She has not rendered the natural form of head, arm, buttock, thigh exactly. But all these lines hold the feeling of a body in them. And as my eyes rest on this image, I can feel my own fear of death, and also, the largeness of grief, how grief will not let you remain insulated from your own feelings, or from life itself. It is as if I knew this girl. And death, too, appears to know her, cradling the fragile body with tenderness; she seems to understand the sorrow of dying. Perhaps this figure has taken into herself all the deaths she has witnessed. And in this way, she has become merciful.

Because Himmler finds it so difficult to witness these deaths, the commandant makes an appeal to him. If it is hard for you, he says, think what it must be for these young men who must carry out these executions, day after day. Shaken by what he has seen and heard, Himmler returns to Berlin resolved to ease the pain of these men. He will consult an engineer and set him to work immediately on new designs. Before the year has ended, he presents the *Einsatzgruppen* with a mobile killing truck. Now the young men will not have to witness death day after day. A hose from the exhaust pipe funnels fumes into a chamber built on the bed of a covered truck, which has a red cross painted on its side so its passengers will not be alarmed as they enter it.

To a certain kind of mind, what is hidden away ceases to exist.

Himmler does not like to watch the suffering of his prisoners. In this sense he does not witness the consequences of his own commands. But the mind is like a landscape in which nothing really ever disappears. What seems to have vanished has only transmuted to another form. Not wishing to witness what he has set in motion, still, in a silent part of himself, he must imagine what takes place. So, just as the child is made to live out the unclaimed imagination of the parent, others under Himmler's power were made to bear witness for him. Homosexuals were forced to witness and sometimes take part in the punishment of other homosexuals, Poles of other Poles, Jews of Jews. And as far as possible, the hands of the men of the SS were protected from the touch of death. Other prisoners were required to bury the bodies, or burn them in the ovens.

Hélène was turned in by a Jewish man who was trying, no doubt, to save his own life, and she was put under arrest by another Jewish man, an inmate of the same camp to which she was taken. She was grateful that she herself had not been forced to do harm. But something haunted her. A death that came to stand in place of her own death. As we walked through the streets of Paris she told me this story.

By the time of her arrest she was married and had a young son. Her husband was taken from their apartment during one of the mass arrests that began in July of 1942. Hélène was out at the time with her son. For some time she wandered the streets of Paris. She would sleep at night at the homes of various friends and acquaintances, leaving in the early morning so that she would not arouse suspicion among the neighbors. This was the hardest time, she told me, because there was so little food, even less than she was to have at Drancy. She had no ration card or any way of earning money. Her whole existence was illegal. She had to be as if invisible. She collected scraps from the street. It was on the street that she told me this story, as we walked from the fourth arrondissement to the fifth, crossing the bridge near Notre Dame, making our way toward the Boulevard St. Michel.

Her husband was a citizen of a neutral country and for this reason legally destined for another camp. From this camp he would not be deported. Instead he was taken to the French concentration camp at Drancy. After his arrest, hoping to help him, Hélène managed to take his papers to the Swiss Consulate. But the papers remained there. After her own arrest she was taken with her son to Drancy, where she was reunited with her husband. He told her that her efforts were useless. But still again and again she found ways to smuggle out letters to friends asking them to take her husband's papers from the Swiss Consulate to the camp at Drancy. One of these letters was to save their lives.

After a few months, preparations began to send Hélène and her family to Auschwitz. Along with many other women, she was taken to have her hair cut short, though those consigned to that task decided she should keep her long, blond hair. Still, she was herded along with the others to the train station and packed into the cars. Then, just two hours before the train was scheduled to leave, Hélène, her son, and her husband were pulled from the train. Her husband's papers had been brought by the Swiss consul to the camp. The Commandant, by assuming Hélène shared the same nationality with her husband, had made a fortuitous mistake.

But the train had to have a specific number of passengers before it could leave. In Hélène's place the guards brought a young man. She would never forget his face, she told me, or his name. Later she tried to find out whether he had lived or died but could learn nothing.

> IN HÉLÈNE'S PLACE THE GUARDS BROUGHT A YOUNG MAN. SHE WOULD NEVER FORGET HIS FACE, SHE TOLD ME, OR HIS NAME. LATER SHE TRIED TO FIND OUT WHETHER HE HAD LIVED OR DIED BUT COULD LEARN NOTHING.

Himmler did not partake in the actual preparations for what he called "the final solution." Nor did he attend the Wannsee Conference where the decision to annihilate millions of human beings was made. He sent his assistant Heydrich. Yet Heydrich, who was there, did not count himself entirely present. He could say that each decision he made was at the bequest of Heinrich Himmler. In this way an odd system of insulation was created. These crimes, these murders of millions, were all carried out in absentia, as if by no one in particular.

This ghostlike quality, the strange absence of a knowing conscience, as if the living creature had abandoned the shell, was spread throughout the entire chain of command. So a French bureaucrat writing a letter in 1942 speaks in detail of the mass arrests that he himself supervised as if he had no other part in these murders except as a kind of spiritless cog in a vast machine whose force compelled him from without. *The German authorities have set aside especially for that purpose enough trains to transport 30,000 Jews*, he writes. *It is therefore necessary that the arrests made should correspond to the capacity of the trains.*

It is August 23, 1943. The first inmates of concentration camp Dora have arrived. Is there some reason why an unusually high percentage of prisoners ordered to work in this camp are homosexuals? They are set to work immediately, working with few tools, often with bare hands, to convert long tunnels carved into the Harz Mountains into a factory for the manufacture of missiles. They work for eighteen hours each day. Six of these hours are set aside for formal procedures, roll calls, official rituals of the camp. For six hours they must try to sleep in the tunnels, on the damp earth, in the same area where the machines, pickaxes, explosions, and drills are making a continually deafening noise, twenty-four hours of every day. They are fed very little. They see the daylight only once a week, at the Sunday roll call. The tunnels themselves are illuminated with faint light bulbs. The production of missiles has been moved here because the factories at Peenemünde were bombed. Because the secret work at Peenemünde had been revealed to the Allies by an informer, after the bombing the Reichsführer SS proposed that the factories should be installed in a concentration camp. Here, he argued, security could be more easily enforced; only the guards had any freedom, and they were subject to the harsh discipline of the SS. The labor itself could be hidden under the soil of the Harz Mountains.

Memory can be like a long, half-lit tunnel, a tunnel where one is likely to encounter phantoms of a self, long concealed, no longer nourished with the force of consciousness, existing in a tortured state between life and death. In his account of his years at Peenemünde, Wernher von Braun never mentions concentration camp Dora. Yet he was seen there more than once by inmates who remembered him. As the designing engineer, he had to supervise many details of production. Conditions at camp Dora could not have escaped his attention. Dora did not have its own crematorium. And so many men and women died in the course of a day that the bodies waiting to be picked up by trucks and taken to the ovens of Buchenwald were piled high next to the entrance to the tunnels.

Perhaps von Braun told himself that what went on in those tunnels had nothing to do with him. He had not wished for these events, had not wanted them. The orders came from someone who had power over him. In the course of this writing I remembered a childhood incident that made me disown myself in the same way. My best friend, who was my neighbor, had a mean streak and because of this had a kind of power over the rest of us who played with her. For a year I left my grandmother's house to live with my mother again. On my return I had been replaced by another little girl, and the two of them excluded me. But finally my chance arrived. My friend had a quarrel with her new friend and enlisted me in an act of revenge. Together we cornered her at the back of a yard, pushing her into the garbage cans, yelling nasty words at her, throwing things at her.

    My friend led the attack, inventing the strategies and the words which were hurled. With part of myself I knew what it was to be the object of this kind of assault. But I also knew this was the way to regain my place with my friend. Later I disowned my acts, as if I had not committed them. Because I was under the sway of my friend's power, I told myself that what I did was really her doing. And in this way became unreal to myself. It was as if my voice threatening her, my own anger, and my voice calling names, had never existed.

I was told this story by a woman who survived the holocaust. The war had not yet begun. Nor the exiles. Nor the mass arrests. But history was on the point of these events, tipping over, ready to fall into the relentless path of consequences. She was then just a child, playing games in the street. And one day she found herself part of a circle of other children. They had surrounded a little boy and were calling him names because he was Jewish. He was her friend. But she thought if she left this circle, or came to his defense, she herself would lose her standing among the others. Then, suddenly, in an angry voice her mother called her in from the street. As soon as the door shut behind her, her mother began to shout, words incomprehensible to her, and slapped her across the face. *Your father*, her mother finally said, after crying, and in a quieter voice, *was Jewish*. Her father had been dead for three years. Soon after this day her mother too would die. As the danger grew worse her gentile relatives would not harbor her any longer, and she joined the fate of those who tried to live in the margins, as if invisible, as if mere shadows, terrified of a direct glance, of recognition, existing at the unsteady boundary of consciousness.

In disowning the effects we have on others, we disown ourselves. My father watched the suffering of my childhood and did nothing. He was aware of my mother's alcoholism and the state of her mind when she drank. He knew my grandmother to be tyrannical. We could speak together of these things almost dispassionately, as if both of us were disinterested witnesses to a fascinating social drama. But after a day's visit with him, spent at the park, or riding horses, or at the movies, he would send me back into that world of suffering we had discussed so dispassionately.

His disinterest in my condition was not heartless. It reflected the distance he kept from his own experience. One could sense his suffering but he never expressed it directly. He was absent to a part of himself. He was closer to tears than many men, but he never shed those tears. If I cried he would fall into a frightened silence. And because of this, though I spent a great deal of time with him, he was always in a certain sense an absent father. Unknowingly I responded in kind, for years, feeling a vaguely defined anger that would neither let me love nor hate him.

My father learned his disinterest under the guise of masculinity. Boys don't cry. There are whole disciplines, institutions, rubrics in our culture which serve as categories of denial.

Science is such a category. The torture and death that Heinrich Himmler found disturbing to witness became acceptable to him when it fell under this rubric. He liked to watch the scientific experiments in the concentration camps. And then there is the rubric of military order. I am looking at a photograph. It was taken in 1941 in the Ukraine. The men of an *einsatzgruppen* are assembled in a group pose. In front of them their rifles rest in ceremonial order, composed into tripods. They stand straight and tall. They are clean-shaven and their uniforms are immaculate, in *apple-pie order*, as we would say in America.

It is not surprising that cleanliness in a profession that sheds blood would become a compulsion. Blood would evidence guilt and fear to a mind trying to escape the consequence of its decisions. It is late in the night when Laura tells me one more story. Her father is about to be sent to Europe, where he will fight in the Battle of the Bulge and become a general. For weeks her mother has prepared a party. The guests begin to arrive in formal dress and sparkling uniforms. The white-gloved junior officers stand to open the doors. Her mother, regal in satin and jewels, starts to descend the staircase. Laura sits on the top stair watching, dressed in her pajamas. Then suddenly a pool of blood appears at her mother's feet, her mother falls to the floor, and almost as quickly, without a word uttered, a junior officer sweeps up the stairs, removes her mother into a waiting car, while another one cleans up the blood. No one tells Laura that her mother has had a miscarriage, and the party continues as if no event had taken place, no small or large death, as if no death were about to take place, nor any blood be spilled.

But the nature of the material world frustrates our efforts to remain free of the suffering of others. The mobile killing van that Himmler summoned into being had some defects. Gas from the exhaust pipes leaked into the cabin where the drivers sat and made them ill. When they went to remove the bodies from the van they were covered with blood and excrement, and their faces bore expressions of anguish. Himmler's engineers fixed the leak, increased the flow of gas so the deaths would be quicker, and built in a drain to collect the bodily fluids that are part of death.

There are times when no engineers can contain death. Over this same landscape through which the mobile killing vans traveled, an invisible cloud would one day spread, and from it would descend a toxic substance that would work its way into the soil and the water, the plants and the bodies of animals, and into human cells, not only in this landscape of the Ukraine, but in the fjords of Norway, the fields of Italy and France, and even here, in the far reaches of California, bringing a death that recalled, more than forty years later, those earlier hidden deaths.

You can see pictures of them. Whole families, whole communities. The fabric on their backs almost worn through. Bodies as if ebbing away before your eyes. Poised on an edge. The cold visible around the thin joints of arms and knees. A bed made in a doorway. Moving then, over time, deeper and deeper into the shadows. Off the streets. Into back rooms, and then to the attics or the cellars. Windows blackened. Given less and less to eat. Moving into smaller and smaller spaces. Sequestered away like forbidden thoughts, or secrets.

Could he have seen in these images of those he had forced into hiding and suffering, into agony and death, an image of the outer reaches of his own consciousness? It is only now that I can begin to see he has become part of them. Those whose fate he sealed. Heinrich Himmler. A part of Jewish history. Remembered by those who fell into the net of his unclaimed life.

Claimed as a facet of the wound, part of the tissue of the scar. A mark on the body of our minds, both those of us who know this history and those who do not.

For there is a sense in which we are all witnesses. Hunger, desperation, pain, loneliness, these are all visible in the streets about us. The way of life we live, a life we have never really chosen, forces us to walk past what we see. And out at the edge, beyond what we see or hear, we can feel a greater suffering, cries from a present or past starvation, a present or past torture, cries of those we have never met, coming to us in our dreams, and even if these cries do not survive in our waking knowledge, still, they live on in the part of ourselves we have ceased to know.

I think now of the missile again and how it came into being. Scientific inventions do not spring whole like Athena from the head of Zeus from the analytic implications of scientific discoveries. Technological advance takes shape slowly in the womb of society and is influenced and fed by our shared imagination. What we create thus mirrors the recesses of our own minds, and perhaps also hidden capacities. Television mimics the ability to see in the mind's eye. And the rocket? Perhaps the night flight of the soul, that ability celebrated in witches to send our thoughts as if through the air to those distant from us, to send images of ourselves, and even our secret feelings, out into an atmosphere beyond ourselves, to see worlds far flung from and strange to us becomes manifest in a sinister fashion in the missile.

Self-portrait in charcoal. Since the earliest rendering she made of her own image, much time has passed. The viewer here has moved closer. Now the artist's head fills the frame. She is much older in years and her features have taken on that androgyny which she thought necessary to the work of an artist. Her hair is white on the paper where the charcoal has not touched it. She is in profile and facing a definite direction. Her eyes look in that direction. But they do not focus on anyone or anything. The portrait is soft, the charcoal rubbed almost gently over the surface, here light, here dark. Her posture is one not so much of resolution as resignation. The portrait was drawn just after the First World War, the war in which her son Peter died. I have seen these eyes in the faces of those who grieve, eyes that are looking but not focused, seeing perhaps what is no longer visible.

After the war, German scientists who developed the V-1 and V-2 rocket immigrate to the United States where they continue to work on rocketry. Using the Vengeance weapon as a prototype, they develop the first ICBM missiles.

On the twenty-third of May 1945, as the war in Europe comes to an end, Heinrich Himmler is taken prisoner by the Allied command. He has removed the military insignia from his clothing, and he wears a patch over one eye. Disguised in this manner, and carrying the identity papers of a man he had condemned to death, he attempts to cross over the border at

Bremervörde. No one at the checkpoint suspects him of being the Reichsführer SS. But once under the scrutiny of the guards, all his courage fails him. Like a trembling schoolboy, he blurts out the truth. Now he will be taken to a center for interrogation, stripped of his clothing and searched. He will refuse to wear the uniform of the enemy, so he will be given a blanket to wrap over his underclothing. Taken to a second center for interrogation, he will be forced to remove this blanket and his underclothes. The interrogators, wishing to make certain he has no poison hidden anywhere, no means by which to end his life and hence avoid giving testimony, will surround his naked body. They will ask him to open his mouth. But just as one of them sees a black capsule wedged between his teeth, he will jerk his head away and swallow. All attempts to save his life will fail. He will not survive to tell his own story. His secrets will die with him.

There were many who lived through those years who did not wish to speak of what they saw or did. None of the German rocket engineers bore witness to what they saw at concentration camp Dora. Common rank and file members of the Nazi Party, those without whose efforts or silent support the machinery could not have gone on, fell almost as a mass into silence. In Berlin and Munich I spoke to many men and women, in my generation or younger, who were the children of soldiers, or party members, or SS men, or generals, or simply believers. Their parents would not speak to them of what had happened. The atmosphere in both cities was as if a pall had been placed over memory. And thus the shared mind of this nation has no roots, no continuous link with what keeps life in a pattern of meaning.

Lately I have come to believe that an as yet undiscovered human need and even a property of matter is the desire for revelation. The truth within us has a way of coming out despite all conscious efforts to conceal it. I have heard stories from those in the generation after the war, all speaking of the same struggle to ferret truth from the silence of their parents so that they themselves could begin to live. One born the year the war ended was never told a word about concentration camps, at home or in school. She began to wake in the early morning hours with nightmares which mirrored down to fine and accurate detail the conditions of the camps. Another woman searching casually through some trunks in the attic of her home found a series of pamphlets, virulently and cruelly anti-Semitic, which had been written by her grandfather, a high Nazi official. Still another pieced together the truth of her father's life, a member of the Gestapo, a man she remembered as playful by contrast to her stern mother. He died in the war. Only over time could she put certain pieces together. How he had had a man working under him beaten. And then, how he had beaten her.

Many of those who survived the holocaust could not bear the memories of what happened to them and, trying to bury the past, they too fell into silence. Others continue to speak as they are able. The manner of speech varies. At an artist's retreat in the Santa Cruz Mountains I met a woman who survived Bergen Belsen and Auschwitz. She inscribes the number eight in many of her paintings. And the number two. This is the story she is telling with those numbers. It was raining the night she arrived with her mother, six brothers and sisters at Auschwitz. It fell very hard, she told me. We were walking in the early evening up a hill brown in the California fall. The path was strewn with yellow leaves illuminated by the sun in its descent. They had endured the long trip from Hungary to Poland, without food or water. They were very tired. Now the sky seemed very black but the platform, lit up with stadium lights, was blinding after the darkness of the train. She would never, she told me, forget the shouting. It is as if she still cannot get the sound out of her ears. The Gestapo gave one shrill order after another, in a language she did not yet understand. They were herded in confusion, blows coming down on them randomly from the guards, past a tall man in a cape. This was Dr. Mengele. He made a single gesture toward all her family and continued it toward her but in a different direction. For days, weeks, months after she had learned what their fate had been she kept walking in the direction of their parting and beyond toward the vanishing point of her vision of them.

There were seven from her family who died there that night. The eighth to die was her father. He was sent to a different camp and died on the day of liberation. Only two lived, she and one brother. The story of one life cannot be told separately from the story of other lives. Who are we? The question is not simple. What we call the self is part of a larger matrix of relationship and society. Had we been born to a different family, in a different time, to a different world, we would not be the same. All the lives that surround us are in us.

· · ● · ·

In the last decade the Soviet Union improves its antiballistic missiles to make them maneuverable and capable of hovering in midair. The United States continues to develop and test the MX missile, with advanced inertial guidance, capable of delivering ten prearmed electronically guided warheads, each with maneuverability, possessing the power and accuracy to penetrate hardened silos. And the Soviet Union begins to design a series of smaller one-warhead mobile missiles, the SS-25, to be driven around by truck, and the SS-X-24, to be drawn on railroad tracks. And the United States develops a new warhead for the Trident missile carrying fourteen smaller warheads that can be released in a barrage along a track or a road.

A train is making its way through Germany. All along its route those who are in the cars can look out and see those who are outside the cars. And those who are outside can see those who are inside. Sometimes words are exchanged. Sometimes there is a plea for water. And sometimes, at the risk of life, water is given. Sometimes names are called out, or curses are spoken, under the breath. And sometimes there is only silence.

Who are those on the inside and where are they going? There are rumors. It is best not to ask. There are potatoes to buy with the last of the rations. There is a pot boiling on the stove. And, at any rate, the train has gone; the people have vanished. You did not know them. You will not see them again. Except perhaps in your dreams. But what do those images mean? Images of strangers. Agony that is not yours. A face that does not belong to you. And so in the daylight you try to erase what you have encountered and to forget those tracks that are laid even as if someplace in your body, even as part of yourself.

• • • ● • • •

QUESTIONS FOR A SECOND READING

1. One of the challenges a reader faces with Griffin's text is knowing what to make of it. It's a long piece, but the reading is not difficult. The sections are short and straightforward. While the essay is made up of fragments, the arrangement is not deeply confusing or disorienting. Still, the piece has no single controlling idea; it does not move from thesis to conclusion. One way of reading the essay is to see what one can make of it, what it might add up to. In this sense, the work of reading is to find one idea, passage, image, or metaphor — something in the text — and use this to organize the essay.

    As you prepare to work back through the text, think about the point of reference you could use to organize your reading. Is the essay "about" Himmler? secrets? fascism? art? Germany? the United States? families and child-rearing? gay and lesbian sexuality? Can one of the brief sections be taken as a key to the text? What about the italicized sections — how are they to be used?

    You should not assume that one of these is the right way to read. Assume, rather, that one way of working with the text is to organize it around a single point of reference, something you could say that Griffin "put there" for you to notice and to use.

    Or you might want to do this in your name rather than Griffin's. That is, you might, as you reread, chart the connections *you* make, connections that you feel belong to you (to your past, your interests, your way of reading), and think about where and how you are drawn into the text (and with what you take to be Griffin's interests and desires). You might want to be prepared to talk about why you sum things up the way you do.

2. Although this is not the kind of prose you would expect to find in a textbook for a history course, and although the project is not what we usually think of as a "research" project, Griffin is a careful researcher. The project is serious and deliberate; it is "about" history, both family history and world history. Griffin knows what she is doing. So what *is* Griffin's project? As you reread, look to those sections where Griffin seems to be speaking to her readers about her work — about how she reads and how she writes, about how she gathers her materials and how she studies them. What is she doing? What is at stake in adopting such methods? How and why might you teach someone to do this work?

· · ● · · ·

ASSIGNMENTS FOR WRITING

1. Griffin's text gathers together related fragments and works on them, but does so without yoking examples to a single, predetermined argument or thesis. In this sense, it is a kind of anti-essay. One of the difficulties readers of this text face is in its retelling. If someone says to you, "Well, what was it about?" the answer is not easy or obvious. The text is so far-reaching, so carefully composed of interrelated stories and reflections, and so suggestive in its implications and in the connections it enables that it is difficult to sum-marize without violence, without seriously reducing the text.

    But, imagine that somebody asks, "Well, what was it about?" Write an essay in which you present your reading of "Our Secret." You want to give your reader a sense of what the text is like (or what it is like to read the text), and you want to make clear that the account you are giving is your reading, your way of working it through. You might, in fact, want to suggest what you leave out or put to the side. (The first second-reading question might help you prepare for this.)

2. Griffin argues that we — all of us, especially all of us who read her essay — are part of a complex web of connections. At one point she says,

    > Who are we? The question is not simple. What we call the self is part of a larger matrix of relationship and society. Had we been born to a different family, in a different time, to a different world, we would not be the same. All the lives that surround us are in us. (p. 411)

    At another point she asks, "Is there any one of us who can count our-selves outside the circle circumscribed by our common past?" She speaks of a "field,"

    > like a field of gravity that is created by the movements of many bodies. Each life is influenced and it in turn becomes an influence. Whatever is a cause is also an effect. Childhood experience is just one element in the determining field. (p. 386)

    One way of thinking about this concept of the self (and of interrelated-ness), at least under Griffin's guidance, is to work on the connections that she implies and asserts. As you reread the selection, look for powerful and surpris-ing juxtapositions, fragments that stand together in interesting and suggestive ways. Think about the arguments represented by the blank space between those sections. (And look for Griffin's written statements about "relatedness.") Look for connections that seem important to the text (and to you) and repre-sentative of Griffin's thinking (and yours). Then write an essay in which you use these examples to think through your understanding of Griffin's claims for this "larger matrix," the "determining field," or our "common past."

3. It is useful to think of Griffin's prose as experimental. She is trying to do something that she can't do in the "usual" essay form. She wants to make a

different kind of argument or engage her reader in a different manner. And so she mixes personal and academic writing. She assembles fragments and puts seemingly unrelated material into surprising and suggestive relationships. She breaks the "plane" of the page with italicized intersections. She organizes her material, but not in the usual mode of thesis-example-conclusion. The arrangement is not nearly so linear. At one point, when she seems to be prepared to argue that German child-rearing practices produced the Holocaust, she quickly says:

> Of course there cannot be one answer to such a monumental riddle, nor does any event in history have a single cause. Rather a field exists, like a field of gravity that is created by the movements of many bodies. Each life is influenced and it in turn becomes an influence. Whatever is a cause is also an effect. Childhood experience is just one element in the determining field. (p. 386)

Her prose serves to create a "field," one where many bodies are set in relationship.

It is useful, then, to think about Griffin's prose as the enactment of a method, as a way of doing a certain kind of intellectual work. One way to study this, to feel its effects, is to imitate it, to take it as a model. For this assignment, write a Griffin-like essay, one similar in its methods of organization and argument. You will need to think about the stories you might tell, about the stories and texts you might gather (stories and texts not your own). As you write, you will want to think carefully about arrangement and about commentary (about where, that is, you will speak to your reader *as* the writer of the piece). You should not feel bound to Griffin's subject matter, but you should feel that you are working in her spirit.

• • ● • •

MAKING CONNECTIONS

1. Is it surprising that prisons resemble factories, schools, barracks, hospitals, which all resemble prisons? (p. 355)
   — MICHEL FOUCAULT, "Panopticism"

The child, Dr. Schreber advised, *should be permeated by the impossibility of locking something in his heart....*

That this philosophy was taught in school gives me an interior view of the catastrophe to follow. It adds a certain dimension to my image of these events to know that a nation of citizens learned that no part of themselves could be safe from the scrutiny of authority, nothing locked in the heart, and at the same time to discover that the head of the secret police of this nation was the son of a schoolmaster. It was this man, after all, Heinrich Himmler, Reichsführer SS, who was later to say, speaking of the mass arrests of Jews, *Protective custody is an act of care.* (p. 388)
   — SUSAN GRIFFIN, "Our Secret"

Both Griffin and Foucault write about the "fabrication" of human life and desire within the operations of history and of specific social institutions — the family, the school, the military, the factory, the hospital. Both are concerned with the relationship between forces that are hidden, secret, and those that are obvious, exposed. Both write with an urgent concern for the history of the present, for the ways our current condition is tied to history, politics, and culture.

And yet these are very different pieces to read. They are written differently — that is, they differently invite a reader's participation and understanding. They take different examples from history. They offer different accounts of the technologies of order and control. It can even be said that they do their work differently and that they work toward different ends.

Write an essay in which you use one of the essays to explain and to investigate the other — where you use Griffin as a way of thinking about Foucault or Foucault as a way of thinking about Griffin. "To explain," "to investigate" — perhaps you would prefer to think of this encounter as a dialogue or a conversation, a way of bringing the two texts together. You should imagine that your readers are familiar with both texts, but have not yet thought of the two together. You should imagine that your readers do not have the texts in front of them, that you will need to do the work of presentation and summary.

2. We might read both Joy Castro's work (p. 263) and Susan Griffin's "Our Secret" as containing elements of autobiography. Each writer relies on stories from her own life to demonstrate the relationship between one individual life and the larger cultural and political implications. Griffin writes, "To a certain kind of mind, what is hidden away ceases to exist" (p. 404). As readers, we are struck by the ways this statement (and so many of Griffin's statements) pertains both to her own life story and to the larger historical narrative of the Holocaust.

    Reread both Castro and Griffin, looking for sentences and phrases that seem to work on two levels (the personal and the political/cultural). Which sentences or phrases suggest to you that they are both about the writer's life *and* about all of our lives, about the world? How can you tell?

    Write an essay in which you illuminate, through the work of these two writers, the relationship between one life and what happens in the world at large. How do these writers help us understand ourselves as individuals and also as parts of larger systems, cultures, or worlds?

3. John Edgar Wideman, in "Our Time" (p. 622), uses personal history to think about and to represent forces beyond the individual that shape human life and possibility — family, national history, and race. Susan Griffin is engaged in a similar project; she explains her motives this way: "One can find traces of every life in each life."

    Perhaps. It is a bold step to think that this is true and to believe that one can, or should, write the family into the national or international narrative. Write an essay in which you read "Our Secret" alongside Wideman's "Our

Time." Your goal is not only to discuss how these writers do what they do, and to what conclusions and to what ends, but also to discuss your sense of what is at stake in each project. How does a skilled writer handle such a project? What are the technical issues? What would lead a writer to write like this? Would you do the same? Where and how? For whose benefit?

4. One way to imagine Susan Griffin's project in "Our Secret" is to think of her study of Heinrich Himmler as a journey through texts. She spends a significant amount of time attending to Himmler's journals and writings, looking at the way he stood in photographs, closely reading the words he chose as a child and later as a Nazi soldier. Griffin says she herself has been "searching" through these documents. She writes:

> Now as I sit here I read once again the fragments from Heinrich's boyhood diary that exist in English. I have begun to think of these words as ciphers. Repeat them to myself, hoping to find a door into the mind of this man, even as his character first forms so that I might learn how it is he becomes himself. (p. 384)

Considering the journals and memoirs he consults, one might think of Richard E. Miller, in "The Dark Night of the Soul" (p. 435), as having a similar project to Griffin's, one of sifting through texts in order to uncover their relationships to the human beings who read and wrote these texts. Miller writes:

> Asking why a Steve Cousins or an Eric Harris or a Dylan Klebold is violent is itself a meaningless act, not because the motivation is too deeply buried or obscurely articulated to ever be known, but because we no longer live in a world where human action can be explained. We have plenty of information; it just doesn't amount to anything. This is the logic of the history of increasing humiliation working itself out over time. (pp. 440–41)

Write an essay in which you discuss Griffin's project of looking at Himmler in relation to Miller's examination of Eric Harris and Dylan Klebold. How do Miller's words above help to illuminate, expand, or complicate Griffin's thoughts in "Our Secret"? What does Griffin mean when she says she thinks of Himmler's words as ciphers? In what ways do Griffin and Miller seem to be engaging in a similar inquiry or investigation? What does each text offer as its theory of writing and reading?

BEN

Lerner

Ben Lerner (b. 1979) is a professor of English at Brooklyn College. He received a BA in political science and an MFA in creative writing from Brown University. And, as you will learn below, he was once the U.S. National High School Champion in Extemporaneous Speaking.

Lerner has been a Fulbright Scholar in Spain, a Howard Foundation Fellow, and a Guggenheim Fellow. In 2015, he won a MacArthur "Genius" Fellowship. He is the cofounder and coeditor of *No: A Journal of the Arts*. His essays of criticism and commentary appear regularly in leading journals and magazines. He is the author of three prize-winning books of poetry: *The Lichtenberg Figures* (2004); *Angle of Yaw* (2006), a finalist for the National Book Award; and *Mean Free Path* (2010). In 2011, Lerner published his first novel, *Leaving the Atocha Station*, which was widely and enthusiastically read and reviewed, and which established his position as one of the leading U.S. writers of his generation. In 2014, he published his second novel, *10:04*, which won *The Paris Review* Terry Southern Prize and which was named one of the Best Books of the Year by *The New Yorker*, the *New York Times Book Review*, the *Wall Street Journal*, the *Boston Globe*, NPR, and *Vanity Fair*, among a long list of others.

"Contest of Words: High School Debate and the Demise of Public Speech" was first published in *Harper's Magazine* in 2012. In his essays and novels, Lerner returns again and again to scenes of reading and writing and schooling: scenes from his high school; his grade school; the local library in Topeka, Kansas, where he grew up; his time as an undergraduate at Brown; or his early career as a poet and novelist. Both *Leaving the Atocha Station* and *10:04* have writers as their central characters.

Lerner's long essay *The Hatred of Poetry* (2016) begins:

> In ninth grade English Mrs. X required us to memorize and recite a poem and so I went and asked the Topeka High librarian to direct me to the shortest poem she knew and she suggested Marianne Moore's "Poetry," which, in the 1967 version, reads in its entirety:

I, too, dislike it.
> Reading it, however, with a perfect contempt for it, one discovers in
> it, after all, a place for the genuine.

I remember thinking my classmates were suckers for having mainly memorized Shakespeare's 18th sonnet whereas I had only to recite twenty-four words. Never mind the fact that a set rhyme scheme and iambic pentameter make fourteen of Shakespeare's lines easier to memorize than Moore's three, each one of which is interrupted by a conjunctive adverb — a parallelism of awkwardness that basically serves as its form. That, plus the four instances of "it," makes Moore sound like a priest begrudgingly admitting that sex has its function while trying to avoid using the word, an effect amplified by the deliberately clumsy enjambment of the second line and the third ("in/it"). In fact, "Poetry" is a very difficult poem to commit to memory, as I demonstrated by failing to get it right each of the three chances I was given by Mrs. X, who was looking down at the text, my classmates cracking up.

Here, and in other instances, you can see how these memories give him a way to examine and make reasonable (or legible) his adult life as a writer. (Why *would* a smart, ambitious adult commit a life to writing?) You can see this in the care he gives to the poems he recalls — the effects of rhyme and rhythm in a sonnet by Shakespeare; the character of the speaker in Marianne Moore's poem "Poetry," a speaker who becomes like a priest talking about sex without ever using the word. In the essay that follows, as in the example above, Lerner thinks about the language by thinking about its instances, its moments of use, as he knows and recalls them most intimately.

Contest of Words: High School Debate and the Demise of Public Speech

Although high school debate is often considered the thinking person's — the nerd's — alternative to sports, my memories of it are primarily somatic: the starched collar of the dress shirt against my recently shaved neck, small cuts and razor bumps deepening the sensation; the constant gentle pressure of the tie; how my gait and posture adjusted under the direction of the suit; the way the slacks always felt high and tight because I normally let my baggy jeans sag to whatever level we white midwestern adolescents had tacitly established as our norm. The constriction in my shoulders would be extreme — less accumulated stress than a kind of constant flexing, an indication of battle-readiness. My hair would be drawn into a ponytail (though the sides of my head were shaved, a disastrous tonsorial compromise between skinhead and hippie that can perhaps stand for the irresolvable tension between the household of my lefty, loving, Jewish psychologist parents and the very red state in which they'd raised me), which heightened the already considerable tension in my temples. I recall a continual low-level nausea, anxiety about the next round mixing with the McDonald's breakfast we would have stopped for on the road; I recall prodigious perspiration independent of temperature, periodic involuntary erection or the fear of it. Understand, I was not the only one who found "competitive speech" so physically trying. I can conjure — cannot not conjure — the image of two young women in nearly matching charcoal pantsuits hyperventilating into paper bags at Washburn Rural High School. I can still see a sophomore vomiting into his file folders soon after learning he'd be facing the defending state champions in a semifinal round.

Our tournaments were held in Kansas public high schools that appeared strangely altered on the weekends, the spaces subtly but profoundly transformed when emptied of students and teachers and severed from the rhythms of a normal day. Each room, with its hortatory posters, its rows of empty desks, equations or dates or stock phrases left on chalk- or dry-erase board, possessed something of the unreality of a theatrical set and yet something of the gravity of a postapocalyptic scene, as though a nuclear disaster had obliterated the population mid-lesson without affecting the building. You could occasionally even pick up traces of Speed Stick or scented lip gloss or other floating signatures of a social order now suspended. I remember trying combinations on the main hall lockers and touching a wrestling state-championship banner in the cafeteria with the distance of an anthropologist or a ghost.

To such a school that was no longer a school a small population of formally dressed adolescents from all over Kansas would travel by bus or van through the early-morning dark. See them arrive, wheeling plastic tubs of evidence through the freezing parking lot. They gather for a brief welcome assembly in a cafeteria redolent of bleach before dispersing in teams to the classrooms where a judge and timekeeper await. The lids come off the tubs, various papers are retrieved from hanging folders, and the round commences. The first few seconds of a speech might sound more or less like oratory, but soon the competitors will be accelerating to nearly unintelligible speeds, pitch and volume rising, spit and sweat flying as they attempt to "spread" their opponents — that is, to make more arguments and marshal more evidence than the other team can respond to within the allotted time, the rule being that a "dropped argument," no matter its quality, is conceded. (The judge, usually a former high school or college debater, hunches over a legal pad, producing a flow sheet of the round along with the competitors, recording argument and counterargument in shorthand, rarely making eye contact with the speakers.)

If you could walk the halls like an anthropologist or a ghost and peer into the rooms mid-round, competitive interscholastic debate would appear to you not as an academic subject but as a full-bodied glossolalic ritual in which participants teeter on the edge of syncope, reducing what is nominally an exchange of ideas to an athletic display of unreason. Whatever its value to the initiated, whatever its jargon and rules, from the outside debate must appear more cultic ecstasy than "public speaking."

> WHATEVER ITS VALUE TO THE INITIATED, WHATEVER ITS JARGON AND RULES, FROM THE OUTSIDE DEBATE MUST APPEAR MORE CULTIC ECSTASY THAN "PUBLIC SPEAKING."

And yet what I most want to describe is how in those weird rooms I experienced occasional accesses of power. I might be in Olathe on a December afternoon enumerating in accelerating succession the various ways implementation of my opponent's health-care plan would lead to holocaust when I would pass a mysterious threshold. I would begin to feel less like I was delivering a speech and more that a speech was delivering me, that the rhythm and intonation of my presentation were beginning to dictate its content, that I no longer had to organize my arguments so much as let them flow through me. Suddenly the physical tension was all focused energy, a transformation that made the event vaguely erotic. I became in these transportative moments an acned rhapsode, and if the song that was coursing through me was about the supposedly catastrophic risks of a single-payer health-care system or the affirmative speaker's failure to prove solvency, I was nevertheless more in the realm of poetry than of prose, my speech stretched by speed and intensity until I felt its referential meaning dissolve into pure form, until I was singing the oldest song, singing the very possibility of language. In a public school closed to the public, in a suit that felt like a costume, while pretending to argue about policy, I, in all my adolescing awkwardness, would be seized, however briefly, by an experience of prosody.

On Saturday evenings I would return home from a tournament, change clothes, have a late dinner with my parents, then get picked up by my best friend, Stephen, who'd drive us to a party. These gatherings tended to take place at the middle-class home of someone whose parents were out of town. Most vivid are my memories of basement spaces, though what most remains with me is their indeterminacy; I can feel myself descending carpeted stairs into a twilit domain of smoke and music. The composite odor of malt liquor, perfume, weed, and maybe cat litter returns — not, it surprises me to say, altogether unpleasantly. The main activity, of course, was getting fucked up; there were drinking games and outsize bongs, and there would eventually be the spectacle of someone puking, passing out, or otherwise committing a severe party foul. There was plenty of making out, and, when possible, couples would absent themselves to private rooms. There were rumored orgiastic scenes I always managed to miss, but I remember sexual activity as secondary to inebriation, though the former was of course all but unimaginable without the latter.

There was always a reasonable expectation of violence, that somebody would get his nose broken or a bottle shattered on his head, usually as a result of talking shit, vaguely disrespecting someone, something; the constriction of my shoulders at parties was extreme. The violence was as a rule weakly motivated, sometimes totally random. I remember one gathering in a basement that had a pool table in its center; nobody was playing. At one point the lights were cut, there was a loud crack, a scream. When the lights were restored one of the partygoers was splayed on the floor in a small puddle of blood; someone from Topeka West had hurled the cue ball through the dark, not caring whom he hit, and fled. Luckily, it struck someone in the jaw and not the temple.

The violence I witnessed tended to arise not from conflicts over traditional American forms of difference or from conventional gendered rights of passage but from an identity vacuum so total that even its vocabulary of brutality had to be borrowed, however awkwardly: I remember watching the son of a prominent businessman working his fingers into an array of gang signs before he hit a rival with a bat — or was it

THE MORE PREPOSTEROUS THE POSE, THE MORE EXTREME THE VIOLENCE REQUIRED TO HOLD IT.

some sort of pipe? — in the driveway of his family's McMansion. The more preposterous the pose, the more extreme the violence required to hold it. Handguns were occasionally flashed, if never discharged, in my presence (though I did once see a freshman pistol-whipped). Our misogynistic language, our manner of dress and address, our ways of abusing substances and one another, were largely modeled on gangsta rap and its videos.

This feedback loop in which middle-class suburban white boys imitated the exaggerated image of urban African-American violence, an image they (or their parents) helped finance through record sales, was largely a response to the cultural poverty of a thoroughly franchised landscape. The downtown had long since fallen to the pressures of a peripheral mall; the neighborhood and family-run restaurants had been replaced by Applebee's ("America's Favorite Neighbor"®) and Olive Garden ("When you're here, you're family"®). Violence was a response to the numbing effects of a suburban standardization so total it solicited increasingly extreme forms of reality testing; violence was a mechanism for "keeping it real." We had to appropriate even our jargon of authenticity.

For me, violence provided a crucial link between the arena of competitive speech and the realm of the white middle-class pseudogangster, the wankster, the wigger, which constituted the upper echelon of Topekan adolescent society. My participation in debate and competitive speech could just barely escape nerdiness if I narrated it to nondebaters as a form of linguistic combat — the only kind of conflict, despite my constant weight lifting and tough friends, into which I was really prepared to enter. Moreover, verbal jousting was as close as I could come to reconciling the culture of my household with the world beyond it. I could never be one of the fighters, and not just because I've always been a physical coward but also because I was my parents' son: I grew up in a home full of books and music; I had been at every moment of my life supported and loved; I was always going to leave Topeka for college and did not feel trapped there. If many of my friends were fake gangsters, I was a fake fake gangster; debate and speech, by transposing conflict to a verbal and comparatively intellectual register, offered at least a partial synthesis of these two worlds. I became a bully, quick and vicious and ready to spread an interlocutor with insults at the smallest provocation; I dominated; I made other debaters cry. If this occasionally brought me to the brink of getting my ass kicked, it generally served as a deterrent.

Fortunately for me, this shifting of aggression to the domain of language was sanctioned by one of the practices the cool kids had appropriated: after several hours of drinking, if nothing had broken up the party, you were likely to encounter some of us freestyling. In many ways this is the most embarrassing of all the poses, the clearest manifestation of a crisis in white masculinity and its representational regimes, a small group of privileged crackers often arrhythmically recycling the genre's dominant and to us totally inapplicable clichés. But it was socially essential for me: the rap battle helped translate my prowess as a public speaker into something cool. Even now it's hard for me to believe my luck, that there was a ritualized poetic insult exchange bridging the gap between my Saturday afternoons and Saturday nights, allowing me to transition from one contest to the other.

And yet during those house parties, as some eighty ounces of Olde English malt liquor coursed through my body, I might again be seized by an experience of prosody that transcended the stolen and perverted materials out of which it was made. "Freestyle" is a misnomer for a radically formal activity in which the pressure of rhyming in real time forces a speaker to prioritize the material attributes of language, its sounds and stresses, while still performing narrative tasks. Freestyling isn't about fitting preexisting content into rhyming and rhythmic forms but rather about discovering content, what's sayable, in the act of composition. I would sometimes manage to rise, I beg you to believe me, above the stupid violence of our battles and enter a zone in which sentences unfolded at a speed I could not consciously control. At that point it didn't matter what words I was plugging into the machinery of syntax, it didn't matter if I was rhyming about bitches or blow or the Canadian health-care system; it didn't matter that I looked like an idiot; what mattered was that language, the fundamental medium of sociality, was being displayed in its abstract capacity, and that my friends and I would catch a glimpse, however fleeting, of grammar as pure possibility.

> FREESTYLING ISN'T ABOUT FITTING PREEXISTING CONTENT INTO RHYMING AND RHYTHMIC FORMS BUT RATHER ABOUT DISCOVERING CONTENT, WHAT'S SAYABLE, IN THE ACT OF COMPOSITION.

The activity in debate and forensics that most closely corresponded to freestyling was Extemporaneous Speaking, not Policy Debate. ("Forensics" refers to competitive interscholastic speaking events other than debate, whereas "Policy Debate" denotes the evidence-heavy team debate in which the spread is dominant; all are governed by the National Forensics League.) I won the National Championship in International Extemp — there was also a Domestic Extemp — my senior year, after having finished second my junior year. I won the state championship all four years. I never became a nationally competitive policy debater; that would have required endless hours of research, filling those plastic tubs with evidence and briefs, summer "institutes," and a similarly committed partner. As the name implies, Extemp emphasizes improvisation: a competitor draws three questions at random — on international affairs if you're in IX, domestic if DX — chooses one, then has thirty minutes to prepare a five- to seven-minute speech that he or she delivers without notes. Topics might be frighteningly particular ("Will the Ukrainian Parliament ratify the new constitution next month?") or frighteningly general ("What is the future of Mexico?"). We Extempers had our own smaller plastic tubs of hanging folders specific to countries or issues that we'd stuffed with articles from magazines and newspapers, and we were supposed to cite sources in our speeches to substantiate our claims, but this was much lighter research than that required by Policy Debate; you just read several magazines a week, highlighted, photocopied.

Extemp required less preparation, but it could be so nightmarish that even serious policy debaters respected it. They scoffed, meanwhile, at Original Oratory, in which you delivered a polished, memorized speech on any topic. Imagine your sixteen-year-old self in a "prep room" before a final round choosing among three questions of almost sadistic obscurity.

(At local tournaments, the prep room was in the high school library, competitors wandering around mumbling to themselves like lunatics as they tried to commit outlines to memory.) You go with the question about water disputes in Djibouti because you at least know what water is, but how are you going to project fluency and authority on a topic about which your tub is horribly silent? Or imagine transitioning to your second major point in the third minute of a speech that's going swimmingly only to realize you've forgotten it; you have no notes, you have no way to call a time-out. I saw novice Extempers begin to stammer, fall silent, flee the room.

Extemp was officially about developing such a command of current affairs that one could speak confidently on a range of topics, but it was of course as much about the opposite: how a teenager in an ill-fitting suit could speak *as if* he had a handle on the crisis in Kashmir, how polish could compensate for substance as one determined the viability of a two-state solution. As in freestyling, the scariest and yet most potentially exhilarating aspect of Extemp was how much of your content you had to discover in the act of speaking, so that when you did catch the right rhythm, it felt like channeling.

I'm not disputing the very real synthetic intelligence of many of Extemp's participants, but the speeches required decisiveness: clear rather than complex answers won rounds, and you learned to stud a speech with sources the way a politician reaches for statistics — to provide the affect of authority more than to illuminate an issue or settle a point of fact. Much of your coaching and practice focused on how to use your body to lend your speech structure, when and where to step to mark transitions, when and how to gesture. Unlike Policy Debate, in which the spread eclipsed all oratorical values, style and presentation remained primary in Extemp, even if the goal was to project an image of erudition. One common defense I heard of Policy Debate's addiction to the spread was that students interested in the niceties of speech could go and do Extemp.

Or they could do L–D. In 1979 a representative of Phillips Petroleum, then the primary corporate sponsor of the National Forensics League, observed a round of Policy Debate at the national tournament and found it incomprehensible. Phillips expressed its concerns about the direction Policy Debate was taking to the executive council of the National Forensics League. The result was the formation of a new, one-on-one debating activity, Lincoln–Douglas Debate, which emphasized *values*, its format intended to prioritize oratorical persuasion. Speakers were expected to argue from a moral framework, not an empirical one. L–D — there were lots of jokes among policy debaters about the initials standing for "learning disabled" — featured resolutions that explicitly invoked justice and morality; e.g., "It is morally permissible to kill one innocent person to save the lives of more innocent people"; "In a democratic society, felons ought to retain the right to vote." In terms of short-circuiting the spread, the content of the resolutions was ultimately less important than the fact that the resolutions changed every couple of months, eliminating the tubs of evidence and encouraging competitors and judges to focus on the quality of delivery.

I'm not interested here in attempting to present these various activities in their considerable internal complexity but rather in noting the fearful symmetry between the ideological compartmentalization of high school debate and what passes for our national political discourse. It almost outpaces parody: in the year of my birth — the year of the Iranian Revolution, the year before "the Great Communicator" thrashed Carter in a televised debate by dismissing points of fact ("There you go again") and focusing on framing — Phillips Petroleum helped formalize the sundering of values from policy in high school interscholastic debate. The parallel isn't perfect, but it's undeniable: the supposedly disinterested policy wonks debate the intricacies of health care or financial regulation in a jargon designed to be inaccessible to the uninitiated while the more presidential speakers test out plain-spoken value claims on "lay judges," i.e., civilians. And this division was underwritten by petrodollars. High school L–D is infinitely more intelligent than our actual presidential debates, and I'm not claiming policy debaters never made an argument about right and wrong, but I can't believe that the existence of a corporately sponsored separation of value and policy in high school debate can be separated from that separation in the political culture at large.

> I'M NOT INTERESTED HERE IN ATTEMPTING TO PRESENT THESE VARIOUS ACTIVITIES IN THEIR CONSIDERABLE INTERNAL COMPLEXITY BUT RATHER IN NOTING THE FEARFUL SYMMETRY BETWEEN THE IDEOLOGICAL COMPARTMENTALIZATION OF HIGH SCHOOL DEBATE AND WHAT PASSES FOR OUR NATIONAL POLITICAL DISCOURSE.

One of the most common criticisms I've heard of the spread was that it detached Policy Debate from the real world, that nobody used language the way policy debaters did, except maybe auctioneers or rappers. Those are significant exceptions, but I'd also note that corporate persons use a version of the spread all the time: think of the spoken warnings at the end of television commercials for prescription drugs, when risk information is disclosed at a speed designed to make it difficult to comprehend. Or think about all the various forms of "fine print" one receives from financial institutions and health-insurance companies; the last thing you're supposed to do with those hundreds of thousands of words is comprehend them. These types of disclosure are designed to conceal; they expose you to information that, should you challenge the institution in question, will be treated like a "dropped argument" in a fast round of debate — you have already conceded the validity of the point by failing to address it when it was presented. It's no excuse that you didn't have the time. Americans are always getting "spread" in their daily lives. Meanwhile our politicians speak very, very slowly about values utterly disconnected from their policies.

When I left Topeka for college in 1997, having graduated as the National Forensics League's all-time point leader, I'd already put debate and speech behind me, and thought of myself as a serious young poet. My college application essay was about moving from debate, which conceived of linguistic exchange as a contest with winners and losers, to a more poetic understanding of the nuances of language in which writer and reader collaborated on the construction of meaning. Or something like that. It was true that I had started reading and writing poetry in high school in part to correct for the combativeness of my wankster/debater profile, in part because I had a vague and hackneyed idea that it could transform my mere sensitivity into romantic genius, thereby making my comparative lack of masculine virtues at least potentially attractive to the opposite sex. I also had a genuine fascination with language, and great mentors, two of them former Topeka High School debaters.

I remember lying in the dark on a dorm-room floor in college beside two fellow freshmen who had just split a horse tranquilizer when someone put on a recording of the British poet Tom Raworth reading one of his poems at an unusually rapid pace. The reading seemed to transpire at a speed that just exceeded comprehension, and yet I had a range of affective responses to the quick juxtapositions and syntactic disjunctions that felt like a species of understanding. If this was new to me as poetry, I nevertheless had a moment of recognition — it reminded me of the first time I'd heard the spread, and certainly resembled fast debate more than any poetry reading I'd attended in Kansas. And I recall sitting in an almost empty black-box theater that first northeastern winter and watching a sound poet perform excerpts from Kurt Schwitters's "Ursonate"; he appeared to me at his most intense like an alien delivering a negative rebuttal.

Poetry, whether or not it could deliver, seemed to my adolescent self to promise both a sensitization to the present moment, a lyric intensity, and a connection to an archival past, a longitudinal community. I thought of poetry as the opposite of debate. What I never anticipated was that poetry would become another domain where I would encounter something like the spread's reduction of reason to an athletic performance of its bankruptcy, as well as something like the experience of real power amid the posing and composing of freestyle and Extemp. Innovative postwar American poets such as Charles Olson, who emphasized the importance of discovering a poem's form and content in the act of writing, reminded me of the transports of Extemp (and freestyle), whereas I had initially thought poetry was about the opposite, about polishing a perfect text that would bear no traces of its manufacture. When I read the Language poets, whose long-form prose poetry used disjunction and non sequitur to subvert the dominant representational orders of the day, or heard them read their poetry aloud, I was reminded of how Extempers and other debaters would often cover syllogistic failures with fluency or speed; transcribed, such basically insane speeches could be mistaken for certain experimental poems.

If I have recognized the spread in drug warnings and financial doublespeak, where the corporate use of language approaches the absurd, where the shell of a communicative form is used to foreclose communication,

I have also recognized it in forms of poetry that deliberately push us to confront the contingency and craziness of our culture's use and abuse of words. When I participated in fast debate or caught the rhythm of free-style or Extemp or discovered in the act of poetic composition energies I did not possess prior to the activity of writing, I was making contact, however briefly, with the generative, transpersonal powers of language. When I was in my Dillard's suit spewing arguments in a largely empty school, when I was a belligerent little wankster rhyming in a basement, when I was an ignorant undergrad abandoning the clichés of my macho midwestern romanticism for the clichés of poetic vanguardism, I was, in all my preposterousness, responding to a very real crisis: the standardiza-tion of landscape and culture, a national separation of value and policy, an impoverished political discourse ("There you go again") that served to naturalize our particular cultural insanity. I was a privileged young subject — white, male, middle class — of an empire in which every avail-able identity was a lie, but when I felt the language breaking down as I spoke it — as it spoke me — I felt, amid a general sense of doom, that other worlds were possible.

And then I was in another dorm room watching the helicopter footage of Columbine as the extent of the massacres became clear and the passion-less nihilism of midwestern white boys achieved its apotheosis in a high school library I couldn't stop imagining as an Extemp prep room. And then George Bush won the millennial election he actually lost, in part because his halting, ungrammatical speech allowed him to present him-self as a NASCAR everyman. And then I watched the towers fall and our military "strategery" unfolded in Afghanistan and Iraq and white boys could once again define themselves in opposition to racialized others and the Foxnewsification of the language outpaced parody and a Bush or Rumsfeld press conference dispensed with logic and linearity more thor-oughly than did experimental poetry. Then he won again, war crimes in plain sight. Then Obama briefly energized the nation by addressing the public like adults and race hatred flared and white people reverse-engineered themselves as a threatened ethnicity as Hussein Obama who wasn't even born in this country advanced his Islamofascist socialist agenda and was elected as the bubble burst despite the warnings of the hockey mom and avid hunter who spoke in slow non sequitur. When she was unable to name a newspaper she read or a Supreme Court case with which she disagreed, she blamed it on "gotcha journalism." The Tea Party, with its assault weapons and slurs and tragicomic signs, with its justified if misguided outrage at the so-called elites, managed to shift the Republi-can base further toward violent unreason while our supposedly commu-nist president oversaw the greatest consolidation of capitalist class power in the country's history, increased drone strikes, and so on. It all seemed to happen so fast.

I know the imperial crack-up is older than all this, at least as old as the '70s, when the country's industrial strength began to wane, when its military was defeated in Vietnam, when oil became a perpetual crisis, when derivatives markets were developed; at least as far back as 1979, the year of my birth, when Phillips separated value and policy in debate, the year before Ronald Reagan was elected and did the same to our politics. As Earl Shorris wrote in this magazine last year:

> [Reagan] removed ethics from politics. Everything followed on his elegant excision, an operation performed so deftly on the body politic that it did not feel the wound.

It's in the incredibly slow speech of politicians, of the new right in particular, of the Bushes and Palins and Bachmanns and others, that I feel the wound, the void: the valorized slowness of fetishized stupidity, politicians flustered in advance by any question that pertains to anything but guns and faith. When a reporter asked Bush to name his biggest mistake since 9/11, he replied:

> I wish you'd have given me this written question ahead of time so I could plan for it. . . . I'm sure something will pop into my head here . . . you just put me under the spot . . . and maybe I'm not as quick on my feet as I should be in coming up with one . . .

There's no need to multiply the examples of gaps and gaffes — which are not aberrations in the speaking style of the far right but rather its basic unit of composition. Their linguistic world is that of the anti-Extemp, where failures in fluency are marks of authenticity, ignorance is often a point of pride, and tautology supplants cogitation. Romney, earlier this year: "I'm not familiar precisely with exactly what I said, but I stand by what I said, whatever it was."

EVERYTHING PUBLIC HAS LONG BEEN UP FOR AUCTION, AND THE POLITICIANS ACROSS OUR VERY NARROW SPECTRUM RUN INTERFERENCE BY SPEAKING SO SLOWLY WE'LL FORGET THEY REPRESENT A CLASS OF AUCTIONEERS.

It is a stubborn slowness that appeals to so many "spread" Americans, particularly white ones, for whom everything seems to be happening too rapidly: suddenly gays are getting married and there's a black president with his hands on my Medicare and all these people speaking Spanish and a perpetual news-crawler's worth of other outrages committed against the greatness of God and country. More generally, the rhetorical and intellectual poverty of the presidential debates, of the national discourse, of both parties, compensates for the disastrous effects of our policies: the lightning-fast trades of bundled debt, the remotely controlled drone strikes, the oil flowing into the Gulf. Everything public has long been up for auction, and the politicians across our very narrow spectrum run interference by speaking so slowly we'll forget they represent a class of auctioneers. Obama himself is such a measured if eloquent public speaker that some on the far right have asserted that his "unnaturally slow" pace is designed to induce mass hypnosis.

But recently I have encountered another kind of slow speech, one that does not attempt to cover for the spreadsheets of Wall Street or tranquilize the public and that incorporates its audience into the speech act itself: the people's mic. The human microphone, wherein people gathered around a speaker repeat back what the speaker says in order to amplify a voice without permit-requiring equipment, is by necessity deliberate, requires breaking a speech into easily repeatable fragments. I admit I always find joining in a little embarrassing, as I have always found chanting and choral speech of whatever form embarrassing: I am embarrassed to yell around others, fear that my voice will be conspicuous somehow or fail to blend in, am embarrassed to yell before I know what the statement we're building toward is.

Nevertheless I do participate and as I participate I feel, despite all my awkwardness and occasional frustration, that this is *poiesis*, "making," an attempt at rebuilding our language in the wake of the various spreads, an attempt distinct from the regressions of our national politics. We are turning away from the thoroughly evacuated public discourse that serves primarily to further the interest of its corporate sponsors in order to form a grassroots corporate person. Because the public mic, no matter what it's being used to say, is saying: This is a corporation of an older and more basic sort, a subject constituted around something other than private gain. No demands are being made within the dominant language of the day, because the demand is for a new language. I'm not claiming that demand can be actualized, I can't prove solvency, as debaters would say, and of course language can always be perverted or co-opted, but I believe its collective haltingness is an eloquent expression of the necessity of our learning as a people how to speak.

— • • • ● • • —

QUESTIONS FOR A SECOND READING

1. Lerner's essay ranges widely, from high school debate to contemporary politics. And it ranges, as well, in its mode of address. There is the ordinary language of, say, a high school party ("getting fucked up," "getting my ass kicked") and there are a number of specialized or uncommon terms. Here are six from the first four paragraphs: *somatic, tonsorial, glossolalic, syncope, rhapsode,* and (as it is used here) *spread.*

   As you reread, circle the most striking or unusual (for you) words or phrases—including words or phrases that seem to be too arcane or too common for an introductory textbook. If you need to, look the hard words up in a dictionary in order to think again about what they might mean here, in the essay, in context.

   What is Lerner doing at these moments? (And it is safe to assume that he is not always doing the same thing.) What is he doing to you, or for you, as his reader? What he is doing on his own behalf—for fun, perhaps, or strategically—or because he can't help himself?

   Think about the writer, Lerner, as a speaker performing for an audience that is meant to include you. This is, after all, an essay about public speech. If there is a lesson here in speaking and writing, in public speech, what might it be?

2. Lerner is a very talented writer. He has established a reputation as an important young essayist, but even more so as an important young poet and novelist. And he writes amazing sentences.

    Here are two remarkable sentences from his essay, sentences that might be called (to use Lerner's terms) "rhapsodic," sentences in which you can feel, however fleetingly, "grammar as pure possibility."

    > I became in these transportative moments an acned rhapsode, and if the song that was coursing through me was about the supposedly catastrophic risks of a single-payer health-care system or the affirmative speaker's failure to prove solvency, I was nevertheless more in the realm of poetry than of prose, my speech stretched by speed and intensity until I felt its referential meaning dissolve into pure form, until I was singing the oldest song, singing the very possibility of language. In a public school closed to the public, in a suit that felt like a costume, while pretending to argue about policy, I, in all my adolescing awkwardness, would be seized, however briefly, by an experience of prosody. (pp. 420–21)

    These sentences give a reader the "experience of prosody." They do what they argue. They "prioritize the material attributes of language, its sounds and stresses, while still performing narrative tasks." You are swept up by the shape and rhythm of the sentences (until meaning dissolves into form), the first sentence pushing forward in its enthusiasm, the second stopping and starting as it tries to bring the energy, briefly, back under intellectual control.

    As you reread, find two sentences that you feel to be similarly expressive or rhapsodic. And write two sentences of your own in imitation, using the same structure and punctuation but with words (and a topic) of your own.

3. Lerner's essay moves from scene to scene — from high school debate to basement parties, from his freshman year at Brown to the more recent Occupy Wall Street public demonstrations. The connections are implied rather than stated. Lerner leaves it up to a reader to think through the connections or to account for the logic in the argument.

    As you reread, mark the key moments of transition in the essay. And then prepare yourself to describe how, for you, the sections are connected. For example, think about what the first section hands off to the second, or what the third section alludes to (or relies upon) in the preceding two sections. And, as you proceed, think about the larger picture, about how Lerner gets (and how you get) from beginning to end. What is the point of the ending? What is the argument here?

4. "Contest of Words" relies upon a reader's knowledge of the "people's mic" and the Occupy movement. In order to prepare for a rereading, research this

moment in our nation's recent history and prepare a brief presentation. You can use the Internet to search out details. It would also be interesting to ask around on campus. Most likely you can find someone with firsthand experience of the movement.

— • • ● • • —

ASSIGNMENTS FOR WRITING

1. As we saw in the third "Question for a Second Reading," Lerner's essay moves from scene to scene—from high school debate to basement parties, from his freshman year at Brown to the more recent Occupy Wall Street public demonstrations. The connections are implied rather than stated. Lerner leaves it up to a reader to think through the connections or to account for the logic in the argument.

    Let's imagine that it is your job to explain Lerner's argument to someone who has read the essay but who is not quite sure what it says, or why it is interesting (or important), someone who isn't quite sure what the implications might be. With paraphrase and some direct (including block) quotation, write an essay to provide your sense of what the essay says and why it might be of consequence to you and to people of your generation. Be sure to take time to explain and interpret the key passages and details of Lerner's essay. And be sure to take time, most likely at the end, to speak for yourself, to extend what he says to your interests, experiences, stories, and concerns.

2. Write an essay that is modeled on (or inspired by) "Contest of Words." Think of your essay as an homage, something that is in conversation with what Lerner has written, something that a knowing reader would recognize as prompted by or related to his essay.

    Ideally, your essay will be similarly voiced and similarly structured. There will be sentences that have a Lerner-like quality to them. Ideally, you would begin with a language lesson, some moment of speaking or writing that was (and remains) meaningful to you, a defining moment. And, from that, ideally, you might reach out to think about the larger contexts of school, friends, family, community, state, and/or nation. Ideally, you might make some direct reference to "Contest of Words"—or you might adopt some of its language.

    But this is a real world, not an ideal one. Do what you can in order to write an essay that you believe in, one that can be compelling, engaging, memorable for both you and your reader.

— • • ● • • —

MAKING CONNECTIONS

1. Like Ben Lerner, Richard E. Miller, in "The Dark Night of the Soul" (p. 435), refers to the school shootings at Columbine, and he links what he calls the "literate arts" with the state of the nation. He speaks about the "practice" of the humanities, about the uses of language that circulate meaningfully and

powerfully (or that don't) in the world of young adults in the contemporary United States. In his book *Writing at the End of the World*, Miller says,

> The practice of the humanities . . . is not about admiration or greatness or appreciation or depth of knowledge or scholarly achievement; it's about the movement between worlds, arms out, balancing: it's about making the connections that count. (p. 198)

Arms out, balancing. The final image in Lerner's essay is of the people's microphone, people together, making connections, and what he calls a "collective haltingness."

Both Lerner and Miller are teachers. Both want to speak on behalf of the nation and its new generations of readers, writers, and speakers. While there are no direct references, one to the other, the two essays are part of a general conversation about the state of the language in the United States today. What does each say? How might they be said to speak to each other? to speak differently?

And, finally, where are you in this? Where are you, and people like you, the group for whom you feel prepared to speak? What examples might you bring to the table? You, too, have been and will continue to be expected to take courses in reading and writing and public speaking, to read, write, and talk in "critical and self-reflective ways," to use Miller's phrase. Where are you in this conversation?

Write an essay in which you explore these questions.

2. Both Ben Lerner and Richard Rodriguez, in "The Achievement of Desire" (p. 533), provide an account of growing up in America, where growing up is intimately related to the use and mastery of language. What is striking, of course, are the differences, although perhaps there are some common experiences or concerns, something they share.

Write an essay in which you use these two essays, along with examples from your own schooling and your own experience in the world, to consider the role that language plays in the lives of young adults today as they grow up in the United States, struggle to speak (or write) and to be heard, and achieve (or fail to achieve) what they desire. You should imagine an essay that breaks roughly into thirds—that is, one where you get as much space as Lerner or Rodriguez.

RICHARD E.
Miller

Richard E. Miller is professor of English and the executive director of the Plangere Writing Center at Rutgers University. He received his BA from St. John's University, his MA from the University of Massachusetts at Boston, and his PhD from the University of Pittsburgh. He is the author of *As If Learning Mattered: Reforming Higher Education* (1998), *Writing at the End of the World* (2005; from which the following selection is drawn), and, with Kurt Spellmeyer, a textbook, *The New Humanities Reader* (fifth edition, 2015).

Throughout his career, Miller has looked at schooling in the United States and, in particular, at the required curriculum in English — a literature course and a composition course — and he has asked big questions. For example, in *Writing at the End of the World*, he says:

> In a secular society, education is the most powerful resource citizens have to ensure a brighter future for themselves. But what is one to do when the future includes a radioactive wasteland in the northern Ukraine? The smoldering ruins of the World Trade Center? Looted museums in a bombed-out Baghdad? No meaningful discussion of the humanities can proceed without confronting such examples of human depravity and indifference. Who, surveying the ruins at Chernobyl, would be persuaded either by Matthew Arnold's argument that we are ennobled by studying the best that has been thought and said in our time or by those who maintain that the work in the humanities provides the foundation for a critical engagement with the world? (pp. ix–x)

Here is what Miller says about his own teaching. Since he is referring, in part, to his teaching in first-year writing courses, a course occupying the same curricular slot as the one you are taking, this is worth quoting at length.

> When I am back in the classroom, I work at getting the students to use their writing not just as a tool for making arguments, but also as a lens for exploring complexity and a vehicle for arriving at nuanced understandings of a lived reality that is inescapably characterized by ambiguities, shades of meaning, contradictions, and gaps. That's a long way to try to take undergraduates in one course in one semester, but this is what I believe the function of a secular public education should

be: to provide training in the arts of solving the problems of this world, training that recognizes that people, who never leave behind their embodied histories and their cherished beliefs, can't be revised the way papers can. (pp. 196–197)

His goal, he says, for himself and for his students, is

learning how to speak in ways that others can hear, in finding a way to move and be in more than one world at once. This isn't the only answer and it isn't always the answer, but learning how to look for such answers and finding out how to implement the evanescent solutions the search itself suggests is the primary function of the humanities as I conceive them. The practice of the humanities, so defined, is not about admiration or greatness or appreciation or depth of knowledge or scholarly achievement; it's about the movement between worlds, arms out, balancing; it's about making the connections that count. (p. 198)

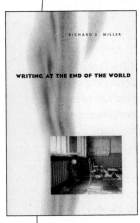

Miller is a brilliant essayist and an innovative thinker. He has turned his attention increasingly to multimedia composition, composition in digital environments, both in his own writing and as a necessary next step for the teaching of English. For an example of this work, search online for the presentation he gave to the Modern Language Association: "This Is How We Dream, Parts 1 and 2."

The Dark Night of the Soul

Though they may already have faded from memory, driven off by more recent and yet more spectacular horrors, for a few short weeks in 1999, the events at Columbine High School mesmerized the nation. There was the live footage of students fleeing in terror across the green, the boy with the bleeding head being dropped from the window, the SWAT teams moving in. There was the discovery of what lay beyond the eye of the camera: fifteen dead, a cache of weapons, a large homemade bomb made with two propane tanks and a gasoline canister, the eventual disclosure of an even more sinister fantasy that involved hijacking a plane and crashing it in New York City.[1] There was the ongoing effort to present fuller and fuller portraits of Eric Harris and Dylan Klebold, the two young men who masterminded the slaughter: they were outsiders, video-game enthusiasts, members of the Trench Coat Mafia, neo-Nazis, two boys who couldn't tell their alcohol-fueled dreams from reality, a leader and a follower, a smart kid and a loser, specimens of a middle-class value system in crisis, proof of the need for stricter gun-control laws. And finally, there were the funerals, the white caskets covered in writing from those left behind, the doves released into the air, and all those inspirational speeches about healing and hope.

Any major social cataclysm produces in its wake two responses; First, there is the search for causes: Why did this happen? Who is to blame? And second, there is an appeal to some greater authority to assist in preventing such upheavals in the future. Following Columbine, fingers were pointed at everyone and everything: inattentive parents, indifferent guidance counselors, insensitive jocks, the entertainment industry, powerful gun lobbyists, the media, the Internet, the military-industrial complex, a president who couldn't keep his pants on.[2] And then, as one would expect, there were calls both for increased external controls — new laws, regulations, supervisory agencies — and for increased internal controls — educational interventions, moral training, prayer. Surely, more laws, more education, and more religious instruction would bring these violent students back into line.

Despite heightened sensitivity and increased security, however, the schoolyard massacre has proven to be a remarkably durable and recurring social cataclysm. In February 1997, a sixteen-year-old in Bethel, Alaska, entered his high school and murdered the principal and another student. In October 1997, another sixteen-year-old, this one living in Pearl, Mississippi, killed his mother, then went to school and killed two more students. In December 1997, a fourteen-year-old took aim at a prayer circle in West Paducah, Kentucky, killing three. In March 1998, two boys, eleven and thirteen, pulled a fire alarm and gunned down students exiting Westside Middle School in Jonesboro, Arkansas, leaving five dead. And the list goes on with additional shootings over the past five years at high schools in Fayetteville, Tennessee; Springfield, Oregon; Richmond, Virginia; Conyers, Georgia; Deming, New Mexico; and Cold Spring, Minnesota. In March 2001, a skinny kid, whom classmates called "Anorexic Andy," walked into his high school in Santee, California, to reenact his version of Columbine. He killed two and wounded thirteen before being subdued. And in April 2002, Robert Steinhaeuser returned to Johann Gutenberg High School in Erfurt, Germany, to avenge his expulsion for forging a doctor's note: he killed two students and thirteen teachers before turning his gun on himself.

It's reassuring to think that either the work of the legal system or the educational system can reduce or eliminate altogether the threat of the unpredictable and the unforeseen. This is why we have childproof medicine bottles, penalties for not buckling up, informational literature on family planning for students in junior high school: these are all examples of reasonable responses to known problems. But the schoolyard massacre seems a problem of a different order. What legal or educational response could be equal to the challenge of controlling the behavior of so many students from such varied backgrounds? Just how much surveillance would be required to bring the marginalized fraction of the student population back into the fold? How invasive would a curricular intervention have to be to succeed in instilling a set of preferable values in those who currently feel so deeply alienated while at school? While the answers to these questions are unknown, what we do know is this: the day after Columbine High School reopened, after all the public and private soul-searching in the community about the killings, after all the media coverage and analysis, after an enormous pep rally replete with bouncing cheerleaders, enthusiastic athletes, and all the mandatory school spirit one could ever hope for, swastikas were found scratched in a stall in one of the high school's newly painted bathrooms.

Eric Harris certainly didn't accept the idea that anyone was to blame for his actions or that anything could have been done to stop him or Dylan Klebold in going forward with their plan. Anticipating speculation of just this kind, Harris wrote in his diary:

> i want to leave a lasting impression on the world, and god damnit do not blame anyone else besides me and V for this. dont blame my family, they had no clue and there is nothing they could have done, they brought me up just fucking fine. dont blame toy stores or any other stores for selling us ammo, bomb materials or anything like that because its not their fault. i dont want no fucking laws on buying fucking PVC pipes. we are kind of a select case here so dont think this will happen again. dont blame the

school. dont fucking put cops all over the place just because we went on a killing spree doesnt mean everyone else will and hardly ever do people bring bombs or guns to school anyway. the admin. is doing a fine job as it is. i dont know who will be left after we kill but dammit don't change any policies just because of us. it would be stupid and if there is any way in this fucked up universe we can come back as ghosts we will haunt the life out of anyone who blames anyone besides me and V.[3]

If one accepts Harris's assertions, then the events at Columbine are largely without motive or meaning: the killing spree was a misguided grab for immortality by two young men at loose ends. If one rejects Harris's assertions, though, and persists in the pursuit for causes, one is left with the inescapable fact that the hierarchical, exclusionary environment of mandatory schooling fosters feelings of rage and helplessness that cannot be contained. The law drives everyone into the schoolhouse; the educational system then sifts and sorts its way through the masses, raising expectations and crushing dreams as it goes. Eventually, something has to give.[4]

What is to be done? What is to be done? Only those utterly indifferent to the suffering of others can forestall asking this question for long. And, after any tragedy that involves the death of young people, it doesn't take long for someone to make the case that the problem lies with advanced technology and all the fantasy factories that it has spawned, which together have blurred the line between fact and fiction. After the Columbine shootings, Pat Schroeder, the former congresswoman from Colorado who now runs the Association of American Publishers, was among those who argued that we've reached the point where suburban kids are becoming mass murderers because we've created domestic spaces that isolate individuals in a technological sea of entertainment — the TV, the VCR, the computer, the entertainment center, the Internet, a different toy for everyone. "*This* is the beautiful family of America living the American dream," Schroeder observed wryly. "But we need some ways to relate to each other as human beings. We need to work on getting connected." Convinced that the virtual connections available in cyberspace tend to be divisive, Schroeder has committed herself to protecting the practice of reading books. Schroeder believes that book clubs and coffee bars provide a kind of embodied community unavailable on the Internet. These places where people go to discuss the printed word are, she says, "among the few civil institutions left. [They are] places to go see other people" (qtd. in Gross).

I share Schroeder's desire for a future where physical communion with others is still an option. You might say, in fact, that Schroeder and I come from the same secular faith tradition, that we share the same belief in reading's potentially redemptive power. And yet, there are dark days when I doubt the activities of reading and writing have much of a future. Indeed, after Columbine, it seems almost ludicrous to suggest that the social, psychological, and biochemical problems that contributed to this massacre might have been peacefully resolved if only Harris and Klebold had spent more time talking about what they were reading. Does reading really possess such curative powers? Does writing? Does group discussion?

Reading, writing, talking, meditating, speculating, arguing: these are the only resources available to those of us who teach the humanities and they are, obviously, resources that can be bent to serve any purpose. Harris and Klebold, in fact, wrote and produced for all different sorts of media; they read a range of material that supported their beliefs and that taught them how to put together their incendiary devices; they hung out with like-minded individuals and discussed their ideas. They relied on writing to post their scathing observations about their peers on Harris's Web site; they composed poems in their creative writing class that their teacher described as "dark and sad"; they created a video for a class project in which they acted out their fantasy of moving through the school gunning down their tormentors (Pooley 30–32). Harris even had the affectation of an English teacher, declaring on his Web site that one of the many habits he found unforgivable in his peers was the tendency to pronounce the "t" in "often": "Learn to speak correctly, you morons," he commands (Barron). They read, they wrote, they talked. And at the end of the process, they tried to kill everyone they could.

For some, it will hardly come as a surprise to learn that reading and writing have no magically transformative powers. But for those of us who have been raised into the teaching and publishing professions, it can be quite a shock to confront the possibility that reading and writing and talking exercise almost *none* of the powers we regularly attribute to them in our favorite stories. The dark night of the soul for literacy workers comes with the realization that training students to read, write, and talk in more critical and self-reflective ways cannot protect them from the violent changes our culture is undergoing. Helen Keller learning to see the world through a language traced into the palm of her hand; Malcolm X in prison memorizing the dictionary word by word; Paulo Freire moving among the illiterate masses in Brazil: we tell ourselves and our students over and over again about the power of reading and writing while the gap between rich and poor grows greater, the Twin Towers come crashing down, and somewhere some other group of angry young men is at work silently stockpiling provisions for the next apocalypse.

If you're in the business of teaching others how to read and write with care, there's no escaping the sense that your labor is increasingly irrelevant. Indeed, one way to understand the dark, despairing character of so much of the critical and literary theory that has come to dominate the humanities over the past two decades is to see this writing as the defensive response of those who have recognized but cannot yet admit that the rise of technology and the emergence of the globalized economy have diminished the academy's cultural significance. And so, to fight off the sense that words exercise less and less power in world affairs, one can declare that discourse plays a fundamental role in the constitution of reality. Rather than concede that reading as an activity has come to consume less and less time in the average person's life, one can insist that the canon wars are the ground upon which the nation's political future is being determined; rather than accept the fact that technological advances have taken control of publishing out of the hands of the few and transformed everyone with access to the Internet into a potential author and critic, one can decry the movement of our culture's critical center from the university to the sound stage of the Oprah Winfrey Show. What is unthinkable in such pronouncements about the centrality of academic work is the possibility that the vast majority of the reading and writing that teachers and their students do about literature and culture more generally might not be all that important. It could all just be a rather labored way of passing the time.

I have these doubts, you see, doubts silently shared by many who spend their days teaching others the literate arts. Aside from gathering and organizing information, aside from generating critiques and analyses that forever fall on deaf ears, what might the literate arts be said to be good for? How — and in what limited ways — might reading and writing be made to matter in the new world that is evolving before our eyes? Is there any way to justify or explain a life spent working with — and teaching others to work with — texts? These are the questions that animate the meditations that follow. Those who have never felt the inner urgency of such questions need read no further.

THE PRINCE OF DARKNESS

In a million millennia, the sun will be bigger. It will feel nearer. In a million millennia, if you are still reading me, you can check these words against personal experience, because the polar ice caps have melted and Norway enjoys the climate of North Africa.

Later still, the oceans will be boiling. The human story, or at any rate, the terrestrial story, will be coming to an end. I don't honestly expect you to be reading me then.

— MARTIN AMIS, *The Information*

In *The Information,* Martin Amis's bleak and scorching send-up of the literary professions, the following beliefs are gleefully debunked: that reading makes you a better person; that writers of merit are driven to write by virtue of their deep insights into the human spirit; that a world filled with artistic creations is superior to one filled with the castoffs of consumer culture; that writing provides access to immortality. To stage his skewering of these cultural commonplaces, Amis pits two writers against each other: Richard Tull, the author of artistic, experimental (that is to say, unreadable) novels; and Gwyn Barry, who is vapid and soulless, but whose eventless, multicultural, utopian novel, *Amelior,* has become an international phenomenon. To the degree that *The Information* has a plot, it revolves around Tull's repeated efforts to punish Barry for having met with popular literary success. To Tull's way of thinking, Barry's greatest literary achievement is a work of no consequence: as he describes it, *Amelior* "was about a group of fair-minded young people who, in an unnamed country, strove to establish a rural community. And they succeeded. And then it ended. Not worth writing in the first place, the finished book was, in Richard's view, a ridiculous failure" (28). And yet, in the world Amis has created for his readers, pretentious, sentimental slop of this kind has adulation heaped upon it, while work like the kind Richard Tull produces — work that strains mightily to achieve a high seriousness, work that is replete with veiled literary references, work that endlessly announces its indebtedness to the earlier classics — actually physically harms the few who can bear to read it, causing migraines, seeing disorders, and even forced hospitalizations.

Tull, who is unable to find a publisher and whose previous novels are out of print, can only view his friend's success as a cruel joke the universe is playing on him, one he's determined to counteract. But, as Tull eventually discovers, there's no fighting the ways of the universe. In the grand scheme of things, he is insignificant, and what lies in store for him is what lies in store for us all — a story of increasing humiliation. In fact, *The History of Increasing Humiliation* is one of the many books for which Tull has received an advance but has yet to write, one which is to contain his theory about "the decline in the status and virtue of literary protagonists" (92). As Tull sees it, there's a direct connection between the decline in the status of heroes in the novel and the growth in our understanding of the dimensions of the universe: with each advance in astronomical studies, "we get smaller" (93). We can see the effects of this in our literary creations, Tull argues: "First gods, then demigods, then kings, then great warriors, great lovers, then burghers and merchants and vicars and doctors and lawyers. Then social realism: you. Then irony: me. Then maniacs and murderers, tramps, mobs, rabble, flotsam, vermin" (92). And indeed, Amis uses Tull as a vehicle to prove this theory, assaulting the pieties of those who would privilege the acts of reading and writing by showing artists to be indistinguishable from criminals. By this, Amis does not mean that all criminals are like Hannibal Lecter, all-knowing virtuosos who transgress and transcend social bonds at will. Rather, as Amis puts it, "the criminal *is* like an artist (though not for the reasons usually given, which merely depend on immaturity and the condition of self-employment): the criminal resembles the artist in his pretension, his incompetence, and his self-pity" (76). One could hardly say that the status of the criminal has been elevated through such a comparison.

When Tull's initial efforts to harm his rival fail, he turns to Steve Cousins, a financially secure, semi-retired criminal, who now entertains himself by pursuing "recreational" adventures in his profession: his specialty, as he defines it, is "fuck[ing] people up" for sport (116). And, for reasons that are never quite clear, "Scozzy," as his mates call him, is determined to hurt a writer, preferably Gwyn Barry. Scozzy may be motivated by his own hatred of *Amelior*, which he refers to as a "total crock" and "complete crap" (114); he may be driven by the autodidact's sense of inferiority (113); he may be acting out the aggressions of an abandoned child (Amis repeatedly links Scozzy to the wild boy of Aveyron). But to seek motivation for Scozzy's actions is, within Amis's cosmology, to misunderstand the criminal's place in the universe and our own as well. Asking why a Steve Cousins or an Eric Harris or a Dylan Klebold is violent is itself a meaningless act, not because the motivation is too deeply buried or obscurely articulated to ever be known, but because we no longer live in a world where human action can be explained. We have plenty of information; it just doesn't amount to anything. This is the logic of the history of increasing humiliation working itself out over time.

At one point in the novel, Tull's wife, Gina, is reading the newspaper in horror, trying to make sense of the actions of a child-murderer. "Words," says Gina, " —words fail me. *Why?* Won't someone tell me?" (123). Amis then interrupts this scene to introduce his own commentary on how we are to make sense of these senseless acts, the ones which rob us of speech, the ones which drive us to ask why. "A contemporary investigator will tell you that he hardly ever thinks about motive. It's no help. He's sorry, but it's no help. Fuck the why, he'll say. Look at the how, which will give you the who. But fuck the why" (124). There is no ultimate explanation for these acts of brutality, which is something the little boy, who apologized to the man who was about to murder him, could not understand: "the little boy was searching for motivation in the contemporary playground. Don't look. You won't find it, because it's gone. I'm sorry. I'm sorry" (124).[5]

As it goes with the world, so it goes with the novel: to seek out what motivates Tull to try to destroy Gwyn Barry, to try to understand why Scozzy would want to hurt Barry, to see some reason in Gina's betrayal of Tull — these are all fruitless acts in Amis's cosmos, where only the naive believe that violence is the result of some ultimately discernable act of volition. Tull understands that he lives in a world defined by random acts of violence and he is afraid, not for his own safety, but for his son's: "violence would come, if it came, from the individual, from left field, denuded of motive. The urban pastoral was all left field. There was no right field. And violence wouldn't come for Richard. It would come for Marco" (99). And, indeed, this very scenario is acted out in the conclusion to *The Information,* with Scozzy, bent on revenge for having been publicly insulted by Tull, heading to Tull's neighborhood determined to kidnap Marco. Unaware of the danger his son is in, drunkenly planning one final plot to bring Barry down, Tull stumbles into his apartment only to discover Barry in the act of sodomizing his wife. Meanwhile, outside in the park, Barry's bodyguards happen to intercept Scozzy before he is able to harm Marco. Broken and defeated, Tull belatedly realizes that he owes his son's life to the man he viewed as being in every way his inferior. As the novel ends, with Barry proudly sauntering off victorious, Tull climbs the stairs back to his apartment "working on a way of forgiving Gina. A form of words. Because if he forgave her, she could never leave him now. Who was he? Who had he been throughout? Who would he always be?" (373). Tull, "a failed book reviewer who comes on like Dr. Johnson" (286), has been shown to be a fool who can't even read the intentions and the capabilities of those closest to him. Barry, the avowed fraud and hypocrite, gets everything — fame, fortune, even "the Profundity Requital," which guarantees him lifetime support so he can devote himself to thinking about the social good.

Although Amis explicitly outlaws such a question, one can't help but wonder why a writer would produce such a scathing portrait of the literary world and its denizens. If this is Amis's assessment both of his peers and of the reading public, then why go on writing? Is he, like Gwyn Barry, just along for the ride, cynically "doing what every man would do if he thought he could get away with it" (286)?[6] *The Information* might best be read as a meditation on the fact that sooner or later all writers encounter something that robs them of their sleep, something that deprives them of feeling that what they do matters. As the novel opens, Richard Tull is crying in his sleep, crying because the night had brought "all its unwelcome information" (4). And when he wakes, he considers calling Gwyn Barry, for whom "there would be no information, or the information, such as it was, would all be good" (5). Tull and Barry are both entering their forties and the information that awaits them on this threshold communicates different messages: Gina has given Tull an additional year to complete his latest and perhaps final novel, *Untitled*, after which time — the novel's failure being a foregone conclusion — Tull will have to commit himself to more gainful employment. Barry, on the other hand, has written two bestsellers; his marriage has been featured on the BBC; he's got an international promotional tour lined up; he's been nominated for the Profundity Requital. Tull is having "a crisis of the middle years," a crisis Amis himself has been through. Citing what are presumably notes from his own writing journal, Amis observes, "intimations of monstrousness are common, are perhaps universal, in early middle age" (44). One form this takes is a preoccupation with the question, "how can I ever play the omniscient, the all-knowing, when I don't know *anything*?" (43).

So the information that comes with age, the information that comes at night, brings news of futility, ignorance, insignificance, humiliation: "When we die, our bodies will eventually go back where they came from: to a dying star, our own, five billion years from now, some time around the year 5,000,001,995" (45). With the aging of the body and the foreclosing of future possibilities, all the inbound information serves to turn one's attention to mortality: "the information is telling me to stop saying *hi* and to start saying *bye*" (89). Throughout the novel, Amis concedes that he is not in control of what is happening, that events are unfolding and characters are developing without reference to any greater design on his part. "I don't come at these people," Amis explains in the middle of the novel, "They come at me. They come at me like information formed in the night. I don't make them. They're already there" (190–91). Whether Amis is genuinely haunted by these characters or is only mocking the terror that lesser writers experience when they lose control of their material is a matter of importance only to those who wish to argue over Amis's own literary achievements. For the purposes of this discussion, though, the salient point is to note the ways in which Amis's novel brings together the aging body, the activity of writing, and the inbound information to explore — and I would say produce — feelings of hopelessness. We live in the Information Age and all the information is telling us that whatever we have done, whatever we are doing, and whatever we plan to do will never have any lasting significance.

FOLLOWING THE WORD

> You know, Eric, you can read about this stuff, but you can't understand it until you live it.
>
> — CHRIS McCANDLESS in Jon Krakauer's *Into the Wild*

Chris McCandless's misadventures in the Alaskan wilderness are now well known, thanks to Jon Krakauer's best-selling account of the young man's disappearance and death in *Into the Wild*. These are the facts: after graduating from Emory in 1990, McCandless donated the remains of his college trust fund to Oxfam, burned what money remained, along with his identification papers, and disappeared. Two years later, in the fall of 1992, his emaciated body was found, along with his favorite books and his journal, in a school bus deep in the Alaskan wilds. Something about McCandless's quest and his ultimate fate captured the imagination of readers across the country. For some, the story is a tragedy, one that concerns a deadly conflict between youthful idealism and a brutal, unforgiving reality. For those reading this version of McCandless's life, the loss of a young man who wanted to commune with the natural world and the disappearance of a world untouched by the mercenary desires of human society are developments to be mourned.

> McCANDLESS STANDS AS EVIDENCE THAT THERE CONTINUE TO BE REAL READERS WHO INVEST THE ACTIVITIES OF READING AND WRITING WITH GREAT SIGNIFICANCE.

For others, though, McCandless's story is just another example of the foolishness of those who believe more in the power of books than in the power of the natural world. For these readers, McCandless is a stock figure, a suburban rube, a dreamer who neither understood nor respected the very forces he sought to embrace. For these readers, McCandless got what he deserved.

I am interested in McCandless not because of the debate his death has sparked, but because he provides us with an opportunity to consider a reader who differs from Amis's characters in one critical regard: regardless of whether or not Amis himself actually believes that knowledge of the size of the cosmos robs the activities of reading and writing of any lasting meaning, McCandless stands as evidence that there continue to be real readers who invest the activities of reading and writing with great significance. In this respect, McCandless is just the kind of reader that Amis's character Richard Tull (and almost every English teacher) is looking for: a reader who savors the words that others have produced, who seeks guidance from the printed page, who dreams of inhabiting the landscapes that his or her most-admired authors describe in such loving detail. While one could argue that some similar utopian longing is there to be found boiling beneath Amis's bleak account of these information-saturated times, it is much more immediately clear that McCandless actually believed that it was possible to escape the bonds of the corporatized world and reach a space of greater calm. He knew this because his books told him so.

What makes *Into the Wild* remarkable is Krakauer's ability to get some purchase on McCandless's actual reading practice, which, in turn, enables him to get inside McCandless's head and speculate with considerable authority about what ultimately led the young man to abandon the comforts of home and purposefully seek out mortal danger. Krakauer is able to do this, in part, because he has access to the books that McCandless read, with all their underlinings and marginalia, as well as to his journals and the postcards and letters McCandless sent to friends during his journey. Working with these materials and his interviews with McCandless's family and friends, Krakauer develops a sense of McCandless's inner life and eventually comes to some understanding of why the young man was so susceptible to being seduced by the writings of London, Thoreau, Muir, and Tolstoy. Who McCandless is and what becomes of him are, it turns out, intimately connected to the young man's approach to reading — both what he chose to read and how he chose to read it.

After graduating from college, McCandless hopped in his car and headed west, embarking on a journey that, since Kerouac, has become a cliché for the dispossessed male. McCandless told no one where he was going or what his plans were. When his car broke down, he abandoned it and began hitchhiking. He renamed himself "Alexander Supertramp." He kept a journal and took photographs to record his adventure. He traveled to California, canoed down into Mexico, made his way toward Alaska. Along the way, he met people who looked out for him and he, more often than not, would return their kindness by encouraging them to read the books that had so moved him. To one, McCandless wrote: "Wayne, you really should read *War and Peace*. I meant it when I said you had one of the highest characters of any man I'd met. That is a very powerful and highly symbolic book. It has things in it that I think you will understand. Things that escape most people" (Krakauer 33). He took a job working at a flea market selling used paperbacks and lost himself in the pleasure of organizing merchandise and assisting in the very kind of commercial transactions he elsewhere despised. His boss reported: "Alex was big on the classics: Dickens, H. G. Wells, Mark Twain, Jack London. London was his favorite. He'd try to convince every snowbird who walked by that they should read *Call of the Wild*" (43–44). In the abandoned bus where McCandless's body was eventually found, there were books by Tolstoy and Thoreau with highlighted passages celebrating chastity and moral purity (65–66). On some plywood he had written what Krakauer calls McCandless's "declaration of independence":

AND NOW AFTER TWO RAMBLING YEARS COMES THE FINAL AND GREATEST ADVENTURE. THE CLIMACTIC BATTLE TO KILL THE

FALSE BEING WITHIN AND VICTORIOUSLY CONCLUDE THE SPIRI-
TUAL PILGRIMAGE. . . . NO LONGER TO BE POISONED BY CIVILIZA-
TION HE FLEES, AND WALKS ALONE UPON THE LAND TO BECOME
LOST IN THE WILD. (163; capitals and italics in original)

Like most readers, McCandless surrounded himself with books that
reinforced his own beliefs — in this case, texts that confirmed his sense
that he was living honorably by attempting to follow his beliefs *to the letter.* Alternately the evangelist and the pilgrim, McCandless moved through
the world trying to convert others to his point of view and turning away
from anyone who sought to make more intimate contact with him personally. As Alex, he was a hobo, a vagabond, the self-defined "super" tramp,
someone who had neither the need nor the desire for human relationships: his books and his solo adventures satisfied his yearnings for connection. Or, as Krakauer puts it in his summary judgment of McCandless's
motivations: "Unlike Muir and Thoreau, McCandless went into the wilderness not primarily to ponder nature or the world at large but, rather, to
explore the inner country of his own soul" (183).

As much as Krakauer admires McCandless for having embarked
upon such a spiritual journey, he is careful to point out that McCandless
was ultimately undone by the great trust he placed in the written word.
The harshest judgment Krakauer offers in his account emerges in his
discussion of McCandless's way of reading Jack London's stories about life
in Alaska: "He was so enthralled by these tales . . . that he seemed to forget
they were works of fiction, constructions of the imagination that had more
to do with London's romantic sensibilities than with the actualities of life
in the subarctic wilderness. McCandless conveniently overlooked the fact
that London himself had spent just a single winter in the North and that
he'd died by his own hand on his California estate at the age of forty, a
fatuous drunk, obese and pathetic, maintaining a sedentary existence that
bore scant resemblance to the ideals he espoused in print" (44). What
most interests me about Krakauer's critique of London is its vehemence:
Krakauer's rage here is for an author whose life and words don't align.
Because McCandless wanted to believe in the world London invented,
because McCandless wanted to be enchanted, he failed to ask the question that Krakauer believes must be of concern to all readers: namely,
what is the relationship between what the author says and the way the
author lives? London used his writing as a place to store his fantasies
about struggling to survive, about lonely battles against the elements, about
the animal within, fantasies that have trapped and — Krakauer's language
suggests — even killed some of those naive enough to believe them.

While Krakauer faults McCandless for being fooled by London's prose,
he goes to great lengths to defend McCandless against charges of reck-
lessness or incompetence. It is true, Krakauer concedes, that McCandless
could have taken any number of actions to avoid dying in the woods. The
young man could have taken a map with him; he could have done a better
job exploring the banks of the suddenly uncrossable river that prevented

him from returning by the route he came in on; he could even have started a forest fire to alert the authorities to his plight. But for those who see McCandless's death by starvation as irrefutable proof of his failure as an outdoorsman, Krakauer has another explanation: McCandless died in the woods not because he couldn't find enough food to survive, but because he ate seeds that no one knew to be poisonous. Relying on *Tanaina Plantlore* to guide his gatherings in the wild, McCandless trusted its author completely. As he grew weaker and as game grew scarcer, McCandless began to eat the roots of a species of wild potato that the book identified as nontoxic. The book said nothing about the seeds of the wild potato and it is Krakauer's hypothesis that, as he grew more desperate, McCandless took the book's silence on the seeds as permission to ingest them. If Krakauer is right, one could say that McCandless was killed off by a reading practice that placed too much faith in books, a practice that forgets that the world in all its infinite complexity and particularity will always exceed the explanatory grasp of any single text and, indeed, of all texts taken in their totality.

Whenever I've taught this book — and I've used it with first-year students, undergraduate literature majors, and advanced graduate students — the issue of trust inevitably arises as a problem. Why accept Krakauer's account when he is so obviously invested in defending McCandless from his critics? The fact that Krakauer is so openly identified with the subject of his research is a sign, I would say, that he is producing a kind of writing that can and should still matter. Because Krakauer has inhabited the same clichés that captured McCandless, because he understands their pull from the inside, he is able to offer an account of the young man's motivations that is simultaneously sympathetic *and* critical. By working on the materials of McCandless's life, Krakauer learns how to do what McCandless was unable or unwilling to do: he comes to understand and respect the thoughts of those who were appalled by his behavior. He is doing the work of making peace with his past. Thus, although Krakauer claims he is just trying to make sense of "why some people seem to despise [McCandless] so intensely for having died" in the Alaskan wilds, the truth is that Krakauer is equally interested in using McCandless as a vehicle for making sense of his own turbulent, and occasionally self-destructive, youth. As it turns out, McCandless and Krakauer had much in common. They read and were moved by many of the same authors; they fell in love, like many lonely, alienated, introspective young men before them, with a stark, unforgiving beauty that they could only find in books and in the natural world; and, finally, when the time was right, they both ran away from a world that did not live up to their expectations.

From a certain vantage point, McCandless's Alaskan odyssey and Krakauer's harrowing attempt to climb the Devils Thumb are clichés of modernity: they are the stories of young men, fed up with society, determined to get away from it all. (One version of this cliché involves heading off into the wild; a more recent version, as we've seen, involves entering the schoolyard armed to the teeth.) Now that he has safely made the passage into middle age, Krakauer can see that there's nothing particularly original about embarking on such a journey and he is reluctant to require that such adventures be treated either with reverence or with scorn. On his own journey, Krakauer discovered just how fleeting the profound and transformative experience of scaling a mountain peak can be. Less than a month after realizing his dream, he found himself back in Colorado, pounding nails into frames for townhouses. Over the years that followed, Krakauer came to a different realization: "I was a raw youth who mistook passion for insight and acted according to an obscure, gap-ridden logic. I thought climbing the Devils Thumb would fix all that was wrong with my life. In the end, of course, it changed almost nothing" (155).

Since Krakauer and McCandless moved through the same experiential world for a time, Krakauer seems to know, intuitively, where to look to find a final explanation for McCandless's aberrant behavior. Why would a young man with so much going for him throw it all away? Unlike Amis, Krakauer cannot accept a world without motive, so he continues to probe until he discovers what he believes to be the series of events that alienated McCandless from his family and friends. The ultimate cause of McCandless's disaffection, it would appear, was that his father had conducted an extended affair when McCandless was a small child. Years later, unbeknownst to his parents, McCandless found out about his father's double life and confided in his sister that this discovery made his "entire childhood seem like a fiction" (121–23). To some, it will seem that in uncovering this information, Krakauer has simply succeeded in moving McCandless from one familiar narrative to another, finding at the heart of his desire to escape nothing more than another primordial example of the Oedipal struggle. However accurate such an assessment might be, I would argue that the true significance of Krakauer's discovery lies elsewhere. Having learned this dark family secret, Krakauer is able to provide us with a glimpse of how McCandless responded when confronted with a reality quite unlike the one contained in the books he had chosen to surround himself with. With his childhood transformed into a fiction, McCandless understood himself to have received a warrant to embark on a new life. He believed he was alone. He believed he owed no one anything. He believed he was free.

ON MEDITATIVE WRITING AND ITS CONSEQUENCES

Several years have now passed since I first realized how numerous were the false opinions that in my youth I had taken to be true, and thus how doubtful were all those that I had subsequently built upon them. And thus I realized that once in my life I had to raze everything to the ground and begin again from the original foundations, if I wanted to establish anything firm and lasting in the sciences.

— RENÉ DESCARTES, *Meditations on First Philosophy*

All these unhappy men, the betrayed and the betrayers, the real and the fictional. Is there any hope for them? Or for the wasted worlds they've left in their wake? Thinking about these lives, so deeply entangled with violence, neglect, and lies; watching the news, which is forever reporting that another angry man has entered some building or schoolyard, guns blazing; feeling the weight of these stories, and knowing their inevitable movement towards death, destruction, and humiliation: such thoughts only serve to plunge one deeper into the darkness. Amis's fiction clearly offers no escape from such ruminations. And Krakauer's real-life account confirms the fact that relying on reading as a mode of escape has its own unique set of dangers. Against the backdrop of Columbine (or Kosovo or Rwanda or September 11 or Afghanistan or Iraq — the news never fails to offer up another example), there is little these authors can do. The senseless loss of life always trumps the efforts of the meaning makers. Why bother with reading and writing when the world is so obviously going to hell?

One could say that the course of Western philosophy was forever altered by an encounter with a differently phrased version of this question. When Descartes reached that point in his life when he felt that nothing he had been told in the past could be trusted, he, too, sealed himself off from the rest of society and contemplated the dark possibility that he might be doomed to live out the rest of his days in a dream world. This, at any rate, is the opening conceit of his *Meditations on First Philosophy*. To rid himself of all the false opinions that he had been fed in his youth, Descartes tells us that he waited until he had both the maturity and the free time necessary to devote to the harrowing task of self-purification. In his mid-forties, he sits by the fire, in his dressing gown, all alone. He is transported by the idea that he can attack his past and demolish it. He, too, wants to be free. And so Descartes settles down to the task of dismantling and reassembling his cosmology, a process that takes him six days to complete.[7]

> **WHY BOTHER WITH READING AND WRITING WHEN THE WORLD IS SO OBVIOUSLY GOING TO HELL?**

On the first day of his meditations, everything collapses under the force of Descartes' determined skepticism. There is nothing Descartes has ever thought or felt that cannot also be doubted. Since everything that comes to him through his senses is misleading, he finds it impossible to distinguish dream states from states of consciousness. He even imagines the possibility that there might well be "an evil genius, supremely powerful and clever" who whiles away his time deceiving him at every turn (62). While the first act of the God of Genesis is to separate light from darkness, Descartes' accomplishment, on his first day, is to plunge his readers into the pitch of night. In the inverted world he has created with his skepticism, one dreams in the light and fears waking to toil "among the inextricable shadows of the difficulties" that have been produced by the workings of his mind (63).

On the second day, Descartes sets out to inhabit the world of doubt he has created: "I suppose that everything I see is false. I believe that none of what my deceitful memory represents ever existed" (63). Shorn of his past, of his body with all its misleading signals and vague impressions, Descartes discovers his true essence: he is first and foremost a "thing that thinks" (*une chose qui pense*) (65). And as a "thing that thinks," he determines that the senses are not to be trusted: in the midst of this meditation, Descartes looks out the window and believes he sees men walking by on the street. "[Y]et," Descartes asks,"but what do I see aside from hats and coats, which could conceal automata?" (68). To get to the essence of any thing, be it a man or a piece of wax, we must strip "it of its clothing" and "look at [it] in its nakedness" (68): we must remove all outward appearances and get to that which does not change.

On the third day, having shut his eyes, stopped up his ears, withdrawn all his senses, and abandoned his past, Descartes surveys the world of his creation and determines that he is alone. The only way out of this bleak environment that is haunted by malicious demons and the illusory reports of the senses is to posit the existence of a firm foundation, which, for reasons we'll discuss shortly, Descartes designates "God." Descartes' "proof" or "discovery" of God's existence is well known: God is the perfection that Descartes can conceive of but does not actually possess in his thoughts. Since Descartes' thoughts cannot be the cause of this state of perfection (because "what is more perfect [that is, what contains in itself more reality] cannot come into being from what is less perfect"), this perfection must exist outside of him (73). From this, "it necessarily follows that I am not alone in the world, but that something else, which is the cause of this idea, also exists" (74).

Alone with his God in the fourth meditation, Descartes turns his thoughts to an issue that has been at the center of our current discussion: how to distinguish between truth and falsity. For Descartes, the crucial task before him is to explain how God, who is perfect, could have created a thinking thing so defective that it struggles to distinguish fact from fiction, truth from lies. Setting to the side the question of *why* his creator elected to design him in this way, Descartes posits that his own errors result from the fact that he has been endowed by his creator with a will that has a much wider scope than his intellect. On the fifth and sixth days of his meditations, in a repetition that bespeaks a certain anxiety, Descartes once again proves the existence of God and then, after some deft negotiations, is returned to his body and the sensuous world. Before resting, Descartes looks back on where his thinking has taken him and concludes that "the hyperbolic doubts of the last few days ought to be rejected as ludicrous" (103). By doubting everything, he has found the firm ground that is necessary for going on: there is a God; everything that happens is not a lie; the mind can provide us with direct access to the truth. Descartes, it would appear, is home free.

Why should the thoughts this lonely man had more than 350 years ago warrant our attention now? Descartes contributed to the larger effort to liberate reason from the prison of religious dogma and he did this, in part, by driving a wedge between the mind, which traffics in clear and distinct ideas, and the body, which transmits and receives the innately imperfect data of the senses. Fearful of how his thoughts might be received at the time, Descartes had his meditations published first in Latin in Paris and only later allowed them to be translated into French and reprinted in Holland where he was staying. He also placed at the front of his meditations an open letter "to the Most Wise and Distinguished Men, the Dean and Doctors of the Faculty of Sacred Theology of Paris," explaining his reasons for seeking to make public the transcripts, as it were, of his own encounter with the darkness. For those readers prone to skipping such front matter and jumping straight to the body of the text, it will probably come as something of a surprise to learn that Descartes' meditations, which seem like such an earnest attempt to find some solid bedrock upon which to build a life free of falsehoods, are actually a ruse. As Descartes makes clear in his letter to the faculty, he never really had any doubts at all about God or the eternal life of the soul: he's simply trying to put together an argument that will persuade the "unbelievers" (*infidèles*) of what he and his fellow believers "believe by faith" (47). So, the darkness, the radical doubt, the mind floating free of the body are all just props to add to the drama of the fiction he's created — ways of getting those outside the circle of believers to share in his illusion.

That's one way to read Descartes' opening remarks to the Faculty of Sacred Theology. There is, however, yet another possibility. (There always is.) Maybe the letter to the deans and doctors is the sham, just Descartes whispering sweet nothings to those in power in hopes of securing a protected space where he can carry out his scientific research without threat of being harassed. And, given that Descartes is so good at creating the illusion of compliance, what can the illustrious deans and faculty do? He's poured it on so thick — he's just doing what any fellow believer would do, contributing to the cause, etc. — that they just have to get out of the way. If the God that emerges from Descartes' meditations is one more likely to be found residing in the theorems of analytical geometry than in the sanctuaries of the Vatican, what's the harm? That's how advertising works: it's just food for the infidels. It poses no threat to the believers, for what true believer would doubt the existence of God or that the soul separates from the body at death?

There's no resolving the question of whether or not Descartes was being completely sincere when he wrote to the deans and doctors of the Faculty of Sacred Theology in Paris seeking their protection. All we can know is that he had good reason to fear their powers and the institution they represented. For our purposes, what matters most is pausing to take note of the intellectual regime that has risen in the wake of Descartes' effort to break free of dogmatic belief by locating the self at the nexus of reason and the will. To resolve his crisis in certainty and construct a working space that is not contaminated by the lies of the past, Descartes established an internal hierarchy that gives primacy to the mind and its universal truths — truths that, like the properties of a triangle, are clear, distinct, and without a history. The body and its voyage through time are without interest: nothing is to be gained by exploring what happens to the body as it moves through the social institutions that govern life. These are just accidents of time and place. The mind is where the action is.

Whether Descartes himself learned anything as a result of writing down these meditations isn't clear. We know only that Descartes' meditations were designed to provide their author with a method for protecting himself from being deceived by the world and its denizens. Encased in this regulatory mechanism, Descartes is, I believe, more alone at the end of his meditations than when he started. For now that he has rid himself of his fictions and screwed himself into the real, he has no need to consider these fundamental matters any further: "I will say in addition that these arguments are such that I believe there is no way open to the human mind whereby better ones could ever be found" (48). True to this claim, Descartes spends much of the rest of his life defending the veracity of his proofs and the cogency of his line of reasoning. He wanders off into the dreamy world of argumentation.

JOINING THE LIARS' CLUB: WRITING AND THE GENERATION OF HOPE

I never knew despair could lie.

— MARY KARR, *The Liars' Club*

It's safe to say that the spirit of our time differs markedly from the spirit of Descartes' time. While he wrote to banish the particular and to revel in the universal, now that we inhabit the age of the memoir, we find ourselves surrounded by those who write to distinguish themselves from the crowd by capturing the deep particularity and pathos of their own past experiences. Frank McCourt describes the grueling poverty of the Irish immigrant; former Princeton professor Michael Ryan records having sex with his dog; Kathryn Harrison, sex with her father; David Denby, sex with himself (while reading the Great Books no less); James McBride, what it's like to grow up black while having a white mother; Susanna Kaysen, what it's like to be institutionalized. The list goes on and on, because every shoe salesman and waitress, every schoolteacher and cop, every politician and pundit has a story to tell and wants to share it now via the Internet, on some television talk show, or on the printed page. The chosen media doesn't seem to matter. The stories will out.

While there has been much fretting in the critical community about this "turn to the personal" and all that it may be said to signify, the memoirs just keep coming, flooding over the outstretched arms of all those who would like to contain the spread of this genre. That the memoirs, in general, return to scenes of violence and violation is worth pondering, for here one finds evidence of one way in which writing continues to matter at the current moment: the memoir allows one to plunge into the darkness of the past; it provides the means both for evoking and for making sense of that past; and it can be made to generate a sense of possibility, a sense that a better, brighter future is out there to be secured. When judged by these criteria, Mary Karr's *The Liars' Club* stands out as one of the most remarkable representatives of the genre.

The Liars' Club opens with fragments of a recovered memory, "a single instant surrounded by dark": Karr, at seven years old, being inspected by her family doctor; the Sheriff and his deputies moving through her house; the backyard on fire; her mother being taken away; the concerted effort to find a place for the children to stay (3). One of the central projects of *The Liars' Club* is to make sense of these fragments, to relocate them in a more coherent, more comprehensive account of Karr's past. What happened that night? Why did no one ever speak of it again? To answer these questions, Karr has to wade through the faulty, inexact evidence that her family — which is its own liars' club — makes available to her and then find a way to tell not only her story, but also the stories of Pete Karr, her father, Charlie Marie Moore Karr, her mother, and Lecia, her sister.

By the middle of Karr's memoir, she has succeeded in finding out what led to the appearance of the police and the firemen in her house. She eventually remembers being with her sister, hiding in the dark, their mother in the bedroom doorway holding a knife and then, moments later, her mother in the hallway calling the police, saying, "Get over here. I just killed them both. Both of them. I've stabbed them both to death" (157). But to get to this moment, Karr must first detail: life among the working poor in Leechfield, Texas; the odd union of her father, an oil worker, and her mother, a highly educated woman with artistic aspirations; her parents' spiral into alcoholism, the violent fights, the long separations; the slow, agonizingly painful death of the grandmother; her own rape by a neighborhood boy. She is participating in a form of revelation, a ritual of purging and purification. She is telling the family secrets, pulling the ghosts out of the closets, waking the dead, and she does so with no overt sign of shame.

At one point, in retaliation for a beating she received in a fight with the boys who lived next door, Karr credits herself with going on "a rampage that prefigured what Charles Whitman — the guy who shot and killed thirteen people from the tower at the University of Texas — would do a few years later" (161). She got a BB gun, climbed a tree, and waited for her victims to walk out into a nearby field. And when the enemy clan appeared, Karr opened fire, hitting one of the children in the neck before the family fled out of range. When one of the boys hid behind his father, Karr reports that her response was as follows: "*You pussy*, I thought, as if Rickey's not wanting to get shot were a defining mark against his manhood" (162). For this activity, Karr received a whipping. She notes, as well, that her "morning as sniper won [her] a grudging respect. Kids stopped mouthing off about Mother" (162). Violence silenced her tormenters and it kept the enemies at bay. Within the psychic economy of the world Karr inhabited at the time, this doubtless seemed the only rational response available to her.

Eventually, Karr recovers the psychically charged world surrounding her memory of that dark night. Trapped in a life she never wanted serving as a "hausfrau" to an oilman in a "crackerbox house," surrounded by people she despised, Charlie Marie Karr tried to set her world on fire. She burned down her studio. She made a bonfire of her paintings, the children's toys, their books, their furniture, their clothes, their shoes.

As Mary and her sister mutely look on, they are transformed by the experience: they are ready to be led into the fire themselves. "We are in the grip of some big machine grinding us along. The force of it simplifies everything. A weird calm has settled over me from the inside out. What is about to happen to us has stood in line to happen. All the roads out of that instant have been closed, one by one" (152).

They are doomed.

No neighbor intervenes to stop what is happening. No one calls the police. The children don't run away to save themselves. The father doesn't appear to rescue them. The mother is not restrained by some maternal instinct. On the familial level, this is the apocalypse: this is a time without hope. And yet, for reasons that are never explained and perhaps never can be, Charlie Marie doesn't actually go through with murdering her children. She only thinks she has. The disaster passes. The mother is institutionalized. Mary takes her BB gun into the tree. And eventually Charlie Marie comes back home.

From a certain vantage point, this would appear to be the logical place for Karr to end her meditation. She's cast light into her memory of that dark night in the bedroom and now knows what happened. Why keep *The Liars' Club* going for another two hundred pages? What else is there to know? The story continues, I would argue, for two interrelated reasons. First, Karr only knows the *how* and the *what* regarding that night; she does not know *why* her mother went over the edge. Second, Karr's writing has not yet delivered her from those memories because she knows only the facts, not the truth of what happened. At the age of seven, thinking magically, she understood only that her mother had tried to kill her for failing to clean up her room. By the middle of the book, she recognizes the inadequacy of such an explanation. Without the *why* she has nothing, just information coming in the dead of night.

Pursuing the question of motivation takes Karr into still darker waters. After her mother's psychotic episode, her parents move to Colorado and eventually divorce. Her mother remarries and sinks deeper into a drunken stupor. Karr walks in on her mother having sex with another man; Karr is raped again; Charlie Marie tries to kill her new husband, buys a bar, stays up late reading French philosophy and "talking in a misty-eyed way about suicide" (230). Eventually, Charlie Marie puts the girls on a plane back to their father, but it's the wrong plane and they end up flying to Mexico. The calamities continue without ever exposing the cause of all this senseless, self-destructive behavior. Why is it that no one seeks help? What is it that fuels Charlie Marie's all-encompassing sense of despair? Why is it that Pete Karr seeks refuge with the other members of "the Liars' Club," a group of men who drink together and tell tall tales that keep their pasts shrouded in darkness?

When Karr finally finds the key that unlocks the mystery of her family's past, it is long after she has grown up and moved away. Her parents have reunited. She has watched her father's steady decline after a stroke, sat by his side during his final days, listened to him ramble on about his life in the war, a time he never before mentioned. She discovers that he was wounded twice, one time stuck with "a bayonet through his forearm, leaving a scar [she'd] seen a thousand times and never once asked about" (307), the other time left for dead under the rubble of a bridge he'd helped to explode. This last news sends Karr up to the family attic in search of military papers that might be used to get her father additional medical assistance. While moving amongst the family's remains, she discovers four jewelry boxes, each containing a wedding ring. She has, quite unexpectedly, found her mother's hidden past and she then finds the strength to use this material evidence to compel her mother to speak. As Karr confronts her ever-reticent mother, she observes: "Few born liars ever intentionally embark in truth's direction, even those who believe that such a journey might axiomatically set them free" (311).

Karr uncovers the systemic violence that defined her mother's past — the sudden, inexplicable disappearance of her first husband and her first two children, the years she spent trying to find her first family, the reunion where she was convinced to leave the children with their father and return to her studio apartment in Texas — and as she does so the fragmented pieces of her own life begin to fall into place. In the end, the mystery is not so mysterious: "Those were my mother's demons, then, two small children, whom she longed for and felt ashamed for having lost." The explanation for Charlie Marie's years of silence about her past is both simple and profound. She tells her daughter that she kept these events a secret because she was afraid that, if Mary knew, she "wouldn't like [her] anymore" (318).

It would be easy to ridicule such an explanation. After all, Charlie Marie has done much in her life that her daughter did know about that would have justified rejection. She neglected her children, placed them in harm's way, tried to kill herself, tried to kill them. Karr herself finds her mother's reasoning to be "pathetic" (318). However one judges Charlie Marie's excuse, though, the fact that she cannot produce a satisfying or reasonable account for her silence is compelling evidence of just how much power stories *can* exercise over the lives of individuals. By clinging to her silence, by keeping her story trapped inside, she invested her untold story with such a monstrous power that she came to believe that speaking it aloud would make her essentially unlikable. Left alone with this story, Charlie Marie transformed a series of events where she was outmatched, unprepared, and cruelly victimized into irrefutable proof of her own unworthiness as a mother. Without some other connection to the world, without some other voice to counter her interpretations, Charlie Marie was left to suffer her own perpetually punishing judgments. Within this psychic economy, the only possible way for Charlie Marie to remain likable was to keep her story a secret. To remain likable, she had to lie.

The revelation of Charlie Marie's story did not produce the anticipated effect, though.

As Karr puts it: "what Mother told absolved us both, in a way. All the black crimes we believed ourselves guilty of were myths, stories we'd cobbled together out of fear. We expected no good news interspersed with the bad. Only the dark aspect of any story sank in. I never knew despair could lie." As the book ends, Karr escapes the darkness that has defined her past and contemplates "the cool tunnel of white light the spirit might fly into at death." Acknowledging that this description of what it's like to die may simply be an account of "death's neurological fireworks, the brain's last light show," Karr insists that this is a lie she can live with. She is content to at least entertain the possibility of a future communion with her loved ones, a time when "all your beloveds hover before you, their lit arms held out in welcome" (320).

In Karr's hands, the memoir thus becomes a vehicle for arriving at an understanding that produces forgiveness. Writing, as she uses it, is a hermeneutic practice that involves witnessing the mundane horrors of the past in order to make peace with that past. And, as the preceding account makes clear, it also becomes, however briefly, a means for gaining access to the light of the universal. While the other writers and events I've discussed here have turned our attention to death and decay, Karr offers an encounter with the prospect of one's mortality that leads neither to despair nor cynicism nor violence nor suicide nor escape. Even if it's a lie, the lie Karr tells herself at the end of *The Liars' Club* is a lie that keeps her inside the realm of social relations, helping her make what she can of what life has put before her.

AN EXPERIMENT IN INSTITUTIONAL AUTOBIOGRAPHY

It might seem that, by organizing these readings in this way, I've been building up to a spirited defense of the social and therapeutic value of writing one's memoirs. After all, this kind of writing worked for Karr, why shouldn't it work for us all? But the genre of the memoir is no more likely to compel a writer to make peace with the past or to find some sense of connection with others than is poetry, fiction, the meditative essay, the policy statement, the well-honed critique, the bulleted memo, the forced confession, the suicide note. When Martin Amis composed his memoirs, for instance, the genre didn't force him to shift his world view: he ends *Experience* with atrocity, Auschwitz, ruminations on the murder of one of his cousins, and "the usual articles of faith for a man of fifty . . . : that the parents are going, the children are staying, and I am somewhere in between" (371). When Eric Harris began his diary with the statement, "I hate the fucking world," he wasn't laying the groundwork for a transformative inner voyage; he was girding himself for battle.

If we accept Amis's bleak view of the future of publishing — and I think we should — then the challenge, for all whose lives are inextricably bound to the literate arts, is to make a compelling case for why writing might be said to matter in the twenty-first century. Amis taking the long view, Alex Supertramp running into the wild, Descartes alone with his thoughts: it is clear that these men knew that writing could be used to articulate and extend one's sense of despair and one's sense of superiority. What isn't clear, though, is whether these men knew what Karr knows — namely, how to use writing as a practice for constructing a sense of hope and optimism atop the ruins of previous worlds. Is it possible to produce writing that generates a greater sense of connection to the world and its inhabitants? Of self-understanding? Writing that moves out from the mundane, personal tragedies that mark any individual life into the history, the culture, and the lives of the institutions that surround us all?

In working my way up to this set of questions, I have unexpectedly found myself relying on words and phrases that immediately produce religious connotations: the dark night of the soul, the generation of hope, the power of forgiveness. While I did not set out to consider religious matters, the language I've fallen into using has inevitably led me to a set of concerns that tends to be avoided by those who share my secular sensibilities. Under normal circumstances, I might find other, less volatile terms. But these aren't normal circumstances. There will never again be a book that can credibly be labeled "great," not because outstanding books are no longer being produced, but because the world is now awash with writing that no one reads, with last year's blockbusters ending up in the dump next to this year's most insightful critiques. If one is in search of fame or truth and one has placed all one's hopes on the activity of writing, this fact can be a devastating blow. But, however painful it may be to admit, it is clear that those of us who remain committed to books are part of a residual culture whose days are numbered. The fetishization of the written word is coming to an end and in its place one finds a fascination with moving what is known from here to there in the shortest amount of time and with the elusive pleasures of religious conviction. One finds as well a haunting sense of disconnection, as one tightly wound individual after another hatches a plot to make others pay for these ambient feelings of placelessness. The world as we have known it is passing away and the world that is emerging is one that appears to be fraught with danger.

> **IS IT POSSIBLE TO PRODUCE WRITING THAT GENERATES A GREATER SENSE OF CONNECTION TO THE WORLD AND ITS INHABITANTS? OF SELF-UNDERSTANDING?**

What to do? These concerns about the diminishing power of reading and writing serve as the launching point for a sustained investigation into the value of humanistic inquiry at the present moment. In fashioning the oxymoronic phrase "institutional autobiography" to describe the collection of meditations that follows,[8] I mean to highlight a brand of intellectual inquiry that is centrally concerned with what might best be termed "the felt experience of the impersonal." The course of any given individual life cuts through or around a set of institutions charged with responsibility for nurturing both a sense of self and a sense of connection between self and society — the family, the school, and, for some, the church or the house of worship. It goes without saying that the relative influence each of these institutions has on any given individual depends on a number of variables, including race, class, and gender. By linking the institutional with the autobiographical, my goal is not to draw attention away from our individual differences, but rather to show that we all internalize institutional influences in ways that are both idiosyncratic and historically situated, open-ended and overdetermined, liberating and confining. We all go to school, bringing both our minds and our embodied histories: what happens there is both utterly predictable and utterly mysterious, the circumscribed movement of a statistical norm and the free flight of aberrant data.

Historically, schooling in the United States has served as the battleground where the nation works out its evolving understanding of social justice — through, for example, busing, affirmative action, the student loan program, the multicultural curriculum. What has changed recently, though, is the power of weaponry that students bring to the schoolyard and the magnitude of the notoriety that accrues to those who show up ready for a fight. The police investigating the actions of Harris and Klebold concluded that the two young men were driven, above all, by a desire for fame: "[A]ll the rest of the justifications are just smoke. They certainly wanted the media to write stories about them every day. And they wanted cult followings. They [were] going to become superstars by getting rid of bad people" (Cullen, "Kill Mankind"). We might say that Harris and Klebold wanted what all writers are said to want, what Richard Tull and Alexander Supertramp dreamed of and what Gwyn Barry, Amis, Krakauer, Descartes, and Karr have all, to varying degrees, achieved. The costs of such fame are quite high and the benefits fleeting at best.

Can secular institutions of higher education be taught to use writing to foster a kind of critical optimism that is able to transform idle feelings of hope into viable plans for sustainable action? Can the first year writing course become a place where we engage productively with the dark realities of our time: violence, suicide, war, and terrorism, as well as fraudulence, complicity, and trauma? Can teachers of first year writing be moved beyond praising students for generating arguments without consequence, thought with no interest in action? If there is to be lasting hope for the future of higher education, that hope can only be generated by confronting our desolate world and its threatening, urgent realities. The only way out is through.

NOTES

[1] The boys' larger plans were laid out in Harris's diary, in which he fantasized about going to an island after the massacre or, "if there isn't such a place," he wrote, "then we will hijack a hell of a lot of bombs and crash a plane into NYC with us inside [f]iring away as we go down." Eric Harris, personal diary. For a discussion of inaccuracies in the initial characterization of the boys' interests and beliefs, see Cullen, "Inside." [All notes are Miller's, unless indicated by Eds.]

[2] Michael Moore's *Bowling for Columbine* rebuts these familiar explanations for the massacre in Littleton and makes the compelling argument that it is a culture of fear, particularly fear of the racialized other, that is the source of America's violent ways.

[3] Harris, personal diary. "V" is short for "Vodka," Harris's code name for Dylan Klebold. For more on the contents of Harris's diary, see Cullen, "Kill Mankind," and Prendergast.

[4] Harris, who was in the final semester of his senior year, had been rejected from a number of colleges in the weeks prior to carrying out the attack on Columbine. And, just before the attack, he had been rejected by the Marine Corps, apparently because he was taking the antidepressant Luvox. Although both Harris and Klebold were considered by their peers to be "brilliant, particularly in math and computers," it was Klebold who seemed to have had everything going for him: unlike Harris, he had had a date for the senior prom and he had just returned from a trip with his parents to visit the University of Arizona, where he had been admitted for the following fall (Pooley 28). Whatever their shared experiences moving through the school system and the juvenile penal system had been, it was clear to both that their paths would begin to diverge radically after graduation.

[5] Kate Battan, lead investigator of the Columbine shootings, is quoted as having said, as she completed her report: "Everybody wants a quick answer. They want an easy answer so that they can sleep at night and know this is not going to happen tomorrow at their school. And there is no such thing in this case. There's not an easy answer. I've been working on this nonstop daily [for six months] since April 20th and I can't tell you why it happened" (qtd. in Cullen, "Inside").

[6] Amis does, in fact, share much in common with his successful character: he thrives on publicity; he made a name for himself early on as a modern Lothario, and his insistence during contract negotiations for *The Information* on receiving the largest advance ever given in Britain for a literary novel earned him the enmity of much of the literary community (Lyall C13).

[7] Descartes was trained by the Jesuits, the religious order founded by Ignatius Loyola who became a committed Christian after a transformative experience reading *The Life of Christ*. Part of the training Descartes received involved going on a series of retreats where initiates meditated on passages from Scripture in the hope that this practice would help them to achieve a deeper understanding of the text and a more loving response to the world. That Descartes returned to the meditational form later in life is evidence of its lasting pedagogical value.

[8] Miller refers to the chapters in *Writing at the End of the World* that follow this one, essays of a similar method. These chapters, some of which draw on his own experience, are not included in this selection. [Eds.]

BIBLIOGRAPHY

Amis, Martin. *Experience: A Memoir*. New York: Hyperion, 2000.

——. *The Information*. New York: Harmony, 1995.

Barron, James. "Warnings from a Student Turned Killer." *New York Times*, May 1, 1999: A12.

Bowling for Columbine. Dir. Michael Moore. United Artists, 2002.

Cullen, Dave. "Inside the Columbine High Investigation." *Salon.com*, Sept. 23, 1999. Feb. 22, 2003 <http://www.salon.com/news/feature/1999/09/23/columbine>.

——. "Kill Mankind. No One Should Survive." *Salon.com*, Sept. 23, 1999. Feb. 19, 2003 <http://www.salon.com/news/feature/1999/09/23/journal>.

Denby, David. *Great Books: My Adventures with Homer, Rousseau, Woolf, and Other Indestructible Writers of the Western World*. New York: Simon, 1996.

Descartes, René. *Discourse on Method and Meditations on First Philosophy*. Trans. Donald A. Cress. 4th ed. Indianapolis: Hackett, 1998.

Gross, Jane. "Out of the House, but Still Focused on Family." *New York Times*, Apr. 29, 1999: B2.

Harris, Eric. Personal diary (excerpts). *Westword.com*, Dec. 12, 2002 <http://www.westword.com/special_reports/columbine/files/index_html>.

Harrison, Kathryn. *The Kiss*. New York: Bard, 1996.

Karr, Mary. *The Liars' Club*. New York: Viking, 1995.

Kaysen, Susanna. *Girl, Interrupted*. New York: Vintage, 1994.

Krakauer, Jon. *Into the Wild*. New York: Villard, 1996.

Lyall, Sarah. "Martin Amis's Big Deal Leaves Literati Fuming." *New York Times*, Jan. 31, 1995: C13.

McBride, James. *The Color of Water: A Black Man's Tribute to His White Mother*. New York: Riverhead, 1996.

McCourt, Frank. *Angela's Ashes: A Memoir*. New York: Scribner, 1996.

Pooley, Eric. "Portrait of a Deadly Bond." *Time*, May 10, 1999: 26–32.

Prendergast, Alan. "I'm Full of Hate and I Love It." *Denver Westword*, Dec. 6, 2001. Feb. 25, 2003 <http://www.westword.com/issues/2001-12-06/news.html/l/index.html>.

Ryan, Michael. *Secret Life: An Autobiography*. New York: Vintage, 1996.

QUESTIONS FOR A SECOND READING

1. "The Dark Night of the Soul" is the first chapter in Miller's book *Writing at the End of the World*. The chapter, which we are inviting you to read as an essay, is organized by subheadings. You might think of these as a way of *punctuating* the essay, and you might think of this technique as a tool for your own toolkit.

   As you reread the essay, pay attention to each unit marked off by a sub-heading, and pay attention to the progression or arrangement of these units. How might they mark stages or strategies for the writer? for the reader? (Are they big paragraphs, for example, or mini-essays, or stanzas, or something else?) How might you describe the principle of selection and organization? Can you imagine bringing this strategy into your own writing?

2. In the final chapter of *Writing at the End of the World*, Miller says the following about his own writing:

   > While the assessments, evaluations, proposals, reports, commentaries, and critiques I produce help to keep the bureaucracy of higher education going, there is another kind of writing I turn to in order to sustain the ongoing search for meaning in a world no one controls. This writing asks the reader to make imaginative connections between disparate elements; it tracks one path among many possible ones across the glistening water. (p. 196)

   We can assume that this is the kind of writing present in "The Dark Night of the Soul." And he says this about English and the humanities:

   > The practice of the humanities ... is not about admiration or greatness or appreciation or depth of knowledge or scholarly achievement; it's about the movement between worlds, arms out, balancing; it's about making the connections that count. (p. 198)

   This latter is a pretty bold statement, since English departments have traditionally defined their job as teaching students to read deeply, to conduct scholarly research, and to appreciate great works of literature. What Miller has to offer, rather, is "movement between worlds, arms out, balancing" or "making the connections that count."

   As you reread "The Dark Night of the Soul," be prepared to talk about connections — about the connections Miller makes, about the ways he makes them, and about the ways you as a reader are (or are not) invited into this process. Is Miller's description of his project, as represented above, accurate or sufficient? If what is represented in Miller's writing can suggest a goal for a curriculum or an imperative for English instruction in high schools and in colleges, what changes would need to be made? What would a course look like? What would its students do? Would you want to take such a course?

3. For the sake of argument, let's say that Jon Krakauer and Mary Karr are the key figures in this essay — Krakauer as a reader, Karr as a writer. As you reread, pay particular attention to these two sections. What are the appropriate

goals and methods for reading, if Krakauer is to serve as a model? What are the appropriate goals and methods for writing, if Karr is to serve as a model? And do you agree with the initial assumption, that Krakauer and Karr are the key figures in this essay?

For further research: Two chapters in *Writing at the End of the World* are, at least in part, autobiographical. In them Miller writes about his own family, and the story he tells is a difficult one. You could read these chapters to add a third key figure to this mix — Miller himself. Does Miller read Karr as an exemplary figure? With this example in mind, how do you read Miller? How might you place his writing in relation to hers?

4. Miller introduces two phrases in the final paragraphs of "The Dark Night of the Soul": "the felt experience of the impersonal" and "critical optimism." He introduces these to set up key terms a reader can use in reading the chapters that follow in his book. You don't have these chapters to refer to. Still, the chapter that you read should serve as suitable preparation for you to make sense of these terms. As you reread "The Dark Night of the Soul," keep these key terms in mind. And be prepared to write one-paragraph definitions of each. What do they mean for Miller? What do they mean in relation to the work he does in "The Dark Night of the Soul"? Each paragraph should include a reference (with a block quotation) to one of Miller's examples.

5. Miller has recently turned his attention to multimedia composition in digital environments, both in his own writing and as a necessary next step for the teaching of English. You can access an example of this work by searching online for the video "This Is How We Dream, Parts 1 and 2." Watch this video presentation, and as you reread, take the notes you will need to be prepared to talk about new media in relation to the concerns expressed in "The Dark Night of the Soul."

. . . ● . . .

ASSIGNMENTS FOR WRITING

1. Miller's essay opens with a list of fatal shootings in schools — troublingly, an incomplete list. As the essay builds to questions — questions for educators and for students — the specters of violence and alienation remain, changing how we think about the reading and writing school endeavors to teach us. "I have these doubts, you see," Miller writes of academic work, "doubts silently shared by many who spend their days teaching others the literate arts. Aside from gathering and organizing information, aside from generating critiques and analyses that forever fall on deaf ears, what might the literate arts be said to be good for?" (p. 439).

Write an essay that takes up this question — "what might the literate arts be good for?" — and that takes it up from your range of reference and from your point of view — or, more properly, from the point of view of you and people like you, the group you feel prepared to speak for. As an exercise in understanding, your essay should be modeled on one (or more) of the sections in "The Dark Night of the Soul." You can choose the text — and the text can be anything that might serve as an example of the literate arts, things in print but also including songs, films, and TV shows. But your presentation and discussion of the text should be in conversation with Miller — with his concerns, his key terms, his examples, and his conclusions.

2. In the final chapter of *Writing at the End of the World*, Miller says the following about English and the humanities:

> The practice of the humanities . . . is not about admiration or greatness or appreciation or depth of knowledge or scholarly achievement; it's about the movement between worlds, arms out, balancing; it's about making the connections that count. (p. 198)

This is a pretty bold statement, since English departments have traditionally defined their job as teaching students to read deeply, to conduct scholarly research, and to appreciate great works of literature. What Miller has to offer, rather, is "movement between worlds, arms out, balancing" or "making the connections that count."

"The Dark Night of the Soul" could be said to be about the teaching of English. Reread it, taking notes and marking sections you might use to think about Miller's concerns and his contributions and about schooling and the teaching of the "literate arts." This is a subject about which you already have some considerable experience. Write an essay in response to "The Dark Night of the Soul," one in which you engage Miller's argument from the point of view of the student. If what is represented in Miller's writing can suggest a goal for a curriculum or an imperative for English instruction in high schools and in colleges, what changes would need to be made? What would a course look like? What would its students do? Would you want to take such a course?

3. In the final chapter of *Writing at the End of the World*, Miller says the following about his own writing:

> While the assessments, evaluations, proposals, reports, commentaries, and critiques I produce help to keep the bureaucracy of higher education going, there is another kind of writing I turn to in order to sustain the ongoing search for meaning in a world no one controls. This writing asks the reader to make imaginative connections between disparate elements; it tracks one path among many possible ones across the glistening water. (p. 196)

We can assume that this is the kind of writing present in "The Dark Night of the Soul."

Reread "The Dark Night of the Soul" with particular attention to Miller's method, which is, in simplest terms, putting one thing next to another. Pay attention to the connections Miller makes, to the ways he makes them, and to the ways as a reader you are (or are not) invited into this process. And write a Miller-like essay. To give the project some shape and limit, let's say that it should bring together at least three "disparate elements," three examples you can use to think about whatever it is you want to think about. You don't need to be constrained to Miller's subject — writing, reading, and schooling — although this subject might be exactly the right one for you. Your writing should, however, be like Miller's in its sense of urgency. Write about something that matters to you — in other words, that you care about, that touches you personally and deeply.

4.   Consider the following passage from Miller's "The Dark Night of the Soul":

> What makes *Into the Wild* remarkable is Krakauer's ability to get some purchase on McCandless's actual reading practice, which, in turn, enables him to get inside McCandless's head and speculate with considerable authority about what ultimately led the young man to abandon the comforts of home and purposefully seek out mortal danger. Krakauer is able to do this, in part, because he has access to the books that McCandless read, with all their underlinings and marginalia, as well as to his journals and the postcards and letters McCandless sent to friends during his journey. Working with these materials and his interviews with McCandless's family and friends, Krakauer develops a sense of McCandless's inner life and eventually comes to some understanding of why the young man was so susceptible to being seduced by the writings of London, Thoreau, Muir, and Tolstoy. Who McCandless is and what becomes of him are, it turns out, intimately connected to the young man's approach to reading — both what he chose to read and how he chose to read it. (p. 444)

When Miller is writing about Krakauer's *Into the Wild*, he seems to suggest that what we read, and how we read, can say something about who we are and about what we might become. This is a very bold claim.

Think of a book that made a difference to you, that captured you, maybe one you have read more than once, maybe one that you've made marks in or that still sits on your bookshelf. Or, if not a book, think of your favorite song or album or movie or TV show, something that engaged you at least potentially as McCandless was engaged by London, Thoreau, Muir, and Tolstoy. What was it that you found there? What kind of reader were you? And what makes this a story in the past tense? How and why did you move on? (Or if it is not a story in the past tense, where are you now, and are you, like McCandless, in any danger?)

· · ● ● ● · ·

MAKING CONNECTIONS

1.   After years spent unwilling to admit its attractions, I gestured nostalgically toward the past. I yearned for that time when I had not been so alone. I became impatient with books. I wanted experience more immediate. I feared the library's silence. I silently scorned the gray, timid faces around me. I grew to hate the growing pages of my dissertation on genre and Renaissance literature. (In my mind I heard

relatives laughing as they tried to make sense of its title.) I wanted something — I couldn't say exactly what. (p. 549)

> — RICHARD RODRIGUEZ, "The Achievement of Desire"

For some, it will hardly come as a surprise to learn that reading and writing have no magically transformative powers. But for those of us who have been raised into the teaching and publishing professions, it can be quite a shock to confront the possibility that reading and writing and talking exercise almost *none* of the powers we regularly attribute to them in our favorite stories. The dark night of the soul for literacy workers comes with the realization that training students to read, write, and talk in more critical and self-reflective ways cannot protect them from the violent changes our culture is undergoing. (p. 438)

> — RICHARD E. MILLER, "The Dark Night of the Soul"

Both Richard E. Miller and Richard Rodriguez are concerned with the limits (and the failures) of education, with particular attention to the humanities and to the supposed benefits to be found in reading and writing. "I have these doubts, you see," Miller writes of academic work, "doubts silently shared by many who spend their days teaching others the literate arts. Aside from gathering and organizing information, aside from generating critiques and analyses that forever fall on deaf ears, what might the literate arts be said to be good for?" (p. 439).

Write an essay that takes up this question — "what might the literate arts be said to be good for?" — and that takes it up with these two essays, Miller's "The Dark Night of the Soul" and Rodriguez's "The Achievement of Desire" (p. 533), as your initial points of reference. What does each say? How might they be said to speak to each other? And, finally, where are you in this? Where are you, and people like you, the group for whom you feel prepared to speak? You, too, have been and will continue to be expected to take courses in reading and writing, to read, write, and talk in "critical and self-reflective ways." Where are you in this conversation?

2. After years spent unwilling to admit its attractions, I gestured nostalgically toward the past. I yearned for that time when I had not been so alone. I became impatient with books. I wanted experiences more immediate. I feared the library's silence. I silently scorned the gray, timid faces around me. I grew to hate the growing pages of my dissertation on genre and Renaissance literature. (In my mind I heard relatives laughing as they tried to make sense of its title.) I wanted something — I couldn't say exactly what. (p. 549)

    > — RICHARD RODRIGUEZ, "The Achievement of Desire"

I could not, in the end, for some blessed reason, turn away from myself. Not at least in this place. The place of desire. I think now of the small lines etching themselves near the eyes of a woman's face I loved. And how, seeing these lines, I wanted to stroke her face. To lean myself, my body, my skin into her. A part of me unravels as I think of this, and I am taken toward longing, and beyond, into another region, past the walls of this house, or all I can see, stretching farther than the horizon where right now sea and sky blend. It is as if my cells are moving in a larger wave, a wave that takes in every history, every story. (p. 180)

— SUSAN GRIFFIN, *A Chorus of Stones*

We typically think of desire as something that leads us toward something, not as an achievement in and of itself, but as a process. Both Richard Rodriguez (p. 533) and Susan Griffin (p. 381) embody desire in different ways in their essays. If Richard E. Miller were to read these writers for their desires, what do you think he would notice?

Write an essay in which you think through the relationship between writing and desire. With Miller in mind, consider how Rodriguez's or Griffin's essay enacts a set of desires. What seems to propel their writing? What interests or concerns move them from one subject to another? At the same time, what desires do they come to as the essay unfolds? What do they seem to move closer to, and what do they seem to leave behind? Use this opportunity to reflect on your own writing and the changing desires that propel you or slow you down, the set of desires that may or may not be found in Miller's ideals, Rodriguez's reflections, or Griffin's imaginings.

3. One way to imagine Susan Griffin's project in "Our Secret" (p. 381) is to think of her study of Heinrich Himmler as a journey through texts. She spends a significant amount of time attending to Himmler's journals and writings, looking at the way he stood in photographs, closely reading the words he chose as a child and later as a Nazi soldier. Griffin says that she has been "searching" through these documents. She writes:

> Now as I sit here I read once again the fragments from Heinrich's boyhood diary that exist in English. I have begun to think of these words as ciphers. Repeat them to myself, hoping to find a door into the mind of this man, even as his character first forms so that I might learn how it is he becomes himself. (p. 384)

Considering the journals and memoirs he consults, one might think of Richard E. Miller as having a similar project to Griffin's, one of sifting through texts in order to uncover their relationships to the human beings who read and wrote these texts. Miller writes:

> Asking why a Steve Cousins or an Eric Harris or a Dylan Klebold is violent is itself a meaningless act, not because the motivation is too deeply buried or obscurely articulated to ever be known, but because we no longer live in a world where human action can be explained. We have plenty of information; it just doesn't amount to anything. This is the logic of the history of increasing humiliation working itself out over time. (pp. 440–41)

Write an essay in which you discuss Griffin's project of looking at Himmler in relation to Miller's examination of Eric Harris and Dylan Klebold. How do Miller's words above help illuminate, expand, or complicate Griffin's thoughts in "Our Secret"? What does Griffin mean when she says she thinks of Himmler's words as ciphers? In what ways do Griffin and Miller seem to be engaging in a similar inquiry or investigation? What does each text offer as its theory of writing and reading?

4. In his essay "Our Time" (p. 622), John Edgar Wideman worries over the problems of representation, of telling his brother's story. He speaks directly to the fundamental problem writers face when they try to represent the lives of others: "I'd slip unaware out of his story and into one of my own. I'd be following him, an obedient shadow, then a cloud would blot the sun and I'd be gone, unchained, a dark form still skulking behind him but no longer in tow" (p. 637). Wideman goes on to say:

> The hardest habit to break . . . would be listening to myself listen to him. That habit would destroy any chance of seeing my brother on his terms; and seeing him in his terms, learning his terms, seemed the whole point of learning his story. . . . I had to teach myself to listen. Start fresh, clear the pipes, resist too facile an identification, tame the urge to take off with Robby's story and make it my own. (p. 637)

Richard E. Miller, in "The Dark Night of the Soul," is also concerned with the problems of representation. He provides readings of the lives of others — from Eric Harris to Chris McCandless to Martin Amis to René Descartes and Mary Karr — who are also engaged with the problems of representation and understanding. Write an essay about writing and representation, about the real world and the world of texts, with Wideman and Miller as your primary points of reference. How do they understand representation as a problem for writers and readers? How is that understanding represented (or enacted) in their own work? Which might have something to learn from the example of the other?

5. Both Richard E. Miller, in "The Dark Night of the Soul," and Judith Butler, in "Beside Oneself: On the Limits of Sexual Autonomy" (p. 238), are concerned with the fundamental question of what, in Butler's terms, "makes for a livable world." How would Miller read, appropriate, and understand Butler's essay?

   "The Dark Night of the Soul" is divided into sections; most sections consider a particular text: Krakauer's *Into the Wild*, Descartes's *Meditations*, Karr's *The Liars' Club*. Reread Miller in order to get a sense of his argument, style, and method, and then write a section that could be added to "The Dark Night of the Soul" with Butler's "Beside Oneself" as its subject.

· · · ● · · ·

ENGAGING WITH STUDENT WRITING

You will find below a couple of responses to Richard E. Miller written by students using the "Assignments for Writing" in *Ways of Reading*. The essays included here are previously unpublished, but we invite you to read them in much the same way as you would read the other essays collected in this book. They are meant to serve not as models or examples, but as opportunities to work on an essay as a reader and as a writer.

Books Aren't Enough
By Austin Crull

Perched on a shelf above my bed are a few dozen novels with worn covers and faded letters written down their spines. These books fit right in with their surroundings. A messy bed, clothes strewn about the room, and a desk with just about any item you could think of spread randomly across it. Yet there is a distinct difference here. The books are worn, but they stand neatly in line. Their spines are cracked, yet they emanate a feeling of composition rather than chaos. In their pages are stories about wizards, elves, and tons of other imaginative creatures that can only be found on the pages of fantasy novels. What can a book say about a person? And how can we discover this answer if that which we are searching for is about ourselves? It seems that self-analysis is the only means of reaching these answers. In a way, we must step outside ourselves in order to truly find what makes us who we are. In this instance, books are the evidence collected for self-inspection, and just as Jon Krakauer studied Chris McCandless in his book *Into the Wild*, we too can gain a wealth of knowledge about ourselves through the books we read.

Stepping over and around the mess on the floor, I step directly in front of the bookshelf of a nineteen-year-old college student. One book stands out from the rest. It is larger than the rest, but that's not what makes it so apparent to me. While the entire collection looks well used, this book in particular looks as though it has been picked up far more than the rest. *The Lord of the Rings* by J. R. R. Tolkien is inscribed down the side in faded golden letters. The story is well known—one of unlikely friendships, good versus evil, and overcoming seemingly insurmountable obstacles. So what does this tell us? That this person has friends? That this person hates evil and maybe has overcome a few obstacles in his life? Were this the case, then it seems we've discovered the identity of just about every kid in the world. It is not these truths that we are searching for. They speak neither to the complexities of a person nor to the depths of human emotion. What about this one book tells something that nothing else in the room could possibly reveal? The fact that it has been read numerous times says something in and of itself. This book is important. Something is locked within the text of these pages that enthralls the reader so much that he comes back and reads it time and time again.

One of these components is the sheer depth of this novel. Its author, Tolkien, spent a lifetime writing the pages of this book, leaving no question unanswered and no detail overlooked. Perhaps this says something about its reader. A book like this may reveal the curiosity of our subject. He is someone who searches for every answer and needs to know every detail. Another component may be the magnitude of the story. In the book the fate of the world rests on the shoulders of some of the smallest and seemingly most insignificant characters. To an outsider this can suggest the insecurities of the reader. Perhaps the reader connects with the insignificance of the characters. There is hope in the story and reassurance that no one is truly insignificant. Our reader no doubt finds comfort in these ideas. In addition to these ideas, one notion is quite evident that our reader may identify with. Adventure. Looking around this room, you can see textbooks everywhere. It is a college kid's dorm after all. This book no doubt offers an escape from the exams, a relief from the readings about molecules and economics. This book provides excitement, and it disconnects readers from mediocre reality.

So what does this all really say about our subject? He has insecurities. Sometimes he wishes to break free from the bonds of reality. These conclusions seem to be similar to the few that were drawn earlier. They are shared by nearly everyone. These conclusions don't seem to create an identity as much as they create the picture of humanity. It is at this point where I notice the problem with our question. There is no sense of individuality when we look upon the books in this room. Thousands of people have read all these books. They provide a blank page when we try to interpret a person through them. It is the mind we are trying to unlock which creates the interpretation for us. Without seeing how someone reacts to the pages of *The Lord of the Rings*, we have no chance of discovering who they are. Our thoughts and actions are what reveal our identities — not those of an author. It is at these moments, when we think we understand someone, that we fall short.

In Richard E. Miller's *Writing at the End of the World*, he mentions that the author of *Into the Wild*, Jon Krakauer, researches who his subject (Chris McCandless) is through his readings. No doubt this is true; however, Krakauer also researches McCandless through interviews with family and friends, his writings, and his actions. That is how Krakauer develops an identity for his subject. The human mind is so complex that it takes more than one medium for us to develop an identity for another person. And even with all the resources at Krakauer's fingertips, who's to say that his suggestions are accurate? It seems an insurmountable challenge to create an identity for someone else no matter what the resources at your disposal.

Austin Crull's essay, "Books Aren't Enough," seems to both enact *and* challenge Miller's arguments about how reading might shape a human mind. Crull speculates about himself through the books he finds in his room, but he also reflects on the room itself and on the condition of the books he finds there. It seems he wants us to consider not only the books but also the context in which they are found. Ultimately, he tells us: "Without seeing how someone reacts to the pages of *The Lord of the Rings*, we have no chance of discovering who they are. Our thoughts and actions are what reveal our identities—not those of an author." What does Crull seem to be arguing in this statement? How does he want to intervene in Miller's questions about literacy and the way reading might reflect one's "inner life"? Why do you suppose Crull wants to focus on "how someone reacts"? Is this issue of reaction one Miller misses or neglects? How might you position Crull and Miller as contributing to the same conversation? How do they converge, collaborate, or challenge each other?

Dreams: The Core of One's Identity?
By Brady Bartlett

Sigmund Freud believed that dreams are the symbolic language of the subconscious mind. So what does that tell us? Are dreams impulses or desires that are too harmful or disturbing to our conscious mind? Are they suppressed feelings that we have shoved deep inside of ourselves? A person's superego keeps the subconscious mind from acting out—one's superego is shut off during the dream state—so are dreams the profound hidden passions that drive and influence somebody?

My roommate keeps a journal of the dreams he has. He wakes up in the morning and writes them down to make sure he doesn't miss any details. What would somebody be able to learn about Obi if they stumbled on his journal of dreams? Is it fair to make assumptions about Obi's motives or thoughts based on complex symbolic dreams? His dreams could be nothing but exaggerations of thoughts and interactions that occurred throughout the day. Is it fair for me to make these assumptions about Obi based on his subconscious mind?

I am on a bridge. It is a brown bridge, and I am running. The city is behind me. Some force starts to push me. I start to fall off the bridge to the left. I am falling in air. Right before I hit the ground, I wake up.

Does Obi live in the city? Maybe he is afraid of the city and does not want to be stuck there his whole life. He feels threatened about his surroundings—he no longer wants to be there—he runs. Obi is on the bridge, on his way out of the city, and then he falls off of the bridge. Obi does not believe in himself. Instead of seeing himself get out of the city, he falls off before he gets away from the danger. He thinks that he will not be able to make it away from the city. He worries that he does not have what it takes to get out.

I'm in the woods with my older brother. We are climbing this big rock in the woods. All of a sudden a few giant robot monkeys start coming toward my brother and me. They have guns! My brother tells me to hide. He starts shooting them, but is shot in the leg. I run up next to him. I grab the gun and start shooting. They are getting closer. I wake up.

Obi's brother takes the normal older brother role in life. His older brother protects him even if it is a life-and-death situation. There is definite trust that his older brother will watch out for him, even against giant robot monkeys. The point right after his older brother gets shot in the leg and Obi runs to his aid shows that the trust and love are mutual. His brother is willing to risk his life to save him, and Obi has his brother's back also. The fact that he grabbed the gun and started shooting back probably means he is pretty brave or at least in the face of danger he stands up. He is not a coward. He is a person who cares greatly about his family.

I'm on a trip to California. I am going to see the Dodgers vs. Indians baseball game. At the game I get the urge to play floor hockey. Next thing I know I am playing floor hockey at USC. While playing, I look up and see my buddy from home (who goes there), and after I finish the game, I go give him a hug. I wake up.

This friend of his is probably pretty close to him. Maybe they have talked about visiting each other, and that is what brought this dream about. He misses his friend and wants to see him. Seeing him reminds him of home, which he also misses, but not enough to go home. He is happy being independent but still wanted to get that sense of home. He is also probably someone who likes sports, seeing as in his dream he both watched one and played one.

I am older; in my thirties if I had to guess. I am dressed in a suit, and my date is wearing a gorgeous blue dress. We are at a fancy restaurant. Suddenly we're in a hot tub at a mansion. Nobody is around but us. It is quiet. The sun is setting, and the view out to the ocean is breathtaking. As I lean in for a kiss, the alarm goes off . . . of course.

From this I get that Obi is ambitious. I think that a normal life is not in his plans for the future. He has bigger plans. This may not be his ideal dream house or girl, but he is hoping that he lives nicely when he is older. He could be high maintenance and used to this type of living, or he does not live like this and aspires to be successful. If he aspires to be like this, his standards are high. Instead of being content with a nice family in the countryside, he goes for the gold. Fancy suit, beautiful girl, expensive restaurant, mansion, ocean view. He thinks this is what will make him happy in life.

Certainly one cannot figure out a great deal about people through their dreams. Think of a dream that you have had more than once. One that sticks with you. What does it say about you? Why do you think you had it? The problem with dreams is that they are not fully understood. Even I cannot tell you what my dreams mean. My guess would be a more educated guess because I know more about myself, but a guess nonetheless. This extends beyond dreams. You cannot judge someone or try to figure them out through dreams, their writing, what they read, or what music they listen to. To understand somebody, you have to communicate with them and try to get to know them.

When you read someone's things to try to get a sense of who they are, too much is left for assumption and interpretation. Too many factors are not taken into consideration by the reader, like their mood. If I write something while I am in an angry mood, what is said will come off a lot differently than if I were in a very happy state of mind. Reading someone else's dreams is very appealing because it is always interesting to see what goes on in somebody's mind when they no longer have control. During dreams your morals are put to the side, and that barrier is no longer there. Your mind is free to do what it likes. Feelings that are so deep that you do not even acknowledge their existence may arise during dreams. The dream could be a fantasy that is not possible to achieve in real life.

Do dreams really mean anything to someone? Perhaps they are just some connections to something still on the conscious mind. Maybe somebody just told Obi a story or he watched a movie, and in his dream state it was taken to a completely different level. In the dream state there are no boundaries. You can fly, be invisible, never die, be wealthy, or even not look the same. You are at the mercy of your subconscious mind. If someone tries to interpret these images made from your subconscious mind, it is simply unfair. You are not even sure what these symbolic messages mean, so how would somebody else know? Next time you have a dream, write it down and think of what might be said about you if a total stranger tried to interpret it.

Brady Bartlett experiments with form in this essay. He moves back and forth between his thinking about Obi's dream journal and quotations from the journal. We might understand Bartlett's essay as experimenting with shifts in perspective, just as Susan Griffin's essay "Our Secret" (p. 381) does. However, rather than writing an essay that engages with a text that Obi reads, Bartlett chooses to engage with a text that Obi *writes*, a text that is intended to record the images and narratives of his subconscious mind. Austin Crull, in his essay "Books Aren't Enough," seems to suggest that reactions might be more telling than merely what one reads. Does Bartlett's essay spend time thinking about reactions as well? What does Bartlett seem to suggest about how literacy practices (reading and writing) shape and reflect lives? Bartlett interprets Obi through his dreams; however, at the close of his essay, he seems to be questioning whether this is a legitimate or fair strategy for interpretation. What appears to be his concern? Does Miller have similar concerns as he offers his interpretations of Eric Harris's journal? Consider Bartlett, Crull, and Miller as three writers who are all trying to tackle the difficult project of representing their own and others' readings. How would you describe each of their approaches? What are they saying *to* one another?

WALKER
Percy

Walker Percy, in his midforties, after a life of relative obscurity as, he said, a "failed physician," wrote his first novel, *The Moviegoer*. It won the National Book Award for fiction in 1962, and Percy emerged as one of this country's leading novelists. Little in his background would have predicted such a career.

After graduating from Columbia University's medical school in 1941, Percy (1916–1990) worked at Bellevue Hospital in New York City. He soon contracted tuberculosis from performing autopsies and was sent to a sanitorium to recover, where, as he said, "I was in bed so much, alone so much, that I had nothing to do but read and think. I began to question everything I had once believed." He returned to medicine briefly but suffered a relapse and during his long recovery began "to make reading a full-time occupation." He left medicine, but not until 1954, almost a decade later, did he publish his first essay, "Symbol as Need."

The essays that followed, including "The Loss of the Creature," all dealt with the relationships between language and understanding or belief. In the later essays, Percy seemed to turn away from academic forms of argument and to depend more and more on stories or anecdotes from daily life — to write, in fact, as a storyteller and to be wary of abstraction or explanation. Robert Coles has said that Percy's failure to find a form that would reach a larger audience may have led him to try his hand at a novel. You will notice in the essay that follows that Percy delights in piling example upon example; he never seems to settle down to a topic sentence, or any sentence for that matter, that sums everything up and makes the examples superfluous.

In addition to *The Moviegoer*, Percy wrote five other novels, including *Lancelot* (1977) and *The Thanatos Syndrome* (1987). He published two books of essays, *The Message in the Bottle: How Queer Man Is, How Queer Language Is, and What One Has to Do with the Other* (1975, from which "The Loss of the Creature" is taken) and *Lost in the Cosmos: The Last Self-Help Book* (1983). Percy died at his home in Covington, Louisiana, on May 10, 1990, leaving a considerable amount of unpublished work, some of which was gathered into a posthumous collection, *Signposts in a Strange Land* (1991). *The Correspondence of Shelby Foote and Walker Percy* was published in 1996.

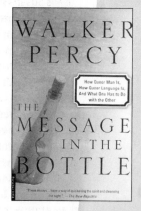

The Loss of the Creature

I

Every explorer names his island Formosa, beautiful. To him it is beautiful because, being first, he has access to it and can see it for what it is. But to no one else is it ever as beautiful — except the rare man who manages to recover it, who knows that it has to be recovered.

Garcia López de Cárdenas discovered the Grand Canyon and was amazed at the sight. It can be imagined: One crosses miles of desert, breaks through the mesquite, and there it is at one's feet. Later the government set the place aside as a national park, hoping to pass along to millions the experience of Cárdenas. Does not one see the same sight from the Bright Angel Lodge that Cárdenas saw?

The assumption is that the Grand Canyon is a remarkably interesting and beautiful place and that if it had a certain value P for Cárdenas, the same value P may be transmitted to any number of sightseers — just as Banting's discovery of insulin can be transmitted to any number of diabetics. A counterinfluence is at work, however, and it would be nearer the truth to say that if the place is seen by a million sightseers, a single sightseer does not receive value P but a millionth part of value P.

> THE THING IS NO LONGER THE THING AS IT CONFRONTED THE SPANIARD; IT IS RATHER THAT WHICH HAS ALREADY BEEN FORMULATED — BY PICTURE POSTCARD, GEOGRAPHY BOOK, TOURIST FOLDERS, AND THE WORDS *GRAND CANYON*.

It is assumed that since the Grand Canyon has the fixed interest value P, tours can be organized for any number of people. A man in Boston decides to spend his vacation at the Grand Canyon. He visits his travel bureau, looks at the folder, signs up for a two-week tour. He and his family take the tour, see the Grand Canyon, and return to Boston. May we say that this man has seen the Grand Canyon? Possibly he has. But it is more likely that what he has done is the one sure way not to see the canyon.

Why is it almost impossible to gaze directly at the Grand Canyon under these circumstances and see it for what it is — as one picks up a strange object from one's back yard and gazes directly at it? It is almost impossible because the Grand Canyon, the thing as it is, has been appropriated by the symbolic complex which has already been formed in the sightseer's mind. Seeing the canyon under approved circumstances is seeing the symbolic complex head on. The thing is no longer the thing as it confronted the Spaniard; it is rather that which has already been formulated — by picture postcard, geography book, tourist folders, and the words *Grand Canyon*. As a result of this preformulation, the source of the sightseer's pleasure undergoes a shift. Where the wonder and delight of the Spaniard arose from his penetration of the thing itself, from a progressive discovery of depths, patterns, colors, shadows, etc., now the sightseer measures his satisfaction *by the degree to which the canyon conforms to the preformed complex*. If it does so, if it looks just like the postcard, he is pleased; he might even say, "Why it is every bit as beautiful as a picture postcard!" He feels he has not been cheated. But if it does not conform, if the colors are somber, he will not be able to see it directly; he will only be conscious of the disparity between what it is and what it is supposed to be. He will say later that he was unlucky in not being there at the right time. The highest point, the term of the sightseer's satisfaction, is not the sovereign discovery of the thing before him; it is rather the measuring up of the thing to the criterion of the preformed symbolic complex.

Seeing the canyon is made even more difficult by what the sightseer does when the moment arrives, when sovereign knower confronts the thing to be known. Instead of looking at it, he photographs it. There is no confrontation at all. At the end of forty years of preformulation and with the Grand Canyon yawning at his feet, what does he do? He waives his right of seeing and knowing and records symbols for the next forty years. For him there is no present; there is only the past of what has been formulated and seen and the future of what has been formulated and not seen. The present is surrendered to the past and the future.

The sightseer may be aware that something is wrong. He may simply be bored; or he may be conscious of the difficulty: that the great thing yawning at his feet somehow eludes him. The harder he looks at it, the less he can see. It eludes everybody. The tourist cannot see it; the bellboy at the Bright Angel Lodge cannot see it: for him it is only one side of the space he lives in, like one wall of a room; to the ranger it is a tissue of everyday signs relevant to his own prospects — the blue haze down there means that he will probably get rained on during the donkey ride.

How can the sightseer recover the Grand Canyon? He can recover it in any number of ways, all sharing in common the stratagem of avoiding the approved confrontation of the tour and the Park Service.

It may be recovered by leaving the beaten track. The tourist leaves the tour, camps in the back country. He arises before dawn and approaches the South Rim through a wild terrain where there are no trails and no railed-in lookout points. In other words, he sees the canyon by avoiding all the facilities for seeing the canyon. If the benevolent Park Service hears about this fellow and thinks he has a good idea and places the following notice in the Bright Angel Lodge: *Consult ranger for information on getting off the beaten track* — the end result will only be the closing of another access to the canyon.

It may be recovered by a dialectical movement which brings one back to the beaten track but at a level above it. For example, after a lifetime of avoiding the beaten track and guided tours, a man may deliberately seek out the most beaten track of all, the most commonplace tour imaginable: he may visit the canyon by a Greyhound tour in the company of a party from Terre Haute — just as a man who has lived in New York all his life may visit the Statue of Liberty. (Such dialectical savorings of the familiar as the familiar are, of course, a favorite stratagem of *The New Yorker* magazine.) The thing is recovered from familiarity by means of an exercise in familiarity. Our complex friend stands behind his fellow tourists at the Bright Angel Lodge and sees the canyon through them and their predicament, their picture taking and busy disregard. In a sense, he exploits his fellow tourists; he stands on their shoulders to see the canyon.

Such a man is far more advanced in the dialectic than the sightseer who is trying to get off the beaten track — getting up at dawn and approaching the canyon through the mesquite. This stratagem is, in fact, for our complex man the weariest, most beaten track of all.

It may be recovered as a consequence of a breakdown of the symbolic machinery by which the experts present the experience to the consumer. A family visits the canyon in the usual way. But shortly after their arrival, the park is closed by an outbreak of typhus in the south. They have the canyon to themselves. What do they mean when they tell the home folks of their good luck: "We had the whole place to ourselves"? How does one see the thing better when the others are absent? Is looking like sucking: the more lookers, the less there is to see? They could hardly answer, but by saying this they testify to a state of affairs which is considerably more complex than the simple statement of the schoolbook about the Spaniard and the millions who followed him. It is a state in which there is a complex distribution of sovereignty, of zoning.

It may be recovered in a time of national disaster. The Bright Angel Lodge is converted into a rest home, a function that has nothing to do with the canyon a few yards away. A wounded man is brought in. He regains consciousness; there outside his window is the canyon.

The most extreme case of access by privilege conferred by disaster is the Huxleyan novel of the adventures of the surviving remnant after the great wars of the twentieth century. An expedition from Australia lands in Southern California and heads east. They stumble across the Bright Angel Lodge, now fallen into ruins. The trails are grown over, the guard rails fallen away, the dime telescope at Battleship Point rusted. But there is the canyon, exposed at last. Exposed by what? By the decay of those facilities which were designed to help the sightseer.

This dialectic of sightseeing cannot be taken into account by planners, for the object of the dialectic is nothing other than the subversion of the efforts of the planners.

The dialectic is not known to objective theorists, psychologists, and the like. Yet it is quite well known in the fantasy-consciousness of the popular arts. The devices by which the museum exhibit, the Grand Canyon, the ordinary thing, is recovered have long since been stumbled upon. A movie shows a man visiting the Grand Canyon. But the movie maker knows something the planner does not know. He knows that one cannot take the sight frontally. The canyon must be approached by the stratagems we have mentioned: the Inside Track, the Familiar Revisited, the Accidental Encounter. Who is the stranger at the Bright Angel Lodge? Is he the ordinary tourist from Terre Haute that he makes himself out to be? He is not. He has another objective in mind, to revenge his wronged brother, counterespionage, etc. By virtue of the fact that he has other fish to fry, he may take a stroll along the rim after supper and then we can see the canyon through him. The movie accomplishes its purpose by concealing it. Overtly the characters (the American family marooned by typhus) and we the onlookers experience pity for the sufferers, and the family experience anxiety for themselves; covertly and in truth they are the happiest of people and we are happy through them, for we have the canyon to ourselves. The movie cashes in on the recovery of sovereignty through disaster. Not only is the canyon now accessible to the remnant: the members of the remnant are now accessible to each other, a whole new ensemble of relations becomes possible — friendship, love, hatred, clandestine sexual adventures. In a movie when a man sits next to a woman on a bus, it is necessary either that the bus break down or that the woman lose her memory. (The question occurs to one: Do you imagine there are sightseers who see sights just as they are supposed to? a family who live in Terre Haute, who decide to take the canyon tour, who go there, see it, enjoy it immensely, and go home content? a family who are entirely innocent of all the barriers, zones, losses of sovereignty I have been talking about? Wouldn't most people be sorry if Battleship Point fell into the canyon, carrying all one's fellow passengers to their death, leaving one alone on the South Rim? I cannot answer this. Perhaps there are such people. Certainly a great many American families would swear they had no such problems, that they came, saw, and went away happy. Yet it is just these families who would be happiest if they had gotten the Inside Track and been among the surviving remnant.)

It is now apparent that as between the many measures which may be taken to overcome the opacity, the boredom, of the direct confrontation of the thing or creature in its citadel of symbolic investiture, some are less authentic than others. That is to say, some stratagems obviously serve other purposes than that of providing access to being — for example, various unconscious motivations which it is not necessary to go into here.

Let us take an example in which the recovery of being is ambiguous, where it may under the same circumstances contain both authentic and unauthentic components. An American couple, we will say, drives down into Mexico. They see the usual sights and have a fair time of it. Yet they are never without the sense of missing something. Although Taxco and Cuernavaca are interesting and picturesque as advertised, they fall short of "it." What do the couple have in mind by "it"? What do they really hope for? What sort of experience could they have in Mexico so that upon their return, they would feel that "it" had happened? We have a clue: Their hope has something to do with their own role as tourists in a foreign country and the way in which they conceive this role. It has something to do with other American tourists. Certainly they feel that they are very far from "it" when, after traveling five thousand miles, they arrive at the plaza in Guanajuato only to find themselves surrounded by a dozen other couples from the Midwest.

Already we may distinguish authentic and unauthentic elements. First, we see the problem the couple faces and we understand their efforts to surmount it. The problem is to find an "unspoiled" place. "Unspoiled" does not mean only that a place is left physically intact; it means also that it is not encrusted by renown and by the familiar (as in Taxco), that it has not been discovered by others. We understand that the couple really want to get at the place and enjoy it. Yet at the same time we wonder if there is not something wrong in their dislike of their compatriots. Does access to the place require the exclusion of others?

Let us see what happens.

The couple decide to drive from Guanajuato to Mexico City. On the way they get lost. After hours on a rocky mountain road, they find themselves in a tiny valley not even marked on the map. There they discover an Indian village. Some sort of religious festival is going on. It is apparently a corn dance in supplication of the rain god.

The couple know at once that this is "it." They are entranced. They spend several days in the village, observing the Indians and being themselves observed with friendly curiosity.

Now may we not say that the sightseers have at last come face to face with an authentic sight, a sight which is charming, quaint, picturesque, unspoiled, and that they see the sight and come away rewarded? Possibly this may occur. Yet it is more likely that what happens is a far cry indeed from an immediate encounter with being, that the experience, while masquerading as such, is in truth a rather desperate impersonation. I use the word *desperate* advisedly to signify an actual loss of hope.

The clue to the spuriousness of their enjoyment of the village and the festival is a certain restiveness in the sightseers themselves. It is given expression by their repeated exclamations that "this is too good to be true," and by their anxiety that it may not prove to be so perfect, and finally by their downright relief at leaving the valley and having the experience in the bag, so to speak — that is, safely embalmed in memory and movie film.

What is the source of their anxiety during the visit? Does it not mean that the couple are looking at the place with a certain standard of performance in mind? Are they like Fabre, who gazed at the world about him with wonder, letting it be what it is; or are they not like the overanxious mother who sees her child as one performing, now doing badly, now doing well? The village is their child and their love for it is an anxious love because they are afraid that at any moment it might fail them.

We have another clue in their subsequent remark to an ethnologist friend. "How we wished you had been there with us! What a perfect goldmine of folkways! Every minute we would say to each other, if only you were here! You must return with us." This surely testifies to a generosity of spirit, a willingness to share their experience with others, not at all like their feelings toward their fellow Iowans on the plaza at Guanajuato!

I am afraid this is not the case at all. It is true that they longed for their ethnologist friend, but it was for an entirely different reason. They wanted him, not to share their experience, but to certify their experience as genuine.

"This is it" and "Now we are really living" do not necessarily refer to the sovereign encounter of the person with the sight that enlivens the mind and gladdens the heart. It means that now at last we are having the acceptable experience. The present experience is always measured by a prototype, the "it" of their dreams. "Now I am really living" means that now I am filling the role of sightseer and the sight is living up to the prototype of sights. This quaint and picturesque village is measured by a Platonic ideal of the Quaint and the Picturesque.

Hence their anxiety during the encounter. For at any minute something could go wrong. A fellow Iowan might emerge from a 'dobe hut; the chief might show them his Sears catalog. (If the failures are "wrong" enough, as these are, they might still be turned to account as rueful conversation pieces. "There we were expecting the chief to bring us a churinga and he shows up with a Sears catalog!") They have snatched victory from disaster, but their experience always runs the danger of failure.

They need the ethnologist to certify their experience as genuine. This is borne out by their behavior when the three of them return for the next corn dance. During the dance, the couple do not watch the goings-on; instead they watch the ethnologist! Their highest hope is that their friend should find the dance interesting. And if he should show signs of true absorption, an interest in the goings-on so powerful that he becomes oblivious of his friends — then their cup is full. "Didn't we tell you?" they say at last. What they want from him is not ethnological explanations; all they want is his approval.

What has taken place is a radical loss of sovereignty over that which is as much theirs as it is the ethnologist's. The fault does not lie with the ethnologist. He has no wish to stake a claim to the village; in fact, he desires the opposite: he will bore his friends to death by telling them about the village and the meaning of the folkways. A degree of sovereignty has been surrendered by the couple. It is the nature of the loss, moreover, that they are not aware of the loss, beyond a certain uneasiness. (Even if they read this and admitted it, it would be very difficult for them to bridge the gap in their confrontation of the world. Their consciousness of the corn dance cannot escape their consciousness of their consciousness, so that with the onset of the first direct enjoyment, their higher consciousness pounces and certifies: "Now you are doing it! Now you are really living!" and, in certifying the experience, sets it at nought.)

Their basic placement in the world is such that they recognize a priority of title of the expert over his particular department of being. The whole horizon of being is staked out by "them," the experts. The highest satisfaction of the sightseer (not merely the tourist but any layman seer of sights) is that his sight should be certified as genuine. The worst of this impoverishment is that there is no sense of impoverishment. The surrender of title is so complete that it never even occurs to one to reassert title. A poor man may envy the rich man, but the sightseer does not envy the expert. When a caste system becomes absolute, envy disappears. Yet the caste of layman-expert is not the fault of the expert. It is due altogether to the eager surrender of sovereignty by the layman so that he may take up the role not of the person but of the consumer.

I do not refer only to the special relation of layman to theorist. I refer to the general situation in which sovereignty is surrendered to a class of privileged knowers, whether these be theorists or artists. A reader may surrender sovereignty over that which has been written about, just as a consumer may surrender sovereignty over a thing which has been theorized about. The consumer is content to receive an experience just as it has been presented to him by theorists and planners. The reader may also be content to judge life by whether it has or has not been formulated by those who know and write about life. A young man goes to France. He too has a fair time of it, sees the sights, enjoys the food. On his last day, in fact as he sits in a restaurant in Le Havre waiting for his boat, something happens. A group of French students in the restaurant get into an impassioned argument over a recent play. A riot takes place. Madame la concierge joins in, swinging her mop at the rioters. Our young American is transported. This is "it." And he had almost left France without seeing "it"!

> WHEN A CASTE SYSTEM BECOMES ABSOLUTE, ENVY DISAPPEARS. YET THE CASTE OF LAYMAN-EXPERT IS NOT THE FAULT OF THE EXPERT. IT IS DUE ALTOGETHER TO THE EAGER SURRENDER OF SOVEREIGNTY BY THE LAYMAN.

But the young man's delight is ambiguous. On the one hand, it is a pleasure for him to encounter the same Gallic temperament he had heard about from Puccini and Rolland. But on the other hand, the source of his pleasure testifies to a certain alienation. For the young man is actually barred from a direct encounter with anything French excepting only that which has been set forth, authenticated by Puccini and Rolland — those who know. If he had encountered the restaurant scene without reading Hemingway, without knowing that the performance was so typically, charmingly French, he would not have been delighted. He would only have been anxious at seeing things get so out of hand. The source of his delight is the sanction of those who know.

This loss of sovereignty is not a marginal process, as might appear from my example of estranged sightseers. It is a generalized surrender of the horizon to those experts within whose competence a particular segment of the horizon is thought to lie. Kwakiutls are surrendered to Franz Boas; decaying Southern mansions are surrendered to Faulkner and Tennessee Williams. So that, although it is by no means the intention of the expert to expropriate sovereignty — in fact he would not even know what sovereignty meant in this context — the danger of theory and consumption is a seduction and deprivation of the consumer.

In the New Mexico desert, natives occasionally come across strange-looking artifacts which have fallen from the skies and which are stenciled: *Return to U.S. Experimental Project, Alamogordo. Reward.* The finder returns the object and is rewarded. He knows nothing of the nature of the object he has found and does not care to know. The sole role of the native, the highest role he can play, is that of finder and returner of the mysterious equipment.

The same is true of the laymen's relation to *natural* objects in a modern technical society. No matter what the object or event is, whether it is a star, a swallow, a Kwakiutl, a "psychological phenomenon," the layman who confronts it does not confront it as a sovereign person, as Crusoe confronts a seashell he finds on the beach. The highest role he can conceive himself as playing is to be able to recognize the title of the object, to return it to the appropriate expert and have it certified as a genuine find. He does not even permit himself to see the thing — as Gerard Hopkins could see a rock or a cloud or a field. If anyone asks him why he doesn't look, he may reply that he didn't take that subject in college (or he hasn't read Faulkner).

This loss of sovereignty extends even to oneself. There is the neurotic who asks nothing more of his doctor than that his symptoms should prove interesting. When all else fails, the poor fellow has nothing to offer but his own neurosis. But even this is sufficient if only the doctor will show interest when he says, "Last night I had a curious sort of dream; perhaps it will be significant to one who knows about such things. It seems I was standing in a sort of alley —" (I have nothing else to offer you but my own unhappiness. Please say that it, at least, measures up, that it is a *proper* sort of unhappiness.)

II

A young Falkland Islander walking along a beach and spying a dead dogfish and going to work on it with his jackknife has, in a fashion wholly unprovided in modern educational theory, a great advantage over the Scarsdale high-school pupil who finds the dogfish on his laboratory desk. Similarly the citizen of Huxley's *Brave New World* who stumbles across a volume of Shakespeare in some vine-grown ruins and squats on a potsherd to read it is in a fairer way of getting at a sonnet than the Harvard sophomore taking English Poetry II.

The educator whose business it is to teach students biology or poetry is unaware of a whole ensemble of relations which exist between the student and the dogfish and between the student and the Shakespeare sonnet. To put it bluntly: A student who has the desire to get at a dogfish or a Shakespeare sonnet may have the greatest difficulty in salvaging the creature itself from the educational package in which it is presented. The great difficulty is that he is not aware that there is a difficulty; surely, he thinks, in such a fine classroom, with such a fine textbook, the sonnet must come across! What's wrong with me?

The sonnet and the dogfish are obscured by two different processes. The sonnet is obscured by the symbolic package which is formulated not by the sonnet itself but by the *media* through which the sonnet is transmitted, the media which the educators believe for some reason to be transparent. The new textbook, the type, the smell of the page, the classroom, the aluminum windows and the winter sky, the personality of Miss Hawkins — these media which are supposed to transmit the sonnet may only succeed in transmitting themselves. It is only the hardiest and cleverest of students who can salvage the sonnet from this many-tissued package. It is only the rarest student who knows that the sonnet must be salvaged from the package. (The educator is well aware that something is wrong, that there is a fatal gap between the student's learning and the student's life: the student reads the poem, appears to understand it, and gives all the answers. But what does he recall if he should happen to read a Shakespeare sonnet twenty years later? Does he recall the poem or does he recall the smell of the page and the smell of Miss Hawkins?)

One might object, pointing out that Huxley's citizen reading his sonnet in the ruins and the Falkland Islander looking at his dogfish on the beach also receive them in a certain package. Yes, but the difference lies in the fundamental placement of the student in the world, a placement which makes it possible to extract the thing from the package. The pupil at Scarsdale High sees himself placed as a consumer receiving an experience-package; but the Falkland Islander exploring his dogfish is a person exercising the sovereign right of a person in his lordship and mastery of creation. He too could use an instructor and a book and a technique, but he would use them as his subordinates, just as he uses his jackknife. The biology student does not use his scalpel as an instrument, he uses it as a magic wand! Since it is a "scientific instrument," it should do "scientific things."

> IT IS ONLY THE HARDIEST AND CLEVEREST OF STUDENTS WHO CAN SALVAGE THE SONNET FROM THIS MANY-TISSUED PACKAGE.

The dogfish is concealed in the same symbolic package as the sonnet. But the dogfish suffers an additional loss. As a consequence of this double deprivation, the Sarah Lawrence student who scores A in zoology is apt to know very little about a dogfish. She is twice removed from the dogfish, once by the symbolic complex by which the dogfish is concealed, once again by the spoliation of the dogfish by theory which renders it invisible. Through no fault of zoology instructors, it is nevertheless a fact that the zoology laboratory at Sarah Lawrence College is one of the few places in the world where it is all but impossible to see a dogfish.

The dogfish, the tree, the seashell, the American Negro, the dream, are rendered invisible by a shift of reality from concrete thing to theory which Whitehead has called the fallacy of misplaced concreteness. It is the mistaking of an idea, a principle, an abstraction, for the real. As a consequence of the shift, the "specimen" is seen as less real than the theory of the specimen. As Kierkegaard said, once a person is seen as a specimen of a race or a species, at that very moment he ceases to be an individual. Then there are no more individuals but only specimens.

To illustrate: A student enters a laboratory which, in the pragmatic view, offers the student the optimum conditions under which an educational experience may be had. In the existential view, however — that view of the student in which he is regarded not as a receptacle of experience but as a knowing being whose peculiar property it is to see himself as being in a certain situation — the modern laboratory could not have been more effectively designed to conceal the dogfish forever.

The student comes to his desk. On it, neatly arranged by his instructor, he finds his laboratory manual, a dissecting board, instruments, and a mimeographed list:

> *Exercise 22: Materials*
> 1 dissecting board
> 1 scalpel
> 1 forceps
> 1 probe
> 1 bottle india ink and syringe
> 1 specimen of *Squalus acanthias*

The clue of the situation in which the student finds himself is to be found in the last item: 1 specimen of *Squalus acanthias*.

The phrase *specimen of* expresses in the most succinct way imaginable the radical character of the loss of being which has occurred under his very nose. To refer to the dogfish, the unique concrete existent before him, as a "specimen of *Squalus acanthias*" reveals by its grammar the spoliation of the dogfish by the theoretical method. This phrase, *specimen of,* example of, instance of, indicates the ontological status of the individual creature in the eyes of the theorist. The dogfish itself is seen as a rather shabby expression of an ideal reality, the species *Squalus acanthias.* The result is the radical devaluation of the individual dogfish. (The *reductio ad absurdum* of Whitehead's shift is Toynbee's employment of it in his historical method. If a gram of NaCl is referred to by the chemist as a "sample of" NaCl, one may think of it as such and not much is missed by the oversight of the act of being of this particular pinch of salt, but when the Jews and the Jewish religion are understood as — in Toynbee's favorite phrase — a "classical example of" such and such a kind of *Voelkerwanderung,* we begin to suspect that something is being left out.)

If we look into the ways in which the student can recover the dogfish (or the sonnet), we will see that they have in common the stratagem of avoiding the educator's direct presentation of the object as a lesson to be learned and restoring access to sonnet and dogfish as beings to be known, reasserting the sovereignty of knower over known.

In truth, the biography of scientists and poets is usually the story of the discovery of the indirect approach, the circumvention of the educator's presentation — the young man who was sent to the *Technikum* and on his way fell into the habit of loitering in book stores and reading poetry;

or the young man dutifully attending law school who on the way became curious about the comings and goings of ants. One remembers the scene in *The Heart Is a Lonely Hunter* where the girl hides in the bushes to hear the Capehart in the big house play Beethoven. Perhaps she was the lucky one after all. Think of the unhappy souls inside, who see the record, worry about scratches, and most of all worry about whether they are *getting it*, whether they are bona fide music lovers. What is the best way to hear Beethoven: sitting in a proper silence around the Capehart or eavesdropping from an azalea bush?

However it may come about, we notice two traits of the second situation: (1) an openness of the thing before one — instead of being an exercise to be learned according to an approved mode, it is a garden of delights which beckons to one; (2) a sovereignty of the knower — instead of being a consumer of a prepared experience, I am a sovereign wayfarer, a wanderer in the neighborhood of being who stumbles into the garden.

One can think of two sorts of circumstances through which the thing may be restored to the person. (There is always, of course, the direct recovery: A student may simply be strong enough, brave enough, clever enough to take the dogfish and the sonnet by storm, to wrest control of it from the educators and the educational package.) First by ordeal: The Bomb falls; when the young man recovers consciousness in the shambles of the biology laboratory, there not ten inches from his nose lies the dogfish. Now all at once he can see it directly and without let, just as the exile or the prisoner or the sick man sees the sparrow at his window in all its inexhaustibility; just as the commuter who has had a heart attack sees his own hand for the first time. In these cases, the simulacrum of everydayness and of consumption has been destroyed by disaster; in the case of the bomb, literally destroyed. Secondly, by apprenticeship to a great man: one day a great biologist walks into the laboratory; he stops in front of our student's desk; he leans over, picks up the dogfish, and, ignoring instruments and procedure, probes with a broken fingernail into the little carcass. "Now here is a curious business," he says, ignoring also the proper jargon of the specialty. "Look here how this little duct reverses its direction and drops into the pelvis. Now if you would look into a coelacanth, you would see that it —" And all at once the student can see. The technician and the sophomore who loves his textbooks are always offended by the genuine research man because the latter is usually a little vague and always humble before the thing; he doesn't have much use for the equipment or the jargon. Whereas the technician is never vague and never humble before the thing; he holds the thing disposed of by the principle, the formula, the textbook outline; and he thinks a great deal of equipment and jargon.

But since neither of these methods of recovering the dogfish is pedagogically feasible — perhaps the great man even less so than the Bomb — I wish to propose the following educational technique which should prove equally effective for Harvard and Shreveport High School. I propose that English poetry and biology should be taught as usual, but that at irregular intervals, poetry students should find dogfishes on their desks and biology students should find Shakespeare sonnets on their dissection boards. I am serious in declaring that a Sarah Lawrence English major who began poking about in a dogfish with a bobby pin would learn more in thirty minutes than a biology major in a whole semester; and that the latter upon reading on her dissecting board

> That time of year Thou may'st in me behold
> When yellow leaves, or none, or few, do hang
> Upon those boughs which shake against the cold —
> Bare ruin'd choirs where late the sweet birds sang

might catch fire at the beauty of it.

The situation of the tourist at the Grand Canyon and the biology student are special cases of a predicament in which everyone finds himself in a modern technical society — a society, that is, in which there is a division between expert and layman, planner and consumer, in which experts and planners take special measures to teach and edify the consumer. The measures taken are measures appropriate to the consumer: the expert and the planner *know* and *plan*, but the consumer *needs* and *experiences*.

There is a double deprivation. First, the thing is lost through its packaging. The very means by which the thing is presented for consumption, the very techniques by which the thing is made available as an item of need-satisfaction, these very means operate to remove the thing from the sovereignty of the knower. A loss of title occurs. The measures which the museum curator takes to present the thing to the public are self-liquidating. The upshot of the curator's efforts are not that everyone can see the exhibit but that no one can see it. The curator protests: Why are they so indifferent? Why do they even deface the exhibit? Don't they know it is theirs? But it is not theirs. It is his, the curator's. By the most exclusive sort of zoning, the museum exhibit, the park oak tree, is part of an ensemble, a package, which is almost impenetrable to them. The archaeologist who puts his find in a museum so that everyone can see it accomplishes the reverse of his expectations. The result of his action is that no one can see it now but the archaeologist. He would have done better to keep it in his pocket and show it now and then to strangers.

The tourist who carves his initials in a public place, which is theoretically "his" in the first place, has good reasons for doing so, reasons which the exhibitor and planner know nothing about. He does so because in his role of consumer of an experience (a "recreational experience" to satisfy a "recreational need") he knows that he is disinherited. He is deprived of his title over being. He knows very well that he is in a very special sort of zone in which his only rights are the rights of a consumer. He moves like a ghost through schoolroom, city streets, trains, parks, movies. He carves his initials as a last desperate measure to escape his ghostly role of consumer. He is saying in effect: I am not a ghost after all; I am a sovereign person. And he establishes title the only way remaining to him, by staking his claim over one square inch of wood or stone.

Does this mean that we should get rid of museums? No, but it means that the sightseer should be prepared to enter into a struggle to recover a sight from a museum.

The second loss is the spoliation of the thing, the tree, the rock, the swallow, by the layman's misunderstanding of scientific theory. He believes that the thing is *disposed of* by theory, that it stands in the Platonic relation of being a *specimen* of such and such an underlying principle. In the transmission of scientific theory from theorist to layman, the expectation of the theorist is reversed. Instead of the marvels of the universe being made available to the public, the universe is disposed of by theory. The loss of sovereignty takes this form: as a result of the science of botany, trees are not made available to every man. On the contrary. The tree loses its proper density and mystery as a concrete existent and, as merely another *specimen* of a species, becomes itself nugatory.

Does this mean that there is no use taking biology at Harvard and Shreveport High? No, but it means that the student should know what a fight he has on his hands to rescue the specimen from the educational package. The educator is only partly to blame. For there is nothing the educator can do to provide for this need of the student. Everything the educator does only succeeds in becoming, for the student, part of the educational package. The highest role of the educator is the maieutic role of Socrates: to help the student come to himself not as a consumer of experience but as a sovereign individual.

The thing is twice lost to the consumer. First, sovereignty is lost: it is theirs, not his. Second, it is radically devalued by theory. This is a loss which has been brought about by science but through no fault of the scientist and through no fault of scientific theory. The loss has come about as a consequence of the seduction of the layman by science. The layman will be seduced as long as he regards beings as consumer items to be experienced rather than prizes to be won, and as long as he waives his sovereign rights as a person and accepts his role of consumer as the highest estate to which the layman can aspire.

As Mounier said, the person is not something one can study and provide for; he is something one struggles for. But unless he also struggles for himself, unless he knows that there is a struggle, he is going to be just what the planners think he is.

• • ● • • •

QUESTIONS FOR A SECOND READING

1. Percy's essay proceeds by adding example to example, one after another. If all the examples were meant to illustrate the same thing, the same general point or idea, then one would most likely have been enough. The rest would have been redundant. It makes sense, then, to assume that each

example gives a different view of what Percy is saying, that each modifies the others, or qualifies them, or adds a piece that was otherwise lacking. It's as though Percy needed one more to get it right or to figure out what was missing along the way. As you read back through the essay, pay particular attention to the *differences* between the examples (between the various tourists going to the Grand Canyon, or between the tourists at the Grand Canyon and the tourists in Mexico). Also note the logic or system that leads from one to the next. What progress of thought is represented by the movement from one example to another, or from tourists to students?

2. The essay is filled with talk about "loss"—the loss of sovereignty, the loss of the creature—but it is resolutely ambiguous about what it is that we have lost. As you work your way back through, note the passages that describe what we are missing and why we should care. Are we to believe, for example, that Cárdenas actually had it (whatever "it" is)—that he had no preconceived notions when he saw the Grand Canyon? Mightn't he have said, "I claim this for my queen" or "There I see the glory of God" or "This wilderness is not fit for man"? To whom, or in the name of what, is this loss that Percy chronicles such a matter of concern? If this is not just Percy's peculiar prejudice, if we are asked to share his concerns, whose interests or what interests are represented here?

3. The essay is made up of stories or anecdotes, all of them fanciful. Percy did not, in other words, turn to first-person accounts of visitors to the Grand Canyon or to statements by actual students or teachers. Why not, do you suppose? What does this choice say about his "method"—about what it can and can't do? As you reread the essay, look for sections you could use to talk about the power and limits of Percy's method.

— • • • • • • • —

ASSIGNMENTS FOR WRITING

1. Percy tells several stories—some of them quite good stories—but it is often hard to know just what he is getting at, just what point he is trying to make. If he's making an argument, it's not the sort of argument that is easy to summarize. And if the stories (or anecdotes) are meant to serve as examples, they are not the sort of examples that lead directly to a single, general conclusion or that serve to clarify a point or support an obvious thesis. In fact, at the very moment when you expect Percy to come forward and pull things together, he offers yet another story, as though another example, rather than any general statement, would get you closer to what he is saying.

    There are, at the same time, terms and phrases to suggest that this is an essay with a point to make. Percy talks, for example, about "the loss of sovereignty," "symbolic packages," "consumers of experience," and "dialectic," and it seems that these terms and phrases are meant to name or comment on key scenes, situations, or characters in the examples.

For this assignment, tell a story of your own, one that is suggested by the stories Percy tells — perhaps a story about a time you went looking for something or at something, or about a time when you did or did not find a dogfish in your Shakespeare class. You should imagine that you are carrying out a project that Percy has begun, a project that has you looking back at your own experience through the lens of "The Loss of the Creature," noticing what Percy would notice and following the paths that he would find interesting. Try to bring the terms that Percy uses — like "sovereign," "consumer," "expert," and "dialectic"—to bear on the story you have to tell. Feel free to imitate Percy's style and method in your essay.

2. Percy charts several routes to the Grand Canyon: you can take the packaged tour, you can get off the beaten track, you can wait for a disaster, you can follow the "dialectical movement which brings one back to the beaten track but at a level above it." This last path (or stratagem), he says, is for the complex traveler.

> Our complex friend stands behind his fellow tourists at the Bright Angel Lodge and sees the canyon through them and their predicament, their picture taking and busy disregard. In a sense, he exploits his fellow tourists; he stands on their shoulders to see the canyon. (p. 474)

The complex traveler sees the Grand Canyon through the example of the common tourists with "their predicament, their picture taking and busy disregard." He "stands on their shoulders" to see the canyon. This distinction between complex and common approaches is an important one in the essay. It is interesting to imagine how the distinction could be put to work to define ways of reading.

Suppose that you read "The Loss of the Creature" as a common reader. What would you see? What would you identify as key sections of the text? What would you miss? What would you say about what you see?

If you think of yourself, now, as a complex reader, modeled after any of Percy's more complex tourists or students, what would you see? What would you identify as key sections of the text? What would you miss? What would you say about what you see?

For this assignment, write an essay with three sections. You may number them, if you choose. The first section should represent the work of a common reader with "The Loss of the Creature," and the second should represent the work of a complex reader. The third section should look back and comment on the previous two. In particular, you might address these questions: Why might a person prefer one reading over the other? What is to be gained or lost with both?

• • ● • •

MAKING CONNECTIONS

1. In her essay "Arts of the Contact Zone" (p. 512), Mary Louise Pratt shares some of Walker Percy's concerns for how we do and don't connect to the world around us. Pratt is interested in attempts — and failures — to connect across differences in culture, language, status, and power. And Percy — well, he is harder to pin down.

   As you reread these two essays, see how and where Pratt's notion of the "contact zone" might provide access to some of the examples and concerns in Percy's essay. What are the "contact zones" that concern him? How are they defined? What "arts" might he be proposing for those who find themselves in such a place or at such a moment?

   Pratt and Percy could be said to be asking similar questions, and they write with similar urgency. What is equally interesting, perhaps, are their differences. Write an essay in which you consider Pratt's concept of the "contact zone" in relation to Percy's argument in "The Loss of the Creature." And in the end, so far as you are concerned, who speaks to you most convincingly? Which essay do you find more compelling?

2. > But the difference lies in the fundamental placement of the student in the world. (p. 480)
   >
   > — WALKER PERCY, "The Loss of the Creature"

   Richard Rodriguez, in "The Achievement of Desire" (p. 533) and Richard Miller, in "The Dark Night of the Soul" (p. 435), both write about students and how they are "placed" in the world by teachers, located in the world through the ways schools characteristically represent knowledge, the novice, and the expert.

   Choose one of these selections to reread alongside Walker Percy's "The Loss of the Creature," and as you reread look for passages and examples that you feel best represent each writer's argument, places where the two essays seem to speak back and forth to each other.

   Write an essay that presents the argument of each to a reader who has not read the essays, a reader who is smart and savvy and, like you, interested in schooling. Your essay should consider the ways these two essays might be said to engage a similar topic, with a particular eye to the differences. And, as a way to finish, think about what bearing these readings, these two authors and their work as you know it, might have on your own thought and experience.

3. Percy develops a metaphor of tourists observing the Grand Canyon to make arguments about the ways in which a preconceived "symbolic complex" prevents tourists from actually seeing the sites they've come to see — in this case, the Grand Canyon itself. The tourists, Percy argues, instead see whatever it is they expect to see.

In his book *After the Last Sky* and in the chapter we have selected from that book, "States" (p. 559), Edward Said documents and reflects upon his return to Palestine, his homeland. He thinks about how hard it is to return, to find the places and the people he left. And Said thinks about how difficult it has been for the Palestinian people to be seen or heard by the rest of the world. With a photographer, Jean Mohr, he sets out to document his trip.

Reread "The Loss of the Creature" alongside "States," looking for a particular section or particular passages in each that seem to speak to the same issues — sight, direct experience, knowledge, preconception, and recovery. Write an essay that considers the ways these two essays might be said to speak back and forth to each other, with a particular eye to the differences in time, place, and argument. And, as a way to end your essay, think about what bearing these readings, these two authors and their work as you know it, might have on your own thought and experience.

4.   But the difference lies in the fundamental placement of the student in the world. (p. 480)

— WALKER PERCY, "The Loss of the Creature"

What I am about to say to you has taken me more than twenty years to admit: *A primary reason for my success in the classroom was that I couldn't forget that schooling was changing me and separating me from the life I enjoyed before becoming a student.* (p. 534)

— RICHARD RODRIGUEZ, "The Achievement of Desire"

Both Walker Percy and Richard Rodriguez, in "The Achievement of Desire" (p. 533), write about students and how they are "placed" in the world by teachers and by the way schools characteristically represent knowledge, the novice, and the expert. And both tell stories to make their points, stories of characteristic students in characteristic situations. Write an essay in which you tell a story of your own, one meant to serve as a corrective or a supplement to the stories Percy and Rodriguez tell. You will want both to tell your story and to use it as a way of returning to and commenting on Percy and Rodriguez and the arguments they make. Your authority can rest on the fact that you are a student and as a consequence have ways of understanding this position that they do not.

MICHAEL
Pollan

Jeff Morgan 08/Alamy

Michael Pollan (b. 1955) is the John S. and James L. Knight Professor of Journalism at the University of California at Berkeley's Graduate School of Journalism, where he also serves as the director of the Knight Program in Science and Environmental Journalism. For nearly three decades, Pollan has been a contributing writer to the *New York Times Magazine*, and his essays have appeared in nationally renowned periodicals like *Harper's Magazine*, *Vogue*, *The New Yorker*, *National Geographic*, and *The Nation*. His work has also been anthologized in collections like *The Best American Essays*, *The Best American Science Writing*, *The Norton Book of Nature Writing*, and *The New Kings of Nonfiction*.

Pollan is the author of many books, including *New York Times* bestsellers *The Botany of Desire: A Plant's-Eye View of the World* (2001), *The Omnivore's Dilemma: A Natural History of Four Meals* (2006), *In Defense of Food: An Eater's Manifesto* (2008), *Food Rules: An Eater's Manual* (2009), and *Cooked: A Natural History of Transformation* (2013). Pollan's work explores the intersections of nature and culture, and he writes regularly on issues connected to health, the environment, agribusiness, and, perhaps most extensively, on food consumption and production. Such work is surely important because, as Pollan writes in *The Omnivore's Dilemma*, "the way we eat represents our most profound engagement with the natural world. Daily, our eating turns nature into culture, transforming the body of the world into our bodies and mind."

The selection that follows comes from Pollan's *In Defense of Food*, a book that explores how food science has changed (and perhaps overcomplicated) the Western diet and that questions how we might better eat to promote both health and environmental sustainability. As you read, consider how Pollan reviews the history of food science and explores how beliefs about food develop, spread, and are then later challenged and dismissed.

Nutritionism Defined

The term isn't mine. It was coined by an Australian sociologist of science by the name of Gyorgy Scrinis, and as near as I can determine first appeared in a 2002 essay titled "Sorry Marge" published in an Australian quarterly called *Meanjin*. "Sorry Marge" looked at margarine as the ultimate nutritionist product, able to shift its identity (*no cholesterol!* one year, *no trans fats!* the next) depending on the prevailing winds of dietary opinion. But Scrinis had bigger game in his sights than spreadable vegetable oil. He suggested that we look past the various nutritional claims swirling around margarine and butter and consider the underlying message of the debate itself: "namely, that we should understand and engage with food and our bodies in terms of their nutritional and chemical constituents and requirements — the assumption being that this is all we need to understand." This reductionist way of thinking about food had been pointed out and criticized before (notably by the Canadian historian Harvey Levenstein, the British nutritionist Geoffrey Cannon, and the American nutritionists Joan Gussow and Marion Nestle), but it had never before been given a proper name: "nutritionism." Proper names have a way of making visible things we don't easily see or simply take for granted.

The first thing to understand about nutritionism is that it is not the same thing as nutrition. As the "-ism" suggests, it is not a scientific subject but an ideology. Ideologies are ways of organizing large swaths of life and experience under a set of shared but unexamined assumptions. This quality makes an ideology particularly hard to see, at least while it's still exerting its hold on your culture. A reigning ideology is a little like the weather — all pervasive and so virtually impossible to escape. Still, we can try.

> IDEOLOGIES ARE WAYS OF ORGANIZING LARGE SWATHS OF LIFE AND EXPERIENCE UNDER A SET OF SHARED BUT UNEXAMINED ASSUMPTIONS.

In the case of nutritionism, the widely shared but unexamined assumption is that the key to understanding food is indeed the nutrient. Put another way: Foods are essentially the sum of their nutrient parts. From this basic premise flow several others.

Since nutrients, as compared with foods, are invisible and therefore slightly mysterious, it falls to the scientists (and to the journalists through whom the scientists reach the public) to explain the hidden reality of foods to us. In form this is a quasireligious idea, suggesting the visible world is not the one that really matters, which implies the need for a priesthood. For to enter a world where your dietary salvation depends on unseen nutrients, you need plenty of expert help.

But expert help to do what exactly? This brings us to another unexamined assumption of nutritionism: that the whole point of eating is to maintain and promote bodily health. Hippocrates' famous injunction to "let food be thy medicine" is ritually invoked to support this notion. I'll leave the premise alone for now, except to point out that it is not shared by all cultures and, further, that the experience of these other cultures suggests that, paradoxically, regarding food as being about things other than bodily health — like pleasure, say, or sociality or identity — makes people no less healthy; indeed, there's some reason to believe it may make them *more* healthy. This is what we usually have in mind when we speak of the French paradox. So there is at least a question as to whether the ideology of nutritionism is actually any good for you.

It follows from the premise that food is foremost about promoting physical health that the nutrients in food should be divided into the healthy ones and the unhealthy ones — good nutrients and bad. This has been a hallmark of nutritionist thinking from the days of Liebig, for whom it wasn't enough to identify the nutrients; he also had to pick favorites, and nutritionists have been doing so ever since. Liebig claimed that protein was the "master nutrient" in animal nutrition, because he believed it drove growth. Indeed, he likened the role of protein in animals to that of nitrogen in plants: Protein (which contains nitrogen) comprised the essential human fertilizer. Liebig's elevation of protein dominated nutritionist thinking for decades as public health authorities worked to expand access to and production of the master nutrient (especially in the form of animal protein), with the goal of growing bigger, and therefore (it was assumed) healthier, people. (A high priority for Western governments fighting imperial wars.) To a considerable extent we still have a food system organized around the promotion of protein as the master nutrient. It has given us, among other things, vast amounts of cheap meat and milk, which have in turn given us much, *much* bigger people. Whether they are healthier too is another question.

It seems to be a rule of nutritionism that for every good nutrient, there must be a bad nutrient to serve as its foil, the latter a focus for our food fears and the former for our enthusiasms. A backlash against protein arose in America at the turn of the last century as diet gurus like John Harvey Kellogg and Horace Fletcher (about whom more later) railed against the deleterious effects of protein on digestion (it supposedly led to the proliferation of toxic bacteria in the gut) and promoted the cleaner, more wholesome carbohydrate in its place. The legacy of that revaluation is the breakfast cereal,

> IT SEEMS TO BE A RULE OF NUTRITIONISM THAT FOR EVERY GOOD NUTRIENT, THERE MUST BE A BAD NUTRIENT TO SERVE AS ITS FOIL, THE LATTER A FOCUS FOR OUR FOOD FEARS AND THE FORMER FOR OUR ENTHUSIASMS.

the strategic objective of which was to dethrone animal protein at the morning meal.

Ever since, the history of modern nutritionism has been a history of macronutrients at war: protein against carbs; carbs against proteins, and then fats; fats against carbs. Beginning with Liebig, in each age nutritionism has organized most of its energies around an imperial nutrient: protein in the nineteenth century, fat in the twentieth, and, it stands to reason, carbohydrates will occupy our attention in the twenty-first. Meanwhile, in the shadow of these titanic struggles, smaller civil wars have raged within the sprawling empires of the big three: refined carbohydrates versus fiber; animal protein versus plant protein; saturated fats versus polyunsaturated fats; and then, deep down within the province of the polyunsaturates, omega-3 fatty acids versus omega-6s. Like so many ideologies, nutritionism at bottom hinges on a form of dualism, so that at all times there must be an evil nutrient for adherents to excoriate and a savior nutrient for them to sanctify. At the moment, trans fats are performing admirably in the former role, omega-3 fatty acids in the latter. It goes without saying that such a Manichaean view of nutrition is bound to promote food fads and phobias and large abrupt swings of the nutritional pendulum.

Another potentially serious weakness of nutritionist ideology is that, focused so relentlessly as it is on the nutrients it can measure, it has trouble discerning qualitative distinctions among foods. So fish, beef, and chicken through the nutritionist's lens become mere delivery systems for varying quantities of different fats and proteins and whatever other nutrients happen to be on their scope. Milk through this lens is reduced to a suspension of protein, lactose, fats, and calcium in water, when it is entirely possible that the benefits, or for that matter the hazards, of drinking milk owe to entirely other factors (growth hormones?) or relationships between factors (fat-soluble vitamins and saturated fat?) that have been overlooked. Milk remains a food of humbling complexity, to judge by the long, sorry saga of efforts to simulate it. The entire history of baby formula has been the history of one overlooked nutrient after another: Liebig missed the vitamins and amino acids, and his successors missed the omega-3s, and still to this day babies fed on the most "nutritionally complete" formula fail to do as well as babies fed human milk. Even more than margarine, infant formula stands as the ultimate test product of nutritionism and a fair index of its hubris.

This brings us to one of the most troubling features of nutritionism, though it is a feature certainly not troubling to all. When the emphasis is on quantifying the nutrients contained in foods (or, to be precise, the *recognized* nutrients in foods), any qualitative distinction between whole foods and processed foods is apt to disappear. "[If] foods are understood only in terms of the various quantities of nutrients they contain," Gyorgy Scrinis wrote, then "even processed foods may be considered to be 'healthier' for you than whole foods if they contain the appropriate quantities of some nutrients."

How convenient.

NUTRITIONISM COMES TO MARKET

No idea could be more sympathetic to manufacturers of processed foods, which surely explains why they have been so happy to jump on the nutritionism bandwagon. Indeed, nutritionism supplies the ultimate justification for processing food by implying that with a judicious application of food science, fake foods can be made even more nutritious than the real thing. This of course is the story of margarine, the first important synthetic food to slip into our diet. Margarine started out in the nineteenth century as a cheap and inferior substitute for butter, but with the emergence of the lipid hypothesis in the 1950s, manufacturers quickly figured out that their product, with some tinkering, could be marketed as better — smarter! — than butter: butter with the bad nutrients removed (cholesterol and saturated fats) and replaced with good nutrients (polyunsaturated fats and then vitamins). Every time margarine was found wanting, the wanted nutrient could simply be added (Vitamin D? *Got it now*. Vitamin A? *Sure, no problem*). But of course margarine, being the product not of nature but of human ingenuity, could never be any smarter than the nutritionists dictating its recipe, and the nutritionists turned out to be not nearly as smart as they thought. The food scientists' ingenious method for making healthy vegetable oil solid at room temperature — by blasting it with hydrogen — turned out to produce unhealthy trans fats, fats that we now know are more dangerous than the saturated fats they were designed to replace. Yet the beauty of a processed food like margarine is that it can be endlessly reengineered to overcome even the most embarrassing about-face in nutritional thinking — including the real wincer that its main ingredient might cause heart attacks and cancer. So now the trans fats are gone, and margarine marches on, unfazed and apparently unkillable. Too bad the same cannot be said of an unknown number of margarine eaters.

By now we have become so inured to fake foods that we forget what a difficult trail margarine had to blaze before it and other synthetic food products could win government and consumer acceptance. At least since the 1906 publication of Upton Sinclair's *The Jungle*, the "adulteration" of common foods has been a serious concern of the eating public and the target of numerous federal laws and Food and Drug Administration regulations. Many consumers regarded "oleomargarine" as just such an adulteration, and in the late 1800s five states passed laws requiring that all butter imitations be dyed pink so no one would be fooled. The Supreme Court struck down the laws in 1898. In retrospect, had the practice survived, it might have saved some lives.

The 1938 Food, Drug and Cosmetic Act imposed strict rules requiring that the word "imitation" appear on any food product that was, well, an imitation. Read today, the official rationale behind the imitation rule seems at once commonsensical and quaint: ". . . there are certain traditional foods that everyone knows, such as bread, milk and cheese, and that when consumers buy these foods, they should get the foods they are expecting . . . [and] if a food resembles a standardized food but does not comply with the standard, that food must be labeled as an 'imitation.'"

Hard to argue with that . . . but the food industry did, strenuously for decades, and in 1973 it finally succeeded in getting the imitation rule tossed out, a little-noticed but momentous step that helped speed America down the path to nutritionism.

Industry hated the imitation rule. There had been such a tawdry history of adulterated foods and related forms of snake oil in American commerce that slapping the word "imitation" on a food product was the kiss of death — an admission of adulteration and inferiority. By the 1960s and 1970s, the requirement that such a pejorative term appear on fake food packages stood in the way of innovation, indeed of the wholesale reformulation of the American food supply — a project that, in the wake of rising concerns about dietary fat and cholesterol, was coming to be seen as a good thing. What had been regarded as hucksterism and fraud in 1906 had begun to look like sound public health policy by 1973. The American Heart Association, eager to get Americans off saturated fats and onto vegetable oils (including hydrogenated vegetable oils), was actively encouraging the food industry to "modify" various foods to get the saturated fats and cholesterol out of them, and in the early seventies the association urged that "any existing and regulatory barriers to the marketing of such foods be removed."

And so they were when, in 1973, the FDA (not, note, the Congress that wrote the law) simply repealed the 1938 rule concerning imitation foods. It buried the change in a set of new, seemingly consumer-friendly rules about nutrient labeling so that news of the imitation rule's repeal did not appear until the twenty-seventh paragraph of *The New York Times'* account, published under the headline F.D.A. PROPOSES SWEEPING CHANGE IN FOOD LABELING: NEW RULES DESIGNED TO GIVE CONSUMERS A BETTER IDEA OF NUTRITIONAL VALUE. (The second deck of the headline gave away the game: PROCESSORS BACK MOVE.) The revised imitation rule held that as long as an imitation product was not "nutritionally inferior" to the natural food it sought to impersonate — as long as it had the same quantities of recognized nutrients — the imitation could be marketed without using the dreaded "i" word.

With that, the regulatory door was thrown open to all manner of faked low-fat products: Fats in things like sour cream and yogurt could now be replaced with hydrogenated oils or guar gum or carrageenan, bacon bits could be replaced with soy protein, the cream in "whipped cream" and "coffee creamer" could be replaced with corn starch, and the yolks of liquefied eggs could be replaced with, well, whatever the food scientists could dream up, because the sky was now the limit. As long as the new fake foods were engineered to be nutritionally equivalent to the real article, they could no longer be considered fake. Of course the operative nutritionist assumption here is that we know enough to determine nutritional equivalence — something that the checkered history of baby formula suggests has never been the case.

Nutritionism had become the official ideology of the Food and Drug Administration; for all practical purposes the government had redefined foods as nothing more than the sum of their recognized nutrients. Adulteration had been repositioned as food science. All it would take now was a push from McGovern's *Dietary Goals* for hundreds of "traditional foods that everyone knows" to begin their long retreat from the supermarket shelves and for our eating to become more "scientific."

. . ● ◉ ● . .

BAD SCIENCE

To understand how nutrition science could have been so spectacularly wrong about dietary fat and health, it's important to understand that doing nutrition science isn't easy. In fact, it's a lot harder than most of the scientists who do it for a living realize or at least are willing to admit. For one thing, the scientific tools at their disposal are in many ways ill suited to the task of understanding systems as complex as food and diet. The assumptions of nutritionism — such as the idea that a food is not a system but rather the sum of its nutrient parts — pose another set of problems. We like to think of scientists as being free from ideological taint, but of course they are as much the product of their ideological environment as the rest of us. In the same way nutritionism can lead to a false consciousness in the mind of the eater, it can just as easily mislead the scientist.

> IN THE SAME WAY NUTRITIONISM CAN LEAD TO A FALSE CONSCIOUSNESS IN THE MIND OF THE EATER, IT CAN JUST AS EASILY MISLEAD THE SCIENTIST.

The problem starts with the nutrient. Most nutritional science involves studying one nutrient at a time, a seemingly unavoidable approach that even nutritionists who do it will tell you is deeply flawed. "The problem with nutrient-by-nutrient nutrition science," points out Marion Nestle, a New York University nutritionist, "is that it takes the nutrient out of the context of the food, the food out of the context of the diet, and the diet out of the context of the lifestyle."

If nutrition scientists know this, why do they do it anyway? Because a nutrient bias is built into the way science is done. Scientists study variables they can isolate; if they can't isolate a variable, they won't be able to tell whether its presence or absence is meaningful. Yet even the simplest food is a hopelessly complicated thing to analyze, a virtual wilderness of chemical compounds, many of which exist in intricate and dynamic relation to one another, and all of which together are in the process of changing from one state to another. So if you're a nutrition scientist you do the only thing you *can* do, given the tools at your disposal: Break the thing down into its component parts and study those one by one, even if that means ignoring subtle interactions and contexts and the fact that the whole may well be more than, or maybe just different from, the sum of its parts. This is what we mean by reduction-ist science.

Scientific reductionism is an undeniably powerful tool, but it can mis-lead us too, especially when applied to something as complex, on the one side, as a food and on the other a human eater. It encourages us to take a simple mechanistic view of that transaction: Put in this nutrient, get out that physiological result. Yet people differ in important ways. We all know that lucky soul who can eat prodigious quantities of fattening food without ever gaining weight. Some populations can metabolize sugars better than others. Depending on your evolutionary heritage, you may or may not be able to digest the lactose in milk. Depending on your genetic makeup, reducing the saturated fat in your diet may or may not move your choles-terol numbers. The specific ecology of your intestines helps determine how efficiently you digest what you eat, so that the same 100 calories of food may yield more or less food energy depending on the proportion of Firmicutes and Bacteroides resident in your gut. In turn, that balance of bacterial species could owe to your genes or to something in your envi-ronment. So there is nothing very machinelike about the human eater, and to think of food as simply fuel is to completely misconstrue it. It's worth keeping in mind too that, curiously, the human digestive tract has roughly as many neurons as the spinal column. We don't yet know exactly what they're up to, but their existence suggests that much more is going on in digestion than simply the breakdown of foods into chemicals.

Also, people don't eat nutrients; they eat foods, and foods can behave very differently from the nutrients they contain. Based on epidemiologi-cal comparisons of different populations, researchers have long believed that a diet containing lots of fruits and vegetables confers some protection against cancer. So naturally they ask, What nutrient in those plant foods is responsible for that effect? One hypothesis is that the antioxidants in fresh produce — compounds like beta-carotene, lycopene, vitamin E, and so on — are the X factor. It makes good theoretical sense: These molecules (which plants produce to protect themselves from the highly reactive forms of oxygen they produce during photosynthesis) soak up the free radicals in our bodies, which can damage DNA and initiate cancers. At least that's how it seems to work in a test tube. Yet as soon as you remove these crucial molecules from the con-text of the whole foods they're found in, as we've done in creating antioxidant supplements, they don't seem to work at all. Indeed, in the case of beta-carotene ingested as a supplement, one study has suggested that in some people it may actually *increase* the risk of certain cancers. Big oops.

What's going on here? We don't know. It could be the vagaries of human digestion. Maybe the fiber (or some other component) in a carrot protects the antioxidant molecule from destruction by stomach acids early in the digestive process. Or it could be we isolated the wrong antioxidant. Beta is just one of a whole slew of carotenes found in common vegetables; maybe we focused on the wrong one. Or maybe beta-carotene works as an antioxidant only in concert with some other plant chemical or process; under other circumstances it may behave as a pro-oxidant.

Indeed, to look at the chemical composition of any common food plant is to realize just how much complexity lurks within it. Here's a list of just the antioxidants that have been identified in a leaf of garden-variety thyme:

> alanine, anethole essential oil, apigenin, ascorbic acid, beta-carotene, caffeic acid, camphene, carvacrol, chlorogenic acid, chrysoeriol, derulic acid, erio-dictyol, eugenol, 4-terpinol, gallic acid, gamma-terpinene, isichlorogenic acid, isoeugenol, isothymonin, kaemferol, labiatic acid, lauric acid, linalyl acetate, luteolin, methionine, myrcene, myristic acid, naringenin, rosmarinic acid, selenium, tannin, thymol, trytophan, ursolic acid, vanillic acid.

This is what you ingest when you eat food flavored with thyme. Some of these chemicals are broken down by your digestion, but others go on to do various as-yet-undetermined things to your body: turning some gene's expression on or off, perhaps, or intercepting a free radical before it disturbs a strand of DNA deep in some cell. It would be great to know how this all works, but in the meantime we can enjoy thyme in the knowledge that it probably doesn't do any harm (since people have been eating it forever) and that it might actually do some good (since people have been eating it forever), and even if it does nothing at all, we like the way it tastes.

It's important also to remind ourselves that what reductive science can manage to perceive well enough to isolate and study is subject to almost continual change, and that we have a tendency to assume that what we *can* see is the important thing to look at. The vast attention paid to cholesterol since the 1950s is largely the result of the fact that for a long time cholesterol was the only factor linked to heart disease that we had the tools to measure. (This is sometimes called parking-lot science, after the legendary fellow who loses his keys in a parking lot and goes looking for them under the streetlight — not because that's where he lost them but because that's where it's easiest to see.) When we learned how to measure different types of cholesterol, and then triglycerides and C-reactive protein, those became the important components to study. There will no doubt be other factors as yet unidentified. It's an old story: When Prout and Liebig nailed down the macronutrients, scientists figured that they now understood the nature of food and what the body needed from it. Then when the vitamins were isolated a few decades later, scientists thought, okay, now we *really* understand food and what the body needs for its health; and today it's the polyphenols and carotenoids that seem to have completed the picture. But who knows what else is going on deep in the soul of a carrot?

THAT'S THE GREAT THING ABOUT EATING FOODS AS COMPARED WITH NUTRIENTS: YOU DON'T NEED TO FATHOM A CARROT'S COMPLEXITY IN ORDER TO REAP ITS BENEFITS.

The good news is that, to the carrot eater, it doesn't matter. That's the great thing about eating foods as compared with nutrients: You don't need to fathom a carrot's complexity in order to reap its benefits.

The mystery of the antioxidants points up the danger in taking a nutrient out of the context of food; scientists make a second, related error when they attempt to study the food out of the context of the diet. We eat foods in combinations and in orders that can affect how they're metabolized. The carbohydrates in a bagel will be absorbed more slowly if the bagel is spread with peanut butter; the fiber, fat, and protein in the peanut butter cushion the insulin response, thereby blunting the impact of the carbohydrates. (This is why eating dessert at the end of the meal rather than the beginning is probably a good idea.) Drink coffee with your steak, and your body won't be able to fully absorb the iron in the meat. The olive oil with which I eat tomatoes makes the lycopene they contain more available to my body. Some of those compounds in the sprig of thyme may affect my digestion of the dish I add it to, helping to break down one compound or stimulate production of an enzyme needed to detoxify another. We have barely begun to understand the relationships among foods in a cuisine.

But we do understand some of the simplest relationships among foods, like the zero-sum relationship: If you eat a lot of one thing, you're probably not eating a lot of something else. This fact alone may have helped lead the diet-heart researchers astray. Like most of us, they assumed that a bad outcome like heart disease must have a bad cause, like saturated fat or cholesterol, so they focused their investigative energies on how these bad nutrients might cause disease rather than on how the absence of something else, like plant foods or fish, might figure in the etiology of the disease. Nutrition science has usually put more of its energies into the idea that the problems it studies are the result of too much of a bad thing instead of too little of a good thing. Is this good science or nutritionist prejudice? The epidemiologist John Powles has suggested this predilection is little more than a Puritan bias: *Bad things happen to people who eat bad things.*

But what people *don't* eat may matter as much as what they do. This fact could explain why populations that eat diets containing lots of animal food generally have higher rates of coronary heart disease and cancer than those that don't. But nutritionism encouraged researchers to look beyond the possibly culpable food itself — meat — to the culpable nutrient in the meat, which scientists have long assumed to be the saturated fat. So they are baffled indeed when large dietary trials like the Women's Health Initiative and the Nurses' Health Study fail to find evidence that reducing fat intake significantly reduces the incidence of heart disease or cancer.

Of course thanks to the low-fat-diet fad (inspired by the same reductionist hypothesis about fat), it is entirely possible to slash your intake of saturated fat without greatly reducing your consumption of animal protein: Just drink the low-fat milk, buy the low-fat cheese, and order the chicken breast or the turkey bacon instead of the burger. So did the big dietary trials exonerate meat or just fat? Unfortunately, the focus on nutrients didn't tell us much about *foods.* Perhaps the culprit nutrient in meat and dairy is the animal protein itself, as some researchers hypothesize. (The Cornell nutritionist T. Colin Campbell argues as much in his recent book, *The China Study*.) Others think it could be the particular kind of iron in red meat (called heme iron) or the nitrosamines produced when meat is cooked. Perhaps it is the steroid growth hormones typically present in the milk and meat; these hormones (which occur naturally in meat and milk but are often augmented in industrial production) are known to promote certain kinds of cancer.

Or, as I mentioned, the problem with a meat-heavy diet might not even be the meat itself but the plants that all that meat has pushed off the plate. We just don't know. But eaters worried about their health needn't wait for science to settle this question before deciding that it might be wise to eat more plants and less meat. This of course is precisely what the McGovern committee was trying to tell us.

The zero-sum fallacy of nutrition science poses another obstacle to nailing down the effect of a single nutrient. As Gary Taubes points out, it's difficult to design a dietary trial of something like saturated fat because as soon as you remove it from the trial diet, either you have dramatically reduced the calories in that diet or you have replaced the saturated fat with something else: other fats (but which ones?), or carbohydrates (but what kind?), or protein. Whatever you do, you've introduced a second variable into the experiment, so you will not be able to attribute any observed effect strictly to the absence of saturated fat. It could just as easily be due to the reduction in calories or the addition of carbohydrates or polyunsaturated fats. For every diet hypothesis you test, you can construct an alternative hypothesis based on the presence or absence of the substitute nutrient. It gets messy.

And then there is the placebo effect, which has always bedeviled nutrition research. About a third of Americans are what researchers call responders — people who will respond to a treatment or intervention regardless of whether they've actually received it. When testing a drug you can correct for this by using a placebo in your trial, but how do you correct for the placebo effect in the case of a dietary trial? You can't: Low-fat foods seldom taste like the real thing, and no person is ever going to confuse a meat entrée for a vegetarian substitute.

Marion Nestle also cautions against taking the diet out of the context of the lifestyle, a particular hazard when comparing the diets of different populations. The Mediterranean diet is widely believed to be one of the most healthful traditional diets, yet much of what we know about it is based on studies of people living in the 1950s on the island of Crete — people who in many respects led lives very different from our own. Yes, they ate lots of olive oil and more fish than meat. But they also did more physical labor. As followers of the Greek Orthodox church, they fasted frequently. They ate lots of wild greens — weeds. And, perhaps most significant, they ate far fewer total calories than we do. Similarly, much of what we know about the health benefits of a vegetarian diet is based on studies of Seventh-Day Adventists, who muddy the nutritional picture by abstaining from alcohol and tobacco as well as meat. These extraneous but unavoidable factors are called, aptly, confounders.

One last example: People who take supplements are healthier than the population at large, yet their health probably has nothing whatsoever to do with the supplements they take — most of which recent studies have suggested are worthless. Supplement takers tend to be better educated, more affluent people who, almost by definition, take a greater than usual interest in personal health — confounders that probably account for their superior health.

But if confounding factors of lifestyle bedevil epidemiological comparisons of different populations, the supposedly more rigorous studies of large American populations suffer from their own arguably even more disabling flaws. In ascending order of supposed reliability, nutrition researchers have three main methods for studying the impact of diet on health: the case-control study, the cohort study, and the intervention trial. All three are seriously flawed in different ways.

In the case-control study, researchers attempt to determine the diet of a subject who has been diagnosed with a chronic disease in order to uncover its cause. One problem is that when people get sick they may change the way they eat, so the diet they report may not be the diet responsible for their illness. Another problem is that these patients will typically report eating large amounts of whatever the evil nutrient of the moment is. These people read the newspaper too; it's only natural to search for the causes of one's misfortune and, perhaps, to link one's illness to one's behavior. One of the more pernicious aspects of nutritionism is that it encourages us to blame our health problems on lifestyle choices, implying that the individual bears ultimate responsibility for whatever illnesses befall him. It's worth keeping in mind that a far more powerful predictor of heart disease than either diet or exercise is social class.

Long-term observational studies of cohort groups such as the Nurses' Health Study represent a big step up in reliability from the case-control study. For one thing, the studies are prospective rather than retrospective: They begin tracking subjects before they become ill. The Nurses' Study, which has collected data on the eating habits and health outcomes of more than one hundred thousand women over several decades (at a cost of more than one hundred million dollars), is considered the best study of its kind, yet it too has limitations. One is its reliance on food-frequency questionnaires (about which more in a moment). Another is the population of nurses it has chosen to study. Critics (notably Colin Campbell) point out that the sample is relatively uniform and is even more carnivorous than the U.S. population as a whole. Pretty much everyone in the group eats a Western diet. This means that when researchers divide the subject population into groups (typically fifths) to study the impact of, say, a low-fat diet, the quintile eating the lowest-fat diet is not all that low — or so dramatically different from the quintile consuming the highest-fat diet. "Virtually this entire cohort of nurses is consuming a high-risk diet," according to Campbell. That might explain why the Nurses' Study has failed to detect significant benefits for many of the dietary interventions it's looked at. In a subject population that is eating a fairly standard

Western diet, as this one is, you're never going to capture the effects, good or bad, of more radically different ways of eating. (In his book, Campbell reports Walter Willett's personal response to this criticism: "You may be right, Colin, but people don't want to go there.")

The so-called gold standard in nutrition research is the large-scale intervention study. In these studies, of which the Women's Health Initiative is the biggest and best known, a large population is divided into two groups. The intervention group changes its diet in some prescribed way while the control group (one hopes) does not. The two groups are then tracked over many years to learn whether the intervention affects relative rates of chronic disease. In the case of the Women's Health Initiative study of dietary fat, a $415 million undertaking sponsored by the National Institutes of Health, the eating habits and health outcomes of nearly forty-nine thousand women (aged fifty to seventy-nine) were tracked for eight years to assess the impact of a low-fat diet on a woman's risk of breast and colorectal cancer and cardiovascular disease. Forty percent of the women were told to reduce their consumption of fat to 20 percent of total calories. When the results were announced in 2006, it made front-page news (*The New York Times* headline said LOW-FAT DIET DOES NOT CUT HEALTH RISKS, STUDY FINDS) and the cloud of nutritional confusion beneath which Americans endeavor to eat darkened further.

Even a cursory examination of the study's methods makes you wonder what, if anything, it proved, either about dietary fat or meat eating. You could argue that, like the Nurses' Health Study, all any such trials prove is that changing one component in the diet at a time, and not by much, does not confer a significant health benefit. But perhaps the strongest conclusion that can be drawn from an analysis of the Women's Health Initiative is about the inherent limitations of this kind of nutrient-by-nutrient nutrition research.

Even the beginning student of nutritionism will immediately spot several flaws: The focus was on dietary fat rather than on any particular food, such as meat or dairy. So women could reach their goal simply by switching to lower-fat animal products. Also, no distinctions were made between different types of fat: Women getting their allowable portion of fat from olive oil or fish were lumped together with women getting their fat from low-fat cheese or chicken breasts or margarine. Why? Because when the study was designed sixteen years ago, the whole notion of "good fats" was not yet on the mainstream scientific scope. Scientists study what scientists can see.

Another problem with the trial was that the low-fat group failed to hit the target of reducing their fat intake to 20 percent of total calories. The best they could manage was 24 percent in the first year, but by the end of the study they'd drifted back to 29 percent, only a few percentage points lower than the control group's fat intake. Which was itself drifting downward as the women allowed to eat as much fat as they wanted presumably read the newspapers and the food product labels and absorbed the culture's enthusiasm for all things low fat. (This corruption of a control group by popular dietary advice is called the treatment effect.) So it's hardly surprising that the health outcomes of the two groups would not greatly differ — by the end, they might have been consuming pretty much the same diet.

I say "might have been" because we actually have little idea what these women were really eating. Like most people asked about their diet, they lied about it — which brings us to what is perhaps the single biggest problem in doing nutrition science. Even the scientists who conduct this sort of research conduct it in the knowledge that people underestimate (let's be generous) their food intake all the time. They have even developed scientific figures for the magnitude of the error. "Validation studies" of dietary trials like the Women's Health Initiative or the Nurses' Study, which rely on "food-frequency questionnaires" filled out by subjects several times a year, indicate that people on average eat between a fifth and a third more than they say they do on questionnaires.[1] How do the researchers know that? By comparing what people report on their food-frequency questionnaires with interviews about their dietary intake over the previous twenty-four hours, thought to be somewhat more reliable. Somewhat. Because as you might expect, these "twenty-four-hour recall" data have their own accuracy problems: How typical of your overall diet is what you ate during any single twenty-four-hour period?

To try to fill out the food-frequency questionnaire used by the Women's Health Initiative, as I recently did, is to realize just how shaky the data on which all such dietary studies rely really are. The survey, which takes about forty-five minutes to complete, starts off with some relatively easy questions. "Did you eat chicken or turkey during the last three months?" Having answered yes, I then was asked, "When you ate chicken or turkey, how often did you eat the skin?" And, "Did you usually choose light meat, dark meat, both?" But the survey soon became harder, as when it asked me to think back over the past three months to recall whether when I ate okra, squash, or yams were they fried, and if so, were they fried in stick margarine, tub margarine, butter, shortening (in which category they inexplicably lumped together hydrogenated vegetable oil and lard), olive or canola oil, or nonstick spray? I would hope they'd take my answers with a grain of salt because I honestly didn't remember and in the case of any okra eaten in a restaurant, even a hypnotist or CIA interrogator could not extract from me what sort of fat it was fried in. Now that we spend half of our food dollars on meals prepared outside of the home, how can respondents possibly know what type of fats they're consuming?

Matters got even sketchier in the second section of the survey, when I was asked to specify how many times in the last three months I'd eaten a half-cup serving of broccoli, among a dizzying array of other fruits and vegetables I was asked to tally for the dietary quarter. I'm not sure Marcel Proust himself could recall his dietary intake over the last ninety days with the sort of precision demanded by the FFQ.

When you get to the meat section, the portion sizes specified haven't been seen in America since the Hoover administration. If a four-ounce portion of steak is considered "medium," was I really going to admit that the steak I enjoyed on an un-recallable number of occasions during the past three months was probably the equivalent of two or three (or in the case of a steak house steak, no fewer than *four*) of these portions? I think not. In fact, most of the "medium serving sizes" to which I was asked to compare my own consumption made me feel like such a pig that I badly wanted to shave a few ounces here, a few there. (I mean, I wasn't under oath or anything.)

These are the sort of data on which the largest questions of diet and health are being decided today. "The most intellectually demanding challenge in the field of nutrition," as Marion Nestle writes in *Food Politics*, "is to determine dietary intake." The uncomfortable fact is that the entire field of nutritional science rests on a foundation of ignorance and lies about the most basic question of nutrition: What are people eating? Over lunch, I asked Nestle if I was perhaps being too harsh. She smiled.

"To really know what a person is eating you'd have to have a second invisible person following them around, taking photographs, looking at ingredients, and consulting accurate food composition tables, which we don't have." When you report on an FFQ that you ate a carrot, the tabulator consults a U.S. Department of Agriculture database to determine exactly how much calcium or beta-carotene that carrot contained. But because all carrots are not created equal, their nutrient content varying with everything from the variety planted and type of soil it was planted in to the agriculture system used (organic? conventional?) and the carrot's freshness, these tables suffer from their own inaccuracies.

I was beginning to realize just how much suspension of disbelief it takes to be a nutrition scientist.

"It's impossible," Nestle continued. "Are people unconsciously underestimating consumption of things they think the researcher thinks are bad or overestimating consumption of things they think the researcher thinks are good? We don't know. Probably both. The issue of reporting is extraordinarily serious. We have to ask, How accurate are the data?"

> **I WAS BEGINNING TO REALIZE JUST HOW MUCH SUSPENSION OF DISBELIEF IT TAKES TO BE A NUTRITION SCIENTIST.**

It's not as though the epidemiologists who develop and deploy FFQs are unaware of their limitations. Some of them, like Walter Willett, strive heroically to repair the faulty data, developing "energy adjustment" factors to correct for the fact that the calories reported on surveys are invariably wrong and complicated "measurement error" algorithms to fix the errors in the twenty-four-hour recall surveys used to fix the errors in the FFQ.

I tracked down Gladys Block, the prominent epidemiologist who developed the FFQ on which the Women's Health Initiative based its own questionnaire. We met for coffee in Berkeley, where she is a professor in the School of Public Health. Nearing retirement, Block is unusually thoughtful about the limits of her field and disarmingly candid. "It's a mess," she said, speaking not of the FFQ itself but of the various formulae and algorithms being used to correct errors in the data. "Because if the energy [i.e., the reported calorie consumption] is off, then the nutrients are off too. So if you're going to correct for calories, do you then also correct for . . ." She paused and then sighed. "No, it's a mess."

Block thinks the problem with nutrition science, which she feels "has led us astray," is not the FFQ itself but mis- and overinterpretation of the data derived from the FFQ, a tool for which she makes realistic but strikingly modest claims: "The real purpose of the FFQ is to rank people" on their relative consumption of, say, fruits and vegetables or total calories. "If someone reports consuming five hundred calories a day, that's not true, obviously, but you *can* say they're probably at the low end of the spectrum. People overworry about accuracy."

This was not the sort of thing I expected to hear from an epidemiologist. But then neither was this: "I don't believe anything I read in nutritional epidemiology anymore. I'm so skeptical at this point."

NOTE

[1] In fact, the magnitude of the error could be much greater, judging by the huge disparity between the total number of food calories produced every day for each American (3,900) and the average number of those calories Americans own up to chomping each day: 2,000. Waste can account for some of this disparity, but not nearly all of it.

· · ● · ·

QUESTIONS FOR A SECOND READING

1. Pollan begins this selection by citing the work of Gyorgy Scrinis, the man who coined the term *nutritionism*. While the citation from Scrinis provides Pollan the central term (and namesake) of his chapter, it also lends Pollan a powerful illustrative example — margarine — to discuss and return to at various points in the chapter. Spend some time thinking about Pollan's choice to make extensive use of this example. Why might margarine be an especially useful and meaningful illustration for conveying the ideas Pollan is exploring? What do you know about margarine and how it has historically been marketed? How might this example help readers understand and envision the claims and histories Pollan introduces?

   Read back through the sections where Pollan discusses margarine and think about the ideas that are communicated in those sections. If Pollan hadn't focused on margarine as a key example, what other product might have been substituted for similar rhetorical impact? How would the piece have been different with the substitute?

2. Early on in this selection, Pollan writes, "Proper names have a way of making visible things we don't easily see or simply take for granted" (p. 490). What do

you think Pollan means by this, and why might this be the case? In what ways might Pollan's text be reread as an account of the powers and dangers of naming?

Read through the text again, and try to identify other moments where Pollan showcases how the naming of something suddenly increased its visibility. Are there moments where Pollan provides a name for something you hadn't thought about or hadn't noticed before? Are there places in the text where you might give a (different) name to the phenomena Pollan describes? Finally, can you think of other examples of instances in your life or in the broader culture when naming has dramatically changed your or the culture's understanding of something?

3. Pollan spends a significant amount of time focusing on the limits of our knowledge, rather than discussing what we *do* know about food and nutrition. There are several places in the text where he explicitly says that food scientists do not know the reasons behind research findings, and throughout the piece you can notice that he relies on words like "possibly," "probably," "might," and "maybe." Such terms are sometimes referred to as *qualifiers* or as *hedges*. They suggest limits to knowledge and only degrees of certainty. Why do you think that Pollan adopts such a writing style? What might be the value of such a rhetorical strategy? What can we learn by exploring what we don't know or what we thought we knew but has turned out to be untrue (or at least incomplete)? Why might such exploration be important?

— • • ● • • —

ASSIGNMENTS FOR WRITING

1. One way of reading this excerpt by Pollan is to see it as a history of how our understanding of food has changed. Pollan examines how different (and often competing) conceptualizations of food are put forward by institutional forces like the Food and Drug Administration and the American Heart Association and also by product marketers and advertisers. In doing this, Pollan showcases how the meaning of food is socially constructed (and reconstructed) through the narratives we associate with it.

The biggest shift in narrative that Pollan explores here is that we increasingly think about food as science, as collections of nutrients necessary for various chemical processes performed by the body. This scientific conceptualization of food is markedly different from other understandings of food that might see food as the source of pleasure or food as central to our heritage and connection to the past.

In product packaging and marketing, though, what is really interesting is to see how these different narratives and conceptualizations of food are operationalized individually or in combination to sell a product. Incorporating ideas from Pollan, write an essay in which you explore how the marketing of a particular food product (or collection of food products) is reliant on certain narrative conceptualizations of food. Work to explain and theorize why that conceptualization might be especially useful for that particular product. In writing this essay, you might pay attention to and discuss the visual design of the product packaging, the narrative accompanying that product, and the commercial advertisements associated with it.

2. Pollan writes that "the history of modern nutritionism has been a history of macronutrients at war: protein against carbs; carbs against proteins, and then fats; fats against carbs. . . . In each age nutritionism has organized most of its energies around an imperial nutrient" (p. 492). He explains that "in the shadow of these titanic struggles, smaller civil wars have raged within the sprawling empires of the big three: refined carbohydrates versus fiber; animal protein versus plant protein; saturated fats versus polyunsaturated fats; and then, deep down within the province of the polyunsaturates, omega-3 fatty acids versus omega-6s" (p. 492).

Write an essay that explores Pollan's use of the metaphor of warfare in this passage. What are the illuminations and constraints of this metaphor in representing debates about food and nutrition? What does the war metaphor teach us about this debate? How can you see this metaphor playing out in the public discourse on food and dieting? After examining Pollan's metaphor, you might challenge it and put forward your own metaphor to help provide additional insights into debates about food and nutrition.

3. Near the end of this selection, Pollan discusses his experience filling out the food-frequency questionnaire used by the Women's Health Initiative. Pollan did this to try to understand the way that nutrition researchers are collecting data about food consumption habits and coming to conclusions about the impact of various dietary practices. Find one of these food-frequency questionnaires online (they are relatively easy to find by typing "food-frequency questionnaire pdf" into an Internet search engine). Fill one out and write an essay about the process of completing it and what you learned or discovered through that process.

In writing your essay, you might consider several of the following questions: What surprised you or was difficult about filling out the questionnaire? What ideologies or conceptions about food seem to shape or influence the questionnaire? How might the findings feed or reinforce existing cultural attitudes about food? What questions aren't asked that you think should be asked? How did thinking about and answering the questions affect you emotionally? Which answers do you think are more or less accurate, and why? What types of contextual information cannot be gathered from such a questionnaire? What other data collection processes might be more beneficial, and why?

4. Consider the difficult situation Pollan is in as a writer. He discusses the complex history and evolution of food science and consumer attitudes, and he attempts to present this material to a broad audience of individuals mainly outside the arena of food science. Pollan is surely aware that much of this material might seem difficult or dense to an average reader. As you reread this piece, note

places in the text where you can see Pollan working to make difficult material more interesting or easier to understand. What sort of strategies does he use to do this? You might identify a section that you find especially engaging and come up with a list of reasons why that section is so effective. Then identify a section that you feel is less engaging, and think about how Pollan might have worked to improve that section. What strategies could he have used? How would you re-present that information in a new way?

Write an essay in which you engage the question of difficulty as writers try to take it on. Discuss Pollan's strategies and propose some ideas of your own. You might consider a time you have had to present difficult materials to others. What strategies did you use? How might you even use those very strategies in this essay you've been asked to write about Pollan?

- - • • ● • • - -

MAKING CONNECTIONS

1. In "Ways of Seeing" (p. 142), John Berger reflects on how our understanding of images changes when we label them "art." Berger writes that "when an image is presented as a work of art, the way people look at it is affected by a whole series of learned assumptions about art. Assumptions concerning: Beauty, Truth, Genius, Civilization, Form, Status, Taste, etc" (p. 144). Berger explains that these assumptions tend to "mystify rather than clarify," and laments that as a result of those assumptions, "[w]orks of art are made unnecessarily remote"; they become removed and distanced from viewers (p. 145).

   Though Michael Pollan is writing about a very different topic, he makes a similar argument, explaining that when food is presented as a work of science, we mystify it and end up distancing food from those who consume it:

   > Since nutrients, as compared with foods, are invisible and therefore slightly mysterious, it falls to the scientists (and to the journalists through whom the scientists reach the public) to explain the hidden reality of foods to us. In form this is a quasireligious idea, suggesting the visible world is not the one that really matters, which implies the need for a priesthood. For to enter a world where your dietary salvation depends on unseen nutrients, you need plenty of expert help. (pp. 490–91)

   Reread the section of Berger's essay on mystification, and consider how his description of the problem connects to the "mysterious" and "quasireligious" dimensions of food science that Pollan is describing in this passage. Write an essay that puts Berger in conversation with Pollan and explores the dangers of mystifying food. Consider what is lost in that process. Like Berger, think about how mystification detaches individuals from history and from place. How does detachment happen with the mystification of food? What are the consequences of this? Who benefits and who loses as food becomes a mysterious substance, increasingly detached from consumers?

2. According to Michael Pollan, two of the biggest research challenges for nutrition science research are capturing context and complexity, and he explains that these challenges exist for understandable reasons:

> Scientists study variables they can isolate; if they can't isolate a variable, they won't be able to tell whether its presence or absence is meaningful. Yet even the simplest food is a hopelessly complicated thing to analyze, a virtual wilderness of chemical compounds, many of which exist in intricate and dynamic relation to one another, and all of which together are in the process of changing from one state to another. So if you're a nutrition scientist you do the only thing you *can* do, given the tools at your disposal: Break the thing down into its component parts and study those one by one, even if that means ignoring subtle interactions and contexts and the fact that the whole may well be more than, or maybe just different from, the sum of its parts. (pp. 495–96)

Like Pollan, Ruth Behar discusses the limits and challenges of disciplinary methodologies in "The Vulnerable Observer" (p. 113). As an anthropologist, Behar explains the impossibility of ever fully capturing and representing observations made during ethnographic fieldwork:

> We try to listen well. We write fieldnotes about all the things we've misunderstood, all the things that later will seem so trivial, so much the bare surface of life. And then it is time to pack our suitcases and return home. And so begins our work, our hardest work — to bring the ethnographic moment back, to resurrect it, to communicate the distance, which too quickly starts to feel like an abyss, between what we saw and heard and our inability, finally, to do justice to it in our representations. Our fieldnotes become palimpsests, useless unless plumbed for forgotten revelatory moments, unexpressed longings, and the wounds of regret. (p. 117)

Write an essay that reflects on the limitations of different disciplinary research methodologies and interpretative paradigms, using examples from Pollan and Behar. Discuss why it is important for researchers to regularly encounter and discuss their disciplines' limitations and challenges and how researchers might learn from the methodologies of other disciplines. How, for instance, might the work in the field of nutrition science benefit from the ethnographic practices discussed by Behar?

3. Michael Pollan spends a significant amount of time discussing the complex challenges facing research in the field of nutrition, and he explains that perhaps the biggest struggle is to accurately capture the dietary intake of individuals. As Pollan explains, "The uncomfortable fact is that the entire field of nutritional science rests on a foundation of ignorance and lies about the most basic question of nutrition: What are people eating?" (p. 503).

When Pollan discusses this problem with Marion Nestle, an expert in nutrition, food studies, and public health, she agrees and explains, "To really know what a person is eating you'd have to have a second invisible person following them around, taking photographs, looking at ingredients, and consulting accurate food composition tables, which we don't have" (p. 503).

Though we do not all have silent and invisible companions following us around and cataloging what we eat, food consumption is often a public act, one seen and evaluated by others. On any trip to the grocery store, others see the items you grab and put into your cart, the juxtaposition of both "healthy" and "unhealthy" food items that progress down the conveyor belt and are scanned by a cashier. Similarly, colleagues often see what you are eating in the break room or in the cafeteria or at the diner on the street corner. Nosey houseguests check refrigerators and silently judge the assortment of goods.

Write an essay that examines food consumption habits through the lenses of surveillance, visibility, power, and discipline that are discussed in Michel Foucault's essay "Panopticism" (p. 328). Channeling the approach of Foucault, think about how the architecture and physical layout of spaces of food consumption are connected to visibility, disciplinary functions, and power relations. Explore how the threat of being seen by others shapes one's eating and food purchasing. What are the consequences of both the visibility and the response to it?

MARY LOUISE

Pratt

Mary Louise Pratt (b. 1948) grew up in Listowel, Ontario, a small Canadian farm town. She got her BA at the University of Toronto and her PhD from Stanford University, where for nearly thirty years she was a professor in the departments of comparative literature and Spanish and Portuguese. At Stanford, she was one of the cofounders of the new freshman culture program, a controversial series of required courses that replaced the old Western civilization core courses. The course she is particularly associated with is called "Europe and the Americas"; it brings together European representations of the Americas with indigenous American texts. As you might guess from the essay that follows, the program at Stanford expanded the range of countries, languages, cultures, and texts that are seen as a necessary introduction to the world; it also, however, revised the very idea of culture that many of us take for granted — particularly the idea that culture, at its best, expresses common values in a common language. Among other awards and honors, Pratt is the recipient of a Guggenheim Fellowship and a Fellowship at the Center for Advanced Study in the Behavioral Sciences, Stanford University. She is Silver Professor in the Department of Spanish and Portuguese at New York University. She served as president of the Modern Language Association for 2003.

Pratt is the author of *Toward a Speech Act Theory of Literary Discourse* (1977) and coauthor of *Women, Culture, and Politics in Latin America* (1990), the textbook *Linguistics for Students of Literature* (1980), *Amor Brujo: The Images and Culture of Love in the Andes* (1990), and *Imperial Eyes: Studies in Travel Writing and Transculturation* (1992). The essay that follows was revised to serve as the introduction to *Imperial Eyes*, which examines European travel writing in the eighteenth and nineteenth centuries, when Europe was "discovering" Africa and the Americas. It argues that travel writing produced "the rest of the world" for European readers. It didn't "report" on Africa or South America; it produced an "Africa" or an "America" for European consumption. Travel writing produced places that could be thought of as barren, empty, undeveloped, inconceivable, needful of European influence and control, ready to serve European industrial, intellectual, and commercial interests. The reports of travelers or, later, scientists and anthropologists are part of a more general process by which the emerging industrial nations took possession of new territory.

The European understanding of Peru, for example, came through Euro-pean accounts, not from attempts to understand or elicit responses from Andeans, Peruvian natives. Such a response was delivered when an Andean, Guaman Poma, wrote to King Philip III of Spain, but his letter was unreadable. Pratt is interested in just those moments of contact between peoples and cul-tures. She is interested in how King Philip read (or failed to read) a letter from Peru, but also in how someone like Guaman Poma prepared himself to write to the king of Spain. To fix these moments, she makes use of a phrase she coined, the "contact zone." She explains:

> I use [this term] to refer to the space of colonial encounters, the space in which peoples geographically and historically separated come into contact with each other and establish ongoing relations, usually involv-ing conditions of coercion, radical inequality, and intractable con-flict. . . . By using the term "contact," I aim to foreground the interactive, improvisational dimensions of colonial encoun-ters so easily ignored or suppressed by diffusionist accounts of conquest and domination. A "contact" perspective empha-sizes how subjects are constituted in and by their relations to each other. It treats the relations among colonizers and colonized, or travelers and "travelees," not in terms of separ-ateness or apartheid, but in terms of copresence, interaction, interlocking understandings and practices. (*Imperial Eyes*, pp. 6–7)

"Arts of the Contact Zone" was first written as a lecture. It was delivered as a keynote address at the second Modern Lan-guage Association Literacy Conference, held in Pittsburgh, Pennsylvania, in 1990.

Arts of the Contact Zone

Whenever the subject of literacy comes up, what often pops first into my mind is a conversation I overheard eight years ago between my son Sam and his best friend, Willie, aged six and seven, respectively: "Why don't you trade me Many Trails for Carl Yats...Yesits...Ya-strum-scrum." "That's not how you say it, dummy, it's Carl Yes...Yes...oh, I don't know." Sam and Willie had just discovered baseball cards. Many Trails was their decoding, with the help of first-grade English phonics, of the name Manny Trillo. The name they were quite rightly stumped on was Carl Yastrzemski. That was the first time I remembered seeing them put their incipient literacy to their own use, and I was of course thrilled.

Sam and Willie learned a lot about phonics that year by trying to decipher surnames on baseball cards, and a lot about cities, states, heights, weights, places of birth, stages of life. In the years that followed, I watched Sam apply his arithmetic skills to working out batting averages and subtracting retirement years from rookie years; I watched him develop senses of patterning and order by arranging and rearranging his cards for hours on end, and aesthetic judgment by comparing different photos, different series, layouts, and color schemes. American geography and history took shape in his mind through baseball cards. Much of his social life revolved around trading them, and he learned about exchange, fairness, trust, the importance of processes as opposed to results, what it means to get cheated, taken advantage of, even robbed. Baseball cards were the medium of his economic life too. Nowhere better to learn the power and arbitrariness of money, the absolute divorce between use value and exchange value, notions of long- and short-term investment, the possibility of personal values that are independent of market values.

Baseball cards meant baseball card shows, where there was much to be learned about adult worlds as well. And baseball cards opened the door to baseball books, shelves and shelves of encyclopedias, magazines, histories, biographies, novels, books of jokes, anecdotes, cartoons, even poems. Sam learned the history of American racism and the struggle against it through baseball; he saw the Depression and two world wars from behind home plate. He learned the meaning of commodified labor, what it means for one's body and talents to be owned and dispensed by another. He knows something about Japan, Taiwan, Cuba, and Central America and how men and boys do things there. Through the history and experience of baseball stadiums he thought about architecture, light, wind, topography, meteorology, the dynamics of public space. He learned the meaning of expertise, of knowing about something well enough that you can start a conversation with a stranger and feel sure of holding your own. Even with an adult — especially with an adult. Throughout his preadolescent years, baseball history was Sam's luminous point of contact with grown-ups, his lifeline to caring. And, of course, all this time he was also playing baseball, struggling his way through the stages of the local Little League system, lucky enough to be a pretty good player, loving the game and coming to know deeply his strengths and weaknesses.

Literacy began for Sam with the newly pronounceable names on the picture cards and brought him what has been easily the broadest, most varied, most enduring, and most integrated experience of his thirteen-year life. Like many parents, I was delighted to see schooling give Sam the tools with which to find and open all these doors. At the same time I found it unforgivable that schooling itself gave him nothing remotely as meaningful to do, let alone anything that would actually take him beyond the referential, masculinist ethos of baseball and its lore.

However, I was not invited here to speak as a parent, nor as an expert on literacy. I was asked to speak as an MLA [Modern Language Association] member working in the elite academy. In that capacity my contribution is undoubtedly supposed to be abstract, irrelevant, and anchored outside the real world. I wouldn't dream of disappointing anyone. I propose immediately to head back several centuries to a text that has a few points in common with baseball cards and raises thoughts about what Tony Sarmiento, in his comments to the conference, called new visions of literacy. In 1908 a Peruvianist named Richard Pietschmann was exploring in the Danish Royal Archive in Copenhagen and came across a manuscript. It was dated in the city of Cuzco in Peru, in the year 1613, some forty years after the final fall of the Inca empire to the Spanish and signed with an unmistakably Andean indigenous name: Felipe Guaman Poma de Ayala. Written in a mixture of Quechua and ungrammatical, expressive Spanish, the manuscript was a letter addressed by an unknown but apparently literate Andean to King Philip III of Spain. What stunned Pietschmann was that the letter was twelve hundred pages long. There were almost eight hundred pages of written text and four hundred of captioned line drawings. It was titled *The First New Chronicle and Good Government.* No one knew (or knows) how the manuscript got to the library in Copenhagen or how long it had been there. No one, it appeared, had ever bothered to read it or figured out how. Quechua was not thought of as a written language in 1908, nor Andean culture as a literate culture.

> **THE LETTER GOT THERE, ONLY 350 YEARS TOO LATE, A MIRACLE AND A TERRIBLE TRAGEDY.**

Pietschmann prepared a paper on his find, which he presented in London in 1912, a year after the rediscovery of Machu Picchu by Hiram Bingham. Reception, by an international congress of Americanists, was apparently confused. It took twenty-five years for a facsimile edition of the work to appear in Paris. It was not till the late 1970s, as positivist reading habits gave way to interpretive studies and colonial elitisms to post-colonial pluralisms, that Western scholars found ways of reading Guaman Poma's *New Chronicle and Good Government* as the extraordinary intercultural tour de force that it was. The letter got there, only 350 years too late, a miracle and a terrible tragedy.

I propose to say a few more words about this erstwhile unreadable text, in order to lay out some thoughts about writing and literacy in what I like to call the *contact zones*. I use this term to refer to social spaces where cultures meet, clash, and grapple with each other, often in contexts of highly asymmetrical relations of power, such as colonialism, slavery, or their aftermaths as they are lived out in many parts of the world today. Eventually I will use the term to reconsider the models of community that many of us rely on in teaching and theorizing and that are under challenge today. But first a little more about Guaman Poma's giant letter to Philip III.

Insofar as anything is known about him at all, Guaman Poma exemplified the sociocultural complexities produced by conquest and empire. He was an indigenous Andean who claimed noble Inca descent and who had adopted (at least in some sense) Christianity. He may have worked in the Spanish colonial administration as an interpreter, scribe, or assistant to a Spanish tax collector — as a mediator, in short. He says he learned to write from his half brother, a mestizo whose Spanish father had given him access to religious education.

Guaman Poma's letter to the king is written in two languages (Spanish and Quechua) and two parts. The first is called the *Nueva corónica*, "New Chronicle." The title is important. The chronicle of course was the main writing apparatus through which the Spanish presented their American conquests to themselves. It constituted one of the main official discourses. In writing a "new chronicle," Guaman Poma took over the official Spanish genre for his own ends. Those ends were, roughly, to construct a new picture of the world, a picture of a Christian world with Andean rather than European peoples at the center of it — Cuzco, not Jerusalem. In the *New Chronicle* Guaman Poma begins by rewriting the Christian history of the world from Adam and Eve (Fig. 1), incorporating the Amerindians into it as offspring of one of the sons of Noah. He identifies five ages of Christian history that he links in parallel with the five ages of canonical Andean history — separate but equal trajectories that diverge with Noah and reintersect not with Columbus but with Saint Bartholomew, claimed to have preceded Columbus in the Americas. In a couple of hundred pages, Guaman Poma constructs a veritable encyclopedia of Inca and pre-Inca history, customs, laws, social forms, public offices, and dynastic leaders. The depictions resemble European manners and customs description, but also reproduce the meticulous detail with which knowledge in Inca society was stored on *quipus* and in the oral memories of elders.

Guaman Poma's *New Chronicle* is an instance of what I have proposed to call an *autoethnographic* text, by which I mean a text in which people undertake to describe themselves in ways that engage with representations others have made of them. Thus if ethnographic texts are those in which European metropolitan subjects represent to themselves their others (usually their conquered others), autoethnographic texts are representations that the so-defined others construct *in response to* or in dialogue with those

EL PRIMER MVNDO 22
ADAN•EVA

Figure 1. Adam and Eve.

texts. Autoethnographic texts are not, then, what are usually thought of as autochthonous forms of expression or self-representation (as the Andean *quipus* were). Rather they involve a selective collaboration with and appropriation of idioms of the metropolis or the conqueror. These are merged or infiltrated to varying degrees with indigenous idioms to create self-representations intended to intervene in metropolitan modes of understanding. Autoethnographic works are often addressed to both metropolitan audiences and the speaker's own community. Their reception is thus highly indeterminate. Such texts often constitute a marginalized group's point of entry into the dominant circuits of print culture. It is interesting to think, for example, of American slave autobiography in its autoethnographic dimensions, which in some respects distinguish it from Euramerican auto-biographical tradition. The concept might help explain why some of the earliest published writing by Chicanas took the form of folkloric manners and customs sketches written in English and published in English-language newspapers or folklore magazines (see Treviño). Autoethnographic representation often involves concrete collaborations between people, as between literate ex-slaves and abolitionist intellectuals, or between Guaman

Poma and the Inca elders who were his informants. Often, as in Guaman Poma, it involves more than one language. In recent decades autoethnography, critique, and resistance have reconnected with writing in a contemporary creation of the contact zone, the *testimonio*.

Guaman Poma's *New Chronicle* ends with a revisionist account of the Spanish conquest, which, he argues, should have been a peaceful encounter of equals with the potential for benefiting both, but for the mindless greed of the Spanish. He parodies Spanish history. Following contact with the Incas, he writes, "In all Castille, there was a great commotion. All day and at night in their dreams the Spaniards were saying, 'Yndias, yndias, oro, plata, oro, plata del Piru'" ("Indies, Indies, gold, silver, gold, silver from Peru") (Fig. 2). The Spanish, he writes, brought nothing of value to share with the Andeans, nothing but armor and guns "con la codicia de oro, plata, oro y plata, yndias, a las Yndias, Piru" ("with the lust for gold, silver, gold and silver, Indies, the Indies, Peru") (p. 372). I quote these words as an example of a conquered subject using the conqueror's language to construct a parodic, oppositional representation of the conqueror's own speech. Guaman Poma mirrors back to the Spanish (in their language,

Figure 2. Conquista. Meeting of Spaniard and Inca. The Inca says in Quechua, "You eat this gold?" Spaniard replies in Spanish, "We eat this gold."

which is alien to him) an image of themselves that they often suppress and will therefore surely recognize. Such are the dynamics of language, writing, and representation in contact zones.

The second half of the epistle continues the critique. It is titled *Buen gobierno y justicia*, "Good Government and Justice," and combines a description of colonial society in the Andean region with a passionate denunciation of Spanish exploitation and abuse. (These, at the time he was writing, were decimating the population of the Andes at a genocidal rate. In fact, the potential loss of the labor force became a main cause for reform of the system.) Guaman Poma's most implacable hostility is invoked by the clergy, followed by the dreaded *corregidores,* or colonial overseers (Fig. 3). He also praises good works, Christian habits, and just men where he finds them, and offers at length his views as to what constitutes "good government and justice." The Indies, he argues, should be administered through a collaboration of Inca and Spanish elites. The epistle ends with an imaginary question-and-answer session in which, in a reversal of hierarchy, the king is depicted asking Guaman Poma questions about how to reform the empire — a dialogue imagined across the many lines that

Figure 3. Corregidor de minas. Catalog of Spanish abuses of indigenous labor force.

divide the Andean scribe from the imperial monarch, and in which the subordinated subject single-handedly gives himself authority in the colonizer's language and verbal repertoire. In a way, it worked — this extraordinary text did get written — but in a way it did not, for the letter never reached its addressee.

To grasp the import of Guaman Poma's project, one needs to keep in mind that the Incas had no system of writing. Their huge empire is said to be the only known instance of a full-blown bureaucratic state society built and administered without writing. Guaman Poma constructs his text by appropriating and adapting pieces of the representational repertoire of the invaders. He does not simply imitate or reproduce it; he selects and adapts it along Andean lines to express (bilingually, mind you) Andean interests and aspirations. Ethnographers have used the term *transculturation* to describe processes whereby members of subordinated or marginal groups select and invent from materials transmitted by a dominant or metropolitan culture. The term, originally coined by Cuban sociologist Fernando Ortiz in the 1940s, aimed to replace overly reductive concepts of acculturation and assimilation used to characterize culture under conquest. While subordinate peoples do not usually control what emanates from the dominant culture, they do determine to varying extents what gets absorbed into their own and what it gets used for. Transculturation, like autoethnography, is a phenomenon of the contact zone.

> **TRANSCULTURATION, LIKE AUTOETHNOGRAPHY, IS A PHENOMENON OF THE CONTACT ZONE.**

As scholars have realized only relatively recently, the transcultural character of Guaman Poma's text is intricately apparent in its visual as well as its written component. The genre of the four hundred line drawings is European — there seems to have been no tradition of representational drawing among the Incas — but in their execution they deploy specifically Andean systems of spatial symbolism that express Andean values and aspirations.[1]

In Figure 1, for instance, Adam is depicted on the left-hand side below the sun, while Eve is on the right-hand side below the moon, and slightly lower than Adam. The two are divided by the diagonal of Adam's digging stick. In Andean spatial symbolism, the diagonal descending from the sun marks the basic line of power and authority dividing upper from lower, male from female, dominant from subordinate. In Figure 2, the Inca appears in the same position as Adam, with the Spaniard opposite, and the two at the same height. In Figure 3, depicting Spanish abuses of power, the symbolic pattern is reversed. The Spaniard is in a high position indicating dominance, but on the "wrong" (right-hand) side. The diagonals of his lance and that of the servant doing the flogging mark out a line of illegitimate, though real, power. The Andean figures continue to occupy the left-hand side of the picture, but clearly as victims. Guaman Poma wrote that the Spanish conquest had produced *"un mundo al revés,"* "a world in reverse."

In sum, Guaman Poma's text is truly a product of the contact zone. If one thinks of cultures, or literatures, as discrete, coherently structured, monolingual edifices, Guaman Poma's text, and indeed any autoethnographic work, appears anomalous or chaotic — as it apparently did to the European scholars Pietschmann spoke to in 1912. If one does not think of cultures this way, then Guaman Poma's text is simply heterogeneous, as the Andean region was itself and remains today. Such a text is heterogeneous on the reception end as well as the production end: it will read very differently to people in different positions in the contact zone. Because it deploys European and Andean systems of meaning making, the letter necessarily means differently to bilingual Spanish-Quechua speakers and to monolingual speakers in either language; the drawings mean differently to monocultural readers, Spanish or Andean, and to bicultural readers responding to the Andean symbolic structures embodied in European genres.

In the Andes in the early 1600s there existed a literate public with considerable intercultural competence and degrees of bilingualism. Unfortunately, such a community did not exist in the Spanish court with which Guaman Poma was trying to make contact. It is interesting to note that in the same year Guaman Poma sent off his letter, a text by another Peruvian was adopted in official circles in Spain as the canonical Christian mediation between the Spanish conquest and Inca history. It was another huge encyclopedic work, titled the *Royal Commentaries of the Incas,* written, tellingly, by a mestizo, Inca Garcilaso de la Vega. Like the mestizo half brother who taught Guaman Poma to read and write, Inca Garcilaso was the son of an Inca princess and a Spanish official, and had lived in Spain since he was seventeen. Though he too spoke Quechua, his book is written in eloquent, standard Spanish, without illustrations. While Guaman Poma's life's work sat somewhere unread, the *Royal Commentaries* was edited and reedited in Spain and the New World, a mediation that coded the Andean past and present in ways thought unthreatening to colonial hierarchy.[2] The textual hierarchy persists; the *Royal Commentaries* today remains a staple item on PhD reading lists in Spanish, while the *New Chronicle and Good Government*, despite the ready availability of several fine editions, is not. However, though Guaman Poma's text did not reach its destination, the transcultural currents of expression it exemplifies continued to evolve in the Andes, as they still do, less in writing than in storytelling, ritual, song, dance-drama, painting and sculpture, dress, textile art, forms of governance, religious belief, and many other vernacular art forms. All express the effects of long-term contact and intractable, unequal conflict.

Autoethnography, transculturation, critique, collaboration, bilingualism, mediation, parody, denunciation, imaginary dialogue, vernacular expression — these are some of the literate arts of the contact zone. Miscomprehension, incomprehension, dead letters, unread masterpieces, absolute heterogeneity of meaning — these are some of the perils of writing in the contact zone. They all live among us today in the transnationalized metropolis of the United States and are becoming more widely visible, more pressing, and, like Guaman Poma's text, more decipherable to those who once would have ignored them in defense of a stable, centered sense of knowledge and reality.

CONTACT AND COMMUNITY

The idea of the contact zone is intended in part to contrast with ideas of community that underlie much of the thinking about language, communication, and culture that gets done in the academy. A couple of years ago, thinking about the linguistic theories I knew, I tried to make sense of a utopian quality that often seemed to characterize social analyses of language by the academy. Languages were seen as living in "speech communities," and these tended to be theorized as discrete, self-defined, coherent entities, held together by a homogeneous competence or grammar shared identically and equally among all the members. This abstract idea of the speech community seemed to reflect, among other things, the utopian way modern nations conceive of themselves as what Benedict Anderson calls "imagined communities."[3] In a book of that title, Anderson observes that with the possible exception of what he calls "primordial villages," human communities exist as *imagined* entities in which people "will never know most of their fellow-members, meet them or even hear of them, yet in the mind of each lives the image of their communion." "Communities are distinguished," he goes on to say, "not by their falsity/genuineness, but by *the style in which they are imagined*" (15; emphasis mine). Anderson proposes three features that characterize the style in which the modern nation is imagined. First, it is imagined as *limited*, by "finite, if elastic, boundaries"; second, it is imagined as *sovereign*; and, third, it is imagined as *fraternal*, "a deep, horizontal comradeship" for which millions of people are prepared "not so much to kill as willingly to die" (15). As the image suggests, the nation-community is embodied metonymically in the finite, sovereign, fraternal figure of the citizen-soldier.

Anderson argues that European bourgeoisies were distinguished by their ability to "achieve solidarity on an essentially imagined basis" (74) on a scale far greater than that of elites of other times and places. Writing and literacy play a central role in this argument. Anderson maintains, as have others, that the main instrument that made bourgeois nation-building projects possible was print capitalism. The commercial circulation of books in the various European vernaculars, he argues, was what first created the invisible networks that would eventually constitute the literate elites and those they ruled as nations. (Estimates are that 180 million books were put into circulation in Europe between the years 1500 and 1600 alone.)

Now obviously this style of imagining of modern nations, as Anderson describes it, is strongly utopian, embodying values like equality, fraternity, liberty, which the societies often profess but systematically fail to realize. The prototype of the modern nation as imagined community was, it seemed to me, mirrored in ways people thought about language and the speech community. Many commentators have pointed out how modern views of language as code and competence assume a unified and homogeneous social world in which language exists as a shared patrimony — as a device, precisely, for imagining community. An image of a universally shared literacy is also part of the picture. The prototypical manifestation of language is generally taken to be the speech of individual adult native speakers face-to-face (as in Saussure's famous diagram) in monolingual, even monodialectal situations — in short, the most homogeneous case linguistically and socially. The same goes for written communication. Now one could certainly imagine a theory that assumed different things — that argued, for instance, that the most revealing speech situation for understanding language was one involving a gathering of people each of whom spoke two languages and understood a third and held only one language in common with any of the others. It depends on what workings of language you want to see or want to see first, on what you choose to define as normative.

In keeping with autonomous, fraternal models of community, analyses of language use commonly assume that principles of cooperation and shared understanding are normally in effect. Descriptions of interactions between people in conversation, classrooms, medical and bureaucratic settings, readily take it for granted that the situation is governed by a single set of rules or norms shared by all participants. The analysis focuses then on how those rules produce or fail to produce an orderly, coherent exchange. Models involving games and moves are often used to describe interactions. Despite whatever conflicts or systematic social differences might be in play, it is assumed that all participants are engaged in the same game and that the game is the same for all players. Often it is. But of course it often is not, as, for example, when speakers are from different classes or cultures, or one party is exercising authority and another is submitting to it or questioning it. Last year one of my children moved to a new elementary school that had more open classrooms and more flexible curricula than the conventional school he started out in. A few days into the term, we asked him what it was like at the new school. "Well," he said, "they're a lot nicer, and they have a lot less rules. But know *why* they're nicer?" "Why?" I asked. "So you'll obey all the rules they don't have," he replied. This is a very coherent analysis with considerable elegance and explanatory power, but probably not the one his teacher would have given.

When linguistic (or literate) interaction is described in terms of orderliness, games, moves, or scripts, usually only legitimate moves are actually named as part of the system, where legitimacy is defined from the point of view of the party in authority — regardless of what other parties might see themselves as doing. Teacher-pupil language, for example, tends to be described almost entirely from the point of view of the teacher and teaching, not from the point of view of pupils and pupiling (the word doesn't even exist, though the thing certainly does). If a classroom is analyzed as a social world unified and homogenized with respect to the teacher, whatever students do other than what the teacher specifies is invisible or anomalous to the analysis. This can be true in practice as well. On several occasions my fourth grader, the one busy obeying all the rules they didn't have, was given writing assignments that took the form of answering a series of questions to build up a paragraph. These questions often asked him to identify with the interests of those in power over him — parents, teachers, doctors, public authorities. He invariably sought ways to resist or subvert these assignments. One assignment, for instance, called for imagining "a helpful invention." The students were asked to write single-sentence responses to the following questions:

> What kind of invention would help you?
> How would it help you?
> Why would you need it?
> What would it look like?
> Would other people be able to use it also?
> What would be an invention to help your teacher?
> What would be an invention to help your parents?

Manuel's reply read as follows:

A grate adventchin

Some inventchins are GRATE!!!!!!!!!!!! My inventchin would be a shot that would put every thing you learn at school in your brain. It would help me by letting me graduate right now!! I would need it because it would let me play with my friends, go on vacachin and, do fun a lot more. It would look like a regular shot. Ather peaple would use to. This inventchin would help my teacher parents get away from a lot of work. I think a shot like this would be GRATE!

Despite the spelling, the assignment received the usual star to indicate the task had been fulfilled in an acceptable way. No recognition was available, however, of the humor, the attempt to be critical or contestatory, to parody the structures of authority. On that score, Manuel's luck was only slightly better than Guaman Poma's. What is the place of unsolicited oppositional discourse, parody, resistance, critique in the imagined classroom community? Are teachers supposed to feel that their teaching has been most successful when they have eliminated such things and unified the social world, probably in their own image? Who wins when we do that? Who loses?

Such questions may be hypothetical, because in the United States in the 1990s, many teachers find themselves less and less able to do that even if they want to. The composition of the national collectivity is changing and so are the styles, as Anderson put it, in which it is being imagined. In the 1980s in many nation-states, imagined national syntheses that had retained hegemonic force began to dissolve. Internal social groups with histories and lifeways different from the official ones began insisting on those histories and lifeways *as part of their citizenship*, as the very mode of their membership in the national collectivity. In their dialogues with dominant institutions, many groups began asserting a rhetoric of belonging that made demands beyond those of representation and basic rights granted from above. In universities we started to hear, "I don't just want you to let me be here, I want to belong here; this institution should belong to me as much as it does to anyone else." Institutions have responded with, among other things, rhetorics of diversity and multiculturalism whose import at this moment is up for grabs across the ideological spectrum.

These shifts are being lived out by everyone working in education today, and everyone is challenged by them in one way or another. Those of us committed to educational democracy are particularly challenged as that notion finds itself besieged on the public agenda. Many of those who govern us display, openly, their interest in a quiescent, ignorant, manipulable electorate. Even as an ideal, the concept of an enlightened citizenry seems to have disappeared from the national imagination. A couple of years ago the university where I work went through an intense and wrenching debate over a narrowly defined Western-culture requirement that had been instituted there in 1980. It kept boiling down to a debate over the ideas of national patrimony, cultural citizenship, and imagined community. In the end, the requirement was transformed into a much more broadly defined course called Cultures, Ideas, Values.[4] In the context of the change, a new course was designed that centered on the Americas and the multiple cultural histories (including European ones) that have intersected here. As you can imagine, the course attracted a very diverse student body. The classroom functioned not like a homogeneous community or a horizontal alliance but like a contact zone. Every single text we read stood in specific historical relationships to the students in the class, but the range and variety of historical relationships in play were enormous. Everybody had a stake in nearly everything we read, but the range and kind of stakes varied widely.

> **THE VERY NATURE OF THE COURSE PUT IDEAS AND IDENTITIES ON THE LINE.**

It was the most exciting teaching we had ever done, and also the hardest. We were struck, for example, at how anomalous the formal lecture became in a contact zone (who can forget Atahuallpa throwing down the Bible because it would not speak to him?). The lecturer's traditional (imagined) task — unifying the world in the class's eyes by means of a monologue that rings equally coherent, revealing, and true for all, forging an ad hoc community, homogeneous with respect to one's own words — this task became not only impossible but anomalous and unimaginable. Instead, one had to work in the knowledge that whatever one said was going to be systematically received in radically heterogeneous ways that we were neither able nor entitled to prescribe.

The very nature of the course put ideas and identities on the line. All the students in the class had the experience, for example, of hearing their culture discussed and objectified in ways that horrified them; all the students saw their roots traced back to legacies of both glory and shame; all the students experienced face-to-face the ignorance and incomprehension, and occasionally the hostility, of others. In the absence of community values and the hope of synthesis, it was easy to forget the positives; the fact, for instance, that kinds of marginalization once taken for granted were gone. Virtually every student was having the experience of seeing the world described with him or her in it. Along with rage, incomprehension, and pain, there were exhilarating moments of wonder and revelation, mutual understanding, and new wisdom — the joys of the contact zone. The sufferings and revelations were, at different moments to be sure, experienced by every student. No one was excluded, and no one was safe.

The fact that no one was safe made all of us involved in the course appreciate the importance of what we came to call "safe houses." We used the term to refer to social and intellectual spaces where groups can constitute themselves as horizontal, homogeneous, sovereign communities with high degrees of trust, shared understandings, temporary protection from legacies of oppression. This is why, as we realized, multicultural curricula should not seek to replace ethnic or women's studies, for example. Where there are legacies of subordination, groups need places for healing and mutual recognition, safe houses in which to construct shared understandings, knowledges, claims on the world that they can then bring into the contact zone.

Meanwhile, our job in the Americas course remains to figure out how to make that crossroads the best site for learning that it can be. We are looking for the pedagogical arts of the contact zone. These will include, we are sure, exercises in storytelling and in identifying with the ideas, interests, histories, and attitudes of others; experiments in transculturation and collaborative work and in the arts of critique, parody, and comparison (including unseemly comparisons between elite and vernacular cultural forms); the redemption of the oral; ways for people to engage with suppressed aspects of history (including their own histories), ways to move *into and out of* rhetorics of authenticity; ground rules for communication across lines of difference and hierarchy that go beyond politeness but maintain mutual respect; a systematic approach to the all-important concept of *cultural mediation*. These arts were in play in every room at the extraordinary Pittsburgh conference on literacy. I learned a lot about them there, and I am thankful.

NOTES

[1] For an introduction in English to these and other aspects of Guaman Poma's work, see Rolena Adorno. Adorno and Mercedes Lopez-Baralt pioneered the study of Andean symbolic systems in Guaman Poma. [All notes are Pratt's.]

[2] It is far from clear that the *Royal Commentaries* was as benign as the Spanish seemed to assume. The book certainly played a role in maintaining the identity and aspirations of indigenous elites in the Andes. In the mid-eighteenth century, a new edition of the *Royal Commentaries* was suppressed by Spanish authorities because its preface included a prophecy by Sir Walter Raleigh that the English would invade Peru and restore the Inca monarchy.

[3] The discussion of community here is summarized from my essay "Linguistic Utopias."

[4] For information about this program and the contents of courses taught in it, write Program in Cultures, Ideas, Values (CIV), Stanford Univ., Stanford, CA 94305.

BIBLIOGRAPHY

Adorno, Rolena. *Guaman Poma de Ayala: Writing and Resistance in Colonial Peru*. Austin: U of Texas P, 1986.

Anderson, Benedict. *Imagined Communities: Reflections on the Origins and Spread of Nationalism*. London: Verso, 1984.

Garcilaso de la Vega, El Inca. *Royal Commentaries of the Incas*. 1613. Austin: U of Texas P, 1966.

Guaman Poma de Ayala, Felipe. *El primer nueva corónica y buen gobierno*. Manuscript. Ed. John Murra and Rolena Adorno. Mexico: Siglo XXI, 1980.

Pratt, Mary Louise. "Linguistic Utopias." *The Linguistics of Writing*. Ed. Nigel Fabb et al. Manchester: Manchester UP, 1987. 48–66.

Treviño, Gloria. "Cultural Ambivalence in Early Chicano Prose Fiction." Diss. Stanford U, 1985.

— • • ● • • —

QUESTIONS FOR A SECOND READING

1. Perhaps the most interesting question "Arts of the Contact Zone" raises for its readers is how to put together the pieces: the examples from Pratt's children, the discussion of Guaman Poma and the *New Chronicle and Good Government*, the brief history of European literacy, and the discussion of curriculum reform at Stanford. The terms that run through the sections are, among others, these: "contact," "community," "autoethnography," "transculturation." As you reread, mark those passages you might use to trace the general argument that cuts across these examples.

2. This essay was originally delivered as a lecture. Before you read Pratt's essay again, create a set of notes on what you remember as important, relevant, or worthwhile. Imagine yourself as part of her audience. Then reread the essay. Where would you want to interrupt her? What questions could you ask her that might make "Arts of the Contact Zone" more accessible to you?

3. This is an essay about reading and writing and teaching and learning, about the "literate arts" and the "pedagogical arts" of the contact zone. Surely the composition class, the first-year college English class, can be imagined as a contact zone. And it seems in the spirit of Pratt's essay to identify (as a student) with Guaman Poma. As you reread, think about how and where this essay might be said to speak directly to you about your education as a reader and writer in a contact zone.

4. There are some difficult terms in this essay: "autochthonous," "autoethnography," "transculturation." The last two are defined in the text; the first you will have to look up. (We did.) In some ways, the slipperiest of the key words in the essay is "culture." At one point Pratt says,

> If one thinks of cultures, or literatures, as discrete, coherently structured, monolingual edifices, Guaman Poma's text, and indeed any autoethnographic work, appears anomalous or chaotic — as it apparently did to the European scholars Pietschmann spoke to in 1912. If one does not think of cultures this way, then Guaman Poma's text is simply heterogeneous, as the Andean region was itself and remains

today. Such a text is heterogeneous on the reception end as well as the production end: it will read very differently to people in different positions in the contact zone. (p. 519)

If one thinks of cultures as "coherently structured, monolingual edifices," the text appears one way; if one thinks otherwise, the text is "simply heterogeneous." What might it mean to make this shift in the way one thinks of culture? Can you do it—that is, can you read the *New Chronicle* from both points of view, make the two points of view work in your own imagining? Can you, for example, think of a group that you participate in as a "community"? Then can you think of it as a "contact zone"? Which one seems "natural" to you? What does Pratt assume to be the dominant point of view now, for *her* readers?

As you reread, not only do you want to get a sense of how to explain these two attitudes toward culture, but you also need to practice shifting your point of view from one to the other. Think, from inside the position of each, of the things you would be expected to say about Poma's text, Manuel's invention, and your classroom.

· • ● • ● • • ·

ASSIGNMENTS FOR WRITING

Here, briefly, are two descriptions of the writing one might find or expect in the "contact zone." They serve as an introduction to the three writing assignments.

Autoethnography, transculturation, critique, collaboration, bilingualism, mediation, parody, denunciation, imaginary dialogue, vernacular expression — these are some of the literate arts of the contact zone. Miscomprehension, incomprehension, dead letters, unread masterpieces, absolute heterogeneity of meaning — these are some of the perils of writing in the contact zone. They all live among us today in the transnationalized metropolis of the United States and are becoming more widely visible, more pressing, and, like Guaman Poma's text, more decipherable to those who once would have ignored them in defense of a stable, centered sense of knowledge and reality. (pp. 519–20)

We are looking for the pedagogical arts of the contact zone. These will include, we are sure, exercises in storytelling and in identifying with the ideas, interests, histories, and attitudes of others; experiments in transculturation and collaborative work and in the arts of critique, parody, and comparison (including unseemly comparisons between elite and vernacular cultural forms); the redemption of the oral; ways for people to engage with suppressed aspects of history (including their own histories), ways to move *into and out of* rhetorics of authenticity; ground rules for communication across lines of difference and hierarchy that go beyond politeness but maintain mutual respect; a systematic approach to the all-important concept of *cultural mediation*. (p. 524)

1. One way of working with Pratt's essay, of extending its project, would be to conduct your own local inventory of writing from the contact zone. You might do this on your own or in teams with others from your class. You will want to gather several similar documents, your "archive," before you make your final selection. Think about how to make that choice. What makes one document stand out as representative? Here are two ways you might organize your search:

   a. You could look for historical documents. A local historical society might have documents written by Native Americans ("Indians") to the white settlers. There may be documents written by slaves to masters or to northern whites explaining their experience with slavery. There may be documents by women (like suffragists) trying to negotiate for public positions and rights. There may be documents from any of a number of racial or ethnic groups — Hispanic, Jewish, Irish, Italian, Polish, Swedish — trying to explain their positions to the mainstream culture. There may, perhaps at union halls, be documents written by workers to owners. Your own sense of the heritage of your area should direct your search.

   b. Or you could look for contemporary documents in the print that is around you, things that you might otherwise overlook. Pratt refers to one of the characteristic genres of the Hispanic community, the *"testimonio."* You could look at the writing of any marginalized group, particularly writing intended, at least in part, to represent the experience of outsiders to the dominant culture (or to be in dialogue with that culture or to respond to that culture). These documents, if we follow Pratt's example, would encompass the work of young children or students, including college students.

   Once you have completed your inventory, choose a document you would like to work with and present it carefully and in detail (perhaps in even greater detail than Pratt's presentation of the *New Chronicle*). You might imagine that you are presenting this to someone who would not have seen it and would not know how to read it, at least not as an example of the literate arts of the contact zone.

2. Another way of extending the project of Pratt's essay would be to write your own autoethnography. It should not be too hard to locate a setting or context in which you are the "other" — the one who speaks from outside rather than inside the dominant discourse. Pratt says that the position of the outsider is marked not only by differences of language and ways of thinking and speaking but also by differences in power, authority, and status. In a sense, she argues, the only way those in power can understand you is in *their* terms. These are terms you will need to use to tell your story, but your goal is to describe your position in ways that "engage with representations others have made of [you]" without giving in or giving up or disappearing in their already formed sense of who you are.

This is an interesting challenge. One of the things that will make the writing difficult is that the autoethnographic or transcultural text calls upon skills not usually valued in American classrooms: bilingualism, parody, denunciation, imaginary dialogue, vernacular expression, storytelling, unseemly comparisons of high and low cultural forms — these are some of the terms Pratt offers. These do not fit easily with the traditional genres of the writing class (essay, term paper, summary, report) or its traditional values (unity, consistency, sincerity, clarity, correctness, decorum).

You will probably need to take this essay (or whatever it should be called) through several drafts. It might be best to begin as Pratt's student, using her description as a preliminary guide. Once you get a sense of your own project, you may find that you have terms or examples to add to her list of the literate arts of the contact zone.

3. Citing Benedict Anderson and what he calls "imagined communities," Pratt argues that our idea of community is "strongly utopian, embodying values like equality, fraternity, liberty, which the societies often profess but systematically fail to realize" (p. 520). Against this utopian vision of community, Pratt argues that we need to develop ways of understanding (even noticing) social and intellectual spaces that are not homogeneous, unified; we need to develop ways of understanding and valuing difference.

Think of a community of which you are a member, a community that is important to you. And think about the utopian terms you are given to name and describe this community. Think, then, about this group in Pratt's terms — as a "contact zone." How would you name and describe this social space? Write an essay in which you present these alternate points of view on a single social group. You will need to present this discussion fully, so that someone who is not part of your group can follow what you say, and you should take time to think about the consequences (for you, for your group) of this shift in point of view, in terms.

· · · ● · · ·

MAKING CONNECTIONS

1. Here, from "Arts of the Contact Zone," is Mary Louise Pratt on the "autoethnographic" text:

> Guaman Poma's *New Chronicle* is an instance of what I have proposed to call an *autoethnographic* text, by which I mean a text in which people undertake to describe themselves in ways that engage with representations others have made of them. Thus if ethnographic texts are those in which European metropolitan subjects represent to themselves their others (usually their conquered others), autoethnographic texts are representations that the so-defined others construct *in response to* or in dialogue with those texts. . . . They involve a selective collaboration with and appropriation of idioms of the metropolis or the conqueror. These are merged or infiltrated to

varying degrees with indigenous idioms to create self-representations intended to intervene in metropolitan modes of understanding. . . . Such texts often constitute a marginalized group's point of entry into the dominant circuits of print culture. It is interesting to think, for example, of American slave autobiography in its autoethnographic dimensions, which in some respects distinguish it from Euramerican autobiographical tradition. (pp. 514–15)

John Edgar Wideman's "Our Time" (p. 622) and the excerpts from Gloria Anzaldúa's "How to Tame a Wild Tongue" (p. 26) could serve as twentieth-century examples of autoethnographic texts. Choose one of these selections and reread it with "Arts of the Contact Zone" in mind. Write an essay that presents the selection as an example of autoethnographic and/or transcultural texts. You should imagine that you are working to put Pratt's ideas to the test (*do* they do what she says such texts must do?), but also add what you have to say concerning this text as a literate effort to be present in the context of difference.

2. In the selection titled "States" (p. 559), Edward Said says,

All cultures spin out a dialectic of self and other, the subject "I" who is native, authentic, at home, and the object "it" or "you," who is foreign, perhaps threatening, different, out there. From this dialectic comes the series of heroes and monsters, founding fathers and barbarians, prized masterpieces and despised opponents that express a culture from its deepest sense of national self-identity to its refined patriotism, and finally to its coarse jingoism, xenophobia, and exclusivist bias. (p. 583)

This is as true of the Palestinians as it is of the Israelis — although, he adds, "For Palestinian culture, the odd thing is that its own identity is more frequently than not perceived as 'other.'"

Citing Benedict Anderson and what he refers to as "imagined communities," Mary Louise Pratt in "Arts of the Contact Zone" argues that our idea of community is "strongly utopian, embodying values like equality, fraternity, liberty, which the societies often profess but systematically fail to realize" (p. 520). Against this utopian vision of community, Pratt argues that we need to develop ways of understanding (noticing or creating) social and intellectual spaces that are not homogeneous or unified — contact zones. She argues that we need to develop ways of understanding and valuing difference.

There are similar goals and objects to these projects. Reread Pratt's essay with Said's "States" in mind. As she defines what she refers to as the "literate arts of the contact zone," can you find points of reference in Said's text? Said's thinking always attended to the importance and the conditions of writing, including his own. There are ways that "States" could be imagined as both "autoethnographic" and "transcultural." How might Said's work allow you to understand the "literate arts of the contact zone" in practice? How might his work allow you to understand the problems and possibilities of such writing beyond what Pratt has imagined, presented, and predicted?

3. In "Arts of the Contact Zone," Mary Louise Pratt defines contact zones as "social spaces where cultures meet, clash, and grapple with each other, often in contexts of highly asymmetrical relations of power" (p. 514). Atul Gawande, in "Slow Ideas" (p. 362), chronicles the ways that lifesaving innovations and changes for childbirth in India and the treatment of cholera in Bangladesh take hold. At one point in his essay, he writes that the physicians involved in these projects want to change systems in cultures so that particular practices and treatments become daily routines or the norm. "To create new norms," he writes, "you have to understand people's existing norms and barriers to change" (p. 368).

    Pratt might argue that those involved in the childbirth and cholera projects interacted in a context of "highly asymmetrical relations of power," where the health-care providers in India and Bangladesh hold the dominant position, trying to get medical treatments to take hold in systems in cultures where neither incentives nor penalties work.

    Write an essay in which you consider how Pratt's concept of the contact zone might be useful in helping us understand the ways that change came about in childbirth practices in India and the treatment of cholera in Bangladesh. What might be the "autoethnographic texts" produced during the evolutions of these changes, and how might you say that the caregivers, including Gawande, learned to read them? And, finally, what conclusions might you draw about Gawande's understanding of systemic or cultural change as the development of social and intellectual understanding in a contact zone?

RICHARD
Rodriguez

Richard Rodriguez, the son of Mexican immigrants, was born in San Francisco in 1944. He grew up in Sacramento, where he attended Catholic schools before going on to Stanford University, Columbia University, the Warburg Institute in London, and the University of California at Berkeley, eventually pursuing a PhD in English Renaissance literature. His essays have been published in *Saturday Review*, *The American Scholar*, *Change*, and elsewhere. He now lives in San Francisco and works as a lecturer, an educational consultant, and a freelance writer. He has published several books: *Hunger of Memory: The Education of Richard Rodriguez* (1981), *Days of Obligation: An Argument with My Mexican Father* (1992), *Brown: The Last Discovery of America* (2002), and *Darling: A Spiritual Autobiography* (2013).

In *Hunger of Memory*, a book of autobiographical essays that the *Christian Science Monitor* called "beautifully written, wrung from a sore heart," Rodriguez tells the story of his education, paying particular attention to both the meaning of his success as a student and, as he says, "its consequent price — the loss." Rodriguez's loss is represented most powerfully by his increased alienation from his parents and the decrease of intimate exchanges in family life. His parents' primary language was Spanish; his, once he became eager for success in school, was English. But the barrier was not only a language barrier. Rodriguez discovered that the interests he developed at school and through his reading were interests he did not share with those at home — in fact, his desire to speak of them tended to threaten and humiliate his mother and father.

This separation, Rodriguez argues, is a necessary part of every person's development, even though not everyone experiences it so dramatically. We must leave home and familiar ways of speaking and understanding in order to participate in public life. On these grounds, Rodriguez has been a strong voice against bilingual education, arguing that classes conducted in Spanish will only reinforce Spanish-speaking students' separateness from mainstream American life. Rodriguez's book caused a great deal of controversy upon publication, particularly in the Hispanic community. As one critic argued, "It is indeed painful that Mr. Rodriguez has come to identify himself so completely with the majority culture that he must propagandize for a system of education which can only produce other deprived and impoverished souls like himself." In his second book, *Days of Obligation: An Argument with My Mexican Father*, Rodriguez continues to explore his relationship with his family and with his Mexican heritage; here, however, he also writes of his life as a gay male and the forms of alienation entailed by his sexuality, including his sense of distance from gay lifestyles and culture, both popular and academic.

The selection that follows, Chapter 2 of *Hunger of Memory*, deals with Rodriguez's experiences in school. "If," he says, "because of my schooling I had grown culturally separated from my parents, my education finally had given me ways of speaking and caring about that fact" (p. 550). This essay is a record of how he came to understand the changes in his life. A reviewer writing in the *Atlantic Monthly* concluded that *Hunger of Memory* will survive in our literature "not because of some forgotten public issues that once bisected Richard Rodriguez's life, but because his history of that life has something to say about what it means to be American . . . and what it means to be human."

The Achievement of Desire

I stand in the ghetto classroom — "the guest speaker" — attempting to lecture on the mystery of the sounds of our words to rows of diffident students. "Don't you hear it? Listen! The music of our words. *'Sumer is icumen in. . . .'* And songs on the car radio. We need Aretha Franklin's voice to fill plain words with music — her life." In the face of their empty stares, I try to create an enthusiasm. But the girls in the back row turn to watch some boy passing outside. There are flutters of smiles, waves. And someone's mouth elongates heavy, silent words through the barrier of glass. Silent words — the lips straining to shape each voiceless syllable: *"Meet meee late errr."* By the door, the instructor smiles at me, apparently hoping that I will be able to spark some enthusiasm in the class. But only one student seems to be listening. A girl, maybe fourteen. In this gray room her eyes shine with ambition. She keeps nodding and nodding at all that I say; she even takes notes. And each time I ask a question, she jerks up and down in her desk like a marionette, while her hand waves over the bowed heads of her classmates. It is myself (as a boy) I see as she faces me now (a man in my thirties).

THE BOY WHO FIRST ENTERED A CLASSROOM BARELY ABLE TO SPEAK ENGLISH, TWENTY YEARS LATER CONCLUDED HIS STUDIES IN THE STATELY QUIET OF THE READING ROOM IN THE BRITISH MUSEUM.

The boy who first entered a classroom barely able to speak English, twenty years later concluded his studies in the stately quiet of the reading room in the British Museum. Thus with one sentence I can summarize my academic career. It will be harder to summarize what sort of life connects the boy to the man.

With every award, each graduation from one level of education to the next, people I'd meet would congratulate me. Their refrain [was] always the same: "Your parents must be very proud." Sometimes then they'd ask me how I managed it — my "success." (How?) After a while, I had several quick answers to give in reply. I'd admit, for one thing, that I went to an excellent grammar school. (My earliest teachers, the nuns, made my success their ambition.) And my brother and both my sisters were very good students. (They often brought home the shiny school trophies I came to want.) And my mother and father always encouraged me. (At every graduation they were behind the stunning flash of the camera when I turned to look at the crowd.)

As important as these factors were, however, they account inadequately for my academic advance. Nor do they suggest what an odd success I managed. For although I was a very good student, I was also a very bad student. I was a "scholarship boy," a certain kind of scholarship boy. Always successful, I was always unconfident. Exhilarated by my progress. Sad. I became the prized student — anxious and eager to learn. Too eager, too anxious — an imitative and unoriginal pupil. My brother and two sisters enjoyed the advantages I did, and they grew to be as successful as I, but none of them ever seemed so anxious about their schooling. A second-grade student, I was the one who came home and corrected the "simple" grammatical mistakes of our parents. ("Two negatives make a positive.") Proudly I announced — to my family's startled silence — that a teacher had said I was losing all trace of a Spanish accent. I was oddly annoyed when I was unable to get parental help with a homework assignment. The night my father tried to help me with an arithmetic exercise, he kept reading the instructions, each time more deliberately, until I pried the textbook out of his hands, saying, "I'll try to figure it out some more by myself."

When I reached the third grade, I outgrew such behavior. I became more tactful, careful to keep separate the two very different worlds of my day. But then, with ever-increasing intensity, I devoted myself to my studies. I became bookish, puzzling to all my family. Ambition set me apart. When my brother saw me struggling home with stacks of library books, he would laugh, shouting: "Hey, Four Eyes!" My father opened a closet one day and was startled to find me inside, reading a novel. My mother would find me reading when I was supposed to be asleep or helping around the house or playing outside. In a voice angry or worried or just curious, she'd ask: "What do you see in your books?" It became the family's joke. When I was called and wouldn't reply, someone would say I must be hiding under my bed with a book.

(How did I manage my success?)

What I am about to say to you has taken me more than twenty years to admit: *A primary reason for my success in the classroom was that I couldn't forget that schooling was changing me and separating me from the life I enjoyed before becoming a student.* That simple realization! For years I never spoke to anyone about it. Never mentioned a thing to my family or my teachers or classmates. From a very early age, I understood enough, just enough about my classroom experiences to keep what I knew repressed, hidden beneath layers of embarrassment. Not until my last months as a graduate student, nearly thirty years old, was it possible for me to think much about the reasons for my academic success. Only then. At the end of my schooling, I needed to determine how far I had moved from my past. The adult finally confronted, and now must publicly say, what the child shuddered from knowing and could never admit to himself or to those many faces that smiled at his every success. ("Your parents must be very proud. . . .")

I

At the end, in the British Museum (too distracted to finish my dissertation) for weeks I read, speed-read, books by modern educational theorists, only to find infrequent and slight mention of students like me. (Much more is written about the more typical case, the lower-class student who barely is helped by his schooling.) Then one day, leafing through Richard Hoggart's *The Uses of Literacy*, I found, in his description of the scholarship boy, myself. For the first time I realized that there were other students like me, and so I was able to frame the meaning of my academic success, its consequent price — the loss.

Hoggart's description is distinguished, at least initially, by deep understanding. What he grasps very well is that the scholarship boy must move between environments, his home and the classroom, which are at cultural extremes, opposed. With his family, the boy has the intense pleasure of intimacy, the family's consolation in feeling public alienation. Lavish emotions texture home life. *Then*, at school, the instruction bids him to trust lonely reason primarily. Immediate needs set the pace of his parents' lives. From his mother and father the boy learns to trust spontaneity and nonrational ways of knowing. *Then*, at school, there is mental calm. Teachers emphasize the value of a reflectiveness that opens a space between thinking and immediate action.

Years of schooling must pass before the boy will be able to sketch the cultural differences in his day as abstractly as this. But he senses those differences early. Perhaps as early as the night he brings home an assignment from school and finds the house too noisy for study.

> He has to be more and more alone, if he is going to "get on." He will have, probably unconsciously, to oppose the ethos of the hearth, the intense gregariousness of the working-class family group. Since everything centres upon the living-room, there is unlikely to be a room of his own; the bedrooms are cold and inhospitable, and to warm them or the front room, if there is one, would not only be expensive, but would require an imaginative leap — out of the tradition — which most families are not capable of making. There is a corner of the living-room table. On the other side Mother is ironing, the wireless is on, someone is singing a snatch of song or Father says intermittently whatever comes into his head. The boy has to cut himself off mentally, so as to do his homework, as well as he can.[1]

The next day, the lesson is as apparent at school. There are even rows of desks. Discussion is ordered. The boy must rehearse his thoughts and raise his hand before speaking out in a loud voice to an audience of classmates. And there is time enough, and silence, to think about ideas (big ideas) never considered at home by his parents.

Not for the working-class child alone is adjustment to the classroom difficult. Good schooling requires that any student alter early childhood habits. But the working-class child is usually least prepared for the change. And, unlike many middle-class children, he goes home and sees in his parents a way of life not only different but starkly opposed to that of the classroom. (He enters the house and hears his parents talking in ways his teachers discourage.)

Without extraordinary determination and the great assistance of others — at home and at school — there is little chance for success. Typically most working-class children are barely changed by the classroom. The exception succeeds. The relative few become scholarship students. Of these, Richard Hoggart estimates, most manage a fairly graceful transition. Somehow they learn to live in the two very different worlds of their day. There are some others, however, those Hoggart pejoratively terms "scholarship boys," for whom success comes with special anxiety. Scholarship boy: good student, troubled son. The child is "moderately endowed," intellectually mediocre, Hoggart supposes — though it may be more pertinent to note the special qualities of temperament in the child. High-strung child. Brooding. Sensitive. Haunted by the knowledge that one *chooses* to become a student. (Education is not an inevitable or natural step in growing up.) Here is a child who cannot forget that his academic success distances him from a life he loved, even from his own memory of himself.

Initially, he wavers, balances allegiance. ("The boy is himself [until he reaches, say, the upper forms] very much of *both* the worlds of home and school. He is enormously obedient to the dictates of the world of school, but emotionally still strongly wants to continue as part of the family circle.") Gradually, necessarily, the balance is lost. The boy needs to spend more and more time studying, each night enclosing himself in the silence permitted and required by intense concentration. He takes his first step toward academic success, away from his family.

From the very first days, through the years following, it will be with his parents — the figures of lost authority, the persons toward whom he feels deepest love — that the change will be most powerfully measured. A separation will unravel between them. Advancing in his studies, the boy notices that his mother and father have not changed as much as he. Rather, when he sees them, they often remind him of the person he once was and the life he earlier shared with them. He realizes what some Romantics also know when they praise the working class for the capacity for human closeness, qualities of passion and spontaneity, that the rest of us experience in like measure only in the earliest part of our youth. For the Romantic, this doesn't make working-class life childish. Working-class life challenges precisely because it is an *adult* way of life.

The scholarship boy reaches a different conclusion. He cannot afford to admire his parents. (How could he and still pursue such a contrary life?) He permits himself embarrassment at their lack of education. And to evade nostalgia for the life he has lost, he concentrates on the benefits education will bestow upon him. He becomes especially ambitious. Without the support of old certainties and consolations, almost mechanically, he assumes the procedures and doctrines of the classroom. The kind of allegiance the young student might have given his mother and father only days earlier, he transfers to the teacher, the new figure of authority. "[The scholarship boy] tends to make a father-figure of his form-master," Hoggart observes.

But Hoggart's calm prose only makes me recall the urgency with which I came to idolize my grammar school teachers. I began by imitating their accents, using their diction, trusting their every direction. The very first facts they dispensed, I grasped with awe. Any book they told me to read, I read — then waited for them to tell me which books I enjoyed. Their every casual opinion I came to adopt and to trumpet when I returned home. I stayed after school "to help" — to get my teacher's undivided attention. It was the nun's encouragement that mattered most to me. (She understood exactly what — my parents never seemed to appraise so well — all my achievements entailed.) Memory gently caressed each word of praise bestowed in the classroom so that compliments teachers paid me years ago come quickly to mind even today.

The enthusiasm I felt in second-grade classes I flaunted before both my parents. The docile, obedient student came home a shrill and precocious son who insisted on correcting and teaching his parents with the remark: "My teacher told us. . . ."

I intended to hurt my mother and father. I was still angry at them for having encouraged me toward classroom English. But gradually this anger was exhausted, replaced by guilt as school grew more and more attractive to me. I grew increasingly successful, a talkative student. My hand was raised in the classroom; I yearned to answer any question. At home, life was less noisy than it had been. (I spoke to classmates and teachers more often each day than to family members.) Quiet at home, I sat with my papers for hours each night. I never forgot that schooling had irretrievably changed my family's life. That knowledge, however, did not weaken ambition. Instead, it strengthened resolve. Those times I remembered the loss of my past with regret, I quickly reminded myself of all the things my teachers could give me. (They could make me an educated man.) I tightened my grip on pencil and books. I evaded nostalgia. Tried hard to forget. But one does not forget by trying to forget. One only remembers. I remembered too well that education had changed my family's life. I would not have become a scholarship boy had I not so often remembered.

Once she was sure that her children knew English, my mother would tell us, "You should keep up your Spanish." Voices playfully groaned in response. *"¡Pochos!"* my mother would tease. I listened silently.

After a while, I grew more calm at home. I developed tact. A fourth-grade student, I was no longer the show-off in front of my parents. I became a conventionally dutiful son, politely affectionate, cheerful enough, even — for reasons beyond choosing — my father's favorite. And much about my family life was easy then, comfortable, happy in the rhythm of our living together: hearing my father getting ready for work; eating the breakfast my mother had made me; looking up from a novel to hear my brother or one of my sisters playing with friends in the backyard; in winter, coming upon the house all lighted up after dark.

But withheld from my mother and father was any mention of what most mattered to me: the extraordinary experience of first-learning. Late afternoon: in the midst of preparing dinner, my mother would come up behind me while I was trying to read. Her head just over mine, her breath warmly scented with food. "What are you reading?" Or, "Tell me all about your new courses." I would barely respond, "Just the usual things, nothing special." (A half smile, then silence. Her head moving back in the silence. Silence! Instead of the flood of intimate sounds that had once flowed smoothly between us, there was this silence.) After dinner, I would rush to a bedroom with papers and books. As often as possible, I resisted parental pleas to "save lights" by coming to the kitchen to work. I kept so much, so often, to myself. Sad. Enthusiastic. Troubled by the excitement of coming upon new ideas. Eager. Fascinated by the promising texture of a brand-new book. I hoarded the pleasures of learning. Alone for hours. Enthralled. Nervous. I rarely looked away from my books — or back on my memories. Nights when relatives visited and the front rooms were warmed by Spanish sounds, I slipped quietly out of the house.

It mattered that education was changing me. It never ceased to matter. My brother and sisters would giggle at our mother's mispronounced words. They'd correct her gently. My mother laughed girlishly one night, trying not to pronounce *sheep* as *ship*. From a distance I listened sullenly. From that distance, pretending not to notice on another occasion, I saw my father looking at the title pages of my library books. That was the scene on my mind when I walked home with a fourth-grade companion and heard him say that his parents read to him every night. (A strange-sounding book — *Winnie the Pooh*.) Immediately, I wanted to know, "What is it like?" My companion, however, thought I wanted to know about the plot of the book. Another day, my mother surprised me by asking for a "nice" book to read. "Something not too hard you think I might like." Carefully I chose one, Willa Cather's *My Ántonia*. But when, several weeks later, I happened to see it next to her bed unread except for the first few pages, I was furious and suddenly wanted to cry. I grabbed up the book and took it back to my room and placed it in its place, alphabetically on my shelf.

"Your parents must be very proud of you." People began to say that to me about the time I was in sixth grade. To answer affirmatively, I'd smile. Shyly I'd smile, never betraying my sense of the irony: I was not proud of my mother and father. I was embarrassed by their lack of education. It was not that I ever thought they were stupid, though stupidly I took for granted their enormous native intelligence. Simply, what mattered to me was that they were not like my teachers.

But, "Why didn't you tell us about the award?" my mother demanded, her frown weakened by pride. At the grammar school ceremony several weeks after, her eyes were brighter than the trophy I'd won. Pushing back the hair from my forehead, she whispered that I had "shown" the *gringos*. A few minutes later, I heard my father speak to my teacher and felt ashamed of his labored, accented words. Then guilty for the shame. I felt such contrary feelings. (There is no simple road-map through the heart of the scholarship boy.) My teacher was so soft-spoken and her words were edged sharp and clean. I admired her until it seemed to me that she spoke too carefully. Sensing that she was condescending to them, I became nervous. Resentful. Protective. I tried to move my parents away. "You both must be very proud of Richard," the nun said. They responded quickly. (They were proud.) "We are proud of all our children." Then this afterthought: "They sure didn't get their brains from us." They all laughed. I smiled.

Tightening the irony into a knot was the knowledge that my parents were always behind me. They made success possible. They evened the path. They sent their children to parochial schools because the nuns "teach better." They paid a tuition they couldn't afford. They spoke English to us.

For their children my parents wanted chances they never had — an easier way. It saddened my mother to learn that some relatives forced their children to start working right after high school. To *her* children she would say, "Get all the education you can." In schooling she recognized the key to job advancement. And with the remark she remembered her past.

As a girl new to America my mother had been awarded a high school diploma by teachers too careless or busy to notice that she hardly spoke English. On her own, she determined to learn how to type. That skill got her jobs typing envelopes in letter shops, and it encouraged in her an optimism about the possibility of advancement. (Each morning when her sisters put on uniforms, she chose a bright-colored dress.) The years of young womanhood passed, and her typing speed increased. She also became an excellent speller of words she mispronounced. "And I've never been to college," she'd say, smiling, when her children asked her to spell words they were too lazy to look up in a dictionary.

Typing, however, was dead-end work. Finally frustrating. When her youngest child started high school, my mother got a full-time office job once again. (Her paycheck combined with my father's to make us — in fact — what we had already become in our imagination of ourselves — middle class.) She worked then for the (California) state government in numbered civil service positions secured by examinations. The old ambition of her youth was rekindled. During the lunch hour, she consulted bulletin boards for announcements of openings. One day she saw mention of something called an "anti-poverty agency." A typing job. A glamorous job, part of the governor's staff. "A knowledge of Spanish required." Without hesitation she applied and became nervous only when the job was suddenly hers.

"Everyone comes to work all dressed up," she reported at night. And didn't need to say more than that her co-workers wouldn't let her answer the phones. She was only a typist, after all, albeit a very fast typist. And an excellent speller. One morning there was a letter to be sent to a Washington cabinet officer. On the dictating tape, a voice referred to urban guerrillas. My mother typed (the wrong word, correctly): "gorillas." The mistake horrified the anti-poverty bureaucrats who shortly after arranged to have her returned to her previous position. She would go no further. So she willed her ambition to their children. "Get all the education you can; with an education you can do anything." (With a good education *she* could have done anything.)

When I was in high school, I admitted to my mother that I planned to become a teacher someday. That seemed to please her. But I never tried to explain that it was not the occupation of teaching I yearned for as much as it was something more elusive: I wanted to *be* like my teachers, to possess their knowledge, to assume their authority, their confidence, even to assume a teacher's persona.

In contrast to my mother, my father never verbally encouraged his children's academic success. Nor did he often praise us. My mother had to remind him to "say something" to one of his children who scored some academic success. But whereas my mother saw in education the opportunity for job advancement, my father recognized that education provided an even more startling possibility: it could enable a person to escape from a life of mere labor.

In Mexico, orphaned when he was eight, my father left school to work as an "apprentice" for an uncle. Twelve years later, he left Mexico in frustration and arrived in America. He had great expectations then of becoming an engineer. ("Work for my hands and my head.") He knew a Catholic priest who promised to get him money enough to study full time for a high school diploma. But the promises came to nothing. Instead there was a dark succession of warehouse, cannery, and factory jobs. After work he went to night school along with my mother. A year, two passed. Nothing much changed, except that fatigue worked its way into the bone; then everything changed.

He didn't talk anymore of becoming an engineer. He stayed outside on the steps of the school while my mother went inside to learn typing and shorthand.

> IT WAS MY FATHER WHO LAUGHED WHEN I CLAIMED TO BE TIRED BY READING AND WRITING.

By the time I was born, my father worked at "clean" jobs. For a time he was a janitor at a fancy department store. ("Easy work; the machines do it all.") Later he became a dental technician. ("Simple.") But by then he was pessimistic about the ultimate meaning of work and the possibility of ever escaping its claims. In some of my earliest memories of him, my father already seems aged by fatigue. (He has never really grown old like my mother.) From boyhood to manhood, I have remembered him in a single image: seated, asleep on the sofa, his head thrown back in a hideous corpselike grin, the evening newspaper spread out before him. "But look at all you've accomplished," his best friend said to him once. My father said nothing. Only smiled.

It was my father who laughed when I claimed to be tired by reading and writing. It was he who teased me for having soft hands. (He seemed to sense that some great achievement of leisure was implied by my papers and books.) It was my father who became angry while watching on television some woman at the Miss America contest tell the announcer that she was going to college. ("Majoring in fine arts.") "College!" he snarled. He despised the trivialization of higher education, the inflated grades and cheapened diplomas, the half education that so often passed as mass education in my generation.

It was my father again who wondered why I didn't display my awards on the wall of my bedroom. He said he liked to go to doctors' offices and see their certificates and degrees on the wall. ("Nice.") My citations from school got left in closets at home. The gleaming figure astride one of my trophies was broken, wingless, after hitting the ground. My medals were placed in a jar of loose change. And when I lost my high school diploma, my father found it as it was about to be thrown out with the trash. Without telling me, he put it away with his own things for safe-keeping.

These memories slammed together at the instant of hearing that refrain familiar to all scholarship students: "Your parents must be proud. . . ." Yes, my parents were proud. I knew it. But my parents regarded my progress with more than mere pride. They endured my early precocious behavior — but with what private anger and humiliation? As their children got older and would come home to challenge ideas both of them held, they argued before submitting to the force of logic or superior factual evidence with the disclaimer, "It's what we were taught in our time to believe." These discussions ended abruptly, though my mother remembered them on other occasions when she complained that our "big ideas" were going to our heads. More acute was her complaint that the family wasn't close anymore, like some others she knew. Why weren't we close, "more in the Mexican style"? Everyone is so private, she added. And she mimicked the yes and no answers she got in reply to her questions. Why didn't we talk more? (My father never asked.) I never said.

I was the first in my family who asked to leave home when it came time to go to college. I had been admitted to Stanford, one hundred miles away. My departure would only make physically apparent the separation that had occurred long before. But it was going too far. In the months preceding my leaving, I heard the question my mother never asked except indirectly. In the hot kitchen, tired at the end of her workday, she demanded to know, "Why aren't the colleges here in Sacramento good enough for you? They are for your brother and sister." In the middle of a car ride, not turning to face me, she wondered, "Why do you need to go so far away?" Late at night, ironing, she said with disgust, "Why do you have to put us through this big expense? You know your scholarship will never cover it all." But when September came there was a rush to get everything ready. In a bedroom that last night I packed the big brown valise, and my mother sat nearby sewing initials onto the clothes I would take. And she said no more about my leaving.

Months later, two weeks of Christmas vacation: the first hours home were the hardest. ("What's new?") My parents and I sat in the kitchen for a conversation. (But, lacking the same words to develop our sentences and to shape our interests, what was there to say? What could I tell them of the term paper I had just finished on the "universality of Shakespeare's appeal"?) I mentioned only small, obvious things: my dormitory life; weekend trips I had taken; random events. They responded with news of their own. (One was almost grateful for a family crisis about which there was much to discuss.) We tried to make our conversation seem like more than an interview.

II

From an early age I knew that my mother and father could read and write both Spanish and English. I had observed my father making his way through what, I now suppose, must have been income tax forms. On other occasions I waited apprehensively while my mother read onion-paper letters airmailed from Mexico with news of a relative's illness or death. For both my parents, however, reading was something done out of necessity and as quickly as possible. Never did I see either of them read an entire book. Nor did I see them read for pleasure. Their reading consisted of work manuals, prayer books, newspaper, recipes.

Richard Hoggart imagines how, at home,

> [the scholarship boy] sees strewn around, and reads regularly himself, magazines which are never mentioned at school, which seem not to belong to the world to which the school introduces him; at school he hears about and reads books never mentioned at home. When he brings those books into the house they do not take their place with other books which the family are reading, for often there are none or almost none; his books look, rather, like strange tools.

In our house each school year would begin with my mother's careful instruction: "Don't write in your books so we can sell them at the end of the year." The remark was echoed in public by my teachers, but only in part: "Boys and girls, don't write in your books. You must learn to treat them with great care and respect."

OPEN THE DOORS OF YOUR MIND WITH BOOKS, read the red and white poster over the nun's desk in early September. It soon was apparent to me that reading was the classroom's central activity. Each course had its own book. And the information gathered from a book was unquestioned. READ TO LEARN, the sign on the wall advised in December. I privately wondered: What was the connection between reading and learning? Did one learn something only by reading it? Was an idea only an idea if it could be written down? In June, CONSIDER BOOKS YOUR BEST FRIENDS. Friends? Reading was, at best, only a chore. I needed to look up whole paragraphs of words in a dictionary. Lines of type were dizzying, the eye having to move slowly across the page, then down, and across. . . . The sentences of the first books I read were coolly impersonal. Toned hard. What most bothered me, however, was the isolation reading required. To console myself for the loneliness I'd feel when I read, I tried reading in a very soft voice. Until: "Who is doing all that talking to his neighbor?" Shortly after, remedial reading classes were arranged for me with a very old nun.

At the end of each school day, for nearly six months, I would meet with her in the tiny room that served as the school's library but was actually only a storeroom for used textbooks and a vast collection of *National Geographics*. Everything about our sessions pleased me: the smallness of the room; the noise of the janitor's broom hitting the edge of the long hallway outside the door; the green of the sun, lighting the wall; and the old woman's face blurred white with a beard. Most of the time we took turns. I began with my elementary text. Sentences of astonishing simplicity seemed to me lifeless and drab: "The boys ran from the rain.... She wanted to sing.... The kite rose in the blue." Then the old nun would read from her favorite books, usually biographies of early American presidents. Playfully she ran through complex sentences, calling the words alive with her voice, making it seem that the author somehow was speaking directly to me. I smiled just to listen to her. I sat there and sensed for the very first time some possibility of fellowship between a reader and a writer, a communication, never *intimate* like that I heard spoken words at home convey, but one nonetheless *personal*.

One day the nun concluded a session by asking me why I was so reluctant to read by myself. I tried to explain; said something about the way written words made me feel all alone — almost, I wanted to add but didn't, as when I spoke to myself in a room just emptied of furniture. She studied my face as I spoke; she seemed to be watching more than listening. In an uneventful voice she replied that I had nothing to fear. Didn't I realize that reading would open up whole new worlds? A book could open doors for me. It could introduce me to people and show me places I never imagined existed. She gestured toward the bookshelves. (Bare-breasted African women danced, and the shiny hubcaps of automobiles on the back covers of the *Geographic* gleamed in my mind.) I listened with respect. But her words were not very influential. I was thinking then of another consequence of literacy, one I was too shy to admit but nonetheless trusted. Books were going to make me "educated." *That* confidence enabled me, several months later, to overcome my fear of the silence.

In fourth grade I embarked upon a grandiose reading program. "Give me the names of important books," I would say to startled teachers. They soon found out that I had in mind "adult books." I ignored their suggestion of anything I suspected was written for children. (Not until I was in college, as a result, did I read *Huckleberry Finn* or *Alice's Adventures in Wonderland*.) Instead, I read *The Scarlet Letter* and Franklin's *Autobiography*. And whatever I read I read for extra credit. Each time I finished a book, I reported the achievement to a teacher and basked in the praise my effort earned. Despite my best efforts, however, there seemed to be more and more books I needed to read. At the library I would literally tremble as I came upon whole shelves of books I hadn't read. So I read and I read and I read: *Great Expectations*; all the short stories of Kipling; *The Babe Ruth Story*; the entire first volume of the *Encyclopedia Britannica* (A–ANSTEY); the *Iliad*; *Moby Dick*; *Gone with the Wind*; *The Good Earth*; *Ramona*; *Forever Amber*; *The Lives of the Saints*; *Crime and Punishment*; *The Pearl*.... Librarians who initially frowned when I checked out the maximum ten books at a time started saving books they thought I might like. Teachers would say to the rest of the class, "I only wish the rest of you took reading as seriously as Richard obviously does."

But at home I would hear my mother wondering, "What do you see in your books?" (Was reading a hobby like her knitting? Was so much reading even healthy for a boy? Was it the sign of "brains"? Or was it just a convenient excuse for not helping about the house on Saturday mornings?) Always, "What do you see . . . ?"

What *did* I see in my books? I had the idea that they were crucial for my academic success, though I couldn't have said exactly how or why. In the sixth grade I simply concluded that what gave a book its value was some major idea or theme it contained. If that core essence could be mined and memorized, I would become learned like my teachers. I decided to record in a notebook the themes of the books that I read. After reading *Robinson Crusoe*, I wrote that its theme was "the value of learning to live by oneself." When I completed *Wuthering Heights*, I noted the danger of "letting emotions get out of control." Rereading these brief moralistic appraisals usually left me disheartened. I couldn't believe that they were really the source of reading's value. But for many more years, they constituted the only means I had of describing to myself the educational value of books.

In spite of my earnestness, I found reading a pleasurable activity. I came to enjoy the lonely good company of books. Early on weekday mornings, I'd read in my bed. I'd feel a mysterious comfort then, reading in the dawn quiet — the blue-gray silence interrupted by the occasional churning of the refrigerator motor a few rooms away or the more distant sounds of a city bus beginning its run. On weekends I'd go to the public library to read, surrounded by old men and women. Or, if the weather was fine, I would take my books to the park and read in the shade of a tree. A warm summer evening was my favorite reading time. Neighbors would leave for vacation and I would water their lawns. I would sit through the twilight on the front porches or in backyards, reading to the cool, whirling sounds of the sprinklers.

I also had favorite writers. But often those writers I enjoyed most I was least able to value. When I read William Saroyan's *The Human Comedy*, I was immediately pleased by the narrator's warmth and the charm of his story. But as quickly I became suspicious. A book so enjoyable to read couldn't be very "important." Another summer I determined to read all the novels of Dickens. Reading his fat novels, I loved the feeling I got — after the first hundred pages — of being at home in a fictional world where I knew the names of the characters and cared about what was going to happen to them. And it bothered me that I was forced away at the conclusion, when the fiction closed tight, like a fortune-teller's fist — the futures of all the major characters neatly resolved. I never knew how to take such feelings seriously, however. Nor did I suspect that these experiences could be part of a novel's meaning. Still, there were pleasures to sustain me after I'd finish my books. Carrying a volume back to the library, I would be pleased by its weight. I'd run my fingers along the edge of the pages and marvel at the breadth of my achievement. Around my room, growing stacks of paperback books reinforced my assurance.

I entered high school having read hundreds of books. My habit of reading made me a confident speaker and writer of English. Reading also enabled me to sense something of the shape, the major concerns, of Western thought. (I was able to say something about Dante and Descartes and Engels and James Baldwin in my high school term papers.) In these various ways, books brought me academic success as I hoped that they would. But I was not a good reader. Merely bookish, I lacked a point of view when I read. Rather, I read in order to acquire a point of view. I vacuumed books for epigrams, scraps of information, ideas, themes — anything to fill the hollow within me and make me feel educated. When one of my teachers suggested to his drowsy tenth-grade English class that a person could not have a "complicated idea" until he had read at least two thousand books, I heard the remark without detecting either its irony or its very complicated truth. I merely determined to compile a list of all the books I had ever read. Harsh with myself, I included only once a title I might have read several times. (How, after all, could one read a book more than once?) And I included only those books over a hundred pages in length. (Could anything shorter be a book?)

There was yet another high school list I compiled. One day I came across a newspaper article about the retirement of an English professor at a nearby state college. The article was accompanied by a list of the "hundred most important books of Western Civilization." "More than anything else in my life," the professor told the reporter with finality, "these books have made me all that I am." That was the kind of remark I couldn't ignore. I clipped out the list and kept it for the several months it took me to read all of the titles. Most books, of course, I barely understood. While reading Plato's *Republic*, for instance, I needed to keep looking at the book jacket comments to remind myself what the text was about. Nevertheless, with the special patience and superstition of a scholarship boy, I looked at every word of the text. And by the time I reached the last word, relieved, I convinced myself that I had read *The Republic*. In a ceremony of great pride, I solemnly crossed Plato off my list.

> THE SCHOLARSHIP BOY PLEASES MOST WHEN HE IS YOUNG — THE WORKING-CLASS CHILD STRUGGLING FOR ACADEMIC SUCCESS.

III

The scholarship boy pleases most when he is young — the working-class child struggling for academic success. To his teachers, he offers great satisfaction; his success is their proudest achievement. Many other persons offer to help him. A businessman learns the boy's story and promises to underwrite part of the cost of his college education. A woman leaves him her entire library of several hundred books when she moves. His progress is featured in a newspaper article. Many people seem happy for him. They marvel. "How did you manage so fast?" From all sides, there is lavish praise and encouragement.

In his grammar school classroom, however, the boy already makes students around him uneasy. They scorn his desire to succeed. They scorn him for constantly wanting the teacher's attention and praise. "Kiss Ass," they call him when his hand swings up in response to every question he hears. Later, when he makes it to college, no one will mock him aloud. But he detects annoyance on the faces of some students and even some teachers who watch him. It puzzles him often. In college, then in graduate school, he behaves much as he always has. If anything is different about him it is that he dares to anticipate the successful conclusion of his studies. At last he feels that he belongs in the classroom, and this is exactly the source of the dissatisfaction he causes. To many persons around him, he appears too much the academic. There may be some things about him that recall his beginnings — his shabby clothes; his persistent poverty; or his dark skin (in those cases when it symbolizes his parents' disadvantaged condition) — but they only make clear how far he has moved from his past. He has used education to remake himself.

It bothers his fellow academics to face this. They will not say why exactly. (They sneer.) But their expectations become obvious when they are disappointed. They expect — they want — a student less changed by his schooling. If the scholarship boy, from a past so distant from the classroom, could remain in some basic way unchanged, he would be able to prove that it is possible for anyone to become educated without basically changing from the person one was.

Here is no fabulous hero, no idealized scholar-worker. The scholarship boy does not straddle, cannot reconcile, the two great opposing cultures of his life. His success is unromantic and plain. He sits in the classroom and offers those sitting beside him no calming reassurance about their own lives. He sits in the seminar room — a man with brown skin, the son of working-class Mexican immigrant parents. (Addressing the professor at the head of the table, his voice catches with nervousness.) There is no trace of his parents in his speech. Instead he approximates the accents of teachers and classmates. Coming from *him* those sounds seem suddenly odd. Odd too is the effect produced when *he* uses academic jargon — bubbles at the tip of his tongue: "*Topos* . . . negative capability . . . vegetation imagery in Shakespearean comedy." He lifts an opinion from Coleridge, takes something else from Frye or Empson or Leavis. He even repeats exactly his professor's earlier comment. All his ideas are clearly borrowed. He seems to have no thought of his own. He chatters while his listeners smile — their look one of disdain.

When he is older and thus when so little of the person he was survives, the scholarship boy makes only too apparent his profound lack of *self*-confidence. This is the conventional assessment that even Richard Hoggart repeats:

> [The scholarship boy] tends to over-stress the importance of examinations, of the piling-up of knowledge and of received opinions. He discovers

a technique of apparent learning, of the acquiring of facts rather than of the handling and use of facts. He learns how to receive a purely literate education, one using only a small part of the personality and challenging only a limited area of his being. He begins to see life as a ladder, as permanent examination with some praise and some further exhortation at each stage. He becomes an expert imbiber and doler-out; his competence will vary, but will rarely be accompanied by genuine enthusiasms. He rarely feels the reality of knowledge, of other men's thoughts and imaginings, on his own pulses. . . . He has something of the blinkered pony about him. . . .

But this is criticism more accurate than fair. The scholarship boy is a very bad student. He is the great mimic; a collector of thoughts, not a thinker; the very last person in class who ever feels obliged to have an opinion of his own. In large part, however, the reason he is such a bad student is because he realizes more often and more acutely than most other students — than Hoggart himself — that education requires radical self-reformation. As a very young boy, regarding his parents, as he struggles with an early homework assignment, he knows this too well. That is why he lacks self-assurance. He does not forget that the classroom is responsible for remaking him. He relies on his teacher, depends on all that he hears in the classroom and reads in his books. He becomes in every obvious way the worst student, a dummy mouthing the opinions of others. But he would not be so bad — nor would he become so successful, a *scholarship* boy — if he did not accurately perceive that the best synonym for primary "education" is "imitation."

Those who would take seriously the boy's success — and his failure — would be forced to realize how great is the change any academic undergoes, how far one must move from one's past. It is easiest to ignore such considerations. So little is said about the scholarship boy in pages and pages of educational literature. Nothing is said of the silence that comes to separate the boy from his parents. Instead, one hears proposals for increasing the self-esteem of students and encouraging early intellectual independence. Paragraphs glitter with a constellation of terms like *creativity* and *originality*. (Ignored altogether is the function of imitation in a student's life.) Radical educationalists meanwhile complain that ghetto schools "oppress" students by trying to mold them, stifling native characteristics. The truer critique would be just the reverse: not that schools change ghetto students too much, but that while they might promote the occasional scholarship student, they change most students barely at all.

From the story of the scholarship boy there is no specific pedagogy to glean. There is, however, a much larger lesson. His story makes clear that education is a long, unglamorous, even demeaning process — *a nurturing never natural to the person one was before one entered a classroom.* At once different from most other students, the scholarship boy is also the archetypal "good student." He exaggerates the difficulty of being a student, but his exaggeration reveals a general predicament. Others are changed by their schooling as much as he. They too must re-form themselves. They must develop the skill of memory long before they become truly critical thinkers. And when they read Plato for the first several times, it will be with awe more than deep comprehension.

The impact of schooling on the scholarship boy is only more apparent to the boy himself and to others. Finally, although he may be laughable — a blinkered pony — the boy will not let his critics forget their own change. He ends up too much like them. When he speaks, they hear themselves echoed. In his pedantry, they trace their own. His ambitions are theirs. If his failure were singular, they might readily pity him. But he is more troubling than that. They would not scorn him if this were not so.

IV

Like me, Hoggart's imagined scholarship boy spends most of his years in the classroom afraid to long for his past. Only at the very end of his schooling does the boy-man become nostalgic. In this sudden change of heart, Richard Hoggart notes:

> He longs for the membership he lost, "he pines for some Nameless Eden where he never was." The nostalgia is the stronger and the more ambiguous because he is really "in quest of his own absconded self yet scared to find it." He both wants to go back and yet thinks he has gone beyond his class, feels himself weighted with knowledge of his own and their situation, which hereafter forbids him the simpler pleasures of his father and mother. . . .

According to Hoggart, the scholarship boy grows nostalgic because he remains the uncertain scholar, bright enough to have moved from his past, yet unable to feel easy, a part of a community of academics.

This analysis, however, only partially suggests what happened to me in my last year as a graduate student. When I traveled to London to write a dissertation on English Renaissance literature, I was finally confident of membership in a "community of scholars." But the pleasure that confidence gave me faded rapidly. After only two or three months in the reading room of the British Museum, it became clear that I had joined a lonely community. Around me each day were dour faces eclipsed by large piles of books. There were the regulars, like the old couple who arrived every morning, each holding a loop of the shopping bag which contained all their notes. And there was the historian who chattered madly to herself. ("Oh dear! Oh! Now, what's this? What? Oh, my!") There were also the faces of young men and women worn by long study. And everywhere eyes turned away the moment our glance accidentally met. Some persons I sat beside day after day, yet we passed silently at the end of the day, strangers. Still, we were united by a common respect for the written word and for scholarship. We did form a union, though one in which we remained distant from one another.

More profound and unsettling was the bond I recognized with those writers whose books I consulted. Whenever I opened a text that hadn't been used for years, I realized that my special interests and skills united me to a mere handful of academics. We formed an exclusive — eccentric! — society, separated from others who would never care or be able to share our concerns. (The pages I turned were stiff like layers of dead skin.) I began to wonder: Who, beside my dissertation director and a few faculty members, would ever read what I wrote? And: Was my dissertation much more than an act of social withdrawal? These questions went unanswered in the silence of the Museum reading room. They remained to trouble me after I'd leave the library each afternoon and feel myself shy — unsteady, speaking simple sentences at the grocer's or the butcher's on my way back to my bed-sitter.

Meanwhile my file cards accumulated. A professional, I knew exactly how to search a book for pertinent information. I could quickly assess and summarize the usability of the many books I consulted. But whenever I started to write, I knew too much (and not enough) to be able to write anything but sentences that were overly cautious, timid, strained brittle under the heavy weight of footnotes and qualifications. I seemed unable to dare a passionate statement. I felt drawn by professionalism to the edge of sterility, capable of no more than pedantic, lifeless, unassailable prose.

Then nostalgia began.

After years spent unwilling to admit its attractions, I gestured nostalgically toward the past. I yearned for that time when I had not been so alone. I became impatient with books. I wanted experience more immediate. I feared the library's silence. I silently scorned the gray, timid faces around me. I grew to hate the growing pages of my dissertation on genre and Renaissance literature. (In my mind I heard relatives laughing as they tried to make sense of its title.) I wanted something — I couldn't say exactly what. I told myself that I wanted a more passionate life. And a life less thoughtful. And above all, I wanted to be less alone. One day I heard some Spanish academics whispering back and forth to each other, and their sounds seemed ghostly voices recalling my life. Yearning became preoccupation then. Boyhood memories beckoned, flooded my mind. (Laughing intimate voices. Bounding up the front steps of the porch. A sudden embrace inside the door.)

For weeks after, I turned to books by educational experts. I needed to learn how far I had moved from my past — to determine how fast I would be able to recover something of it once again. But I found little. Only a chapter in a book by Richard Hoggart. . . . I left the reading room and the circle of faces.

I came home. After the year in England, I spent three summer months living with my mother and father, relieved by how easy it was to be home. It no longer seemed very important to me that we had little to say. I felt easy sitting and eating and walking with them. I watched them, nevertheless, looking for evidence of those elastic, sturdy strands that bind generations in a web of inheritance. I thought as I watched my mother one night: of course a friend had been right when she told me that I gestured and laughed just like my mother. Another time I saw for myself: my father's eyes were much like my own, constantly watchful.

But after the early relief, this return, came suspicion, nagging until I realized that I had not neatly sidestepped the impact of schooling. My desire to do so was precisely the measure of how much I remained an academic. *Negatively* (for that is how this idea first occurred to me): my need to think so much and so abstractly about my parents and our relationship was in itself an indication of my long education. My father and mother did not pass their time thinking about the cultural meanings of their experience. It was I who described their daily lives with airy ideas. And yet, *positively*: the ability to consider experience so abstractly allowed me to shape into desire what would otherwise have remained indefinite, meaningless longing in the British Museum. If, because of my schooling, I had grown culturally separated from my parents, my education finally had given me ways of speaking and caring about that fact.

My best teachers in college and graduate school, years before, had tried to prepare me for this conclusion, I think, when they discussed texts of aristocratic pastoral literature. Faithfully, I wrote down all that they said. I memorized it: "The praise of the unlettered by the highly educated is one of the primary themes of 'elitist' literature." But, "the importance of the praise given the unsolitary, richly passionate and spontaneous life is that it simultaneously reflects the value of a reflective life." I heard it all. But there was no way for any of it to mean very much to me. I was a scholarship boy at the time, busily laddering my way up the rungs of education. To pass an examination, I copied down exactly what my teachers told me. It would require many more years of schooling (an inevitable miseducation) in which I came to trust the silence of reading and the habit of abstracting from immediate experience — moving away from a life of closeness and immediacy I remembered with my parents, growing older — before I turned unafraid to desire the past, and thereby achieved what had eluded me for so long — the end of education.

NOTE

[1] All quotations in this essay are from Richard Hoggart, *The Uses of Literacy* (London: Chatto and Windus, 1957), chapter 10. [Note is Rodriguez's.]

• • • ● • • •

QUESTIONS FOR A SECOND READING

1. In *Hunger of Memory*, the book from which "The Achievement of Desire" is drawn, Rodriguez says several times that the story he tells, although it is very much his story, is also a story of our common experience — growing up, leaving home, becoming educated, entering the world. When you reread this essay, look particularly for sections or passages you might bring forward as evidence that this is, in fact, an essay that can give you a way of looking at your own life, and not just his. And look for sections that defy universal application. To what degree *is* his story the story of our common experience? Why might he (or his readers) want to insist that his story is everyone's story?

2.   At the end of the essay, Rodriguez says:

> It would require many more years of schooling (an inevitable mis-
> education) in which I came to trust the silence of reading and the
> habit of abstracting from immediate experience — moving away from
> a life of closeness and immediacy I remembered with my parents,
> growing older — before I turned unafraid to desire the past, and
> thereby achieved what had eluded me for so long — the end of educa-
> tion. (p. 550)

What do you think, as you reread this essay, is the "end of education"? And
what does that end (that goal? stopping point?) have to do with "miseducation," "the silence of reading," "the habit of abstracting from immediate experience," and "desir[ing] the past"?

—————————————— • • • ● • • ——————————————

ASSIGNMENTS FOR WRITING

1.   You could look at the relationship between Richard Rodriguez and Richard
Hoggart as a case study of the relation of a reader to a writer or a student to
a teacher. Look closely at Rodriguez's references to Hoggart's book, *The Uses
of Literacy*, and at the way Rodriguez made use of that book to name and
describe his own experience as a student. What did he find in the book? How
did he use it? How does he use it in his own writing?

   Write an essay in which you discuss Rodriguez's use of Hoggart's *The
Uses of Literacy*. How, for example, would you compare Rodriguez's version of
the "scholarship boy" with Hoggart's? (At one point, Rodriguez says that
Hoggart's account is "more accurate than fair" (p. 547). What might he have
meant by that?) And what kind of reader is the Rodriguez who is writing "The
Achievement of Desire" — is he still a "scholarship boy," or is that description
no longer appropriate?

   Note: You might begin your research with what may seem to be a
purely technical matter, examining how Rodriguez handles quotations and
works Hoggart's words into paragraphs of his own. On the basis of
Rodriguez's use of quoted passages, how would you describe the relationship between Hoggart's words and Rodriguez's? Who has the greater authority? Who is the expert, and under what conditions? What "rules" might
Rodriguez be said to follow or to break? Do you see any change in the
course of the essay in how Rodriguez uses block quotations? in how he
comments on them?

2.   Rodriguez insists that his story is also everyone's story. Take an episode from
your life, one that seems in some way similar to one of the episodes in "The
Achievement of Desire," and cast it into a shorter version of Rodriguez's essay.
Your job here is to look at your experience in Rodriguez's terms, which
means thinking the way he does, noticing what he would notice, interpreting details in a similar fashion, using his key terms, seeing through his point

4. After years spent unwilling to admit its attractions, I gestured nostal-
    gically toward the past. I yearned for that time when I had not been
    so alone. I became impatient with books. I wanted experience more
    immediate. I feared the library's silence. I silently scorned the gray,
    timid faces around me. I grew to hate the growing pages of my dis-
    sertation on genre and Renaissance literature. (In my mind I heard
    relatives laughing as they tried to make sense of its title.) I wanted
    something — couldn't say exactly what. (p. 549)

    — RICHARD RODRIGUEZ, "The Achievement of Desire"

    For some, it will hardly come as a surprise to learn that reading and
    writing have no magically transformative powers. But for those of us
    who have been raised into the teaching and publishing professions,
    it can be quite a shock to confront the possibility that reading and
    writing and talking exercise almost *none* of the powers we regularly
    attribute to them in our favorite stories. The dark night of the soul for
    literacy workers comes with the realization that training students to
    read, write, and talk in more critical and self-reflective ways cannot
    protect them from the violent changes our culture is undergoing.
    (p. 438)

    — RICHARD E. MILLER, "The Dark Night of the Soul"

Both Richard E. Miller and Richard Rodriguez are concerned with the limits
(and the failures) of education, with particular attention to the humanities
and to the supposed benefits to be found in reading and writing. "I have
these doubts, you see," Miller writes of academic work, "doubts silently
shared by many who spend their days teaching others the literate arts. Aside
from gathering and organizing information, aside from generating critiques
and analyses that forever fall on deaf ears, what might the literate arts be
said to be good for?" (p. 439).

Write an essay that takes up this question — "what might the literate arts
be said to be good for?" — and that takes it up with these two essays, Miller's
"The Dark Night of the Soul" and Rodriguez's "The Achievement of Desire," as
your initial points of reference. What does each say? How might they be said
to speak to each other? And, finally, where are you in this? Where are you,
and people like you, the group for whom you feel prepared to speak? You,
too, have been and will continue to be expected to take courses in reading
and writing, to read, write, and talk in "critical and self-reflective ways."
Where are you in this conversation?

EDWARD
Said

© Ulf Andersen/Getty Images

Edward Said (1935–2003) was one of the world's most distinguished literary critics and scholars, distinguished (among other things) for his insistence on the connectedness of art and politics, literature and history. As he argues in his influential essay "The World, the Text, the Critic,"

> Texts have ways of existing, both theoretical and practical, that even in their most rarefied form are always enmeshed in circumstance, time, place, and society — in short, they are in the world, and hence worldly. The same is doubtless true of the critic, as reader and as writer.

Said (pronounced "sigh-eed") was a "worldly" reader and writer, and the selection that follows is a case in point. It is part of his long-term engagement with the history and politics of the Middle East, particularly of the people we refer to as Palestinians. His critical efforts, perhaps best represented by his most influential book, *Orientalism* (1978), examine the ways the West has represented and understood the East ("They cannot represent themselves; they must be represented"), demonstrating how Western journalists, writers, artists, and scholars have created and preserved a view of Eastern cultures as mysterious, dangerous, unchanging, and inferior.

Said was born in Jerusalem, in what was at that time Palestine, to parents who were members of the Christian Palestinian community. In 1947, as the United Nations was establishing Israel as a Jewish state, his family fled to Cairo. In the introduction to *After the Last Sky: Palestinian Lives* (1986), the book from which the following selection was taken, he says,

> I was twelve, with the limited awareness and memory of a relatively sheltered boy. By the mid-spring of 1948 my extended family in its entirety had departed, evicted from Palestine along with almost a million other Palestinians. This was the *nakba*, or catastrophe, which heralded the destruction of our society and our dispossession as a people.

Said was educated in English-speaking schools in Cairo and Massachusetts; he completed his undergraduate training at Princeton and received his PhD from Harvard in 1964. He was a member of the English department at Columbia University in New York from 1963 until his death from leukemia.

In the 1970s, he began writing to a broad public on the situation of the Palestinians; from 1977 to 1991, he served on the Palestinian National Council, an exile government. In 1991, he split from the Palestine Liberation Organization (PLO) over its Gulf War policy (Yasser Arafat's support of Saddam Hussein) and, as he says, for "what I considered to be its new defeatism."

The peculiar and distinctive project represented by *After the Last Sky* began in the 1980s, in the midst of this political engagement. "In 1983," Said writes in the introduction,

> while I was serving as a consultant to the United Nations for its International Conference on the Question of Palestine (ICQP), I suggested that photographs of Palestinians be hung in the entrance hall to the main conference site in Geneva. I had of course known and admired Mohr's work with John Berger, and I recommended that he be commissioned to photograph some of the principal locales of Palestinian life. Given the initial enthusiasm for the idea, Mohr left on a special UN-sponsored trip to the Near East. The photographs he brought back were indeed wonderful; the official response, however, was puzzling and, to someone with a taste for irony, exquisite. You can hang them up, we were told, but no writing can be displayed with them.

In response to a UN mandate, Said had also commissioned twenty studies for the participants at the conference. Of the twenty, only three were accepted as "official documents." The others were rejected "because one after another Arab state objected to this or that principle, this or that insinuation, this or that putative injury to its sovereignty." And yet, Said argues, the complex experience, history, and identity of the people known as Palestinians remained virtually unknown, particularly in the West (and in the United States). To most, Said says, "Palestinians are visible principally as fighters, terrorists, and lawless pariahs." When Jean Mohr, the photographer, told a friend that he was preparing an exhibition on the Palestinians, the friend responded, "Don't you think the subject's a bit dated? Look, I've taken photographs of Palestinians too, especially in the refugee camps . . . it's really sad! But these days, who's interested in people who eat off the ground with their hands? And then there's all that terrorism. . . . I'd have thought you'd be better off using your energy and capabilities on something more worthwhile."

For both Said and Mohr, these rejections provided the motive for *After the Last Sky*. Said's account, from the book's introduction, is worth quoting at length for how well it represents the problems of writing:

> Let us use photographs and a text, we said to each other, to say something that hasn't been said about Palestinians. Yet the problem of writing about and representing — in all senses of the word — Palestinians in some fresh way is part of a much larger problem. For it is not as if no one speaks about or portrays the Palestinians. The difficulty is that everyone, including the Palestinians themselves, speaks a very great deal. A huge body of literature has grown up, most of it polemical, accusatory, denunciatory. At this point, no one writing about

Palestine — and indeed, no one going to Palestine — starts from scratch: We have all been there before, whether by reading about it, experiencing its millennial presence and power, or actually living there for periods of time. It is a terribly crowded place, almost too crowded for what it is asked to be by way of history or interpretation of history.

The resulting book is quite a remarkable document. The photos are not the photos of a glossy coffee-table book, and yet they are compelling and memorable. The prose at times leads to the photos; at times it follows as meditation or explanation, an effort to get things right — "things like exile, dispossession, habits of expression, internal and external landscapes, stubbornness, poignancy, and heroism." It is a writing with pictures, not a writing to which photos were later added. Said had, in fact, been unable to return to Israel/Palestine for several years. As part of this project, he had hoped to be able to take a trip to the West Bank and Gaza in order to see beyond Mohr's photographs, but such a trip proved to be unsafe and impossible — both Arab and Israeli officials had reason to treat him with suspicion. The book was written in exile; the photos, memories, books, and newspapers, these were the only vehicles of return.

After the Last Sky is, Said wrote in 1999, "an unreconciled book, in which the contradictions and antinomies of our lives and experiences remain as they are, assembled neither (I hope) into neat wholes nor into sentimental ruminations about the past. Fragments, memories, disjointed scenes, intimate particulars." The Palestinians, Said wrote in the introduction, fall between classifications. "We are at once too recently formed and too variously experienced to be a population of articulate exiles with a completely systematic vision and too voluble and trouble making to be simply a pathetic mass of refugees." And he adds, "The whole point of this book is to engage this difficulty, to deny the habitually simple, even harmful representations of Palestinians, and to replace them with something more capable of capturing the complex reality of their experience."

Furthermore, he says, "just as Jean Mohr and I, a Swiss and a Palestinian, collaborated in the process, we would like you — Palestinians, Europeans, Americans, Africans, Latin Americans, Asians — to do so also." This is both an invitation and a challenge. While there is much to learn about the Palestinians, the people and their history, the opening moment in the collaborative project is to learn to look and to read in the service of a complex and nuanced act of understanding.

Said is the author of many books and collections, including *Joseph Conrad and the Fiction of Autobiography* (1966), *Beginnings: Intention and Method* (1975), *Orientalism* (1978), *The Question of Palestine* (1979), *Covering Islam: How the Media and the Experts Determine How We See the Rest of the World* (1981), *Blaming the Victims* (1988), *Musical Elaborations* (1991), *Culture and Imperialism* (1993), *The Politics of Dispossession: The Struggle for Palestinian Self-Determination, 1989–1994* (1994), *Representations of the Intellectual* (1994), *Peace and Its Discontents: Essays on Palestine in the Middle East Peace Process* (1995), *Out of Place: A Memoir* (2000),

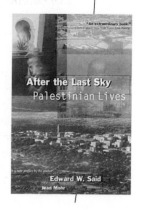

Reflections on Exile (2000), *The Edward Said Reader* (2000), *The End of the Peace Process: Oslo and After* (2001), *Power, Politics, and Culture* (2001), *Mona Hatoum: The Entire World as a Foreign Land* (2001), *On Late Style: Music and Literature Against the Grain* (2006), and *Music at the Limits* (2007).

Jean Mohr has worked as a photographer for UNESCO, the World Health Organization, and the International Red Cross. He has collaborated on four books with John Berger: *Ways of Seeing* (1972; see excerpt on p. 142), *A Seventh Man* (1975), *Another Way of Telling* (1982), and *A Fortunate Man* (1967).

States

Caught in a meager, anonymous space outside a drab Arab city, outside a refugee camp, outside the crushing time of one disaster after another, a wedding party stands, surprised, sad, slightly uncomfortable. Palestinians — the telltale mixture of styles and attitudes is so evidently theirs — near Tripoli in northern Lebanon. A few months after this picture was taken their camp was ravaged by intra-Palestinian fighting. Cutting across the wedding party's path here is the ever-present Mercedes, emblazoned with its extra mark of authenticity, the proud *D* for *Deutschland*. A rare luxury in the West, the Mercedes — usually secondhand and smuggled in — is the commonest of cars in the Levant. It has become what horse, mule, and camel were, and then much more. Universal taxi, it is a symbol of modern technology domesticated, of the intrusion of the West into traditional life, of illicit trade. More important, the Mercedes is the all-purpose conveyance, something one uses for everything — funerals, weddings, births, proud display, leaving home, coming home, fixing, stealing, reselling, running away in, hiding in. But because Palestinians have no state of their

Tripoli, Badawi camp, May 1983.

own to shield them, the Mercedes, its provenance and destination obscure, seems like an intruder, a delegate of the forces that both dislocate and hem them in. "The earth is closing on us, pushing us through the last passage," writes the poet Mahmoud Darwish.

The paradox of mobility and insecurity. Wherever we Palestinians are, we are not in our Palestine, which no longer exists. You travel, from one end of the Arab world to the other, in Europe, Africa, the Americas, Australia, and there you find Palestinians like yourself who, like yourself, are subject to special laws, a special status, the markings of a force and violence not yours. Exiles at home as well as abroad, Palestinians also still inhabit the territory of former Palestine (Israel, the West Bank, Gaza), in sadly reduced circumstances. They are either "the Arabs of Judea and Samaria," or, in Israel, "non-Jews." Some are referred to as "present absentees." In Arab countries, except for Jordan, they are given special cards identifying them as "Palestinian refugees," and even where they are respectable engineers, teachers, business people, or technicians, they know that in the eyes of their host country they will always be aliens. Inevitably, photographs of Palestinians today include this fact and make it visible.

Memory adds to the unrelieved intensity of Palestinian exile. Palestine is central to the cultures of Islam, Christianity, and Judaism; Orient and Occident have turned it into a legend. There is no forgetting it, no way of overlooking it. The world news is often full of what has happened in Palestine-Israel, the latest Middle East crisis, the most recent Palestinian

© Jean Mohr

© Jean Mohr

Tel Sheva, 1979. A village of settled nomads near Bersheeba. Some years ago, these people still lived in a tent, under the desert sky. The carpet on the ground is the only reminder of that earlier period.

diffusion

exploits. The sights, wares, and monuments of Palestine are the objects of commerce, war, pilgrimage, cults, the subjects of literature, art, song, fantasy. East and West, their high and their commercial cultures, have descended on Palestine. Bride and groom wear the ill-fitting nuptial costumes of Europe, yet behind and around them are the clothes and objects of their native land, natural to their friends and attendants. The happiness of the occasion is at odds with their lot as refugees with nowhere to go. The children playing nearby contrast starkly with the unappealing surroundings; the new husband's large workman's hands clash with his wife's delicate, obscuring white. When we cross from Palestine into other territories, even if we find ourselves decently in new places, the old ones loom behind us as tangible and unreal as reproduced memory or absent causes for our present state.

Sometimes the poignancy of resettlement stands out like bold script imposed on faint pencil traces. The fit between body and new setting is not good. The angles are wrong. Lines supposed to decorate a wall instead form an imperfectly assembled box in which we have been put. We perch on chairs uncertain whether to address or evade our interlocutor. This child is held out, and yet also held in. Men and women re-express the unattractiveness around them: The angle made across her face by the woman's robe duplicates the ghastly wall pattern, the man's crossed feet repeat and contradict the outward thrust of the chair leg [p. 560]. He seems unsettled, poised for departure. Now what? Now where? All at once it is our transience and impermanence that our visibility expresses, for we can be seen as figures forced to push on to another house, village, or region. Just as we once were taken from one "habitat" to a new one, we can be moved again.

Exile is a series of portraits without names, without contexts. Images that are largely unexplained, nameless, mute. I look at them without precise anecdotal knowledge, but their realistic exactness nevertheless makes a deeper impression than mere information. I cannot reach the actual people who were photographed, except through a European photographer who saw them for me. And I imagine that he, in turn, spoke to them through an interpreter. The one thing I know for sure, however, is that they treated him politely but as someone who came from, or perhaps acted at the direction of, those who put them where they so miserably are. There was the embarrassment of people uncertain why they were being looked at and recorded. Powerless to stop it.

When A. Z.'s father was dying, he called his children, one of whom is married to my sister, into his room for a last family gathering. A frail, very old man from Haifa, he had spent his last thirty-four years in Beirut in a state of agitated disbelief at the loss of his house and property. Now he murmured to his children the final faltering words of a penniless, helpless patriarch. "Hold on to the keys and the deed," he told them, pointing to a battered suitcase near his bed, a repository of the family estate salvaged from Palestine when Haifa's Arabs were expelled. These intimate mementos of a past irrevocably lost circulate among us, like the genealogies and fables of a wandering singer of tales. Photographs, dresses, objects severed

Amman, 1984. A visit to the former mayor of Jerusalem and his wife, in exile in Jordan.

from their original locale, the rituals of speech and custom: Much reproduced, enlarged, thematized, embroidered, and passed around, they are
strands in the web of affiliations we Palestinians use to tie ourselves to
our identity and to each other.

Sometimes these objects, heavy with memory — albums, rosary beads,
shawls, little boxes — seem to me like encumbrances. We carry them about,
hang them up on every new set of walls we shelter in, reflect lovingly on
them. Then we do not notice the bitterness, but it continues and grows
nonetheless. Nor do we acknowledge the frozen immobility of our attitudes.

Ramallah, 1979. An everyday street scene, banal and reassuring. And yet, the tension is constant. A passing military jeep, a flying stone — the incident, the drama, can occur at any moment.

© Jean Mohr

In the end the past owns us. My father spent his life trying to escape these objects, "Jerusalem" chief among them — the actual place as much as its reproduced and manufactured self. Born in Jerusalem, as were his parents, grandparents, and all his family back in time to a distant vanishing point, he was a child of the Old City who traded with tourists in bits of the true cross and crowns of thorn. Yet he hated the place; for him, he often said, it meant death. Little of it remained with him except a fragmentary story

or two, an odd coin or medal, one photograph of his father on horseback, and two small rugs. I never even saw a picture of my grandmother's face. But as he grew older, he reverted to old Jerusalemite expressions that I did not understand, never having heard them during the years of my youth.

Identity — who we are, where we come from, what we are — is difficult to maintain in exile. Most other people take their identity for granted. Not the Palestinian, who is required to show proofs of identity more or less constantly. It is not only that we are regarded as terrorists, but that our existence as native Arab inhabitants of Palestine, with primordial rights there (and not elsewhere), is either denied or challenged. And there is more. Such as it is, our existence is linked negatively to encomiums about Israel's democracy, achievements, excitement; in much Western rhetoric we have slipped into the place occupied by Nazis and anti-Semites; collectively, we can aspire to little except political anonymity and resettlement; we are known for no actual achievement, no characteristic worthy of esteem, except the effrontery of disrupting Middle East peace. Some Israeli settlers on the West Bank say: "The Palestinians can stay here, with no rights, as resident aliens." Other Israelis are less kind. We have no known Einsteins, no Chagall, no Freud or Rubinstein to protect us with a legacy of glorious achievements. We have had no Holocaust to protect us with the world's compassion. We are "other," and opposite, a flaw in the geometry of resettlement and exodus. Silence and discretion veil the hurt, slow the body searches, soothe the sting of loss.

A zone of recollected pleasure surrounds the few unchanged spots of Palestinian life in Palestine. The foodsellers and peddlers — itinerant vendors of cakes or corn — are still there for the casual eye to see, and they still provoke the appetite. They seem to travel not only from place to place, but from an earlier time to the present, carrying with them the same clientele — the young girls and boys, the homeward-bound cyclist, the loitering student or clerk — now as then. We buy their wares with the same surreptitiously found change (who can remember the unit? was it a piaster? fils? shilling?) spent on the same meager object, neither especially good nor especially well prepared. The luxurious pleasure of tasting the vendor's *sim-sim*, the round sesame cakes dipped in that tangy mixture of thyme and sumac, or his *durra*, boiled corn sprayed with salt, surpasses the mere act of eating and opens before us the altogether agreeable taste of food not connected with meals, with nourishment, with routine. But what a distance now actually separates me from the concreteness of that life. How easily traveled the photographs make it seem, and how possible to suspend the barriers keeping me from the scenes they portray.

For the land is further away than it has ever been. Born in Jerusalem in late 1935, I left mandatory Palestine permanently at the end of 1947. In the spring of 1948, my last cousin evacuated our family's house in West Jerusalem; Martin Buber subsequently lived there till his death, I have been told. I grew up in Egypt, then came to the United States as a student. In 1966 I visited Ramallah, part of the Jordanian West Bank, for a family wedding. My father, who was to die five years later, accompanied my sister and me. Since our visit, all the members of my family have resettled — in Jordan, in Lebanon, in the United States, and in Europe. As far as I know, I have no relatives who still live in what was once Palestine. Wars, revolutions, civil struggles have changed the countries I have lived in — Lebanon, Jordan, Egypt — beyond recognition. Until thirty-five years ago I could travel from Cairo to Beirut overland, through territories held or in other ways controlled by rival colonial powers. Now, although my mother lives in Beirut, I have not visited her since the Israeli invasion of 1982: Palestinians are no longer welcome there. The fact is that today I can neither return to the places of my youth, nor voyage freely in the countries and places that mean the most to me, nor feel safe from arrest or violence even in the countries I used to frequent but whose governments and policies have changed radically in recent times. There is little that is more unpleasant for me these days than the customs and police check upon entering an Arab country.

Consider the tremendous upheavals since 1948 each of which effectively destroyed the ecology of our previous existence. When I was born, we in Palestine felt ourselves to be part of a small community, presided over by the majority community and one or another of the outside powers holding sway over the territory. My family and I, for example, were members of a tiny Protestant group within a much larger Greek Orthodox Christian minority, within the larger Sunni Islam majority; the important

> WHAT A DISTANCE NOW ACTUALLY SEPARATES ME FROM THE CONCRETENESS OF THAT LIFE. HOW EASILY TRAVELED THE PHOTOGRAPHS MAKE IT SEEM.

outside power was Britain, with its great rival France a close second. But then after World War II Britain and France lost their hold, and for the first time we directly confronted the colonial legacy — inept rulers, divided populations, conflicting promises made to resident Arabs and mostly European Jews with incompatible claims. In 1948 Israel was established; Palestine was destroyed, and the great Palestinian dispossession began. In 1956 Egypt was invaded by Britain, France, and Israel, causing what was left of the large Levantine communities there (Italian, Greek, Jewish, Armenian, Syrian) to leave. The rise of Abdel Nasser fired all Arabs — especially Palestinians — with the hope of a revived Arab nationalism, but after the union of Syria with Egypt failed in 1961, the Arab cold war, as it has been called, began in earnest; Saudi Arabia versus Egypt, Jordan versus Syria, Syria versus Iraq. . . . A new population of refugees, migrant workers, and traveling political parties crisscrossed the Arab world. We Palestinians immersed ourselves in the politics of Baathism in Syria and Iraq, of Nasserism in Egypt, of the Arab Nationalist Movement in Lebanon.

The 1967 war was followed shortly after by the Arab oil boom. For the first time, Palestinian nationalism arose as an independent force in the Middle East. Never did our future seem more hopeful. In time, however, our appearance on the political scene stimulated, if it did not actually cause, a great many less healthy phenomena: fundamentalist Islam, Maronite nationalism, Jewish zealotry. The new consumer culture, the computerized economy, further exacerbated the startling disparities in the Arab world between rich and poor, old and new, privileged and disinherited. Then, starting in 1975, the Lebanese civil war pitted the various Lebanese sects, the Palestinians, and a number of Arab and foreign powers against each other. Beirut was destroyed as the intellectual and political nerve center of Arab life; for us, it was the end of our only important, relatively independent center of Palestinian nationalism, with the Palestinian Liberation Organization at its heart. Anwar Sadat recognized Israel, and Camp David further dismantled the region's alliances and disrupted its balance. After the Iranian revolution in 1979 came the Iran-Iraq war. Israel's 1982 invasion of Lebanon put more Palestinians on the move, as the massacres in the Palestinian refugee camps of Sabra and Shatila reduced the community still further. By the end of 1983, Palestinians were fighting each other, and Syria and Libya were directly involved, supporting Palestinian dissidents against PLO loyalists. With the irony typical of our political fate, however, in mid-1985 we were united together in Sabra and Shatila to fight off a hostile Shi'ite militia patronized by Syria.

The stability of geography and the continuity of land — these have completely disappeared from my life and the life of all Palestinians. If we are not stopped at borders, or herded into new camps, or denied reentry and residence, or barred from travel from one place to another, more of our land is taken, our lives are interfered with arbitrarily, our voices are prevented from reaching each other, our identity is confined to frightened little islands in an inhospitable environment of superior military force sanitized by the clinical jargon of pure administration. On the West Bank and in Gaza we confront several Zionist "master plans" — which, according to Meron Benvenisti, ex-deputy mayor of Jerusalem, are "explicitly sectarian." He continues:

> The criteria established to determine priorities of settlement regions are "*interconnection [havirah]* between existing Jewish areas for the creation of [Jewish] settlement continuity" and "*separation [hayitz]* to restrict uncontrolled Arab settlement and the prevention of Arab settlement blocs"; "*scarcity [hesech]* refers to areas devoid of Jewish settlement." In these criteria "pure planning and political planning elements are included."
>
> *(The West Bank Data Project:*
> *A Survey of Israeli Policies)*

Continuity for *them*, the dominant population; discontinuity for *us*, the dispossessed and dispersed.

The circle is completed, though, when we Palestinians acknowledge that much the same thesis is adhered to by Arab and other states where sizable Palestinian communities exist. There too we are in dispersed camps, regions, quarters, zones; but unlike their Israeli counterparts, these places are not the scientific product of "pure planning" or "political planning." The Baqa'a camp in Amman, the Palestinian quarter of Hawaly in Kuwait, are simply there.

All forms of Palestinian activity, all attempts at unity, are suspect. On the West Bank and Gaza, "development" (the systematic strengthening of Palestinian economic and social life) is forbidden, whereas "improvement" is tolerated so long as there isn't too much of it; so long as it doesn't become development. The colors of the Palestinian flag are outlawed by

© Jean Mohr

Tyre, South Lebanon, 1983. Bourj el-Shemali camp. The car bears witness to a drama, circumstances unknown. The flowers: the month of May, it is spring. The children: wearing smart clothes, almost certainly donated by a charity. They are refugees — the children of refugees.

© Jean Mohr

Bedouin encampment near Bersheeba, 1979.

Israeli military law; Fathi Gabin of Gaza, an artist, was given a six-month prison sentence for using black, green, red, and white in one of his works. An exhibit of Palestinian culture at al-Najah University in Nablus earned the school a four-month closing. Since our history is forbidden, narratives are rare; the story of origins, of home, of nation is underground. When it appears it is broken, often wayward and meandering in the extreme, always coded, usually in outrageous forms — mock-epics, satires, sardonic parables, absurd rituals — that make little sense to an outsider. Thus Palestinian life is scattered, discontinuous, marked by the artificial and imposed arrangements of interrupted or confined space, by the dislocations and unsynchronized rhythms of disturbed time. Across our children's lives, in the open fields in which they play, lie the ruins of war, of a borrowed or imported industrial technology, of cast-off or abandoned forms. How odd the conjuncture, and yet for Palestinians, how fitting. For where no straight line leads from home to birthplace to school to maturity, all events are accidents, all progress is a digression, all residence is exile. We linger in nondescript places, neither here nor there; we peer through windows without glass, ride conveyances without movement or power. Resourcefulness and receptivity are the attitudes that serve best.

The difference between the new generation of Palestinians and that of 1948 is striking. Our parents bore on their faces the marks of disaster uncomprehended. Suddenly their past had been interrupted, their society obliterated, their existence radically impoverished. Refugees, all of them. Our children know no such past. Cars are equally for riding or, ruined, for playing in. Everything around them seems expendable, impermanent, unstable, especially where — as in Lebanon — Palestinian communities have been disastrously depleted or destroyed, where much of their life is undocumented, where they themselves are uncounted.

No Palestinian census exists. There is no line that can be drawn from one Palestinian to another that does not seem to interfere with the political designs of one or another state. While all of us live among "normal" people, people with complete lives, they seem to us hopelessly out of reach, with their countries, their familial continuity, their societies intact. How does a Palestinian father tell his son and daughter that Lebanon (Egypt, Syria, Jordan, New York) is where we are, but not where we are *from*? How does a mother confirm her intimate recollections of childhood in Palestine to her children, now that the facts, the places, even the names, are no longer allowed to exist?

So we borrow and we patch things together. Palestinians retain the inflections of Jaffa, of Hebron, of Jerusalem and other cities left behind, even as their dialect becomes that of Beirut, Detroit, or Paris. I have found out much more about Palestine and met many more Palestinians than I ever did, or perhaps could have, in pre-1948 Palestine. For a long time I thought that this was so because I was a child then, somewhat sheltered, a member of a minority. But my experience is confirmed by my oldest and closest Palestinian friend, Ibrahim Abu-Lughod. Although he was more in and of pre-1948 Palestine — because older, more conscious and active — than I ever was, he too says that he is much more in contact with Palestinians today than when he was in Palestine. He writes,

> Thanks to modern technological progress, Palestinian families, and Palestinian society as a whole, have been able to forge very numerous human, social, and political links. By getting on a plane I can see the majority of my friends. It's because of this that our family has remained unified. I see all the members of my family at least once or twice a year. Being in Jaffa, I could never have seen relatives who lived in Gaza, for example.

© Jean Mohr

Gaza, 1979. Refugee camp. A boy of unknown age.

But Ibrahim does not celebrate this sociability: "I constantly experience the sense that something is missing for me. To compensate for this lack, I multiply and intensify human contacts."

Over the missing "something" are superimposed new realities. Plane travel and phone conversations nourish and connect the fortunate; the symbols of a universal pop culture enshroud the vulnerable.

There can be no orderly sequence of time. You see it in our children who seem to have skipped a phase of growth or, more alarming, achieved an out-of-season maturity in one part of their body or mind while the rest remains childlike. None of us can forget the whispers and occasional proclamations that our children are "the population factor" — to be feared, and hence to be deported — or constitute special targets for death. I heard it said in Lebanon that Palestinian children in particular should be killed because each of them is a potential terrorist. Kill them before they kill you.

Tel Sheva, 1979. A group portrait, taken at the request of the children.

How rich our mutability, how easily we change (and are changed) from one thing to another, how unstable our place — and all because of the missing foundation of our existence, the lost ground of our origin, the broken link with our land and our past. There are no Palestinians. Who are the Palestinians? "The inhabitants of Judea and Samaria." Non-Jews. Terrorists. Troublemakers. DPs.* Refugees. Names on a card. Numbers on a list. Praised in speeches — *el pueblo palestino, il popolo palestino, le peuple*

*****DPs** Displaced persons or displaced people. [Eds.]

palestinien — but treated as interruptions, intermittent presences. Gone from Jordan in 1970, now from Lebanon.

None of these departures and arrivals is clean, definitive. Some of us leave, others stay behind. Remnants, new arrivals, old residents. Two great images encapsulate our unresolved existence. One is the identity card (passport, travel document, laissez-passer), which is never Palestinian but always something else; it is the subject of our national poem, Mahmoud Darwish's "Bitaqit Hawia": "Record! I am an Arab / Without a name — without title / patient in a country / with people enraged." And the second is Emil Habiby's invention the Pessoptimist (*al-mutasha'il*), the protagonist of a disorderly and ingenious work of Kafkaesque fiction, which has become a kind of national epic. The Pessoptimist is being half here, half not here, part historical creature, part mythological invention, hopeful and hopeless, everyone's favorite obsession and scapegoat. Is Habiby's character fiction, or does his extravagant fantasy only begin to approximate the real? Is he a made-up figure or the true essence of our existence? Is Habiby's jamming-together of words — *mutafa'il* and *mutasha'im* into *mutasha'il*, which repeats the Palestinian habit of combining opposites like *la* ("no") and *na'am* ("yes") into *la'am* — a way of obliterating distinctions that do not apply to us, yet must be integrated into our lives?

Emil Habiby is a craggy, uncompromisingly complex, and fearsomely ironic man from Haifa, son of a Christian family, Communist party stalwart, long-time Knesset member, journalist, editor. His novel about the Pessoptimist (whose first name, incidentally, is Said) is chaotic because it

© Jean Mohr

Bersheeba, 1979. Near a Bedouin encampment, a little kitchen garden — and its scarecrow of bits and pieces.

mixes time, characters, and places; fiction, allegory, history, and flat statement, without any thread to guide the reader through its complexities. It is the best work of Palestinian writing yet produced, precisely because the most seemingly disorganized and ironic. In it we encounter characters whose names are of particular significance to Palestinians: The name of Yuaad, the work's female lead, means "it shall be repeated," a reference to the string of defeats that mark our history, and the fatalistic formulae that color our discourse. One of the other characters is Isam al-Bathanjani — Isam the Eggplant, a lawyer who is not very helpful to Said but who keeps turning up just the same. So it is with eggplants in Palestine. My family — my father in particular — has always been attached to eggplants from Battir, and during the many years since any of us had Battiri eggplants the seal of approval on good eggplants was that "they're almost as good as the Battiris."

Today when I recall the tiresome paeans to Battiris, or when in London and Paris I see the same Jaffa oranges or Gaza vegetables grown in the *bayarat* ("orchards") and fields of my youth, but now marketed by Israeli export companies, the contrast between the inarticulate rich *thereness* of what we once knew and the systematic export of the produce into the hungry mouths of Europe strikes me with its unkind political message. The land and the peasants are bound together through work whose products seem always to have meant something to other people, to have been destined for consumption elsewhere. This observation holds force not just because the Carmel boxes and the carefully wrapped eggplants are emblems of the power that rules the sprawling fertility and enduring human labor of Palestine, but also because the discontinuity between me, out here, and the actuality there is so much more compelling now than my receding memories and experiences of Palestine.

Another, far more unusual, item concerning this vegetable appears in an article by Avigdor Feldman, "The New Order of the Military Government: State of Israel Against the Eggplant," which appeared in the journal *Koteret Rashit*, August 24, 1983. Laws 1015 and 1039, Feldman reports, stipulate that any Arab on the West Bank and Gaza who owns land must get written permission from the military governor before planting either a new vegetable — for example, an eggplant — or fruit tree. Failure to get permission risks one the destruction of the tree or vegetable plus one year's imprisonment.

Exile again. The facts of my birth are so distant and strange as to be about someone I've heard of rather than someone I know. Nazareth — my mother's town. Jerusalem — my father's. The pictures I see display the same produce, presented in the same carelessly plentiful way, in the same rough wooden cases. The same people walk by, looking at the same posters and trinkets, concealing the same secrets,

EXILE AGAIN. THE FACTS OF MY BIRTH ARE SO DISTANT AND STRANGE AS TO BE ABOUT SOMEONE I'VE HEARD OF RATHER THAN SOMEONE I KNOW.

Gaza, 1979. Farm using refugee labor.

searching for the same profits, pleasures, and goals. The same as what? There is little that I can truly remember about Jerusalem and Nazareth, little that is specific, little that has the irreducible durability of tactile, visual, or auditory memories that concede nothing to time, little — and this is the "same" I referred to — that is not confused with pictures I have seen or scenes I have glimpsed elsewhere in the Arab world.

Palestine is exile, dispossession, the inaccurate memories of one place slipping into vague memories of another, a confused recovery of general wares, passive presences scattered around in the Arab environment. The story of Palestine cannot be told smoothly. Instead, the past, like the present, offers only occurrences and coincidences. Random. The man enters a quiet alley where he will pass cucumbers on his right, tomatoes on his left; a priest walks down the stairs, the boy dashes off, satchel under arm, other boys loiter, shopkeepers look out for business; carrying an airline bag, a man advances past a display of trinkets, a young man disappears around the corner, two boys idle aimlessly. Tomatoes, watermelons, arcades, cucumbers, posters, people, eggplants — not simply there, but represented by photographs as being there — saturated with meaning and memory, and still very far away. Look more closely and think through these possibilities: The poster is about Egypt. The trinkets are made in Korea or Hong Kong. The scenes are surveyed, enclosed, and surrounded by Israelis. European and Japanese tourists have more access to Jerusalem and Nazareth than I do. Slowly, our lives — like Palestine itself — dissolve into something else. We can't hold to the center for long.

Nazareth, 1979. Portrait of Om Kalsoum.

© Jean Mohr

Jerusalem, 1979. A snapshot.

© Jean Mohr

Jerusalem, 1979. A snapshot.

Exile. At a recent conference in America featuring a "dialogue" between Israeli and Palestinian intellectuals with reconciliation high on the agenda, a man rises from the audience to pose a question. "I am a Palestinian, a peasant. Look at my hands. I was kicked out in 1948 and went to Lebanon. Then I was driven out, and went to Africa. Then to Europe. Then to here. Today [he pulls out an envelope] I received a paper telling me to leave this country. Would one of you scholars tell me please: Where am I supposed to

© Jean Mohr

Old City of Jerusalem, 1984. A tourist shop. Customers are rare. Will they be American, Swiss, or Israeli?

go now?" No one had anything to tell him. He was an embarrassment, and I have no idea what in fact he did, what became of him. My shame.

The Palestinian's claims on Israel are generally unacknowledged, much less seen as directly connected to the founding of the state. On the Arabs there is an ambivalent Palestinian claim, recognized in Arab countries by countless words, gestures, threats, and promises. Palestine, after all, is the centerpiece of Arab nationalism. No Arab leader since World

© Jean Mohr

Jerusalem, 1979.

War II has failed to make Palestine a symbol of his country's nationalist foreign policy. Yet, despite the avowals, we have no way of knowing really how they — all the "theys" — feel about us. Our history has cost every one of our friends a great deal. It has gone on too long.

Let Ghassan Kanafani's novella *Men in the Sun* stand for the fear we have that unless we press "them" they will allow us to disappear, and the equal worry that if we press them they will either decry our hectoring presence, and quash it in their states, or turn us into easy symbols of their nationalism. Three refugees concealed in the belly of a tanker truck are being transported illegally across the border into Kuwait. As the driver converses with the guards, the men (Palestinians) die of suffocation — in the sun, forgotten. It is not the driver's forgetfulness that nags at him. It is their silence. "Why didn't you knock on the sides of the tank? Why didn't you bang the sides of the tank? Why? Why? Why?" Our fear to press.

The Palestinians as commodity. Producing ourselves much as the *masabih*, lamps, tapestries, baskets, embroideries, mother-of-pearl trinkets are produced. We turn ourselves into objects not for sale, but for scrutiny. People ask us, as if looking into an exhibit case, "What is it you Palestinians want?" — as if we can put our demands into a single neat phrase. All of us speak of *awdah*, "return," but do we mean that literally, or do we mean "we must restore ourselves to ourselves"? The latter is the real point, I think, although I know many Palestinians who want their houses and their way of life back, exactly. But is there any place that fits us, together with our accumulated memories and experiences?

Do we exist? What proof do we have?

The further we get from the Palestine of our past, the more precarious our status, the more disrupted our being, the more intermittent our presence. When did we become "a people"? When did we stop being one? Or are we in the process of becoming one? What do those big questions have to do with our intimate relationships with each other and with others? We frequently end our letters with the mottoes "Palestinian love" or "Palestinian kisses." Are there really such things as Palestinian intimacy and embraces, or are they simply intimacy and embraces, experiences common to everyone, neither politically significant nor particular to a nation or a people?

The politics of such a question gets very close to our central dilemma: We all know that we are Arabs, and yet the concept, not to say the lived actuality, of Arabism — once the creed and the discourse of a proud Arab nation, free of imperialism, united, respected, powerful — is fast disappearing, cut up into the cautious defensiveness of relatively provincial Arab states, each with its own traditions — partly invented, partly real — each with its own nationality and restricted identity. In addition, Palestine has been replaced by an Israel whose aggressive sense of itself as the state of the Jewish people fuels the exclusivity of a national identity won and maintained to a great extent at our expense. We are not Jews, we have no place there except as resident aliens, we are outsiders. In the Arab states we are in a different position. There we are Arabs, but it is the process of nationalization that excludes us: Egypt is for and by Egyptians, Iraq is for and by Iraqis, in ways that cannot include Palestinians whose intense national revival is a separate phenomenon. Thus we are the same as other Arabs, and yet different. We cannot exist except as Arabs, even though "the Arabs" exist otherwise as Lebanese, Jordanians, Moroccans, Kuwaitis, and so forth.

Add to this the problems we have of sustaining ourselves as a collective unit and you then get a sense of how *abstract*, how very solitary and unique, we tend to feel.

Strip off the occasional assertiveness and stridency of the Palestinian stance and you may catch sight of a much more fugitive, but ultimately quite beautifully representative and subtle, sense of identity. It speaks in languages not yet fully formed, in settings not completely constituted, like the shy glance of a child holding her father's knee while she curiously and tentatively examines the stranger who photographs her. Her look conjures up the unappreciated fact of birth, that sudden, unprepared-for depositing of a small bundle of self on the fields of the Levant after which comes the trajectory of dispossession, military and political violence, and that constant, mysterious entanglement with monotheistic religion at its most profound — the Christian Incarnation and Resurrection, the Ascension to heaven of the Prophet Mohammed, the Covenant of Yahweh with his people — that is knotted definitively in Jerusalem, center of the world, *locus classicus* of Palestine, Israel, and Paradise.

A secular world of fatigue and miraculously renewed energies, the world of American cigarettes and an unending stream of small papers pulled out of miscellaneous notebooks or "blocnotes," written on with

© Jean Mohr

Village of Ramah, Galilee, 1979. A secular high school with students from thirty-six neighboring villages.

disposable pens, messages of things wanted, of people missing, of requests to the bureaucracy. The Palestinian predicament: finding an "official" place for yourself in a system that makes no allowances for you, which means endlessly improvising solutions for the problem of finding a missing loved one, of planning a trip, of entering a school, on whatever bit of paper is at hand. Constructed and deconstructed, ephemera are what we negotiate with, since we authorize no part of the world and only influence increasingly small bits of it. In any case, we keep going.

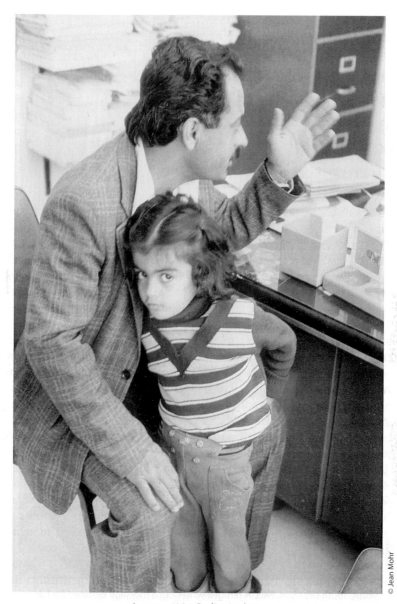

Amman, 1984. Pediatric clinic.

The striking thing about Palestinian prose and prose fiction is its formal instability: Our literature in a certain very narrow sense *is* the elusive, resistant reality it tries so often to represent. Most literary critics in Israel and the West focus on what is said in Palestinian writing, who is described, what the plot and contents deliver, their sociological and political meaning. But it is *form* that should be looked at. Particularly in fiction, the struggle to achieve form expresses the writer's efforts to construct a coherent scene, a narrative that might overcome the almost metaphysical impossibility of representing

© Jean Mohr

Jerusalem, 1979. A dialogue between left-wing Israeli and Arab intellectuals.

better the tension than the peace of passivity, or the unresisting assent to authority.

The pressures of the here and now require an answer to the Palestinian crisis here and now. Whereas our interlocutors, our "others"—the Arab states, the United States, the USSR, Israel, our friends and enemies—have the luxury of a state in which institutions do their work undisturbed by the question of existence-or-not, we lead our lives under a sword of Damocles, whose dry rhetorical form is the query "When are you Palestinians going to accept a solution?"—the implication being that if we don't, we'll disappear. This, then, is our midnight hour.

It is difficult to know how much the often stated, tediously reiterated worries about us, which include endless lectures on the need for a clear Palestinian statement of the desire for peace (as if we controlled the decisive factors!), are malicious provocation and how much genuine, if sympathetic, ignorance. I don't think any of us reacts as impatiently to such things as we did, say, five years ago. True, our collective situation is more precarious now than it was, but I detect a general turning inward among Palestinians, as if many of us feel the need to consolidate and collect the shards of Palestinian life still present and available to us. This is not quietism at all, nor is it resignation. Rather, it springs from the natural impulse to stand back when the headlong rush of events gets to be too much, perhaps, for us to savor life as life, to reflect at some distance from politics on where we came from and where we are, to regrasp, revise, recomprehend the tumultuous experiences at whose center, quite without our consent, we have been made to stand.

Jean Mohr's photograph [p. 592] of a small but clearly formed human group surrounded by a dense and layered reality expresses very well what

Nazareth, 1979. A municipal kindergarten, looked after by nuns.

© Jean Mohr

we experience during that detachment from an ideologically saturated world. This image of four people seen at a distance near Ramallah, in the middle of and yet separated from thick foliage, stairs, several tiers of terraces and houses, a lone electricity pole off to the right, is for me a private, crystallized, almost Proustian evocation of Palestine. Memory: During the summer of 1942 — I was six — we rented a house in Ramallah. My father, I recall, was ill with high blood pressure and recovering from a nervous breakdown. I remember him as withdrawn and constantly smoking. My mother took me to a variety show at the local Friends school. During the second half I left the hall to go to the toilet, but for reasons I could not (and still do not) grasp, the boy-scout usher would not let me back in. I recall with ever-renewed poignancy the sudden sense of distance I experienced from what was familiar and pleasant — my mother, friends, the show; all at once the rift introduced into

© Jean Mohr

Amman, 1984. Camp at Baqa'a, one of the oldest in Jordan. The YWCA looks after some of the kindergartens.

Jerusalem, 1984.

the cozy life I led taught me the meaning of separation, of solitude, and of anguished boredom. There was nothing to do but wait, although my mother did appear a little later to find out what had happened to me. We left immediately, but not before I furtively took a quick look back through the door window at the lighted stage. The telescoped vision of small figures assembled in a detached space has remained with me for over forty years, and it reappears in the adjusted and transformed center of Jean's 1983 picture. I never ventured anywhere near that part of Ramallah again. I would no more know it than I would the precise place of this photo; and yet I am sure it would be familiar, the way this one immediately seemed.

> I NEVER VENTURED ANYWHERE NEAR THAT PART OF RAMALLAH AGAIN. I WOULD NO MORE KNOW IT THAN I WOULD THE PRECISE PLACE OF THIS PHOTO; AND YET I AM SURE IT WOULD BE FAMILIAR.

My private past is inscribed on the surface of this peaceful but somehow brooding pastoral scene in the contemporary West Bank. I am not the only one surveying the scene. There is the child on the left who looks on. There are also the Swiss photographer, compassionate, curious, silent, and of course the ever-present Israeli security services, who hold the West Bank and its population in the vise of occupation. As for those terraces and multiple levels: Do they serve the activities of daily life or are they the haunted stairs of a prison which, like Piranesi's, lead nowhere, confining their human captives? The dense mass of leaves, right and left, lend their

Near Senjel, a village between Ramallah and Nablus, 1979.

bulk to the frame, but they too impinge on the slender life they surround, like memory or a history too complex to be sorted out, bigger than its subject, richer than any consciousness one might have of it.

The power grid recalls the Mercedes in Tripoli. Unassimilated, its modernity and power have been felt with considerable strength in our lives here and there throughout the Third World. Another childhood memory: Driving through the Sinai from Egypt into Palestine, we would see the row of telephone and electricity pylons partnering the empty macadamized road that cut through an even emptier desert. Who are they, I would ask myself. What do they think when we are not here? When we stopped to stretch our legs, I would go up to a pole and look at its dull brown surface for some sign of life, identity, or awareness. Once I marked one with my initials EWS, hoping to find it again on the trip back. All of them looked exactly the same as we hurtled by. We never stopped. I never drove there again, nor can I now. Futile efforts to register my presence on the scene.

Intimate memory and contemporary social reality seem connected by the little passage between the child, absorbed in his private, silent sphere, and the three older people, who are the public world of adults, work, and community. It is a vacant, somewhat tenuously maintained space, however; sandy, pebbly, and weedy. All the force in the photograph moves dramatically from trees left to trees right, from the visible enclave of domesticity (stairs, houses, terrace) to the unseen larger world of power and authority beyond. I wonder whether the four people are in fact connected, or whether as a group they simply happen to be in the way of unseen forces totally indifferent to the dwelling and living space these people inhabit. This is also, then, a photograph of latent, of impending desolation, and once again I am depressed by the transience of Palestinian life, its vulnerability and all too easy dislocation. But another movement, another feeling, asserts itself in response, set in motion by the two strikingly marked openings in the buildings, openings that suggest rich, cool interiors which outsiders cannot penetrate. Let us enter.

· · ● · · ·

QUESTIONS FOR A SECOND READING

1. The first three paragraphs provide a "reading" of the opening photograph, "Tripoli, Badawi camp, May 1983." Or, to put it another way, the writing evolves from and is in response to that photograph. As you reread these paragraphs, pay close attention to what Said is doing, to what he notices, to what prompts or requires commentary. How would you describe and explain the writing that follows? What is he doing with the photo? What is he doing as a writer? What is he doing for a reader? (How does he position a reader?)

    It might be useful to begin by thinking about what Said is *not* doing. It is not, for example, the presentation one might expect in a slide show on travel in Lebanon. Nor is it the kind of presentation one might expect while seeing the slides of family or friends, or slides in an art history or art appreciation class.

    Once you have worked through the opening three paragraphs, reread the essay paying attention to Said's work with all the photographs. Is there a pattern? Do any of the commentaries stand out for their force, variety, innovation?

2. Here is another passage from the introduction to *After the Last Sky*:

    > Its style and method — the interplay of text and photos, the mixture of genres, modes, styles — do not tell a consecutive story, nor do they constitute a political essay. Since the main features of our present existence are dispossession, dispersion, and yet also a kind of power incommensurate with our stateless exile, I believe that essentially unconventional, hybrid, and fragmentary forms of expression should be used to represent us. What I have quite consciously designed, then, is an alternative mode of expression to the one usually encountered in the media, in works of social science, in popular fiction. (p. 6)

    And later:

    > The multifaceted vision is essential to any representation of us. Stateless, dispossessed, de-centered, we are frequently unable either to speak the "truth" of our experience or to make it heard. We do not

usually control the images that represent us; we have been confined to spaces designed to reduce or stunt us; and we have often been distorted by pressures and powers that have been too much for us. An additional problem is that our language, Arabic, is unfamiliar in the West and belongs to a tradition and civilization usually both misunderstood and maligned. Everything we write about ourselves, therefore, is an interpretive translation — of our language, our experience, our senses of self and others. (p. 6)

And from "States":

The striking thing about Palestinian prose and prose fiction is its formal instability: Our literature in a certain very narrow sense *is* the elusive, resistant reality it tries so often to represent. Most literary critics in Israel and the West focus on what is said in Palestinian writing, who is described, what the plot and contents deliver, their sociological and political meaning. But it is *form* that should be looked at. Particularly in fiction, the struggle to achieve form expresses the writer's efforts to construct a coherent scene, a narrative that might overcome the almost metaphysical impossibility of representing the present. (pp. 581–82)

As you reread, think about form — organization, arrangement, and genre. What *is* the order of the writing in this essay? (We will call it an essay for lack of a better term.) How might you diagram or explain its organization? By what principle(s) is it ordered and arranged? The essay shifts genres — memoir, history, argument. It is, as Said says, "hybrid." What surprises are there? or disappointments? How might you describe the writer's strategy as he works on his audience, on readers? And, finally, do you find Said's explanation sufficient or useful — does the experience of exile produce its own inevitable style of report and representation?

3. The essay is filled with references to people (including writers), places, and events that are, most likely, foreign to you. Choose one that seems interesting or important, worth devoting time to research. Of course the Internet will be a resource, but you should also use the library, if only to become aware of the different opportunities and materials it provides. Compile a report of the additional information; be prepared to discuss how the research has served or changed your position as a reader of "States."

4. The final chapter of *After the Last Sky* ends with this:

I would like to think, though, that such a book not only tells the reader about us, but in some way also reads the reader. I would like to think that we are not just the people seen or looked at in these photographs: We are also looking at our observers. (p. 166)

Read back through Said's essay by looking at the photos with this reversal in mind — looking in order to see yourself as the one who is being looked at, as the one observed. How are you positioned by the photographer, Jean Mohr?

How are you positioned by the person in the scene, always acknowledging your presence? What are you being told?

Once you have read through the photographs, reread the essay with a similar question in mind. This time, however, look for evidence of how Said positions you, defines you, invents you as a presence in the scene.

• • ● • •

ASSIGNMENTS FOR WRITING

1. Compose a similar project, a Said-like reading of a set of photos. These can be photos prepared for the occasion (by you or a colleague); they could also be photos already available. Whatever their source, they should represent people and places, a history and/or geography that you know well, that you know to be complex and contradictory, and that you know will not be easily or readily understood by others, both the group for whom you will be writing (most usefully the members of your class) and readers more generally. You must begin with a sense that the photos cannot speak for themselves; you must speak for them.

    In preparation, you should reread closely to come to a careful understanding of Said's project. (The first and second "Questions for a Second Reading" should be useful for this.) To prepare a document that is Said-like (one that shows your understanding of what Said is doing), you will need an expert's sense of how to write from and to photographs, and you will need to consider questions of form — of order, arrangement, and genre.

2. While "States" does not present itself as polemical writing — an argument in defense of Palestinian rights, an argument designed to locate blame or propose national or international policy — it is, still, writing with a purpose. It has an argument, it has a particular project in mind, and it wants something to happen.

    Write an essay that represents the argument or the project of "States" for someone who has not read it. You will need, in other words, to establish a context and to summarize. You should also work from passages (and images) to give your reader a sense of the text, its key terms and language. And write about "States" as though it has something to do with you.

    Your essay is not just summary, in other words, but summary in service of statement, response, or extension. As you are invited to think about the Palestinians, or about exile more generally, or about the texts and images that are commonly available, what do you think? What do you have to add?

3. The final chapter of *After the Last Sky* ends with this:

    > I would like to think, though, that such a book not only tells the reader about us, but in some way also reads the reader. I would like to think that we are not just the people seen or looked at in these photographs: We are also looking at our observers. (p. 166)

The fourth question in "Questions for a Second Reading" sets a strategy for rereading with this passage in mind — looking in order to see yourself as the one who is being looked at, as the one observed. Write an essay in which you think this through by referring specifically to images and to text. How are you positioned? by whom and to what end?

4. Said insists upon our recognizing the contemporary social, political, and historic context for intimate scenes he (and Jean Mohr) present of people going about their everyday lives. The Palestinian people are still much in the news — photographs of scenes from their lives are featured regularly in newspapers, in magazines, and on the Internet. Collect a series of these images from a particular and defined recent period of time — a week or a month, say, when the Palestinians have been in the news. Using these images, and putting them in conversation with some of the passages and images in "States," write an essay in the manner of Said's essay, with text and image in productive relationship. The goal of your essay should be to examine how Said's work, in "States," can speak to us (or might speak to us) today.

- • • ● • • -

MAKING CONNECTIONS

1. Edward Said talks about the formal problems in the writing of "States" (and for more on this, see the second of the "Questions for a Second Reading"):

> The striking thing about Palestinian prose and prose fiction is its formal instability: Our literature in a certain very narrow sense *is* the elusive, resistant reality it tries so often to represent. Most literary critics in Israel and the West focus on what is said in Palestinian writing, who is described, what the plot and contents deliver, their sociological and political meaning. But it is form that should be looked at. Particularly in fiction, the struggle to achieve *form* expresses the writer's efforts to construct a coherent scene, a narrative that might overcome the almost metaphysical impossibility of representing the present. (pp. 581–82)

And here is a similar discussion from the introduction to *After the Last Sky*:

> The multifaceted vision is essential to any representation of us. Stateless, dispossessed, de-centered, we are frequently unable either to speak the "truth" of our experience or to make it heard. We do not usually control the images that represent us; we have been confined to spaces designed to reduce or stunt us; and we have often been distorted by pressures and powers that have been too much for us. An additional problem is that our language, Arabic, is unfamiliar in the West and belongs to a tradition and civilization usually both misunderstood and maligned. Everything we write about ourselves, therefore, is an interpretive translation — of our language, our experience, our senses of self and others. (p. 6)

Edward Said's sense of his project as a writing project, a writing project requiring formal experimentation, is similar to Gloria Anzaldúa's in *Borderlands / La Frontera*. In the chapter represented in *Ways of Reading*, "How to Tame a Wild Tongue" (p. 26), Anzaldúa is also writing (and resisting) "interpretive translation." In place of the photographs in "States," she offers poems, stories, and myths, as well as passages in Spanish.

Write an essay in which you consider these selections as writing projects. The formal experimentation in each is said by the writers to be fundamental, necessary, a product of the distance between a particular world of experience and the available modes of representation. In what ways are the essays similar? In what ways are they different? Where and how is a reader (where and how are you) positioned in each? What is the experience of reading them? What does one need to learn to be their ideal reader?

2. There are several writers in *Ways of Reading* whose writing could be called unconventional, even experimental. A short list includes Gloria Anzaldúa, Ben Lerner, Susan Griffin, and John Edgar Wideman. (We can imagine arguments for several other selections as well.)

    Choose a selection from one of these writers to read alongside Edward Said's "States." As you read the two, pay particular attention to what the writing does, to how it works. This is not quite the same as paying attention to what it says. What does this way of writing allow each writer to do that another style, perhaps "topic sentence, examples, and conclusion," would not? What does it offer a reader — or what does it allow a reader to do? Write an essay in which you compare the styles of these two selections. Is there one that you find compelling or attractive? If each provides a textbook example, what are you invited to think about as you consider the possibilities and limits of your own style? of "standard" or "school" style? In what ways might this work be seen as a way of working on the problems of writing? And what might this work have to do with you, a student in a writing class?

3. Edward Said says,

    > All cultures spin out a dialectic of self and other, the subject "I" who is native, authentic, at home, and the object "it" or "you," who is foreign, perhaps threatening, different, out there. From this dialectic comes the series of heroes and monsters, founding fathers and barbarians, prized masterpieces and despised opponents that express a culture from its deepest sense of national self-identity to its refined patriotism, and finally to its coarse jingoism, xenophobia, and exclusivist bias. (p. 583)

    This is as true of the Palestinians as it is of the Israelis — although, he adds, "For Palestinian culture, the odd thing is that its own identity is more frequently than not perceived as 'other.'"

    Citing Benedict Anderson and what he refers to as "imagined communities," Mary Louise Pratt in "Arts of the Contact Zone" (p. 512) argues that our idea of community is "strongly utopian, embodying values like equality, fraternity, liberty, which the societies often profess but systematically fail to realize" (p. 520). Against this utopian vision of community, Pratt argues that we need to develop ways of understanding (noticing or creating) social and intellectual spaces that are not homogeneous or unified—contact zones. She argues that we need to develop ways of understanding and valuing difference.

There are similar goals and objects to these projects. Reread Pratt's essay with Said's "States" in mind. Recalling what she refers to as the "literate arts of the contact zone," can you find points of reference in Said's text? Said's thinking always attended to the importance and the conditions of writing, including his own. There are ways that "States" could be imagined as both "autoethnographic" and "transcultural." How might his work allow you to understand the "literate arts of the contact zone" in practice? How might his work allow you to understand the problems and possibilities of such writing beyond what Pratt has imagined, presented, and predicted?

4. Jean Mohr's collaboration with John Berger was important to Edward Said, particularly in the 1975 book *A Seventh Man*, a photographic essay on migrant workers in Europe. Find a copy of *A Seventh Man* (in a library or a bookstore or online) and write an essay on what you think it was in Mohr's work, and in his collaboration with Berger, that was most compelling to Said.

5. In Edward Said's essay "States," he theorizes about the notion of exile in relation to Palestinian identity, offering a study of exile and dislocation through his analysis of photographs taken by Jean Mohr. Consider the following passage:

> We turn ourselves into objects not for sale, but for scrutiny. People ask us, as if looking into an exhibit case, "What is it you Palestinians want?"—as if we can put our demands into a single neat phrase. All of us speak of *awdah*, "return," but do we mean that literally, or do we mean "we must restore ourselves to ourselves"? (p. 578)

When Said talks about being looked at as though in an exhibit case, we might understand him as being concerned with the problem of dehumanization. After all, to be in an exhibit case is to be captured, trapped, or even dead. In her essay "Beside Oneself: On the Limits of Sexual Autonomy" (p. 238), Judith Butler might be understood to be considering a similar problem. She writes, "I would like to start, and to end, with the question of the human, of who counts as the human, and the related question of whose lives count as lives, and with a question that has preoccupied many of us for years: what makes for a grievable life?" (p. 238).

Write an essay in which you consider the ways Said and Butler might be said to be speaking with each other. How might the condition of exile be like the condition of being *beside oneself*? What kind of connections—whether you see them as productive or problematic, or both at once—can be made between the ways Said talks about nation, identity, and home, and the ways Butler talks about gender and sexuality? What passages from each seem to have the other in mind? How does each struggle with reference, with pronouns like "we" and "our"?

6. Like Edward Said in "States," Ta-Nehisi Coates includes photographs in "Between the World and Me" (p. 277). (One image is included in our selection. You might look through a copy of the book *Between the World and Me* at your library to see the others.) Both Said and Coates are trying to represent a world — present, past, and future — and both rely on visual images. Write an essay in which you consider the different uses of the photograph in these two selections. How do they function for you, as a reader? What do you imagine the authors had in mind when they selected these images and brought them into the text?

Joe Kohen/Getty Images

MICHAEL
Specter

Michael Specter (b. 1955) received his BA from Vassar and began a career as a journalist with a position at the *Washington Post*, first covering local news and then reporting on national developments in science, medicine, and public health. He later worked for the *New York Times*, where he served as a foreign correspondent, reporting from Russia, Europe, and Africa. In 1996, he was awarded an Overseas Press Club Citation of Excellence for his coverage of the war in Chechnya.

Specter is currently a staff writer at *The New Yorker*, where he covers science, technology, and public health. He has written articles about the global AIDS epidemic, avian influenza, malaria, the world's diminishing freshwater resources, genetically modified food, synthetic biology, and the debate over the meaning of our carbon footprint, among other subjects. He has also published profiles of Lance Armstrong, Sean (P. Diddy) Combs, and Manolo Blahnik. In 2012, he became a visiting professor of environmental and urban studies at Bard College.

One of Specter's recent books is *Denialism: How Irrational Thinking Hinders Scientific Progress, Harms the Planet, and Threatens Our Lives* (2009). The title alone provides an insight into the urgency Specter brings to his analysis of current debates over science and public policy. He is defending science from those whom he sees to be irrational and irresponsible in their rejection of its findings and arguments — as, for example, in the case of those who refuse to immunize their children because of the fear of autism. His writing has brought him several major awards, including two Excellence in Media awards from the Global Health Council (for his reporting on HIV/AIDS), a Science Journalism Award from the American Association for the Advancement of Science, and the Robert P. Balles Annual Prize in Critical Thinking (for *Denialism*) from the Committee for Skeptical Inquiry.

For Specter, "denialists" are those who reject the findings of scientific research when those findings are inconvenient, or when they run counter to belief or intuition. In the introduction to his book, he says denialists "replace the rigorous and open-minded skepticism of science with the inflexible certainty of ideological commitment." If the data of scientific research fails to "fit neatly into an already formed theory," Specter continues, "a denialist doesn't see it as data at all. This enables him to dismiss even the most compelling evidence as just another point of view."

The article that follows, "The Gene Hackers," was first published in *The New Yorker* (November 2015). While it turns to argument at the end, it is primarily objective reporting on the work of a group of young scientists, researchers working on gene therapies. It introduces us to individuals, their labs, their funding sources, and their struggles as professionals. It brings us close to their lives and their research—the settings, the discoveries, and the controversies.

Like all important science journalism, the writing in "The Gene Hackers" represents an impossible task. The article is designed to help us understand what we can't understand (because we lack the knowledge and the training). It attempts to translate advanced research into everyday terms. The article represents (and, we believe, represents at its best) journalism's efforts to promote scientific literacy. The article is meant to bring us closer to science and its methods, and it does this in the hope that we can make informed decisions in matters of personal choice and public policy.

The Gene Hackers

At thirty-four, Feng Zhang is the youngest member of the core faculty at the Broad Institute of Harvard and M.I.T. He is also among the most accomplished. In 1999, while still a high-school student, in Des Moines, Zhang found a structural protein capable of preventing retroviruses like H.I.V. from infecting human cells. The project earned him third place in the Intel Science Talent Search, and he applied the fifty thousand dollars in prize money toward tuition at Harvard, where he studied chemistry and physics. By the time he received his doctorate, from Stanford, in 2009, he had shifted gears, helping to create optogenetics, a powerful new discipline that enables scientists to use light to study the behavior of individual neurons.

Zhang decided to become a biological engineer, forging tools to repair the broken genes that are responsible for many of humanity's most intractable afflictions. The following year, he returned to Harvard, as a member of the Society of Fellows, and became the first scientist to use a modular set of proteins, called TALEs, to control the genes of a mammal. "Imagine being able to manipulate a specific region of DNA ... almost as easily as correcting a typo," one molecular biologist wrote, referring to TALEs, which stands for transcription activator-like effectors. He concluded that although such an advance "will probably never happen," the new technology was as close as scientists might get.

Having already helped assemble two critical constituents of the genetic toolbox used in thousands of labs throughout the world, Zhang was invited, at the age of twenty-nine, to create his own research team at the Broad. One day soon after his arrival, he attended a meeting during which one of his colleagues mentioned that he had encountered a curious region of DNA in some bacteria he had been studying. He referred to it as a CRISPR sequence.

"I had never heard that word," Zhang told me recently as we sat in his office, which looks out across the Charles River and Beacon Hill. Zhang has a perfectly round face, its shape accentuated by rectangular wire-rimmed glasses and a bowl cut. "So I went to Google just to see what was there," he said. Zhang read every paper he could; five years later, he still seemed surprised by what he found. CRISPR, he learned, was a strange cluster of DNA sequences that could recognize invading viruses, deploy a special enzyme to chop them into pieces, and use the viral shards that remained to form a rudimentary immune system. The sequences, identical strings of nucleotides that could be read the same way backward and forward, looked like Morse code, a series of dashes punctuated by an occasional dot. The system had an awkward name — clustered regularly interspaced short palindromic repeats — but a memorable acronym.

CRISPR has two components. The first is essentially a cellular scalpel that cuts DNA. The other consists of RNA, the molecule most often used to transmit biological information throughout the genome. It serves as a guide, leading the scalpel on a search past thousands of genes until it finds and fixes itself to the precise string of nucleotides it needs to cut. It has been clear at least since Louis Pasteur did some of his earliest experiments into the germ theory of disease, in the nineteenth century, that the immune systems of humans and other vertebrates are capable of adapting to new threats. But few scientists had considered the possibility that single bacterial cells could defend themselves in the same way. The day after Zhang heard about CRISPR, he flew to Florida for a genetics conference. Rather than attend the meetings, however, he stayed in his hotel room and kept Googling. "I just sat there reading every paper on CRISPR I could find," he said. "The more I read, the harder it was to contain my excitement."

It didn't take Zhang or other scientists long to realize that, if nature could turn these molecules into the genetic equivalent of a global positioning system, so could we. Researchers soon learned how to create synthetic versions of the RNA guides and program them to deliver their cargo to virtually any cell. Once the enzyme locks onto the matching DNA sequence, it can cut and paste nucleotides with the precision we have come to expect from the search-and-replace function of a word processor. "This was a finding of mind-boggling importance," Zhang told me. "And it set off a cascade of experiments that have transformed genetic research."

With CRISPR, scientists can change, delete, and replace genes in any animal, including us. Working mostly with mice, researchers have already deployed the tool to correct the genetic errors responsible for sickle-cell anemia, muscular dystrophy, and the fundamental defect associated with cystic fibrosis. One group has replaced a mutation that causes cataracts; another has destroyed receptors that H.I.V. uses to infiltrate our immune system.

The potential impact of CRISPR on the biosphere is equally profound. Last year, by deleting all three copies of a single wheat gene, a team led by the Chinese geneticist Gao Caixia created a strain that is fully resistant to powdery mildew, one of the world's most pervasive blights. In September, Japanese scientists used the technique to prolong the life of tomatoes by turning off genes that control how quickly they ripen. Agricultural researchers hope that such an approach to enhancing crops will prove far less controversial than using genetically modified organisms, a process that requires technicians to introduce foreign DNA into the genes of many of the foods we eat.

The technology has also made it possible to study complicated illnesses in an entirely new way. A few well-known disorders, such as Huntington's disease and sickle-cell anemia, are caused by defects in a single gene. But most devastating illnesses, among them diabetes, autism, Alzheimer's, and cancer, are almost always the result of a constantly shifting dynamic that can include hundreds of genes. The best way to understand those connections has been to test them in animal models, a process of trial and error that can take years. CRISPR promises to make that process easier, more accurate, and exponentially faster.

Inevitably, the technology will also permit scientists to correct genetic flaws in human embryos. Any such change, though, would infiltrate the entire genome and eventually be passed down to children, grandchildren, great-grandchildren, and every subsequent generation. That raises the possibility, more realistically than ever before, that scientists will be able to rewrite the fundamental code of life, with consequences for future generations that we may never be able to anticipate. Vague fears of a dystopian world, full of manufactured humans, long ago became a standard part of any debate about scientific progress. Yet not since J. Robert Oppenheimer realized that the atomic bomb he built to protect the world might actually destroy it have the scientists responsible for a discovery been so leery of using it.

> FOR MUCH OF THE PAST CENTURY, BIOLOGY HAS BEEN CONSUMED WITH THREE ESSENTIAL QUESTIONS: WHAT DOES EACH GENE DO? HOW DO WE FIND THE GENETIC MUTATIONS THAT MAKE US SICK? AND HOW CAN WE OVERCOME THEM?

For much of the past century, biology has been consumed with three essential questions: What does each gene do? How do we find the genetic mutations that make us sick? And how can we overcome them? With CRISPR, the answers have become attainable, and we are closing in on a sort of grand unified theory of genetics. "I am not sure what a Golden Age looks like," Winston Yan, a member of Zhang's research team, told me one day when I was with him in the lab, "but I think we are in one."

At least since 1953, when James Watson and Francis Crick characterized the helical structure of DNA, the central project of biology has been the effort to understand how the shifting arrangement of four compounds — adenine, guanine, cytosine, and thymine — determines the ways in which humans differ from each other and from everything else alive. CRISPR is not the first system to help scientists pursue that goal, but it is the first that anyone with basic skills and a few hundred dollars' worth of equipment can use.

"CRISPR is the Model T of genetics," Hank Greely told me when I visited him recently, at Stanford Law School, where he is a professor and the director of the Center for Law and the Biosciences. "The Model T wasn't the first car, but it changed the way we drive, work, and live. CRISPR has made a difficult process cheap and reliable. It's incredibly precise. But an important part of the history of molecular biology is the history of editing genes."

Scientists took the first serious step toward controlling our genes in the early nineteen-seventies, when they learned to cut chains of DNA by using proteins called restriction enzymes. Suddenly, genes from organisms that would never have been able to mate in nature could be combined in the laboratory. But those initial tools were more hatchet than scalpel, and, because they could recognize only short stretches within the vast universe of the human genome, the editing was rarely precise. (Imagine searching through all of Shakespeare for Hamlet's soliloquy on suicide, relying solely on the phrase "to be." You'd find the passage, but only after landing on several hundred unrelated citations.)

When the first draft of the Human Genome Project was published, in 2001, the results were expected to transform our understanding of life. In fundamental ways, they have; the map has helped researchers locate thousands of genes associated with particular illnesses, including hundreds that cause specific types of cancer. To understand the role that those genes play in the evolution of a disease, however, and repair them, scientists need to turn genes on and off systematically and in many combinations. Until recently, though, altering even a single gene took months or years of work.

That began to change with the growing use of zinc fingers, a set of molecular tools that, like CRISPR clusters, were discovered by accident. In 1985, scientists studying the genetic code of the African clawed frog noticed a finger-shaped protein wrapped around its DNA. They soon figured out how to combine that tenacious grip with an enzyme that could cut the DNA like a knife. Two decades later, geneticists began using TALEs, which are made up of proteins secreted by bacteria. But both engineering methods are expensive and cumbersome. Even Zhang, who published the first report on using TALEs to alter the genes of mammals, realized that the system was little more than an interim measure. "It is difficult to use," he told me. "I had to assign a graduate student just to make the proteins and test them before I could begin to use them in an experiment. The procedure was not easy."

Zhang's obsession with science began in middle school, when his mother prodded him to attend a Saturday-morning class in molecular biology. "I was thirteen and had no idea what molecular biology was," he said one evening as we walked across the M.I.T. campus on the way to the fiftieth-anniversary celebration of the Department of Brain and Cognitive Sciences, where Zhang is also a faculty member. "It really opened my imagination." His parents, both engineers, moved the family to Iowa when he was eleven. They stayed largely because they thought he would get a better education in the United States than in China.

In 1997, when Zhang was fifteen, he was offered an internship in a biosafety facility at the Des Moines Human Gene Therapy Research Institute — but he was told that federal law prohibited him from working in a secure lab until he was sixteen. "So I had to wait," he said. On his birthday, Zhang went to the lab and met the scientists. "I was assigned to a man who had a Ph.D. in chemistry but trained as a molecular biologist," he continued. "He had a lot of passion for science, and he had a very big impact on me and my research." On his first day, Zhang spent five hours in the lab, and nearly as much time every day after school until he graduated.

Zhang is unusually reserved, and he speaks in low, almost sleepy tones. I asked him if he considered himself to be mellow, a characteristic rarely associated with prize-winning molecular biologists. "You came to the lab meeting, right?" he replied. Earlier that morning, I had caught the tail end of a weekly meeting that Zhang holds for his group. I watched as he gently but relentlessly demolished a presentation given by one of the people on his team. When I mentioned it to one of the scientists who was at the meeting, he responded, "That was nothing. You should have been there from the start."

At his Saturday-morning classes, Zhang learned how to extract DNA from cells and determine the length of each sequence. But that isn't what he remembers best. "They showed us 'Jurassic Park,'" he said, his voice moving up a register. "And it was amazing to me. The teacher explained the different scientific concepts in the movie, and they all seemed completely feasible."

We had reached the cocktail party, a tepid affair crowded with men in khakis and women wearing sensible shoes. Zhang left after barely twenty minutes and headed back to the lab. He retains his position on the cognitive-sciences faculty, because he hopes that his research will help neuroscientists study the brain in greater detail. He told me that when he was young he had a friend who suffered from serious depression, and he had been surprised to find that there was almost no treatment available. It spurred a lasting interest in psychiatry. "People think you are weak if you are depressed," he said. "It is still a common prejudice. But many people suffer from problems we cannot begin to address. The brain is still the place in the universe with the most unanswered questions."

The Broad Institute was founded, in 2003, by the entrepreneur Eli Broad and his wife, Edythe, to foster research into the molecular components of life and their connections to disease. One afternoon in Zhang's laboratory, Winston Yan offered to walk me through the mechanics of using CRISPR to edit a gene. "We need to be able to break DNA in a very precise place in the genome," he said as I watched him at work. He swivelled in his chair and pointed to a row of vials that contained DNA samples to be analyzed and edited. Yan, a thin, bespectacled man, wore black laboratory gloves and a white Apple Watch; he clapped his hands and shrugged, as if to suggest that the work was simple.

ORDERING THE GENETIC PARTS REQUIRED TO TAILOR DNA ISN'T AS EASY AS BUYING A PAIR OF SHOES FROM ZAPPOS, BUT IT SEEMS TO BE HEADED IN THAT DIRECTION.

Ordering the genetic parts required to tailor DNA isn't as easy as buying a pair of shoes from Zappos, but it seems to be headed in that direction. Yan turned on the computer at his lab station and navigated to an order form for a company called Integrated DNA Technologies, which synthesizes biological parts. "It takes orders online, so if I want a particular sequence I can have it here in a day or two," he said. That is not unusual. Researchers can now order online almost any biological component, including DNA, RNA, and the chemicals necessary to use them. One can buy the parts required to assemble a working version of the polio virus (it's been done) or genes that, when put together properly, can make feces smell like wintergreen. In Cambridge, I.D.T. often makes same-day deliveries. Another organization, Addgene, was established, more than a decade ago, as a nonprofit repository that houses tens of thousands of ready-made sequences, including nearly every guide used to edit genes with CRISPR. When researchers at the Broad, and at many other institutions, create a new guide, they typically donate a copy to Addgene.

The RNA that CRISPR relies upon to guide the molecular scalpel to its target is made of twenty base pairs. Humans have twenty thousand genes, and twenty base pairs occupy roughly the same percentage of space in a single gene as would one person standing in a circle that contained the entire population of the United States. CRISPR is better at locating specific genes than any other system, but it isn't perfect, and sometimes it cuts the wrong target. Yan would order a ready-made probe from Addgene. When it arrives, he pairs it with a cutting enzyme and sends it to the designated gene.

Yan joined Zhang's lab just before what he described as "the CRISPR craze" began. But, he added, the technology has already transformed the field. "For many years, there was a reductionist approach to genetics," he said. "A kind of wishful thinking: 'We will find the gene that causes cancer or the gene that makes you prone to heart disease.' It is almost never that simple."

The next morning, I walked over to the Broad's new Stanley Building and rode the elevator to the top floor, where I emptied my pockets, put on a mask and gown, and slipped booties over my shoes. Then I passed through an air chamber that was sealed with special gaskets and had a fan blowing continuously to keep out foreign microbes. I entered the vivarium, a long, clean floor that looked like a combination of research unit and hospital ward. The vivarium, which opened last year, provides thousands of mice with some of the world's most carefully monitored accommodations.

Despite our growing knowledge of the way that cancer develops in human cells, mutations can't be studied effectively in a petri dish, and, since the late nineteen-eighties, genetically modified mice have served as the standard proxy. What cures (or kills) a mouse won't necessarily have the same effect on a human, but the mouse genome is surprisingly similar to our own, and the animals are cheap and easy to maintain. Like humans, and many other mammals, mice develop complex diseases that affect the immune system and the brain. They get cancer, atherosclerosis, hypertension, and diabetes, among other chronic illnesses. Mice also reproduce every three weeks, which allows researchers to follow several generations at once. Typically, technicians would remove a stem cell from the mouse, then edit it in a lab to produce a particular gene or to prevent the gene from working properly. After putting the stem cell back into the developing embryo of the mouse, and waiting for it to multiply, they can study the gene's effect on the animal's development. The process works well, but it generally allows for the study of only one characteristic in one gene at a time.

The vivarium at the Broad houses an entirely different kind of mouse, one that carries the protein Cas9 (which stands for CRISPR-associated nuclease) in every cell. Cas9, the part of the CRISPR system that acts like a genetic scalpel, is an enzyme. When scientists originally began editing DNA with CRISPR, they had to inject both the Cas9 enzyme and the probe required to guide it. A year ago, Randall Platt, another member of Zhang's team, realized that it would be possible to cut the CRISPR system in two. He implanted the surgical enzyme into a mouse embryo, which made it a part of the animal's permanent genome. Every time a cell divided, the Cas9 enzyme would go with it. In other words, he and his colleagues created a mouse that was easy to edit. Last year, they published a study explaining their methodology, and since then Platt has shared the technique with more than a thousand laboratories around the world.

The "Cas9 mouse" has become the first essential tool in the emerging CRISPR arsenal. With the enzyme that acts as molecular scissors already present in every cell, scientists no longer have to fit it onto an RNA guide. They can dispatch many probes at once and simply make mutations in the genes they want to study.

To demonstrate a potential application for cancer research, the team used the Cas9 mouse to model lung adenocarcinoma, the most common form of lung cancer. Previously, scientists working with animal models had to modify one gene at a time or cross-breed animals to produce a colony with the needed genetic modifications. Both processes were challenging and time-consuming. "Now we can activate CRISPR directly in the cells we're interested in studying, and modify the genome in whatever way we want," Platt said, as he showed me around the vivarium. We entered a small exam room with a commanding view of Cambridge. I watched as a technician placed a Cas9 mouse in a harness inside a biological safety cabinet. Then, peering through a Leica microscope, she used a fine capillary needle to inject a single cell into the mouse's tail.

"And now we have our model," Platt said, explaining that the mouse had just received an injection that carried three probes, each of which was programmed to carry a mutation that scientists believe is associated with lung cancer. "The cells will carry as many mutations as we want to study. That really is a revolutionary development."

"In the past, this would have taken the field a decade, and would have required a consortium," Platt said. "With CRISPR, it took me four months to do it by myself." In September, Zhang published a report, in the journal *Cell*, describing yet another CRISPR protein, called Cpf1, that is smaller and easier to program than Cas9.

The lab employs a similar approach to studying autism. Recent experiments suggest that certain psychiatric conditions can be caused by just a few malfunctioning neurons out of the trillions in every brain. Studying the way neurons function within the brain is difficult. But by re-creating, in the lab, genetic mutations that others have linked to autism and schizophrenia Zhang's team has been able to investigate faulty neurons that may play a role in those conditions.

As the price of sequencing plunges, cancer clinics throughout the United States have begun to study their patients' tumors in greater detail. Tumors are almost never uniform; one may have five mutations or fifty, which means, essentially, that every cancer is a specific, personal disease. Until CRISPR became available, the wide genetic variations in cancer cells often made it hard to develop effective treatments.

"What I love most about the CRISPR process is that you can take any cancer-cell line, knock out every gene, and identify every one of the cell's Achilles' heels," Eric Lander, the fifty-eight-year-old director of the Broad, told me recently. Lander, who was among the leaders of the Human Genome Project, said that he had never encountered a more promising research tool. "You can also use CRISPR to systematically study the ways that a cancer cell can escape from a treatment," he said. "That should make it possible to build a comprehensive road map for cancer."

Lander went on to say that each vulnerability of a tumor might be attacked by a single drug. But cancer cells elude drugs in many ways, and, to succeed, a therapy may need to block them all. That strategy has proved effective for infectious diseases like AIDS. "Remember the pessimism about H.I.V.," he said, referring to the early years of the AIDS epidemic, when a diagnosis was essentially a death sentence. Eventually, virologists developed a series of drugs that interfere with the virus's ability to replicate. The therapy became truly successful, however, only when those drugs, working together, could block the virus completely.

The same approach has proved successful in treating tuberculosis. Lander is convinced that it will also work for many cancers: "With triple-drug therapy," for H.I.V., "we reached an inflection point: we were losing badly, and one day suddenly we were winning."

He stood up and walked across the office toward his desk, then pointed at the wall and described his vision for the future of cancer treatment. "There will be an enormous chart," he said. "Well, it will be electronic, and it will contain the therapeutic road map of every trick that cancer cells have — how they form, all the ways you can defeat them, and all the ways they can escape and defeat a treatment. And when we have that we win. Because every cancer cell starts naïve. It doesn't know what we have waiting in the freezer for it. Infectious diseases are a different story; they share their knowledge as they spread. They learn from us as they move from person to person. But every person's cancer starts naïve. And this is why we will beat it."

Developing any technology as complex and widely used as CRISPR invariably involves contributions from many scientists. Patent fights over claims of discovery and licensing rights are common. Zhang, the Broad Institute, and M.I.T. are now embroiled in such a dispute with Jennifer Doudna and the University of California; she is a professor of chemistry and of molecular biology at Berkeley. By 2012, Doudna, along with Emmanuelle Charpentier, a medical microbiologist who studies pathogens at the Helmholtz Centre for Infection Research, in Germany, and their lab teams, demonstrated, for the first time, that CRISPR could edit purified DNA. Their paper was published that June. In January of 2013, though, Zhang and George Church, a professor of genetics at both Harvard Medical School and M.I.T., published the first studies demonstrating that CRISPR could be used to edit human cells. Today, patents are generally awarded to the first people to file — in this case, Doudna and Charpentier. But Zhang and the Broad argued that the earlier success with CRISPR had no bearing on whether the technique would work in the complex organisms that matter most to scientists looking for ways to treat and prevent diseases.

Zhang was awarded the patent, but the University of California has requested an official reassessment, and a ruling has not yet been issued. Both he and Doudna described the suit to me as "a distraction" that they wished would go away. Both pledged to release all intellectual property to researchers without charge (and they have). But both are also involved in new companies that intend to develop CRISPR technology as therapies, as do many pharmaceutical firms and other profit-seeking enterprises.

CRISPR research is becoming big business: venture-capital firms are competing with one another to invest millions, and any patent holder would have the right to impose licensing fees.

> CRISPR RESEARCH IS BECOMING BIG BUSINESS: VENTURE-CAPITAL FIRMS ARE COMPETING WITH ONE ANOTHER TO INVEST MILLIONS, AND ANY PATENT HOLDER WOULD HAVE THE RIGHT TO IMPOSE LICENSING FEES. WHOEVER WINS STANDS TO MAKE A FORTUNE.

Whoever wins stands to make a fortune. Other achievements are also at stake, possibly including a Nobel Prize. (Doudna's supporters have described her as America's next female Nobel Prize winner, and at times the publicity war seems a bit like the battles waged by movie studios during Academy Award season.) Last year, the National Science Foundation presented Zhang with its most prestigious award, saying that his fundamental research "moves us in the direction" of eliminating schizophrenia, autism, and other brain disorders. A few months later, Doudna and Charpentier received three million dollars each for the Breakthrough Prize, awarded each year for scientific achievement. The prize was established, in 2012, by several Silicon Valley billionaires who are seeking to make science a more attractive career path. The two women also appeared on *Time*'s annual list of the world's hundred most influential people.

In fact, neither group was involved in the earliest identification of CRISPR or in the first studies to demonstrate how it works. In December, 1987, biologists at the Research Institute of Microbial Diseases, in Osaka, Japan, published the DNA sequence of a gene taken from the common intestinal bacterium *E. coli*. Those were early days in the genomic era, and thousands of labs around the world had embarked on similar attempts to map the genes of species ranging from fruit flies to humans. In an effort to better understand how this particular gene functioned, the Japanese scientists also sequenced some of the DNA that surrounded it. When they examined the data, they were surprised to see cellular structures that none of them recognized: they had no idea what to make of the strange phenomenon, but they took note of it, writing in the final sentence of their report, published in the *Journal of Bacteriology*, that the "biological significance of these sequences is not known."

The mystery remained until 2005, when Francisco Mojica, a microbiologist at the University of Alicante, who had long sought to understand CRISPR, decided to compare its DNA with the DNA of tens of thousands of similar organisms. What he saw amazed him: every unknown sequence turned out to be a fragment of DNA from an invading virus.

The pace of research quickened. In 2007, Rodolphe Barrangou and Philippe Horvath, microbiologists then working for Danisco, the Danish food company, had noticed that some of its yogurt cultures were routinely destroyed by viruses and others were not. They decided to find out why. The scientists infected the microbe *Streptococcus thermophilus*, which is widely used to make yogurt, with two viruses. Most of the bacteria died, but those which survived had one property in common: they all contained CRISPR molecules to defend them.

"No single person discovers things anymore," George Church told me when we met in his office at Harvard Medical School. "The whole patent battle is silly. There has been much research. And if anybody should be making a fuss about this I should be making a fuss. But I am not doing that, because I don't think it matters. They are all nice people. They are all doing important work. It's a tempest in a teapot."

From the moment that manipulating genes became possible, many people, including some of those involved in the experiments, were horrified by the idea of scientists in lab coats rearranging the basic elements of life. In 1974, David Baltimore, the pioneering molecular biologist, who was then at M.I.T., and Paul Berg, of Stanford, both of whom went on to win a Nobel Prize for their research into the fundamentals of viral genetics, called for a moratorium on gene-editing research until scientists could develop safety principles for handling organisms that contained recombinant DNA. That meeting, which took place in 1975, at a conference center in Asilomar, California, has come to be regarded as biotechnology's Constitutional Convention.

Roughly a hundred and fifty participants, most of them scientists, gathered to discuss ways to limit the risks of accidentally releasing genetically modified organisms. At the time, the possibility of creating "designer babies" — a prospect that, no matter how unlikely, is attached to almost everything written or said about CRISPR — was too remote to consider. Nevertheless, the technology seemed frightening. In Cambridge, home to both M.I.T. and Harvard, the city council nearly banned such research altogether. The work went on, but decoding sequences of DNA wasn't easy. "In 1974, thirty base pairs" — thirty rungs on the helical ladder of the six billion nucleotides that make up our DNA — "was a good year's work," George Church told me. Now the same work would take seconds.

At least for the foreseeable future, CRISPR's greatest impact will lie in its ability to help scientists rapidly rewrite the genomes of animal and plant species. In laboratories, agricultural companies have already begun to use CRISPR to edit soybeans, rice, and potatoes in an effort to make them more nutritious and more resistant to drought. Scientists might even be able to edit allergens out of foods like peanuts.

Normally, it takes years for genetic changes to spread through a population. That is because, during sexual reproduction, each of the two versions of any gene has only a fifty per cent chance of being inherited. But a "gene drive" — which is named for its ability to propel genes through populations over many generations — manages to override the traditional rules of genetics. A mutation made by CRISPR on one chromosome can copy itself in every generation, so that nearly all descendants would inherit the change. A mutation engineered into a mosquito that would block the parasite responsible for malaria, for instance, could be driven through a large population of mosquitoes within a year or two. If the mutation reduced the number of eggs produced by that mosquito, the population could be wiped out, along with any malaria parasites it carried.

Kevin Esvelt, an evolutionary biologist at Harvard, was the first to demonstrate how gene drives and CRISPR could combine to alter the traits of wild populations. Recently, he has begun to study the possibility of using the technology to eliminate Lyme disease by rewriting the genes of mice in the wild. Lyme disease is caused by a bacterium and transmitted by ticks, and more than eighty-five per cent of the time they become infected after biting a mouse. Once exposed, however, some mice naturally acquire resistance or immunity. "My idea is to take the existing genes that confer resistance to Lyme and make sure that all mice have the most effective version," Esvelt said. To do that, scientists could encode the most protective genes next to the CRISPR system and force them to be passed on together. Esvelt stressed that such an approach would become possible only after much more research and a lengthy series of public discussions on the risks and benefits of the process.

The promise of CRISPR research becomes more evident almost every month. Recently, Church reported that he had edited sixty-two genes simultaneously in a pig cell. The technique, if it proves accurate and easy to repeat, could help alleviate the constant shortage of organ donors in the U.S. For years, scientists have tried to find a way to use pig organs for transplants, but a pig's DNA is filled with retroviruses that have been shown in labs to infect human cells. Church and his colleagues discovered that those viruses share a common genetic sequence. He deployed CRISPR to their exact locations and snipped them out of the genome. In the most successful of the experiments, the CRISPR system deleted all sixty-two of the retroviruses embedded in the pig's DNA. Church then mixed those edited cells with human cells in the laboratory, and none became infected.

While CRISPR will clearly make it possible to alter our DNA, serious risks remain. Jennifer Doudna has been among the most vocal of those calling for caution on what she sees as the inevitable march toward editing human genes. "It's going to happen," she told me the first time we met, in her office at Berkeley. "As a research tool, CRISPR could hardly be more valuable — but we are far from the day when it should be used in a clinical setting." Doudna was a principal author of a letter published in *Science* this spring calling for a temporary research moratorium. She and others have organized a conference to discuss the ethics of editing DNA, a sort of Asilomar redux. The conference, to be attended by more than two hundred scientists — from the U.S., England, and China, among other countries — will take place during the first week of December at the National Academy of Sciences, in Washington.

Until April, the ethical debate over the uses of CRISPR technology in humans was largely theoretical. Then a group at Sun Yat-sen University, in southern China, attempted to repair, in eighty-six human embryos, the gene responsible for betathalassemia, a rare but often fatal blood disorder. If those disease genes, and genes that cause conditions like cystic fibrosis, could be modified successfully in a fertilized egg, the alteration could not only protect a single individual but eventually eliminate the malady from that person's hereditary lineage. Given enough time, the changes would affect all of humanity. The response to the experiment was largely one of fear and outrage. The *Times* carried the story under the headline "CHINESE SCIENTISTS EDIT GENES OF HUMAN EMBRYOS, RAISING CONCERNS."

Critics called the experiment irresponsible and suggested that the scientists had violated an established code of conduct. "This paper demonstrates the enormous safety risks that any such attempt would entail, and underlines the urgency of working to forestall other such efforts," Marcy Darnovsky, of the Center for Genetics and Society, told National Public Radio when the report was published. "The social dangers of creating genetically modified human beings cannot be overstated."

There seems to be little disagreement about that. But the Chinese researchers were not trying to create genetically modified humans. They were testing the process, and every CRISPR researcher I spoke to considered the experiment to have been well planned and carried out with extraordinary care. The scientists also agreed that the results were illuminating. "That was an ethical paper, and a highly responsible project," Lander told me. "What did they do? They took triploid zygotes" — a relatively common genetic aberration — "from I.V.F. clinics. They deliberately chose those because they knew no human could ever develop from them. And what did the paper say? 'Boy, we see problems everywhere.' That was good science, and it was cautionary."

Fewer than half the embryos were edited successfully, and, of those, most retained none of the new DNA that was inserted into the genes. The experiment, which was published in the Beijing-based journal *Protein & Cell*, demonstrated clearly that the day when scientists could safely edit humans is far off. The CRISPR system also made unintended cuts and substitutions, the potential effects of which are unknown. In other cases, it made the right changes in some cells of the embryo but not in all of them, which could cause other problems. "These authors did a very good job, pointing out the challenges," Dieter Egli, a stem-cell researcher at Columbia University, said when the study was published. "They say themselves that this type of technology is not ready for any kind of application."

Doudna agreed that the Chinese experiment yielded valuable results. She is fifty-one, and has been at Berkeley since 2002, when she and her husband, the biochemist Jamie Cate, were offered joint appointments to the departments of chemistry and molecular and cell biology. Their offices are next to each other, with the same commanding view of San Francisco Bay and the Golden Gate Bridge. Doudna's work, unlike that of the scientists at the Broad, has been focussed on molecules, not mammalian genetics. For years, she has been leading investigations into the shape, structure, and capabilities of RNA, and in 2011 Charpentier asked for her help in exploring the mechanism of CRISPR. Doudna is tall, with graying blond hair and piercing blue eyes. She grew up in Hawaii, where her parents were academics; when it was time for college, she decided to leave the island and study in California, at Pomona. She earned her doctorate at Harvard and then moved on to Yale. "I have always been a bit of a restless soul," she said. "I may spend too much time wondering what comes next."

Doudna is a highly regarded biochemist, but she told me that not long ago she considered attending medical school or perhaps going into business. She said that she wanted to have an effect on the world and had begun to fear that the impact of her laboratory research might be limited. The promise of her work on CRISPR, however, has persuaded her to remain in the lab. She told me that she was constantly amazed by its potential, but when I asked if she had ever wondered whether the powerful new tool might do more harm than good she looked uncomfortable. "I lie in bed almost every night and ask myself that question," she said. "When I'm ninety, will I look back and be glad about what we have accomplished with this technology? Or will I wish I'd never discovered how it works?"

Her eyes narrowed, and she lowered her voice almost to a whisper. "I have never said this in public, but it will show you where my psyche is," she said. "I had a dream recently, and in my dream" — she mentioned the name of a leading scientific researcher — "had come to see me and said, 'I have somebody very powerful with me who I want you to meet, and I want you to explain to him how this technology functions.' So I said, Sure, who is it? It was Adolf Hitler. I was really horrified, but I went into a room and there was Hitler. He had a pig face and I could only see him from behind and he was taking notes and he said, 'I want to understand the uses and implications of this amazing technology.' I woke up in a cold sweat. And that dream has haunted me from that day. Because suppose somebody like Hitler had access to this — we can only imagine the kind of horrible uses he could put it to."

Nobody is going to employ CRISPR technology to design a baby, let alone transform the genetic profile of humanity, anytime soon. Even if scientists become capable of editing human embryos, it would take years for the genetically modified baby to grow old enough to reproduce — and then many generations for the alteration to disseminate throughout the population.

But there are long-term consequences to consider. Modern medicine already shapes our genome, by preserving genes that might otherwise have been edited out of our genome by natural selection. Today, millions of people suffer from myopia, and many of them are legally blind. Were it not for the invention of glasses, which have turned poor eyesight largely into a nuisance rather than an existential threat, the genes responsible for myopia might be less prevalent than they are today. The same could be said about many infectious diseases, and even chronic conditions like diabetes.

Humans also carry genes that protect us from one disease but increase our susceptibility to others, and it's impossible to predict the impact of changing all or even most of them. The AIDS virus often enters our blood cells through a protein called CCR5. One particular genetic variant of that protein, called the Delta32 mutation, prevents H.I.V. from locking onto the cell. If every person carried that mutation, nobody would get AIDS. So why not introduce that mutation into the human genome? Several research teams are working to develop drugs that do that in people who have already been infected.

Yet it's important to note that, while such a procedure would prevent H.I.V. infection, it would also elevate our susceptibility to West Nile virus. Today, that trade-off may seem worth the risk, but there's no way of knowing whether it would be true seven or ten generations from now. For example, sickle cells, which cause anemia, evolved as a protection against malaria; the shape of the cell blocks the spread of the parasite. If CRISPR technology had been available two hundred thousand years ago, it might have seemed sensible to edit sickle cells into the entire human population. But the results would have been devastating.

> TODAY, THAT TRADE-OFF MAY SEEM WORTH THE RISK, BUT THERE'S NO WAY OF KNOWING WHETHER IT WOULD BE TRUE SEVEN OR TEN GENERATIONS FROM NOW.

"This is a little bit like geoengineering," Zhang told me, referring to attempts to deliberately alter the climate to offset damages associated with global warming. "Once you go down that path, it may not be so reversible."

George Church disagrees. "It strikes me as a fake argument to say that something is irreversible," he told me. "There are tons of technologies that are irreversible. But genetics is not one of them. In my lab, we make mutations all the time and then we change them back. Eleven generations from now, if we alter something and it doesn't work properly we will simply fix it."

In 1997, Scottish scientists shocked the world by announcing that they had cloned a lamb, which they named Dolly. Scores of journalists (including me) descended on Edinburgh, and wrote that the achievement, while wondrous, also carried the ominous implication that scientists had finally pried open Pandora's box. Many articles about cloning and the value of human life were published. Evil people and dictators would clone themselves, their children, their pets. A new class of humans would arise.

Eighteen years later, the closest we have come to cloning a person was a failed attempt at a monkey, in 2007. Nobody spends much time worrying about it today. In Cambridge this summer, one of the researchers at the Broad told me that he and Louise Brown, the first success of in-vitro fertilization, were both born in 1978. "Did that set off an uproar?" he asked. It did. Even seven years earlier, James Watson had written, in *The Atlantic*, that the coming era of designer babies might overwhelm us all. Today, though, with more than five million children on earth born through in-vitro fertilization, that particular furor, too, seems to have passed.

CRISPR technology offers a new outlet for the inchoate fear of tinkering with the fundamentals of life. There are many valid reasons to worry. But it is essential to assess both the risks and the benefits of any new technology. Most people would consider it dangerous to fundamentally alter the human gene pool to treat a disease like AIDS if we could cure it with medicine or a vaccine. But risks always depend on the potential result. If CRISPR helps unravel the mysteries of autism, contributes to a cure for a form of cancer, or makes it easier for farmers to grow more nutritious food while reducing environmental damage, the fears, like the many others before them, will almost certainly disappear.

• • ● • •

QUESTIONS FOR A SECOND READING

1. Writers punctuate sentences. They use commas, semicolons, periods, parentheses, and dashes to organize the units that make up a sentence.

    Writers also punctuate essays, and you will see an example of this in "The Gene Hackers." As you read, you'll notice that Specter divides his essay into sections. You can assume that each section has a particular job to do. And you can assume that in the space between sections, in the jump from one to the other, there is space for you to stop and take stock, to think about where you have been and where you are going. Be prepared to talk about two of the transitions from section to section, two that seem representative of this method. And be prepared to speak about what you see to be the essay's overall structure or strategy.

2. "The Gene Hackers" begins with this sentence: "At thirty-four, Feng Zhang is the youngest member of the core faculty at the Broad Institute of Harvard and M.I.T."

   It could have begun with this sentence:

   > At least since 1953, when James Watson and Francis Crick character-ized the helical structure of DNA, the central project of biology has been the effort to understand how the shifting arrangement of four compounds — adenine, guanine, cytosine and thymine — determines the ways in which humans differ from each other and from every-thing else alive. (p. 604)

   The first sentence focuses on an individual, the hero of our story; the second focuses on "the central project of biology." It is not at all unusual for science writers, in a general-interest magazine like *The New Yorker*, to lure a reader in and keep a reader's attention by examining a general topic through the story (or the experience or the point of view) of an individual — up close and personal. As you reread, pay attention to the movement from the profile of an individual to the exploration of a general topic, from interview to research (or "reporting"). How does Specter do this? How does the move-ment in and out of the personal serve you (or fail to serve you) as his reader? What happens to "science"? scientific knowledge? objectivity?

3. "The Gene Hackers" is filled with words and concepts that are not in common use: "transcription activator-like effectors," "interspaced short palindromic repeats," "restriction enzymes," to list just a few. As you reread, look for the ways that Specter works to translate, to transform technical terms and diffi-cult concepts into more familiar language and more recognizable examples. Choose three methods that seem to be the most effective, and be prepared to talk about them as methods that can be part of any writer's toolkit. Is there any particular moment in the essay where the translation fails?

4. You often hear that the first person, the use of "I," is not appropriate in seri-ous, professional, academic writing. It is the subject that matters, not the writer and his or her opinion — or so the argument goes. As you reread, pay particular attention to where and when (and how and why) Specter brings himself (as a character) into the essay.

   It is safe to say that "The Gene Hackers" is not *about* Michael Specter. And yet he does appear regularly as a character, using the first-person pro-noun "I." This is a very common strategy in most contemporary narrative nonfiction. (And, it is worth adding, most contemporary narrative nonfiction avoids the use of footnotes or endnotes or any form of MLA-style citation.) Why and when does Specter use this strategy? What happens to "objectivity" in the essay? credibility? scientific knowledge?

5. While this essay is relatively recent (2015), things move quickly in the world of scientific research. Using the Internet (and, if possible, faculty and graduate students on your campus), see what you can find about more recent

developments in CRISPR research, or in Feng Zhang's or Jennifer Doudna's careers. (This might become a group project.) Be prepared to present your findings in class.

• • • ● • • •

ASSIGNMENTS FOR WRITING

1. Write a summary of "The Gene Hackers" that provides an account of CRISPR technology, its history and its future.

    Let's imagine that it is your job to explain Specter's essay to someone who has not yet had the chance to read it, someone who is smart and informed but who doesn't yet know what the essay says or why it is interesting (or important) — or, for that matter, someone who doesn't yet know why it is wrongheaded or not worth reading.

    With paraphrase and some direct (including block) quotation, write an essay to provide your sense of what the essay says and why it might be of consequence to others, in particular to those of your generation. Be sure to take time to explain and interpret the key passages and details. And be sure to take time, most likely at the end, to speak for yourself, to extend what Specter says to your interests, experiences, stories, and concerns.

2. With this essay as your primary resource (even as your only resource), write an essay that provides an insight into contemporary science — its researchers, its funding, its institutions, its audiences, its discoveries, its controversies, its failures, and its successes. What did you learn from this essay about the workings of science and scientists? How does that world work? What does it take to be successful?

3. "The Gene Hackers" provides an example of a certain form of reporting — of gathering information and preparing it for a general audience. Prepare a similar article, one where you take something you know well, something you know better (or more deeply) than most, and write an article like Specter's, one designed to explain what you know to those who are outsiders.

    Your article will most likely be shorter than his, but it should follow his method and style. It should be written in sections. It should combine scenes and stories with facts or concepts. If possible, you should also include statements by other experts. The "Questions for a Second Reading" should help as you prepare for this project.

• • • ● • • •

MAKING CONNECTIONS

1. In "The Vulnerable Observer" (p. 113), Ruth Behar writes about anthropology (a field that combines science and narrative) and about the difficult work of writing as an ethnographer — telling the truth about others through close observation. Michael Specter's essay, "The Gene Hackers," is about a different,

"harder" science—biochemistry. Specter is a journalist. He is not writing from the inside; he, like Behar, is fundamentally an observer. Is he a "vulnerable observer"?

If you read (or reread) "The Gene Hackers" through the lens of Behar's essay—in terms of both what it says and what it does (how it is written)—what do you see to be the significant differences between science journalism and ethnography? If these two essays could be said to represent two different career paths, two different routes to knowledge, which might you choose for a vocation—and why?

2. Michael Pollan in "Nutritionism Defined" (p. 490) and Atul Gawande in "Slow Ideas" (p. 362), like Michael Specter, write about science and public policy. Pollan and Specter are journalists; Gawande is a physician; all three are writers.

Write an essay that looks at one of these two selections, either "Nutritionism Defined" or "Slow Ideas," from the perspective of "The Gene Hackers." Where and how might they be said to speak to each other? How do they each understand the key issues in science as they relate to public policy? How do they represent the role of the essay as a form of engagement with science and with public policy? If you had to choose one of the two as exemplary—as an example of what we need more of if, as a nation, we are going to be able to make informed decisions about scientific research—which would you choose? and why?

One possible shape for your essay is to present your take, your point of view, on each reading, with summary and block quotation, and then to turn, in a third section, to the larger questions about journalism, science, and public policy.

3. Like all important science journalism, the writing in "The Gene Hackers" represents an impossible task. The article is designed to help us understand what we can't understand (because we lack the knowledge and the training). It attempts to translate advanced research into everyday terms.

There are several selections in this textbook that represent advanced research or advanced thought. They are difficult and challenging and yet are meant to speak to broad concerns. Here are three (you might choose others): John Berger, "Ways of Seeing" (p. 142); Judith Butler, "Beside Oneself: On the Limits of Sexual Autonomy" (p. 238); and Michel Foucault, "Panopticism" (p. 328). Choose one and, with Specter's essay as your point of reference, think about how it does and doesn't translate, tries and succeeds (or tries and fails) to translate, advanced thinking into everyday terms.

Think of this as an essay, then, on the difficult task of bringing a reader to understand something difficult. What are the significant achievements or failures in these two examples? What lessons can you draw—lessons that might apply to student writers (and readers) in an academic setting?

Anthony Barboza/Getty Images

JOHN EDGAR

Wideman

John Edgar Wideman was born in 1941 in Washington, D.C., but spent most of his youth in Homewood, a neighborhood in Pittsburgh. He earned a BA from the University of Pennsylvania and taught at the University of Wyoming and the University of Massachusetts at Amherst. He is currently Asa Messer Professor and professor of Africana studies and English at Brown University and sits on the board of the literary journal *Conjunctions*. In addition to the nonfiction work *Brothers and Keepers* (1984), from which this selection is drawn, Wideman has published a number of critically acclaimed works of fiction, including *The Lynchers* (1986); *Reuben* (1989); *Fever: Twelve Stories* (1989); *Philadelphia Fire: A Novel* (1991); and a series of novels set in Homewood: *Damballah* (1981), *Hiding Place* (1982), and *Sent for You Yesterday* (which won the 1984 PEN/Faulkner Award). The latter novels have been reissued as a set, titled *The Homewood Trilogy*. His most recent books include *The Cattle Killing* (1996), *Two Cities* (1998), *Hoop Roots* (2001), *The Island, Martinique* (2003), *God's Gym* (2005), *Fanon* (2008), and *Briefs* (2010). In 1994, Wideman published another work of nonfiction, *Fatheralong: A Meditation on Fathers and Sons, Race and Society*.

In the preface to *The Homewood Trilogy*, Wideman writes,

The value of black life in America is judged, as life generally in this country is judged, by external, material signs of success. Urban ghettoes are dangerous, broken-down, economically marginal pockets of real estate infected with drugs, poverty, violence, crime, and since black life is seen as rooted in the ghetto, black people are identified with the ugliness, danger, and deterioration surrounding them. This logic is simpleminded and devastating, its hold on the American imagination as old as slavery; in fact, it recycles the classic justification for slavery, blaming the cause and consequences of oppression on the oppressed. Instead of launching a preemptive strike at the flawed assumptions that perpetuate racist thinking, blacks and whites are doomed to battle endlessly with the symptoms of racism.

In these three books again bound as one I have set myself to the task of making concrete those invisible planes of existence that bear witness to the fact that black life, for all its material impoverishment, continues to thrive, to generate alternative styles, redemptive strategies, people who hope and cope. But more than attempting to prove a "humanity," which should be self-evident anyway to those not blinded by racism, my goal is to celebrate and affirm. *Where did I come from? Who am I? Where am I going?*

Brothers and Keepers is a family story; it is about Wideman and his brother Robby. John went to Oxford as a Rhodes Scholar, and Robby went to prison for his role in a robbery and a murder. In the section that follows, "Our Time," Wideman tries to understand his brother, their relationship, where they came from, where they are going. In this account, you will hear the voices of Robby, John, and people from the neighborhood, but also the voice of the writer, speaking about the difficulty of writing and the dangers of explaining away Robby's life.

Brothers and Keepers is not the first time Wideman has written to or about his brother. The first of the Homewood series, *Damballah*, is dedicated to Robby. The dedication reads:

> Stories are letters. Letters sent to anybody or everybody. But the best kind are meant to be read by a specific somebody. When you read that kind you know you are eavesdropping. You know a real person somewhere will read the same words you are reading and the story is that person's business and you are a ghost listening in.

> Remember. I think it was Geral I first heard call a watermelon a letter from home. After all these years I understand a little better what she meant. She was saying the melon is a letter addressed to us. A story for us from down home. Down Home being everywhere we've never been, the rural South, the old days, slavery, Africa. That juicy, striped message with red meat and seeds, which always looked like roaches to me, was blackness as cross and celebration, a history we could taste and chew. And it was meant for us. Addressed to us. We were meant to slit it open and take care of business.

> Consider all these stories as letters from home. I never liked watermelon as a kid. I think I remember you did. You weren't afraid of becoming instant nigger, of sitting barefoot and goggle-eyed and Day-Glo black and drippy-lipped on massa's fence if you took one bite of the forbidden fruit. I was too scared to enjoy watermelon. Too self-conscious. I let people rob me of a simple pleasure. Watermelon's still tainted for me. But I know better now. I can play with the idea even if I can't get down and have a natural ball eating a real one.

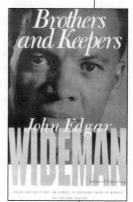

> Anyway . . . these stories are letters. Long overdue letters from me to you. I wish they could tear down the walls. I wish they could snatch you away from where you are.

Our Time

You remember what we were saying about young black men in the street-world life. And trying to understand why the "square world" becomes completely unattractive to them. It has to do with the fact that their world is the GHETTO and in that world all the glamour, all the praise and attention is given to the slick guy, the gangster especially, the ones that get over in the "life." And it's because we can't help but feel some satisfaction seeing a brother, a black man, get over on these people, on their system without playing by their rules. No matter how much we have incorporated these rules as our own, we know that they were forced on us by people who did not have our best interests at heart. So this hip guy, this gangster or player or whatever label you give these brothers that we like to shun because of the poison that they spread, we, black people, still look at them with some sense of pride and admiration, our children openly, us adults somewhere deep inside. We know they represent rebellion — what little is left in us. Well, having lived in the "life," it becomes very hard — almost impossible — to find any contentment in joining the status quo. Too hard to go back to being nobody in a world that hates you. Even if I had struck it rich in the life, I would have managed to throw it down the fast lane. Or have lost it on a revolutionary whim. Hopefully the latter.

I have always burned up in my fervent passions of desire and want. My senses at times tingle and itch with my romantic, idealistic outlook on life, which has always made me keep my distance from reality, reality that was a constant insult to my world, to my dream of happiness and peace, to my people-for-people kind of world, my easy-cars-for-a-nickel-or-a-dime sorta world. And these driving passions, this sensitivity to the love and good in people, also turned on me because I used it to play on people and their feelings. These aspirations of love and desire turned on me when I wasn't able to live up to this sweet-self morality, so I began to self-destruct, burning up in my sensitivity, losing direction, because nowhere could I find this world of truth and love and harmony.

In the real world, the world left for me, it was unacceptable to be "good," it was square to be smart in school, it was jive to show respect to people outside the street world, it was cool to be cold to your woman and the people that loved you. The things we liked we called "bad." "Man, that was a bad girl." The world of the angry black kid growing up in the sixties was a world in which to be in was to be out — out of touch with the square world and all of its rules on what's right and wrong. The thing was to make your own rules, do your own thing, but make sure it's contrary to what society says or is.

I SHALL ALWAYS PRAY

Garth looked bad. Real bad. Ichabod Crane anyway, but now he was a skeleton. Lying there in the bed with his bones poking through his skin, it made you want to cry. Garth's barely able to talk, his smooth, medium-brown skin yellow as pee. Ichabod legs and long hands and long feet, Garth could make you laugh just walking down the street. On the set you'd see him coming a far way off. Three-quarters leg so you knew it had to be Garth the way he was split up higher in the crotch than anybody else. Wilt the Stilt with a lean bird body perched on top his high waist. Size-fifteen shoes. Hands could palm a basketball easy as holding a pool cue. Fingers long enough to wrap round a basketball, but Garth couldn't play a lick. Never could get all that lankiness together on the court. You'd look at him sometimes as he was trucking down Homewood Avenue and think that nigger ain't walking, he's trying to remember how to walk. Awkward as a pigeon on roller skates. Knobby joints out of whack, arms and legs flailing, going their separate ways, his body jerking to keep them from going too far. Moving down the street like that wouldn't work, didn't make sense if you stood back and watched, if you pretended you hadn't seen Garth get where he was going a million times before. Nothing funny now, though. White hospital sheets pulled to his chest. Garth's head always looked small as a tennis ball way up there on his shoulders. Now it's a yellow, shrunken skull.

Ever since Robby had entered the ward, he'd wanted to reach over and hide his friend's arm under the covers. For two weeks Gar had been wasting away in the bed. Bad enough knowing Gar was dying. Didn't need that pitiful stick arm reminding him how close to nothing his main man had fallen. So fast. It could happen so fast. If Robby tried to raise that arm it would come off in his hand. As gentle as he could would not be gentle enough. The arm would disintegrate, like a long ash off the end of a cigarette.

Time to leave. No sense in sitting any longer. Garth not talking, no way of telling whether he was listening either. And Robby has nothing more to say. Choked up the way he gets inside hospitals. Hospital smell and quiet, the bare halls and bare floors, the echoes, something about all that he can't name, wouldn't try to name, rises in him and chills him. Like his teeth are chattering the whole time he's inside a hospital. Like his entire body is trembling uncontrollably, only nobody can see it or hear it but him. Shaking because he can't breathe the stuffy air. Hot and cold at the same time. He's been aching to leave since he entered the ward. Aching to get up and bust through the big glass front doors. Aching to pounce on that spidery arm flung back behind Gar's head. The arm too wasted to belong to his friend. He wants to grab it and hurl it away.

Robby pulls on tight white gloves the undertaker had dealt out to him and the rest of the pallbearers. His brown skin shows through the thin material, turns the white dingy. He's remembering that last time in Garth's ward. The hospital stink. Hot, chilly air. A bare arm protruding from the sleeve of the hospital gown, more dried-up toothpick than arm, a withered twig, with Garth's fingers like a bunch of skinny brown bananas drooping from the knobby tip.

Robby had studied the metal guts of the hospital bed, the black scuff marks swirling around the chair's legs. When he'd finally risen to go, his chair scraping against the vinyl floor broke a long silence. The noise must have roused Garth's attention. He'd spoken again.

You're good, man. Don't ever forget, Rob. You're the best.

Garth's first words since the little banter back and forth when Robby had entered the ward and dragged a chair to the side of Gar's bed. A whisper scarcely audible now that Robby was standing. Garth had tried to grin. The best he could manage was a pained adjustment of the bones of his face, no more than a shadow scudding across the yellow skull, but Robby had seen the famous smile. He hesitated, stopped rushing toward the door long enough to smile back. Because that was Gar. That was the way Gar was. He always had a smile and a good word for his cut buddies. Garth's grin was money in the bank. You could count on it like you could count on a good word from him. Something in his face would tell you you were alright, better than alright, that he believed in you, that you were, as he'd just whispered, "the best." You could depend on Garth to say something to make you feel good, even though you knew he was lying. With that grin greasing the lie you had to believe it, even though you knew better. Garth was the gang's dreamer. When he talked, you could see his dreams. That's why Robby had believed it, seen the grin, the bright shadow lighting Garth's face an instant. Out of nothing, out of pain, fear, the certainty of death gripping them both, Garth's voice had manufactured the grin.

Now they had to bury Garth. A few days after the visit to the hospital the phone rang and it was Garth's mother with the news of her son's death. Not really news. Robby had known it was just a matter of time. Of waiting for the moment when somebody else's voice would pronounce the words he'd said to himself a hundred times. *He's gone. Gar's dead.* Long gone before the telephone rang. Gar was gone when they stuck him up in the hospital bed. By the time they'd figured out what ailed him and admitted him to the hospital, it was too late. The disease had turned him to a skeleton. Nothing left of Garth to treat. They hid his messy death under white sheets, perfumed it with disinfectant, pumped him full of drugs so he wouldn't disturb his neighbors.

The others had squeezed into their pallbearers' gloves. Cheap white cotton gloves so you could use them once and throw them away like the rubber ones doctors wear when they stick their fingers up your ass. Michael, Cecil, and Sowell were pallbearers, too. With Robby and two men from Garth's family they would carry the coffin from Gaines Funeral Parlor to the hearse. Garth had been the dreamer for the gang. Robby counted four black fingers in the white glove. Garth was the thumb. The hand would be clumsy, wouldn't work right without him. Garth was different. But everybody else was different, too. Mike, the ice man, supercool. Cecil indifferent, ready to do most anything or nothing and couldn't care less which it was. Sowell wasn't really part of the gang; he didn't hang with them, didn't like to take the risks that were part of the "life." Sowell kept a good job. The "life" for him was just a way to make quick money. He didn't shoot up; he thought of himself as a businessman, an investor not a partner in their schemes. They knew Sowell mostly through Garth. Perhaps things would change now. The four survivors closer after they shared the burden of Gar's coffin, after they hoisted it and slid it on steel rollers into the back of Gaines's Cadillac hearse.

Robby was grateful for the gloves. He'd never been able to touch anything dead. He'd taken a beating once from his father rather than touch the bloody mousetrap his mother had nudged to the back door with her toe and ordered him to empty. The brass handle of the coffin felt damp through the glove. He gripped tighter to stop the flow of blood or sweat, whatever it was leaking from him or seeping from the metal. Garth had melted down to nothing by the end so it couldn't be him nearly yanking off Robby's shoulder when the box shifted and its weight shot forward. Felt like a coffin full of bricks. Robby stared across at Mike but Mike was a soldier, eyes front, riveted to the yawning rear door of the hearse. Mike's eyes wouldn't admit it, but they'd almost lost the coffin. They were rookie pallbearers and maneuvering down the carpeted front steps of Gaines Funeral Parlor they'd almost let Garth fly out their hands. They needed somebody who knew what he was doing. An old, steady head to show them the way. They needed Garth. But Garth was long gone. Ashes inside the steel box.

They began drinking later that afternoon in Garth's people's house. Women and food in one room, men hitting the whiskey hard in another. It was a typical project apartment. The kind everybody had stayed in or visited one time or another. Small, shabby, featureless. Not a place to live. No matter what you did to it, how clean you kept it or what kind of furniture you loaded it with, the walls and ceilings were not meant to be home for anybody. A place you passed through. Not yours, because the people who'd been there before you left their indelible marks everywhere and you couldn't help adding your bruises and knots for the next tenants. You could rent a kitchen and bedroom and a bathroom and a living room, the project flats were laid out so you had a room for each of the things people did in houses. Problem was, every corner was cut. Living cramped is one thing and people can get cozy in the closest quarters. It's another thing to live in a place designed to be just a little less than adequate. No slack, no space to personalize, to stamp the flat with what's peculiar to your style. Like a man sitting on a toilet seat that's too small and the toilet too close to the bathtub so his knees shove against the enamel edge. He can move his bowels that way and plenty of people in the world have a lot less but he'll never enjoy sitting there, never feel the deep down comfort of belonging where he must squat.

Anyway, the whiskey started flowing in that little project apartment. Robby listened, for Garth's sake, as long as he could to old people reminiscing about funerals they'd attended, about all the friends and relatives they'd escorted to the edge of Jordan, old folks sipping good whiskey and moaning and groaning till it seemed a sin to be left behind on this side of the river after so many saints had crossed over. He listened to people express their grief, tell sad, familiar stories. As he got high he listened less closely to the words. Faces and gestures revealed more than enough. When he split with Mike and Cecil and their ladies, Sowell tagged along. By then the tacky, low-ceilinged rooms of the flat were packed. Loud talk, laughter, storytellers competing for audiences. Robby half expected the door he pushed shut behind himself to pop open again, waited for bottled-up noise to explode into the funky hallway.

Nobody thinking about cemeteries now. Nobody else needs to be buried today, so it was time to get it on. Some people had been getting close to rowdy. Some people had been getting mad. Mad at one of the guests in the apartment, mad at doctors and hospitals and whites in general who had the whole world in their hands but didn't have the slightest idea what to do with it. A short, dark man, bubble-eyed, immaculately dressed in a three-piece, wool, herringbone suit, had railed about the callousness, the ignorance of white witch doctors who, by misdiagnosing Garth's illness, had sealed his doom. His harangue had drawn a crowd. He wasn't just talking, he was testifying, and a hush had fallen over half the room as he dissected the dirty tricks of white folks. If somebody ran to the hospital and snatched a white-coated doctor and threw him into the circle surrounding the little fish-eyed man, the mourners would tear the pale-faced devil apart. Robby wished he could feed them one. Remembered Garth weak and helpless in the bed and the doctors and nurses flitting around in the halls, jiving the other patients, ignoring Gar like he wasn't there. Garth was dead because he had believed them. Dead because he had nowhere else to turn when the pain in his gut and the headaches grew worse and worse. Not that he trusted the doctors or believed they gave a flying fuck about him. He'd just run out of choices and had to put himself in their hands. They told him jaundice was his problem, and while his liver rotted away and pain cooked him dizzy Garth assured anyone who asked that it was just a matter of giving the medicine time to work. To kill the pain he blew weed as long as he had strength to hold a joint between his lips. Take a whole bunch of smoke to cool me out these days. Puffing like a chimney till he lost it and fell back and Robby scrambling to grab the joint before Garth torched hisself.

When you thought about it, Garth's dying made no sense. And the more you thought the more you dug that nothing else did neither. The world's a stone bitch. Nothing true if that's not true. The man had you coming and going. He owned everything worth owning and all you'd ever get was what he didn't want anymore, what he'd chewed and spit out and left in the gutter for niggers to fight over. Garth had pointed to the street and said, If we ever make it, it got to come from there, from the curb. We got to melt that rock till we get us some money. He grinned then, Ain't no big thing. We'll make it, brother man. We got what it takes. It's our time.

Something had crawled in Garth's belly. The man said it wasn't nothing. Sold him some aspirins and said he'd be alright in no time. The man
killed Garth. Couldn't kill him no deader with a .357 magnum slug, but
ain't no crime been committed. Just one those things. You know, everybody
makes mistakes. And a dead nigger ain't really such a big mistake when
you think about it. Matter of fact you mize well forget the whole thing.
Nigger wasn't going nowhere, nohow. I mean he wasn't no brain surgeon
or astronaut, no movie star or big-time athlete. Probably a dope fiend or
gangster. Wind up killing some innocent person or wasting another nigger. Shucks. That doctor ought to get a medal.

Hey, man. Robby caught Mike's eye. Then Cecil and Sowell turned to
him. They knew he was speaking to everybody. Late now. Ten, eleven, because it had been dark outside for hours. Quiet now. Too quiet in his pad.
And too much smoke and drink since the funeral. From a bare bulb in the
kitchen ceiling light seeped down the hallway and hovered dimly in the
doorway of the room where they sat. Robby wondered if the others felt as
bad as he did. If the cemetery clothes itched their skin. If they could smell
grave dust on their shoes. He hoped they'd finish this last jug of wine and
let the day be over. He needed sleep, downtime to get the terrible weight
of Garth's death off his mind. He'd been grateful for the darkness. For the
company of his cut buddies after the funeral. For the Sun Ra tape until it
ended and plunged them into a deeper silence than any he'd ever known.
Garth was gone. In a few days people would stop talking about him. He
was in the ground. Stone-cold dead. Robby had held a chunk of crumbly
ground in his white-gloved fingers and mashed it and dropped the dust
into the hole. Now the ground had closed over Garth and what did it
mean? Here one day and gone the next and that was that. They'd bury
somebody else out of Gaines tomorrow. People would dress up and cry
and get drunk and tell lies and next day it'd be somebody else's turn to die.
Which one of the shadows in this black room would go first? What did it
matter? Who cared? Who would remember their names; they were ghosts
already. Dead as Garth already. Only difference was, Garth didn't have it
to worry about no more. Garth didn't have to pretend he was going anywhere cause he was there. He'd made it to the place they all were headed
fast as their legs could carry them. Every step was a step closer to the
stone-cold ground, the pitch-black hole where they'd dropped Garth's
body.

Hey, youall. We got to drink to Garth one last time.

They clinked glasses in the darkness. Robby searched for something
to say. The right words wouldn't come. He knew there was something
proper and precise that needed to be said. Because the exact words eluded
him, because only the right words would do, he swallowed his gulp of
heavy, sweet wine in silence.

He knew he'd let Garth down. If it had been one of the others dead,
Michael or Cecil or Sowell or him, Garth wouldn't let it slide by like this,
wouldn't let it end like so many other nights had ended, the fellows nodding off one by one, stupefied by smoke and drink, each one beginning to

trace the seemingly random inconveniences and impositions coloring her life to their source in a master plan.

I first heard Garth's story in the summer of 1975, the summer my wife carried our daughter Jamila in her belly, the summer before the robbery and killing. The story contained all the clues I'm trying to decipher now. Sitting in the kitchen vaguely distracted by gospel music from the little clock radio atop the table, listening as my mother expressed her sorrow, her indignation at the way Garth was treated, her fears for my brother, I was hearing a new voice. Something about the voice struck me then, but I missed what was novel and crucial. I'd lost my Homewood ear. Missed all the things unsaid that invested her words with special urgency. People in Homewood often ask: You said that to say what? The impacted quality of an utterance either buries a point too obscurely or insists on a point so strongly that the listener wants the meat of the message repeated, wants it restated clearly so it stands alone on its own two feet. If I'd been alert enough to ask that question, to dig down to the root and core of Garth's story after my mother told it, I might have understood sooner how desperate and dangerous Homewood had become. Six years later my brother was in prison, and when he began the story of his troubles with Garth's death, a circle completed itself; Robby was talking to me, but I was still on the outside, looking in.

That day six years later, I talked with Robby three hours, the maximum allotted for weekday visits with a prisoner. It was the first time in life we'd ever talked that long. Probably two and a half hours longer than the longest, unbroken, private conversation we'd ever had. And it had taken guards, locks, and bars to bring us together. The ironies of the situation, the irony of that fact, escaped neither of us.

I WAS HEARING A NEW VOICE. SOMETHING ABOUT THE VOICE STRUCK ME THEN, BUT I MISSED WHAT WAS NOVEL AND CRUCIAL. I'D LOST MY HOMEWOOD EAR.

I listened mostly, interrupting my brother's story a few times to clarify dates or names. Much of what he related was familiar. The people, the places. Even the voice, the words he chose were mine in a way. We're so alike, I kept thinking, anticipating what he would say next, how he would say it, filling in naturally, easily with my words what he left unsaid. Trouble was our minds weren't interchangeable. No more than our bodies. The guards wouldn't have allowed me to stay in my brother's place. He was the criminal. I was the visitor from outside. Different as night and day. As Robby talked I let myself forget that difference. Paid too much attention to myself listening and lost some of what he was saying. What I missed would have helped define the difference. But I missed it. It was easy to half listen. For both of us to pretend to be closer than we were. We needed the closeness. We were brothers. In the prison visiting lounge I acted toward my brother the way I'd been acting toward him all my life, heard what I wanted to hear, rejected the rest.

When Robby talked, the similarity of his Homewood and mine was a trap. I could believe I knew exactly what he was describing. I could relax into his story, walk down Dunfermline or Tioga, see my crippled grandmother sitting on the porch of the house on Finance, all the color her pale face had lost blooming in the rosebush beneath her in the yard, see Robby in the downstairs hall of the house on Marchand, rapping with his girl on the phone, which sat on a three-legged stand just inside the front door. I'd slip unaware out of his story into one of my own. I'd be following him, an obedient shadow, then a cloud would blot the sun and I'd be gone, unchained, a dark form still skulking behind him but no longer in tow.

The hardest habit to break, since it was the habit of a lifetime, would be listening to myself listen to him. That habit would destroy any chance of seeing my brother on his terms; and seeing him in his terms, learning his terms, seemed the whole point of learning his story. However numerous and comforting the similarities, we were different. The world had seized on the difference, allowed me room to thrive, while he'd been forced into a cage. Why did it work out that way? What was the nature of the difference? Why did it haunt me? Temporarily at least, to answer these questions, I had to root my fiction-writing self out of our exchanges. I had to teach myself to listen. Start fresh, clear the pipes, resist too facile an identification, tame the urge to take off with Robby's story and make it my own.

I understood all that, but could I break the habit? And even if I did learn to listen, wouldn't there be a point at which I'd have to take over the telling? Wasn't there something fundamental in my writing, in my capacity to function, that depended on flight, on escape? Wasn't another person's skin a hiding place, a place to work out anxiety, to face threats too intimidating to handle in any other fashion? Wasn't writing about people a way of exploiting them?

A stranger's gait, or eyes, or a piece of clothing can rivet my attention. Then it's like falling down to the center of the earth. Not exactly fear or panic but an uneasy, uncontrollable momentum, a sense of being swallowed, engulfed in blackness that has no dimensions, no fixed points. That boundless, incarcerating black hole is another person. The detail grabbing me functions as a door and it swings open and I'm drawn, sucked, pulled in head over heels till suddenly I'm righted again, on track again and the peculiarity, the ordinariness of the detail that usurped my attention becomes a window, a way of seeing out of another person's eyes, just as for a second it had been my way in. I'm scooting along on short, stubby legs and the legs are not anybody else's and certainly not mine, but I feel for a second what it's like to motor through the world atop these peculiar duck thighs and foreshortened calves and I know how wobbly the earth feels under those run-over-at-the-heel, split-seamed penny loafers. Then just as suddenly I'm back. I'm me again, slightly embarrassed, guilty because I've been trespassing and don't know how long I've been gone or if anybody noticed me violating somebody else's turf.

Do I write to escape, to make a fiction of my life? If I can't be trusted with the story of my own life, how could I ask my brother to trust me with his?

The business of making a book together was new for both of us. Difficult. Awkward. Another book could be constructed about a writer who goes to a prison to interview his brother but comes away with his own story. The conversations with his brother would provide a stage for dramatizing the writer's tortured relationship to other people, himself, his craft. The writer's motives, the issue of exploitation, the inevitable conflict between his role as detached observer and his responsibility as a brother would be at the center of such a book. When I stopped hearing Robby and listened to myself listening, that kind of book shouldered its way into my consciousness. I didn't like the feeling. That book compromised the intimacy I wanted to achieve with my brother. It was as obtrusive as the Wearever pen in my hand, the little yellow sheets of Yard Count paper begged from the pad of the guard in charge of overseeing the visiting lounge. The borrowed pen and paper (I was not permitted into the lounge with my own) were necessary props. I couldn't rely on memory to get my brother's story down and the keepers had refused my request to use a tape recorder, so there I was. Jimmy Olson, cub reporter, poised on the edge of my seat, pen and paper at ready, asking to be treated as a brother.

We were both rookies. Neither of us had learned very much about sharing our feelings with other family members. At home it had been assumed that each family member possessed deep, powerful feelings and that very little or nothing at all needed to be said about these feelings because we all were stuck with them and talk wouldn't change them. Your particular feelings were a private matter and family was a protective fence around everybody's privacy. Inside the perimeter of the fence each family member resided in his or her own quarters. What transpired in each dwelling was mainly the business of its inhabitant as long as nothing generated within an individual unit threatened the peace or safety of the whole. None of us knew how traditional West African families were organized or what values the circular shape of their villages embodied, but the living arrangements we had worked out among ourselves resembled the ancient African patterns. You were granted emotional privacy, independence, and space to commune with your feelings. You were encouraged to deal with as much as you could on your own, yet you never felt alone. The high wall of the family, the collective, communal reality of other souls, other huts like yours eliminated some of the dread, the isolation experienced when you turned inside and tried to make sense out of the chaos of your individual feelings. No matter how grown you thought you were or how far you believed you'd strayed, you knew you could cry *Mama* in the depths of the night and somebody would tend to you. Arms would wrap round you, a soft soothing voice lend its support. If not a flesh-and-blood mother then a mother in the form of song or story or a surrogate, Aunt Geral, Aunt Martha, drawn from the network of family numbers.

Privacy was a bridge between you and the rest of the family. But you had to learn to control the traffic. You had to keep it uncluttered, resist the temptation to cry wolf. Privacy in our family was a birthright, a union card granted with family membership. The card said you're one of us but also certified your separateness, your obligation to keep much of what defined your separateness to yourself.

An almost aesthetic consideration's involved. Okay, let's live together. Let's each build a hut and for security we'll arrange the individual dwellings in a circle and then build an outer ring to enclose the whole village. Now your hut is your own business, but let's in general agree on certain outward forms. Since we all benefit from the larger pattern, let's compromise, conform to some degree on the materials, the shape of each unit. Because symmetry and harmony please the eye. Let's adopt a style, one that won't crimp anybody's individuality, one that will buttress and enhance each member's image of what a living place should be.

So Robby and I faced each other in the prison visiting lounge as familiar strangers, linked by blood and time. But how do you begin talking about blood, about time? He's been inside his privacy and I've been inside mine, and neither of us in thirty-odd years had felt the need to exchange more than social calls. We shared the common history, values, and style developed within the tall stockade of family, and that was enough to make us care about each other, enough to insure a profound depth of mutual regard, but the feelings were undifferentiated. They'd seldom been tested specifically, concretely. His privacy and mine had been exclusive, sanctioned by family traditions. Don't get too close. Don't ask too many questions or give too many answers. Don't pry. Don't let what's inside slop out on the people around you.

The stories I'd sent to Robby were an attempt to reveal what I thought about certain matters crucial to us both. Our shared roots and destinies. I wanted him to know what I'd been thinking and how that thinking was drawing me closer to him. I was banging on the door of his privacy. I believed I'd shed some of my own.

We were ready to talk. It was easy to begin. Impossible. We were neophytes, rookies. I was a double rookie. A beginner at this kind of intimacy, a beginner at trying to record it. My double awkwardness kept getting in the way. I'd hidden the borrowed pen by dropping my hand below the level of the table where we sat. Now when in hell would be the right moment to raise it? To use it? I had to depend on my brother's instincts, his generosity. I had to listen, listen.

Luckily there was catching up to do. He asked me about my kids, about his son, Omar, about the new nieces and nephews he'd never seen. That helped. Reminded us we were brothers. We got on with it. Conditions in the prisons. Robby's state of mind. The atmosphere behind the prison walls had been particularly tense for over a year. A group of new, younger guards had instituted a get-tough policy. More strip searches, cell shakedowns, strict enforcement of penny-ante rules and regulations. Grown men treated like children by other grown men. Inmates yanked out of line and punished because a button is undone or hair uncombed. What politicians demanded in the free world was being acted out inside the prison. A crusade, a war on crime waged by a gang of gung-ho guards against men who were already certified casualties, prisoners of war. The walking wounded being beaten and shot up again because they're easy targets. Robby's closest friends, including Cecil and Mike, are in the hole. Others who were considered potential troublemakers had been transferred to harsher prisons. Robby was warned by a guard. We ain't caught you in the shit yet, but we will. We know what you're thinking and we'll catch you in it. Or put you in it. Got your buddies and we'll get you.

The previous summer, 1980, a prisoner, Leon Patterson, had been asphyxiated in his cell. He was an asthma sufferer, a convicted murderer who depended on medication to survive the most severe attacks of his illness. On a hot August afternoon when the pollution index had reached its highest count of the summer, Patterson was locked in his cell in a cell block without windows and little air. At four o'clock, two hours after he'd been confined to the range, he began to call for help. Other prisoners raised the traditional distress signal, rattling tin cups against the bars of their cells. Patterson's cries for help became screams, and his fellow inmates beat on the bars and shouted with him. Over an hour passed before any guards arrived. They carted away Patterson's limp body. He never revived and was pronounced dead at 10:45 that evening. His death epitomized the polarization in the prison. Patterson was seen as one more victim of the guards' inhumanity. A series of incidents followed in the ensuing year, hunger strikes, melees between guards and prisoners, culminating in a near massacre when the dog days of August hung once more over the prison.

One of the favorite tactics of the militant guards was grabbing a man from the line as the prisoners moved single-file through an archway dividing the recreation yard from the main cell blocks. No reason was given or needed. It was a simple show of force, a reminder of the guards' absolute power, their right to treat the inmates any way they chose, and do it with impunity. A sit-down strike in the prison auditorium followed one of the more violent attacks on an inmate. The prisoner who had resisted an arbitrary seizure and strip search was smacked in the face. He punched back and the guards jumped him, knocked him to the ground with their fists and sticks. The incident took place in plain view of over a hundred prisoners and it was the last straw. The victim had been provoked, as-saulted, and surely would be punished for attempting to protect himself, for doing what any man would and should do in similar circumstances. The prisoner would suffer again. In addition to the physical beating they'd administered, the guards would attack the man's record. He'd be written up. A kangaroo court would take away his *good time*, thereby lengthening the period he'd have to wait before becoming eligible for probation or parole. Finally, on the basis of the guards' testimony he'd probably get a sixty-day sojourn in the hole. The prisoners realized it was time to take a stand. What had happened to one could happen to any of them. They rushed into the auditorium and locked themselves in. The prisoners held out till armed state troopers and prison guards in riot gear surrounded the building. Given the mood of that past year and the unmistakable threat in the new warden's voice as he repeated through a loudspeaker his refusal to meet with the prisoners and discuss their grievances, everybody inside the building knew that the authorities meant business, that the forces of law and order would love nothing better than an excuse to turn the auditorium into a shooting gallery. The strike was broken. The men filed out. A point was driven home again. Prisoners have no rights the keepers are bound to respect.

That was how the summer had gone. Summer was bad enough in the penitentiary in the best of times. Warm weather stirred the prisoners' blood. The siren call of the streets intensified. Circus time. The street blooming again after the long, cold winter. People outdoors. On their stoops. On the corners. In bright summer clothes or hardly any clothes at all. The free-world sounds and sights more real as the weather heats up. Confinement a torture. Each cell a hotbox. The keepers take advantage of every excuse to keep you out of the yard, to deprive you of the simple pleasure of a breeze, the blue sky. Why? So that the pleasant weather can be used as a tool, a boon to be withheld. So punishment has a sharper edge. By a perverse turn of the screw something good becomes something bad. Summer a bitch at best, but this past summer as the young turks among the guards ran roughshod over the prisoners, the prison had come close to blowing, to exploding like a piece of rotten fruit in the sun. And if the lid blew, my brother knew he'd be one of the first to die. During any large-scale uprising, in the first violent, chaotic seconds no board of inquiry would ever be able to reconstruct, scores would be settled. A bullet in the back of the brain would get rid of troublemakers, remove potential leaders, uncontrollable prisoners the guards hated and feared. You were supremely eligible for a bullet if the guards couldn't press your button. If they hadn't learned how to manipulate you, if you couldn't be bought or sold, if you weren't into drug and sex games, if you weren't cowed or depraved, then you were a threat.

Robby understood that he was sentenced to die. That all sentences were death sentences. If he didn't buckle under, the guards would do everything in their power to kill him. If he succumbed to the pressure to surrender dignity, self-respect, control over his own mind and body, then he'd become a beast, and what was good in him would die. The death sentence was unambiguous. The question for him became: How long could he survive in spite of the death sentence? Nothing he did would guarantee his safety. A disturbance in a cell block halfway across the prison could provide an excuse for shooting him and dumping him with the other victims. Anytime he was ordered to go with guards out of sight of other prisoners, his escorts could claim he attacked them, or attempted to escape. Since the flimsiest pretext would make murdering him acceptable, he had no means of protecting himself. Yet to maintain sanity, to minimize their opportunities to destroy him, he had to be constantly vigilant. He had to discipline himself to avoid confrontations, he had to weigh in terms of life and death every decision he made; he had to listen and obey his keepers' orders, but he also had to determine in certain threatening situations whether it was better to say no and keep himself out of a trap or take his chances that this particular summons was not the one inviting him to his doom. Of course to say no perpetuated his reputation as one who couldn't be controlled, a bad guy, a guy you never turn your back on, one of the prisoners out to get the guards. That rap made you more dangerous in the keepers' eyes and therefore increased the likelihood they'd be frightened into striking first. Saying no put you in no less jeopardy than going along with the program. Because the program was contrived to kill you. Directly or indirectly, you knew where you were headed. What you didn't know was the schedule. Tomorrow. Next week. A month. A minute. When would one of them get itchy, get beyond waiting a second longer? Would there be a plan, a contrived incident, a conspiracy they'd talk about and set up as they drank coffee in the guards' room or would it be the hair-trigger impulse of one of them who held a grudge, harbored an antipathy so elemental, so irrational that it could express itself only in a burst of pure, unrestrained violence?

If you're Robby and have the will to survive, these are the possibilities you must constantly entertain. Vigilance is the price of survival. Beneath the vigilance, however, is a gnawing awareness boiling in the pit of your stomach. You can be as vigilant as you're able, you can keep fighting the good fight to survive, and still your fate is out of your hands. If they decide to come for you in the morning, that's it. Your ass is grass and those minutes, and hours, days and years you painfully stitched together to put off the final reckoning won't matter at all. So the choice, difficult beyond words, to say yes or say no is made in light of the knowledge that in the end neither your yes nor your no matters. Your life is not in your hands.

The events, the atmosphere of the summer had brought home to Robby the futility of resistance. Power was absurdly apportioned all on one side. To pretend you could control your own destiny was a joke. You learned to laugh at your puniness, as you laughed at the stink of your farts lighting up your cell. Like you laughed at the seriousness of the masturbation ritual that romanticized, cloaked in darkness and secrecy, the simple, hungry shaking of your penis in your fist. You had no choice, but you always had to decide to go on or stop. It had been a stuttering, stop, start, maybe, fuck it, bitch of a summer, and now, for better or worse, we were starting up something else. Robby backtracks his story from Garth to another beginning, the house on Copeland Street in Shadyside where we lived when he was born.

I know that had something to do with it. Living in Shadyside with only white people around. You remember how it was. Except for us and them couple other families it was a all-white neighborhood. I got a thing about black. See, black was like the forbidden fruit. Even when we went to Freed's in Homewood, Geraldine and them never let me go no farther than the end of the block. All them times I stayed over there I didn't go past Mr. Conrad's house by the vacant lot or the other corner where Billy Shields and them stayed. Started to wondering what was so different about a black neighborhood. I was just a little kid and I was curious.

I really wanted to know why they didn't want me finding out what was over there. Be playing with the kids next door to Freed, you know, Sonny and Gumpy and them, but all the time I'm wondering what's round the corner, what's up the street. Didn't care if it was *bad* or good or dangerous or what, I had to find out. If it's something bad I figured they would have told me, tried to scare me off. But nobody said nothing except, No. Don't you go no farther than the corner. Then back home in Shadyside nothing but white people so I couldn't ask nobody what was special about black. Black was a mystery and in my mind I decided I'd find out what it was all about. Didn't care if it killed me, I was going to find out.

One time, it was later, I was close to starting high school, I overheard Mommy and Geraldine and Sissy talking in Freed's kitchen. They was talking about us moving from Shadyside back to Homewood. The biggest thing they was worried about was me. How would it be for me being in Homewood and going to Westinghouse? I could tell they was scared. Specially Mom. You know how she is. She didn't want to move. Homewood scared her. Not so much the place but how I'd act if I got out there in the middle of it. She already knew I was wild, hard to handle. There'd be too much mess for me to get into in Homewood. She could see trouble coming.

And she was right. Me and trouble hooked up. See, it was a question of being somebody. Being my own person. Like youns had sports and good grades sewed up. Wasn't nothing I could do in school or sports that youns hadn't done already. People said, Here comes another Wideman. He's gon be a good student like his brothers and sister. That's the way it was spozed to be. I was another Wideman, the last one, the baby, and everybody knew how I was spozed to act. But something inside me said no. Didn't want to be like the rest of youns. Me, I had to be a rebel. Had to get out from under youns' good grades and do. Way back then I decided I wanted to be a star. I wanted to make it big. My way. I wanted the glamour. I wanted to sit high up.

Figured out school and sports wasn't the way. I got to thinking my brothers and sister was squares. Loved youall but wasn't no room left for me. Had to figure out a new territory. I had to be a rebel.

Along about junior high I discovered Garfield. I started hanging out up on Garfield Hill. You know, partying and stuff in Garfield cause that's where the niggers was. Garfield was black, and I finally found what I'd been looking for. That place they was trying to hide from me. It was heaven. You know. Hanging out with the fellows. Drinking wine and trying anything else we could get our hands on. And the ladies. Always a party on the weekends. Had me plenty sweet little soft-leg Garfield ladies. Niggers run my butt off that hill more than a couple times behind messing with somebody's piece but I'd be back next weekend. Cause I'd found heaven. Looking back now, wasn't much to Garfield. Just a rinky-dink ghetto up on a hill, but it was the street. I'd found my place.

Having a little bit of a taste behind me I couldn't wait to get to Homewood. In a way I got mad with Mommy and the rest of them. Seemed to me like they was trying to hold me back from a good time. Seemed like they just didn't want me to have no fun. That's when I decided I'd go on about my own business. Do it my way. Cause I wasn't getting no slack at home. They still expected me to be like my sister and brothers. They didn't know I thought youns was squares. Yeah. I knew I was hipper and groovier than youns ever thought of being. Streetwise, into something. Had my own territory and I was bad. I was a rebel. Wasn't following in nobody's footsteps but my own. And I was a hip cookie, you better believe it. Wasn't a hipper thing out there than your brother, Rob. I couldn't wait for them to turn me loose in Homewood.

Me being the youngest and all, the baby in the family, people always said, ain't he cute. That Robby gon be a ladykiller. Been hearing that mess since day one so ain't no surprise I started to believing it. Youns had me pegged as a lady's man so that's what I was. The girls be talking the same trash everybody else did. Ain't he cute. Be petting me and spoiling me like I'm still the baby of the family and I sure ain't gon tell them stop. Thought I was cute as the girls be telling me. Thought sure enough, I'm gon be a star. I loved to get up and show my behind. Must have been good at it too cause the teacher used to call me up in front of the class to perform. The kids'd get real quiet. That's probably why the teacher got me up. Keep the class quiet while she nods off. Cause they'd listen to me. Sure nuff pay attention.

Performing always come natural to me. Wasn't nervous or nothing. Just get up and do my thing. They liked for me to do impressions. I could mimic anybody. You remember how I'd do that silly stuff around the house. Anybody I'd see on TV or hear on a record I could mimic to a T. Bob Hope, Nixon, Smokey Robinson, Ed Sullivan. White or black. I could talk just like them or sing a song just like they did. The class yell out a famous name and I'd do the one they wanted to hear. If things had gone another way I've always believed I could have made it big in show business. If you could keep them little frisky kids in Liberty School quiet you could handle any audience. Always could sing and do impressions. You remember Mom asking me to do them for you when you came home from college.

I still be performing. Read poetry in the hole. The other fellows get real quiet and listen. Sing down in there too. Nothing else to do, so we entertain each other. They always asking me to sing or read. "Hey, Wideman. C'mon man and do something." Then it gets quiet while they waiting for me to start. Quiet and it's already dark. You in your own cell and can't see nobody else. Barely enough light to read by. The other fellows can hear you but it's just you and them walls so it feels like being alone much as it feels like you're singing or reading to somebody else.

Yeah. I read my own poems sometimes. Other times I just start in on whatever book I happen to be reading. One the books you sent me, maybe. Fellows like my poems. They say I write about the things they be thinking. Say it's like listening to their own self thinking. That's cause we all down there together. What else you gonna do but think of the people on the outside. Your woman. Your kids or folks, if you got any. Just the same old sad shit we all be thinking all the time. That's what I write and the fellows like to hear it.

Funny how things go around like that. Go round and round and keep coming back to the same place. Teacher used to get me up to pacify the class and I'm doing the same thing in prison. You said your teachers called on you to tell stories, didn't they? Yeah. It's funny how much we're alike. In spite of everything I always believed that. Inside. The feeling side. I always believed we was the most alike out of all the kids. I see stuff in your books. The kinds of things I be thinking or feeling.

Your teachers got you up, too. To tell stories. That's funny, ain't it.

I listen to my brother Robby. He unravels my voice. I sit with him in the darkness of the Behavioral Adjustment Unit. My imagination creates something like a giant seashell, enfolding, enclosing us. Its inner surface is velvet-soft and black. A curving mirror doubling the darkness. Poems are Jean Toomer's petals of dusk, petals of dawn. I want to stop. Savor the sweet, solitary pleasure, the time stolen from time in the hole. But the image I'm creating is a trick of the glass. The mirror that would swallow Robby and then chime to me: You're the fairest of them all. The voice I hear issues from a crack in the glass. I'm two or three steps ahead of my brother, making fiction out of his words. Somebody needs to snatch me by the neck and say, Stop. Stop and listen, listen to him.

The Behavioral Adjustment Unit is, as one guard put it, "a maximum-security prison within a maximum-security prison." The "Restricted Housing Unit" or "hole" or "Home Block" is a squat, two-story cement building containing thirty-five six-by-eight-foot cells. The governor of Pennsylvania

> **I LISTEN TO MY BROTHER ROBBY.**
> **HE UNRAVELS MY VOICE.**

closed the area in 1972 because of "inhumane conditions," but within a year the hole was reopened. For at least twenty-three hours a day the prisoners are confined to their cells. An hour of outdoor exercise is permitted only on days the guards choose to supervise it. Two meals are served three hours apart, then nothing except coffee and bread for the next twenty-one. The regulation that limits the time an inmate can serve in the BAU for a single offense is routinely sidestepped by the keepers. "Administrative custody" is a provision allowing officials to cage men in the BAU indefinitely. Hunger strikes are one means the prisoners have employed to protest the harsh conditions of the penal unit. Hearings prompted by the strikes have produced no major changes in the way the hole operates. Law, due process, the rights of the prisoners are irrelevant to the functioning of this prison within a prison. Robby was sentenced to six months in the BAU because a guard suspected he was involved in an attempted escape. The fact that a hearing, held six months later, established Robby's innocence, was small consolation since he'd already served his time in the hole.

Robby tells me about the other side of being the youngest: Okay, you're everybody's pet and that's boss, but on the other hand you sometimes feel you're the least important. Always last. Always bringing up the rear. You learn to do stuff on your own because the older kids are always busy, off doing their things, and you're too young, left behind because you don't fit, or just because they forget you're back here, at the end, bringing up the rear. But when orders are given out, you sure get your share. "John's coming home this weekend. Clean up your room." Robby remembers being forced to get a haircut on the occasion of one of my visits. Honor thy brother. Get your hair cut, your room rid up, and put on clean clothes. He'll be here with his family and I don't want the house looking like a pigpen.

I have to laugh at the image of myself as somebody to get a haircut for. Robby must have been fit to be tied.

Yeah, I was hot. I mean, you was doing well and all that, but shit, you were my brother. And it was my head. What's my head got to do with you? But you know how Mommy is. Ain't no talking to her when her mind gets set. Anything I tried to say was "talking *back*," so I just went ahead to the man and got my ears lowered.

I was trying to be a rebel but back then the most important thing still was what the grown-ups thought about me. How they felt meant everything. Everything. Me and Tish and Dave were the ones at home then. You was gone and Gene was gone so it was the three of us fighting for attention. And we fought. Every crumb, everytime something got cut up or parceled out or it was Christmas or Easter, we so busy checking out what the other one got wasn't hardly no time to enjoy our own. Like a dogfight or cat fight all the time. And being the youngest I'm steady losing ground most the time. Seemed like to me, Tish and Dave the ones everybody talked about. Seemed like my time would never come. That ain't the way it really was, I know. I had my share cause I was the baby and ain't he cute and lots of times I know I got away with outrageous stuff or got my way cause I could play that baby mess to the hilt. Still it seemed like Dave and Tish was the ones really mattered. Mommy and Daddy and Sis and Geral and Big Otie and Ernie always slipping some change in their pockets or taking them to the store or letting them stay over all night in Homewood. I was a jealous little rascal. Sometimes I thought everybody thought I was just a spoiled brat. I'd say damn all youall. I'd think, Go on and love those square turkeys, but one day I'll be the one coming back with a suitcase full of money and a Cadillac. Go on and love them good grades. Robby gon do it his own way.

See, in my mind I was Superfly. I'd drive up slow to the curb. My hog be half a block long and these fine foxes in the back. Everybody looking when I ease out the door clean and mean. Got a check in my pocket to give to Mom. Buy her a new house with everything in it new. Pay her back for the hard times. I could see that happening as real as I can see your face right now. Wasn't no way it wasn't gon happen. Rob was gon make it big. I'd be at the door, smiling with the check in my hand and Mommy'd be so happy she'd be crying.

Well, it's a different story ain't it. Turned out different from how I used to think it would. The worst thing I did, the thing I feel most guilty behind is stealing Mom's life. It's like I stole her youth. Can't nothing change that.

I can't give back what's gone. Robbing white people didn't cause me to lose no sleep back then. Couldn't feel but so bad about that. How you gon feel sorry when society's so corrupt, when everybody got their hand out or got their hand in somebody else's pocket and ain't no rules nobody listens to if they can get away with breaking them? How you gon apply the rules? It was dog eat dog out there, so how was I spozed to feel sorry if I was doing what everybody else doing. I just got caught is all. I'm sorry about that, and damned sorry that guy Stavros got killed, but as far as what I did, as far as robbing white people, ain't no way I was gon torture myself over that one.

I tried to write Mom a letter. Not too long ago. Should say I did write the letter and put it in a envelope and sent it cause that's what I did, but I be crying so much trying to write it I don't know what wound up in that letter. I wanted Mom to know I knew what I'd done. In a way I wanted to say I was sorry for spoiling her life. After all she did for me I turned around and made her life miserable. That's the wrongest thing I've done and I wanted to say I was sorry but I kept seeing her face while I was writing the letter. I'd see her face and it would get older while I was look- ing. She'd get this old woman's face all lined and wrinkled and tired about the eyes. Wasn't nothing I could do but watch. Cause I'd done it and knew I done it and all the letters in the world ain't gon change her face. I sit and think about stuff like that all the time. It's better now. I think about other things too. You know like trying to figure what's really right and wrong, but there be days the guilt don't never go away.

I'm the one made her tired, John. And that's my greatest sorrow. All the love that's in me she created. Then I went and let her down.

When you in prison you got plenty of time to think, that's for damned sure. Too much time. I've gone over and over my life. Every moment. Every little thing again and again. I lay down on my bed and watch it happening over and over. Like a movie. I get it all broke down in pieces then I break up the pieces then I take the pieces of the pieces and run them through my hands so I remember every word a person said to me or what I said to them and weigh the words till I think I know what each and every one meant. Then I try to put it back together. Try to understand where I been. Why I did what I did. You got time for that in here. Time's all you got in here.

Going over and over things sometimes you can make sense. You know. Like the chinky-chinky Chinaman sittin' on the fence. You put it together and you think, yes. That's why I did thus and so. Yeah. That's why I lost that job or lost that woman or broke that one's heart. You stop thinking in terms of something being good or being evil, you just try to say this hap- pened because that happened because something else came first. You can spend days trying to figure out just one little thing you did. People out there in the world walk around in a daze cause they ain't got time to think. When I was out there, I wasn't no different. Had this Superfly thing and that was the whole bit. Nobody could tell me nothing.

Seems like I should start the story back in Shadyside. In the house on Copeland Street. Nothing but white kids around. Them little white kids had everything, too. That's what I thought, anyway. Nice houses, nice clothes. They could buy pop and comic books and candy when they wanted to. We wasn't that bad off, but compared to what them little white kids had I always felt like I didn't have nothing. It made me kinda quiet and shy around them. Me knowing all the time I wanted what they had. Wanted it bad. There was them white kids with everything and there was the black world Mommy and them was holding back from me. No place to turn, in a way. I guess you could say I was stuck in the middle. Couldn't have what the white kids in Shadyside had, and I wasn't allowed to look around the corner for something else. So I'd start the story with Shadyside, the house on Copeland.

Another place to start could be December 29, 1950 — the date of Robby's birth. For some reason — maybe my mother and father were feuding, maybe we just happened to be visiting my grandmother's house when my mother's time came — the trip to the hospital to have Robby began from Finance Street, from the house beside the railroad tracks in Homewood. What I remember is the bustle, people rushing around, yelling up and down the stairwell, doors slammed, drawers being opened and shut. A cold winter day so lots of coats and scarves and galoshes. My mother's face was very pale above the dark cloth coat that made her look even bigger than she was, carrying Robby the ninth month. On the way out the front door she stopped and stared back over her shoulder like she'd forgotten something. People just about shoving her out the house. Lots of bustle and noise getting her through the crowded hallway into the vestibule. Somebody opened the front door and December rattled the glass panes. Wind gusting and whistling, everybody calling out last-minute instructions, arrangements, goodbyes, blessings, prayers. My mother's white face calm, hovering a moment above it all as she turned back toward the hall, the stairs where I was planted, halfway to the top. She didn't find me, wasn't looking for me. A thought had crossed her mind and carried her far away. She didn't know why so many hands were rushing her out the door. She didn't hear the swirl of words, the icy blast of wind. Wrapped in a navy-blue coat, either Aunt Aida's or an old one of my grandmother's, which didn't have all its black buttons but stretched double over her big belly, my mother was wondering whether or not she'd turned off the water in the bathroom sink and deciding whether or not she should return up the stairs to check. Something like that crossing her mind, freeing her an instant before she got down to the business of pushing my brother into the world.

Both my grandfathers died on December 28. My grandmother died just after dawn on December 29. My sister lost a baby early in January. The end of the year has become associated with mournings, funerals; New Year's Day arrives burdened by a sense of loss, bereavement. Robby's birthday became tainted. To be born close to Christmas is bad enough in and of itself. Your birthday celebration gets upstaged by the orgy of gift giving on Christmas Day. No matter how many presents you receive on

December 29, they seem a trickle after the Christmas flood. Plus there's too much excitement in too brief a period. Parents and relatives are exhausted, broke, still hung over from the Christmas rush, so there just isn't very much left to work with if your birthday comes four short days after Jesus'. Almost like not having a birthday. Or even worse, like sharing it with your brothers and sister instead of having the private oasis of your very own special day. So Robby cried a lot on his birthdays. And it certainly wasn't a happy time for my mother. Her father, John French, died the year after Robby was born, one day before Robby's birthday. Fifteen years and a day later Mom would lose her mother. The death of the baby my sister was carrying was a final, cruel blow, scaring my mother, jinxing the end of the year eternally. She dreaded the holiday season, expected it to bring dire tidings. She had attempted at one point to consecrate the sad days, employ them as a period of reflection, quietly, privately memorialize the passing of the two people who'd loved her most in the world. But the death of my father's father, then the miscarriage within this jinxed span of days burst the fragile truce my mother had effected with the year's end. She withdraws into herself, anticipates the worst as soon as Christmas decorations begin appearing. In 1975, the year of the robbery and murder, Robby was on the run when his birthday fell. My mother was sure he wouldn't survive the deadly close of the year.

Robby's birthday is smack dab in the middle of the hard time. Planted like a flag to let you know the bad time's arrived. His adult life, the manhood of my mother's last child, begins as she is orphaned, as she starts to become nobody's child.

I named Robby. Before the women hustled my mother out the door into a taxi, I jumped down the stairs, tugged on her coattail, and reminded her she'd promised it'd be Robby. No doubt in my mind she'd bring me home a baby brother. Don't ask me why I was certain. I just was. I hadn't even considered names for a girl. Robby it would be. Robert Douglas. Where the Douglas came from is another story, but the Robert came from me because I liked the sound. Robert was formal, dignified, important. Robert. And that was nearly as nice as the chance I'd have to call my little brother Rob and Robby.

He weighed seven pounds, fourteen ounces. He was born in Allegheny Hospital at 6:30 in the evening, December 29, 1950. His fingers and toes were intact and quite long. He was a plump baby. My grandfather, high on Dago Red, tramped into the maternity ward just minutes after Robby was delivered. John French was delighted with the new baby. Called him Red. A big fat little red nigger.

December always been a bad month for me. One the worst days of my life was in December. It's still one the worst days in my life even after all this other mess. Jail. Running. The whole bit. Been waiting to tell you this a long time. Ain't no reason to hold it back no longer. We into this telling-the-truth thing so mize well tell it all. I'm still shamed, but there it is. You know that TV of youall's got stolen from Mommy's. Well, I did it. Was me and Henry took youall's TV that time and set the house up to look like a robbery. We did it. Took my own brother's TV. Couldn't hardly look you in the face for a long time after we done it. Was pretty sure youall never knowed it was me, but I felt real bad round youns anyway. No way I was gon confess though. Too shamed. A junkie stealing from his own family. See. Used to bullshit myself. Say I ain't like them other guys. They stone junkies, they hooked. Do anything for a hit. But me, I'm Robby. I'm cool. I be believing that shit, too. Fooling myself. You got to bullshit yourself when you falling. Got to do it to live wit yourself. See but where it's at is you be doing any goddam thing for dope. You hooked and that's all's to it. You a stone junkie just like the rest.

Always wondered if you knew I took it.

Mom was suspicious. She knew more than we did then. About the dope. The seriousness of it. Money disappearing from her purse when nobody in the house but the two of you. Finding a syringe on the third floor. Stuff like that she hadn't talked about to us yet. So your stealing the TV was a possibility that came up. But to me it was just one of many. One of the things that could have happened along with a whole lot of other possibilities we sat around talking about. An unlikely possibility as far as I was concerned. Nobody wanted to believe it was you. Mom tried to tell us how it *could* be but in my mind you weren't the one. Haven't thought about it much since then. Except as one of those things that make me worry about Mom living in the house alone. One of those things making Homewood dangerous, tearing it down.

I'm glad I'm finally getting to tell you. I never could get it out. Didn't want you to think I'd steal from my own brother. Specially since all youall done to help me out. You and Judy and the kids. Stealing youall's TV. Don't make no sense, does it? But if we gon get the story down mize well get it all down.

It was a while ago. Do you remember the year?

Nineteen seventy-one was Greens. When we robbed Greens and got in big trouble so it had to be the year before that, 1970. That's when it had to be. Youns was home for Christmas. Mommy and them was having a big party. A reunion kinda cause all the family was together. Everybody home for the first time in a long time. Tish in from Detroit. David back from Philly. Youns in town. My birthday, too. Party spozed to celebrate my birthday too, since it came right along in there after Christmas. Maybe that's why I was feeling so bad. Knowing I had a birthday coming and knowing at the same time how fucked up I was.

Sat in a chair all day. I was hooked for the first time. Good and hooked. Didn't know how low you could feel till that day. Cold and snowing outside. And I got the stone miseries inside. Couldn't move. Weak and sick. Henry too. He was wit me in the house feeling bad as I was. We was two desperate dudes. Didn't have no money and that Jones down on us.

Mommy kept asking, What's wrong with you two? She was on my case all day. What ails you, Robby? Got to be about three o'clock. She come in the room again: You better get up and get some decent clothes on. We're leaving for Geral's soon. See cause it was the day of the big Christmas party. Geral had baked a cake for me. Everybody was together and they'd be singing Happy Birthday Robby and do. The whole bit an I'm spozed to be guest of honor and can't even move out the chair. Here I go again disappointing everybody. Everybody be at Geral's looking for me and Geral had a cake and everything. Where's Robby? He's home dying cause he can't get no dope.

Feeling real sorry for myself but I'm hating me too. Wrapped up in a blanket like some damned Indin. Shivering and wondering how the hell Ima go out in this cold and hustle up some money. Wind be howling. Snow pitching a bitch. There we is. Stuck in the house. Two pitiful junkies. Scheming how we gon get over. Some sorry-assed dudes. But it's comical in a way too, when you look back. To get well we need to get money. And no way we gon get money less we go outside and get sicker than we already is. Mom peeking in the room, getting on my case. Get up out that chair, boy. What are you waiting for? We're leaving in two minutes.

So I says, Go on. I ain't ready. Youns go on. I'll catch up with youns at Geral's.

Mommy standing in the doorway. She can't say too much, cause youns is home and you ain't hip to what's happening. C'mon now. We can't wait any longer for you. Please get up. Geral baked a cake for you. Everybody's looking forward to seeing you.

Seem like she stands there a hour begging me to come. She ain't mad no more. She's begging. Just about ready to cry. Youall in the other room. You can hear what she's saying but you can't see her eyes and they tearing me up. Her eyes begging me to get out the chair and it's tearing me up to see her hurting so bad, but ain't nothing I can do. Jones sitting on my chest and ain't no getup in me.

Youns go head, Mommy. I'll be over in a little while. Be there to blow them candles out and cut the cake.

She knew better. Knew if I didn't come right then, chances was I wasn't coming at all. She knew but wasn't nothing she could do. Guess I knew I was lying too. Nothing in my mind cept copping that dope. Yeah, Mom. Be there to light them candles. I'm grinning but she ain't smiling back. She knows I'm in trouble, deep trouble. I can see her today standing in the doorway begging me to come with youns.

But it ain't meant to be. Me and Henry thought we come up with a idea. Henry's old man had some pistols. We was gon steal em and hock em. Take the money and score. Then we be better. Wouldn't be no big thing to hustle some money, get the guns outa hock. Sneak the pistols back in Henry's house, everything be alright. Wouldn't even exactly be stealing from his old man. Like we just borrowing the pistols till we score and take care business. Henry's old man wouldn't even know his pistols missing. Slick. Sick as we was, thinking we slick.

A hundred times. Mom musta poked her head in the room a hundred times.

What's wrong with you?

Like a drum beating in my head. What's wrong with you? But the other thing is stronger. The dope talking to me louder. It says get you some. It says you ain't never gon get better less you cop.

We waited long as we could but it didn't turn no better outside. Still snowing. Wind shaking the whole house. How we gon walk to Henry's and steal them pistols? Henry live way up on the hill. And the way up Tokay then you still got a long way to go over into the projects. Can't make it. No way we gon climb Tokay. So then what? Everybody's left for Geral's. Then I remembers the TV youns brought. A little portable Sony black-and-white, right? You and Judy sleeping in Mom's room and she has her TV already in there, so the Sony ain't unpacked. Saw it sitting with youall's suitcases over by the dresser. On top the dresser in a box. Remembered it and soon's I did I knew we had to have it. Sick as I was that TV had to go. Wouldn't really be stealing. Borrow it instead of borrowing the pistols. Pawn it. Get straight. Steal some money and buy it back. Just borrowing youall's TV.

Won't take me and Henry no time to rob something and buy back the TV. We stone thieves. Just had to get well first so we could operate. So we took youns TV and set the house up to look like a robbery.

I'm remembering the day. Wondering why it had slipped completely from my mind. I feel like a stranger. Yet as Robby talks, my memory confirms details of his recollection. I admit, yes. I was there. That's the way it was. But *where* was I? Who was I? How did I miss so much?

His confessions make me uncomfortable. Instead of concentrating on what he's revealing, I'm pushed into considering all the things I could be confessing, should be confessing but haven't and probably won't ever. I feel hypocritical. Why should I allow my brother to repose a confidence in me when it's beyond my power to reciprocate? Shouldn't I confess that first? My embarrassment, my uneasiness, the clinical, analytic coldness settling over me when I catch on to what's about to happen.

I have a lot to hide. Places inside myself where truth hurts, where incriminating secrets are hidden, places I avoid, or deny most of the time. Pulling one piece of that debris to the surface, airing it in the light of day doesn't accomplish much, doesn't clarify the rest of what's buried down there. What I feel when I delve deeply into myself is chaos. Chaos and contradiction. So how up front can I get? I'm moved by Robby's secrets. The heart I have is breaking. But what that heart is and where it is I can't say. I can't depend on it, so he shouldn't. Part of me goes out to him. Heartbreak is the sound of ice cracking. Deep. Layers and layers muffling the sound.

I listen but I can't trust myself. I have no desire to tell everything about myself so I resist his attempt to be up front with me. The chaos at my core must be in his. His confession pushes me to think of all the stuff I should lay on him. And that scares the shit out of me. I don't like to feel dirty, but that's how I feel when people try to come clean with me.

Very complicated and very simple too. The fact is I don't believe in clean. What I know best is myself and, knowing what I know about myself, clean seems impossible. A dream. One of those better selves occasionally in the driver's seat but nothing more. Nothing to be depended upon. A self no more or less in control than the countless other selves who each, for a time, seem to be running things.

Chaos is what he's addressing. What his candor, his frankness, his confession echo against. Chaos and time and circumstances and the old news, the bad news that we still walk in circles, each of us trapped in his own little world. Behind bars. Locked in our cells.

But my heart can break, does break listening to my brother's pain. I just remember differently. Different parts of the incident he's describing come back. Strange thing is my recollections return through the door he opened. My memories needed his. Maybe the fact that we recall different things is crucial. Maybe they are foreground and background, propping each other up. He holds on to this or that scrap of the past and I listen to what he's saved and it's not mine, not what I saw or heard or felt. The pressure's on me then. If his version of the past is real, then what's mine? Where does it fit? As he stitches his memories together they bridge a vast emptiness. The time lost enveloping us all. Everything. And hearing him talk, listening to him try to make something of the nothing, challenges me. My sense of the emptiness playing around his words, any words, is intensified. Words are nothing and everything. If I don't speak I have no past. Except the nothing, the emptiness. My brother's memories are not mine, so I have to break into the silence with my own version of the past. My words. My whistling in the dark. His story freeing me, because it forces me to tell my own.

I'm sorry you took so long to forgive yourself. I forgave you a long time ago, in advance for a sin I didn't even know you'd committed. You lied to me. You stole from me. I'm in prison now listening because we committed those sins against each other countless times. I want your forgiveness. Talking about debts you owe me makes me awkward, uneasy. We remember different things. They set us apart. They bring us together searching for what is lost, for the meaning of difference, of distance.

For instance, the Sony TV. It was a present from Mort, Judy's dad. When we told him about the break-in and robbery at Mom's house, he bought us another Sony. Later we discovered the stolen TV was covered by our homeowner's policy even though we'd lost it in Pittsburgh. A claim was filed and eventually we collected around a hundred bucks. Not enough to buy a new Sony but a good portion of the purchase price. Seemed a lark when the check arrived. Pennies from heaven. One hundred dollars free and clear since we already had the new TV Mort had surprised us with. About a year later one of us, Judy or I, was telling the story of the robbery and how well we came out of it. Not until that very moment when I caught a glimpse of Mort's face out of the corner of my eye did I realize what we'd done. Judy remembers urging me to send Mort that insurance check and she probably did, but I have no recollection of an argument. In my mind there had never been an issue. Why shouldn't we keep the money? But when I saw the look of surprise and hurt flash across Mort's face, I knew the insurance check should have gone directly to him. He's a generous man and probably would have refused to accept it, but we'd taken advantage of his generosity by not offering the check as soon as we received it. Clearly the money belonged to him. Unasked, he'd replaced the lost TV. I had treated him like an institution, one of those faceless corporate entities like the gas company or IRS. By then, by the time I saw the surprise in Mort's face and understood how selfishly, thoughtlessly, even corruptly I'd behaved, it was too late. Offering Mort a hundred dollars at that point would have been insulting. Anything I could think of saying sounded hopelessly lame, inept. I'd fucked up. I'd injured someone who'd been nothing but kind and generous to me. Not intentionally, consciously, but that only made the whole business worse in a way because I'd failed him instinctively. The failure was a measure of who I was. What I'd unthinkingly done revealed something about my relationship to Mort I'm sure he'd rather not have discovered. No way I could take my action back, make it up. It reflected a truth about who I was.

That memory pops right up. Compromising, ugly. Ironically, it's also about stealing from a relative. Not to buy dope, but to feed a habit just as self-destructive. The habit of taking good fortune for granted, the habit of blind self-absorption that allows us to believe the world owes us everything and we are not responsible for giving anything in return. Spoiled children. The good coming our way taken as our due. No strings attached.

Lots of other recollections were triggered as Robby spoke of that winter and the lost TV. The shock of walking into a burgled house. How it makes you feel unclean. How quickly you lose the sense of privacy and security a house, any place you call home, is supposed to provide. It's a form of rape. Forced entry, violation, brutal hands defiling what's personal, and precious. The aftershock of seeing your possessions strewn about, broken. Fear gnawing at you because what you thought was safe isn't safe at all. The worst has happened and can happen again. Your sanctuary has been destroyed. Any time you walk in your door you may be greeted by the same scene. Or worse. You may stumble upon the thieves themselves. The symbolic rape of your dwelling place enacted on your actual body. Real screams. Real blood. A knife at your throat. A stranger's weight bearing down.

Mom put it in different words but she was as shaken as I was when we walked into her house after Geral's party. Given what I know now, she must have been even more profoundly disturbed than I imagined. A double bind. Bad enough to be ripped off by anonymous thieves. How much worse if the thief is your son? For Mom the robbery was proof Robby was gone. Somebody else walking round in his skin. Mom was wounded in ways I hadn't begun to guess at. At the root of her pain were your troubles, the troubles stealing you away from her, from all of us. The troubles thick in the air as that snow you are remembering, the troubles falling on your head and mine, troubles I refused to see....

Snowing and the hawk kicking my ass but I got to have it. TV's in a box under my arm and me and Henry walking down Bennett to Homewood Avenue. Need thirty dollars. Thirty dollars buy us two spoons. Looking for One-Arm Ralph, the fence. Looking for him or that big white Cadillac he drives.

Wind blowing snow all up in my face. Thought I's bout to die out there. Nobody on the avenue. Even the junkies and dealers inside today. Wouldn't put no dog out in weather like that. So cold my teeth is chattering, talking to me. No feeling in my hands but I got to hold on to that TV. Henry took it for a little while so's I could put both my hands in my pockets. Henry lookin bad as I'm feeling. Thought I was gon puke. But it's too goddamn cold to puke.

Nobody in sight. Shit and double shit's what I'm thinking. They got to be somewhere. Twenty-four hours a day, seven days a week somebody doing business. Finally we seen One-Arm Ralph come out the Hi Hat.

This TV, man, Lemme hold thirty dollars on it.

Ralph ain't goin for it. Twenty-five the best he say he can do. Twenty-five don't do us no good. It's fifteen each for a spoon. One spoon ain't enough. We begging the dude now. We got to have it, man. Got to get well. We good for the money. Need thirty dollars for two hits. You get your money back.

Too cold to be standing around arguing. The dude go in his pocket and give us the thirty. He been knowing us. He know we good for it. I'm telling him don't sell the TV right away. Hold it till tomorrow we have his money. He say, You don't come back tonight you blow it. Ralph a hard mother-fucker and don't want him changing his mind again about the thirty so I say, We'll have the money tonight. Hold the TV till tonight, you get your money.

Now all we got to do is find Goose. Goose always be hanging on the set. Ain't nobody else dealing, Goose be out there for his people. Goose an alright dude, but even Goose ain't out in the street on no day like this. I know the cat stays over the barbershop on Homewood Avenue. Across from Murphy's five-and-ten. I goes round to the side entrance, the alleyway tween Homewood and Kelly. That's how you get to his place. Goose lets me in and I cop. For some reason I turn up the alley and go toward Kelly instead of back to Homewood the way I came in. Don't know why I did it. Being slick. Being scared. Henry's waiting on the avenue for me so I go round the long way just in case somebody pinned him. I can check out the scene before I come back up the avenue. That's probably what I'm thinking. But soon's I turn the corner of Kelly, Bam. Up pops the devil.

Up against the wall, Squirrel.

It's Simon and Garfunkel, two jive undercover cops. We call them that, you dig. Lemme tell you what kind of undercover cops these niggers was. Both of em wearing Big Apple hats and jackets like people be wearing then but they both got on police shoes. Police brogans you could spot a mile away. But they think they slick. They disguised, see. Apple hats and hippy-dip jackets. Everybody knew them chumps was cops. Ride around in a big Continental. Going for bad. Everybody hated them cause everybody knew they in the dope business. They bust a junkie, take his shit and sell it. One them had a cousin. Biggest dealer on the Hill. You know where he getting half his dope. Be selling again what Simon and Garfunkel stole from junkies. Some rotten dudes. Liked to beat on people too. Wasn't bad enough they robbing people. They whipped heads too.

Soon's I turn the corner they got me. Bams me up against the wall. They so lame they think they got Squirrel. Think I'm Squirrel and they gon make a big bust. We got you, Squirrel. They happy, see, cause Squirrel dealing heavy then. Thought they caught them a whole shopping bag of dope.

Wearing my double-breasted pea coat. Used to be sharp but it's raggedy now. Ain't worth shit in cold weather like that. Pockets got holes and the dope dropped down in the lining so they don't find nothing the first time they search me. Can tell they mad. Thought they into something big and don't find shit. Looking at each other like, What the fuck's going on here? We big-time undercover supercops. This ain't spozed to be happening to us. They roughing me up too. Pulling my clothes off and shit. Hands all down in my pockets again. It's freezing and I'm shivering but these fools don't give a fuck. Rip my goddamn pea coat off me. Shaking it. Tearing it up. Find the two packs of dope inside the lining this time. Ain't what they wanted but they pissed off now. Take what they can get now.

What's this, Squirrel? Got your ass now.

Slinging me down the alley. I'm stone sick now. Begging these cats for mercy. Youall got me. You got your bust. Lemme snort some the dope, man. Little bit out each bag. You still got your bust. I'm dying. Little taste fore you lock me up.

Rotten motherfuckers ain't going for it. They see I'm sick as a dog. They know what's happening. Cold as it is, the sweat pouring out me. It's sweat but it's like ice. Like knives cutting me. They ain't give back my coat. Snowing on me and I'm shaking and sweating and sick. They can see all this. They know what's happening but ain't no mercy in these dudes. Henry's cross the street watching them bust me. Tears in his eyes. Ain't nothing he can do. The street's empty. Henry's bout froze too. Watching them sling my ass in their Continental. Never forget how Henry looked that day. All alone on the avenue. Tears froze in his eyes. Seeing him like that was a sad thing. Last thing I saw was him standing there across Homewood Avenue before they slammed me up in the car. Like I was in two places. That's me standing there in the snow. That's me so sick and cold I'm crying in the empty street and ain't a damn thing I can do about it.

By the time they get me down to the Police Station, down to No. 5 in East Liberty, I ain't no more good, sure nuff. Puking. Begging them punks not to bust me. Just bout out my mind. Must have been a pitiful sight. Then's when Henry went to Geral's house and scratched on the window and called David out on the porch. That's when youall found out I was in trouble and had to come down and get me. Right in the middle of the party and everything. Henry's sick too and he been walking round Homewood in the cold didn't know what to do. But he's my man. He got to Geral's so youall could come down and help me. Shamed to go in so he scratched on the window to get Dave on the porch.

Party's over and youns go to Mommy's and on top everything else find the house broke in and the TV gone. All the stuff's going through my mind. I'm on the bottom now. Low as you can go. Had me in a cell and I was lying cross the cot staring at the ceiling. Bars all round. Up cross the ceiling too. Like in a cage in the zoo. Miserable as I could be. All the shit staring me in the face. You're a dope fiend. You stole your brother's TV. You're hurting Mommy again. Hurting everybody. You're sick. You're nothing. Looking up at the bars on the ceiling and wondering if I could tie my belt there. Stick my neck in it. I wanted to be dead.

Tied my belt to the ceiling. Then this guard checking on me he starts to hollering.

What you doing? Hey, Joe. This guy's trying to commit suicide.

They take my clothes. Leave me nothing but my shorts. I'm lying there shivering in my underwear and that's the end. In a cage naked like some goddamn animal. Shaking like a leaf. Thinking maybe I can beat my head against the bars or maybe jump down off the bed head first on the concrete and bust my brains open. Dead already. Nothing already. Low as I can go.

Must have passed out or gone to sleep or something, cause it gets blurry round in here. Don't remember much but they gave back my clothes and took me Downtown and there was a arraignment next morning.

Mommy told me later, one the cops advised her not to pay my bond. Said the best thing for him be to stay in jail awhile. Let him see how it is inside. Scare im. But I be steady beggin. Please, please get me out here. Youns got soft-hearted. Got the money together and paid the bond.

What would have happened if you left me to rot in there till my hearing? Damned if I know. I probably woulda went crazy, for one thing. I do know that. Know I was sick and scared and cried like a baby for Mommy and them to get me out. Don't think it really do no good letting them keep me in there. I mean the jail's a terrible place. You can get everything in jail you get in the street. No different. Cept in jail it's more dangerous cause you got a whole bunch of crazies locked up in one little space. Worse than the street. Less you got buddies in there they tear you up. Got to learn to survive quick. Cause jail be the stone jungle. Call prison the House of Knowledge cause you learns how to be a sure nuff criminal. Come in lame you leave knowing all kinds of evil shit. You learn quick or they eats you up. That's where it's at. So you leave a person in there, chances are they gets worse. Or gets wasted.

But Mom has that soft heart anyway and she ain't leaving her baby boy in no miserable jail. Right or wrong, she ain't leaving me in no place like that. Daddy been talking to Simon and Garfunkel. Daddy's hip, see. He been out there in the street all his life and he knows what's to it. Knows those guys and knows how rotten they is. Ain't no big thing they catch one pitiful little junkie holding two spoons. They wants dealers. They wants to look good Downtown. They wants to bust dealers and cop beaucoup dope so's they can steal it and get rich. Daddy makes a deal with them rats. Says if they drop the charges he'll make me set up Goose. Finger Goose and then stay off Homewood Avenue. Daddy says I'll do that so they let me go.

No way Ima squeal on Goose but I said okay, it's a deal. Soon's I was loose I warned Goose. Pretend like I'm trying to set him up so the cops get off my ass but Goose see me coming know the cops is watching. Helped him, really. Like a lookout. Them dumb motherfuckers got tired playing me. Simon got greedy. Somebody set him up. He got busted for drugs. Still see Garfunkel riding round in his Continental but they took him off the avenue. Too dangerous. Everybody hated them guys.

My lowest day. Didn't know till then I was strung out. That's the first time I was hooked. Started shooting up with Squirrel and Bugs Johnson when Squirrel be coming over to Mom's sometimes. Get up in the morning, go up to the third floor, and shoot up. They was like my teachers. Bugs goes way back. He started with Uncle Carl. Been shooting ever since. Dude's old now. Call him King of the Junkies, he been round so long. Bugs seen it all. You know junkies don't hardly be getting old. Have their day then they gone. Don't see em no more. They in jail or dead. Junkie just don't have no long life. Fast life but your average dopehead ain't round long. Bugs different. He was a pal of Uncle Carl's back in the fifties. Shot up together way back then. Now here he is wit Squirrel and me, still doing this thing. Everybody knows Bugs. He the King.

Let me shoot up wit em but they wouldn't let me go out in the street and hustle wit em. Said I was too young. Too green.

Learning from the King, see. That's how I started the heavy stuff. Me and Squirrel and Bugs first thing in the morning when I got out of bed. Mom was gone to work. They getting themselves ready to hit the street. Make that money. Just like a job. Wasn't no time before I was out there, too. On my own learning to get money for dope. Me and my little mob. We was ready. Didn't take us no time fore we was gangsters. Gon be the next Bugs Johnson. Gon make it to the top.

Don't take long. One day you the King. Next day dope got you and it's the King. You ain't nothing. You lying there naked bout to die and it don't take but a minute. You fall and you gone in a minute. That's the life. That's how it is. And I was out there. I know. Now they got me jammed up in the slammer. That's the way it is. But nobody could tell me nothing then. Hard head. You know. Got to find out for myself. Nobody could tell me nothing. Just out of high school and my life's over and I didn't even know it. Too dumb. Too hardheaded. I was gon do it my way. Youns was square. Youns didn't know nothing. Me, I was gon make mine from the curb. Hammer that rock till I was a supergangster. Be the one dealing the shit. Be the one running the junkies. That's all I knew. Street smarts. Stop being a chump. Forget that nickel-dime hoodlum bag. Be a star. Rise to the top.

You know where that got me. You heard that story. Here I sit today behind that story. Nobody to blame but my ownself. I know that now. But things was fucked up in the streets. You could fall in them streets, Brother. Low. Them streets could snatch you bald-headed and turn you around and wring you inside out. Streets was a bitch. Wake up some mornings and you think you in hell. Think you died and went straight to hell. I know cause I been there. Be days I wished I was dead. Be days worser than that.

• • ● ● ● • •

QUESTIONS FOR A SECOND READING

1. Wideman frequently interrupts this narrative to talk about the problems he is having as a writer. He says, for example, "The hardest habit to break, since it was the habit of a lifetime, would be listening to myself listen to him. That habit would destroy any chance of seeing my brother on his terms; and seeing him in his terms, learning his terms, seemed the whole point of learning his story" (p. 637). What might Wideman mean by this — listening to himself listen? As you reread "Our Time," note the sections in which Wideman speaks to you directly as a writer. What is he saying? Where and how are you surprised by what he says?

   Wideman calls attention to the problems he faces. How does he try to solve them? Are you sympathetic? Do the solutions work, so far as you are concerned?

2. Wideman says that his mother had a remarkable capacity for "[trying] on the other person's point of view" (p. 631). Wideman tries on another point of view himself, speaking to us in the voice of his brother Robby. As you reread this selection, note the passages spoken in Robby's voice and try to infer Robby's point of view from them. If you look at the differences between John and Robby as evidenced by the ways they use language to understand and represent the world, what do you notice?

3. Wideman talks about three ways he could start Robby's story: with Garth's death, with the house in Shadyside, and with the day of Robby's birth. What difference would it make in each case if he chose one and not the others? What's the point of presenting all three?

• • ● ● ● • •

ASSIGNMENTS FOR WRITING

1. At several points in the essay, Wideman discusses his position as a writer, telling Robby's story, and he describes the problems he faces in writing this piece (or in "reading" the text of his brother's life). You could read this selection, in other words, as an essay about reading and writing.

   Why do you think Wideman talks about these problems here? Why not keep quiet and hope that no one notices? Choose three or four passages in which Wideman refers directly or indirectly to his work as a writer, and write an essay defining the problems Wideman faces and explaining why you think he raises them as he does. Finally, what might this have to do with your work as a writer — or as a student in this writing class?

2. Wideman tells Robby's story in this excerpt, but he also tells the story of his neighborhood, Homewood; of his mother; and of his grandfather John French. Write an essay retelling one of these stories and explaining what it might have to do with Robby and John's.

3. "Our Time" is a family history, but it is also a meditation on the problems of writing family histories — or, more generally, the problems of writing about the "real" world. There are sections in "Our Time" where Wideman speaks directly about the problems he faces as a writer. And the unusual features in the prose stand as examples of how he tried to solve these problems — at certain points Wideman writes as an essayist, at others like a storyteller; at certain points he switches voices; the piece breaks up into sections, it doesn't move from introduction to conclusion. Think of these as part of Wideman's method, as his way of working on the problems of writing as practical problems, where he is trying to figure out how to do justice to his brother and his story.

As you prepare to write this assignment, read back through the selection to think about it as a way of doing one's work, as a project, as a way of writing. What are the selection's key features? What is its shape or design? How does Wideman, the writer, do what he does? And you might ask: What would it take to learn to write like this? How is this writing related to the writing taught in school? Where and how might it serve you as a student?

Once you have developed a sense of Wideman's method, write a Wideman-like piece of your own, one that has the rhythm and the moves, the shape and the design of "Our Time." As far as subject matter is concerned, let Wideman's text stand as an invitation (inviting you to write about family and neighborhood), but don't feel compelled to follow his lead. You can write about anything you want. The key is to follow the essay as an example of a *way* of writing — moving slowly, turning this way and that, combining stories and reflection, working outside of a rigid structure of thesis and proof.

· · ● · ·

MAKING CONNECTIONS

1. Various selections in this textbook can be said to be "experimental" in their use of nonfiction prose. These are essays that don't do what essays are supposed to do. They break the rules. They surprise. The writers work differently from most writers. They imagine a different project (or they imagine their project differently).

Although any number of the selections in *Ways of Reading* might be read alongside "Our Time," here are some that have seemed interesting to our students: Gloria Anzaldúa, "How to Tame a Wild Tongue" (p. 26); Susan Griffin, "Our Secret" (p. 381); and Richard E. Miller, "The Dark Night of the Soul" (p. 435).

    Choose one selection to compare with John Edgar Wideman's and write an essay in which you both explain and explore the projects represented by the two pieces of writing. How do they address a reader's expectations? How do they manipulate the genre? How do they reimagine the features we take for granted in the genre of the essay — sentences and paragraphs; introductions and conclusions; argument, narrative, and exposition? And what is to be gained (or what is at stake) in writing this way? (Would you, for example, argue that these forms of writing should be taught in college?) You should assume that you are writing for someone who is a sophisticated reader but who is not familiar with these particular essays. You will need, that is, to be careful in choosing and presenting examples.

2.   Both John Edgar Wideman's "Our Time" and Kwame Anthony Appiah's "Racial Identities" (p. 42) call attention to the difficulties of representing and understanding the experience of those whom we call "African Americans" — the difficulty of telling their story, of getting it right, of recovering experience from the representations of others.

    Write an essay in which you represent these two texts as examples of writers working on a problem that has a particular urgency for all Americans, not just black Americans. How might you name this problem? What do you find compelling in each of these approaches to the problem? And what might this problem have to do with you — as a writer, a thinker, a person, and a citizen?

3.   In his essay "Our Time," John Edgar Wideman worries over the problems of representation, of telling his brother's story. He speaks directly to the fundamental problem writers face when they try to represent the lives of others: "I'd slip unaware out of his story and into one of my own. I'd be following him, an obedient shadow, then a cloud would blot the sun and I'd be gone, unchained, a dark form still skulking behind him but no longer in tow" (p. 637). Wideman goes on to say:

> The hardest habit to break . . . would be listening to myself listen to him. That habit would destroy any chance of seeing my brother on his terms; and seeing him in his terms, learning his terms, seemed the whole point of learning his story. . . . I had to teach myself to listen. Start fresh, clear the pipes, resist too facile an identification, tame the urge to take off with Robby's story and make it my own. (p. 637)

Richard E. Miller, in "The Dark Night of the Soul" (p. 435), is also concerned with the problems of representation. He provides readings of the lives of others — from Eric Harris to Chris McCandless to Martin Amis to René Descartes and Mary Karr — who are also engaged with the problems of representation and understanding. Write an essay about writing and representation, about the real world and the world of texts, with Wideman and Miller as your primary points of reference. How do they understand representation as a problem for writers and readers? How is that understanding represented (or enacted) in their own work? Which writer might have something to learn from the example of the other?

4.   Both John Edgar Wideman in "Our Time" and Ta-Nehisi Coates in "Between the World and Me" (p. 277) can be seen as writing to understand the places in which they grew up and the ideas about the world and family that circulated in those places at those times. Wideman takes on this work by writing *about* his brother (sometimes in the voice of his brother), while Coates takes on this work by writing *to* his son. Write an essay in which you consider the following questions: What ideas, arguments, or approaches do Wideman and Coates have in common, despite more than thirty years between the publications of their books? What do their commonalities suggest to you? How does Wideman's writing about his brother make his work different from Coates's writing, in which Coates is talking to his son? How might Coates's perspective address Wideman's concerns about getting to the truth of his brother's story?

Assignment

SEQUENCES

had the last word on the subject of education. It is not as though, by working on one of the essays, you have wrapped the subject up, ready to be put on the shelf.

The sequences are designed, then, so that you will be working not only on essays but on a subject, like education (or history, or culture, or the autobiography), a subject that can be examined, probed, and understood through the various frames provided by your reading. Each essay becomes a way of seeing a problem or a subject; it becomes a tool for thinking, an example of how a mind might work, a way of using language to make a subject rich and alive. In the assignment sequences, your reading is not random. Each sequence provides a set of readings that can be pulled together into a single project.

The sequences allow you to participate in an extended academic project, one with several texts and several weeks' worth of writing. You are not just adding one essay to another (Rodriguez + Pratt = ?) but trying out an approach to a subject by revising it, looking at new examples, hearing what someone else has to say, and beginning again to take a position of your own. Projects like these take time. It is not at all uncommon for professional writers to devote weeks or even months to a single essay, and the essay they write marks not the end of their thinking on the subject, but only one stage. Similarly, when readers are working on a project, the pieces they read accumulate on their desks and in their minds and become part of an extended conversation with several speakers, each voice offering a point of view on a subject, a new set of examples, or a new way of talking that resonates with echoes from earlier reading.

A student may read many books, take several courses, write many papers; ideally each experience becomes part of something larger, an education. The work of understanding, in other words, requires time and repeated effort. The power that comes from understanding cannot be acquired quickly — by reading one essay or working for a few hours. A student, finally, is a person who choreographs such experiences, not someone who passes one test only to move on to another. And the assignment sequences are designed to reproduce, although in a condensed period of time, the rhythm and texture of academic life. They invite you to try on its characteristic ways of seeing, thinking, and writing. The work you do in one week will not be lost when it has bearing on the work you do in the next. If an essay by Susan Griffin has value for you, it is not because you proved to a teacher that you read it, but because you have put it to work and made it a part of your vocabulary as a student.

WORKING WITH A SEQUENCE

Here is what you can expect as you work with a sequence. You begin by working with a single reading. You will need to read each piece twice, the second time with the "Questions for a Second Reading" and the assignment sequence in mind. Before rereading the selection, in other words, you should read through the assignments to get a sense of where you will be headed. And you should read the questions at the end of each selection. (You can use those questions to help frame questions of your own.) The purpose of all these questions, in a sense, is to prepare the text to speak — to bring it to life and insist that it respond to your attention, answer your questions. If you think of the authors as people you can talk to, if you think of their pages as occasions for dialogue (as places where you get to ask questions and insist on responses), if you prepare your return to those pages in these ways, you are opening up the essays or stories (not closing them down or finishing them off) and creating a scene where you get to step forward as a performer.

While each sequence moves from selection to selection in *Ways of Reading*, the most significant movement in the sequence is defined by the essays you write. Your essays provide the other major texts for the course. In fact, when we teach these sequences, we seldom have any discussion of the assigned readings before our students have had a chance to write. When we talk as a group about Atul Gawande's "Slow Ideas," for example, we begin by reproducing one or two student essays, handing them out to the class, and using them as the basis for discussion. We want to start, in other words, by looking at ways of reading Gawande's article — not at his article alone.

The essays you write for each assignment in a sequence might be thought of as works-in-progress. Your instructor will tell you the degree to which each essay should be finished — that is, the degree to which it should be revised and copyedited and worked into a finished performance. In our classes, most writing assignments go through at least one revision. After we have had a chance to see a draft (or after a draft has been seen by others in the class), and after we have had some discussion of sample student essays, we ask students to read the assigned text one more time and to rework their essays to bring their work one step further — not necessarily to finish the essays (as though there would be nothing else to say) but to finish up this stage in their work and to feel their achievement in a way a writer simply cannot the first time through. Each assignment, then, really functions as two assignments in the schedule for the course. As a consequence, we don't "cover" as many essays in a semester as students might in another class. But coverage is not our goal. In a sense, we are teaching our students how to read slowly and closely, to return to a text rather than set it aside, to take the time to reread and rewrite and to reflect on what these activities entail. Some of these sequences, then, contain more readings or more writing assignments than you can address in a quarter or semester. Different courses work at different paces. It is important, however, to preserve time for rereading and rewriting. The sequences were written with the assumption that they would be revised to meet the needs of teachers, students, and programs. As you look at your syllabus, you may find, then, that reading or writing assignments have been changed, added, or dropped. There are alternative selections and assignments at the end of most of these sequences so that the sequences can be customized. Your instructor may wish to replace some of the selections and assignments in the sequence with alternatives.

You will be writing papers that can be thought of as single essays. But you will also be working on a project, something bigger than its individual parts. From the perspective of the project, each piece you write is part of a larger body of work that evolves over the term. You might think of each sequence as a revision exercise, where the revision looks forward to what comes next as well as backward to what you have done. This form of revision asks you to do more than complete a single paper; it invites you to re-see a subject or reimagine what you might say about it from a new point of view. You should feel free, then, to draw on your earlier essays when you work on one of the later assignments. There is every reason for you to reuse ideas, phrases, sentences, even paragraphs as your work builds from one week to the next. The advantage of works-in-progress is that you are not starting over completely every time you sit down to write. You've been over this territory before. You've developed some expertise in your subject. There is a body of work behind you.

Most of the sequences bring together several essays from the text and ask you to imagine them as an extended conversation, one with several speakers. The assignments are designed to give you a voice in the conversation as well, to allow you to speak in turn and to take your place in the company of other writers. This is the final purpose of the assignment sequence: after several weeks' work on the essays and on the subject that draws them together, you will begin to establish your own point of view. You will develop a position from which you can speak with authority, drawing strength from the work you have done as well as from your familiarity with the people who surround you.

This book brings together some of the most powerful voices of our culture. They speak in a manner that asks for response. The assignments at the end of each selection and, with a wider range of reference, the assignment sequences here at the end of the book demonstrate that there is no reason for a student, in such company, to remain silent.

Exploring Identity, Exploring the Self

Kwame Anthony Appiah
Edward Said
Judith Butler
Susan Griffin

ALTERNATIVES:

John Edgar Wideman
Richard E. Miller
Ruth Behar

This sequence invites you to explore some complicated questions about identity — questions about who we are as human beings, about our relationships to others, and about the narratives we tell about ourselves and others. The sequence is particularly challenging because it asks you to be self-reflexive and to think critically about representations of race, sexuality, gender, and class. These categories are ways of characterizing identity, but as with all categories, the characterizations they produce are partial, flawed, and incomplete. Each of these authors asks you to think about different aspects of identity, and the questions in this sequence ask you to draw from the readings and from your own experience, at times, to explore the question: who are we?

In the first two assignments, you'll get the chance to think about two ways identity might be said to be expressed or enacted: narrative and representation. We tell stories about who we are. Inevitably, we also tell stories about others. In those narratives, we find representations. You might think of the sequence as moving from those specific examples of narrative and representation to more philosophical and political questions about what it means to be human, and how the concept of the human is employed to make some identities seem more legitimate or compelling than others. To work with this sequence, you have to be willing to imagine other ways of being outside whatever your own ways of being might be; you have to be able to look closely at the texts at hand to raise questions about what they reveal and how their assertions might be connected to your own life. The final assignment asks you to respond to Susan Griffin's assertion that we are part of a complex web of connections. If Griffin is right that "all the lives that surround us are in us," this would suggest that we might have some responsibility to think about lives other than our own as a way of thinking about ourselves.

ASSIGNMENT 1

Narrative and Identity

KWAME ANTHONY APPIAH

Consider this passage from "Racial Identities":

> Collective identities, in short, provide what we might call scripts: narratives that people can use in shaping their life plans and in telling their life stories. In our society (though not, perhaps, in the England of Addison and Steele) being witty does not in this way suggest the life script of "the wit." And that is why what I called the personal dimensions of identity work differently from the collective ones.
>
> This is not just a point about modern Westerners: cross-culturally it matters to people that their lives have a certain narrative unity; they want to be able to tell a story of their lives that makes sense. The story — my story — should cohere in the way appropriate by the standards made available in my culture to a person of my identity. In telling that story, how I fit into the wider story of various collectivities is, for most of us, important. (pp. 57–58)

Your project in this assignment is to consider the terms, the stages, the conclusions, and the consequences of Kwame Anthony Appiah's argument in his essay "Racial Identities." If, as a mental exercise (or because you are convinced), you accept Appiah's notion that "collective identities, in short, provide what we might call scripts: narratives that people can use in shaping their life plans and in telling their life stories," how might you tell a story that places yourself in relation to the available scripts, to the life stories available to a person like you — a person of your culture (or collectivity), a person of your age, now, in the twenty-first century?

You are not required to write in the genre of the memoir (as though you were writing a chapter of your autobiography), but many find that an inviting way to begin. What a reader wants is a view of you and your world, not in the pen-pal sense of what you look like or what you prefer in music, but with the goal of understanding something more general, something about people like you, something about what it is that shapes and defines a person or an identity in this place and at this point in time. In Appiah's terms, your writing will negotiate the competing demands of a life and a "script," of the personal and the collective, of individual freedom and the politics of identity.

We are trying to avoid the word "essay" in describing this project, since that word carries certain generic restrictions. Our advice is for you to begin not with a generalization but with some specific scene or scenes. Begin with a story (or stories) rather than with an argument. If people are speaking, you may choose to let them speak as characters speak in fiction. You may write in the first person if you find it helpful to do so.

ASSIGNMENT 2

Identity and Representation

EDWARD SAID

The final chapter of Edward Said's *After the Last Sky* ends with this:

> I would like to think, though, that such a book not only tells the reader about us, but in some way also reads the reader. I would like to think that we are not just the people seen or looked at in these photographs: We are also looking at our observers.

Read back through Said's essay "States" (p. 559) by looking at the photos with this reversal in mind — looking in order to see yourself as the one who is being looked at, as the one observed. How are you positioned by the photographer, Jean Mohr? How are you positioned by the person in the scene, always acknowledging your presence? What are you being told?

Once you have read through the photographs, reread the essay with a similar question in mind. This time, however, look for evidence of how Said positions you, defines you, invents you as a presence in the scene.

ASSIGNMENT 3

The Concept of Human

JUDITH BUTLER

The opening lines of Judith Butler's essay might be understood as an invitation to participate with her in one of the traditions of philosophy. She writes:

> What makes for a livable world is no idle question. It is not merely a question for philosophers. It is posed in various idioms all the time by people in various walks of life. If that makes them all philosophers,

then that is a conclusion I am happy to embrace. It becomes a question for ethics, I think, not only when we ask the personal question, what makes my own life bearable, but when we ask, from a position of power, and from the point of view of distributive justice, what makes, or ought to make, the lives of others bearable? Somewhere in the answer we find ourselves not only committed to a certain view of what life is, and what it should be, but also of what constitutes the human, the distinctively human life, and what does not. (p. 238)

Write an essay that takes up this invitation — and that takes it up in specific reference to what Butler has offered in "Beside Oneself: On the Limits of Sexual Autonomy." You will need, then, to take some time to represent her essay — both what it says and what it does. The "Questions for a Second Reading" (p. 256) should be helpful in preparing for this. Imagine an audience of smart people, people who may even know something about Butler, but who have not read this essay. You have read it, and you want to give them a sense of how and why you find it interesting and important. You'll also need to take time to address her questions in your own terms: What makes for a livable world? What constitutes the human? Don't slight this part of your essay. Give yourself as many pages as you gave Butler. You should, however, make it clear that you are writing in response to what you have read. You'll want to indicate, both directly and indirectly, how your thoughts are shaped by, indebted to, or in response to hers.

ASSIGNMENT 4

The Politics of Dehumanization

JUDITH BUTLER, EDWARD SAID

In his essay "States," Edward Said theorizes about the notion of exile in relation to Palestinian identity, offering a study of exile and dislocation through his analysis of photographs taken by Jean Mohr. Consider the following passage:

We turn ourselves into objects not for sale, but for scrutiny. People ask us, as if looking into an exhibit case, "What is it you Palestinians want?" — as if we can put our demands into a single neat phrase. All of us speak of *awdah*, "return," but do we mean that literally, or do we mean "we must restore ourselves to ourselves"? (p. 578)

When Said talks about being looked at as though in an exhibit case, we might understand him as being concerned with the problem of dehumanization. After all, to be in an exhibit case is to be captured, trapped, even dead. We might understand Judith Butler as also wrestling with the problem of dehumanization. In her essay "Beside Oneself: On the Limits of Sexual Autonomy," she writes: "I would like to start, and to end, with the question of the human, of who counts as the human, and the related question of whose lives count as lives, and with a question that has preoccupied many of us for years: what makes for a grievable life?" (p. 238).

Write an essay in which you consider the ways Said and Butler might be said to be speaking with each other. How might the condition of exile be like the condition of being *beside oneself*? What kind of connections — whether you see them as productive or problematic, or both at once — can be made between the ways Said talks about nation, identity, and home, and the ways Butler talks about gender and sexuality? What passages from each seem to have the other in mind? How does each struggle with reference, with pronouns like "we" and "our"?

ASSIGNMENT 5

Interconnectedness and Identity

SUSAN GRIFFIN

Susan Griffin argues that we — all of us, especially all of us who have read her essay — are part of a complex web of connections. At one point she says,

> Who are we? The question is not simple. What we call the self is part of a larger matrix of relationship and society. Had we been born to a different family, in a different time, to a different world, we would not be the same. All the lives that surround us are in us. (p. 411)

At another point she asks, "Is there any one of us who can count ourselves outside the circle circumscribed by our common past?" She speaks of a "field,"

> like a field of gravity that is created by the movements of many bodies. Each life is influenced and it in turn becomes an influence. Whatever is a cause is also an effect. Childhood experience is just one element in the determining field. (p. 386)

One way of thinking about this concept of the self and of interrelatedness, at least under Griffin's guidance, is to work on the connections that she implies and asserts. As you reread the selection, look for powerful and surprising juxtapositions, fragments that stand together in interesting and suggestive ways. Think about the arguments represented by the blank space between those sections. (And look for Griffin's written statements about "relatedness.")

Look for connections that seem important to the text (and to you) and representative of Griffin's thinking (and yours). Then, write an essay in which you use these examples to think through your understanding of Griffin's claims for this "larger matrix," the "determining field," or our "common past."

ALTERNATIVE ASSIGNMENT

A Writer's Identity, A Writer's Position

JOHN EDGAR WIDEMAN

At several points in his essay "Our Time" (p. 622), John Edgar Wideman discusses his position as a writer, telling Robby's story, and he describes the problems he faces in writing this piece (or in "reading" the text of his brother's life). You could read this selection, in other words, as an essay about reading and writing.

Why do you think Wideman talks about these problems here? Why not keep quiet and hope no one notices? Choose three or four passages in which Wideman refers directly or indirectly to his work as a writer, and write an essay defining the problems Wideman faces and explaining why you think he raises them as he does. Finally, what might this have to do with your work as a writer — or as a student in this writing class?

ALTERNATIVE ASSIGNMENT

What We Read and Its Connection to Who We Are

RICHARD E. MILLER

Consider the following passage from Richard E. Miller's "The Dark Night of the Soul":

> What makes *Into the Wild* remarkable is Krakauer's ability to get some purchase on McCandless's actual reading practice, which, in turn, enables him to get inside McCandless's head and speculate with considerable authority about what ultimately led the young man to abandon the comforts of home and purposefully seek out mortal danger. Krakauer is able to do this, in part, because he has access to the books that McCandless read, with all their underlinings and marginalia, as well as to his journals and the postcards and letters McCandless sent to friends during his journey. Working with these materials and his interviews with McCandless's family and friends, Krakauer develops a sense of McCandless's inner life and eventually comes to some understanding of why the young man was so susceptible to being seduced by the writings of London, Thoreau, Muir, and Tolstoy. Who McCandless is and what becomes of him are, it turns out, intimately connected to the young man's approach to reading — both what he chose to read and how he chose to read it.
> (p. 444)

When Miller is writing about Krakauer's *Into the Wild*, he seems to suggest that what we read and how we read can say something about who we are and about what we might become. This is a bold claim.

Think of a book that made a difference to you, that captured you, maybe one you have read more than once, maybe one that you've made marks in, or one that still sits on your bookshelf. Or, if not a book, think of your favorite song, album, movie, or TV show, something that engaged you at least potentially as McCandless was engaged by London, Thoreau, Muir, and Tolstoy. What was it that you found there? What kind of reader were you? And what makes this a story in the past tense? How and why did you move on? (Or if it is not a story in the past tense, where are you now, and are you, like McCandless, in any danger?)

ALTERNATIVE ASSIGNMENT

Representing Others

JOHN EDGAR WIDEMAN

In his essay "Our Time," John Edgar Wideman worries over the problems of representation, of telling his brother's story. He speaks directly to the fundamental problem writers face when they try to represent the lives of others: "I'd slip unaware out of his story and into one of my own. I'd be following him, an obedient shadow, then a cloud would blot the sun and I'd be gone, unchained, a dark form still skulking behind him but no longer in tow" (p. 637). Wideman goes on to say:

> The hardest habit to break ... would be listening to myself listen to him. That habit would destroy any chance of seeing my brother on his terms; and seeing him in his terms, learning his terms, seemed the whole point of learning his story. . . . I had to teach myself to listen. Start fresh, clear the pipes, resist too facile an identification, tame the urge to take off with Robby's story and make it my own. (p. 637)

Richard E. Miller, in "The Dark Night of the Soul" (p. 435), is also concerned with the problems of representation. He provides readings of the lives of others — from Eric Harris to Chris McCandless to Martin Amis to René Descartes and Mary Karr — who are also engaged with the problems of representation and understanding. Write an essay about writing and representation, about the real world and the world of texts, with Wideman and Miller as your primary points of reference. How do they understand representation as a problem for writers and readers? How is that understanding represented (or enacted) in their own work? Which writer might have something to learn from the example of the other?

ALTERNATIVE ASSIGNMENT

The Reflexive Self

RUTH BEHAR

Early on in the "The Vulnerable Observer," Ruth Behar discusses the anxieties many academic writers feel about acknowledging their personal investment in or relation to the subjects about which they are writing. Behar cites Kay Redfield Jamison's *An Unquiet Mind* as a text that deals with these anxieties extensively. Jamison asks some very difficult questions:

> Will my work now be seen by my colleagues as somehow biased because of my illness? . . . If, for example, I am attending a scientific meeting and ask a question, or challenge a speaker, will my question be treated as though it is coming from someone who has studied and treated mood disorders for many years, or will it instead be seen as a highly subjective, idiosyncratic view of someone who has a personal ax to grind? (Jamison as cited in Behar, p. 118)

Think about a moment in your life when you worried that your impartiality or investment in an issue might have affected how you were interpreting a situation or how your interpretation of a situation might be read and interpreted by others. Write an essay about that experience, the limits of objectivity, and the potential value and usefulness of subjective experience. Engage with passages from Behar and perhaps also from Jamison to help you explore these issues and the personal example you are using. Though this assignment asks you to identify an experience similar to those of Behar and Jamison, be mindful of the differences between your experiences and theirs. You might even discuss how those differences shape the meaning and significance of the narratives that construct your life and theirs.

SEQUENCE TWO

The Aims of Education

W. E. B. Du Bois
Joy Castro
Mary Louise Pratt
Richard Rodriguez
Richard E. Miller
Ta-Nehisi Coates

ALTERNATIVE:
Susan Griffin

You have been in school for many years, long enough for your experiences in the classroom to seem natural, inevitable. The purpose of this sequence is to invite you to step outside a world you may have begun to take for granted, to look at the ways you have been taught and at the unspoken assumptions behind your education. The nine assignments that follow bring together six essays that discuss how people (and particularly students) become trapped inside habits of thought. These habits of thought become invisible (or seem natural) because of the ways our schools work or because of the ways we have traditionally learned to use language when we speak, read, or write.

ASSIGNMENT 1
Agents of Change
W. E. B. DU BOIS

W. E. B. Du Bois writes to reform American education. There are many other writers in *Ways of Reading* who write as agents of change, although with different starting points, different concerns, and different agendas: Joy Castro, in "Hungry" and "On Becoming Educated" (p. 263, 266); Mary Louise Pratt, in "Arts of the Contact Zone"

(p. 512); Richard Rodriguez, in "The Achievement of Desire" (p. 533); and Richard E. Miller, in "The Dark Night of the Soul" (p. 435), are just a few examples.

Write an essay in which you put one of these essays (or another from *Ways of Reading*) into conversation with the three chapters from *The Souls of Black Folk*. Where and how do they speak to the same issues? Where and how do they differ in their arguments and in their approach? How are they different as pieces of writing—different in style and in intent? You will need to represent carefully the positions of each. You will need to think about differences as well as similarities. And you should think about how and why the differences might be attributed to history, to race, or to gender.

ASSIGNMENT 2

The Contact Zone

MARY LOUISE PRATT

> The idea of the contact zone is intended in part to contrast with ideas of community that underlie much of the thinking about language, communication, and culture that gets done in the academy. (p. 520)
>
> — MARY LOUISE PRATT, "Arts of the Contact Zone"

Citing Benedict Anderson and what he calls "imagined communities," Mary Louise Pratt argues that our idea of community is "strongly utopian, embodying values like equality, fraternity, liberty, which the societies often profess but systematically fail to realize." Against this utopian vision of community, Pratt argues that we need to develop ways of understanding (even noticing) social and intellectual spaces that are not homogeneous, unified; we need to develop ways of understanding and valuing difference. And, for Pratt, the argument extends to schooling. She asks:

> What is the place of unsolicited oppositional discourse, parody, resistance, critique in the imagined classroom community? Are teachers supposed to feel that their teaching has been most successful when they have eliminated such things and unified the social world, probably in their own image? Who wins when we do that? Who loses? (p. 522)

"Such questions," she says, "may be hypothetical, because in the United States in the 1990s, many teachers find themselves less and less able to do that even if they want to."

"In the United States in the 1990s." "The imagined classroom community." From your experience, what scenes might be used to represent schooling in the 1990s and beyond? How are they usually imagined (idealized, represented, interpreted, valued)? What are the implications of Pratt's argument?

Write an essay in which you use Pratt's terms to examine a representative scene from your own experience with schools and schooling. What examples, stories, or images best represent your experience? How might they be inter-preted as examples of community? as examples of "contact zones"? As you pre-pare your essay, you will want to set the scene as carefully as you can, so that someone who was not there can see it fully. Think about how someone who has not read Pratt might interpret the scene. And think through the various ways *you* might interpret your example. And you should also think about your position in an argument about school as a contact zone. What do you (or people like you) stand to gain or lose when you adopt Pratt's point of view?

ASSIGNMENT 3

The Pedagogical Arts
of the Contact Zone
MARY LOUISE PRATT

Meanwhile, our job in the Americas course remains to figure out how to make that crossroads the best site for learning that it can be. We are looking for the pedagogical arts of the contact zone. These will include, we are sure, exercises in storytelling and in identifying with the ideas, interests, histories, and attitudes of others; experiments in transculturation and collaborative work and in the arts of critique, parody, and comparison (including unseemly comparisons between elite and vernacular cultural forms); the redemption of the oral; ways for people to engage with suppressed aspects of history (including their own histories), ways to move *into and out of* rhetorics of authen-ticity; ground rules for communication across lines of difference and hierarchy that go beyond politeness but maintain mutual respect; a systematic approach to the all-important concept of *cultural media-tion*. (p. 524)

> — MARY LOUISE PRATT, "Arts of the Contact Zone"

Mary Louise Pratt writes generally about culture and history, but also about read-ing and writing and teaching and learning, about the "literate" and "pedagogical" arts of this place she calls the contact zone. Think about the class you are in — its position in the curriculum, in the institution. Think about its official goals (and its unofficial goals). Think about the positions represented by the students, the teacher. Think about how to think about the class, in Pratt's terms, as a contact zone.

And think about the unusual exercises represented by her list: "storytelling," "experiments in transculturation," "critique," "parody," "unseemly comparisons," moving into and out of "rhetorics of authenticity" — these are some of them. Take one of these suggested exercises, explain what you take it to mean, and then go on to discuss how it might be put into practice in a writing class. What would students do? to what end? How would their work be evaluated? What place would the exercise have in the larger sequence of assignments over the term, quarter, or semester? In your terms, and from your point of view, what might you learn from such an exercise?

Or you could think of the question this way: What comments would a teacher make on one of the papers you have written so far in order that its revision might stand as one of these exercises? How would the revision be different from what you are used to doing?

Write an essay in which you present and discuss an exercise designed to serve the writing class as a contact zone.

ASSIGNMENT 4

Ways of Reading, Ways of Speaking, Ways of Caring

RICHARD RODRIGUEZ

> What I am about to say to you has taken me more than twenty years to admit: *A primary reason for my success in the classroom was that I couldn't forget that schooling was changing me and separating me from the life I enjoyed before becoming a student.* (p. 534)

> If, because of my schooling, I had grown culturally separated from my parents, my education finally had given me ways of speaking and caring about that fact. (p. 550)
>
> — RICHARD RODRIGUEZ, "The Achievement of Desire"

As you reread Richard Rodriguez's essay, what would you say are his "ways of speaking and caring"? One way to think about this question is to trace how the lessons he learned about reading, education, language, family, culture, and class shifted as he moved from elementary school through college and graduate school to his career as a teacher and a writer. What scholarly abilities did he learn that provided him with "ways of speaking and caring" valued in the academic community? Where and how do you see him using them in his essay?

Write an essay in which you discuss how Rodriguez reads (reviews, summarizes, interprets) his family, his teachers, his schooling, himself, and his books. What differences can you say such reading makes to those ways of speaking and caring that you locate in the text?

A Story of Schooling

RICHARD RODRIGUEZ

Richard Rodriguez insists that his story is also everyone's story. Take an episode from your life, one that seems in some way similar to one of the episodes in "The Achievement of Desire" (p. 533), and cast it into a shorter version of Rodriguez's essay. Your job here is to look at your experience in Rodriguez's terms, which means thinking the way he does, noticing what he would notice, interpreting details in a similar fashion, using his key terms, seeing through his point of view; it could also mean imitating his style of writing, working with quotations from other writers, doing whatever it is you see him doing characteristically while he writes. Imitation, Rodriguez argues, is not necessarily a bad thing; it can, in fact, be one of the powerful ways in which a person learns.

Note: This assignment can also be used to read against "The Achievement of Desire." Rodriguez insists on the universality of his experience leaving home and community and joining the larger public life. You could highlight the differences between your experience and his. You should begin by imitating Rodriguez's method; you do not have to arrive at his conclusions, however.

The Literate Arts

RICHARD E. MILLER

Richard E. Miller's essay opens with a list of fatal shootings in school — troublingly, an incomplete list. As the essay builds to questions — questions for educators and for students — the specters of violence and alienation remain, changing how we think about the reading and writing school endeavors to teach us. "I have these doubts, you see," Miller writes of academic work, "doubts silently shared by many who spend their days teaching others the literate arts. Aside from gathering and organizing information, aside from generating critiques and analyses that forever fall on deaf ears, what might the literate arts be said to be good for?" (p. 439).

Write an essay that takes up this question — "what might the literate arts be said to be good for?" — and that takes it up from your range of reference and from your point of view — or, more properly, from the point of view of you and people like you, the group you feel prepared to speak for. As an exercise in understanding, your essay should be modeled on one (or more) of the sections in "The Dark Night of the Soul." You can choose the text — and the text can be anything that might serve as an example of the literate arts, things in print but also including songs, films, and TV shows. But your presentation and discussion of the text should be in conversation with Miller — with his concerns, his key terms, his examples, and his conclusions.

ASSIGNMENT 7

Entering the Conversation

MARY LOUISE PRATT, RICHARD RODRIGUEZ,

RICHARD E. MILLER

> After years spent unwilling to admit its attractions, I gestured nostal-
> gically toward the past. I yearned for that time when I had not been
> so alone. I became impatient with books. I wanted experience more
> immediate. I feared the library's silence. I silently scorned the gray,
> timid faces around me. I grew to hate the growing pages of my dis-
> sertation on genre and Renaissance literature. (In my mind I heard
> relatives laughing as they tried to make sense of its title.) I wanted
> something—I couldn't say exactly what. (p. 549)
>
> — RICHARD RODRIGUEZ, "The Achievement of Desire"

> For some, it will hardly come as a surprise to learn that reading and
> writing have no magically transformative powers. But for those of us
> who have been raised into the teaching and publishing professions, it
> can be quite a shock to confront the possibility that reading and writing
> and talking exercise almost *none* of the powers we regularly attribute
> to them in our favorite stories. The dark night of the soul for literacy
> workers comes with the realization that training students to read, write,
> and talk in more critical and self-reflective ways cannot protect them
> from the violent changes our culture is undergoing. (p. 438)
>
> — RICHARD E. MILLER, "The Dark Night of the Soul"

"I have these doubts, you see," Richard E. Miller writes of academic work, "doubts silently shared by many who spend their days teaching others the literate arts. Aside from gathering and organizing information, aside from generating critiques and analyses that forever fall on deaf ears, what might the literate arts be said to be good for?"

These questions are repeated, in different contexts and with different inflections, by all of the writers you have been reading: Mary Louise Pratt, Richard Rodriguez, and Richard E. Miller. All are concerned with the limits (and the failures) of education, with particular attention to the humanities and to the supposed benefits to be found in reading and writing.

Write an essay that takes up this question—"what might the literate arts be said to be good for?"—and that takes it up with these writers and these essays as your initial point of reference. What do they say? How might they be said to speak to one another? And, finally, where are you in this? Where are you, and people like you, the group for whom you feel prepared to speak? You, too, have been and will continue to be expected to take courses in reading and writing, to read, write, and talk in critical and self-reflective ways. Where are you in this conversation?

ASSIGNMENT 8

Race and Education

W. E. B. DU BOIS

In "The Forethought," the introduction to *The Souls of Black Folk*, W. E. B. Du Bois writes:

> Herein lie buried many things which if read with patience may show the strange meaning of being black here in the dawning of the Twentieth Century. This meaning is not without interest to you, Gentle Reader; for the problem of the Twentieth Century is the problem of the color-line.

While we have chosen only three of the fourteen chapters in *The Souls of Black Folk*, we chose these three because they seem to ask to be read together. How and why might they *now* require "patience" of their readers? How might they be read, together, as an attempt to lead a reader to an understanding of the "strange meaning of being black . . . in the dawning of the Twentieth Century"? What do they say about notions of race? What do they have to say to the twenty-first century?

Write an essay that looks at these three chapters in light of the project and the concerns outlined by Du Bois in "The Forethought." You should imagine that your reader is interested in knowing something about Du Bois and, through his writing, about the experience of African Americans almost 100 years ago and how that experience might connect to our current moment. You should think of yourself as a historian, using this text (not only what it says but *how* it says what it says) as your primary document. And, as you help someone think through these chapters, you should ask: How might this writing be significant now, more than 100 years later? Where and how are Du Bois's concerns represented today, for example, in the curriculum of your university? If you look at the structures of education today, what might you say, following Du Bois, about the problems of the color-line?

ASSIGNMENT 9

Gender, Race, and Education

W. E. B. DU BOIS

There is an interesting and characteristic sentence toward the end of the chapter "Of the Training of Black Men" that nicely illustrates a difficulty Du Bois has in writing women into his account of education. He says:

> Comparing them as a class [black students educated in the South] with my fellow students in New England and in Europe, I cannot hesitate in saying that nowhere have I met men and women with a broader spirit of helpfulness, with deeper devotion to their life-work, or with more consecrated determination to succeed in the face of bitter difficulties than among Negro college-bred men. (p. 316)

The "men and women" at the opening of the sentence become "college-bred men" by its close. Go back and reread these three chapters, looking carefully to see how and where women are represented. Where are Du Bois's sympathies? What does he take for granted? What does he struggle to acknowledge? (It might also be useful to do some research for this assignment — to find out, for example, about the educational opportunities available to women and, in particular, to black women at the turn of the century, or to read other pieces by Du Bois on the status of women. For the latter, the collection of essays and articles in the Library of America edition, *W. E. B. Du Bois: Writings*, is particularly useful.)

Write an essay in which you represent and discuss the ways Du Bois figures women into his account of the issues confronting the education of black Americans in the South at the turn of the century. Where and how are they present? Where and how are they absent? And how would you account for their position in these texts?

A word of caution: it should be clear that it is not enough to claim in absolute terms that Du Bois is sexist or that he is a product of his time. It serves no good purpose to reduce Du Bois to a stick figure (and it would be wrong); texts are all in one way or another products of their times, and a student would have to do a considerable amount of work to be able to speak responsibly about what Americans thought or said in 1903. Your work here is to locate in Du Bois's writing passages that will allow you to think about his efforts to write about gender, race, and education.

ALTERNATIVE ASSIGNMENT
Writing against the Grain
SUSAN GRIFFIN

As you reread "Our Secret" (p. 381), think of Susan Griffin's prose as experimental, as deliberate and crafted. She is trying to do something that she can't do in the "usual" essay form. She wants to make a different kind of argument and engage her reader in a different manner. And so she mixes personal and academic writing. She assembles fragments and juxtaposes seemingly unrelated material in surprising and suggestive relationships. She breaks the "plane" of the page with italicized intersections. She organizes her material, that is, but not in the usual mode of thesis-example-conclusion. The arrangement is not nearly so linear. At one point, when she seems to be prepared to argue that German child-rearing practices produced the Holocaust, she quickly says:

> Of course there cannot be one answer to such a monumental riddle, nor does any event in history have a single cause. Rather a field exists, like a field of gravity that is created by the movements of many bodies. Each life is influenced and it in turn becomes an influence. Whatever is a cause is also an effect. Childhood experience is just one element in the determining field. (p. 386)

Her prose serves to create a "field," one where many bodies are set in relationship.

It is useful, then, to think about Griffin's prose as the enactment of a method, as a way of doing a certain kind of intellectual work. One way to study this, to feel its effects, is to imitate it, to take it as a model. For this assignment, write a Griffin-like essay, one similar in its methods or organization and argument. You will need to think about the stories you might tell, about the stories and texts you might gather (stories and texts not your own). As you write, you will want to think carefully about arrangement and about commentary (about where, that is, you will speak to your reader as the writer of the piece). You should not feel bound to Griffin's subject matter, but you should feel that you are working in her spirit.

ALTERNATIVE ASSIGNMENT
The Task of Attention
SUSAN GRIFFIN

> I am looking now at the etching called *Poverty*, made in 1897. Near the center, calling my attention, a woman holds her head in her hands. (p. 390)
>
> — SUSAN GRIFFIN, "Our Secret"

This is one of the many moments when Susan Griffin speaks to us as though in the midst of her work. The point of this assignment is to think about that work — what it is, how she does it, and what it might have to do with schools and schooling. She is, after all, doing much of the traditional work of scholars — going to the archive, studying old materials, traveling and interviewing subjects, learning and writing history.

And yet this is not the kind of prose you would expect to find in a textbook for a history course. Even if the project is not what we usually think of as a research project, Griffin is a careful researcher. Griffin knows what she is doing. Go back to look again (this time with a writer's eye) at both the features of Griffin's prose and the way she characterizes her work as a scholar, gathering and studying her materials.

Write an essay in which you present an account of *how* Griffin does her work. You should use her words and examples from the text, but you should also feel that it is your job to explain what you present and to comment on it from the point of view of a student. As you reread, look to those sections where Griffin seems to be speaking to her readers about her work — about how she reads and how she writes, about how she gathers her materials and how she studies them. What is she doing? What is at stake in adopting such methods? How might they be taught? Where in the curriculum might (should?) such lessons be featured?

SEQUENCE THREE

The Arts of the
Contact Zone

Mary Louise Pratt
Gloria Anzaldúa
John Edgar Wideman
Edward Said

ALTERNATIVE:

Ruth Behar

This sequence allows you to work closely with the argument of Mary Louise Pratt's "Arts of the Contact Zone," not so much through summary (repeating the argument) as through extension (working under its influence, applying its terms and protocols). In particular, you are asked to try your hand at those ways of reading and writing Pratt defines as part of the "literate arts of the contact zone," ways of reading and writing that have not historically been taught or valued in American schools.

Pratt is one of the country's most influential cultural critics. In "Arts of the Contact Zone," she makes the argument that our usual ways of reading and writing assume identification — that is, we learn to read and write the texts that express our own position and point of view. As a result, texts that reproduce different ways of thinking, texts that allude to different cultural systems, seem flawed, wrong, or inscrutable. As a counterposition, Pratt asks us to imagine scenes of reading, writing, teaching, and learning as "contact zones," places of contact between people who can't or don't or won't necessarily identify with one another.

In the first assignment, you are asked to search for or produce a document to exemplify the arts of the contact zone, working in library archives, searching the streets, surfing the Internet, or writing an "autoethnography." This is a big job, and probably new to most students; it is a project you will want to come back to and revise. The remaining assignments outline a project in which you examine other selections from *Ways of Reading* that exemplify or present moments of cultural contact.

ASSIGNMENT 1

The Literate Arts of the Contact Zone

MARY LOUISE PRATT

Here, briefly, are two descriptions of the writing one might find or expect in the contact zone:

> Autoethnography, transculturation, critique, collaboration, bilingualism, mediation, parody, denunciation, imaginary dialogue, vernacular expression — these are some of the literate arts of the contact zone. Miscomprehension, incomprehension, dead letters, unread masterpieces, absolute heterogeneity of meaning — these are some of the perils of writing in the contact zone. They all live among us today in the transnationalized metropolis of the United States and are becoming more widely visible, more pressing, and, like Guaman Poma's text, more decipherable to those who once would have ignored them in defense of a stable, centered sense of knowledge and reality. (pp. 519–20)

> We are looking for the pedagogical arts of the contact zone. These will include, we are sure, exercises in storytelling and in identifying with the ideas, interests, histories, and attitudes of others; experiments in transculturation and collaborative work and in the arts of critique, parody, and comparison (including unseemly comparisons between elite and vernacular cultural forms); the redemption of the oral; ways for people to engage with suppressed aspects of history (including their own histories), ways to move *into and out of* rhetorics of authenticity; ground rules for communication across lines of difference and hierarchy that go beyond politeness but maintain mutual respect; a systematic approach to the all-important concept of *cultural mediation.* (p. 524)

Here are two ways of working on Mary Louise Pratt's idea of the contact zone. Choose one.

1. One way of working with Pratt's essay, of extending its project, would be to conduct your own local inventory of writing from the contact zone. You might do this on your own or in teams, with others from your class. You will want to gather several similar documents, your "archive," before you make a final selection. Think about how to make that choice. What makes one document stand out as representative? Here are two ways you might organize your search:

    a. You could look for historical documents. A local historical society might have documents written by Native Americans ("Indians") to the white settlers. There may be documents written by slaves to masters or to northern whites explaining their experience. There may be documents written by women (suffragists, for example) trying to negotiate for public positions or rights. There may be documents from any of a number of racial or ethnic groups — Hispanic, Jewish, Irish, Italian, Polish, Swedish — trying to explain their positions to the mainstream culture. There may, perhaps at union halls, be documents written by workers to owners. Your own sense of the heritage of your area should direct your search.

b.   Or you could look at contemporary documents in the print that is around you, texts that you might otherwise overlook. Pratt refers to one of the characteristic genres of the Hispanic community, the "*testimonio.*" You could look for songs, testimonies, manifestos, statements by groups on campus, stories, autobiographies, interviews, letters to the editor, web pages. You could look at the writing of any marginalized group, particularly writing intended, at least in part, to represent the experience of outsiders to the dominant culture (or to be in dialogue with that culture or to respond to that culture). These documents, if we follow Pratt's example, would encompass the work of young children or students, including college students.

Once you have completed your inventory, choose a document you would like to work with and write an essay that presents it carefully and in detail (perhaps in even greater detail than Pratt's presentation of the *New Chronicle*). You will, in other words, need to set the scene, summarize, explain, and work block quotations into your essay. You might imagine that you are presenting this to someone who would not have seen it and would not know how to read it, at least not as an example of the literate arts of the contact zone.

2. Another way of extending the project of Pratt's essay would be to write your autoethnography. It should not be too hard to locate a setting or context in which you are the "other" — the one who speaks from outside rather than inside the dominant discourse. Pratt says that the position of the outsider is marked not only by differences of language and ways of thinking and speaking but also by differences in power, authority, status. In a sense, she argues, the only way those in power can understand you is in *their* terms. These are terms you will need to use to tell your story, but your goal is to describe your position in ways that "engage with representations others have made of [you]" without giving in or giving up or disappearing in their already formed sense of who you are.

   This is an interesting challenge. One of the things that will make the writing difficult is that the autoethnographic or transcultural text calls upon skills not usually valued in American classrooms: bilingualism, parody, denunciation, imaginary dialogue, vernacular expression, storytelling, unseemly comparisons of high and low cultural forms — these are some of the terms Pratt offers. These do not fit easily with the traditional genres of the writing class (essay, term paper, summary, report) or its traditional values (unity, consistency, sincerity, clarity, correctness, decorum).

You will probably need to take this essay (or whatever it should be called) through several drafts. (In fact, you might revise this essay after you have completed assignments 2 and 3.) It might be best to begin as Pratt's student, using her description as a preliminary guide. Once you get a sense of your own project, you may find that you have terms or examples to add to her list of the literate arts of the contact zone.

ASSIGNMENT 2

Borderlands

MARY LOUISE PRATT, GLORIA ANZALDÚA

In "Arts of the Contact Zone" (p. 512), Mary Louise Pratt talks about the "auto-ethnographic" text, "a text in which people undertake to describe themselves in ways that engage with representations others have made of them," and about "transculturation," the "processes whereby members of subordinated or marginal groups select and invent from the materials transmitted by a dominant or metropolitan culture."

Write an essay in which you present a reading of Gloria Anzaldúa's "How to Tame a Wild Tongue" (p. 26) as an example of an autoethnographic and/or transcultural text. You should imagine that you are writing to someone who is not familiar with either Pratt's argument or Anzaldúa's thinking. Part of your work, then, is to present Anzaldúa's text to readers who don't have it in front of them. You have the example of Pratt's reading of Guaman Poma's *New Chronicle and Good Government*. And you have her discussion of the literate arts of the contact zone. Think about how Anzaldúa's text might be similarly read and about how her text does and doesn't fit Pratt's description. Your goal should be to add an example to Pratt's discussion and to qualify it, to alter or reframe what she has said now that you have had a chance to look at an additional example.

ASSIGNMENT 3

Counterparts

JOHN EDGAR WIDEMAN

Here, from "Arts of the Contact Zone," is Mary Louise Pratt on the autoethnographic text:

> Guaman Poma's *New Chronicle* is an instance of what I have proposed to call an *autoethnographic* text, by which I mean a text in which people undertake to describe themselves in ways that engage with representations others have made of them. Thus if ethnographic texts are those in which European metropolitan subjects represent to themselves their others (usually their conquered

The Essay as a Contact Zone

RUTH BEHAR

Ruth Behar spends a significant amount of time throughout "The Vulnerable Observer" discussing the genres she has explored and the one she has eventually settled on — the essay. As Behar explains, "Unconsciously at first, but later with more direction, I chose the essay as a genre through which to *attempt* (the original meaning of *essai* or essay) the dialectic between connection and otherness that is at the center of all forms of historical and cultural representation" (p. 124). Behar goes on to explain that the essay is "an amorphous, open-ended, even rebellious genre that desegregates the boundaries between self and other, [which] has been the genre of choice for radical feminists and cultural critics pursuing thick description" (p. 124).

Behar's discussion of the etymology of the word *essay*, emerging from the French infinitive *essayer*, meaning "to attempt" or "to try," might be unfamiliar to you and different from how you have conceptualized the "essay." Write an essay that explores this denotative definition of the word *essay*, in which you attempt to understand the significance and potential uses of that definition for writers like Behar and for the "radical feminists and cultural critics" Behar associates herself with. Why might the form, conceived of in such a way, be of use to such writers? What does it allow for? In your essay, also consider how Behar's employment of that understanding of the genre is reflected in her text, both in terms of the type of argument and structure she utilizes and in terms of the stylistic features she relies on in her writing.

Autobiographical Explorations

Richard Rodriguez

Edward Said

Susan Griffin

Richard E. Miller

Gloria Bird

ALTERNATIVES:

John Edgar Wideman

Alison Bechdel

Joy Castro

Autobiographical writing has been a regular feature of writing courses since the nineteenth century. There are a variety of reasons for the prevalence of autobiography, not the least of which is the pleasure students take in thinking about and writing about their lives and their world. There is also a long tradition of published autobiographical writing, particularly in the United States. The title of this sequence puts a particular spin on that tradition, since it points to a more specialized use of autobiography, phrased here as "exploration." What is suggested by the title is a use of writing (and the example of one's experience, including intellectual experience) to investigate, question, explore, inquire. Often the genre is not used for these purposes at all. Autobiographical writing is often used for purposes of display or self-promotion, or to further (rather than question) an argument (about success, about how to live a good or proper or fulfilling life).

There are two threads to this sequence. The first is to invite you to experiment with the genre of "autobiographical exploration." The second is to foreground the relationship between your work and the work of others, to think about how and why and where you are prepared to write autobiographically (prepared not only by the lessons you've learned in school but also by the culture and the way it invites you to tell — and live — the story of your life). And, if you are working inside a conventional field, a predictable way of writing, the sequence asks where and how you might make your mark or assert your position — your identity as a person (a character in a life story) and as a writer (someone working with the conventions of life-writing).

The alternative assignments that follow provide similar assignments but with different readings. They can be substituted for or added to the assignments in this sequence.

ASSIGNMENT 1

Desire, Reading, and the Past
RICHARD RODRIGUEZ

In "The Achievement of Desire" (p. 533), Richard Rodriguez tells stories of home but also stories of reading, of moments when things he read allowed him a way of reconsidering or revising ("framing," he calls it) the stories he would tell himself about himself. It is a very particular account of neighborhood, family, ethnicity, and schooling.

At the same time, Rodriguez insists that his story is also everyone's story — that his experience is universal. Take an episode from your life, one that seems in some ways similar to one of the episodes in "The Achievement of Desire," and cast it into a shorter version of Rodriguez's essay. Try to make use of your reading in ways similar to his. Think about what you have read lately in school, perhaps in this anthology.

In general, however, your job in this assignment is to look at your experience in Rodriguez's terms, which means thinking the way he does, noticing what he would notice, interpreting details in a similar fashion, using his key terms, seeing through his point of view; it could mean imitating his style of writing, doing whatever it is you see him doing characteristically when he writes. Imitation, Rodriguez argues, is not necessarily a bad thing; it can, he argues, be one of the powerful ways a person learns. Let this assignment serve as an exercise.

ASSIGNMENT 2

A Photographic Essay
EDWARD SAID

Edward Said, in the introduction to *After the Last Sky*, says of his method in "States":

> Its style and method — the interplay of text and photos, the mixture of genres, modes, styles — do not tell a consecutive story, nor do they

constitute a political essay. Since the main features of our present existence are dispossession, dispersion, and yet also a kind of power incommensurate with our stateless exile, I believe that essentially unconventional, hybrid, and fragmentary forms of expression should be used to represent us. What I have quite consciously designed, then, is an alternative mode of expression to the one usually encountered in the media, in works of social science, in popular fiction. (*After the Last Sky*, p. 6)

And later:

The multifaceted vision is essential to any representation of us. Stateless, dispossessed, de-centered, we are frequently unable either to speak the "truth" of our experience or to make it heard. We do not usually control the images that represent us; we have been confined to spaces designed to reduce or stunt us; and we have often been distorted by pressures and powers that have been too much for us. An additional problem is that our language, Arabic, is unfamiliar in the West and belongs to a tradition and civilization usually both misunderstood and maligned. Everything we write about ourselves, therefore, is an interpretive translation — of our language, our experience, our senses of self and others. (*After the Last Sky*, p. 6)

Reread "States" (p. 559), paying particular attention to the relationship of text and photograph, and paying attention to form. What *is* the order of the writing in this essay? (We will call it an essay for lack of a better term.) How might you diagram or explain its organization? By what principle(s) is it ordered and arranged? The essay shifts genres — memoir, history, argument. It is, as Said comments, "hybrid." What surprises are there? or disappointments? How might you describe the writer's strategy as he works on his audience, on readers? And, finally, do you find Said's explanation sufficient or useful — does the experience of exile produce its own inevitable style of report and representation?

For this assignment, compose a similar project, a Said-like reading of a set of photos. These can be photos prepared for the occasion (by you or a colleague); they could also be photos already available. Whatever their source, they should represent people and places, a history and/or geography that you know well, that you know to be complex and contradictory, and that you know will not be easily or readily understood by others, both the group for whom you will be writing (most usefully the members of your class) and readers more generally. You must begin with a sense that the photos cannot speak for themselves; you must speak for them.

In preparation, you should reread closely to come to a careful understanding of Said's project. The first and second "Questions for a Second Reading" (pp. 593–94) should be useful for this.

ASSIGNMENT 3

The Matrix

SUSAN GRIFFIN

At several points in her essay "Our Secret," Susan Griffin argues that we — all of us — are part of a complex web of connections. We live in history, and history is determining. At one point she says:

> Who are we? The question is not simple. What we call the self is part of a larger matrix of relationship and society. Had we been born to a different family, in a different time, to a different world, we would not be the same. All the lives that surround us are in us. (p. 411)

At another point she asks, "Is there any one of us who can count ourselves outside the circle circumscribed by our common past?" She speaks of a "field"

> like a field of gravity that is created by the movements of many bodies. Each life is influenced and it in turn becomes an influence. Whatever is a cause is also an effect. Childhood experience is just one element in the determining field. (p. 386)

One way of thinking about this concept of the self (and of interrelatedness), at least under Griffin's guidance, is to work on the connections that she implies and asserts. As you reread the selection, look for powerful and surprising juxtapositions, fragments that stand together in interesting and suggestive ways. Think about the arguments represented by the blank spaces on the page or the jumps from section to section. (And look for Griffin's written statements about relatedness.) Look for connections that seem important to the text (and to you) and to be representative of Griffin's thinking (and useful to yours).

Write an essay in which you use these examples to think through the ways Griffin answers the question she raises: Who are we?

ASSIGNMENT 4

The Experience of Thought

RICHARD E. MILLER

In the final chapter of *Writing at the End of the World*, Richard E. Miller says the following about his own writing:

> While the assessments, evaluations, proposals, reports, commentaries, and critiques I produce help to keep the bureaucracy of higher education going, there is another kind of writing I turn to in order to sustain the ongoing search for meaning in a world no one controls. This

writing asks the reader to make imaginative connections between disparate elements; it tracks one path among many possible ones across the glistening water. (*Writing at the End of the World*, p. 196)

We can assume that this is the kind of writing present in "The Dark Night of the Soul."

Reread "The Dark Night of the Soul" (p. 435) with particular attention to Miller's method, which is, in simplest terms, putting one thing next to another. Pay attention to the connections Miller makes, to the ways he makes them, and to the ways as a reader you are (or are not) invited into this process. And write a Miller-like essay. To give the project some shape and limit, let's say that it should bring together at least three "disparate elements," three examples you can use to think about whatever it is you want to think about. You don't need to be constrained to Miller's subject — writing, reading, and schooling — although this subject might be exactly the right one for you. Your writing should, however, be like Miller's in its sense of urgency. In other words, write about something that matters to you, that you care about, that touches you personally and deeply.

ASSIGNMENT 5

The "I" of the Personal Essay

RICHARD RODRIGUEZ, EDWARD SAID, RICHARD E. MILLER

The assignments in this sequence have been designed to prompt autobiographical writing. They have been invitations for you to tell your story and to think about the ways stories represent a person and a life. They have also, of course, been exercises in imitation, in writing like Richard Rodriguez, Edward Said, and Richard E. Miller, in casting your story in their terms. These exercises highlight the ways in which your story is never just your own but also written through our culture's sense of what it means to be a person, to live, grow, change, learn, experience. No writer simply gets to invent childhood. Childhood, like adulthood, is a category already determined by hundreds of thousands of representations of life — in books, in songs, on TV, in paintings, in the stories we tell ourselves about ourselves. As you have written these four personal narratives, you have, of course, been telling the truth, just as you have also, of course, been creating a character, setting scenes, providing certain representations that provide a version of (but that don't begin to sum up) your life.

Read back over the essays you have written (and perhaps revised). As you read, look for examples of where you feel you were doing your best work, where you are proud of the writing and interested in what it allows you to see or to think (where the "investigations" seem most worthwhile).

And think about what is *not* contained in these essays. What experiences are missing? what point of view? what ways of speaking or thinking or writing? If you were to go back to assemble these pieces into a longer essay, what would you keep, and what would you add or change? What are the problems facing a writer, like you, trying to write a life, to take experience and represent it in sentences?

With these questions in mind, reread the essays you have written and write a preface, a short piece introducing a reader to what you have written (to your work — and perhaps work you may do on these essays in the future).

ASSIGNMENT 6

Theories of Autobiography

GLORIA BIRD

Many of the essays in this collection make use of or raise questions about autobiography as a way of thinking about social justice, political questions, and cultural representation. For example, we might understand writers like John Edgar Wideman, Joy Castro, Richard Rodriguez, Susan Griffin, Edward Said, Richard E. Miller, Alison Bechdel, and, of course, Gloria Bird, as addressing questions about autobiography.

Choose two or three of these writers and begin to develop your own theory of autobiography, using specific passages from each writer's work to interrogate, develop, and support your own claims about autobiography. Your essay could consider questions such as the following: What does it mean to do the work of autobiography? How do you understand the relationship between personal experience and intellectual ideas? What work can autobiography do for the writer and/or readers? What does your own experience writing about your own life tell you about these questions? And, finally, what are the difficulties and rewards of writing autobiographical essays?

ALTERNATIVE ASSIGNMENT

Old Habits

JOHN EDGAR WIDEMAN

John Edgar Wideman frequently interrupts the narrative in "Our Time" to talk about the problems he is having as a writer. He says, for example, "The hardest habit to break, since it was the habit of a lifetime, would be listening to myself listen to him. That habit would destroy any chance of seeing my brother on his terms; and seeing him in his terms, learning his terms, seemed the whole point of learning his story" (p. 637).

Wideman gives you the sense of a writer who is aware from the inside, while writing, of the problems inherent in the personal narrative. This genre always shades and deflects; it is always partial and biased; in its very attempts to be complete, to understand totally, it reduces its subject in ways that are unacceptable. And so you can see Wideman's efforts to overcome these problems — he writes in Robby's voice; he starts his story three different times, first with Garth, later with the neighborhood, hoping that a variety of perspectives will overcome the limits inherent in each; he stops and speaks to us not as the storyteller but as the writer, thinking about what he is doing and not doing.

Let Wideman's essay provide a kind of writing lesson. It highlights problems; it suggests alternatives. Using Wideman, then, as your writing teacher, write a family history of your own. Yours will most likely be shorter than Wideman's, but let its writing be the occasion for you also to work on a personal narrative as a writing problem, an interesting problem that forces a writer to think about the limits of representation and point of view (about who gets to speak and in whose terms, about who sums things up and what is left out in this accounting).

ALTERNATIVE ASSIGNMENT

Graphic Autobiography

ALISON BECHDEL

Alison Bechdel writes, "Of course the point at which I began to write the story is not the same as the point at which the story begins" (p. 79). We might read this statement as a commentary on the work of composing autobiography or memoir. She remarks later, "Another difficulty is the fact that the story of my mother and me is unfolding even as I write it" (p. 82).

Consider Bechdel's comments about writing this book and about herself. What does she seem to be suggesting about the difficulties of writing autobiographical work? How would it be different if her work were composed of only words, or if it were a more conventional memoir of mother and daughter? How does her chosen form of graphic memoir enable and limit what she is able to do in writing about herself and her family?

Think of an autobiographical narrative you are familiar with, perhaps in literature or film. You might want to think of a story that involves a mother and daughter, like Bechdel's does. Write an essay in which you discuss the differences between this familiar narrative and Bechdel's work. In your discussion, you'll want to provide particular sets of frames or clusters from Bechdel's work and specific moments in the narrative as examples. What is the relationship between the two autobiographical approaches? What does Bechdel's graphic work do that the other narrative does not do? What can you say about Bechdel's approach from looking at it alongside this other example?

ALTERNATIVE ASSIGNMENT

A Single Life, a Multiple World

JOY CASTRO, SUSAN GRIFFIN

We might read Joy Castro's "Hungry" and "On Becoming Educated" (pp. 263, 266) and Susan Griffin's "Our Secret" (p. 381) as containing elements of autobiography.

Each writer relies on stories from her own life to demonstrate the relationship between one individual life and the larger cultural and political implications. Susan Griffin writes, "To a certain kind of mind, what is hidden away ceases to exist" (p. 404). As readers, we are struck by the ways this statement (and so many of Griffin's statements) pertains both to her own life story and to the larger historical narrative of the Holocaust.

Reread both Castro and Griffin, looking for sentences and phrases that seem to work on two levels (the personal and the political/cultural). Which sentences or phrases suggest to you that they are both about the writer's life *and* about all of our lives, about the world? How can you tell?

Write an essay in which you illuminate, through the work of these two writers, the relationship between one life and what happens in the world at large. How do these writers help us understand ourselves as individuals and also as parts of larger systems, cultures, or worlds?

SEQUENCE FIVE

Experts and Expertise

Judith Butler
Edward Said
Walker Percy

ALTERNATIVES:

Richard E. Miller
Atul Gawande
Michael Specter

The first two assignments in this sequence give you the chance to think about familiar settings or experiences through the work of writers who have had a significant effect on contemporary thought: Judith Butler and Edward Said.

In each case, you will be given the opportunity to work alongside these thinkers as an apprentice, carrying out work they have begun. The final assignment in the sequence will ask you to look back on what you have done, to take stock, and, with Walker Percy's account of the oppressive nature of expertise in mind, to draw some conclusions about the potential and consequences of this kind of intellectual apprenticeship. There are three alternative assignments following the sequence. Any of these could be used in place of the assignments in the sequence.

ASSIGNMENT 1

A Question for Philosophers

JUDITH BUTLER

The opening lines of Judith Butler's essay "Beside Oneself: On the Limits of Sexual Autonomy" might be understood as an invitation to participate with her in one of the traditions of philosophy.

What makes for a livable world is no idle question. It is not merely a question for philosophers. It is posed in various idioms all the time by people in various walks of life. If that makes them all philosophers, then that is a conclusion I am happy to embrace. It becomes a question for ethics, I think, not only when we ask the personal question, what makes my own life bearable, but when we ask, from a position of power, and from the point of view of distributive justice, what makes, or ought to make, the lives of others bearable? Somewhere in the answer we find ourselves not only committed to a certain view of what life is, and what it should be, but also of what constitutes the human, the distinctively human life, and what does not. (p. 238)

Write an essay that takes up this invitation — and that takes it up in specific reference to what Butler has offered in "Beside Oneself: On the Limits of Sexual Autonomy." You will need, then, to take some time to represent her essay — both what it says and what it does. The "Questions for a Second Reading" (p. 256) should be helpful in preparing for this. Imagine an audience of smart people, people who may even know something about Butler, but who have not read this essay. You have read it, and you want to give them a sense of how and why you find it interesting and important.

But you'll also need to take time to address her questions in your own terms: What makes for a livable world? What constitutes the human? Don't slight this part of your essay. Give yourself as many pages as you gave Butler. You should, however, make it clear that you are writing in response to what you have read. You'll want to indicate, both directly and indirectly, how your thoughts are shaped by, indebted to, or in response to hers.

ASSIGNMENT 2

On Representation

EDWARD SAID

In his essay "States" (p. 559), Edward Said insists on our recognizing the contemporary social, political, and historical context for intimate scenes he (and Jean Mohr) present of people going about their everyday lives. The Palestinian people are still much in the news — photographs of scenes from their lives are featured regularly in newspapers, in magazines, and on the Internet. Collect a series of these images from a particular and defined recent period of time — a week or a month, say, when the Palestinians have been in the news. Using these images, and putting them in conversation with some of the passages and images in "States," write an essay in the manner of Said's essay, with text and image in productive relationship. The goal of your essay should be to examine how Said's work in "States" can speak to us (or might speak to us) today.

ASSIGNMENT 3

On Experts and Expertise

JUDITH BUTLER, EDWARD SAID, WALKER PERCY

The whole horizon of being is staked out by "them," the experts. The highest satisfaction of the sightseer (not merely the tourist but any layman seer of sights) is that his sight should be certified as genuine. The worst of this impoverishment is that there is no sense of impoverishment. (p. 477)

I refer to the general situation in which sovereignty is surrendered to a class of privileged knowers, whether these be theorists or artists. A reader may surrender sovereignty over that which has been written about, just as a consumer may surrender sovereignty over a thing which has been theorized about. The consumer is content to receive an experience just as it has been presented to him by theorists and planners. The reader may also be content to judge life by whether it has or has not been formulated by those who know and write about life. (p. 478)

— WALKER PERCY, "The Loss of the Creature"

In the last two assignments you were asked to try on other writers' ways of seeing the world. You looked at what you had read or done, and at scenes from your own life, casting your experience in the terms of others.

Walker Percy, in "The Loss of the Creature," offers what might be taken as a critique of such activity. "A reader," he says, "may surrender sovereignty over that which has been written about, just as a consumer may surrender sovereignty over a thing which has been theorized about." Judith Butler and Edward Said have been presented to you as, in a sense, "privileged knowers." You have been asked to model your own work on their examples.

It seems safe to say that, at least so far as Percy is concerned, surrendering sovereignty is not a good thing to do. If Percy were to read over your work in these assignments, how do you think he would describe what you have done? If he were to take your work as an example in his essay, where might he place it? And how would his reading of your work fit with your sense of what you have done? Would Percy's assessment be accurate, or is there something he would be missing, something he would fail to see?

Write an essay in which you describe and comment on your work in this sequence, looking at it both from Percy's point of view and from your own, but viewing that work as an example of an educational practice, a way of reading (and writing) that may or may not have benefits for the reader.

Note: You will need to review carefully those earlier papers and mark sections that you feel might serve as interesting examples in your discussion. You want to base your conclusions on the best evidence you can. When you begin writing, it might be useful to refer to the writer of those earlier papers as a "he" or a "she" who played certain roles and performed his or her work in certain characteristic ways. You can save the first person, the "I," for the person who is writing this assignment and looking back on those texts.

A Story of Reading

RICHARD E. MILLER

Consider the following passage from Richard E. Miller's "The Dark Night of the Soul":

> What makes *Into the Wild* remarkable is Krakauer's ability to get some purchase on McCandless's actual reading practice, which, in turn, enables him to get inside McCandless's head and speculate with considerable authority about what ultimately led the young man to abandon the comforts of home and purposefully seek out mortal danger. Krakauer is able to do this, in part, because he has access to the books that McCandless read, with all their underlinings and marginalia, as well as to his journals and the postcards and letters McCandless sent to friends along his journey. Working with these materials and his interviews with McCandless's family and friends, Krakauer develops a sense of McCandless's inner life and eventually comes to some understanding of why the young man was so susceptible to being seduced by the writings of London, Thoreau, Muir, and Tolstoy. Who McCandless is and what becomes of him are, it turns out, intimately connected to the young man's approach to reading — both what he chose to read and how he chose to read it. (p. 444)

When Miller is writing about Krakauer's *Into the Wild*, he seems to suggest that what we read, and how we read, can say something about who we are and about what we might become. This is a very bold claim.

Think of a book that made a difference to you, that captured you, maybe one you have read more than once, maybe one that you've made marks in or that still sits on your bookshelf. Or, if not a book, think of your favorite song or album or movie or TV show, something that engaged you at least potentially as McCandless was engaged by London, Thoreau, Muir, and Tolstoy. What was it that you found there? What kind of reader were you? And what makes this a story in the past tense? How and why did you move on? (Or, if it is not a story in the past tense, where are you now, and are you, like McCandless, in any danger?)

A Slow Pedagogy

ATUL GAWANDE

Atul Gawande's "Slow Ideas" (p. 362) can be thought of as a teaching tool. Gawande has things for us to learn about innovation and change in medical practices. He also has things for us to learn about the teaching and learning that made innovation and successful change possible in life-and-death situations. This assignment invites you to write about Gawande's arguments for best practices in teaching for innovation and change and to situate those practices in the conditions for learning that you might call necessary or at least helpful to the success of the teaching.

When you reread "Slow Ideas," mark the moments when Gawande seems to be drawing lessons about best teaching practices from his case examples. It might be that the teaching practices are specific to the cases, or it might be that he's making larger claims about what's effective for teaching others. You'll have to decide how to situate his claims for best teaching practices, but you should at the least situate them in the conditions that seem to be necessary for learning to occur. What is it, in other words, about learners and their situations that has to be present for the best teaching practices to take hold?

Write an essay in which you make a case for what you think Gawande is saying about the best teaching practices for supporting others to innovate and change. Work closely from Gawande's case examples and situate your thinking in the conditions for learning that seem to be necessary for the best practices to work, to take hold.

Reporting as an Expert

MICHAEL SPECTER

"The Gene Hackers" (p. 602) provides an example of a certain form of reporting — of gathering information and preparing it for a general audience. Prepare a similar article, one where you take something you know well, something you know better (or more deeply) than most, and write an article like Michael Specter's, one designed to explain what you know to those who are outsiders.

Your article will most likely be shorter than his, but it should follow his method and style. It should be written in sections. It should combine scenes and stories with facts or concepts. If possible, you should also include statements by other experts. The "Questions for a Second Reading" (p. 616) should help as you prepare for this project.

SEQUENCE SIX

Reading Culture

John Berger
Susan Bordo
Gloria Bird
Michael Pollan

ALTERNATIVES:

Richard E. Miller
Michael Pollan
Ben Lerner

In this sequence, you will be reading and writing about culture. Not "Culture," something you get if you go to the museum or a concert on Sunday, but culture—the images, words, and sounds that pervade our lives and organize and represent our common experience. This sequence invites your reflection on the ways culture "works" in and through the lives of individual consumers.

The difficulty of this sequence lies in the way it asks you to imagine that you are not a sovereign individual, making your own choices and charting the course of your life. This is conceptually difficult, but it can also be distasteful, since we learn at an early age to put great stock in imagining our own freedom. Most of the readings that follow ask you to imagine that you are the product of your culture—that your ideas, feelings, and actions, your ways of thinking and being, are constructed for you by a large, organized, pervasive force (sometimes called history, sometimes called culture, sometimes called ideology). You don't feel this to be the case, but that is part of the power of culture, or so the argument goes. These forces hide themselves. They lead you to believe that their constructions are naturally, inevitably there, that things are the way they are because that is just "the way things are." The assignments in this sequence ask you to read against your common sense. You will be expected to try on the role of the critic—to see how and where it might be useful to recognize complex motives in ordinary expressions.

The authors in this sequence all write as though, through great effort, they could step outside culture to see and criticize its workings. The assignments in this sequence will ask you both to reflect on this type of criticism and to participate in it.

ASSIGNMENT 1

Looking at Pictures

JOHN BERGER

> Original paintings are silent and still in a sense that information never is. Even a reproduction hung on a wall is not comparable in this respect for in the original the silence and stillness permeate the actual material, the paint, in which one follows the traces of the painter's immediate gestures. This has the effect of closing the distance in time between the painting of the picture and one's own act of looking at it. . . . What we make of that painted moment when it is before our eyes depends upon what we expect of art, and that in turn depends today upon how we have already experienced the meaning of paintings through reproductions. (p. 158)
>
> — JOHN BERGER, "Ways of Seeing"

While John Berger describes original paintings as silent in this passage, it is clear that these paintings begin to speak if one approaches them properly, if one learns to ask "the right questions of the past." Berger demonstrates one route of approach, for example, in his reading of the Hals paintings, where he asks questions about the people and objects and their relationship to the painter and the viewer. What the paintings might be made to say, however, depends on the viewer's expectations, his or her sense of the questions that seem appropriate or possible. Berger argues that because of the way art is currently displayed, discussed, and reproduced, the viewer expects only to be mystified.

For this assignment, imagine that you are working against the silence and mystification Berger describes. Go to a museum — or, if that is not possible, to a large-format book of reproductions in the library (or, if that is not possible, to the Internet) — and select a painting that seems silent and still, yet invites conversation. Your job is to figure out what sorts of questions to ask, to interrogate the painting, to get it to speak, to engage with the past in some form of dialogue. Write an essay in which you record this process and what you have learned from it. Somewhere in your essay, perhaps at the end, turn back to Berger's chapter to talk about how this process has or hasn't confirmed what you take to be Berger's expectations.

Note: If possible, include with your essay a reproduction of the painting you select. (Check the postcards at the museum gift shop.) In any event, you want to make sure that you describe the painting in sufficient detail for your readers to follow what you say.

ASSIGNMENT 2

Berger and After

JOHN BERGER, SUSAN BORDO

In "Beauty (Re)discovers the Male Body" (p. 186), Susan Bordo refers to John Berger and his work in *Ways of Seeing*, although she refers to a different chapter from the one included here (p. 142). In general, however, both Berger and Bordo are concerned with how we see and read images; both seek to correct the ways images are used and read; both trace the ways images serve the interests of money and power; both are written to teach readers how and why they should pay a different kind of attention to the images around them.

For this assignment, use Bordo's work to reconsider Berger's. Write an essay in which you consider the two chapters as examples of an ongoing project. Berger's essay precedes Bordo's by about a quarter of a century. If you look closely at one or two of their examples, and if you look at the larger concerns of their arguments, are they saying the same things? doing the same work? If so, how? And why is such work still necessary? If not, how do their projects differ? And how might you explain those differences?

ASSIGNMENT 3

Reading the Body

SUSAN BORDO

In "Beauty (Re)discovers the Male Body" (p. 186), Susan Bordo looks back to the history of advertising (the "cultural genealogy of the ads I've been discussing") and works directly with the ads that prompted and served this chapter in her book. These images are a key part of the writing.

Bordo also speaks directly to you and invites you into her project: "So the next time you see a Dockers or a Haggar ad, think of it not only as an advertisement for khakis but also as an advertisement for a certain notion of what it means to be a man" (p. 211). You don't have to be limited to Dockers, Haggar, or khaki, but as you reread the essay and prepare for this writing assignment, keep your eye out for advertisements that come your way, advertisements that seem perfect for thinking along with Bordo (or advertisements that seem like interesting counterexamples). Clip these or copy them so that you can use them, as she does, as material for writing.

Write an essay in which you take up Bordo's invitation. You should assume an audience that has not read Bordo (or not read her work recently), so you will need to take time to present the terms and direction of her argument. Your goal, however, is to extend her project to your moment in time, when advertising may very well have moved on to different images of men and strategies of presentation.

Bordo is quite specific about her age and experience, her point of view. You should be equally specific. You, too, should establish your point of view. You are placed at a different moment in time; your experience is different; your exposure to images has prepared you differently. You write from a different subject position. Your job, then, is not simply to reproduce Bordo's project but to extend it, to refine it, to put it to the test.

ASSIGNMENT 4

Reading Media

GLORIA BIRD

In "Autobiography as Spectacle: An Act of Liberation or the Illusion of Liberation?" (p. 173), Gloria Bird provides us with an extensive discussion of and excerpt from Ronald Reagan's comments on Native Americans from 1988. Additionally, she provides examples of representations of Native Americans in film. She offers readings of her examples, providing her interpretations and perspective on what she hears and sees in these examples. We might think of Bird, in these moments, as "reading culture," as looking closely at how the subject at hand (Native Americans) is discussed, represented, and understood by others.

Bird worked on this essay in the late 1990s; one question worth thinking about is what Bird might notice about our current moment in history. Do some research in which you try to look for current examples of how Native Americans are discussed, represented, and understood by others. To help you get started, you might consider looking at discussions of professional sports logos or the problematic town seal of Whitesboro, New York. These are just two examples of when and how Native Americans have been discussed, represented, and understood by those outside their communities.

Write an essay in which you choose two to three examples you find in the media. What might Bird say about these examples? How does her essay help you "read culture" so that you can provide the readers of your essay with interpretations and critiques of what you find? You should quote both from the representations you find and from Bird's essay as a way of giving your readers both a window into Bird's essay and a sense of how Bird's essay might help us "read culture."

ASSIGNMENT 5

War on Food

MICHAEL POLLAN

Michael Pollan, in his essay "Nutritionism Defined," writes that "the history of modern nutritionism has been a history of macronutrients at war: protein against carbs; carbs against proteins, and then fats; fats against carbs. . . . In each age nutritionism has organized most of its energies around an imperial nutrient" (p. 492). He explains that "in the shadow of these titanic struggles, smaller civil wars have raged within the sprawling empires of the big three: refined carbohydrates versus fiber; animal protein versus plant protein; saturated fats versus polyunsaturated fats; and then, deep down within the province of the polyunsaturates, omega-3 fatty acids versus omega-6s" (p. 492).

Write an essay that explores Pollan's use of the metaphor of warfare in this passage. What are the illuminations and constraints of this metaphor in representing debates about food and nutrition? What does the war metaphor teach us about this debate? How can you see the this metaphor playing out in the public discourse on food and dieting? After examining Pollan's metaphor, you might challenge it and put forward your own metaphor to help provide additional insights into debates about food and nutrition.

ALTERNATIVE ASSIGNMENT

What Is It Good For?

RICHARD E. MILLER

Richard E. Miller's essay "The Dark Night of the Soul" opens with a list of fatal shootings in schools—troublingly, an incomplete list. As the essay builds to questions—questions for educators and for students—the specters of violence and alienation remain, changing how we think about the reading and writing that school endeavors to teach us. "I have these doubts, you see," Miller writes of academic work, "doubts silently shared by many who spend their days teaching others the literate arts. Aside from gathering and organizing information, aside from generating critiques and analyses that forever fall on deaf ears, what might the literate arts be said to be good for?" (p. 439).

Write an essay that takes up this question—"what might the literate arts be said to be good for?"—and that takes it up from your range of reference and from your point of view—or, more properly, from the point of view of you and people like you, the group you feel prepared to speak for. As an exercise in understanding, your essay should be modeled on one (or more) of the sections in "The Dark Night of the Soul." You can choose the text—and the text can be anything that might serve as an example of the literate arts, things in print but also including songs, films, and TV shows. But your presentation and discussion of the text should be in conversation with Miller—with his concerns, his key terms, his examples, and his conclusions.

ALTERNATIVE ASSIGNMENT

The Food Market

MICHAEL POLLAN

One way of reading Michael Pollan's "Nutritionism Defined" (p. 490) is to see it as a history of how our understanding of food has changed. Pollan examines how different (and often competing) conceptualizations of food are put forward by institutional forces like the Food and Drug Administration and the American Heart Association and also by product marketers and advertisers. In doing this, Pollan showcases how the meaning of food is socially constructed (and reconstructed) through the narratives we associate with it.

The biggest shift in narrative that Pollan explores here is that we increasingly think about food as science, as collections of nutrients necessary for various chemical processes performed by the body. This scientific conceptualization of food is markedly different from other understandings of food, which might see food as the source of pleasure or food as central to our heritage and connection to the past.

In product packaging and marketing, though, what is really interesting is to see how these different narratives and conceptualizations of food are operationalized individually or in combination to sell a product. Incorporating ideas from Pollan, write an essay in which you explore how the marketing of a particular food product (or collection of food products) is reliant on certain narrative conceptualizations of food. Work to explain and theorize why that conceptualization might be especially useful for that particular product. In writing this essay, you might pay attention to and discuss the visual design of the product packaging, the narrative accompanying that product, and the commercial advertisements associated with it.

ALTERNATIVE ASSIGNMENT

Why Read Anything?

BEN LERNER, RICHARD E. MILLER

Like Ben Lerner, in "Contest of Words: High School Debate and the Demise of Public Speech" (p. 419), Richard E. Miller, in "The Dark Night of the Soul" (p. 435), refers to the school shootings at Columbine, and he links what he calls the "literate arts" with the state of the nation. He speaks about the "practice" of the humanities, about the uses of language that circulate meaningfully and powerfully (or that don't) in the world of young adults in the contemporary United States. In his book *Writing at the End of the World,* Miller says,

> The practice of the humanities . . . is not about admiration or greatness or appreciation or depth of knowledge or scholarly achievement;

it's about the movement between worlds, arms out, balancing: it's about making the connections that count. (*Writing at the End of the World*, p. 198)

Arms out, balancing. The final image in Lerner's essay is of the people's microphone, people together, making connections, and what he calls a "collective haltingness."

Both Lerner and Miller are teachers. Both want to speak on behalf of the nation and its new generations of readers, writers, and speakers. While there are no direct references, one to the other, the two essays are part of a general conversation about the state of the language in the United States today. What does each say? How might they be said to speak to each other? to speak differently?

And, finally, where are you in this? Where are you, and people like you, the group for whom you feel prepared to speak? What examples might you bring to the table? You, too, have been and will continue to be expected to take courses in reading and writing and public speaking, to read, write, and talk in "critical and self-reflective ways," to use Miller's phrase. Where are you in this conversation?

Write an essay in which you explore these questions.

SEQUENCE SEVEN

On Difficulty

Michel Foucault
Judith Butler
Kwame Anthony Appiah
Michael Pollan

ALTERNATIVES:

Alison Bechdel
John Edgar Wideman

The assignments in this sequence invite you to consider the nature of difficult texts and how the problems they pose might be said to belong simultaneously to language, to readers, and to writers. The sequence presents four difficult essays (and two alternatives, should you wish to alter the sequence). The assumption the sequence makes is that they are difficult for all readers, not just for students, and that the difficulty is necessary, strategic, and not a mistake or evidence of a writer's failure.

ASSIGNMENT 1

Foucault's Fabrication
MICHEL FOUCAULT

About three-quarters of the way into his chapter "Panopticism," Michel Foucault says,

> Our society is one not of spectacle, but of surveillance; under the surface of images, one invests bodies in depth; behind the great abstraction of exchange, there continues the meticulous, concrete training of useful forces; the circuits of communication are the supports of an accumulation and a centralization of knowledge; the play of signs defines the

anchorages of power; it is not that the beautiful totality of the individual is amputated, repressed, altered by our social order, it is rather that the individual is carefully fabricated in it, according to a whole technique of forces and bodies. (p. 347)

This prose is eloquent and insists on its importance to our moment and our society; it is also very hard to read or to paraphrase. Who is doing what to whom? How do we think about the individual's being carefully fabricated in the social order?

Take this chapter as a problem to solve. What is it about? What are its key arguments? its examples and conclusions? Write an essay that summarizes "Panopticism." Imagine that you are writing for readers who have read the chapter (although they won't have the pages in front of them). You will need to take time to present and discuss examples from the text. Your job is to help your readers figure out what it says. You get the chance to take the lead and be the teacher. You should feel free to acknowledge that you don't understand certain sections even as you write about them.

So, how do you write about something you don't completely understand? Here's a suggestion: when you have completed your summary, read it over and treat it as a draft. Ask questions like these: What have I left out? What was I tempted to ignore or finesse? Go back to those sections of the chapter that you ignored and bring them into your essay. Revise by adding discussions of some of the very sections you don't understand. You can write about what you think Foucault *might* be saying — you can, that is, be cautious and tentative; you can admit that the text is what it is, hard to read. You don't have to master this text. You do, however, need to see what you can make of it.

ASSIGNMENT 2

Concept and Example

JUDITH BUTLER

Judith Butler's "Beside Oneself: On the Limits of Sexual Autonomy" (p. 238) is a philosophical essay, and one of the difficulties it presents to a reader is its emphasis on conceptual language. The sentences most often refer to concepts or ideas rather than to people, places, or events in the concrete, tangible, observable world. It refers to the *human* or to the *body*, but without telling the stories of particular humans or particular bodies. In fact, as a reader, you can feel her pull back at the very moments when she begins to speak in the first person, to personalize the essay. Without something concrete, without some situation or context in which the conceptual can take shape, these conceptual terms can lose their force or meaning. (If there is a story in this essay, it is not the story of the loss of a particular friend or love; it is the "story" of a struggle to understand and to articulate a response to the essay's opening question: what makes for a livable world?)

Reread this essay, noting particular moments (sentences, passages, and paragraphs) that make things hard for you, that are difficult for you as a reader. Choose four that seem to you to be the most representative. How are they hard? How would you characterize the difficulties they present? Where and how do you see Butler trying to help her readers? Where and how does she leave you on your own?

As an exercise, prepare a brief paraphrase or translation of each of these four representative moments: "What I think Butler is saying is . . ." And, finally, write an essay in which you discuss the essay, its argument, its methods, and the difficulties it presents to a reader.

ASSIGNMENT 3

A Reader-Friendly Text

KWAME ANTHONY APPIAH

Compared to Judith Butler's "Beside Oneself: On the Limits of Sexual Autonomy" (p. 238), Kwame Anthony Appiah's "Racial Identities" (p. 42) is a reader-friendly text. But it is also a learned text. It contains casual references to writers and scholars whom you may not recognize: W. E. B. Du Bois, Ian Hacking, Matthew Arnold, Charles Taylor, Thomas Sowell — to list just a few. The essay works with complicated ideas and poses an argument that not only runs against common assumptions, but also raises difficult political questions about race and identity.

As you reread, take note of the places in the text where the writer addresses you or, even if not using direct address, seems to have you in mind. And take note of those places where you find yourself to be most challenged, where the text becomes difficult to read.

When you are done, go back over your notes to see if there are distinct strategies, to see if your examples cluster into types. And write an essay in which you discuss "Racial Identities," its argument, its methods, and the difficulties it presents to a reader. If it is helpful, you might draw on passages from Foucault or Butler for additional examples.

ASSIGNMENT 4

A Theory of Difficulty

MICHEL FOUCAULT, JUDITH BUTLER, KWAME ANTHONY APPIAH

Now that you have worked with these three texts, you are in a good position to review what you have written about each of them in order to say something more general about difficulty — difficulty in writing, difficulty in reading.

Write an essay in which you present a theory of difficulty, a kind of guide, something that might be useful to students who are regularly asked to confront difficult assignments. You will want to work from your previous essays — pulling out sections, revising, reworking examples for this new essay. Don't let your earlier work go unacknowledged. But, at the same time, feel free to move out from these readings to other materials, examples, or situations.

ASSIGNMENT 5

Science Is Hard

MICHAEL POLLAN

Consider the difficult situation Michael Pollan is in as a writer. In "Nutritionism Defined" (p. 490), he discusses the complex history and evolution of food science and consumer attitudes, and he attempts to present this material to a broad audience of individuals mainly outside the arena of food science. Pollan is surely aware that much of this material might seem difficult or dense to an average reader. As you reread this piece, note places in the text where you can see Pollan working to make difficult material more interesting or easier to understand. What sort of strategies does he use to do this? You might identify a section that you find especially engaging and come up with a list of reasons why that section is so effective. Then, identify a section that you feel is less engaging, and think about how Pollan might have worked to improve that section. What strategies could he have used? How would you re-present that information in a new way?

   Write an essay in which you engage the question of difficulty as writers try to take it on. Discuss Pollan's strategies and propose some ideas of your own. You might consider a time you have had to present difficult materials to others. What strategies did you use? How might you even use those very strategies in this essay you've been asked to write about Pollan?

ALTERNATIVE ASSIGNMENT

The Graphic Challenge

ALISON BECHDEL

Some readers might find Alison Bechdel's work difficult to read. Many of us (except for those who might be avid comic book readers) might not be accustomed to reading graphic essays or graphic novels. Because Bechdel's work requires us to perhaps enact a new way of reading a text or thinking about a text, some difficulty or discomfort might arise as we are reading it. As you read "The Ordinary Devoted Mother" (p. 73), think carefully about what the form of her graphic work asks of you. What challenges present themselves as you read Bechdel's work? What difficulties does the graphic excerpt present? And how, as readers, might we adapt, adjust, and learn to be better readers of graphic work? Write an essay that describes the difficulties you faced while reading Bechdel. You'll want to consider the following questions: What about *your* reading strategies makes Bechdel's text difficult for you to read? How might Bechdel's work teach you how to read it? What new strategies might you invent to rise to the graphic challenge?

   If you find, however, that Bechdel's piece seems *less* difficult for you to read than other texts in this sequence, you may instead compose an essay in which you describe the methods of reading you use that might make you more prepared to read a piece like Bechdel's. What about your strategies or practices of reading makes this text *less* difficult than others you have been reading in this sequence?

ALTERNATIVE ASSIGNMENT

A Story of Reading

JOHN EDGAR WIDEMAN

At several points in "Our Time" (p. 622), John Edgar Wideman interrupts the narrative to discuss his position as a writer telling Robby's story. He describes the problems he faces in writing this piece (or in reading the text of his brother's life). You could read this selection, in other words, as an essay about reading and writing. It is Wideman's account of his work.

As a narrative, "Our Time" is made up of sections, fragments, different voices. It is left to the reader, in a sense, to put the pieces together and complete the story. There is work for a reader to do, in other words, and one way to account for that work is to call it "practice" or "training." Wideman wants to force a reader's attention by offering a text that makes unusual demands, a text that teaches a reader to read differently. If you think of your experience with the text, of how you negotiated its terrain, what is the story of reading you might tell? In what way do your difficulties parallel Wideman's — at least those he tells us about when he stops to talk about the problems he faces as a writer?

Write an essay in which you tell the story of what it was like to read "Our Time" and compare your experience working with this text with Wideman's account of his own.

A story of reading — this is not a usual school exercise. Usually you are asked what texts mean, not what it was like to read them. As you prepare for this assignment, think back as closely as you can to your experience the first time through. And you will want to reread, looking for how and where Wideman seems to be deliberately working on his reader, defying expectation and directing response. You want to tell a story that is rich in detail, precise in accounting for moments in the text. You want to bring forward the features that can make your story a good story to read — suspense, action, context, drama. Since this is your story, you are one of the characters. You will want to refer to yourself as you were at the moment of reading while also reserving a space for you to speak from your present position, as a person thinking about what it was like to read the text, and as a person thinking about Wideman and about reading. You are telling a story, but you will need to break the narrative (as Wideman breaks his) to account in more general terms for the demands Wideman makes on readers. What habits does he assume a reader will bring to this text? How and why does he want to break them?

SEQUENCE EIGHT

The Art of Argument

Alison Bechdel
Edward Said
Susan Bordo
Joy Castro
Atul Gawande
Michael Specter

Writing courses have traditionally included a unit on argumentation. The assignments in this sequence ask you to consider arguments in unusual settings. The assignments ask you not only to identify and explore writers' arguments but also to explore how they are enacted. You don't need technical terms for these assignments (like *induction* and *deduction*); you will be asked to develop your own terms, your own ways of describing the arguments you find.

ASSIGNMENT 1

Engaging Visual Pathways

ALISON BECHDEL, EDWARD SAID, SUSAN BORDO

Although Alison Bechdel is exclusively a cartoonist, you might consider her alongside some of the other authors in this book who pair their textual writing with images. Edward Said, in "States" (p. 559), and Susan Bordo, in "Beauty (Re) discovers the Male Body" (p. 186), each make use of images as they compose their individual writing projects. Although each of these writers' texts differs from the other ones in many ways, all of them try to engage both visual and textual pathways in order to enact their various lines of inquiry.

    Write an essay in which you try to describe the multiple ways in which these authors utilize images. How do photographs of bodies or places affect you in comparison to Bechdel's drawings in "The Ordinary Devoted Mother" (p. 73)? How exactly does each of these writers work with images, and what are the purposes of those images? What would it be like if Bechdel offered actual photographs of her family instead of cartoons? How might such a change affect our reading of the piece? Conversely, what if Bordo's images were satirical cartoons or comic strips? Another way to think about this topic is to pose the question: do images convey a kind of argument in the way writing does? If they do convey an argument, how might you describe that process to other readers?

ASSIGNMENT 2

Story as Argument
JOY CASTRO

One way to read Castro's pieces is to see them as narrative, as two short essays that tell the stories of Castro's journey as a student and education. But another way to understand Castro's writing is to imagine these essays as making an argument (or several arguments) about many different things: education, race, class, higher education, social justice, gender, and any other subjects you might have thought of while you considered the fourth "Question for a Second Reading" (p. 272).

Write an essay in which you make an argument about what the most urgent argument of Castro's essays seems to be. Of course, she makes more than one argument. But for the essay you will write, try to prioritize. What is her central argument? Or which of her arguments are most central to you? Why? How can you tell? What passages would you point to in order to support your own argument about what is most important in Castro's work? What is Castro's work *really* about in this selection?

ASSIGNMENT 3

Best Practices
ATUL GAWANDE

Atul Gawande's "Slow Ideas" (p. 362) can be thought of as a teaching tool. Gawande has things for us to learn about innovation and change in medical practices. He also has things for us to learn about the teaching and learning that made innovation and successful change possible in life-and-death situations. This assignment invites you to write about Gawande's arguments for best practices in teaching for innovation and change and to situate those practices in the conditions for learning that you might call necessary or at least helpful to the success of the teaching.

When you reread "Slow Ideas," mark the moments when Gawande seems to be drawing lessons about best teaching practices from his case examples. It might be that the teaching practices are specific to the cases, or it might be that he's making larger claims about what's effective for teaching others. You'll have to decide how to situate his claims for best teaching practices, but you should at the least situate them in the conditions that seem to be necessary for learning to occur. What is it, in other words, about learners and their situations that has to be present for the best teaching practices to take hold?

   Write an essay in which you make a case for what you think Gawande is saying about the best teaching practices for supporting others to innovate and change. Work closely from Gawande's case examples and situate your thinking in the conditions for learning that seem to be necessary for the best practices to work, to take hold.

ASSIGNMENT 4

Arguing as an Expert

MICHAEL SPECTER

"The Gene Hackers" (p. 602) provides an example of a certain form of reporting — of gathering information and preparing it for a general audience. Prepare a similar article, one where you take something you know well, something you know better (or more deeply) than most, and write an article like Michael Specter's, one designed to explain what you know to those who are outsiders.

   Your article will most likely be shorter than his, but it should follow his method and style. It should be written in sections. It should combine scenes and stories with facts or concepts. If possible, you should also include statements by other experts. The "Questions for a Second Reading" (p. 616) should help as you prepare for this project.